MAXWELL
THE OUTSIDER

MAXWELL
THE OUTSIDER

Tom Bower

VIKING

To Veronica

VIKING
Published by the Penguin Group
Viking Penguin, a division of Penguin Books USA Inc.,
375 Hudson Street, New York, New York 10014, U.S.A.
Penguin Books Ltd, 27 Wrights Lane,
London W8 5TZ, England
Penguin Books Australia Ltd, Ringwood,
Victoria, Australia
Penguin Books Canada Ltd, 10 Alcorn Avenue, Suite 300,
Toronto, Ontario, Canada M4V 3B2
Penguin Books (N.Z.) Ltd, 182–190 Wairau Road,
Auckland 10, New Zealand

Penguin Books Ltd, Registered Offices:
Harmondsworth, Middlesex, England

This edition first published in 1992 by Viking Penguin,
a division of Penguin Books USA Inc.

1 3 5 7 9 10 8 6 4 2

Picture research by Valerie Boyd

CIP data available.

ISBN 0-670-84654-6

Printed in the United States of America
Set in Times Roman

CONTENTS

*He that has much to do will do something wrong, and
of that wrong must suffer the consequences; and if it were
possible that he should always act rightly, yet when such
numbers are to judge of his conduct, the bad will censure
and obstruct him by malevolence, and the good sometimes by mistake.*

—Samuel Johnson, *Rasselas*

*Whatever his weight in pounds, shillings and ounces,
He always seems bigger because of his bounces.*

—A. A. Milne, *The House at Pooh Corner*

PREFACE

Robert Maxwell's first writ came as no surprise, but no one expected that eleven more writs would follow. It was Robert Maxwell's style: don't rely upon a sniper if a howitzer might perform the task.

His target was this book which, long before the text was even printed, he had condemned as "malicious and defamatory." The writ was dated February 23, 1988, and the book was due for publication three weeks later. He had not read the book or even seen the cover. It was the first climax of a bizarre battle between a biographer and his subject.

Conceived by Belinda Harley as a launching pad for a new publishing company called Aurum Press, the book's production had been planned with military precision. Under the codename "Robin Hood," the book was typeset in Singapore, printed in Finland and flown to Britain in circumstances which eluded those who broke into the publisher's offices searching for clues.

Not surprisingly, in the months before its publication, Maxwell had sought to discover my intentions. The coordinator of his counter-intelligence network was Peter Jay, the office manager. Those whom I interviewed about Maxwell were asked by Jay—about one hundred people, he confided—to submit full reports. Those, like Lady Falkender, who had initially refused to meet me, were invited to reverse their objections and offer their availability. Lady Falkender's report to Jay did not accord with my recollection of our meeting but amateur sleuths are sadly unreliable.

This same network approached virtually every person I quoted, asking them to say whether they were correctly quoted, thoughtfully telling them they would not be sued if they cooperated.

Even Maxwell's professional spies made mistakes. My lunch with his former secretary and confidante, Anne Robertson, was unknowingly watched by a private detective. As we left the restaurant, I pointed out that her handbag was open. Mrs. Robertson asked me to hold an envelope while she closed the bag. When Maxwell's writ for breach of confidence arrived, the evidence he produced was the detective's eye-witness account of Mrs. Robertson handing over secret papers.

My only advantage was surprise. Some time after Maxwell heard about my intentions to write the book, he commissioned an authorized biography. Since I had deliberately "leaked" in September 1987 that publication was due in July 1988, Maxwell's trusted author felt that time was not pressing. That changed in January 1988 when the serialization agreement with the *Sunday Times* became known. The race began. Since Maxwell owned Europe's largest printing company, he found few production problems hindering his bid to catch up.

Naturally Maxwell wanted to stop the *Sunday Times* endorsing my book. Repeatedly he telephoned the editor, Andrew Neil, and the owner, Rupert Murdoch. Neil manfully resisted the pressure while Maxwell's own book was serialized every day in the *Daily Mirror,* supported, according to his publicity, by a £500,000 budget. That was more than Aurum's turnover!

By then the ownership of Aurum had been transferred. Andrew Lloyd Webber's Really Useful Group had become the publishers. As the curtain fell in New York after the premiere of *Phantom of the Opera,* the telephone rang in Lloyd Webber's box. It was Maxwell urging the composer to dump his author. When his persuasion failed, he defamed Lloyd Webber in an "exclusive" article in the *Sunday Mirror.*

Throughout this saga, Andrew Lloyd Webber's support, which has cost a substantial amount of money and time, has been generous, re-markable and principled. I am particularly grateful to him and to the Really Useful Group's executives, especially Keith Turner, for their continued endorsement. "Bullies," as the *Independent* supportingly wrote at the beginning of this epic, "thrive on the cowardice and weak-ness in their victims." The ability to resist Maxwell's attempt to suppress the freedom of expression depended upon RUG.

The battle seemed equal until Maxwell used his own newspapers to publish defamations about myself. My retort was to issue writs against him. Bower v. Maxwell had a particularly suicidal resonance until those that produce *Private Eye* supported my cause. Christopher Silvester, Ian Hislop and Richard Ingrams may not be everyone's friends, but their interest and encouragement were invaluable to me.

Maxwell's first writ had been issued before Christmas in relation to an article in the *Listener*. Bravely, the BBC stood its ground so that by the time the second writ arrived, just before the *Sunday Times* publication, repeated discussions with lawyers were becoming a way of life.

Fortunately, the judge, Michael Davies, declined Maxwell's application for an injunction. Before he retired from the bench, Mr. Justice Davies would see us all many more times and his decisions would be queried all the way to the House of Lords. "Bower v. Maxwell" or "Maxwell v. Bower" established legal precedents on obscure matters and I wish the lawyers well who depend upon them.

Maxwell's writs transformed the book into an author's dream—a "Number One Best Seller." The only handicap was that the book was gradually no longer on sale. Having failed in the courts, the subject turned his guns on the trade which supplied the alleged poison.

Letters, phone calls, telegrams and writs cascaded upon a trade reeling before the outrage of a publisher. The first to fall were the wholesale distributors, followed by the shops. Individual phone calls and individual letters on the notepaper of his own publisher Macdonald falsely alleged that he had obtained an injunction against the book. Every bookshop in the land was a recipient and those who dared to continue displaying the book were rewarded with a Maxwellian writ. Led by Julian Blackwell, some tried to fight back.

Courageous booksellers responded by refusing to deal with Macdonald's representatives, which provoked another letter from Macdonald closing their credit. In retaliation, those shops refused to stock the authorized biography. That refusal combined with Maxwell's repeated failure in the courts prompted another Maxwell letter defaming me and instructing the recipients that bookshops had a duty to sell the authorized biography which "tells the truth." Only Hatchards of Piccadilly bravely continued sales.

One year later there was little progress. Maxwell's promise of 100 pages of complaints had been reduced to 30. A two-day hearing in February 1989, employing eight lawyers, produced legal precedents but no remedy. The writ against the book soon withered because Maxwell feared the public investigation it would provoke. Successfully, three times, he prevented the paperback appearing. On one occasion he even bought the paperback company to prevent publication. Thankfully, the brave managing director revoked the rights hours before the take-over.

Maxwell's attempts to stop the book were not limited to Britain. Having successfully pressured all the leading publishers in New York and Germany not to buy the rights, he believed his influence extended to France. Fortunately, he was mistaken. But after the book's publication, he issued four writs against me in Paris and elsewhere, including an action for the invasion of his privacy. He complained that I had reported that he had lost a lung and demanded 100,000 francs in compensation for that disclosure. Characteristically, he ignored mention of exactly the same point in his authorized biography. Thanks to the diligence of Maître Zylberstein, Maxwell not only lost his actions but was even ordered to pay me 10,000 francs' damages.

Maxwell's litigation employed at least twelve lawyers, several accountants and two private detectives. I received several anonymous calls warning me of investigations into my past life. I thank those good folk for their warnings and would ask the investigators to send me their results.

Throughout this battle, I realized the value of the experience. Thanks to Maxwell, I have become even more fearless. Whenever I am given a price, I immediately consider, am I buying or selling? Whenever a professional adviser submits his account, I offer him half and hope to settle for less. Whenever a situation suggests fear, I recall Lex Maxwelliana: the answer to threats is counter-threats for there is no such thing as fear. Above all, I have learnt that Lex Maxwelliana is to savor the sheer enjoyment of life.

Lest it should be misunderstood, despite my criticisms of Robert Maxwell, he had qualities which I admire. I met him in 1973 when, with Max Hastings, we agreed to produce a television documentary about him. We fashioned it on *Citizen Kane* which he, unfortunately, did not consider complimentary. After six weeks together, the relationship between Maxwell and me terminated. The relationship between Bower and Hastings became ever closer. Energetic attempts by Maxwell to stop the film's transmission on editorial grounds failed. But during the night before the transmission an unprecedented event occurred. The room where the film had been edited was entered and the sound track was stolen. Fortunately, the thief failed to realize that the film editor, John Williams, had stored a copy elsewhere.

Because of all the above, I never failed to follow Maxwell's activities and today I miss my daily search in the financial pages for his latest ploys. Although I spent little time with him, I felt that I knew him intimately and understood him perfectly. That was why he disliked this book so much, especially the title.

Over the past three years, I have received enormous help and support from many people. In the roll call of honor stand Aurum's original publishers Michael Alcock and Tim Chadwick whose professional skills, good humor and determination were invaluable while their money was essential.

David Hooper, our libel lawyer, saved us from many mistakes and, in his inimicable way, delighted us all with his display of legal skills to outwit Maxwell's batallions. He was ably assisted by Kathryn Garbett.

Michael Shaw of Curtis Brown was a pillar of strength and a good friend.

I am particularly grateful to people at *Private Eye,* the Really Useful Group, Brian McArthur, Belinda Harley, Derek Terrington and all those who, having declined to speak, eventually prefaced their remarks by saying, "It's off the record . . ."

The additions were produced within eighteen days. That would have been impossible without the tremendous help of Israel Goldvitch in Jerusalem, Adele Gooch in Madrid, Robert Fink in New York, Tim Witcher in Paris and Rod Pouncet and Kemlin Furley in Moscow. Lara Marlowe was responsible for the excellent research in France for chapter fifteen. In London, I am grateful to John Ware, Nisha Pillai and especially to my BBC colleague Paul Hamann.

Thanks to Michael Kinsella and Bob Royer for their support and hospitality in Washington and New York.

Finally, one of the essentials of a writer's life are his friends and family. I am particularly fortunate in that regard. Survival would have been impossible without all of them. Especially without the support of my best friend, my wife.

INTRODUCTION

In the calm Atlantic swell, the naked body was quite recognizable. The hunt was over. The pilot swung the Superpuma helicopter toward the setting sun, reduced his speed and tilted his craft toward the sea. At the door, the loader was strapped and ready to be lowered into the water. "We've found it," snapped the pilot to his controller in Madrid. "The location is 27 degrees 46.6 north, 16 degrees 0.6 west." To the layman, the corpse had been found twenty-eight miles off the coast of Gran Canaria, an idyllic Spanish island which is a comfortable retreat for Europe's wealthier citizens.

It was 6:46 p.m. on November 5, 1991. As the loader's feet touched the warm sea, he grunted with displeasure. His task would not be easy. The corpse was enormous—nearly 300 pounds, he later learned. Strangely, it was floating face up, while normally the faces were submerged in the water. There was no time for any other observations. Jerking the collar around the body was a struggle, but the helicopter's winch was soon turning.

Above, the Superpuma's pilot was receiving his instructions. His load was to be taken to Gando military airport on the island. The corpse's description was again confirmed: an enormous man with dark hair, probably dyed; his age, about seventy; no other identification; few wrinkles on the skin, so not long in the water.

As the solitary helicopter fluttered in a north-easterly direction, the world's airwaves exploded. Radio traffic, telephone calls, fax machines, television broadcasts, satellite beams and computed news wires competed to announce the unexpected and therefore astonishing news: a tycoon was dead amid mysterious circumstances. The excitement was provoked by the surprise. Throughout the world, television stations interrupted their programs, radio broadcasters breathlessly promised more news by the minute, and newspaper editors bellowed changes and deployments.

In the White House, the Kremlin, the Elysee and 10 Downing Street, officials rushed to tell their political masters that Robert Maxwell, chairman and owner of Maxwell Communications Corporation, one of the world's biggest media conglomerates, was dead.

On the ninth floor of Maxwell's corporate headquarters in London's Holborn Circus, women sobbed and men froze, gazing at the historic skyline. For years the chairman or the publisher, as he was known, had bullied, humiliated and terrorized his staff. Yet his death robbed them of a giant in their lives and threatened uncertainty.

As the corpse was wheeled from the helicopter to a temporary morgue, speculation about the death ranged from murder to suicide. Few could believe that a man so reviled, so immersed in conspiracies, so discredited by fraud, could have simply died from natural causes.

Suspected of links to a web of competing intelligence agencies; of embittering an army of businessmen; and of perilous brinkmanship with a galaxy of banks, there was, it was agreed, no shortage of reasons why Robert Maxwell should not have committed suicide—or been murdered.

The widow's arrival on the small island on board his personal jet momentarily silenced the speculation. Respect was paid to the woman whose loyalty throughout her husband's innumerable scandals had never been in doubt. Yet as she identified the corpse, allowing the pathologists to commence their grisly task, the obituaries disagreed on whether to mourn a hero or praise the passing of a villain.

Controversial in life, the corpse provoked outrage in death. Regaled at his graveside by the Israeli government as a hero, he was condemned in London as a fraud. No sooner had three pathologists decided that his death was due to natural causes than the foundations of his empire began to totter. Five billion dollars was missing, and the thief had been given a hero's farewell in Jerusalem.

Attention focused upon his last days aboard his luxury yacht. Nothing would be a topic of greater dispute than whether, as he enjoyed the privileges of enormous wealth, he realized that his life's task—to metamorphose from an outsider into an insider—was on the verge of dissolution with the inevitability of public disgrace as an international leper.

His last hours provoked more speculation. Unseen, in the darkness, he had toppled into the sea. Pushed, thrown or fallen, no one knew.

For six hours neither his crew nor his 20,000 employees knew that he was missing. The mystery of the legend entered a new phase.

Just four years earlier, on the first floor of the red-topped *Daily Mirror* building in Holborn, central London, Robert Maxwell had unveiled a new era.

At six minutes past noon on June 17, 1987, he had stood calmly at the entrance of a crowded conference room. His mere appearance had silenced his audience.

Over one hundred people had spotted the man who desired immortality but would compromise with glorification. Tall, bronzed and immaculately dressed (bright blue suit, white shirt and dazzling red bow tie), Robert Maxwell, alias "the publisher," glanced at his watch to judge whether the precise moment had struck for his next public appearance. Behind him stood four uniformed security guards. Hovering in front was his chief of staff, clasping a portable telephone. The publisher placed a premium upon instant communications. Noticeably erect on his left, attempting to peer into the room, were two secretaries. Their employer prided himself on churning out decisions at a faster rate than most can speak and required their constant attendance to transmit his thoughts instantly. At the rear of the hall waited a photographer. Like recent Presidents of the United States of America, the chairman of the British Printing and Publishing Corporation wanted a visual record of history-in-the-making and the photographer was on permanent call to satisfy his single-minded zeal for self-promotion. Eight floors above hummed the nucleus of a growing empire. Even higher, on an adjoining building, was a heliport for the publisher's favored mode of transport to and from the capital. In the garage below was an immaculate Rolls-Royce. The publisher had always displayed a penchant for the biggest and the most expensive cars. Scattered elsewhere was a mansion, apartments, offices, factories, a luxury yacht and twenty thousand employees.

Sixty-four years earlier, the dollar billionaire was born into a community whose poverty and hardship would be unimaginable for those who were now witness to his ease amid wealth and power. Most in the room regarded him with puzzled awe because his path to fame and fortune was as spectacular and peculiar as the mystery of his origins. None could understand how a self-educated peasant could become a redoubtable financier, publisher, politician, industrialist and tycoon extraordinary. The enigma of his inexhaustible tenacity, energy and bravado inflated their deepest suspicions. His huge frame, his piercing eyes and his subliminally alert gestures as he glanced around the room confirmed that he was a hunter and to be feared. For forty-five years the hunter had sought acceptance but remained an outsider. Undeterred, his ambition for the last quarter of his life was to impose himself not only upon Britain but upon the entire world. Time was pressing for this aspiring superstar for he was determined to score a chapter rather than a mere footnote in history.

On cue, Robert Maxwell began squeezing behind a row of sober-suited men who nodded their welcome as he took his place in their midst. Quietly, he called to order the twenty-fourth annual general meeting of the British Printing and Publishing Corporation. In his lifetime, Maxwell chaired hundreds of similar meetings and followed the routine as prescribed by law. The accounts were "read" and approved, directors were recommended and re-elected and questions could be asked. On some notable occasions, in the more turbulent episodes of his career, the timetable was delayed by outbursts of enmity and screams of abuse. But on this occasion, the smooth, genial but slightly impatient chairman had no fear of interruption or of embarrassment. As befits the hailed savior of Europe's biggest printing company, he exuded the self-confidence of a man convinced that his manifest destiny was to command one of the world's biggest communications corporations.

The highlight on this occasion was Maxwell's announcement that in the course of the previous year the corporation had passed important milestones on its way to becoming "a global information communications company before the end of the decade, with annual revenues of £3–5 billion and earnings per share to match." For a company which was bankrupt five years earlier, Maxwell's ambitions were audacious. He was promising nothing less than an eleven- to eighteen-fold rate of expansion in just four years. In the past, he was officially censured for his reckless optimism but he never conceded any wrongdoing. On the contrary, he always pleaded that he had been the victim of willful misunderstanding and much worse. It is a measure of his defiance that his accusers never enjoyed long-lasting satisfaction. Nevertheless, on this occasion from the audience one shareholder was sufficiently bold to challenge his latest prophecy. To the laymen, the shareholder's query was technical but the cognoscenti gathered in the room immediately recognized its pertinence. Would Maxwell actually promise, he asked, that the share earnings would increase eleven-fold? Maxwell began to answer when a young lawyer interrupted and there were whispered consultations. Maxwell's eyes were suddenly covered by a sheen: "I'm afraid that I cannot give any assurances because it would be in breach of the law." The shareholder was puzzled because he had just read that very assurance on the first page of the corporation's glossy annual report. But he found no sympathy among others in the audience. No one present would dare to challenge the chairman. "Next business," smiled Maxwell.

A clutch of directors were re-elected and the meeting was drawing to a close when from the edge of the room a stocky, bespectacled, gray-suited middle-aged man interrupted. It was Henry Poole, an analyst at the brokerage firm of Alexanders, Laing and Cruickshank who, as an expert on the printing industry and BPPC's broker, had recently written laudatory reports about the publisher's "sense of vision." His opening remarks made it clear that the intervention had in fact been carefully planned. "Mr. Maxwell," said Poole, "had given me some notes of what to say but I threw them away." Alternating his gaze between his client and their audience, Poole then uttered the most grievous heresy: "Sixteen years ago the chairman was judged to be a man who was unfit to be the steward of a public company. . . ." A ripple of embarrassment extended across the room as eyes darted from Poole to Maxwell and back again. Maxwell's eyes were covered again by a sheen as he feared that something untoward was occurring which was beyond his control. "It seems that Robert Maxwell has borne every accusation, apart from being drunk in the House of Commons, that was borne by Mr. Melmotte." The silence intensified. Melmotte is described as a "horrid big rich scoundrel . . . a bloated swindler . . . a vile city ruffian" who came from a mysterious background to make a fortune in the City from dealing which included Russia. Melmotte had been destroyed by a financial scandal. The tension had increased. "Mr. Maxwell is not a Melmotte." Whatever eulogy he had intended could not have surpassed what followed. "But I say to those who are here today who manage the pension and investment funds that they are unfit to be the managers of those funds if they do not recognize the achievements of Mr. Maxwell and invest in this company." Relief and a weak smile from the publisher. The embarrassment was neatly averted and the tension passed. The homage was over. Fifteen minutes later, at the lunch, Poole would sit on the publisher's right hand as the honored guest.

This is a story about a man who used and abused people, who aroused fervent loyalty, fear and disdain among otherwise rational and strong human beings, and whose reputation suffered the misfortune of his best attempts to offer his truth. His impatience for reform was matched by his aggressive search for the power to dictate the pace of an erratic agenda for change. Unlike in the United States, the trail in modern

Britain from log cabin to mansion is a perilous saga. The Isles' ruling gentry look askance at brazen ambition and uninherited wealth. They loathe immodesty more than dishonesty. Robert Maxwell's story is about the tenacity of a man who not long ago approved the superimposition of a halo highlight upon an old photo-portrait of himself for a magazine. The caption beneath read, "Multi-faceted talent." Maxwell courted publicity too eagerly to be of profound interest to independently thinking men. His earnest desire to sit in the eye of the world tickled the media's interest but suggested an empire built upon sand. Even the most robust qualities of the most upright citizen are eventually eroded by vanity. Twice in his career Maxwell's vainglory consigned him to commercial oblivion but the same vanity propelled his recovery. The debacle of his third attempt was only revealed in the weeks following his mysterious death. Throughout his life the pattern remained consistent. His personality and methods never changed. The portents for his last dash for glory were both favorable and ominous.

GLOSSARY

AGM	Annual General Meeting
BBC	British Broadcasting Corporation
BIM	Bishopsgate Investment Management
BIT	Bishopsgate Investment Trust
BNPC	British Newspaper Printing Corporation
BOAC	British Overseas Airways Corporation
BPC	British Printing Corporation
BPCC	British Printing and Communications Corporation
DPP	Director of Public Prosecutions
DTI	Department of Trade and Industry
EGM	Extraordinary General Meeting
EPC	European Printing Corporation
EPPAC	European Periodicals, Publicity and Advertising Corporation
FOC	Father of Chapel
HMSO	Her Majesty's Stationery Office
IBM	International Business Machines
ICI	Imperial Chemical Industries
ILSC	International Learning Systems Corporation Limited
IPC	International Publishing Corporation
JEIA	Anglo-American Joint Export-Import Agency
LMS	Lange, Maxwell & Springer
L & BII	London & Bishopsgate International Investment
L & BIIM	London & Bishopsgate International Investment Management
MCC	Maxwell Communications Corporation
MGH	Mirror Group Holdings
MGN	Mirror Group Newspapers
MIMC	Microforms International Marketing Corporation
MSI (1964)	Maxwell Scientific International (1964)
MSI Inc.	Maxwell Scientific International Inc.
MSI (DS)	Maxwell Scientific International (Distribution Services) Limited
NASA	National Aeronautics and Space Administration
NGA	National Graphical Association
NUJ	National Union of Journalists
PPI	Pergamon Press Incorporated
PRISC	Public Relations and Information Services Control
R.M. & Co.	Robert Maxwell & Co.
SOE	Special Operations Executive
SOGAT	Society of Graphical and Allied Trades
TUC	Trades Union Congress
UNESCO	United Nations Educational, Scientific and Cultural Organization

MAXWELL COMPANIES (1987)

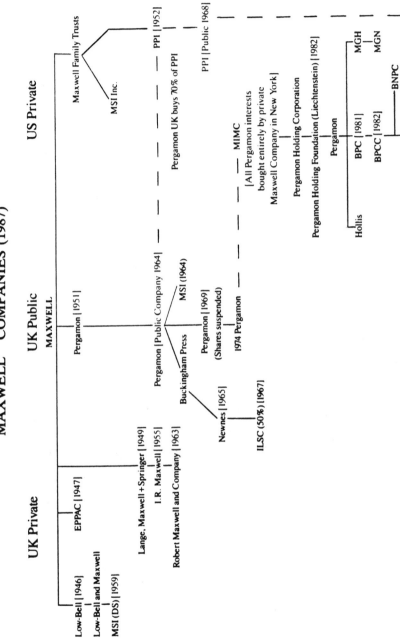

UK Private

Low-Bell [1946]
Low-Bell and Maxwell
MSI (DS) [1959]

EPPAC [1947]

Lange, Maxwell + Springer [1949]
I.R. Maxwell [1955]
Robert Maxwell and Company [1963]

UK Public

MAXWELL

Pergamon [1951]

Buckingham Press

Newnes [1965]

ILSC (50%) [1967]

Pergamon [Public Company 1964]

MSI (1964)

Pergamon [1969]
(Shares suspended)

1974 Pergamon

US Private

Maxwell Family Trusts

MSI Inc.

PPI [1952]

Pergamon UK buys 70% of PPI

PPI [Public 1968]

MIMC
[All Pergamon interests
bought entirely by private
Maxwell Company in New York]

Pergamon Holding Corporation

Pergamon Holding Foundation (Liechtenstein) [1982]

Pergamon

Hollis

BPC [1981]

BPCC [1982]

BNPC

MGH

MGN

MCC [1987]

MCC (US)

MAXWELL COMPANIES (1991)

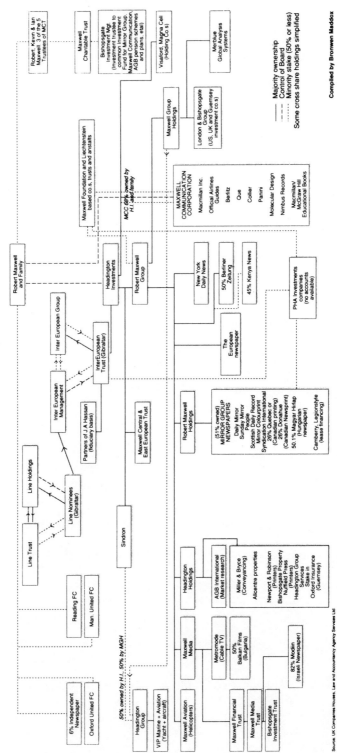

Robert Kevin & Ian Maxwell 3 of the 5 Trustees of MCT

Maxwell Charitable Trust

Bishopsgate Investment Mgt (investment trustee to common investment Fund for Mirror Group, Maxwell Communication, AGB pension schemes and plans, etal)

Visaford, Magna Cell (Holding Co's)

Meriblue Global Analysis Systems

Robert Maxwell and Family

Maxwell Foundation and Liechtenstein based co.s, trusts and anstalts

Maxwell Group Holdings

London & Bishopsgate Group (US, UK and Guernsey investment co's)

MCC 68% owned by H.I. and family

MAXWELL COMMUNICATION CORPORATION

Macmillan Inc.
Official Airlines Guides
Berlitz
Que
Collier
Panini
Molecular Design
Nimbus Records
Macmillan/ McGraw Hill Educational Books

Headington Investments

Robert Maxwell Group

New York Daily News

50% Berliner Zeitung

45% Kenya News

Inter European Group

Inter European Management

Inter/European Trust (Gibraltar)

Partners of J A Hassan (fiduciary basis)

Maxwell Central & East European Trust

Sindron

The European newspaper

PHA Investments companies (no accounts available)

Line Holdings

Line Trust

Line Nominees (Gibraltar)

Reading FC

Man. United FC

Robert Maxwell Holdings

(51% owned) MIRROR GROUP NEWSPAPERS
Daily Mirror
Sunday Mirror
People
Scottish Daily Record
Mirror Colourprint
Syndication International
26% Quebec or (Canadian printing)
26% Donahue (Canadian Newsprint)
50.1% Magyar Hirlap (Hungarian newspaper)
Camberry, Legionstyle (lease financing)

Headington Holdings

AGB International (Market research)

Miller & Bryce (Conveyancing)

Allcentre properies

Newport & Robinson (Printers)
Bishopsgate Property
Nuffield Press (Printers)
Headington Group Services
Stake in Oxford Insurance (Guernsey)

6% Independent Newspaper

Oxford United FC

50% owned by H.I., 50% by MGH

Headington Group

VIP Marine + Avation (Yacht + aircraft)

Maxwell Aviation (Helicopters)

Maxwell Financial Trust

Maxwell Media Trust

Bishopsgate Investment Trust

Maxwell Media

Metromode (Cable TV)

50% Balkan Films (Bulgaria)

82% Modiin (Israeli Newspaper)

Majority ownership
Control of Board
Minority stake (50% or less)
Some cross share holdings simplified

Compiled by Bronwen Maddox

Source: UK Companies House; Law and Accountancy Agency Services Ltd

MAXWELL
THE OUTSIDER

1

Robert Maxwell was born on June 10, 1923, in Slatinske Doly (or Aknazlatina), a small Ruthenian village in the midst of extensive, dark forests wedged between the jagged Carpathian mountains and the River Tisza, which marked the Czech-Romanian border. The region of his birthplace was probably the most primitive and impoverished on the whole European continent. According to legend, the six thousand inhabitants of Slatinske Doly could not even afford a cemetery—either they emigrated or the birds ate their corpses from the gallows. Life for these people resembled that of villagers in western Europe a century before. In 1923, Slatinske Doly was part of the new Czechoslovakian state, but to the Prague government the citizens eking a meager existence in Carpo-Ruthenia were little better than serfs or vagabonds. Spiritually, however, the region was unique. Since the beginning of the nineteenth century, there had grown up a thriving Jewish community, whose attitudes and instincts were inherited by Maxwell and were to propel him through life.

Most of the two thousand Jews who lived in Slatinske Doly, a quarter of the population, were docile and uncommercial, simple peasants who were castigated by the more entrepreneurial Jews in the neighboring town of Sziget as *Luftmenschen*—people who live on air. Most of the villagers failed to earn a regular income but somehow found ways to survive. Among the poorest was Maxwell's own father, Mechel Hoch, a tall, hard-working peasant who earned a pittance buying cattle from farmers for resale to local butchers and later selling the hides to leatherworkers. When times were hard, he supplemented his income by casual work as a woodcutter or a farm laborer especially at harvest time. Mechel was religious though not ultra-Orthodox; occasionally he taught the Talmud to local children and served as an official in one of the village's wooden synagogues. Maxwell's relationship with his father was not particularly close, partly because Mechel spent much of his time traveling around the countryside looking for cattle deals and partly because he was very attached to his mother and her father.

Mechel's wife Hannah Schlomovitch was the classic Jewish mother, managing and ruling the household. Undaunted by the struggle that was her daily life, she was fiercely ambitious for her two sons and five daughters and was renowned for her enormous curiosity. Her nephew Alex Pearl remembers that "She picked up every piece of newspaper in the street to discover what was going on. She was always interested in everything." Her cousin Lazar Schlomovitch, now a professor in Los Angeles, recalls that she was "an exception in the village because she read books. She was almost an intellectual." Like all wives in the Orthodox Jewish community, Hannah cooked only kosher food and ensured that her children regularly attended the local religious school and went daily to the synagogue.

The Hochs and their seven children lived in two rooms in a rented house. The wooden building, heated by a wooden stove, could only boast earthen floors. There were two beds, one for the parents, the other for the children. Water was drawn from a well some distance from the house. The lavatory was a hut at the back of the house; a simple hole in a wooden plank was suspended over a pit, which was emptied annually by gypsies. During the winter their staple diet was potatoes but in summer there were other vegetables from the garden, a monotony that was lightened on Saturdays and religious holidays by meat and occasionally gefillte fish. In summer all the children walked barefoot. In winter, the shoes were normally shared: one child would wear a pair to school in the morning while another wore the same shoes in the afternoon. "We didn't understand 'happiness,' " says Pearl, "except on Saturdays when there was different food on our plates." Maxwell's childhood was dominated by the poverty and by the ineradicable conditioning of purist Judaism.

The genesis of the family name Hoch is characteristic of the culture which surrounded Maxwell. The leading Jewish families of Slatinske Doly bore classic names like Schlomovitch, Shaiovitch and Kra'ama'are. The poor families, especially the new arrivals, were usually nameless. Before 1914, that defect was remedied at regular intervals by Hungarian officials who visited isolated communities to complete a census. For one whole day, the villagers had to remain inside their houses while officials interviewed each family. Invariably among the arrivals were Jews who bore no family name recognizable to the

Hungarians. Accordingly, the officials assigned the family a "name" prompted by the Jew's trade or by any remarkable peculiarity. According to legend, one census in the region was executed on the eve of Yom Kippur, the holiest of Jewish holidays. That evening in synagogue, the village discovered that those families "named" at the end of the day were all called Weiss (white): the census officials had noted that those Jews, already dressed for the evening service, were wearing their long, white tallis and named them accordingly. In the case of Maxwell's forefathers, the census officials noticed that the head of the family was tall or (in German) *hoch*. Maxwell's father was in fact known as "Mechel der Lange," Mechel the Tall, because he was 6 ft. 5 in.

Carpo-Ruthenia's change of nationality in 1919 from Hungarian to Czech directly affected Maxwell's forename. At birth, his father called him Abraham Lajbi but on registration at the local town hall the Czech government official insisted that the birth certificate record a Czech name. Hence Lajbi became Ludvik and the name "Jan" was added to establish that the newborn boy was a true Czech citizen.

Although Jan Ludvik Hoch personally lived amid gross material poverty, throughout his short childhood he witnessed his isolated community undergoing the most dramatic changes: the Jews were winning their struggle to survive; the hitherto closeknit Orthodox community was bitterly divided by political and religious disagreements; and some Jews in the locality were enjoying an unexpected windfall from smuggling, which earned the village the title of *klein Amerika*. So Maxwell experienced a century's evolution compressed into half a generation. His attitudes toward people, business, authority and family life were all fashioned by the revolution which was affecting the Jews in that remote strip of Ruthenia.

The first Jewish settlers had arrived in the area in 1526 as refugees from the Turkish invasion of Hungary but the bedrock of the community were those who fled Polish Galicia in 1648 to escape the vicious pogroms provoked by the Chmielnicki revolt. Although Slatinske Doly was a refuge, they were still subject to rigid anti-Jewish laws. Maxwell's family, like most of his neighbors, were Maramaros Jews who, according to an historical survey, are distinguished by their particularly "conservative, strongly Jewish character, strong physique, and their sane though simple viewpoint, as well as their ability and willingness to work." Jacob Taba became the first Jew to be registered in the village in 1728 after renting a smallholding from an absent landowner. One hundred years later, the registered Jewish community had grown to forty-three families (218 people), most of whom worked for local farmers and owned privately one cow and one horse. United by their religion and by their common language, Yiddish, they lived apart from the indigenous and equally poverty-stricken Russian Orthodox Ruthenian peasants.

Life began to change during the nineteenth century when the huge saltmines in the neighboring village were expanded to supply the mineral to most of the Austro-Hungarian empire. Jews were banned by law from working in the mines, but they could service the workers who were pouring into the area. Three well-established families in Slatinske Doly were permitted to open a salt mill, a flour mill and a lumber mill. Selected Jews were licensed to sell alcohol and meat while others supplemented their income by selling groceries, household goods and clothes. All of them subsisted on bread made of oats and maize, except on the Sabbath when they ate white challah bread, with meat and gefillte fish on holidays. The peasants' diet hardly changed over two centuries.

Despite its economic deprivations, the region enjoyed a diversity of cultures from the steady flow of transients. Over the centuries, Slovaks, Ukrainians, Germans, Romanians, Gypsies, Hungarians and Jews settled amid the Ruthenians and were ruled in turn by the Russians and the Hungarians. Hence Maxwell was born into a world where languages were not a barrier and living among different nationalities was normal. But his religion was quite special.

Endemic anti-Semitism pervaded the whole of central Europe, but the Jews in Slatinske Doly led relatively peaceful lives except when Russian Orthodox priests delivered Easter sermons attacking the murderers of Christ. At the time of Maxwell's birth, most of Slatinske Doly's Jews were devoutly religious Hassidim who had abandoned their peasant clothes for long beards, frock coats and the large, round Shtreimel hat which is edged with pieces of fur. The Hochs were not Hassidic Jews but, like all the boys in the village, Maxwell wore a black skull cap day and night, with long ringlets of hair dangling in front of his ears. Under the disciplined leadership of the rabbis, Maxwell grew up amid the distinctive rituals of an Orthodox sect. With his parents and friends, he spoke Yiddish; at the daily religious classes, he learned Hebrew; and he duly learned a smattering of Hungarian and Ruthenian to converse with the neighboring goyim and some Czech in his teens.

The village's life had been abruptly changed in 1919, four years before Maxwell's birth, by the Allied leaders at the Versailles peace conference redrawing the map of Europe. Tomas Masaryk, Czechoslovakia's founding father, had arrived in France to negotiate the creation of the new state without contemplating the inclusion of Carpo-Ruthenia because its inhabitants were neither Czechs nor Slovaks. But, to his surprise, lobbyists representing the Carpo-Ruthenians who had recently emigrated to America pressured his delegation to embrace their homeland. Masaryk calculated that there were considerable advantages in pleasing the new Americans and agreed to their demands. Ninety thousand Jews who thought they were to become nationals of the Autonomous Soviet Republic of Pedkarpatska Rus, or Sub-Carpathian Russia, became instead citizens of the federal state of Sub-Carpathian Ruthenia within Czechoslovakia's stable democracy. The effect on Slatinske Doly's Jews was considerable. Suddenly, they were cut off from their neighbors in Sziget on the other side of the River Tisza and they had to shift their focus from Budapest to Bratislava and Prague. Slovaks and Czechs, eager for business, quickly began to search for opportunities, and the Jews, especially those in Slatinske Doly, soon suffered from the influx of investment.

Overnight, the Jews also experienced a fundamental change in their status. To avoid nationalistic tensions and remove any sense of allegiance toward Hungary, Masaryk's government granted the Jews Czech nationality but also allowed them to register as Jewish nationals. The recognition of Jews as a separate nationality coincided with an outburst of Zionism in eastern Europe by which Slatinske Doly, a transit center for Ukrainian and Polish refugees en route to Palestine, was particularly affected. The new Zionists, who were often also Communists, clashed passionately with Slatinske Doly's Jews. Maxwell grew up amid this unprecedented upheaval among the faithful.

The education of one's children, regardless of poverty, is an important pillar of Jewish tradition; although Maxwell maintained that he was "self-educated," he, like all the children of the village, received seven years' schooling albeit of a kind unlike any present-day model. To the irritation of the Jews, the Ruthenian schools in Slatinske Doly emphasized Christianity and the indigenous culture; so, since the village was too small to attract government funds, the Jewish community organized its own parallel education. Maxwell, like the other children, attended a local religious elementary school, the Heder, in the early morning, then went to the government school until 1 p.m. before returning to the Heder, which was held in a private house. Accordingly, unlike the Ruthenians, Maxwell was literate by the age of eight, initially in the Hebrew alphabet only. Throughout his life, he found handwriting difficult and his efforts were practically illegible. In the summers after school, Maxwell joined other children to play football with a rag ball, throw stones into the river, or climb mountains that in the wintertime they skied on primitively shaped pieces of wood. Children attended the village school only up to the age of eleven; thereafter most families sent their children to secondary religious schools known as Yeshivos in the larger towns. Mechel Hoch could not afford to send his son to the towns nor was he prepared to accept charity of another Jewish household. Maxwell was sent to an inferior Yeshivo in the village, where he is remembered by his friends as precocious, energetic and intelligent. But during the holidays, because the family was so big, Maxwell was sent to stay with relatives in nearby Kosice who worked in the timber business. Occasionally he remained in Kosice beyond the holidays and attended the local Hebrew school. The pressure for self-improvement, characteristic enough of Jewish families, had become more intense as a result of the village's birth-rate explosion coupled with a lower incidence of infant mortality. For Maxwell, one of seven children, it was obvious that he would need to make his own way since there was no family business. "We always knew that he would leave and make his fortune somewhere else," says Pearl. "He would have probably gone to his uncle in America because we all knew that there was no future in the village."

Maxwell became fond of ascribing his socialism to his mother's explanation for their extreme poverty. She blamed his father's "unemployment," says Maxwell, upon the government in Prague and upon the world's economic system. There was of course no such thing as "unemployment" in a peasant society. It was just that the gaps between Mechel's cattle deals had become longer, because Slatinske Doly was suffering a double crisis. There was a flood of cheap merchandise from Czechoslovakia which had undercut and bankrupted most of the Jewish artisans, with consequent effects on traders like Mechel; at the same time there was the worldwide economic depression. The people of Carpo-Ruthenia probably suffered more than most Europeans since their historical destitution left them without any resources to draw upon. All families in the village, including the Hochs, could rely upon the plethora of Jewish community charities which collected clothes and food and received a steady trickle of donations from the émigrés in America. But Pearl, and Hannah Hoch's cousin Lazar Schlomovitch, are convinced that Mechel was never destitute, especially after 1937 when Hannah's brother arrived from America and bought the family a three-room house. Moreover, as the village's general plight worsened there was a major source of relief—smuggling.

Although Sziget, the nearest town to Slatinske Doly, had become

Romanian, contact with its eight thousand Jews, one-third of the population, had been maintained despite the frontier and the River Tisza. Food and clothing prices, however, were never the same on both sides of the border because the Romanian government imposed different taxes. The tax on the slaughter of animals and on the sale of meat was usually higher in Romania and, as the price of meat rose, the obvious source for cheaper supplies was across the border.

For both the Jews and the Ruthenians in Slatinske Doly smuggling was, according to Rabbi Hugo Gryn who also lived in the area, "an honored trade" in which the whole community was involved. The village's butchers and cattle dealers were natural suppliers. Undoubtedly Maxwell, watching how the meat smugglers negotiated with their customers, would have been enormously intrigued.

Beneath a full moon, both horses and cattle were taken on to rafts, their hoofs wrapped in sacks and a bag of oats or other food fastened across their mouths. After the beasts had been landed on the other side, the real business began. Horse dealers, like their successors, car salesmen, are notorious for their promises, their exaggerated sales talk and their haggling. Smugglers negotiating in the moonlight would be engaged in even tougher and more ruthless dealings since their customers were well aware that the Czech Jew had little alternative but to sell his beast. The moonlit river-banks of Carpo-Ruthenia were an extraordinary site for a business school, but it was one location where Maxwell witnessed an unusual style of business, and his teacher was his grandfather, Yaacov Schlomovitch, who in many ways substituted for Mechel as Maxwell's father.

Schlomovitch was a dealer, a trader and a middle man. Whenever someone in the region had a need, he would seek to satisfy it by buying and selling the commodity in question, making his profit "on the turn." Watching his grandfather ceaselessly looking for business and haggling the two sides at both ends to increase the margin imbued Maxwell with the instinctive sense for dealing which refined businessmen in London and New York came to loathe and fear. The business philosophy that Maxwell learnt was quite simple: only the fittest can survive, and morality has no influence on a business deal.

Even if Adolf Hitler had not become Germany's Chancellor in 1933 and unleashed murderous waves of anti-Semitism across the continent, it is likely that Maxwell would have employed those skills. In jest, he has suggested that had the war not erupted he would have remained in the village and have become a rabbi. In fact, as Pearl, his closest friend in 1939, says, "We all would have left for a better life." The Holocaust caused unparalleled misery, but for a fortunate few the Jewish nation's terrible fate accelerated their careers.

The apprehension of the Nazi threat among the population in Carpo-Ruthenia was gradual. Slatinske Doly was so remote and the Czech government so uniquely protective that the region became a haven, albeit temporary, for Jewish refugees from Germany. By 1938, the climate had changed noticeably. Hitler was demanding the Sudetenland, the German-speaking part of Czechoslovakia, and the widespread attacks on Jews in Austria and in Germany caused the Czech Jews to realize the consequences if Hitler's demands were met. And met they were, under the Munich agreement that September. The following year the dismemberment of Czechoslovakia was complete. By March 1939, when Hitler drove triumphantly into Prague, only the poorer Jews, especially those in the east, remained behind. Most of the others had fled.

Under an agreement with Hitler, that part of Carpo-Ruthenia which included Slatinske Doly was returned to Hungary, and a company of Hungarian soldiers marched into the village on March 17. Although the Hungarian government would be generally more tolerant than other Nazi puppet states, the Jews were nevertheless targeted by new, virulently anti-semitic laws which included immediate conscription into labor battalions for most Jews of military age. The fate of those recruited was easy to imagine and the Hoch family, like many of their neighbors, recognized that there was no future for their sixteen-year-old son in the village. After the Passover holiday in April, Mechel and Hannah agreed that their son should look for work in Budapest. There was no heartbreak about his departure since everyone believed he would return for weekend visits. Both Maxwell and Alex Pearl were given money to buy a train ticket and they arrived in the Hungarian capital after a ten-hour journey. "We were amazed," recalls Pearl. "We had never seen paved roads, street cars, big houses or anything like it. It was terribly exciting." Maxwell was overwhelmed by the wealth he saw. They looked for a room to rent, then found jobs as delivery boys for shops. Soon they were set on breaking with their past. "We took off our 'cuples' and cut our hair so we didn't look so Jewish," says Pearl. "After all, when in Rome . . ." Maxwell had abandoned Orthodoxy and Slatinske Doly forever and was looking at the prizes which the big city could offer.

Maxwell and Pearl were together almost daily until Maxwell suddenly disappeared. Pearl says that he discovered "days later" that Maxwell had secretly left the city. In the version which Maxwell told Pearl in 1945, he had met a group of Czech soldiers in Budapest who intended to make their way to France. Maxwell lied that he was nineteen years old and, since he looked that age, they agreed that he might join them, on condition that he did not say farewell to his friends. In absolute secrecy, he traveled by train with the Czechs to Zagreb in Yugoslavia and continued on to Palestine.

In the 1960s, another version was issued in a press release on Maxwell's behalf: "The 16-year-old Hoch/Maxwell joined the Czech army, fought the Germans and the Russians in eastern Europe, made a fighting retreat across Europe to the Black Sea with the Czech forces and back to France via Bulgaria and Greece, in time for another crack at the Germans, was wounded and captured by the Nazis in Orleans and then escaped."

In 1969, Maxwell told the *Sunday Times* that in December 1939 he had been "tapped on the shoulder at a street corner" in Budapest after he had helped some Czech refugees who were escaping to Yugoslavia. He suggested that at the time he was part of the resistance and escaped a shooting squad for committing treason only because he was under eighteen.

Many other accounts were issued over the following years, until in July 1987 he was the guest on the BBC radio program *Desert Island Discs*. He explained, "I led Czech volunteers out of what was Czechoslovakia across Hungary into Yugoslavia on their way to joining the voluntary Czech army in France." He said that he was arrested, "tortured and beaten up and sentenced to death as a spy" but escaped the death penalty thanks to the intervention of the French ambassador and subsequently escaped imprisonment because his guard was handicapped with only one arm. Maxwell then escaped "into Yugoslavia, then Greece, Bulgaria, Turkey, Syria and Palestine to France and into the Czech army."

The differing accounts are confusing. First, there was no Czech resistance in 1939 fighting the Germans in Ruthenia or Budapest. In fact, there were no German soldiers at that time stationed in Hungary. Secondly, it is hard to understand why a sixteen-year-old Ruthenian who had never previously traveled through Hungary should have been involved in facilitating escapes since in 1939 many Czechs were paying to leave their homeland and traveled through Hungary. It was a favored route for many Jews heading for the safety of Palestine. Thirdly, since the train journey south from Budapest was legitimate, it is puzzling that adults should need a sixteen-year-old to "guide them by train."

Fourthly, by recently adding that he actually arrived in France via Palestine, it suggests that Maxwell followed the well-established route of thousands of Czechs who wanted to join the Czech Legion and eventually sailed for France, under British auspices, as an organized army. Fifthly, his latest version conflicts with the account he gave his best friend Pearl in 1945.

The confusion ends at Agde, west of Marseille. In all the versions, it is clear that he landed or arrived in France in early 1940. He told the *Sunday Times* that it was only then that he formally joined the Second Regiment of the Czech Legion in the name of Ludvik Hoch, but clearly if he sailed from Palestine he was already a member of the Legion. At all events, the Legion fought an undistinguished campaign before evacuating from Sète in May 1940 and sailing to Liverpool on an Egyptian ship, the *Mers el Kebir*.

Jan Horal, a Czech air force pilot, met the young Maxwell soon after his arrival in Britain at the Legion's base outside Dover. Horal was recruiting mechanics and was approached by Maxwell who explained that he was desperate to escape from the dreary camp life. According to Horal, Maxwell had every reason for trying to leave: "His fellow Czechs were chauvinist and anti-Semitic and had instinctively little fondness for an uneducated Ruthenian who looked like a ruffian and spoke a smattering of bad Czech." Horal, who saw Maxwell in Czech clubs several times subsequently during the war, had no doubt that Maxwell was "deeply disliked but was also not very likeable." When he turned down Maxwell's application "because you know nothing about engines," Maxwell persisted: "I can learn very fast." But Horal was adamant. The youth's chutzpah was disagreeable. It is the first recorded instance of Maxwell's ambition and self-confidence.

Horal's impressions are confirmed by a Legionnaire who told the *Sunday Times* in 1969 that the scarcely literate Maxwell seemed like "a wild young man from the mountains . . . quite unruly, like a young bull." Another remembered his astonishing curiosity: "He used to drive everyone wild, because he would follow you like a dog—trying to do anything one had just done, and to do it slightly better. If you jumped over a ditch, he would do so. He has this talent for taking what someone else has conceived and improving it slightly. It's a basic trait."

In 1941 Maxwell, realizing that his future with the Legion was limited, took the exceptional decision of applying to join the Pioneer Corps, known throughout the military as the "British army's coolies" because there was nothing lower. It was a gamble because the Corps offered only frustrating chores and no chance of fighting, yet it was Maxwell's only opportunity to escape from prejudice and insularity. Posted to a camp in Sutton Coldfield, Maxwell said that he learned English from a local woman in six weeks. Certainly by the end of two years, he had perfected the British mannerisms which he displayed from then on. Unlike many refugees, he had consciously and completely discarded his background and had become a student of the British way of life. His reward, in October 1943, was a posting to the Sixth Battalion of the North Staffs Regiment which was then based in Cliftonville on the south coast of England.

For a Czech national to be admitted as a private to a British regiment, even in wartime, was unusual. The Sixth was preparing for the Normandy landings and needed German-speaking officers to translate the enemy's intercepted radio messages. Maxwell had volunteered on the basis of his languages for precisely that duty but he had also, during the previous two years, become a fully trained soldier and, in particular, a marksman. Brigadier Gary Carthew-Yourston, the individualistic commanding officer of the 176th Infantry Brigade, which included the North Staffs, took an instant liking to the reformed ruffian and approved his recruitment to the battalion's Intelligence or "I" section. Carthew-Yourston's decision opened the way for Maxwell's subsequent career.

Maxwell arrived in Cliftonville as Private Leslie du Maurier, a name he had chosen from the brand of cigarettes, to disguise his true identity from the Germans. His serial number was 13051410. Most of the privates and NCOs in the battalion were potters and miners who lived around Stoke-on-Trent and were types with whom Maxwell could strike a friendly rapport since their limited education and narrow horizons mirrored his own. Major Albert Mitchell remembers du Maurier's arrival well: "He looked dark and slim just like his sons now. He spoke nearly fluent English and was assigned to the sniper section. We watched him very carefully in practice sessions and he showed great initiative, moving with agility." Recollections of the young du Maurier among the ranks are typified by Walter Smith, a sniper. He remembers Maxwell's interesting lectures about escaping from Europe, his keen interest in football and his regular wrestling bouts: "He was as strong as an ox." Maxwell acclimatized quickly and, unlike most of the battalion, used his weekend leave to travel regularly to London, earning himself a reputation, according to Mitchell, as "a great socializer."

By his twenty-first birthday in June 1944, Maxwell had been promoted to corporal with responsibility over seven men in a sniper unit; it was unusual for a Czech to be in command of British soldiers. Smith noticed how he relished the insignia of authority and the dispensation of power:

"Commanding people seemed to come naturally to him." The battalion was denied the excitement of the D-Day landings that June. Delayed by storms in the Channel, the battalion sailed in two groups on D + 16 from Margate and Tilbury, landing near Arromanches.

RSM Norman Champ traveled with Maxwell via Douvres toward the 59th Division, which was located opposite the German lines north of Caen. For the Staffordshire professional soldier, du Maurier was an "unusual character," especially because he took "quite unnecessary risks" as a field intelligence NCO. Champ recalls that most nights Maxwell disappeared across the German lines and reappeared at daybreak, often in a German uniform. "I told him," says Champ, "that he'd get himself shot. And then I became suspicious. I went to Colonel McWilkins [the battalion commander] and asked him straight out: 'This du Maurier, is he one of them or one of us?' " McWilkins agreed to "keep an eye on du Maurier" and promoted him shortly afterward to sergeant.

At 4:20 a.m. on July 8, the battalion launched its first attack against the German lines at La Bijoud. The fighting against dug-in Tiger tanks and 75mm anti-tank guns was bitter and confused, and it remained intense over the following four weeks. After skirting Caen to the west, the division fought against the German Panzers at Thury-Harcourt before heading southeast toward the Falaise Gap. Throughout the battle, the various reported sightings of Maxwell reveal an impassioned and energetic soldier. Jimmy Warrington spotted him in a dip organizing the salvage of a Wehrmacht truck; Walter Smith witnessed his fury when he discovered that a group of captured enemy troops whom he was interrogating were Czechs in German uniform; while RSM Champ saw Maxwell, occasionally using the name of "Jones," working directly for the "I" chief Captain Terry, "constantly disappearing across the lines." In the battle for Falaise, the casualties were enormous. "Apart from facing every known form of German weapon," says Champ, "we were also rocketed by our own Thunderbolts, machine-gunned from the air and were unpleasantly close to 500 lb bombs dropped on the wrong target." Champ was soon badly wounded, and both Colonel McWilkins and Terry were killed outright when a lorry filled with mines exploded. Maxwell fortunately survived unscathed and arrived in Paris soon after its liberation in September, renamed by then "Private Leslie Jones."

Few Allied soldiers who passed through the French capital en route to the Rhine left the city without lifelong memories of romance and splendor. Unlike London, the city was barely scarred by bombs, and everyone there, both liberators and liberated, was overwhelmed by emotion. For Maxwell, there was a happy reunion. Brigadier Carthew-Yourston, who had been relieved of his command of 176th Brigade, arrived in Paris to take command of British troops in the capital. Maxwell reintroduced himself and once again endeared himself to his mentor, who recommended that the young NCO should seek companionship from a French group called the Welcome Committee for Allied Personnel. Among the French personnel, acting as an interpreter, was Elisabeth (Betty) Meynard, the twenty-three-year-old daughter of a Protestant silk manufacturer from Lyon who during the war had traded in vegetables. Reminiscing about the circumstances of their meeting, Betty described the encounter as "love at first sight." During the weeks Maxwell remained in Paris, they made plans for the future. "When we realized that we were attracted to each other," recalled Betty, "one of the first things he ever said to me was that if anything ever happened out of our romance, it would happen in England." Then aged just twenty-one, Maxwell expounded his ambitions to his future wife. "The very first thing he told me was that he wanted to work in England, for England." His strategy was bold: "I want to make my fortune," he told Betty, "and then I want to go into Parliament." Thirty years later, Mrs. Maxwell was still astonished that the impoverished refugee had the determination to conceive and realize those ambitions.

Maxwell's ambition also deeply impressed Major-General L. O. Lyne, of the 59th (Staffordshire) Division, who recommended his promotion to second lieutenant. Simultaneously, Carthew-Yourston suggested that du Maurier and Jones were no longer suitable names. The Brigadier proposed a Scottish one, Robert Maxwell. Jan Hoch was not quite prepared to lose his identity completely and therefore adopted Ian as his first Christian name. Long after the war, Ian Robert Maxwell could not quite decide which Christian name to use.

It was usual for a soldier promoted from the ranks to be transferred to another regiment. Maxwell was posted to the Fifth Battalion of Queen's Royal Regiment (West Surrey) then stationed near Brussels. Carthew-Yourston's letter of introduction to the regiment was flattering: "This man has a very strong personality. He is well disciplined but will for various reasons give far better results if he has a certain amount of freedom of choice and movement than in a post where he is surrounded by too many rules and restrictions. His sense of duty is outstanding and his desire to kill Huns a driving force. I hope you will enjoy his company. I know that you have acquired a most valuable officer." While waiting for the next battle, Maxwell regularly traveled, on a captured German motorbike with a sidecar attached, from Belgium down to Paris to court Betty. Their relationship was interrupted in December when the regiment moved up toward Holland. In the midst of bitter, snowy weather he arrived at Vloed and introduced himself to his new commanding officer, Major D. J. Watson of "A" Company.

Watson remembers Second Lieutenant Maxwell as a "popular and outstanding officer" who quickly displayed the qualities which Carthew-Yourston described. The Fifth were preparing for a push toward the River Roer on a twelve-mile front, codenamed "Operation Blackcock," which would be supported by three armored groups. Conditions were worsening as Maxwell's battalion moved forward at 2 a.m. on January 17, 1945. A thaw had turned the snow into thick mud which, combined with fog and the darkness, frustrated their attempts to move their guns across the dykes. By daylight, the Germans were counter-attacking and in the fierce fighting many British lives were lost. During the day, the British position worsened, their casualties increased and the tanks sank further into the mud. It was twelve days into the attack that Maxwell's moment of destiny occurred. During the night of 29th/30th a large number of German troops crossed the river and successfully attacked a village which was occupied by Maxwell's battalion. It was a critical battle which was closely monitored by the senior staff at Corps headquarters. In fierce fighting, two platoons found themselves under heavy fire and effectively cut off. Maxwell, according to Watson, "splendidly led" his platoon in a frontal assault against the Germans now ensconced in the houses. By all accounts, Maxwell rushed a window under withering fire, and after killing the machine-gunner led a counter-attack, forcing the Germans to retreat with heavy losses. Major Watson was impressed by the "brisk and spirited action which is not mentioned in any history book" and recommended the young officer for an award. His citation read:

During the attack on Paarlo on January 29, 1945, Lieutenant Maxwell was leading his platoon when a heavy artillery concentration fell on and near the platoon killing and wounding several men. The attack was in danger of losing momentum, but this officer showing powers of leadership of the highest order controlled his men with great skill and kept up the advance. During the night another platoon of this company was counterattacked and partially overrun. An attempt to restore the position with another platoon failed but Lieutenant Maxwell repeatedly asked to be allowed to lead another attempt which request was eventually granted.

This officer then led two of his sections across bullet-swept ground with great dash and determination and succeeded in contacting the platoon who had been holding out in some buildings.

Showing no regard for his own safety he led his sections in the difficult job of clearing the enemy out of the buildings, inflicting many casualties on them, and causing the remainder to withdraw. By his magnificent example and offensive spirit this officer was responsible for the relief of the platoon; and the restoration of the situation.

Maxwell had fought courageously. The critical action had been so particularly closely followed by anxious chiefs at headquarters that they warmly endorsed Watson's recommendation. In March, Maxwell was awarded the Military Cross by Montgomery in person. He then drove to Paris, where on March 14 at the townhall of the sixteenth arrondissement, he married Betty. Carthew-Yourston was among the guests who watched the bride in a traditional white dress and veil, which Maxwell had raced around Paris to procure, pledge her vows. Possibly to impress his new in-laws, Maxwell told the deputy mayor to record in the marriage certificate that his father was an engineer rather than a cattle dealer.

Two weeks later, Maxwell was again in the midst of battle. His battalion formed part of Montgomery's final thrust across northern Germany toward Hamburg. On April 8, the battalion began a pincer movement against a company of the SS Training Division. Maxwell's own platoon killed no fewer than fifteen SS soldiers and took fourteen prisoners. After disjointed fighting against lackluster resistance, the regiment entered Hamburg on May 3. "When Hamburg was reached," records the official history, "the Battalion was weary, but the casualties had been so few that the fighting strength was hardly affected." Hostilities officially ceased five days later. For Maxwell, it had been a glorious war.

Because he was wounded soon after "Blackcock," Watson had not witnessed Maxwell's receipt of the MC but he does remember when they next met, soon after the German surrender. Maxwell was based at Iserlohn in the Ruhr interrogating prisoners of war. Maxwell's sister Sylvia, who had learned of her brother's whereabouts, arrived at the regiment's temporary headquarters but Maxwell had already moved on to Berlin. Sylvia and her sister Brana had remained hidden in Hungary throughout the war, but the remainder of the Hoch family had perished. The Holocaust had ravaged Slatinske Doly, but only in 1944. For the previous five years, the villagers had suffered increasing hardship. Most males were forced into labor units where many died, some as the victims of sadistic games played by the Hungarian guards, such as hosing water on to the workers in winter and watching their painful, freezing deaths. In the village itself, the women were compelled to watch a succession of executions, including those of some rabbis. Increasingly, they heard accounts from Polish refugees of the production-line killing through the gas chambers, but escape was by then too difficult. The true horror began on April 17, 1944, shortly after Adolf Eichmann's visit to Budapest. A ghetto was built in the center of the village and five thousand people were crammed inside; fifteen to twenty people were assigned to each room of the small houses. The brutality, sadism and torture which the villagers suffered during the ensuing four weeks was, according to the survivors, worse than anything they endured at Auschwitz extermination camp, to which they were transported on May 20 and 23. Most of those who tumbled out of the packed cattle trucks and saw the flames spouting from the crematoria's chimneys were gassed the same day. Among them was Hannah Hoch. Her husband escaped the gas but was shot dead. Maxwell learned of his parents' deaths when he drove to Prague in the summer of 1945 to discover the fate of his family. Strangely, for the next forty years he showed little public interest in the Holocaust, but felt guilt that while he had survived and enjoyed a "good" war, his family had suffered so catastrophically.

For all refugees, the end of the war produced a mixture of emotions—the joy of victory was tinged by sorrow for those who had been murdered. Until May 1945, there is little doubt that Maxwell, like most front-line soldiers, accepted that he would quite probably die in battle. But having escaped the poverty of Slatinske Doly, the Holocaust and the perils of the battlefield, he sensed that he was thereafter living on borrowed time. All the anguish, the humiliations and the defeats which he would endure during the remainder of his life could always be rationalized by the thought that fate, or in his words "the Gods," had been particularly kind. It is a sentiment which can only be properly appreciated by those who have shared his experience. Consequently, during those first weeks in Berlin, Maxwell's hitherto exclusive preoccupation with survival was replaced, despite the self-confident image which developed in later years, by a temporary uncertainty about his future. Unlike the majority of his fellow officers, there was no home beckoning to him. As a penniless nobody, he was unsure about his ambitions. Only the army, where his status was established, offered glowing prospects.

After Germany's defeat the victors could enjoy almost unlimited spoils. For a single packet of cigarettes, the officers of the occupying armies could buy an extravagant lifestyle. A simple scrap of paper decorated with a military stamp and signature was sufficient to requisition any house, its entire contents and the Mercedes in the garage. Throughout Germany, the most menial Allied officer lived in a style to which he was unaccustomed. Copious supplies of food, alcohol and entertainment were on tap while the Germans themselves struggled to survive starvation and illness. Understandably, for the Allied soldiers who had survived the war and seen the horrors of the concentration camps, there were few pangs of conscience about the way their enemy was treated. Maxwell had more reason than most to dislike the Germans and to relish the privileges which would disappear like melting butter if he returned to London and demobilization. If he remained in the army in Berlin, however, there were unrivaled opportunities which an ambitious and talented officer could exploit.

The government of occupied Germany (and, separately, of the city of Berlin) was divided between the four Allies. In its own zone, each Allied army wielded sovereign power, subject only to the Four Power agreement concluded at Potsdam in August 1945. In each of the three western zones, there was a sharp distinction between the regular army of occupation which was responsible for security and combat in any future conflict, and the section of the military which had replaced all the former civilian ministries of the deposed German government. That section was called the military government, known in the British zone as the Control Commission. Politically, the Control Commission was answerable to the Foreign Office in London but it was staffed by military officers, who either were on secondment from the regular army or, as was increasingly the case, were civilians enjoying temporary military rank. By October 1945, there were no less than twenty-four thousand British officers employed by the Control Commission whose responsibilities covered education, health, the judiciary, transportation, de-Nazification and housing. In effect, the military government officers were dictators who wielded enormous power with little occasion to answer for their decisions. In the exercise of this almost unfettered discretion they could either enrich or impoverish a German individual or business.

The quality of those temporary British civil servants was dramatically uneven. Initially, among the higher echelons were talented and impassioned idealists who were dedicated to the rebuilding of a sound democracy. Many were middle-aged men unfit for combat but deemed to possess the special talents needed to govern the defeated enemy. After inadequate briefing during the last months of the war, they arrived in Germany ill prepared for their task, if only because no Allied planner had foreseen the sheer scale of devastation and demoralization which would be inflicted upon the enemy. But as demobilization rapidly robbed the Commission of those qualified staff, many of their replacements were less able men attracted by the promise of privilege and high reward which would be barred to them in Britain. Unmotivated by any higher calling, they exploited their power. It was in that atmosphere that Maxwell had to work during the summer of 1945.

Initially, Maxwell had continued with Field Security duties of interrogating Germans but he possessed one talent which enjoyed an important premium in the British occupation army—his ability to make himself understood in nine languages. His claim to fluency in so many languages was, characteristically, an exaggeration that survived unchallenged, since few British officers spoke German and hardly any spoke Czech, Hungarian, Russian, Polish, Ruthenian and Romanian. His languages, war record and self-presentation made him an ideal candidate for the army's information control section, which in the British sector in Berlin was organized by a section of the Control Commission known as the Public Relations and Information Services Control or PRISC, situated in Berlin's Klaus Grothstrasse. PRISC's more important task was acting as a cultural licensing agency. Germans who wanted to show films, stage plays or publish books and newspapers had to obtain permission from PRISC, whose discretion was guided by two objectives: first, the eradication of every vestige of Nazi philosophy from Germany's cultural life, and second, the reintroduction among the Germans of democratic aspirations. To that end, priority was given to the re-establishment of diverse and liberal newspapers edited by German journalists. Maxwell was appointed Berlin's press chief by Colonel "Red" Edwards, head of PRISC in the city. It represented the end of his association with any British Intelligence activities and his introduction to a profession which would shape the rest of his life.

Among those who applied for a license to publish a newspaper in the British sector of Berlin was Arno Scholz, then forty-one years old, whose proposed newspaper would be called *Der Telegraf.* Scholz was an independent socialist who until 1933 had written for *Vorwärts,* a left-wing newspaper. Soon after Hitler's election he had been arrested and, although later released, he was forbidden to work throughout most of the war. His application was considered by Nicholas Huijsman, the South African-born PRISC officer who was in charge of the press section for the whole British zone, and then by Edwards. After careful vetting, a license was issued on March 12, 1946. Maxwell's role in that process is uncertain. In 1969, Maxwell told the *Sunday Times,* "I had nothing to do with licenses. I certainly could do no such thing as help get a license for *Der Telegraf.* It had a license already." The actual dates are at variance with Maxwell's version, and Huijsman says that the recommendation for awarding the license was forwarded to him by Maxwell. Maxwell's reluctance to take any credit remains puzzling.

To obtain the precious permit, Scholz guaranteed to PRISC that both he and his journalists would submit to total censorship by the Control Commission. It was Scholz's good fortune that the officer appointed to supervise the *Telegraf*'s operations in their ramshackle premises spread over the suburb of Wilmersdorf was Robert Maxwell, recently promoted to captain. In theory Maxwell's job was, in Huijsman's words, "completely negative." Each article of the newspaper had to be vetted to exclude any offensive comments about the four Allied powers or the Control Commission. The temptation for any British officer was to control the newspaper's balance very strictly but Huijsman is certain that Maxwell was generously restrained and intervened on only a minimum of occasions. At 3 a.m. the young officer would solemnly "press the button for democracy" and the printing presses would roll. In retrospect, Maxwell's determinedly laissez-faire attitude contrasts oddly with his later interventionist behavior, but this liberalism was undoubtedly spawned by his admiration for Scholz, with whom he formed a friendship which was to prove as important as his earlier relationship with Carthew-Yourston.

Maxwell's contemporaries in the Control Commission had by then recognized his intelligence, energy and instinct, but they were also suspicious of his successful transformation into an ostensibly impeccable Englishman. Yet, inevitably, because of his apparent fluency and self-confidence, they overlooked his emotional need for a mentor and father-figure. Denied a respected male teacher (other than his grandfather) whose example and advice he could depend upon during his childhood, Maxwell was naturally attracted in Berlin to anyone who could compensate for that lack. Although Scholz was not Jewish, he did share a certain common heritage with Maxwell, and by all accounts the Berliner spent many hours talking to the Czech, molding his political outlook and trying to satisfy his appetite for a vehicle which would provide him with both a fortune and power. Like so many others in Berlin, Scholz was besieged by Maxwell's requests for introductions to important people which he obliged because he liked Maxwell, upon whom he depended daily to further his own ambition to create a successful newspaper.

PRISC's license permitted Scholz to publish the newspaper but did not guarantee him the means for printing and distribution. In common with all German industry amid the postwar chaos, Scholz faced an hourly struggle. Production was constantly interrupted by breakdowns and by the absence of replacements for broken parts of the printing presses. Paper and ink were severely rationed and there were strict daily limits on the allocation of electricity. Often, even these slender quotas could not be fulfilled. Scholz was entirely dependent upon the British military government in the person of Maxwell, who would have to use his influence and ingenuity to find a solution somewhere in the city's devastation. In Huijsman's view, "Maxwell was marvelous at it." In addition, to give "his" newspaper an advantage, Maxwell acted for the first and only time as a journalist, using his rank (according to Huijsman) to "worm out" from military government officials good stories which the *Telegraf* could publish.

The results were hugely successful. According to a confidential Control Commission survey, up to 260,000 copies of the eight-page tabloid were sold six days a week, making it the best-selling newspaper in the British sector. Sixty thousand copies were sold daily in the Soviet zone and a reported 300 copies were flown to Moscow. Within two months of its launch, it incorporated its competitor, *Der Berliner*. Scholz, with firm British support, was destined to build a flourishing business, coincidentally inspiring Maxwell's appetite to own a newspaper. Maxwell did not always reflect his subsequent image as an energetic, nascent newspaper owner, especially in his dealings with Soviet officers who were based in the eastern zone of the city. Maxwell's relationship with the Russians in Berlin has often excited curiosity due to the paucity of information. Since his childhood had been spent near the Soviet border, it was natural that Maxwell would have found much in common with Russian soldiers, especially since he spoke their language and shared many of their customs and attitudes. As relief from the austere, class-conscious British officers, Maxwell escaped for entertainment to drink with his former neighbors, some of whom he met when he subsequently traveled to Russia on business. That camaraderie was witnessed on one of the more official occasions by Detlev Raymond, who later became one of Maxwell's employees.

Elections were due to be held on October 20, 1946, for the city's assembly and each military power was entitled to appoint observers in the other three zones to monitor the voting. Maxwell was chosen as the British representative in the Soviet sector. According to Raymond, Maxwell was found on election day to be ensconced with a Russian colonel completing a three-day alcoholic and gastronomic orgy. When his supervisory task was completed, according to Raymond, Maxwell returned to his standard duties in the British sector. But his relationship with the Russians, according to the KGB, was not simply social.

Apparently, at one stage during his posting in Berlin, either willingly or unwillingly, Maxwell compromised himself with the Russians. The KGB claim that the young officer signed a document which promised to assist the security agency if required. Since everyone involved in the incident is said to be dead, the circumstances are unclear but the existence of a document seems certain, although it was soon forgotten by both sides.

Maxwell in the meantime was laying the foundations for a stable family life. Betty had arrived in Berlin and was living in a requisitioned flat in what was known among the British staff as the "ghetto"—an area exclusively reserved for Allied officers. Other than work, most of his fellow officers felt there was little more to do than to enjoy the endless succession of parties hosted by the military representatives of one of the four powers and by his fellow British officers. Huijsman remembers seeing Maxwell, "a very handsome and personally very charming officer," at least twice a week at social and formal gatherings, and the two became quite close. When Maxwell's first child Michael was born, both Scholz and Huijsman became his godfather. At the christening party, Huijsman's subordinate confessed his true ambition: "He confided to me that he wanted to become a millionaire." Huijsman was apparently unaware that Maxwell had already made his first steps in that direction.

In July 1946, Maxwell was demobbed from the army, but he had already agreed to continue working for PRISC in Berlin as a Control Commission officer wearing a military uniform and retaining the rank of captain. While in Britain during the summer, completing his formal demobilization, Maxwell consummated an arrangement he had made months earlier. On September 18, 1945, a small, £100 company had been incorporated in London. It was called Low-Bell Limited, and its founding director was a Czech refugee called Arnos Lobl. The history of Low-Bell is puzzling but it is fitting that the very first company of which Maxwell became a director should be shrouded in a mystery which would be consistently reproduced on so many occasions during his commercial career.

Although Low-Bell was a trading company, during its first year Lobl did not carry out any business. On August 22, 1946, the directors of Low-Bell, notably Arnos Lobl, held an extraordinary meeting and passed two resolutions: first, to double the number of shares issued by the company to two hundred, and then to grant the power to increase the number of shares to a total of 10,000. The following month, on September 12, Maxwell was formally recorded as owning ninety shares in Low-Bell, while Lobl personally retained a majority of 110 shares. Although Maxwell was still at the time employed by the Control Commission in Berlin and was not living in London, he described himself on the formal document as a merchant who was resident at 21 Stanley Gardens, London W11. The mystery deepened in December when three additional shareholders appeared; again this is consistent with the procedure in Maxwell's later business career, with people casually entering and exiting as directors and employees of his companies. On this first occasion, they were a retired bank manager called John Stratton-Ferrier, a family friend, Paul Raque from Paris and Ladislau Skaloud, described as a merchant who lived in Prague. Their object was to start trading between Britain and Europe.

Lobl, like many Jewish refugees in Britain, lacked any professional qualifications, but appreciated the enormous opportunities for earning a living in straightforward business deals. Like continental Europe, Britain was suffering acute shortages and there was a demand for anything which was manufactured, imported or grown. Even a modest entrepreneur could earn a decent income simply by knowing where and how to buy. Selling was never a problem.

Maxwell returned to Germany and Lobl rented tiny premises in Grand Buildings, Trafalgar Square. Low-Bell's office was crowded even with only two people inside. There was no daylight because the window was covered by an advertising billboard for cinema films. When Low-Bell occupied the office the ad was for Ivor Novello's musical *Perchance to Dream*—a fitting motto for the shareholder resident in Berlin.

Whether Maxwell, on his return to Germany, immediately started dealing on Low-Bell's behalf is unknown—although always suspected by British officers in Berlin—but two months later he became the company's majority shareholder, owning three hundred shares over Lobl's two hundred. Even Maxwell himself could never explain how he identified his first business opportunities. The critical ingredient in his transformation from peasant to tycoon was his remarkable ability to speedily absorb information and learn from the examples of others. Simultaneously, he targeted and then seduced those individuals whose position and influence could advance his career. Driven by inordinate ambition, and fearless of failure, he understood how to exploit the possibilities in occupied Germany that most others ignored. While Scholz built up his newspaper, Maxwell constantly hunted for opportunities, traveling frequently into the Soviet zone, on one occasion visiting the relaunched Leipzig book fair which in the pre-Hitler period had had the same status as the present annual Frankfurt fair. The trip awakened his interest in the business of books, but when he formally resigned from the Commission on March 15, 1947, he was still unsure how he was to make his fortune.

Maxwell explained his resignation to the *Sunday Times* in 1969 as having been caused by a clash with his superiors. He claimed that he was opposed to the Soviet dismantling of German industry and consequently allowed the *Telegraf* to publish anti-Soviet stories which in the period before the Cold War was against Allied laws. His decision, he said, provoked a row with his superiors but Huijsman recalls a friendly parting of the ways occasioned by Maxwell's desire to construct his peacetime career. In any event, Maxwell packed for his return to England armed with his army gratuity and an idea. On the eve of his departure, he telephoned John Kisch, another Czech working for PRISC as the press chief in Düsseldorf. Although the two had never met, they had occasionally spoken on the telephone and Kisch knew Maxwell's reputation as a man with the ability to "fix the impossible." Maxwell suggested to his fellow Czech that they might join forces in a business venture when Kisch returned to London. Kisch agreed.

Kisch arrived at Low-Bell's offices in Trafalgar Square in the summer of 1947 to discover that Maxwell had established a new company, the European Periodicals, Publicity and Advertising Corporation. EPPAC's initial business was to import German newspapers to Britain for sale to German prisoners of war anxious for information about their homeland. Maxwell had seen the value of the idea at the beginning of the year when George Houghton, a senior officer in Berlin, had asked him to negotiate the sale of the *Telegraf* with another London company. But Huijsman had agreed, just before Maxwell left Berlin, that he would be granted the concession, and EPPAC was registered with the military government as an official distributor. Maxwell was in business. Recognizing that his future would never be in editing or writing for a newspaper, he had started as a trader.

Using a huge, gray Dodge still bearing its Berlin military registration plates, Maxwell or Kisch regularly collected the newspapers from Victoria railway station and wearily toured around Britain's POW camps, driving as far as Bridgend in South Wales, where the top Nazi generals were incarcerated. Although sales were healthy, both realized that their business suffered the fatal flaw of a diminishing clientele. Maxwell nevertheless applied on EPPAC's behalf to join the Publishers Association, the elite club of British book publishers. His request was promptly rejected.

Kisch noticed that Maxwell regarded the newspaper distribution as just one of several ventures. Every month, as the director of Low-Bell, Maxwell obtained one ton of caustic soda from ICI for £47. Like every commodity, caustic soda was in short supply and Maxwell found no difficulty in reselling his precious allocation in the Far East for £98. That was a monthly income nowadays worth £1,000, ample for a comfortable living.

Maxwell evidently thrived on those first business ventures, applying—it seemed to some eyewitnesses—the same reckless bravery to his pursuit of fortune as had earned him such commendation in wartime. He displayed a natural talent for trading and a bull-like determination to overcome the confusing multitude of banking and Customs controls which dominated international trade in the post-war era. Yet those who knew him in 1947 are convinced that he was, despite his deals, living way beyond his means. They did not know that his uncle was sending regular payments from America. Nevertheless, Maxwell left Kisch and others in cold fear. Only those who understood that his primitive background excluded any sense of embarrassment or fear of poverty could understand the style. But even they found the pace he set daunting.

In autumn 1947, Maxwell traveled to Berlin. He returned with a new venture which was his key to becoming a millionaire. The business needed new premises and he moved out of Grand Buildings and into ¾ Studio Place, off Kinnerton Street in Knightsbridge. The annual rent at £350 was more than either Maxwell or his partner had ever possessed. Kisch, his nerves outstripped, bid fond farewell and headed for Fleet Street. Maxwell was unmoved. He had new partners in mind for his fortune-making venture.

2

On October 16, 1947, Maxwell arrived at the dilapidated headquarters of the world's largest scientific publishers Ferdinand Springer in West Berlin's Jebenstrasse. At that moment, Ferdinand Springer's business was in ruins, both literally and metaphorically. According to Vernon Baxter, who worked for Maxwell in the early post-war years, it was Arno Scholz who had explained to his protégé the value of German scientific book exports. "Scholz told him," recalls Baxter, "if you help re-establish the trade, the trade will kiss your feet." What followed would change Maxwell's life forever.

The origins of the Springer publishing house, which has no connection with the Axel Springer newspaper group, were laid in May 1842 when Julius Springer opened a bookshop in Berlin. By 1907, when Julius' grandson Ferdinand inherited the small family business, the revolution in science and engineering was gathering momentum throughout the world. Perceiving that German scientists lacked a specialist publisher, Ferdinand personally introduced himself to selected leading experts and offered his services. Within twenty years, because of Germany's position as a pathfinder in science, industry and engineering, Springer swiftly developed a very lucrative world market for his books. Among his stars, including several Nobel Prize winners, were the first works written by Paul Ehrlich, Karl von Frisch, Max Born, Max Planck and Albert Einstein. But his fortune was earned not only in single volumes, but in publishing whole series of books edited by eminent panels of German experts. Springer's Beilstein series on chemistry, medicine, psychology, mathematics, engineering and physics was purchased by every reputable library throughout the world. For practitioners, Springer's publications on the natural sciences were standard textbooks, and after each regular revision the demand for the books was renewed.

Simultaneously, Springer began publishing a wide range of learned journals containing short articles by doctors, scientists and researchers which described their most recent work and their discoveries. Springer found that the same libraries which subscribed to the books were eager customers for his journals. The economics were also extremely attractive: unlike most business payments, subscriptions to journals were paid in advance of delivery, which guaranteed a healthy and positive cash flow.

As the world's interest in science expanded and the demand for Springer's books and journals grew, the publisher realized another bonus. New libraries and universities opening around the world not only started buying Springer's current books and journals, but also wanted to stock their shelves with their past publications. Known as "back issues," the older journals were by definition rarer than the current issues and consequently more valuable. The earnings on trading single, rare issues or buying incomplete sets at reduced rates and adding the missing journals for resale as a prestigious investment were high. To capitalize on growing demand, Springer printed more journals than he could immediately sell as a calculated speculation that the surplus stock would be sold in the future at considerable profit. In 1932, the last year of free trade, Springer's sales were bigger than the combined total of the remaining world's scientific publishers.

Hitler's accession to power in January 1933 changed Springer's business overnight. An immediate ban was imposed on sharing Germany's scientific secrets with the rest of the world. Although articles describing experiments and theories would still be written, their circulation would be strictly limited. But Ferdinand and his cousin Julius, who was a partner in the business, had a more pressing problem. Both were part-Jewish. By applying the detailed criteria established by the Nazis to determine a German's racial origins, Ferdinand was deemed a half-Jew and Julius three-quarters. For completely assimilated and loyal Germans like the Springers, the shock of being branded an enemy by one's own countrymen was considerable. Like so many German Jews, Ferdinand immediately sought allies among his Aryan friends to protect himself and his business from the law. Initially, because of his worldwide reputation as a prestige exporter, Ferdinand's efforts were successful and the Nazis granted a special permit for him to continue as before. But in 1935, following the enactment of the Nuremberg Laws which explicitly discriminated against Jews, Julius was forced to sell his shares in his company.

The purchaser was Tönjes Lange, a senior manager in the company who had been exclusively concerned with managing the business while the Springers had maintained direct contacts with their authors. Lange, as Maxwell would discover in 1947, was an exceptionally sensitive and generous person. His arrangement with Julius was that, should they both survive the Nazi era, Julius could repurchase his interest in the company. Soon after, Julius was arrested and sent to Oranienburg concentration camp from which he would later be released. In the meantime, Ferdinand and Lange managed the business. In November 1942, Ferdinand too was finally forced to sell his own shares. He made the same unofficial agreements with Lange as Julius had concluded. At this juncture, Springer's Vienna branch was officially sold to Tönjes's brother Otto Lange for 600,000 marks. Only a fraction of the amount was paid and Otto solemnly promised to return the business to Ferdinand after the war. For a time, while Springer was managed by the two Lange brothers, Ferdinand stayed in Berlin, but in 1944 he fled to a remote farm in Pomerania until he was arrested by the advancing Red Army.

By then Lange, with Ferdinand's agreement, had organized the physical survival of Springer's business. As the Allied bombing of the capital intensified, sixty-three thousand books, the tens of thousands of handbooks and invaluable antiquarian series and journals, together worth in pre-war prices £6 million, had been transported out of the city for safe-keeping. Some went by road to a huge warehouse one hundred kilometers south of Berlin in Lausitz and, to spread the risk, the remaining stock was sent to several other sites, especially to Vienna, where under Otto's supervision the "iron reserves" were safely hidden in Starein for the remainder of the war.

By the end of the war, Lange's efforts had proved invaluable. Not only had Springer's warehouses in Berlin suffered like most of the city from bombs, fire and flooding, but the publishing headquarters in the Linkstrasse, which had, although damaged, miraculously survived, was sited precisely on the border between the Soviet and British sectors. The building was located in Soviet territory while the front door opened on to the pavement in the British sector. Diplomatic niceties were irrelevant during the first weeks of peace when the Red Army exclusively occupied Berlin, and Lange watched helplessly as a specialist Soviet plunder squad arrived to load £1 million worth of books on to a convoy of trucks for shipment to Moscow. By the time the western Allies arrived, little of Springer's stock in Berlin remained to be looted.

The Allies' interest in Springer's books was not surprising. At the beginning of the war, both British and American soldiers, sailors and airmen had suffered serious disadvantages because the military chiefs' chauvinism had falsely convinced them of the superiority of their own weapons. Yet with the possible exception of radar, German scientists and engineers had outclassed their Allied competitors in the design of military hardware from airframes, jets and tanks to submarines, guns and rockets. German superiority was reflected not only in the new weapons thrown against the Allies, but also in the revolutionary new chemicals, metals, fuels and gases which German industry had invented. In the period between Montgomery's victory at Alamein and the invasion of France, an Anglo-American plan was conceived to plunder German science and industry. Hence, following close behind the waves of Allied soldiers who landed on the Normandy beaches were the first of thousands of specialists whose principal task over the next three years was to investigate the wealth of Germany's scientific secrets. Naturally, Springer's old customers also wanted to know what progress German experts in their particular areas had covered during the twelve years of the Third Reich and Springer was understandably keen to satisfy their demands.

Ferdinand returned to Berlin as a Russian prisoner in April 1945 but he was released one month later. Reunited with Lange, he agreed that they should divide the ownership of the business. Both quickly realized the gigantic hurdles they faced to restart their business. The chaos and devastation in Berlin were overwhelming and everything was tightly controlled by the occupying armies. The Allies, as General Eisenhower proclaimed, were conquerors. They felt little compassion for the Germans and officially none whatsoever for those who had prospered under the Nazis. Nevertheless, Allied policy was to encourage the reopening of non-military industries to prevent Germany becoming a heavy financial burden on the Allies themselves. Springer's new headquarters, in the Reichpietschufer, were located in the British sector, but their initial application for a license to PRISC in summer 1945 was unsuccessful. Some Springer executives believed that the British were suspicious that Ferdinand, despite his Jewish background, must have collaborated at a high level with the Nazis to survive in Berlin until 1944. There were even suggestions that Lange had made a serious attempt to obtain a testimonial from a Vatican bishop that Springer was not a Nazi sympathizer. But in this case, since it was British policy to encourage scientific publishing, for both Britain's and Germany's benefit, PRISC was ordered to ignore the past and Springer was awarded a license on October 24, 1945. In practice the license meant very little. Without telephones, petrol, paper or access to printing presses, Springer's business remained paralyzed. Yet orders were beginning to arrive from all over the world for Springer's back issues and new journals. In November 1946, when Maxwell was still an officer in Berlin, the Control Office in London had telexed that there was "concern about the lack of scientific learned journals coming from Germany to UK. We consider that this should be pressed forward vigorously." However hard Maxwell attempted to implement that directive, he failed because the resources were unavailable. But he had registered the implications of the urgent messages.

In 1946, Tönjes Lange believed that Springer's best hopes for recovery lay in the Russian zone. In the pre-Cold War period, travel between the zones was relatively easy and Lange's assistant Paul Hövel began negotiating with the Soviet authorities to start printing a series of journals and books which had been planned during the last year of the war. Simultaneously, Lange personally began discussions with the Soviets for releasing Springer's stocks in Lausitz, which was in the Russian zone. But Ferdinand decided that Berlin's isolation hampered his relations with his authors and he moved near to the home of Karl Jaspers in Heidelberg in the American zone to establish a new editorial headquarters.

It is not quite clear exactly when Maxwell met Lange and Springer for the first time but Hövel remembers that during 1946 Maxwell was often approached by Ferdinand or Lange at PRISC for help in obtaining allocations, especially paper. Maxwell's duties would have been to judge the assistance Springer should receive and the company's success in securing its share of the rations depended upon the personal relationship developed with Captain Maxwell. Ferdinand and Tönjes Lange, who were both by nature traditional and conservative, were hugely impressed by the handsome, self-confident, German-speaking British captain. By all accounts, by the time Maxwell formally resigned from the Control Commission, his relationship with the two men was quite close, especially that with Tönjes Lange, whom Maxwell would later come to regard as a father-figure and address with fondness as "Onkel."

By October 1947, when Maxwell returned to Berlin, Lange had become desperate. The war had ended more than two years before but his business suffered an insurmountable obstacle. A few new journals were being printed in the Soviet zone and the demand for back issues and antiquarian books was overwhelming not only from libraries but also from astute investors as a hedge against the worthless German currency. Yet he was unable to send the journals and books out of Germany to his customers. An attempt in July to dispatch some parcels had been frustrated by the Allied insistence that all exports had to be in bulk rather than sent as single items. Springer needed someone outside Germany who could distribute the journals to its customers in over twenty countries. On October 16, 1947, with Maxwell's arrival, Springer Verlag was blessed with a golden opportunity denied to its competitors. Maxwell proposed that he should act as their representative abroad. "Maxwell's arrival and offer," recalled Paul Hövel, "was at a most opportune moment." According to Lange, Maxwell's offer was "the only hope for rebuilding our company." Others believe that a tentative agreement had already been concluded between Maxwell and Lange in spring 1947 and that this was the cause of his resignation from PRISC to establish the export network. Maxwell's own account is that the initial offer was made by Lange and that his interest in scientific publishing was purely scientific, sparked by the atomic explosion at Hiroshima. Since Hövel's version was recorded shortly after the event, it is likely to be the most reliable.

Despite all the tension and conflict which would follow, Springer was forever grateful to Maxwell: over the following nine years their joint business was worth DM 20 million. "Never will the Springer Publishing House," recorded an internal memorandum written in July 1959,

> forget the help which Captain Maxwell gave us. . . . Throughout that time, Captain Maxwell always had good advice, solved the most difficult problems and was the person who was primarily responsible between 1947 and 1949 for re-establishing us as publishers. . . . In those terribly difficult times after Maxwell made his first offer, the drastic and successful methods invented by the British Captain (with an MC) produced unimaginably successful solutions to overcome those conditions so we could start exporting again.

Springer faced three fundamental problems: first, to produce new journals; secondly, to regain control over its huge stocks which had survived the war; and thirdly, to obtain permission to trade outside Germany. On the first problem, as we have seen, Maxwell as a PRISC officer gave Springer help in the course of his duties. It was Maxwell's successful efforts to solve the second and third problems which became controversial.

The reason why Hövel described Maxwell's arrival as "opportune" was that Lange had just negotiated with the Russians the release of the valuable stock in Lausitz. Hövel is unclear about the details of transporting the books and journals by truck to West Berlin but it is certain that during the October visit Maxwell and Lange agreed that EPPAC should own the exclusive worldwide distribution rights of Springer's journals and books. Ferdinand, who was always wary of Maxwell, hesitated before endorsing the agreement because he feared Maxwell's total inexperience. The young ex-officer, Ferdinand felt, lacked the staff to wrap and address the packets and lacked the refinement to develop the personal contacts with Springer's traditional and valuable customers. Before signing, he insisted that Lange should try to organize another mass mailing operation of a few copies of its new journals to its most important pre-war customers. With Maxwell's help, a special dispensation was secured to dispatch 369 separate packets from Germany to EPPAC in London for onward shipment. The results, both sides agreed, proved that it was not a realistic, long-term solution. Therefore with Ferdinand's wholehearted support, Lange formally registered the publisher's agreement with Maxwell on November 18, 1947. It fell to Maxwell to secure the crucial export permits and arrange the transport for the contents of the Lausitz warehouse. He launched himself like a whirlwind, desperately keen for his new venture to succeed. "Undoubtedly," recalled Hövel, "it would not have been possible to start exporting on that scale without the influence which Captain Maxwell could exert over key officials."

Under the Allied laws of the occupation, all Germany's trade was controlled by the Anglo-American Joint Export-Import Agency (JEIA), based in Frankfurt. As part of the Allies' rigorous control of the German economy, everything which was bought and sold abroad had to be filtered through British and American officials at JEIA. The agency regularly published details of Germany's import needs and awaited tenders for their supply from Allied industrialists and businessmen. Similarly, nothing could be exported without JEIA's permission and at an agreed price. Since the only credible currency in Germany was cigarettes or chocolate, JEIA had to ensure that German industry obtained a fair price for its exports and, similarly, that its Allied competitors were not undercut. Consequently the true price depended upon the exchange rate between the discredited Reichsmark and the pound or dollar. The rates in 1947 were not officially fixed, but JEIA's normal rate was thirteen marks to one pound. Although the details of Maxwell's negotiations are no longer available, it is indisputable that Maxwell, after obtaining JEIA permission to export Springer's journals, obtained in early December 1947 the exchange rate of twenty-one marks for each pound, a 60 per cent advantage which would substantially increase Maxwell's profits. As later episodes demonstrate, Maxwell probably used the contacts which he had forged as a Control Commission officer to obtain the satisfactory terms. He most likely convinced officials that since it was Allied policy rapidly to disseminate German scientific knowledge, the journals' prices should be kept quite low. On the export license itself, an official noted that the special rate was agreed "after discussion." But Springer would not get any of the benefits of that exchange rate. Nor their customers. "Captain Maxwell," commented an astounded Hövel, "obtained an extraordinarily favorable exchange rate."

Within days of Maxwell's coup, a formal protest about Springer's contract was sent from a Dutch publisher to PRISC's director Kenneth Kirkness at his headquarters in Berlin. Frans von Eugen, the owner of *Excerpta Medica* of Amsterdam, had been granted by UNESCO the rights to publish medical abstracts for specialists and among them were Ferdinand's new journals officially published in Heidelberg, in the American zone. Maxwell's exclusive deal destroyed the Dutch hopes for a monopoly. "I sincerely hope," von Eugen wrote to Kirkness, "that you will use all your influence to frustrate this agreement and any such agreements which would be made in the future as they are ill suited for turning the intercourse between nations in the right channels." Following his letter, von Eugen arrived in Berlin armed with the claim that even the American authorities condemned both the agreement and the exchange rate. Kirkness evidently was unimpressed since less than one month later Maxwell and the Germans formalized and registered their new deal. By January 1948, it would be worth £2,387. By the end of the year, EPPAC had purchased books and journals valued at over one million marks which, converted at the special rate, equalled £47,750. Converted at present-day values, Maxwell had secured a contract worth over half a million pounds.

By early 1948, Springer's journals and books were arriving in London, transported, according to Hövel and Henrik Salle, another veteran Springer employee, by train from Berlin to Bielefeld and from there by truck. Since all transport was controlled by the British military, it is probable that Maxwell bribed British officials for both the permits and trucks to transport the books. To ensure the transport of 150 tons of journals and 150 tons of books, and to provide for future production, Maxwell had negotiated with the British authorities that Springer should be allocated 200 kilowatt hours of electricity, 20,000 kilos of coal for heating, 150,000 sheets of paper, 500 wooden crates and 50 kilos of nails. Springer was back in business and fast moving ahead of its competitors.

Distribution in London was the responsibility of Vernon Baxter, a German refugee whose original name was Blumenfeld and whom Maxwell had recruited on his return from Berlin in October 1947. When Baxter reported for work on his first day Maxwell had forgotten why he had been hired. "Maxwell asked me whether I could set up a book department," says Baxter. "With great cheek I said that I could, but I had no idea." Maintaining an accurate mailing list and sending accounts punctually required considerable organization, and more staff were hired. Most of the employees were Jewish refugees from central Europe, some of them successful professionals before the war and thus over-qualified, but nevertheless grateful for employment despite the low rates of pay and the spartan conditions. Maxwell felt comfortable surrounded by people who shared a similar background and it was important to have German-speakers to handle German publications. "We were bursting at the seams," recalls Baxter, "and then a new recruit arrived. He or she was expected to find a plank of wood and a chair and begin to work." Over the babble of German, Polish and Yiddish, the young Maxwell ruled serenely, nonchalantly ignoring the blatant improvisation. Sooner rather than later, all his employees recognized that Maxwell would brook no challenge. "He was the sun," commented an early transgressor, "and we were either planets or had to leave." The only exception was his partner, Peter Orton.

In contrast with Maxwell's extravagant character, Orton was a quiet-spoken intellectual who in Berlin before the war had been a member of the Communist Party. Peter Oppenheim, as he was then called, had gained comical notoriety as the cadre who had successfully robbed a cake shop to fill the party funds only to be arrested on a tip-off from the taxi driver who had driven him to the shop. He had met Maxwell in the Queen's Regiment, where Orton had been the sergeant to Second Lieutenant Maxwell. Their relationship would never change. "Orton hero-worshiped Maxwell," recalls another Berliner who worked in the office. "For Orton, as for everyone else, Maxwell was a born leader." But behind Maxwell's back, Orton often voiced dislike and criticism of his senior partner's brash gambles. Long before his first major crisis, Orton compared Maxwell to Ivar Kreuger, the Swedish match king whose empire had collapsed amid bloodshed. Orton would die in a car crash before he saw his prophecy come true. Yet together they made a good team. "The difference between the two," recalls Baxter, "was

that Maxwell recognized the advantage of holding someone's coat."
While Maxwell addressed himself to the strategic decisions, alternately
blustering or charming officials while wheeler-dealing, Orton tried to
fashion the sales organization which Springer needed.

Ferdinand was at first delighted by Maxwell's efficient transport of
the stock to Britain but soon felt that his original misgivings were
justified. Whereas the Springers had, over a century, meticulously cultivated a venerable style befitting the publishers of the famous and had
constructed a fastidious distribution system, EPPAC's staff and its management, complained Ferdinand, were "amateur" and their inexperience was provoking Springer's old customers to complain that deliveries
were too slow. Maxwell, Ferdinand complained to Lange, did not love
books and authors like a traditional publisher but was a trader: he
happened to be dealing in books but it might as well have been cattle.
Maxwell's system for their distribution was "inadequate," he told
Lange. "He seems to believe that forwarding a bundle of journals is
nothing more than acting as a postman." Lange did not share his partner's anger.

In summer 1948, when Maxwell arrived again in Berlin, his blooming
exuberance and self-importance reinforced Tönjes Lange's favorable
impression. His young benefactor reported that he had secured orders
from the British government and British universities to buy German
scientific journals from EPPAC and had also arranged that Lord Pak-
enham, the Foreign Office minister responsible for Germany, would
open an exhibition of German books in London which Maxwell had
organized. Lange, who knew the details of Maxwell's impoverished
youth, could not fail to be overwhelmed. In the midst of the Soviet
blockade of Berlin which cut the city's road and rail connections to the
West, and the Cold War, he was sure that Springer's future depended
upon the Englishman. Uncertainty prevailed and he could not possibly
have envisaged the prosperity which would explode in the new Federal
Republic just one year later. Consequently, during that visit, Lange
offered Maxwell another huge slice of Springer's assets. He explained
that his brother Otto Lange had successfully recovered control over
Springer stock stored in Austria, which could be exploited to expand
the publisher's exports. But there was a problem. When the books had
arrived in 1944 from Berlin, Austria had been part of the German
Reich. At the end of the war, Allied laws banned commercial contacts
between Austria and Germany as a criminal offense. Legally, Springer
was denied control over what they had called their "iron reserves."
Lange believed that Maxwell was a possible savior. If the Austrian

company would sell the books to Maxwell in pounds sterling, Springer in Germany could eventually recoup its money. Understandably, Maxwell readily agreed to Lange's plan that the Austrian stock be officially sold to EPPAC, transported to London and resold on Springer's behalf to the rest of the world.

In September 1948, the arrangement was formalized when Ferdinand and the two Langes came to London to sign the agreement with EPPAC. On the same day, EPPAC moved again to larger premises— above a rat-infested banana warehouse in Neal Street, Covent Garden. Within two years Neal Street was to be a mini-empire of fifty employees, and still growing.

Both Otto and Ferdinand were soon unhappy about the proposed deal. Otto feared that he might lose the financial benefits of his legal ownership and be tarnished as a criminal while Ferdinand had become still more upset about EPPAC's incompetence. Throughout the year, as world trading gradually normalized, inquiries and subscriptions had increased, but simultaneously, according to a Springer executive, "The difficulties and the continuous stream of complaints about EPPAC's methods did not stop." EPPAC was certainly not the sole cause of all the problems. Both the Bank of England and British Customs succeeded in injecting obstructions at every level; in any case, some foreign customers were jealous that an upstart like Maxwell had secured a valuable monopoly. But, in Ferdinand's view, Maxwell was much to blame. Instead of remaining in London to smooth out any problems, he had dashed around Europe opening subsidiary offices in Paris, Brussels and Basle, so compounding the difficulties. In addition, he had approached Springer's competitors and offered similar deals to distribute their journals and books. His restless ambitions irritated Ferdinand all the more because Maxwell had inherited Springer's invaluable mailing list, which had been carefully compiled in the course of one century and had targeted sixty thousand individuals in universities, institutes and industry. Overnight, Maxwell could use it for the benefit of Springer's competitors. Yet, despite his reservations, Ferdinand acknowledged that he had no option but to signal his agreement if the stocks in Vienna were to be sold.

The "iron reserves" in Vienna were worth in 1945 prices about £100,000. Springer knew that if the true value were disclosed to the authorities, their export would be banned. At the meeting in London, the three Germans told Maxwell they had decided to undervalue the stock. Springer's contract with EPPAC dated September 16 shows an invoiced price as £4,000 which was later increased to £12,000.

Two weeks later, Maxwell reported that he had removed every bureaucratic obstacle between Vienna, Berlin, Frankfurt and London and was waiting for the first shipment. On October 7 about seventy boxes of books and journals were loaded into a railway wagon destined for London. Among the titles were books on atomic physics, pharmacology, jet engines and medical specialties. But even before the wagon crossed the Channel, the harmony between the three German confederates fell apart. Otto Lange bitterly protested that Ferdinand had broken his wartime promise and had deprived him of reward for all his work and risks. He threatened to renege on the whole deal and blamed his brother in Berlin for allowing Maxwell to benefit handsomely from the favorable exchange rate. Finally, he accused Maxwell of not paying the amount which had been orally agreed in London. Irritated, Maxwell flew to Vienna, accused Otto of breaking his wartime "gentleman's agreement and his word of honor" to Ferdinand and then flew to Frankfurt. With the three Germans warring among themselves, Maxwell's own position had immeasurably strengthened.

While in Frankfurt, Maxwell negotiated with JEIA a new, special dispensation for Springer to dispatch books without the time-consuming need for Customs' clearance for each consignment; he then flew on to Berlin to negotiate an improved discount on the purchase price for EPPAC—50 per cent on books and 40 per cent on journals. With his special exchange rate, Tönjes Lange calculated, Maxwell had by then effectively obtained an unusually high 70 per cent discount. As his success and wealth soared, Maxwell's horizons broadened. During his visit to Berlin in October 1948, he told Lange that he was planning a sales trip to Tokyo to exploit Springer's contacts with Japan's leading book-dealers, Maruzen and Nankodo. For a recently impoverished refugee aged just twenty-five even to contemplate a flight to the Far East just three years after the end of the war staggered the Germans. But by February 15, 1949, when Wagon No. 455 596, the seventh and last of the consignment, left Vienna, Maxwell already had under his control a reservoir of books and journals which would attract the attention of the whole world of learning.

Yet ostensibly Springer received no gratitude from London. Instead, Maxwell forcefully complained that Otto had broken his agreement, which gave EPPAC the sole distribution rights, in "a most unethical manner"; apparently Otto had supplied other British dealers. Maxwell sent Otto a menacing letter: after accusing Otto of breach of the agreement and denying that he owed any more money, Maxwell suggested that since he had sold a mere £150 worth of books so far, he might ship all seven wagon-loads back to Vienna and in future place his orders like other booksellers. Otto did not reply.

For those who knew Maxwell in London, the smooth self-confidence which supported that threat was characteristic of the image that the handsome businessman presented. Despite the stringent post-war austerity under which the majority of Britons suffered, Maxwell never seemed to be affected by the Labour government's rationing of everything from bread and eggs to petrol and clothes. As he dashed around London, dressed in well-tailored suits, he seemed to have settled upon a lifestyle which few could afford. In 1949, he possessed a petrol-guzzling red Chrysler which he had brought back from Prague, and he would soon exchange that status symbol for a Cadillac which, because such cars were still banned for British subjects, was acquired on temporary import license and owned by a foreign friend. Maxwell himself rarely drove his cars, but was chauffeured by an enigmatic and swarthy cockney, Bob Oglanby, whose antecedents were, to Maxwell's staff, mysterious. His insatiable appetite for luxury cars reflected his noticeable desire to impress everyone.

If Maxwell's poor childhood had instilled in him an appreciation of money and taught him the simple delight of grinding down his business partner by exhausting negotiations, it remained true that, in post-war Britain, wealth did not enhance one's social status. Maxwell's only social attributes in 1945 were the MC and his wartime rank. Although by custom only professional officers retain their rank in civilian life, Maxwell clung to his and to those bare letters as if his very survival were dependent upon them. Rigidly, Maxwell insisted on being addressed as "Captain" for nearly two decades after the war. Even in 1969, Springer executives still addressed him in the fashion which, twenty-five years earlier, he had judged would earn some social status among Britain's uniquely class-prejudiced society. In 1949, Maxwell had not finally settled upon his identity. The confusion is evident on his various business notepapers. The heading of EPPAC notepaper showed Capt. R. Maxwell MC, on Springer's letterhead he was R. I. Maxwell MC, yet his private notepaper was headed Capt. I. R. Maxwell MC. To complete the confusion, even when the letterhead stated R. I. Maxwell, he signed the letter I. R. Maxwell.

On one matter, however, there was no confusion. Maxwell was devoted to his family. By 1949, a second child, Anne, had been born. Like the remainder of his nine children, Anne was born at the maternity home, Maisons Laffitte, in a suburb of Paris, France, delivered by Betty's sister, a gynecologist. All the Maxwell children are French citizens by birth, and have remained so. After Anne's birth, the family had moved into a larger flat in Kensington. The amount of time he spent with his family was limited by his work, but never, by all accounts, by play. His only recreations were the cinema and, on Saturday afternoons, watching Arsenal football club play at Highbury. "I would love to own a football club," he told a friend at that time. But in work, despite enormous energy and dedication, the results were still confused. Yaacov Schlomovitch had taught his grandson the talent of negotiating, to buy and sell, but not how to organize an office and staff. Haggling in the fields around Ruthenia did not require chains of management command of the type which Ferdinand Springer required.

In the summer of 1949, Ferdinand's dissatisfaction revived. It had taken one year to unpack, store and catalog the Vienna stock, and EPPAC's inexperienced staff were still failing to keep proper records, to dispatch orders rapidly and, understandably for the inexperienced refugees, to grasp the importance of advertising. In Germany, Springer's staff, who reverently described Ferdinand as *Der Kaiser,* jealously watched Maxwell's windfall and his encroachment upon their work. Some harbored fears that he might ultimately inherit the whole business. To alleviate their complaints, Lange had decided to send his best dealers to help the London operation. At Springer's expense, Maxwell was learning the business, and he now conceived a scheme which would endow him with increased respectability.

On July 14, 1949, Maxwell suggested to Springer that EPPAC was "not really suitable for the distribution of your world renowned publications" and proposed to create a new company which would be called Lange, Maxwell & Springer in which the Germans were offered 49 per cent of the shares for £10,000. Tönjes Lange would be the unpaid chairman, Maxwell the managing director and Orton the secretary. The Springer directors were interested in the idea. Although the Berlin blockade had been lifted and Konrad Adenauer would soon be appointed Chancellor, they were still unsure about their prospects and felt that they might gain more direct control over their business. One week later, Lange agreed and effusively thanked Maxwell for the "honor" of becoming the chairman. Jubilant, Maxwell sent to Lange, whom he now called Charlie, the proposed articles of association with the quip: "If you are clever enough to understand what they mean, then I lift my hat to you. I think the lawyer's language used in these things is appalling. However no doubt you will send me a complete translation in Chinese, in which case I shall, of course, understand it."

Maxwell's conception of LMS was a quintessential example of his business acumen. Under his proposed scheme, Maxwell was the manager of two companies which, while theoretically they would work together, could place him in an embarrassing conflict of interest. Under the agreement, EPPAC contracted with Springer that their joint company, LMS, would distribute all Springer books outside Germany. But EPPAC would not cease to trade since it was EPPAC which was officially importing Springer's books from Germany. So EPPAC would sell its stock to LMS but would continue to trade under Maxwell's management while promising not to compete with LMS for the next ten years. It was a simple arrangement which revealed the essence of Maxwell's future operations: namely, compartmentalization. "Everyone works in blinkers except Maxwell," said one of his trusted advisers twenty years later. "Only he knows the master plan and that keeps changing." Securing Springer's agreement to that duopoly was a masterstroke which launched Maxwell closer toward the millionaire status which he craved.

To establish LMS on a sound footing needed finance. Whereas nowadays almost anyone may approach a bank for a loan, in 1949 it was the privilege of the rich and the respected. Since status was a commodity which Maxwell did not naturally command, it was a major coup when he obtained an interview with the merchant banker, Sir Charles Hambro, to discuss a loan. Although there are suggestions that Hambro, who was attached during the war to Special Operations Executive, the British sabotage organization, had met Maxwell in an Intelligence role (since Maxwell would occasionally hint at his connections with British Intelligence), Maxwell says that the meeting was in fact arranged through Major John Whitlock, a former SOE officer and executive of the publisher Butterworths who enjoyed a reputation as a freemason and "likeable rogue." Hambro was interested in both science and publishing, so Maxwell, who eloquently portrayed LMS's glowing future, was not disappointed. Hambro agreed to a loan of £25,000, the present-day equivalent of a quarter of a million pounds. Maxwell left the Bishopsgate building ecstatic, and cabled Lange the good news that their new company was firmly operational. He had found a new godfather. "It was Charles Hambro," Maxwell told Gunther Heyden, an employee in later years, "who taught me the importance of having a chauffeur. You must think about the business, not about getting to the meeting."

Yet within days of the new company's incorporation in October, there was a crisis. Writing from Berlin, Tönjes complained to Maxwell that he felt isolated, uncomfortable and helpless and feared that Maxwell was more than ever exploiting Springer's reputation and keeping his

German partners in the dark. Maxwell, wrote Tönjes, seemed to ignore advice and was even signing letters as "chairman." Worst of all, Tönjes had confided to Orton that he could not always trust what Maxwell said.

Deliberately deceiving Springer, Maxwell seemed genuinely hurt by the reprimand. "I value your personal friendship and esteem more than anything else in the world," he replied to Tönjes, whom he felt had not understood the enormous obstacles he had faced in establishing the business. Even if London was not as physically destroyed as Berlin, there were myriad problems, which Maxwell listed: inexperienced staff, tax disputes, overcoming the legacy of wartime and socialist regulations. "It doesn't feel good," Maxwell scribbled at the end of his five-page explanation, "to receive such scoldings from one's 'father' and teacher." Tönjes's distrust irked: "Should you ever in any way or manner whatsoever feel or say that you cannot trust my statements, then immediately from that minute I would wish to resign from that association." The crisis was, for the time being, resolved and, as Lange would often repeat, "Maxwell gave us enormous and valuable help over those years."

But Ferdinand and Tönjes were convinced that some of Maxwell's more far-reaching ambitions should be curbed. Maxwell had proposed that LMS should also become a publisher. The idea was flatly rejected. Instead, Springer opted for an invitation from Butterworths, one of Britain's most venerable publishers, founded in 1818, to form a joint company. Ferdinand's motives were simple. Maxwell had proved to be a trader not a publisher, so he would be confined in the new joint venture to simple distribution.

The link between Springer and Butterworths was Dr. Paul Rosbaud, a 53-year-old Austrian metallurgist who was the prewar adviser of Springer's major journal *Naturwissenschaft*. To this day, Rosbaud's wartime career remains a mystery. Although he was credited with aiding the destruction of Nazi Germany's heavy-water program, some suspect that he was also the source in 1939 of the famous "Oslo" report which provided British Intelligence with a detailed insight into unimagined inventions which German scientists had placed at the disposal of the German military. Because the report was so authoritative and suggested German developments which far surpassed British achievements, it was disbelieved, but in the course of the war it proved to be totally accurate. Its authorship has never been officially revealed. Nevertheless, Rosbaud clearly enjoyed good connections with senior British personalities because on November 25, 1946, he was present at a meeting in the Cabinet

Office in Great George Street under the chairmanship of Sir John Anderson, an under-secretary.

The government, having belatedly recognized the importance of science, hoped to encourage the development of journals similar to Springer's and wished Butterworths to be the publisher. Most of those gathered at the November meeting were senior representatives of the British scientific establishment and members of the new Scientific Advisory Board. Others present were the merchant banker Sir Charles Hambro, Hugh Quennell, the mercurial representative of Butterworths who, as a Control Commission officer, had met Maxwell in Germany, and Count Frederick Vanden Heuvel, alias "Fanny the Fixer." During the war, Vanden Heuvel had been a senior British intelligence officer in Switzerland. Since 1945 he had posed as a colorful businessman whereas in reality he was the M.I.6 officer responsible for monitoring, recruiting and gathering reports from Westerners traveling in communist Europe. Vanden Heuvel's meager knowledge of science nevertheless elevated him to the status of expert when compared with the other laymen present who included former officers in SOE. Many years later it would be suggested that Maxwell was being employed by M.I.6 deliberately to gather scientific journals from Russia but the evidence is speculative and circumstantial.

The result of that meeting was the foundation of Butterworth Scientific Publications. But the company failed to flourish and so, in 1949, after Ferdinand had rejected Maxwell's suggestion, a joint company was created called Butterworth-Springer. Rosbaud was appointed the editor of the scientific journals and it was agreed that they would be distributed by LMS.

After just two years, Maxwell was the managing director of an important book distributor which was recognized by the City, the publishing world and the government. But it was not enough. Fifteen years earlier, Maxwell had observed that his grandfather Yaacov Schlomovitch never confined himself to a single deal. Unlike his father Mechel who just dealt in cattle, Yaacov always managed a collection of parallel but unconnected deals. He was constantly juggling, keeping as many deals going simultaneously as he could. Instinctively, Maxwell searched for the same.

Tönjes was possibly the first to recognize Maxwell's inheritance of that talent. In later years, he recalled eating in a Berlin restaurant in 1950 with Maxwell when he noticed his associate listening to the conversation in a foreign language at the neighboring table. Afterward Maxwell explained that the Hungarians were discussing a barter deal and if he acted quickly he might profit from the information. Tönjes was bewildered but admiring. He had not realized that Springer's worldwide manager was also a player in the barter trade—a testament to Maxwell's natural compartmentalization.

Barter is the oldest form of trade, used before coinage was invented. For poorer countries, who after 1945 either had no hard currencies or faced politically motivated trade embargoes, bartering their own produce was the only means of obtaining important foreign goods. In its essence, barter is a simple bilateral exchange, but by the early 1950s Maxwell would become involved in hugely complicated, multilateral deals which would embrace several countries and many different commodities—pork bellies were exchanged for wood which was bartered for silk which might be exchanged for a metal. Success in those barter deals required all the skills and guile of a businessman, and more. So much depended on racing to close the circle before any of the interdependent deals collapsed. Like a juggler, the dealer's success was to keep a huge number of balls in the air which required exceptional mental agility. Throughout his career, his adversaries and friends alike have commented upon Maxwell's phenomenal capacity to retain and instantly recall information. Combined with his charm, fluent sales talk and tireless determination, this facility made him exceptionally skillful in constructing the circle for a barter deal. Lange and Springer were eyewitnesses to one refined brand of Maxwell's style, but Gunther Heyden saw another.

In 1948, Gunther Heyden was just twenty years old. Born in Cologne, he had spent the war in hiding in Germany after his Jewish mother had committed suicide. After the war, he found menial jobs with both the American and British armies until he was employed by PRISC in Berlin to supervise the licensing of cultural activities. Over the following two years, he "quite often" saw Maxwell in Berlin, occasionally dressed in uniform even after he had officially resigned. "Maxwell dropped into the Commission's press club, discussing business with contacts," Heyden remembers. "He was always in and out doing deals." The deals had no connection with books or scientific publishing but were, on behalf of Low-Bell, for unaesthetic commodities such as brushes and cotton waste. No deal was better remembered than Maxwell's coup to sell paint to German railways.

The German requirement for paint was, as usual, formally issued by JEIA in Frankfurt. At the former headquarters of IG Farben, the German chemical conglomerate, Maxwell was a familiar figure, especially to Paul Lassen, a British officer attached to JEIA who was responsible for vetting contracts in the food and agriculture section. Lassen's office was situated on the so-called "Polish corridor" where everyone who wanted a slice of the lucrative business congregated. Lassen candidly admits that the potential for anybody to benefit by corruption was enormous: "I vetted every contract and could have made a fortune." Lassen's friend, Bill Hickey, who was responsible for the paint contract, was visited by Maxwell and Louis Berger, the paint manufacturer. Twenty years ago, Berger told the *Sunday Times* how impressed he had been by Maxwell's dynamic organization, by his ability to obtain visas and transport and by his winning $40 in a poker game with American soldiers to pay for their expenses in Frankfurt. Most of all, Berger was thrilled that Maxwell obtained the enormous $1 million contract for the paint. While Lassen believes that Berger never delivered and was never paid, Heyden says that Maxwell delivered not only the paint but also the brushes. The two JEIA officials impressed Maxwell and when their contracts ended in 1950 both were employed by him to implement his more intricate deals.

By then, Heyden, hired by Orton, had arrived from Berlin. On his first day at Neal Street on January 2, 1950, he received a familiar welcome: "They'd forgotten what they wanted me for." The confusion was symptomatic but transitory. Maxwell's businesses were booming and Heyden was detailed to supervise LMS's publicity, its mailing list and the printing of ten thousand copies of LMS's first catalogue, which featured 1,000 books and 1,200 different journals. His lack of any experience was overlooked.

On that same day, the new company LMS began formal trading. Besides the five-year agreement which gave LMS exclusive rights to the worldwide sales of Springer's books and journals, Maxwell also enjoyed very favorable terms for the return of all unsold books; most importantly, Maxwell's own company, EPPAC, could sell its stock of Springer rare books and old journals to the new company on advantageous terms.

The first LMS board meeting, which was held in January and which the Germans attended, was a notable occasion. Maxwell was representing the competing interests of EPPAC and LMS. It was a pattern of intercompany trading which would be repeated many times over the following years. At that moment, any reluctance the Germans might have felt was dissipated: they were grateful for Maxwell's services, they believed that the intercompany sales would be simple transactions, and they knew that moving the stock back to Germany was fraught with difficulties, not the least of them legal.

Springer, however, was disquieted. The previous year, Maxwell had signed exclusive distribution agreements with his competitors Urban & Schwarzenberg, Ernst & Sohn, Verlag Chemie, Thieme and an East German publisher, Akademie-Verlag. JEIA had agreed that the same hugely advantageous exchange rates could be applied to the new contracts. Ferdinand complained to Lange that he, Springer, was bearing the cost and "taking a great risk" to promote his competitors: "For Maxwell, it was the means to build for himself a huge business in London and he achieved that in an astonishingly short period." Springer was worried that it had placed so much of its future in Maxwell's hands. Yet at its early regular monthly board meetings, Maxwell successfully charmed the very precise Germans with evidence of his success, produced by the "great intensity" of work by his staff of sixty-five. Everything, he claimed, was rapidly becoming more efficient and rationalized, and the empire was expanding. A new ten-thousand-name mailing list had been compiled, a system of Adrema name plates had been completed to speed the dispatch of circulars, and a new warehouse had been rented in the Elephant and Castle district of London. The Germans thought the innovations were "exceptionally good" but their demeanor changed when the very reason for their special relationship with Maxwell suddenly disappeared.

In early 1950, the new government of the Federal Republic of Germany announced that the Allies' vast network of regulations and controls would rapidly vanish and direct exports would be allowed. Anxious to earn dollars, the Bonn government urged companies like Springer to dismantle their artificial arrangements.

Both Ferdinand and Lange realized that, despite the irksome duplication, Springer's prestige and sales had become too enmeshed with the London operation to be abruptly terminated. Moreover, the Maxwell connection placed them at an enormous advantage over their competitors since Germans were still unable to travel to most countries. Through Maxwell, they could still contact their old customers. At that moment, he was on their behalf energetically traveling around the world, opening new offices and selling Springer's books and journals in Japan, Italy, Spain and Austria and opening new offices in Basle and Paris. Both were born inauspiciously as symbols to satisfy Maxwell's dream of the self-styled international entrepreneur rather than as substantial business operations. The French company was grafted onto the remnants of Betty's father's defunct vegetable business, the grandiosely named "Comptoir Industriel et Commercial d'Importation et Exportation" which had been established in 1946 in the rue de Rivoli. On

January 25, 1949, the Comptoir Industriel was renamed EPPAC with Louis Paul Meynard remaining as its managing director and Nassim Zacouto, a carpet dealer, named as a second director. In the same year, Meynard, under Maxwell's direction, moved the new company's head-quarters to a shop with offices above at 24 rue des Écoles, which Maxwell would enthusiastically describe to Lange as "a scientific bookshop." For the Germans, the commercial advantages still outweighed any irritations.

In the cause of Springer, legend relates, Maxwell became the British airline BOAC's first passenger to clock up one million miles. His frequent dashes to Northolt aerodrome were accompanied by pleas from his devoted secretary Anne Dove to "hold the plane for Captain Maxwell" while Oglanby raced along the Great West Road. If the loyalty of most of Maxwell's staff was won by a mixture of love and fear, Anne Dove was the exception. "A superior lady, out of the top drawer, with excellent breeding," is the general recollection of the Jewish refugees who observed their boss's alter ego. "Dove was more than a secretary to Maxwell," recalls Heyden, "she was the most powerful influence on him." Dove, all the refugees suspected, was the source of Maxwell's phenomenal success in British society. Others were convinced that no one could have influenced Maxwell's performance.

Besides his wife, Maxwell relied upon two women in his life. Both were secretaries. Anne Dove was the first. During the war, she had worked as a secretary for SOE, first in Baker Street, then in Cairo and later in Italy. Since that organization appealed to an extraordinary mixture of entrepreneurs, individualists and above all ambitious members of the Establishment who would play important roles in post-war Britain, she had collected during that decade a notable list of contacts ranging across the worlds of finance, politics and culture. In 1950, she returned to Britain and saw an advertisement in the *Daily Telegraph* for a secretary. She applied and after waiting for two hours outside the director's office was on the verge of leaving when she was ushered inside. On one wall of the huge book-lined, mahogany-colored office, she remembers, there was a "huge map of the world with all the capitals pinpointed by red lights. Behind a huge desk which didn't seem large enough for him, I saw a big man with jet black hair and large greenish eyes. But what I noticed most was the very warm and beautifully timbred voice." During the interview, Dove recalls how Maxwell turned the map lights on and "Whenever I would say, 'Have you got an office here or there?' pointing to the various capitals, he would immediately say, 'Of course.' Some of the offices had not even been thought of yet, but Maxwell went on the maxim that nothing was impossible." Dove took the job because she was attracted to the idea of constant travel to all the "offices" and the thought of an endless supply of bananas, her favorite fruit, from the warehouse downstairs. Her boss, she realized, was a man for whom "there was never enough time to achieve all the things he wished for. His own life was planned in his mind several jumps ahead—ambition being the driving force—and as each ambition was achieved then the next plan was already being formulated." Dove was quite prepared to place her impressive list of contacts at her boss's disposal. Among them was Charles Hambro, whom she knew from her service in SOE. "Charles told me that he was pleased that I was with Maxwell looking after things," she recalls, "and Maxwell minded very much what Charles thought of him."

All those meeting Maxwell in 1950 were left breathless by what Dove describes as his "tremendous life-force." The size of his desk, they quipped, matched his ambitions. Visitors discovered that their attempts at conversation were constantly frustrated by their host picking up one of his four telephones and ordering calls to China, America or Russia and then switching from one language to another without a blink. Some staff insist that at least two of the telephones were not even connected but were important props for his role as the international tycoon. "Every time I walked in," remembers one frequent and skeptical visitor, "he was shouting down the phone to New York and one minute later picked up another phone and was screaming at Moscow." According to Heyden, "You could hear Maxwell's voice booming down the length of Neal Street as he alternately harangued or charmed somebody into a profitable deal."

His staff were not so much skeptical as suspended between amusement and fright. Maxwell's senses of humor, fun and generosity were engaging qualities. At Christmas he paid for many staff to return to their families in Germany. But the moods easily changed. His appearance in the general office was usually accompanied by the question: "And what are you doing?" If inadequately answered, there was another dismissal. Those who attempted to temper his approach met with no success. One senior executive who told Maxwell that his staff were quivering on their seats with insecurity was cut off in mid-sentence with a deep growl: "Rubbish, while they work for me they have complete security." "But look at this list of all those who you've fired!" countered the bold employee. "They're ex-employees and ex-employees have no security," was the crushing reply.

Springer employees were less intimidated by the extravagant style.

After a period of relative calm, they were once again sending their complaints to London, especially about the failure to send money which was owed. By November 1950 the outstanding bills amounted to £115,000 (£27,585 in October alone) and the debt was growing. Although Maxwell was not solely to blame—customers were invariably reluctant to pay their accounts, and compliance with the Bank of England's rigid currency controls presented endless difficulties—Springer's suspicious staff constantly scrutinized every detail of London's operations.

Triumphantly, in November they found some evidence to justify their unease. By chance, Springer staff had seen a document, inadvertently sent from London to Berlin, which showed that Maxwell's distribution deals with their competitors Ernst & Sohn and Urban & Schwarzenberg were signed, not as they believed with LMS, but with Maxwell's own company, EPPAC. Both Lange and Ferdinand were shocked since in their view this was a clear contravention of their agreement with Maxwell which forbade EPPAC to compete with LMS for ten years. They were due to travel to London in mid-November and a showdown seemed inevitable. To avert the crisis, at twelve noon on November 1, Maxwell went to Bishopsgate and successfully obtained a further £25,000 loan from Sir Charles Hambro. But it was not enough to prevent the Germans demanding concessions.

At a meeting on November 14, Maxwell agreed that Springer could begin exporting books directly from Germany and that he would repay DM 1.1 million in five monthly installments. The following afternoon, Lange, Ferdinand and Maxwell went to Hambro to confirm the recapitalization of their company. It was a useful opportunity for Maxwell to demonstrate the support he enjoyed in the City. Relations improved and Maxwell once again addressed a letter to Tönjes as "My dear Onkel." Springer, he knew, still depended upon him.

One problem in early 1951 which needed his help was to find a route out of their original agreement. The demand for Springer's books was growing but the supply was hindered by an unpleasant truth that their exports were based on a fundamental deception. Springer had never disclosed to German Customs the true value of the books and journals in the boxes: the value of their exports which were declared on the ECDs (Exchange Control Documents) did not match the true value. Whereas the current certificate was worth DM 30,000, the shipments awaiting dispatch were worth DM 600,000. Lange and Hövel confided to Maxwell that their deception was in danger of exposure.

At first it was argued that the Customs officers would never check the real value of the books, but he was persuaded to the contrary. Then both sides formulated a ruse which they believed to be legal. One hundred boxes awaiting shipment in Berlin and Würzburg would be repacked, relabeled and sold in three parts: Springer would sell to LMS and EPPAC, while Lange & Springer (a separate German company) would sell to LMS. It was the provision of that kind of help which earned Maxwell their gratitude. But the respite was again short-lived.

On November 28, 1950, Maxwell arrived in Berlin reporting that business was booming. He disclosed that he had secured a massive £150,000 order for books from Guozi Shudian, the Communist Chinese book-dealer, and that he had been paid in advance. Ferdinand was less pleased. He claimed that Maxwell had overcharged Springer's old customer and warned that the Chinese would eventually discover the truth. Six weeks later, the crisis deepened.

On November 3, three weeks before Maxwell's confident report to Ferdinand, the directors of LMS in Paris had met and began proceedings to declare the company bankrupt. It was a surprising decision since only five months earlier they had voted to quintuple the company's capital. Now, however, Meynard and the other directors blamed Springer who they erroneously claimed had halved discounts on the sales as the cause of their demise. In contrast, Maxwell's letters to Lange blamed French tariffs, currency restrictions and the state of the French economy.

In quick succession, Maxwell's difficulties were compounded; the LMS operation in Basle also collapsed because the Swiss insisted on buying direct from Berlin and adamantly refused to place their orders in London; and Maxwell's much vaunted deal with Sansoni of Florence, which featured as a considerable profit in that year's accounts, was proving to be disastrous. Shipping books from Germany to Italy via London was costly, and Springer was faced with Sansoni's complaint that excessive stock had been delivered which he insisted Springer should repurchase. For the conservative Springer team, each case was a major crisis. Together, they seemed to presage the *Götterdämmerung*.

Ferdinand, galled that he should have surrendered so much control over his company's reputation and future, reflected his staff's irritation about the London operation. In early 1951, he sent Maxwell a long reprimand criticizing his failure to appreciate the invaluable mailing list. But more revealing were the guidelines which Springer listed as important for a publisher's behavior: adhere to the prices quoted in the catalogs; do not quote a rare-book price for standard books; and treat a customer in such a way that he will return for a further sale. The more memorable cautionary rules have in retrospect a piquancy. A publisher, Maxwell was told, should not promise more than he can fulfill; it is more important to serve a customer than exploit him; one shouldn't buy more than one can pay for; and one shouldn't offer more than one can deliver. "You are making the mistake that you are expecting good results based on faulty methods," concluded Ferdinand. Their personal relationship, he said, was terminated.

The first consequence of the break was a letter from Springer's accountants to Maxwell disclosing that they wanted to scrutinize LMS's accounts. The initial summary sent from London for the year 1949/50 showed a loss of £225. In June 1951 R. A. Meilicke, Springer's lawyer, and Fritz Fuhrmann, an accountant, arrived in London to check the books, especially the sales of EPPAC's stock to LMS. There were good grounds for their suspicions. Maxwell's own accountants had also discovered irregularities.

Over the past year, Frank Beckwith, a qualified chartered secretary and LMS's accounts manager, had been grappling with dozens of untidy files containing invoices and receipts, in an effort to end the chaotic system he had inherited on his recruitment. Reconciling the intercompany trading between EPPAC, LMS and Low-Bell was complicated by the never-ending flow of foreign currencies in and out of their bank accounts and through smaller companies privately owned by Maxwell. Together with Tom Clark, an accountant who would stay with Maxwell for over twenty-five years, Beckwith discovered that their predecessor had been obtaining Maxwell's signature for checks against false invoices which were in fact payments to himself. Defrauding Maxwell, the two new accountants decided, had not been difficult. "Maxwell's style of business," recalls Beckwith, "was like a golfer who liked to hit the big drive down the green but was uninterested in the small strokes at the end." Others suspected that Maxwell had not shown sufficient care to prevent the chaos developing. Among those was Ferdinand Springer.

Fuhrmann's first impression on landing at Northolt aerodrome was favorable. Oglanby graciously chauffeured the German in the Cadillac to the Shaftesbury Hotel. Compared to Berlin, London was a sanctuary with plenty of food and not totally devastated by bombing. Fuhrmann's attitude changed a few hours later when he heard from Meilicke that LMS's accountants, Moodie & Epstein, had reported that LMS's accumulated losses were £22,618, considerably worse than expected. Fuhrmann suspected the accountants of "manipulation."

Fuhrmann met Maxwell at 2 p.m. the following day when Maxwell explained that the proper accounts were not yet ready. Instead of staying in London, Maxwell suggested that the German should fly immediately to Basle. Fuhrmann refused and prepared his own assessment which confirmed that, although the official accounts would show a £22,000 loss, the real loss was only £4,486. The accounts were nevertheless unsatisfactory and the two Germans secretly appointed a solicitor, considered initiating a private investigation, and finally returned home dissatisfied.

The relationship between Maxwell and Ferdinand now exploded. In May 1951, Butterworths decided that their joint venture with Springer was grossly unprofitable although Rosbaud had established three highly respected journals—*Spectrochimica Acta, Journal of Atmospheric and Terrestrial Physics* and *Geochimica et Cosmochimica Acta*—and published two standard textbooks. Maxwell bought their shares but it is not clear how much he paid nor whether Springer knew in advance that he had bought the interest. However, on October 10, 1951, he wrote to Springer requesting £7,500 for the Butterworth-Springer shares he had just bought. Ferdinand's reply was stinging and shows that he felt misled. Maxwell's proposals, he wrote, were an "embarrassing shock" because they broke all the previous agreements. It was "disreputable for a gentleman and businessman to make those type of demands which were contrary to his previous promises." Future relations, he wrote, "were very doubtful," and he ended, "I deeply regret having to write this letter." Within an hour of its receipt, Maxwell telephoned Springer in Heidelberg but the secretary was under orders not to transfer any calls: "Dr. Springer doesn't want to speak to you, Captain Maxwell," she told the evidently hurt caller from London.

Maxwell claimed that he paid £13,000 for all the shares. In February 1969, at a graduate seminar on business studies held at the London School of Economics, he said that he paid "a relatively small sum of money." Pertinently, the self-made millionaire also outlined to the students how he raised the money to buy Rosbaud's infant publishing house in 1951: "As I had no other capital other than my gratuity [i.e. on demobilization from the army in 1947], the capital was provided from three sources. First a loan from Hambros Bank; secondly, a contribution by some of my relatives and friends in America; thirdly, a contract with Her Majesty's Stationery Office to supply them with out-of-print wartime German scientific material for which they paid in advance."

Rosbaud and his three staff joined Maxwell in Neal Street without celebration. They were given a small office and were instantly forgotten.

The only formality was to produce a name for the new company. Orton toyed at first with Athena Press after the goddess of wisdom, but discovered that the name was already registered. He then suggested Pergamon, the Greek town in Asia Minor where stood the Altar of Pergamon, dedicated to Athena. Maxwell summarily approved the suggestion and soon after received from Heinz Götz, a friend, a reproduction of the Pergamon coin found at Herakleia which shows the head of Athena. He gave it to Rosbaud, commenting that it could be the company's symbol. That settled, Pergamon barely featured in Maxwell's thoughts for the next four years. He had embarked on an adventurous scheme which would win him the fame which he desired.

3

The members of the Garrick Club in London are predominantly men of letters—actors, writers and publishers—and lawyers. It was the natural rendezvous in early 1951 for Arthur Coleridge, the great-grandson of England's Lord Chief Justice and a relative of the nineteenth-century poet, to meet an acquaintance for an early-evening drink. Coleridge, who during the war had worked in the Cabinet Office, was the managing director of an ailing book-wholesaler called Simpkin Marshall which was owned by Pitmans, then one of Britain's major publishers. His host at the Garrick was Count Vanden Heuvel, Charles Hambro's business scout, whose elegant, foreign appearance impressed Coleridge as it did everyone else. Heuvel had suggested that he might have a buyer for Simpkins called Robert Maxwell.

Simpkin Marshall was a unique British institution, acting as the wholesale intermediary between publishers and the retail bookshops. The book trade was, then as now, fragmented, and the cost of ordering and distributing single copies of books to every shop in the country was high. Simpkin Marshall, like their only competitor W. H. Smith, offered bookshops a central warehouse from which to obtain books from every publisher. In the trade it was known as the "single copy wholesale." Simpkins' pride was that it stocked nearly every book in print and many books which had been long forgotten, and that any telephone order could be delivered by the following day. Since the bookshop paid the same price buying from Simpkins as it paid buying direct from the publisher, Simpkins earned its profits by obtaining the books from the publisher at a lower price than the shop. With an annual turnover of over £1 million, Simpkins' profits before the war were quite acceptable. That state of affairs came to an abrupt end on December 29, 1940, during one of the worst nights of the Blitz, when Simpkins' warehouse in the City of London was hit and four million books were destroyed. Demoralized, Simpkins' owners decided voluntarily to liquidate their business.

A group of leading publishers were anxious to maintain the institution. They bought Simpkins' goodwill and urged the publisher James Pitman to lease part of a new warehouse which he had built out of speculative philanthropy in Neasden, north London, called the Book Centre. Initially, the publishers and Pitman hoped that the new venture could be run as a cooperative for the book trade but they found little support. Most publishers, before the war, had become unhappy with the narrower profit margin received on the sales which went through Simpkins rather than direct from their own warehouses.

Nevertheless, Pitman, committed to the notion of a central warehouse, tried to rebuild the business at his own risk. A new, more centrally located warehouse was rented in 1944 at Rossmore Court in Marylebone and stocks were gradually rebuilt. Yet by 1947 the new company's modest annual profits had turned to huge losses and the prospects were grim. The warehouse was too small, too much of its stock was printed on poor-quality wartime paper, and its labor costs were rocketing. Moreover, in the new era, the civilized cohesion which had cemented the industry for generations was disintegrating. While the book trade unanimously and piously paid tribute to the importance of Simpkin Marshall, individually most publishers in the face of growing competition took a selfish view of their interests. Increasingly they were unwilling to give Simpkins special discounts and preferred to deliver direct to shops. Even those who sat on Simpkins' board were undermining the business by squeezing its profit margins. By 1951, when Simpkins' debts to Pitmans amounted to more than £250,000, James decided to dispose of the institution. It fell to Coleridge to make the first contact with a prospective purchaser, Maxwell.

Since the Garrick was not appropriate for a business meeting, Coleridge and Heuvel took a taxi to the Savoy Hotel and met Maxwell in the bar. Coleridge, the only Englishman of the three, was immediately impressed. Maxwell, wearing fine-cut tweed, looked and sounded the proverbial English gentleman. The dark, handsome young man with clipped moustache and huge bushy eyebrows gave out a hypnotic quality which "magnetized" Coleridge. Even compared to Heuvel, dressed in a Savile Row suit, Maxwell shone. The only flaw which Coleridge noticed on that first day was a slight imperfection in the Captain's English: he used plural nouns when singular were required.

Heuvel had judged Maxwell's interest in Simpkins perfectly. Several

Jewish refugees had recently established themselves in London as successful publishers because they had spotted the deficiencies of the crusty, arch-conservative scions of the British trade. For Maxwell, Simpkin Marshall was a typical example of a good idea which, because of bad management, had turned sour. He recognized that whatever notable qualities the British possessed, they were not blessed with an aggressive sense of business and viewed money-making with distaste. For the refugee, the British disdain for ruthless negotiations and trading reflected an ineptitude which he could exploit. Buoyed with immeasurable self-confidence, he was certain that his energy and talent could revive any bankrupt businesses. In Simpkins' case, he needed only to persuade the publishers not to be shortsighted: after all, German publishers had long supported a central warehouse for book distribution. As he explained to Coleridge in the Savoy bar, he hoped to create the same institution in Britain. His only question to Coleridge was: would he help? Coleridge agreed and without any further questions Maxwell began negotiating the purchase of the bankrupt company from Pitmans. It was a decision which would never cease to haunt him.

One indicator seemed to be favorable. Over the previous financial year Pitman had turned a £23,000 loss into a £17,000 profit. On balance, the deal which was struck seemed advantageous to Maxwell—although, according to one accountant's investigation four years later, Simpkins had actually lost £34,261 that year.

Maxwell paid Pitmans £160,000 for the total ownership of Simpkins, whose assets Pitmans had valued at £250,000. But Maxwell was required to pay only £50,000 (part of which he borrowed from Hambros Bank) immediately. The remaining £110,000 was due in nine half yearly installments over the following years. Significantly, the whole £160,000 was immediately entered in Simpkins' accounts as a debt owed by the company to Maxwell although he had paid only £50,000. Until its eventual collapse, Simpkins' accounts would always show a debt owing to its managing director. That accounting procedure was commented upon adversely a few years later. Pitmans was also owed about £108,000 by Simpkins; this debt was dealt with by Pitmans agreeing to write off £35,637 of its losses completely and account for the remaining £72,590 of the money by using the services of the Book Centre in Neasden. In theory, Maxwell had negotiated a bargain which, if properly managed, would secure for him respectability and a voice among the power-brokers.

Soon after the transfer was finalized, Maxwell issued his very first press statement to the trade magazine, the *Bookseller*. Like thousands of other statements over the next decades, his first was characterized by its optimism, ambition and promises: "I am determined that this will prove to be a long and successful chapter, founded on an even greater improvement in services to both booksellers and publishers. . . . Nothing will be spared to promote the completeness and efficiency of this service in every way." After explaining how Simpkins would be expanded, especially by export sales, Maxwell pledged "all my energies" to develop goodwill. Two weeks later his confidence was rewarded by the trade. Under the headline "Man of the Hour," the *Bookseller* sought to dispel the fears of those who were evidently "a trifle startled" about "the burning question in the book trade just now: Who is Robert Maxwell?"

The magazine's answer to its own question was glowing. After mentioning Maxwell's courageous war record, it described how "he was asked by a number of prominent German publishers to help them restart their exports" and how the business had expanded ever since although "there was nothing to prevent them, had they so wished, from thanking Maxwell for his services and then politely bidding him good-day. The fact that no German publisher has chosen to exert this independence is itself eloquent testimony to the efficiency of Lange, Maxwell and Springer as a selling agency." Trusted by the Germans, Maxwell was also said to be dynamic, having traveled 800,000 miles since 1947 to speak to his customers in any of his nine languages. All that and more, said the *Bookseller,* would be placed at Simpkins' disposal; "in particular the remarkable publicity machine which he has built up at Lange, Maxwell and Springer, and which regularly and continuously feeds up-to-the-minute information to the 480,000 people in all parts of the world who have reported their specialized book requirements to L.M. & S., will be placed fully at Simpkins' service." Maxwell now had to match his promises with performance.

Maxwell's first weeks at Rossmore Court are remembered by Coleridge and others as enjoyable. For those accustomed to the pace of traditional managers, Maxwell's dynamism and especially his speed of calculation—"always on the back of an envelope"—was inspiring. After two weeks he announced a survival plan which involved selling all of Simpkins' stock, negotiating bigger discounts and persuading publishers to deposit books at Simpkins on sale or return. Everything depended upon overcoming the publishers' prejudice and shortsightedness.

Coleridge was appointed as Maxwell's "ambassador" to arrange the blitz of introductions. The clubbable heir of a judge and the ambitious offspring of a peasant attended many meetings but won few converts. "They were a severe, tight community who lived in the Garrick," recalls Coleridge, "and couldn't stand the sight of an upstart, especially someone who was so brash." Nevertheless, Simpkins' turnover did begin to increase and that year's profits headed toward £50,000, but Maxwell was impatient. At the beginning of 1952, he decided that the cause of Simpkins' shortcomings was the division of the warehouses between Rossmore Court, which was too small, and Neasden, which was badly located. His recipe was to bring all his businesses, including LMS, under one roof by procuring bigger and more impressive premises.

The site chosen as the headquarters of the whole Maxwell empire was a former bottling plant, abandoned by the brewers Fullers, situated on the Marylebone Road in central London which was later rebuilt as the headquarters of Woolworths. Maxwell overlooked its obvious deficiencies—it was old, was built of wood, had few telephones and as a former bottling plant was totally unsuited for a book warehouse which needed vast shelving. He also ignored Simpkins' insolvency. He was impressed by its major advantage which was that it was very big and matched his ambitions. Soon after the purchase, he renamed the warehouse "Maxwell House," brushing aside those who tried to dissuade him because of the comical comparisons with the brand of instant coffee. But he was unable to ignore the loud demands by the local authorities who threatened to close the site immediately as a fire hazard. He had bought the lease without estimating the price of the necessary extensive rebuilding, which he would later claim had cost £63,000 although Orton confided to Tönjes Lange that the real cost was £140,000.

Those who moved the tens of thousands of books into Maxwell House in summer 1952 have one predominant recollection: "Maxwell was always shouting, 'I want it done yesterday.' " Impatiently he strode through the new warehouse tipping up boxes of carefully packed books, cursing about the loss of a day's business. The newly appointed manager of the warehouse, who is today still fond of his former boss, was amazed: "His personality was like a sledgehammer. He could not adjust it to match his partners." Within days, Simpkin Marshall was back in business with a lot of goodwill from the staff. "He represented Simpkins' only hope for salvation," recalls another manager, who initially wished him well. Another decided after two and a half days that he would prefer another job and went to Maxwell to submit his resignation. "Resign? After two and a half days," shouted the employer. "Never! You're fired."

Maxwell House was a pot-pourri of nationalities. On the first three floors were four hundred partially unionized Simpkin Marshall employees who worked amid stacking shelves which were strung between old bottling machines. Above them were the staff and stock of LMS. Most of those storemen were former Czech and Polish soldiers who regularly fought among themselves but were convinced that their boss had arrived in Britain with "pips in his pocket." On the top floor, across gangplanks laid over the open roofs, was an office set aside for Rosbaud and Pergamon, while over another roof was an office housing Lassen and Hickey, who were deeply immersed in barter deals. Maxwell House would have been better named "Maxwell's Bazaar": under one roof, deals were being struck in German scientific journals, Argentinian pork bellies and practically every book currently published in Britain. Gunther Heyden, working for LMS, can remember "a mad combination of refugees speaking Yiddish, cockneys and English aristocrats from Oxbridge. A lot of suspicion between everyone. There were cliques and factions and everyone was convinced that Anne Dove was keeping them out." Heyden's awareness is substantiated by the confessions of Simpkins' sales manager, who worked on the next floor down and deliberately behaved "more British than the British" to avoid any taint of the "Mitteleuropa above us." Maxwell, of course, was oblivious to any tensions or to the notion that Maxwell House was a high-risk social experiment. Bringing all his businesses under one roof made, he believed, good commercial sense. The rambling building might create confusion but that was ideal for maintaining rigid compartmentalization and protecting his secrecy. "He would never want his right hand to know what his left hand was doing," says Anne Dove. "Sometimes I'm not quite sure that he knew himself. But it was part of his success which was built by making all his instincts work for him." Ensconced in a huge office, Maxwell presented himself to the outside world as a tycoon—late-night dinners were often delivered from the Savoy—and ordered Coleridge to relaunch Simpkins with a lavish party.

Throughout his life in Britain, Maxwell was fond of hosting big receptions. Gauging their success is not easy or even fair because so much depends upon the attitude of those invited. As unashamed snobs, some of those who arrived at Maxwell's parties in the early 1950s might have been reluctant to make a pretense of enjoyment, but even fewer attempted the civil gesture when they were invited to the launch of Simpkins which was "the biggest party the book trade had probably ever seen." A huge marquee was erected inside the warehouse and, though the atmosphere was stuffy, there was ample to eat and drink. Suddenly a booming voice was heard from hitherto undetected tannoys introducing "the managing director of Simpkin Marshall, Captain Ian Robert Maxwell MC," and Maxwell began to address his guests from another room. At great length, in a deep cavernous voice, he extolled the virtues of using Simpkins' services. He wanted publishers to change the basis of their relationship with Simpkins and urged them to deposit their books on sale or return. At the end, most of his audience were fidgeting in the fetid atmosphere and beginning to conclude that their prejudice was justified. "The general attitude was, 'We don't have to trust this man, so why should we?' " recalls one publisher. Maxwell returned to the marquee, ebullient and convinced that his guests had been impressed. "It did him more harm than good" was the reaction of one staid guest. But John Brown, one of the younger publishers who would later become Publisher of Oxford University Press, was enthusiastic: "I was making my way as well and I admired his courage for taking on the impossible."

Maxwell won some successes but the turnover of books was stubbornly stuck. Simpkins' recovery was slower than he had anticipated while his labor costs were mounting. The bloated workforce with its rigid twice-daily tea break and regular strikes was, he decided, an easy target for savings.

For someone of Maxwell's background, the British unions' inflexible habits and the absence of a recognizable work ethic was, to say the least, frustrating. Simpkins' four hundred employees had little sympathy for the financial plight of their employer and reacted accordingly when Maxwell informed their shop steward that he wanted, immediately, 150 layoffs. The shop steward, Bill Pescott, summoned his local SOGAT official, Bill Keyes, then a young trade unionist, whose career over the following thirty years would be peppered by bitter and emotional fights against Maxwell's bulldog resolve.

Unlike most other union leaders whom Maxwell would physically confront in his career, Keyes had something more in common with him than just a stubborn ambition to succeed. Both were tall, forceful men who possessed an ability to control their naturally volatile tempers to suit the occasion. Both enjoyed their battles and detested contemplating defeat. Like all whose public image is aggressive and uncompromising, both believed themselves to be at heart soft, emotional and caring. As a left-wing trade unionist, Keyes had spent a lifetime fighting on his members' behalf the inaptly named press barons of Fleet Street. Fortunately for Keyes, over most of that era the battle was tilted in his favor because the barons routinely succumbed to union demands. By deploying ruthlessness, brinkmanship and a saving dose of reality,

Keyes succeeded in frustrating most of the management's attempts to demolish the print workers' restrictive practices. Accordingly, when Keyes was telephoned late one Friday night in 1952 and told that a certain Robert Maxwell, the new managing director of Simpkin Marshall, not only was threatening 150 dismissals but was planning to lay off exclusively trade union members, Keyes warmed to the prospect of teaching the newcomer the facts of life. What followed was the curtain raiser to a long and respectful relationship; Maxwell himself once said, "Look, we both come from the same sort of background"—to which the unionist replied, "Yes, but I haven't forgotten mine."

Keyes arrived in Marylebone Road at 8:30 on a Saturday morning. At first Maxwell refused to see him, but he relented soon after. "He was arrogant when I walked into his office," recalls Keyes, "and he just told me that he wasn't going to be told what he could do." Keyes's response to such a taunt was to threaten a total shutdown. Maxwell's counter-response, which Keyes would hear repeated over the years, was categoric: "I haven't got any time. I've got to catch a plane to Russia." Keyes was equally dogmatic: "Go to Russia, but you won't have a business when you come back."

Like high-stakes poker, successful negotiations about money among tycoons or with union leaders depend upon many ingredients, but ultimately the outcome is decided by whose nerve cracks first. On this occasion, seeking to impress a left-wing union official by referring to a visit to Moscow positively rebounded. Keyes coolly waited while Maxwell fretted about missing his plane and then conceded the union's demands. "It was my first fight and first victory against Maxwell," recalls Keyes.

Keyes's victory contributed to Simpkins' immediate financial plight. The huge rebuilding costs had wiped out the previous year's £50,000 profit and left the company with a massive £98,000 loss. But that year's accounts would also reveal an unexpected item. Maxwell had repaid the £110,000 which he personally owed to Pitmans although under the original agreement it was to have been repaid by installments over nine years. The reasons for the accelerated repayment will be explained later, but the methods Maxwell used would become controversial.

According to the accounts, it was Simpkins and not Maxwell who repaid Maxwell's personal debt. Because repayment was accelerated, Pitmans agreed to accept £98,000 instead of £110,000. The accounting methods used were ingenious but totally legal. With the help of Hambros, special preference shares had been issued to increase Simpkins' capital, but the cash which Maxwell had invested by purchasing the shares was immediately repaid to him by the company. The result of the money chase was that Simpkins paid Maxwell's debts to Pitmans and left Maxwell in complete control of the company, though he had paid no more than the initial £50,000. The extra money had come from Simpkins' own cash flow.

Maxwell had demonstrated his mastery of accountancy, a characteristic which recurs throughout his life. Accountancy, it must be emphasized, is not a science but an art, and the classification of any money is, within certain limits, quite legitimately subject to considerable personal discretion by the accountants. The immediate result of Maxwell's exercise of his discretion was that Simpkins' reserves were £45,000 poorer in actual cash than they had been at the beginning of the year. Since the company was still hovering on the verge of insolvency, it was a bold decision to take.

There was no secret why Maxwell was in such haste to repay the debt. In his bid to build an empire, he wanted a base in America where there was undoubtedly a huge market for British books and for Springer's journals. In 1952, he wanted to buy the British Book Center in New York, which was for sale. Pitmans, who had a power of veto over any investment while Maxwell still owed money, could see no commercial sense in the venture. So Maxwell paid off the debt and was free to bid for the Book Center.

Pitmans' disapproval appeared to be well founded because the American company was bankrupt. The Book Center had been founded at the end of the war by B. T. Batsford, a British publisher, with the support of other companies, and ambitiously housed in a five-story office block on the relatively fashionable East 55th Street. After three years the founders' hopes began to fade and Batsfords sold part of its controlling interest to a Conservative Member of Parliament, Captain Peter Baker MC, a well-known socialite who, everyone agreed, had fought "a wonderful war." After demobilization, Baker had embarked on a mercurial career of establishing a publishing company, investing in a film studio and winning a seat in Parliament. Maxwell was very attracted to Baker, showing no obvious disdain for his politics. For at the turn of the decade Maxwell, who had never lost sight of his ambition to become a Member of Parliament, was in contact with several Tory politicians. Possibly Maxwell saw in Baker an entrée into politics, but his friend's dazzling success was very brief.

In early 1952, Baker was drinking heavily and suffering financial problems. Maxwell lent him £13,500. Just months later, in May, Maxwell agreed to cancel the debt in return for Baker's 1,215 shares in the

Book Center, which gave Maxwell a major interest. There still remained a $78,000 (£27,857) debt which the Center owed Batsfords. Maxwell's negotiations produced an apparently good deal. For £7,000 and a further £3,606 he obtained Batsfords' 334 shares and complete control. Although the shares were bought by Maxwell personally, a check for £9,666 was paid by Simpkins and charged to the debt owed to Maxwell. It was totally legal because, according to the accounts, Simpkins was still in debt to Maxwell, but the sagacity of that transaction would soon be queried by independent accountants. However, in mid-1952 it seemed to outsiders that Maxwell's success was impressive.

Within one year of the meeting at the Savoy, Maxwell was operating from a major property in central London, and controlled Simpkin Marshall, LMS and the Book Center. He seemed set to become a major international book-distributor, with a lifestyle to match. He had moved from suburban Chiswick to Claygate, a substantial detached residence in Esher which housed his family (now expanded to four children with the birth of girl twins). His business interests were accompanied by intense socializing. Through Anne Dove he was introduced to a succession of luminaries including two Labour politicians who also seemed set on stardom. The first was Francis Noel-Baker, son of the Labour veteran, and the second was Hugh Gaitskell, the Labour Party leader. Many of Maxwell's former employees remember the stir that Gaitskell's arrival at Maxwell House caused, but none remembers it better than Bill Keyes who watched it from outside. Keyes was on picket duty in one of the regular strikes for a wage increase. As Gaitskell approached the entrance, Keyes asked him to respect their picket. "He just ignored us," says Keyes.

Coleridge understood why Maxwell was currying friendship with politicians. During one conversation Maxwell confided that his ambition was now to become Prime Minister of Britain. His self-confidence was shared by Betty. "My husband," she told Coleridge, "can do anything," and that included governing the country. Endearingly, Maxwell did not believe that his birthplace and religion were obstacles. Few of those around him, however, especially his fellow refugees, could see any suggestion that Maxwell embraced any particular political philosophy: he seemed to be motivated largely by the desire to increase his wealth. But others like Anne Dove believed that Maxwell wanted power, particularly political power.

Anne Dove understood his ambitions better than anyone and often held parties for him to meet the influential people whom she knew. Admiringly, she watched her boss in action: "He always made a point of learning something from everybody. It was his instinct." He always made a beeline for those who were important and, with the skill of a seasoned actor, played a matching role: "He had respect for power, which was a natural outcome of his character." He was also, she recognized, abrasive in handling people. Dove pointedly states, "I often made him undo unfair things like dismissals. It was his best quality. He always knew when he was wrong and quite humble." But in the euphoria of his success, no one else noticed that characteristic or the appearance of the first cracks in his ambitions. The initial cause emanated from Heidelberg.

Tönjes Lange's first reaction to Maxwell's purchase of Simpkin Marshall had been cautiously optimistic. Although the take-over was effected without his knowledge and was contrary to their agreement about his exclusive employment for LMS, the publicity Maxwell had attracted in London convinced both Lange and even Ferdinand that they were associated with someone who was rising very fast in British society. In particular, they were impressed by the *Bookseller*'s prediction that LMS would become part of Simpkin Marshall and "480,000 clients all over the world will be served specialist books and up-to-the-minute information." Despite the fear that LMS's fortunes might suffer because Maxwell's efforts would be diverted to his new interests, both believed that there might be advantages in the massive amount of new capital which Maxwell would presumably have at his disposal. Consequently, throughout 1952, they tried to help and advise Maxwell in the organization of his new business, although to their disappointment he ignored their suggestions. His very ambition, they felt, was a major cause of the friction.

In May 1952, Maxwell opened a LMS office in New York at the Book Center's premises despite Ferdinand's and Tönjes Lange's objections. His motives were to challenge Springer's two American competitors, Walter Johnson and Stechert. To staff the new office, Maxwell hired Albert Daub, a German refugee who was Stechert's sales director. Explaining his tactics to Lange, Maxwell declared his assumption that with Daub he would inherit most of Stechert's customers. He was quickly disillusioned. His prey had no influence with the customers and his former employers were delighted to be rid of him. Another attempt by Maxwell to hire expertise also misfired but in a different way. Charles Hutt was recruited from Butterworths and brought enormous expertise. But months later, he was lured away by Johnson with all his inside knowledge.

These miscalculations were exposed toward the end of 1952 just when Springer's staff were searching through the London files for other reasons to reopen their bid to recover control of Springer's exports. Among their discoveries was the payment of £10,000 for a series of lackluster "Book of the Month"–type promotion campaigns which had little connection with scientific books; moreover, sales of Springer's new publications were static, and Shudian of China, Springer's old customer, was refusing to place any new orders because half of his order made eighteen months previously had not been delivered. The case they made against the London connection seemed convincing.

Maxwell ignored Springer's complaints. He was preoccupied by the uncertain finances of Simpkin Marshall, as those in his office recall: "He was forever on the phone to Sir Charles Hambro." The banker had loaned Simpkins £74,000 and was still personally well disposed toward Maxwell. But his fellow directors had become uneasy about the bank's link and wanted to end the commitment. At first Hambro resisted and negotiated to secure the loans against Simpkins' assets. But even that was insufficient for Hambro's colleagues and in early 1953 Maxwell was asked to find a new source of finance. Some years earlier he had borrowed money from an Armenian carpet dealer called Nassim Sakuto, whom he had met in Berlin. Sakuto claimed to have sold carpets to Goering and was trying to reclaim his property. It was an unlikely story but he was prepared to lend Maxwell money in return for a share of future profits. On Orton's advice the relationship was terminated and Maxwell now needed an alternative source of money. He turned to Kurt Wallersteiner, a German refugee, with whom he was closely involved in barter deals.

Wallersteiner was a talented organic chemist and chartered chemical engineer who had developed a series of international trading companies, most notably the Watford Chemical Company and the Anglo-Continental Exchange. They met at a lunch at the Athenaeum Club in spring 1952 hosted by Major John Whitlock, the clubbable Butterworths executive with an interest in science.

The two refugees immediately achieved a close rapport, especially since Maxwell still retained an interest in barter. Wallersteiner at the time was supplying pharmaceuticals and chemicals to East Germany, which, like all Communist countries, had little convertible currency and paid instead with East German products. Wallersteiner was attracted to the precarious trade by the big profits earned by deals with the Communist countries at the height of the Cold War. But the perpetual juggling act required skill, and Wallersteiner would occasionally come unstuck, as when he was stranded with one and a half million babies' feeding bottles in a Hamburg warehouse. When the two men met, Maxwell also had a pressing problem. He needed to liquidate the barter "payments" made by the Chinese and Yugoslavs for the supply of Springer journals, although he seemed better able than Wallersteiner to terminate the juggling act profitably.

Throughout the post-embryo period of building his book-marketing interests, Maxwell had nurtured Low-Bell's business. The era of extreme shortages still prevailed and fortunes could be earned by skillfully negotiating through the tangle of government controls to supply a much needed commodity. Soon after they met, Maxwell offered Wallersteiner the services of his own team, Bill Hickey and Paul Lassen. Lassen, the junior of the duo, recalls that while "Waller would set the deals up, Maxy would have to rescue him from the mess." In recognition of his services, Lassen's wages would sometimes be paid by the Watford Chemical Co.

The deals invariably involved a triangle formed by west Europe, China and East Germany. Occasionally, everything went through smoothly, one such transaction being the supply of indigo-blue dye to China via East Germany. Other deals were initiated through LMS's supply of British and American books and journals, which would be part of a normal barter deal. But Lassen remembers a series of transactions which ended in desperate phone calls, frantic flights across Europe, threats to extract money which was owed and endless negotiations to sell a bewildering and occasionally exotic array of foods, chemicals and hardware which were located in Customs' warehouses at ports around the world. Lassen particularly remembers shipments from China of silk, egg-yolk spray and tea. It was a characteristic of the period that obtaining import permits was a precious skill which in the barter trade became invaluable when Maxwell or Wallersteiner wanted to close the circle and collect the money. Lassen was often the fireman who rushed off to "liquidate" the deal. Successfully he negotiated for the silk, worth more than £1 million, to be sold to Debenhams, and for the egg yolk to be bought by cake manufacturers in the Midlands; while the tea, which had been obtained in exchange for cement, was, he proudly recalls, liquidated within three days: "I knew nothing about tea but I found a broker in London who put his nose into the sample and said it was excellent. I flew to Rotterdam and air-freighted the cargo to Britain within three days. Maxy was very pleased and gave me a one hundred pound bonus."

Lassen unsuccessfully fought shy of Wallersteiner's more dubious deals, especially the purchase of the antibiotic streptomycin in America, which were done without Maxwell's knowledge. Washington has always been sensitive about its trade with the Communist bloc and its prejudices were never more intense than at the height of the Korean War. For the sly entrepreneur who managed to break the American trade embargo and supply the Communists' urgent needs, the profits were commensurate with the risk. In 1952, Wallersteiner had bought streptomycin in America, which had been shipped to Holland. Surreptitiously, the boxes were relabeled and, with false shipping documents, forwarded to China. In return more silk arrived in Europe. Lassen collected the payment in East Berlin from "Diamond Jim" in bundles of dollar notes. According to Lassen, who was "unhappy" about crossing into the east, "Waller was caught on that deal and someone in Europe was imprisoned."

No deal however reached the bizarre proportions of Wallersteiner's shipment of chemicals to East Germany bartered for an assortment of china, glass and textiles which were shipped to Argentina. The Argentinians in turn shipped two thousand tons of pork bellies to Britain but to Wallersteiner's horror the British Ministry of Food condemned the meat as substandard. With his costs mounting daily, Wallersteiner searched for a solution. Part of the shipment was sent to Holland for canning while the remainder was sold to Austria under the guise of a bilateral barter deal between two nations. Anne Dove stayed with Maxwell at the Hotel Sacher in Vienna for that complicated transaction. "It was absolutely hilarious," she recalls, "like a music-hall comedy where strange men were constantly coming in and out and hiding behind doors and curtains while Maxwell and Wallersteiner argued about the deal." It was one of the rare occasions when Dove realized that Maxwell's right hand did not know what his left hand was doing. "The meat was so old," says Dove, "that I warned Wallersteiner that he would poison a whole nation but everyone just thought it was a hoot." Among the strange cast helping Maxwell and Wallersteiner to conclude the deal was Sir George Franckenstein, GCVO, an Austrian-born nobleman, diplomat and financier who was naturalized as a British citizen in 1938 and received a knighthood in the same year. Franckenstein had fallen on hard times but still had enough connections in his homeland to convince Austrian officials that they should accept that Wallersteiner was the representative of the fictitious state of the Oceania Republic and agree to exchange the pork for prefabricated houses. It fell to Hickey and Lassen to find customers for the houses.

In typical Maxwell style, the new project was attacked with gusto. Since the lack of housing in post-war Britain was an emotive political issue, Maxwell had high hopes of profits. A prototype, installed with electricity and plumbing, was erected in High Wycombe and government officials were invited for inspection tours. Nobody responded. Four months later, Maxwell's team finally secured an interview at the Ministry where, according to Lassen, "We were treated like children." Rejected by the government and also by the building societies, their efforts were deployed to selling the houses to Canada, America and Cyprus.

Meanwhile, the pork, after canning in Holland, was sold to East Germany in return for some thousands of tons of cement. After the British government refused to grant an import license, the cement was sold to Canada for the foundations of the wooden houses. The chain seemed finally complete, but en route to Canada one Liberty ship sprang a leak that set the cement rock hard. On that transaction there were no profits for either Low-Bell or the Watford Chemical Company.

To the staff in the Marylebone Road, the antics of Hickey and Lassen were barely comprehensible, and, in the compartmentalized world which Maxwell created, that was the intention. Heyden remembers only the "shadowy" Wallersteiner, who was forever coming in and out, while others jibed about the "mysterious foreigner." For those engrossed in rescuing Simpkin Marshall, the managing director's endless meetings with the ubiquitous Wallersteiner were frustrating. Some surmised that Maxwell was "keeping his cards close to his chest" because he was reluctant, as an aspiring socialite and book magnate, to be seen in the grubby and unaesthetic world of pork and chemicals. In line with compartmentalization, Simpkins' accountants did not prepare Low-Bell accounts. "Barter was not the image he wanted to cultivate," recalls one of his financial staff.

There were, however, pressing reasons for Maxwell's relationship with Wallersteiner. With Simpkins losing money, Wallersteiner's business was an enticing prospect for easily earned income. One year after their first meeting, on July 3, 1953, Maxwell was formally appointed "confidential manager" of Wallersteiner's companies and was to be paid 20 per cent of their net profits. In 1969 Maxwell explained his motives: "I would be able to control him and prevent him from doing any unsavory business in Iron Curtain countries." He added that this would add to his own profit and be to the benefit of the national economy. Within five weeks, on August 14, Maxwell had persuaded Wallersteiner to take over Hambros' secured charge which by then had mounted to £320,000. Wallersteiner paid by way of a debenture which was not redeemable until 1958. Since Wallersteiner had already lent Simpkins £50,000, his commitment to Simpkins' success was greater than Maxwell's own. According to Wallersteiner, they celebrated their partnership by dining together at Les Ambassadeurs in Mayfair.

The following month, on September 28, Maxwell asked Wallersteiner for more money. Wallersteiner claims that Maxwell assured him that Simpkins was thriving, and on that basis he lent a further £100,000, although Maxwell, by a special share issue, still retained control over the company. But Simpkins' costs continued to mount. A successful strike had led to increased wages while the volume of Simpkins' trade had barely increased. Yet there were limited successes. Two weeks after Wallersteiner's third loan, Maxwell persuaded thirty-five publishers to deliver their books on sale or return. Although he had achieved a singularly important breakthrough, "The trade was simply suspicious," says one of Simpkins' executives, "and they had some grounds."

In the summer of 1953, Coleridge suddenly resigned, so sparking a crisis of confidence. In the trade, the gossip was that the company was virtually insolvent. Publishers personally demanded that their accounts be settled. The behavior of Otto Kyllmann of Constable was typical: he arrived at Maxwell House, told the taxi to wait, and burst into Maxwell's office, refusing to leave until he had received a check. There were also rumors that books which had been bought for export at a 50 per cent discount and ostensibly shipped to the Book Center in New York had been sold in Britain where the publisher's discount would have been 33 per cent. The fiddle, if it existed, was deemed to be the brainchild of a Simpkins employee who had joined the company before the war, and Maxwell would never have known what the trade long suspected. Although Simpkins had little prospect of recovering from bankruptcy, some observers claim that Maxwell was "deeply worried," while others assert that there was no visible sign of concern. Simpkins' impending collapse might have been less alarming if his relationship with Springer, which supplied the bulk of Maxwell House's income, had not again been endangered.

Earlier in the year, Lange had summoned Maxwell to Berlin for a weekend discussion, in particular about the delay in payments. Maxwell, it was felt, was spending too much of his time on Simpkins' business at the expense of LMS'. Lange had heard privately from Orton that while Simpkins' costs had increased by 300 per cent, its turnover was up by only 180 per cent. But Maxwell arrived, employed his customary mixture of persuasive charm and salesmanship and departed after convincing his "uncle" that the suspicions were unfounded because "sales and profits had increased during the previous year by 24 per cent."

But by September the reservoir of goodwill had practically disappeared. Orton told Hövel that the local authority in London was once again threatening to order the closure of Maxwell House on the grounds that it was a fire hazard. Maxwell's only hope of reprieve, said Orton, was to use his influence at the Ministry of Labour. Hövel was particularly struck by Coleridge's resignation and by Maxwell's refusal to "properly exploit" the Germans' advice. "We regretfully came to the conclusion," says Hövel, "that too many sales were being lost by poor advertising. It was not completely Maxwell's fault that we felt that it was time for a friendly divorce."

The formal letter, couched in mournful terms, was sent in November. The official reason cited for the break was the new German exchange regulations which required payment in dollars for exports to America. Tönjes noted with regret that they rarely saw or even heard from Maxwell anymore. Ferdinand, however, was delighted by the break. In a letter to his nephew Bernhard, who was attempting to establish a Springer publishing house in New York, Ferdinand warned against any relationship with Maxwell and Bernhard accepted the advice: "Maxwell has proved to be a difficult person to do business with." Maxwell had proposed to Bernhard that he invest in the new company, but Bernhard's rejection was emphatic: "We don't want him as a person who wields any influence here."

Legally, Maxwell could have forestalled the break for one year but since he had bought Simpkins without Springer's approval he was on weak ground. That weekend Maxwell and Lange agreed to an amicable, partial separation under which Maxwell relinquished his exclusive selling rights throughout the world but was allowed to represent LMS in some areas. The new arrangement would amply suit his latest ambition: to tap the vast reservoir of scientific journals published in the Communist bloc countries which had never been read in the West.

The first public hint of the strategy which would earn its architect his first million pounds was a small article in *Der Telegraf,* Maxwell's old newspaper, on January 19, 1954. After long negotiations, the Soviet government had agreed to consider Maxwell's proposals to translate and print Russian scientific papers in the West. Since there were no direct flights, the easiest route was via East Berlin. Maxwell arrived at Tempelhof airport in West Berlin, where he gave an interview to the newspaper. He described himself as the publisher and director of the "world's biggest bookseller, Simpkin Marshall," as the director of a "London merchant bank" which hoped to conclude some barter deals with the Russians (presumably Wallersteiner's Anglo-Continental Exchange) and as the first publisher from the free world to negotiate for the sale of scientific books with the Soviets.

Anne Dove walked alongside Maxwell in the middle of the night across the snow-covered Kurfürstendamm, watched by armed Russian soldiers, into the Soviet zone. By arrangement a taxi was waiting to take them to the airport. These were pioneering forays behind the Iron Curtain but Maxwell was by then a seasoned traveler. Maxwell and Dove stayed in Moscow for two weeks. The Russians constantly refused to answer Maxwell's questions and to give a date for the next round of negotiations. Between the meetings, Maxwell was confined to the hotel with a minder with whom he played chess. During the negotiations themselves, Maxwell and Dove were plied with vodka. But Maxwell, according to Dove, was always well prepared. "He ate loads of yogurt to line his stomach. I ate caviar. He knew all the tricks." At the end, Maxwell could wait no longer and returned to England without a firm contract. "As we crossed the Channel he breathed a sigh of relief and said how pleased he was to be home. Being British meant more to him than anything else. 'I feel safe,' he would say to me."

The contrast between his patriotism and the long trips to the Iron Curtain countries did not pass unnoticed by the British security services. Soon after their return, Anne Dove received a private call from a source she well recognized. She was invited to come for a "discreet chat with an anonymous man in an unnumbered room in the War Office." It was the cover address for M.I.5., the British internal security service. The purpose was explicit. "They wanted me to vouch for his loyalty. Of course they trusted my judgment." It was not the last occasion that Maxwell's good business contacts with the Communist bloc were suspected as a cover for sinister activities, especially after Mezhdunarodnaya Kniga, the Soviet publishing house, granted him an exclusive contract for the Western world. But that did not prevent Dickie Franks, the head of M.I.6's DP4 section, approaching Maxwell. Franks' task was to recruit British travelers to the Communist bloc and he approached Maxwell for assistance and information. Maxwell gave Franks the benefit of his observations but little more.

In Neal Street Maxwell was triumphant and began circulating the enormous new offering to potential customers using the LMS subscribers' list. "As a result of Captain Maxwell's visit to Moscow last January," it read, "a wide range of Soviet scientific books is now available." The letter was written on LMS paper and among the first recipients of his advertisement in June was Ferdinand Springer, who claimed that he knew nothing about the deal. It was another crucial moment in Springer's relationship with Maxwell since they were on the verge of signing a new agreement.

Tönjes Lange had felt considerable doubts about any new arrangement because Maxwell had proved uncontrollable and had avoided summoning a board meeting for the past two years. Nevertheless sentiment and Maxwell's irrepressible charm had always swayed his doubts and he had agreed that Maxwell could retain some exclusive world selling rights. The new advertisement arrived as the lawyers were clarifying some final details. Ferdinand was apoplectic. "We demand," he wrote to Maxwell, "an immediate and complete break between us and LMS." Condemning the "serious breach of trust," Springer wrote that he regretted taking the final step but blamed Maxwell's "misuse of our loyalty."

Maxwell personally negotiated the break on July 2, 1954, in Heidelberg, under which he agreed to dissolve LMS and operate under the name I. R. Maxwell & Co. Ltd. Springer gave Maxwell exclusive rights until 1959 in the British Empire, France, China and Indonesia at the same discounts. Maxwell, seemingly unconcerned, asked only that the break be kept a strict secret and flew directly to New York. On his return he wrote to "My dear Onkel Lange" and promised "a smooth handover" at the beginning of 1955.

The divorce was not smooth. Within four weeks Maxwell was protesting that Springer had broken the agreement. Lange counter-charged that Maxwell was guilty of the same; in particular that Maxwell, instead of ensuring the swift disappearance of the name Lange, Maxwell & Springer had actually printed his new notepaper with the subtitle "Formerly Lange, Maxwell & Springer Ltd," a clear breach of his promise not to use the name in the future. Over the following months, Springer would repeatedly complain that Maxwell's staff were trying to hang on to old contracts or offer cut-rate terms in territories where they no longer enjoyed exclusivity. But by then Maxwell was fighting for his reputation in London.

The discord with Springer coincided with Simpkins' unstoppable slide into insolvency. In the book trade, the easiest method of directly influencing the apparent financial state of a company was through the accountant's valuation of the stock. Tom Clark, Simpkins' accountant, tried within the law to paint the best picture of the company's financial state, but his view proved to be too optimistic because one year later the stock which he had valued at £180,000 was written off as worthless. Clearly, the accountants were fighting a losing battle. Only Maxwell's determination delayed the inevitable. On May 3, 1954, he turned again to Wallersteiner for help. In a late-night meeting in Marylebone, according to Wallersteiner, Maxwell presented a predated contract which extended his own control of the German's companies in exchange for more shares in Simpkins and a right to 20 per cent of Simpkins' profits. Wallersteiner claims that he signed the following day. The background to what seems like inexplicable generosity or folly appears in Wallersteiner's own explanation to the *Sunday Times* in 1969. The businessman claimed that he feared retribution from Western governments and Intelligence agencies for his barter deals with the Communist bloc and that Maxwell had promised him protection. His account must be read with caution because he has subsequently been convicted and imprisoned for several frauds. For his part, Maxwell claimed that Wallersteiner's "investment" was actually his own money earned by the Watford Co. from the barter deals.

Whatever the truth, soon after signing, the partners had a bitter argument which ended with Wallersteiner, whose total investment in Simpkins was by that time £470,000, threatening to call a creditors' meeting. This was clearly a tense moment for Maxwell because it could have provoked Simpkins' immediate closure. In a pattern which would be repeated on many occasions over the coming years, Maxwell called Isidore Kerman, his solicitor. That night, Maxwell swore a twelve-page affidavit. It was unequivocal: "Based upon their present trading position, their goodwill and their prospects . . . [Simpkin Marshall] are not only capable of carrying on their present business, but can look forward to considerable improvement and increase of their trade." Then Maxwell swore that Simpkins, "apart from their considerable fixed assets, have an excess of current assets over current liabilities of approximately £450,000." The following morning Kerman obtained a High Court injunction which forbade Wallersteiner to endanger Simpkins' survival by alleging that the company was bankrupt. Here was an astonishing state of affairs. Subsequently Maxwell always correctly asserted that Simpkins was insolvent throughout his ownership, yet his sworn statement suggested the contrary.

In an uneasy truce over the following days, a new agreement was fashioned which froze their respective claims. Maxwell had an effective call on all Watford's profits and Wallersteiner would have to wait four years for repayment of the loans. But Maxwell did agree to accept Brigadier Alfred Critchley as Simpkins' chairman. Wallersteiner had met Critchley, a Canadian soldier and the first chairman of BOAC, through Count Vanden Heuvel and hoped to use his Establishment contacts for future barter deals in North America.

Critchley immediately hired the prestigious accountancy firm Peat, Marwick, Mitchell to investigate Simpkins' plight. Simultaneously, Maxwell hired a smaller firm of accountants, Chalmers Wade, who had direct experience of the publishing trade, "to investigate [Simpkins'] trading arrangements" but not the company's finances. Chalmers' recommendations were identical to Maxwell's own survival plan, which he had presented to London's publishers four years earlier. But the report did contain one observation of future relevance. A sale of books from Simpkins to another company owned by Maxwell had been entered in the accounts as worth £105,000. But investigation revealed that the Maxwell company had the right to return the books, which somewhat colored the accuracy of the entry as an irrevocable "sale." Fifteen years later, the same queries about accountancy practices would be raised during the investigation of Pergamon's affairs.

A third investigation was undertaken by Wallersteiner's own accountants. Like Peat, Marwick, they would eventually declare the company insolvent but they also reported an unforeseen discovery. Simpkins' biggest single debt, no less than £111,335 (it would subsequently increase to £117,000), was owed by Maxwell's own company, the Book Center in New York.

Peat's report also revealed similar inter-company transactions. In the previous year, Simpkins, despite its parlous state, had lent £211,599 to other companies which were controlled by Maxwell himself and had charged no interest. The money, commented Peat, Marwick, was not a normal trading loan, but amounted to "financial assistance." They also reported that Maxwell's affidavit describing Simpkins' surplus as £450,000 was erroneous. He had ignored Simpkins' debts of £524,813 which, after various computations, left an actual deficit, in their opinion, of £12,173 in net tangible assets. Although every assessment depended on an individual accountant's interpretation, the sharp contradiction between Peat, Marwick's report and Maxwell's unequivocally optimistic version was seized upon by London's publishers.

Before the report was finalized, events moved swiftly. In November, Maxwell admitted that Simpkins was insolvent and appealed to the Publishers Association for support by adopting Chalmers' recommendations. His argument, as explained in two articles for *Time and Tide,* seems thirty-five years later reasonable and sane. "British publishers," he wrote, "are now issuing a record number of more than 24,000 books each year. This is larger even than the United States with three times our population. Yet here in Britain publishing is still largely regarded as an occupation for gentlemen. In the United States it is a very big business run on hard economic commercial lines. Why are British publishers so reluctant at facing the facts?"

The facts were, wrote Maxwell, that the publishing industry needed to "modernize itself and take seriously the promise of giving a better service to authors and the book-buying public . . . otherwise the United Kingdom publishers will lose a great deal of their traditional export markets." In June 1954 there was to be a World Book Fair in Earls Court, but Britain's leading publishers, including Macmillan and Heinemann, were refusing to exhibit, which reflected their old-fashioned, undynamic attitude toward exporting. "Many British publishers are now congratulating themselves that the American attempt to take over the British publishing houses has been repulsed. But they are wrong in adopting this self-congratulatory attitude. The truth is the American publishers have now decided that there is hardly anything here worth buying." His ardor for reform was unlikely to endear itself to the Association, whose xenophobia would bar all refugee publishers from a seat on their council for some years. In January, the Association rejected the survival plan. The writing was on the wall, but Maxwell was well prepared. Frank Beckwith was sent to New York to arrange that the assets of Book Center and LMS were legally separated from Simpkins. The earlier appointment of Maxwell's sister Brana Natkin, who was an American citizen, as a Book Center director would effectively prevent the British receiver from gaining access to the company's records. In London, a new office and headquarters for Maxwell's other businesses had already been purchased in Fitzroy Square. The news on April 14 that a petition for the winding up of Simpkins had been presented to the High Court triggered his evacuation plan.

During the night, Beckwith and Clark, helped by Maxwell, loaded LMS's filing cabinets in Maxwell's Humber, shuttling to and from Fitzroy Square. Simultaneously, Lassen moved Low-Bell's files to the new headquarters. Gunther Heyden remembers the "frantic activity to disentangle the companies and get our assets out of Simpkin Marshall's premises before it collapsed." During the controlled panic, a fire broke out in the basement, but it was quickly extinguished. The following day, the receiver arrived and Heyden and others would spend hours arguing that furniture and stock did not belong to Simpkins. In the confusion, it was not easy for the receiver to disprove the counterclaims of LMS, EPPAC, Robert Maxwell and Co., Pergamon, International Encyclopedias, Low-Bell and a host of smaller trading companies all registered at the same address. Even the accountants had not always been certain which of the companies was responsible for which payment.

For Maxwell, based the following day in Fitzroy Square, it was practically business as usual. Once again ensconced in a huge room with a large oil portrait of an English gentleman behind him ("That's my august uncle, Moshe Schlemiel," he would joke), he seemed to those around him supremely confident. While Lassen fixed the central heating, Heyden was still selling Springer's stock, and in a small office Paul Rosbaud was unobtrusively planning Pergamon's new journals. There seemed sufficient opportunities for the future—despite the excitement, Maxwell had even squeezed in a trip to China. Probably only Anne Dove appreciated Maxwell's real concerns. Resting in the Himalayas on account of a "blood disorder," she received an endless stream of letters and telegrams from Maxwell about his plight. "He was really quite worried," she says. But to others it seemed that Maxwell was unconcerned when the time came for Simpkins to be accorded a proper funeral at a formal meeting of creditors for the bankrupt company.

On June 15, nearly two hundred publishers, their representatives and lawyers crowded into Winchester House, Old Broad Street to hear the official receiver's report. Every account agrees that there was considerable antagonism toward Maxwell, who was sitting on the platform next to the receiver. "He was very shocked by the atmosphere," recalls his former sales manager. "It was a bruising experience for him," says another, who vividly recalls how the atmosphere soured and Maxwell's demeanor changed as he was confronted publicly with the consequences of his business management.

To protect themselves from the possibility of Simpkins' bankruptcy, the majority of publishers had agreed to give Simpkins their books on sale or return in the belief that they remained the owners until the books were sold. Maxwell, they felt, had personally assured them that they were safe. But according to the legal advice obtained by the receiver, the stock was in fact owned by Simpkins. The publishers, accordingly, had lost their money. Simpkins owed £656,388 and had just £70,000 in assets to repay its creditors. The receiver announced that he had found one puzzling debt owed to Simpkins, namely £113,000 from the Book Center in New York which he believed was one cause of Simpkins' collapse. "Captain Maxwell," the receiver told his restless audience, "has informed the official receiver that the debt is not recoverable beyond about £10,000. . . . As Captain Maxwell was aware of the financial difficulties of both the British Book Center Inc. and Simpkins when Simpkins was supplying the books and the debt was mounting, [that deal would] require close investigation." The only reassurance for the creditors was that Maxwell had assured the receiver that he was trying to sell the Book Center and intended to hand over the proceeds rather than cover his own losses. "It appears doubtful," said the receiver, "whether the company was at any time solvent. The directors concerned were at fault in acquiring the Marylebone premises and financing British Book Center Inc. at a time when the company was insolvent without making satisfactory arrangements for the introduction of sufficient further capital." Maxwell was criticized for not having "considered and decided upon liquidation at a much earlier date."

Bill Keyes remembers Harold Macmillan, whose family firm was one of Simpkins' creditors, leaving Winchester House outraged. "We have lost a fortune," confided the future Prime Minister, "but my lawyers say we'll never get our money back." Macmillan never forgot or forgave the circumstances of Simpkins' collapse. Nor did several members of the future Labour government. But Maxwell quickly recovered his composure. In a statement which would add notoriety to the existing dislike, he told the editor of the *Bookseller,* "I've come down flat on my arse, but I'm going up again and this time I'm staying up." The Bouncing Czech was born and many British publishers were reluctant to deal with him again.

Right up until his death, Maxwell felt that the enormous antagonism which the collapse provoked was unfair. "I took over an insolvent company," he told the author in 1973, "and I did the best possible." He was, he felt, a misunderstood but well-intentioned reformer. But Frank Beckwith, who was Simpkins' company secretary, noticed a fatal flaw soon after the original purchase: "Selling books is based on counting halfpennies and Maxwell's style was not suited to that sort of care about precise costs." In the publishers' view, Maxwell's great sin was his cavalier interpretation of the director's role in a company. "His problem," says one of his executives, "was that he couldn't distinguish between his interests and the interests of others. He saw himself as autonomous and not as a trustee of shareholders' interests." The fate of the Book Center is proof of that view. Eventually the receiver would be paid £14,829 by William Curtis, Maxwell's former manager at the Book Center, as settlement of the £113,000 debt, but the New York building itself remained the hub of Maxwell's future and fast-expanding American operations.

4

Until the collapse of Simpkin Marshall, Maxwell had shown barely any interest in Pergamon, an aloofness which was welcomed by Paul Rosbaud and his twenty-two-year-old assistant Maria Sachs. Rosbaud and Maxwell had nothing in common other than being refugees involved in scientific publishing. But even in that slender mutuality lay fierce differences. Rosbaud was a cultured, Austrian atomic scientist who, according to Sachs, was "contemptuous of Maxwell whom he saw as an uneducated Hungarian," and their approaches to scientific publishing were sharply contrasting. While Rosbaud considered himself a true publisher who, in the old tradition, identified with the experiences of "my authors," Maxwell's reading, Rosbaud alleged, was exclusively confined to books of accounts. "Rosbaud believed in science," says Sachs, "while Maxwell believed in money."

Rosbaud had therefore been dejected when Butterworth-Springer had agreed in 1951 to Maxwell's purchase of their shares, but since his own efforts to buy the company had failed, he reluctantly accepted his fate. Ferdinand Springer had urged Rosbaud to leave Pergamon, but both were persuaded by Maxwell not to upset the arrangement to save Pergamon from collapse. On Ferdinand's insistence, Maxwell agreed to give Rosbaud a 20 per cent stake in Pergamon, but that does not seem to have been effected on account of Rosbaud's refusal. After the take-over, Rosbaud's fears dwindled. He had been given a small office in Studio Place, which he occupied with Maria Sachs and Eric Buckley, his production manager. Buckley thought Maxwell was an ideal employer. They had met a few years earlier when Maxwell had offered Butterworths the services of his book-binding subsidiary, Maxsons, and ever since they had shared a common interest in improving the technology of printing and had discussed plans for expansion. Even for

Sachs, who was deeply devoted to Rosbaud, Maxwell was "generous, good-natured, with a Balkan sense of humor." Caught in the middle, she realized that the relationship between the two men was "doomed from the outset." But, until they moved into Marylebone Road, the three employees saw little of Maxwell and rather more of the actress Hermione Gingold standing on the doorstep of her nearby house in a dressing-gown.

Rosbaud's asset was his reputation among those scientists who had fled Nazi Germany. He found no difficulty in attracting Otto Frisch, Laurence Wager and L. H. Ahrens (who were unknown to Ferdinand Springer) to his new publishing house in London. Simultaneously, he pinpointed the British scientists whose work was still relatively unpublicized and offered the formula which Springer had perfected. Among the early recruits were Sir Edward Appleton, Sir Harold Thompson, Rodney Hill, Peter Danckwerts and Kenneth Denbigh, who all envied the proliferation of scientific journals in Germany and were irritated by the monopoly of American scientists in English-speaking publications. They resented, as did many of the younger American academics, the exclusion of their work by the editors of the established journals who, they believed, did not understand their discoveries and were prejudiced against newcomers. The reaction of Denbigh, a pioneer in chemical engineering at Cambridge University, to Rosbaud was typical: "He offered us something quite special." He was impressed during Rosbaud's visit to his laboratories by the Austrian's grasp of the theoretical and experimental advances which the British scientists had accomplished. Rosbaud proposed, according to Denbigh, "a journal which emphasized European achievements. He was the driving force to launch the *Journal of Chemical Engineering Science* and it has remained one of the most successful journals in the field." Payment, of course, was never an issue. "There was deep loyalty toward Rosbaud," recalls Maria Sachs, "but his commercial sense was zero."

Throughout their stay in Marylebone Road, that weakness remained unimportant. During brief and irregular meetings, Maxwell cast a quick eye over Pergamon's uncomplicated balance sheet and, according to Sachs, showed "no interest in the journals' content but only in the financial principles of scientific publishing." Pergamon was just profitable but remained a very small publisher. During those three years, only two other journals were added to Pergamon's list: the *Journal of Nuclear Physics* and the *Journal of Mechanics and Physics of Solids*, and fourteen books. Like Denbigh, all the editors were personally attracted by Rosbaud and had no contact with Maxwell.

After Simpkins' crash, Maxwell's attitude toward his fledgling company changed. Pergamon enjoyed a good but limited reputation, earning profits of £5,000 a year, which he decided to expand in direct competition with Springer. Sachs recalls that when Maxwell's serious interest in the business started, "he was surprised by our success, especially because we were selling book rights to big publishers like McGraw-Hill in New York." She remembers the McGraw-Hill deal in particular because Maxwell insisted on renegotiating the terms. Rosbaud argued that Maxwell's increased demands would destroy his relationships but, according to Sachs, "Maxwell couldn't leave it alone and in the end McGraw pulled out."

Maxwell had long realized that it did not require scientific talent to establish a new journal. With a modicum of research, a heavy measure of flattery and plenty of organizational skill, anyone of acumen could identify a field of science which was enjoying particular attention but was not yet served by an established journal. It was then a matter of locating a collection of scientists whose work was the most respected and invite them to form an editorial board whose task would be to commission, select and edit papers for publication in their own journal. This was self-motivated, vanity publishing which depended upon Maxwell's talents to sell. With access to LMS's huge mailing list, the availability of Pergamon's new journals was widely advertised and, although each journal's sales in the early 1950s did not exceed more than a few hundred, the sales figures were less crucial since subscriptions were paid in advance. Financial management could be carefully controlled and there were the back issues as an investment for the future. The formula was well established when Rosbaud first tasted Maxwell's ambitions just a few weeks after the move to Fitzroy Square. A large villa, Maxwell announced, had been rented on Pergamon's behalf in Geneva.

What ensued was the first Geneva conference on the peaceful use of atomic energy organized by the United Nations in 1955. Rosbaud's natural interest in the subject dictated that he should attend. In the wake of Hiroshima, the launching of the world's first nuclear submarine and the earliest construction programs of atomic power stations for domestic electricity, the conference was a natural magnet for every atomic scientist in the world, if only to meet the American pioneers from Oak Ridge and Los Alamos. It was also a magnet for every other scientific publisher who, like Pergamon, hoped to capitalize on the sudden declassification of America's atomic secrets and commission books for a fast-growing market. To Rosbaud's irritation, Maxwell, whose knowledge of atomic science was limited to recognizing the mushroom cloud of an explosion, also wanted to attend, not to listen to speeches but to test the commercial opportunities.

Among the scientists invited to the conference was John Dunworth, the head of the reactor department at Britain's atomic research center at Harwell who had been recruited by Rosbaud to be the editor-in-chief of Pergamon's *Journal of Nuclear Energy*. Shortly before leaving for Geneva, Maxwell and Dunworth met to agree on special arrangements for the conference. In Dunworth's name, Maxwell would stage a series of receptions in his rented villa to which every scientist attending the conference would be invited. Dunworth understood the purpose. Maxwell, he says, was "an enormously engaging companion who was determined to make a lot of money." At the parties, Maxwell systematically engaged each guest in conversation to establish a relationship and discover the potential for new publications. Geneva, in Dunworth's opinion, "opened Maxwell's eyes very quickly to the commercial opportunities of scientific journals." Buckley also could only look on in awe as Maxwell, having absorbed the jargon, held seemingly high-powered conversations with the fathers of atomic science. Maria Sachs watched Maxwell's technique: "He was smart because he always knew what to offer to buy the person—fame or money." Rosbaud, however, was inconsolably piqued, infuriated that a businessman should speak as an equal to a scientist and full of scorn for the "so-called polyglot" who "spoke a lot of languages, all equally badly." If Maxwell was even aware of Rosbaud's mood, he was invariably oblivious to others' sensitivities, and he brushed it aside because he was too preoccupied in scooping the commercial benefits for himself.

In the normal course of events, the United Nations, as the conference organizers, would eventually publish all of the 1,100 papers prepared for the occasion in bound volumes—"undigested and unedited." Maxwell perceived that here was a natural and unexploited extension to the journal business. Pergamon would publish and sell the most important papers in "critically revised" volumes under the general title "Progress in Nuclear Energy." Purposefully, he approached the most eminent of the scientists and invited them to create six editorial boards which would select and supervise the publication of those series. By the end of the conference, he had recruited the cream of American, British and French nuclear scientists. Among the editors of the series entitled the "Economics of Nuclear Power" was Maxwell himself. He returned from Geneva euphoric, determined that the Pergamon series should appear before the official volumes. "We worked fast and furious," recalls Buckley, "and came out long ahead." Pergamon was dramatically transformed. "Overnight we were involved in huge production schedules," says Buckley. Maxwell also appreciated the lucrative possibilities of taking two bites of the cherry. While the Geneva conference was published under one title, the same papers but "revised to include later developments" were also sold in another series entitled "Physics and Mathematics."

By the end of 1955, in one year under Maxwell's direction, Pergamon was no longer a small publisher. Its output had grown to fifty journals and eighteen books. The production planned for the following year was nearly double. By the end of 1957, Pergamon was publishing over one hundred journals and books. Among its prestigious contributors whose past papers were collected and presented as Pergamon publications were the physicists Max Born and Niels Bohr. The range of topics was also impressive: electrolytic and chemical polishing of metals; the Aurorae and the Airglow; atmospheric pollution; irradiation colors and luminescence; psychosomatic research; neurochemistry and the chemistry of solids. In addition, Maxwell began to take over the business management of established but unexploited specialist journals from learned societies, such as the *British Abstracts of Medical Sciences,* and placed the Pergamon imprint on their cover. It was the prelude to a life of constantly flying around the world to scientific conferences on every conceivable subject to repeat his success at Geneva. Destinations from Stockholm to Santiago, Moscow to Montreal and Peking to Paris were regular stops in his itinerary to offer Pergamon's services to scientific conferences as the official publisher of their papers and proceedings and to present to the scientists the opportunity to create editorial boards to establish new journals. Gunther Heyden recalls his "total exhaustion. We traveled nonstop and at night, because he didn't need any sleep, he would either talk or play practical jokes to prevent me sleeping. He just drove himself and all of us on and on and, if someone was no longer wanted, he would be fired."

Relentlessly, universities throughout the world were being offered an increasing range of journals which, because of the prestige of the editorial boards, their librarians were initially eager to buy. Selling depended upon image and Maxwell was a master of presentation. Pergamon was presented as an international company with offices at the British Book Center in New York, in Los Angeles and in Paris. The foreword to Pergamon's catalog was a three-page description of the history of Pergamon's birthplace in ancient Greece culled from *Encyclopaedia Britannica.* There was even a motto. Amid great laughter, Maxwell directed Heyden to find the Latin for "We shall find a way or we shall make one." *Invenimus viam aut faciemus* was thereafter printed on Pergamon's catalogs. Once the initial subscription target had been met and the money taken, there was always the opportunity at the end of the year to fill out the last issue with a collection of papers from an obscure conference or from another Pergamon journal and keep the choicest papers for the new year and another subscription. Rosbaud's intimate business was transformed beyond recognition. In 1958, utterly isolated from the business itself, he left, full of resentment that he was not due a penny.

By then, Maxwell had also capitalized upon his close personal relationship with the President of the Soviet Academy of Sciences. No other Western publisher had invested the time and energy in repeated journeys to Moscow to cultivate the Russians. In the midst of the Cold War, few would have dared and the remainder would have seen little purpose. Maxwell, who grew up physically closer to the Soviet Union than most publishers in the West, was pragmatic and understanding about the Communist system. He understood the Russian way of life and could speak the language both literally and metaphorically. Among the first to meet Maxwell in 1954 was Yuri Leonov, a general director at Mezhdunarodnaya Kniga, the Soviet state publishing organization. Leonov recalls the young and handsome Maxwell with a "clever approach to publishers." Negotiating in English, because his Russian was not perfect, Maxwell explained that since Russia was not a signatory to the international copyright convention, he could take any scientific books and journals he wanted and republish them in the West without paying any royalties. In fact, he had been doing that for some time. But he was now prepared, explained Maxwell, to pay the authors a royalty direct. Leonov was certainly impressed with his "countryman's" approach, partly because of his charm and also because in their political discussions, Maxwell "expressed sympathy toward the Soviet Union."

At Maxwell's request, Leonov approached his superiors and especially Yuri Gradov, the legal adviser of Mezhdunarodnaya Kniga, to negotiate an exclusive deal for Pergamon. Gradov felt immediate sympathy toward the man whom he met on the windy street outside the foreign ministry building: "There were no precedents for the agreement but my orders were to do a deal with Maxwell." In fact, Gradov was ordered to conclude a deal at any price. "I was told to forget about making money. Maxwell was to have the rights to the journals for ideological purposes. My superiors wanted a source of propaganda in the West to prove that the Russians were not idiotic bears. So Maxwell was to get anything he wanted at no cost."

Before starting the negotiations, Gradov checked with the KGB: "They told me that Maxwell was all right. Otherwise they wouldn't have let him into the country." The KGB's assurance confirmed Gradov's impression of Maxwell's special status. The publisher had been allocated a Communist shrine in the then exclusive National Hotel situated opposite the Kremlin. Room 107, where Maxwell stayed, was the room used by Lenin in 1917 after his arrival from St. Petersburg and before he moved into the Kremlin: "It seemed that only an important person would get that hallowed room," concludes Gradov.

While Maxwell sat, legs up on a huge table drinking tea and smoking cigarettes in an enormous conference room in the foreign ministry, Gradov drafted their agreement. At the end of four days, the publisher had secured an advantageous contract which was endorsed by Academician Topchiev, the General Secretary of the Soviet Academy of Science. Gradov had taken Maxwell to meet Topchiev and could not fail to be impressed by the Academician's sentiment toward the publisher: "Take anything you want. Translate it and don't bother about the royalties." On Topchiev's recommendation that Maxwell was solid, Russia's scientists, anxious to be published in the West and to receive some hard currency, offered the publisher their work. Although Maxwell would have been tempted to take Topchiev's offer literally, his agreement with Mezhdunarodnaya Kniga stipulated payments of about 20 per cent royalties for the publication rights.

With the agreement signed, Maxwell sought a representative in Moscow. He was introduced to Victor Louis, an English-speaking journalist who used his own apartment as the Pergamon office. Louis, who became famous in Britain during that era for his supply of scoops about Russian politics to the *London Evening News,* could only have worked for Maxwell and the British press with the agreement of the KGB. Although the precise nature of Maxwell's relationship with the KGB in that period remains unclear, it is certain that he was sponsored by the Soviet security service. Maxwell returned to Britain with the foundations to create his first millions. Under his agreement with Mezhdunarodnaya Kniga (the Soviet publishing organization), Pergamon enjoyed the exclusive rights to a wide range of journals which had not hitherto been seen in the West. After translation in Fitzroy Square by "two Poles and two Cossacks," they were sold in a variety of packages, but demand remained limited until the unexpected launch of the Sputnik in 1957. Overnight, Western scientists, prompted by worried politicians, sought every source of information about Soviet science and it was Pergamon which owned the monopoly. As interest increased and Pergamon's profits multiplied, Maxwell restlessly traveled through eastern Europe, particularly Poland, Hungary and East Germany, obtaining similar concessions for their scientific journals and winning their goodwill by placing orders to print Pergamon publications because they were cheaper than British tenders. By 1962, Maxwell's declared annual profit from his trade with Russia amounted to £50,000 and was increasing. With the assistance of the publishers of the *Great Soviet Encyclopaedia,* he had obtained the rights to edit and publish *Information USSR* which was automatically purchased by most libraries throughout the West. Proudly, he announced that he was the only British publisher to have a stand at the British trade fair in Moscow and claimed to have personally persuaded Khrushchev to soften the strict Soviet attitudes toward Western copyrights, although nothing in fact transpired. Maxwell's relationship with the Communists blossomed. He would become a uniquely trusted Westerner who was received in the Kremlin by successive Soviet leaders and would publish their autobiographies in translated versions throughout the West. Each volume in the autobiography series was accompanied by an interview with Maxwell, although the questions were often nearly the same length as the answers. But, curiously, many of those Soviet-bloc journals were offered for sale not directly by Pergamon, but through the Pergamon Institute in New York which was described as a "Non-profit-making foundation under the Presidency of Sir Robert Robinson OM FRS." In Britain, however, there was barely any suggestion that Pergamon was not enjoying the profits of its monopoly.

Despite the illusion that Pergamon was totally based in London, America was in fact the financial center of its operations. In about 1951, Maxwell had established a family trust in Liechtenstein which in turn owned a series of private companies in New York. There were significant tax and legal advantages in dividing the business between London, New York and Liechtenstein and the structure satisfied Maxwell's most fundamental principle of compartmentalization, whereby employees knew only about their own function and Maxwell alone personally understood the overall operation. The most important private company trading on his behalf in New York was Pergamon Press Inc. (PPI), which was founded in 1952. PPI was based at the British Book Center in East 55th Street under Detlev Raymond, a German whom Orton and Maxwell had recruited in Berlin. In parallel with Pergamon in Britain, Raymond, helped by Maria Sachs, established contacts with

American scientists, fostered relationships to create new American editorial boards and bought established journals such as *Acta Metallurgica* which enjoyed large circulations.

On his frequent flights to America, Maxwell was often accompanied by his secretary, Anne Dove. Unlike Britain, America could not offer Maxwell the commercial and political opportunities he sought because there were thousands of similar hustling entrepreneurs in this nation of immigrants. Dove could see the true Maxwell at the center of his family and she was surprised. During their first years traveling together, Dove had often asked her employer whether he was Jewish. "He never gave a direct answer," says Dove. "He would jokingly reply, 'Can a Jew read the Sunday lesson?' referring to his attendance at the local church in Esher." But in New York, Dove met his family and notably his cousin, Irving Schlomovitch, who worked for Maxwell. "One Friday, Irving said to me that Maxwell was going to celebrate Shabbat with him and I said, 'But is Mr. Maxwell Jewish?' I got an odd stare." Understandably, Maxwell had decided that unlike in New York, in Britain there was no premium on being Jewish.

America was also a country where the respected British publisher could still trade without fear of embarrassment. Anne Dove was equipped with a facsimile set of the stamp collection of King George V, bound in sheepskin, and she criss-crossed America to sell the collection to American philatelists. "It was a great success," she recalls, "especially in Dallas where Maxwell had notified the British consul to arrange a conference. Hundreds turned up."

In the smaller, more compact quarters of Fitzroy Square, it was much easier for the staff to observe how Maxwell operated. The hall outside his office was usually filled with people waiting for a long-delayed appointment and often anxious to attract Maxwell into a prospective deal. Those who managed to get inside met a man whose self-confidence had never been greater. He exuded a mixture of generosity and affection for those whom he saw as both talented and loyal, and utter contempt for those who were deemed dispensable. Often the talented and loyal were the same individuals who were deemed to be dispensable. Few observed Maxwell closer than Gunther Heyden, who besides selling Springer's stock was also on a commission to sell *Encyclopaedia Britannica* on behalf of Maxwell's company, International Encyclopaedias Ltd., which owned the agency for sales in Belgium, France, Germany and South Africa. Heyden was challenged by Maxwell to sell one thousand sets with the promise of a £1,000 bonus. "Maxwell believed that in business you can't be democratic. He would want to see how far he could push people and then they would be dismissed. When the person was on the floor, he would start weeping."

Like all of Maxwell's employees, Heyden could not fathom the complexity of his employer's emotions, and he gained no further insight when Maxwell was taken critically ill to University College Hospital. Maxwell was suffering from suspected cancer of the lung and was awaiting an operation for the removal of a lobe. He had been warned that he might not recover from the surgery. Among his visitors was Anne Dove, who found Maxwell in his room interviewing a Christian Science leader, "trying to find an acceptable truth about life." The visitor was one in a succession of Jewish, Catholic and Church of England ministers who failed to provide an acceptable answer to his question. After his recovery, the fact that he might have died had not apparently changed his attitudes toward mortals or eternity.

His life remained a series of hectic travel schedules and new ventures. In 1952, he had established Harmony Films, whose directors included the producer Paul Czinner, his wife the actress Elizabeth Bergner and the impoverished Sir George Franckenstein. In 1954, Czinner directed the filming of Mozart's *Don Giovanni* from the live performance at the Salzburg Festival and used the same techniques three years later for the visit of the Bolshoi ballet to London. Maxwell arranged with Buckingham Palace that the première should be a Royal Gala Charity performance to which the Duchess of Kent was invited. It was a glittering occasion, which he barely had time to enjoy before flying to China on business.

The Palace was not the only casualty of Maxwell's unremitting pace, and the consequences were costly. On December 15, 1958, Tönjes Lange wrote that Springer wanted to terminate all its connections with Maxwell. After explaining that Springer would always be "grateful" for his help in the post-war period, Lange explained that too many customers were "dissatisfied" with the service from London to continue any further relationship. The verdict was a body-blow and Maxwell's reaction reflected his confusion.

His first reply on January 2 was a straightforward acknowledgment that while he was "naturally sad and disappointed" there would be "a great many points to settle" which he hoped would be done in a "friendly, efficient and fair way." The following day, however, he sent another letter which was markedly different. "Your letter," he wrote, "caused me a great deal of anguish and surprise. Anguish because it means official notice to sever our special relations which have existed over a decade and which have been so dear to my heart. Everything I know, everything that I have built up, everything that I have learned and acquired spring in one way or another from the joint fountain of Dr. Ferdinand Springer and yourself and the splendid House of Springer Verlag." The letter continued with the statement that he would be returning to Springer "in accordance with our distribution agreement" books worth DM 300,000 and journals worth DM 200,000. Maxwell asked, "Do you propose to raise any difficulty about their return and credit?"

Lange certainly did raise difficulties. The correspondence, which lasted one year, was inaugurated in twelve detailed pages in which Lange denied that their latest agreement signed on November 13, 1956, supported Maxwell's claim to the money or his proposed return of the old journals. Lange realized that Maxwell was irritated about losing Springer's lucrative trade especially since his warehouse was still full of old, unsaleable stock. But Lange took particular exception to Maxwell's reference to their "strictly confidential" post-war agreements which was code that Springer's false Customs declarations after 1950 had weakened their ability to make demands. It could have been the beginning of an ugly divorce except that Maxwell was emotionally attached to Lange and did not want a break with his surrogate father. "Please, my dear uncle Lange," he wrote on December 23, 1959, "let's agree to break the Gordian knot in the new year in a friendly and generous fashion." They compromised, but barely met again before Lange's death in 1960. It was the end of an era but it caused only a slight hiccup in Pergamon's profits.

By 1959, Pergamon's two hundred employees had already outgrown numbers 4 and 5 Fitzroy Square and, following the expiry of the lease of the warehouse in Elephant and Castle, Maxwell decided to move to Oxford for both cheaper accommodation and prestige. In May he rented Headington Hill Hall, on the outskirts of the old town, for £2,000 a year. The mansion, which was formerly the home of Lady Ottoline Morrell, would also serve as the Maxwell family home. The previous tenants, the Red Cross, had built four single-story office buildings in the grounds and they were ideal for Pergamon's staff. The move was completed during 1960 but Fitzroy Square was kept to house I. R. Maxwell & Co. who were described as "international university and industrial booksellers." The compartmentalization between the two businesses, selling and publishing, was physically complete.

Oxford was an ideal location to launch Pergamon's expansion in the 1960s, the decade of a boom in education. With the prospect of the Robbins report and the consequent building of a range of new universities, there were endless opportunities for huge profits to supply new schools and universities. In anticipation, Pergamon embarked on new ventures such as a one-thousand-volume library of original works on science, technology and engineering which was sold in paperback supported by a prestigious team of editorial advisers, principally Sir Robert Robinson, Sir John Cockcroft and Sir Edward Appleton. Called "The Commonwealth and International Library of Science, Technology, Engineering and Literature," it aimed to provide books for African and Asian students in competition with Communist-supplied books which Maxwell believed to be politically slanted. "I want to help the man in the factory," he explained, "who is anxious to educate himself." Executives at the competing Oxford University Press were surprised by Maxwell's promotion since their own one-thousand-volume "Commonwealth Library" had been offering similar courses for many years. On that occasion, executives decided to take no action, but in 1977 they did issue an injunction to prevent the sale of another Maxwell publication, *Pergamon's Oxford Dictionary*, which they complained had plagiarized their own standard work. Maxwell quickly retreated but inside the publishing world, where memories of the Simpkins crash were still fresh, the latest juggle added to a new wave of criticisms against a man widely viewed as an upstart.

The major complaint concerned Pergamon's pricing and publication policy. Editorials published in the *Lancet,* the medical journal, in *Nature* and in the *Archives of Internal Medicine* complained that Pergamon's monopoly and its high prices, which were often three times greater than those of other publishers, were draining libraries of scarce funds. Philip Wade, in a letter to the *Lancet,* complained that as a librarian he was paying for Pergamon journals three or four times as much as individuals were being charged. Wade further complained that, having paid an inflated subscription for the journal *Biochemical Pharmacology,* he expected to receive as promised an abstract of the proceedings of an international conference in Stockholm because Pergamon was publishing all the papers in a nine-volume set to which he had also subscribed. Instead, he found that the journal was filled out with the papers of the conference and, more irritatingly, a brand new journal to which the library had also subscribed, the *International Journal of Neopharmacology,* contained in its first issue exactly the same papers. "I may stupidly have missed some warning of that [first] duplication," wrote Wade, "but I see little justification for a new journal if its first issue must be padded with papers from a congress held eighteen months before a journal began. . . . It is wrong that libraries should be so burdened; and they should be spared buying the same material twice over." Maxwell replied that instructions had been issued to prevent duplication in the future.

Some authors were also complaining of minimal fees, and, in an unusual and prominent announcement in the *Author* magazine, readers were warned about signing contracts with Pergamon. "The printed form of contract," the announcement in the Spring 1963 issue stated, "was in many . . . respects unsatisfactory. . . . The advantages to such an author, from the point of view of academic prestige, of having a published book to his credit may well tempt him to sign a contract which he will subsequently regret. Authors who have been offered contracts by this firm are strongly advised to consult the Society before committing themselves."

Maxwell rebutted those criticisms from an industry which he condemned as ultra-conservative, uninnovative and self-destructive as "sour grapes." Both the professional institutes and traditional publishers had failed science and scientists, he said, and they were jealous about his personal and professional success. "I don't make a penny from any of the journals," he told the *Sunday Times,* and when asked why he did it for nothing, he replied, "I do it because it ought to be done." This was plainly nonsense, although many of his authors felt genuinely grateful for his generous support. Among them was Sir Harold "Tommy" Thompson, an eminent and highly decorated professor of organic chemistry and late Master of St. John's College, Oxford. Thompson appreciated Maxwell's style since he also had wide-ranging interests, including the editorship of Pergamon's most prestigious journal, *Spectrochimica Acta.* Thompson was also a keen footballer and a chairman of the Football Association. During their many hours together, Thompson introduced Maxwell to the politics of the British sport and so stimulated his later interest.

By the early 1960s, Maxwell felt that he could afford to ignore critics. He was a millionaire with a Rolls-Royce and a mansion. His family life was much closer than in the previous decade when Betty had relied upon nannies and a train of other employees to look after the home and all of her children. There would have been perfect contentment had Michael, his eldest son, not been critically injured in a motor accident in 1961. He would be kept alive on a support system in Oxford until 1968. A daughter had died of leukemia in infancy. Seven children survived. He introduced into his home life the same mercurial discipline he imposed upon his employees. It was a homespun philosophy called "The three Cs—consideration, concentration and conciseness." Maxwell expected his children's behavior to be in stark contrast to his own. Showing politeness, speaking in respectful tones and diligently obeying rules were precisely what Maxwell senior had steadfastly and proudly rejected. Yet he expected those qualities from both employees and his family. Betty Maxwell has described those years of running a home with seven children as "always running behind [him] trying to catch up." Psychologists describe that peculiar condition of demanding from others the opposite of your own character as "projected identification." Maxwell, one can assume, unconsciously disliked some aspects of his personality and reacted violently if he perceived it in others. In his children, he wanted to forestall the development of his own characteristics. Since by all accounts his children are in some respects the antithesis of their father, he was clearly successful. The pain inflicted upon his sons, especially Kevin and Ian, was noticeable. Their headmaster at Marlborough often reflected upon the severe beatings that their father unmercifully applied. It is unlikely that Maxwell was personally beaten as a child, or that he would have tolerated accepting the same pain. But he strove toward realizing his ambitions, carried forward by the sheer individualism which he could not tolerate among others. His next goal was to fulfill the ambition he had confided to Betty in 1944—to become a politician.

5

Anne Dove has no doubts why Maxwell became a Member of Parliament for the Labour Party: "The Tories wouldn't have had him." Although there is no evidence that he applied to join the Conservative Party, it would have seemed the natural citadel to match his lifestyle and business activities. Under Harold Macmillan, the nation was riding the crest of a boom which had enjoyed the innovation of jet airliners, LP records, transistors, sleek cars and the first computers. Maxwell was as enraptured by that era's affluence which was associated with the Conservatives as he was irritated by Labour's agonized doctrinal disputes about nationalization and defense, its cloth-cap image and its Little Englander prejudice against business. Some interpreted his friendship with Peter Baker as a prelude to applying to Central Office to become a Conservative candidate. If he had been so minded, there would have been one insuperable obstacle: Harold Macmillan. The Prime Minister had vowed never to forgive or forget Maxwell's stewardship of Simpkin Marshall. If he was to become a politician, there was therefore no alternative but to join the Opposition.

Maxwell's first approach to the Labour Party was in late spring 1959 when the newspapers had begun to speculate that a general election would be held in the autumn. He applied to the local party in Esher which, because of the overwhelming Conservative majority in the constituency, was a relatively moribund association. Paul Vanson, the nominated Labour candidate, remembers the "big impression" Maxwell created when he first arrived because "he was interested in being active." The party's finances were precarious and Maxwell offered to organize a fund-raising dance. "It lifted our eyes," recalls Vanson, "because we weren't used to it." Vanson "thinks" that he can recall enrolling Maxwell as a party member.

Cyril Smith, the local party's chairman, relates a very different account of Maxwell's first appearance at the Esher party: "The rumbustious Ian Maxwell got up to make a point at a pre-election debate in the King George's Hall and just didn't stop speaking, which made me intensely annoyed." Smith does not believe that Maxwell became a member of the Esher party. Certainly, Maxwell never produced his Esher membership card.

In summer 1959, Maxwell was therefore possibly not a member. It was at this time that an employee confided to him that she was pregnant and, although unmarried, intended to have the child. The father was an American who had been temporarily employed by Pergamon and was returning home. She further told Maxwell that her decision to become a single parent would prevent her remaining as the prospective Labour candidate for Aylesbury and she was resigning her candidacy.

Maxwell encouraged the employee to marry the recently divorced American, requesting her to recommend him to the Aylesbury Selection Committee. She agreed but the Committee did not put Maxwell on the short-list. According to Albert Birch and Freda Roberts, both members, the committee had already made alternative arrangements. But Maxwell clearly made a good impression because an Aylesbury official suggested that he might try for the seat in the neighboring constituency of North Buckinghamshire where the Labour candidate, Dr. Gordon Evans, had just resigned after a serious road accident.

North Buckinghamshire, which was a mixture of "hunting, shooting and fishing" villages, plus the towns of Bletchley and Wolverton, was an attractive proposition. The sitting Tory member had won in 1955 by only 1,140 votes, making it one of the country's most marginal seats. With the election announcement imminent, there was already a rush of applicants for the nomination although the national polls pointed to the Tories as favorites to win. First reports in Buckinghamshire's local papers spoke of a short-list of fifteen, but only five, including Maxwell, were finally interviewed when the party executive met on Saturday, August 22, 1959. Four were local men who represented the constituency's two major industries, farming and the railways; among them was the party's vice-president, who could boast a long record of service in the constituency. In every sense, Maxwell was the outsider.

In the week before the selection, Maxwell gave local newspapers the material for a short biographical profile. As was the case throughout his life, in Maxwell's perception of himself, he regularly introduced new interpretations of identical events.

In the summer of 1959, Maxwell described himself as a publisher, speaking nine languages, who employed five hundred people and produced 250 books and 50 journals a year. There was mention of the Pergamon Institute, which disseminated "research carried out in Russia and other people's democratic republics" and a statement that he had produced a film of the Bolshoi ballet. The full account of his war record was: "got into the army when he was 16, was wounded in the battle of France in 1940, escaped from a POW camp, was commissioned in the field for bravery during the Normandy invasion and awarded the MC in 1945. He was later with the Foreign Office in West Berlin and helped launch three socialist democrat newspapers [sic]." To the uninformed, it would seem that Maxwell had fought throughout the war in the British army.

Persuading the committee was not an easy task for Maxwell. Candidates normally must show long membership and a laudable record of working for the party. He could show neither. According to the local newspaper, he told the committee that the Esher Labour Party was dormant but he had become a member "twelve months" earlier. In 1973 he said that he joined "some time after the war. I don't have any specific time or date." He also agreed that it "may well be true" that he joined "only a few weeks before nomination." Since he was not officially registered at Esher or at Aylesbury, and certainly did not apply for membership just before the selection meeting, it is probable that Maxwell was not even a member when he faced the committee. He did assure its members, however, that he had been "an active supporter of the party since 1945" and a Fabian since 1956.

The opposition against him was vocal. Some were frankly unsympathetic to a foreign-born millionaire as a Labour Member, while others clearly favored one of the local candidates. The day before the selection, the sitting Tory MP Sir Frank Markham advised the Labour committee to choose a local man because "This constituency has never yet been won in any contested election other than by a North Bucks man." Most of the committee probably agreed with him. But after the five candidates had made their speeches and had been questioned, the stalwarts were deeply divided. Maxwell had, according to Bryan Barnard, the constituency's agent, "outshone them all by his delivery, the content of the speech and the way he dealt with questions." Frank Atter, a fitter from Wolverton, a member of the committee and later a bitter opponent, remembers that Maxwell spoke "very well." After a marathon eleven hours and three ballots the committee announced that "Captain Ian Robert Maxwell MC" was their choice.

Hours later Maxwell made a rousing speech, commenting on the "magnificent turnout of delegates" and defiantly declaring war against his opponent: "From here on Sir Frank can expect unrelentless [sic] trouble and fight. He had better get up early in the morning if he wants to hold on to his seat. Due to Gordon Evans's dreadful accident, he [Sir Frank] has been feeling pretty sure he will walk away once again by fooling the people as he usually does at election time by talking our kind of philosophy and selling the socialist line to the people. But let us not forget that he was a turncoat." The meaning of the last comment was unclear. After predicting a "four to six thousand majority" at the election, he promised to "hold on to the seat for an eternity." At a press conference on the same day, he handed out a release in which his background was described as a man "of farm laboring stock [who], with only his army gratuity behind him, started a scientific publishing business." His brief membership of the party was not mentioned and, when asked about the recent purchase of Headington Hall, he replied that they were "business premises and I shall not live there."

The controversy about Maxwell's nomination broke nationally within hours of its announcement. The *Daily Telegraph* reported a NEC meeting at Transport House where Dan McGarvey, a trade union leader, and Tom Agar, a Co-Op representative, allegedly moved motions to oppose Maxwell's candidacy because it broke the rule that candidates needed two years' membership of the party to qualify for nomination. James Callaghan was also reported to be critical that Maxwell had not served "an apprenticeship the hard way," but the party leader Hugh Gaitskell marshalled the majority to approve Maxwell's candidacy. Since James Callaghan cannot recollect the meeting and since the others mentioned are dead, it is impossible to confirm the report's accuracy. But, inevitably, the Conservative newspapers saw political capital in the new candidate's background—he was foreign, rich and lived in a mansion in Oxford.

The second source of discord was more wounding. His biographical sketches had not mentioned his birthplace and the local newspapers carried articles suggesting that his foreign background had been concealed even from the selection committee. Atter believes that Maxwell's Czech birth was not known at the meeting but is equally certain that it would have made no difference. Barnard believes that the committee knew. Maxwell admitted to the local newspaper that he had not mentioned his past publicly because "I have come to look on Britain as my country and did not think it worth mentioning," and he insisted that the selection committee possessed "all my antecedents." The local paper was properly sympathetic to the omission, quoting a supporter:

"Captain Maxwell is no more a foreigner than Prince Philip. Like him he was born abroad, came here as a boy, fought for this country and has been working for its interests ever since."

At his adoption meeting in Wilton Hall, three hundred Labour supporters stood and applauded their candidate. Gordon Evans, despite his injuries, spoke for Maxwell in a tape-recording and praised the party for choosing a candidate "from another small country" who had risked his life for Britain. Maxwell responded with a grand gesture, the "Buckingham Plan for Nuclear Disarmament," which proposed that the nuclear powers should place their weapons "in trust for the United Nations" and that they should pledge themselves not to test or use their bombs and ultimately to hand them over to the UN. Copies of his anti-unilateralist plan, he told his new supporters, had already been sent to President Eisenhower, Nikita Khrushchev and Hugh Gaitskell. North Bucks had not previously been a launching pad for the world stage but its new Labour candidate was ambitious. The following day, the election was called for October 8.

Barnard describes the party's organization as "poor." The constituency covered a large area containing the two towns, Bletchley and Wolverton, and dozens of villages. Over the previous years, canvassing of the electorate to discover Labour supporters had been patchy and the organization of the party in the villages was practically nonexistent. For a marginal candidate, where every vote counted, it was a serious handicap. But Maxwell was undaunted and set off in military style, driving a Humber Super Snipe, with his headquarters, a caravan, trailing behind. At night, a tent could be attached to provide sleeping accommodation. His campaign would not suffer from a lack of energy or determination, but any aspirations to lofty ideals were dashed within the first twenty-four hours. Maxwell's ambitious peace initiative was buried and forgotten beneath an onslaught against his personal credibility. He became the victim of unadulterated racial prejudice.

The first intimation of trouble was the news that Tom Mitchinson, the vice-president of the local Labour Party who had been rejected as the candidate, had signed the nomination papers of the Conservative MP, Frank Markham. Mitchinson claimed that Maxwell had definitely not told the selection committee that he was born in Czechoslovakia and that he, Mitchinson, was therefore "dissatisfied" with the procedures. The Tories naturally jumped for joy over the defection and began openly to solicit support for their candidate on the basis that he was "English through and through."

By the second day, Mitchinson's desertion sparked a wider whispering campaign which questioned Maxwell's business reputation and the collapse of Simpkin Marshall, and even raised doubts whether he had really won the MC. By the third day, a printed list of questions had been compiled by Markham's team which Tory supporters were urged to put to Maxwell at his meetings. All were personally damaging— about his experiences in the Czech army, his name when he won the MC, about Simpkins, and why he employed nonunion labor at Pergamon. Wounded, Maxwell protested that he was the helpless "victim of a smear campaign," but clearly his original autobiographical account had contributed to the suspicion.

His quickly prepared rebuttal fueled the controversy. The Military Cross, he explained, was awarded when serving in the "7th Armoured Division (the Desert Rats)"; he obtained a letter from James Pitman declaring that there was "no blemish attached to Captain Maxwell's career in the matter of his scientific book career," which was not relevant to the collapse of Simpkins; and he said that Pergamon's staff were "all encouraged to join their trade unions," which the Tories disputed. The election campaign degenerated into what was politely described as a "fierce" fight and by locals as a brawl, since Maxwell took his defense into his enemies' camp by personally attending Markham's meetings to hurl questions at his detractor. Their battle formally ended at the count in Buckingham's council chamber, the day after the election, amid "unprecedented . . . noise and din."

Since Harold Macmillan's Conservative government was returned to office with an increased majority, Maxwell had no chance of winning his own election. Sir Frank Markham was re-elected with a slightly increased majority of 1,746 votes, although proportionately the vote for both Markham and Maxwell fell. But Maxwell could console himself with the knowledge that while nationally the swing to the Tories was just over 1 per cent, in North Bucks it was less at 0.6 per cent—which was a positive reflection of the campaign he had fought. At the end of the count, Maxwell was undaunted, but he was still bitter and refused to shake the victor's hand. To loud cheers and even louder boos he tried to make the traditional thanks but his voice was drowned when he claimed that victory would have belonged to him "had the Tories fought cleanly." When the uproar finally subsided, Maxwell shouted, "Long live socialism and victory!," and after revealing that he had served writs alleging defamation on three Conservatives attending the count, he went to a meeting of rail-workers where he pledged himself to "stick with you."

Like all defeated candidates, Maxwell suffered an anticlimax after the defeat but it was brief. Barnard recalls that "Elisabeth was particularly hurt but the bitterness had made him more determined than ever." The prospect of waiting four years for another election was not a depressing one since, unlike most aspiring candidates, he had not had to suffer the tedious process of establishing his credentials with successive constituency associations and with the party leaders. He had started at the top and needed only to fertilize his new roots in Bucks and at Transport House.

By the turn of the year he had found a small house in the constituency and with Barnard's guidance began attending the necessary functions to court his supporters and to prove that he would be a worthy candidate at the next election. Simultaneously, he and Barnard organized an elaborate canvas of every voter; it would take four years to complete but could be guaranteed to pay rich dividends. Under Maxwell, the constituency would be managed like all his other businesses.

At the national level, Maxwell was already known and admired. Merlyn Rees, subsequently to become Home Secretary, who had just been defeated for the third time and despaired of ever entering the Commons, recalls asking a senior party official in 1959 whether he knew of any suitable work for a failed candidate. "I was told that a brilliant chap, very similar to Stafford Cripps, had recently come into the party and taken it by storm. He planned an encyclopedia on social sciences which seemed ideal for me." Rees took the job after an interview with Maxwell and anticipated moving his family to Oxford. After the first day, he telephoned his wife and ordered, "Halt. This isn't going to work." Rees felt unable to work for someone with "so many balls in the air who played God on five telephones."

Richard Marsh, who would also become a Cabinet minister, recalls first meeting Maxwell after the election defeat at the party conference in Brighton. "I couldn't forget the first meeting. Outside was his red Rolls-Royce with personalized number plates which were my initials and he kept asking me, 'How did you become a Labour candidate?' as if it was like a business transaction. It seemed to me very strange because he had no history in the party." As the two became better acquainted Marsh concluded that "they didn't come any tougher but he had limitless charm when necessary and he needed it because in the Labour Party there was a predisposition against wealth."

There was also a strong hint of the messianic in Maxwell's first major appearance at a Labour Party rally in Vauxhall Gardens in 1962. Hugh Gaitskell was addressing the Festival of Labour when an aide whispered that "Captain Robert Maxwell MC is arriving to deliver a message from the electors of North Bucks." The leader nodded and then heard that the messenger was arriving by helicopter. "He was," said another future minister who witnessed the arrival, "like a Harrier jet: all power down to get upward thrust."

But Tam Dalyell, like other young Labour politicians, "liked him from the word go for his boundless energy" after they first met at the party conference in 1963. Maxwell had by then established his credentials as a specialist in science, an area which Harold Wilson, who had become the party leader after Gaitskell's sudden death, intended to emphasize in Labour's next election manifesto. With Dalyell, Maxwell was co-opted on to Labour's science committee, which was chaired by Richard Crossman, the brilliant and unpredictable academic who instinctively admired mavericks. For Crossman, "any man of foreign birth who had fathered nine children and who was decorated in the field must be exceptional." The senior politician was impressed by Maxwell's "tremendous organizing capacity . . . An explosive, enormously dynamic man." Maxwell and Dalyell met regularly as they toured the country attending conferences arranged by Dalyell at which Crossman could meet scientists and university teachers. But Crossman, whom Maxwell occasionally described as his mentor, never thought of his protégé as a socialist or even as a natural politician. "You've got to understand the Labour Party, Bob, if you want to succeed inside it," said Crossman in 1963, but he felt that his advice had fallen on deaf ears.

The proof of that obtuseness was a speech Maxwell delivered in 1967 to a party conference about Labour's education policy, during which he attempted to justify sending two of his children to public schools. "I only send those who are in need of going there" because of inadequate family circumstances or low aptitude. His views would be greeted with incredulity and catcalls by Labour party stalwarts who realized that he failed to understand the intellectual philosophy which required the complete comprehensivization of British education. From the outset, his insensitivity plagued his relationship with the majority of the party. Even those, like Crossman, who might otherwise have been sympathetic admirers came away confounded by the sophistry. He was a millionaire who drove a Rolls-Royce and had moved into a lavish home having spent £350,000 on building works. Visitors to the aspiring socialist politician were met by peacocks strutting across the lawn and booming loudspeakers, summoning employees to the phone or to urgent meetings. Yet he apparently championed the cause of the underdogs against financiers like himself. Regularly, he attacked the Conservative government's proposals to remove Resale Price Maintenance which, he claimed, would cause the "murder" of small traders. On one occasion he began his speech by disclosing that, only hours earlier, "I cancelled my flight to Miami to be with you tonight." His audience, a group of poor farm workers, were told, "I know what it is like to go hungry because for over twenty years my father was on the dole." Some in the party were enthralled by the singular power of an individual who could crush any expression of doubts about the contradictions. Others accepted that, while he was not an ideological socialist, these were the sentiments of a radical pledged to reform who was against inherited privilege and wanted the poor to have a fair chance. But overall, the party's meek acceptance of Maxwell the millionaire as a member reflected the innate indolence—often misdescribed as good-natured tolerance—of the British, which Maxwell would capitalize on until the end of his life.

To soften the edges and modify the image, in 1963 he presented his business activities more as philanthropic dedications. He bought and subsidized *Isis,* the Oxford University newspaper (of which his son Philip became an editor), he funded a scholarship at Balliol College and established a chain of bookshops on university campuses to be launched with the rousing flourish "Books must replace bombs." Yet all his bookshops eventually failed, the *Isis* subsidy was withdrawn, but four of his children did graduate from Balliol—"The same as Asquith," he would boast. Altogether, his multifarious activities created confusion about what he represented. But in 1964 his self-confidence knew no limits.

In July, Ansbachers, the merchant bank, floated Pergamon as a public company. Twenty years' work was capitalized by selling 1.1 million shares to the public for $3.5 million. Maxwell and his family trusts retained 2.9 million shares. Legally, they were owned by Liechtenstein trusts, which concealed Maxwell's wealth, protected him from paying taxes, and would allow him the excuse, when necessary, of denying control of the company's affairs. The sale showed that Maxwell's stake in Pergamon was worth roughly £10 million. His other interests in America can be valued at several more millions but their true worth was hidden in the secrecy of Liechtenstein trusts.

With that money secured, Maxwell began looking for new business opportunities. His motives, he explained, were his altruism and his ambition for influence. In 1964, the *Daily Herald,* a staunchly pro-Labour Party newspaper, was suffering huge losses. Fifty-one per cent of its shares were owned by the International Publishing Corporation

(IPC) and the remainder by the TUC. IPC's chairman Cecil King had announced that its shares were for sale since the company wanted to launch a new paper, the *Sun*. When no buyers appeared, King delivered an ultimatum that the newspaper would be handed to the TUC for nothing. The Labour movement, who deemed it vital that the party should enjoy the unequivocal support of at least one Fleet Street newspaper, was shocked. The problem was how to save the *Herald*. Maxwell produced a survival plan.

His proposal, which stood out as a sensible balance between capitalist reality and socialist principles, was his first attempt to break the costly stranglehold of the print unions over Fleet Street. He suggested that a new print plant should be established with a government subsidy in an area of high unemployment. During the day, when the presses were not printing the *Herald,* they would be used for general contracts, especially a slice of the £11 million which was spent annually by the trade unions. If his plan were accepted, he predicted, the TUC would earn £750,000 profits annually. Since the trade union movement had never managed to engage itself in business ventures, it was convenient to ignore his plan.

It was a passing rebuff in what was certain to be a momentous election year and an era of political and social upheaval exemplified in the Orpington by-election and Beatlemania. The Conservative government in autumn 1964 seemed worn out by office and shattered by a series of embarrassing scandals which had culminated in the resignations of John Profumo and Harold Macmillan. The new Prime Minister, Sir Alec Douglas-Home, who seemed as relevant to the Swinging Sixties as a penny-farthing bicycle, stubbornly refused to call an election. The Old World seemed to be dying while Wilson promised a Kennedyesque vision of technological revolution which he had called "the conscious, planned, purposive use of scientific progress." Maxwell felt that he epitomized that brave new world and his conviction was reinforced when George Brown, the deputy leader of the Labour Party, visited his constituency. Party members were assured by Brown that Maxwell "was bound to play a very major role indeed in a new Labour government" because he "represented very much the kind of new look which we think has to be brought into the country." Maxwell had every reason to believe that Brown spoke for the party leader and that his talents would soon be used for the nation's benefit. He felt, in Christopher Booker's phrase, that he would be part of "the dream after the storm."

When the election was finally announced, Maxwell was automatically nominated as the candidate. Over the previous five years, he had earned an impressive reputation in the constituency for his hard work, while nationally it was recognized that he had revamped Labour's National Fund Raising Organization at Transport House to improve the party's finances. Even Tom Mitchinson was quoted as saying that he would vote Labour because Maxwell had proved himself worthwhile. The local association's coffers were full thanks to Barnard's regular lotteries, and the agent could report a record 90 per cent canvass of voters. In the biographical-profile material provided for the local papers Maxwell described his birthplace as Slovakia, mentioned that he had traveled two million miles to win export orders and to attend scientific meetings and listed his presidency of the National Labour Party working committee to improve productivity as evidence of his contribution to the party's manifesto.

At his adoption meeting on September 25, 1964, he made a long, rousing speech promising that the campaign would be fought on issues which he spelled out in the most patriotic terms. "I cannot believe that the British people have become so content with their betting shops and bingo clubs that they are prepared to watch our once great nation slip into third-rate obscurity." He appealed for the expansion of business and the "zest for a fight" in a mixture of images evoking the buccaneer and Churchill: "We were only recently the richest nation on the globe. During the last twenty years we have shrunk back in terms of world-power to our condition before Trafalgar and Waterloo, a small country with a smallish population among greater and more powerful nations. Now we are back with Drake and Nelson, with Cromwell, Marlborough and Wellington, living hard and dangerously and surviving as a nation only if, like them, we are tougher, more austere, better at our jobs than our competitors." Maxwell believed that a Labour government would radically galvanize Britain's lethargic industrial performance.

Politically, he could not quite subscribe to every aspect of Labour's policy. There would be no "foolish renationalization," he promised, beyond steel, and he expressly excluded British Road Services from state ownership. "We will not interfere with the right and liberty of the individual who can do a job that is vital to the community." His promise that grammar schools would not be abolished similarly reflected Maxwell's own views rather than the party's. Yet on defense he was leftish: "We are prepared to give up the pretense of an independent nuclear deterrent which is neither independent and doesn't deter." Finally, he expressed the hope that personalities and smears would not feature because the "constituency had a basinful of that type of campaign in the last election." He beamed as his supporters stood and cheered, certain that the next of his ambitions would be realized within three weeks.

The major local issue was the survival of the Wolverton railway workshops which under the Beeching reorganization plan to reduce the rail network's losses was threatened with closure. "Now," he bitterly complained, "our prized workshops are going to Steptoe's Knacker's Yard for pennies." Yet one of those benefiting was Maxwell himself, who had negotiated to buy a part of the very same Wolverton workshops.

His acquisition had only been discovered in September. A local newspaper confronted Maxwell and obtained an admission and a promise. Robert Maxwell and Co., he conceded, had bought workshops and land from British Rail with an option to buy more. He refused to confirm that the price was £360,000 but pledged that the buildings would be used to provide "1,200 jobs in twelve to eighteen months," mostly for engineering workers living in Wolverton, although "the nature of the product is for the moment confidential." It was the type of "regeneration" which Labour was promising, but it looked surprisingly similar to a plan which he had announced six months earlier for a printing plant for 1,200 employees in Dundee which was not yet realized.

For sheer energy alone, Maxwell deserved to win the election. His daily whistle-stop dash around the villages of Buckinghamshire in a red Land Rover, and occasionally in a helicopter, delivering impromptu speeches, generated unprecedented enthusiasm. His organization and self-presentation as plain "Bob" (the "Captain" had been dropped), demoralized his new Conservative opponent, Elaine Kellet. Even when his birthplace became an issue with the jibe "You're not going to vote for a bloody foreigner, are you?" Maxwell had his rebuttal ready: "I am as British as His Royal Highness Prince Philip and so far as I know the Queen seems to be very happy with his services and so is the country." The cheers continued until long after the result was declared.

Despite the microphones, the returning officer's voice could barely be heard above the roar when the crowd realized that Maxwell was elected. His majority of 1,481 was a resounding victory, a 6 per cent swing, much higher than the national average to Labour and the first time that Labour had held the seat since 1951. The headlines in the local newspaper spelled out his great success. Under the headline, "Party Workers' Tumultuous Welcome for Mr. Maxwell," the report described "scenes of great enthusiasm" as, engulfed by his supporters, he and Betty marched through the center of Buckingham to the party headquarters. There he told the cheering crowd, "Harold Wilson has watched the result with great care and it will be a great relief to him that Labour has kept its promise and won the seat." The Labour government had won by the slender majority of four seats and one of those vital seats was his own. Robert Maxwell had little doubt, as he spoke, that the nation's collective attention was fixed upon him and was concluding that, as destiny had ordained, he was indeed the man of the hour. If he looked, according to the local newspaper editor, surprisingly calm, it was, he later admitted, because he felt "humble, grateful and very tired." To reaffirm that he would not forget why he was elected, he promised that he would fight to keep a local station open and that a maternity hospital would be built at Bletchley before the end of the following year.

The new MP arrived at Westminster on the first day of the new Parliament, determined to make his contribution to save the nation from bankruptcy. His relationship with the new Prime Minister encouraged his confident belief that he would be offered an appointment. Wilson had been "stunned by Maxwell's formidable achievement of winning Buckingham." But Maxwell mistook Wilson's respect for colorful, self-made risk-takers as indicating that he was being considered for ministerial office. He could not see that his pushy and flamboyant personality offended Wilson's natural bureaucratic caution, nor did he take into account the fact that among his fellow politicians were many Labour Members who had worked over the previous twenty years for the opportunity of office. Among them was Crossman. Only days after the election, Crossman had taken his friend aside at a bar in New College, Oxford, and told him, on the basis of his knowledge of Wilson, "You have no chance whatsoever of a job in this government." Crossman explained that both as a newcomer and "with your past and your temperament, you'll have to be satisfied with the backbenches." According to Crossman, Maxwell was "very, very crestfallen" but he was "grateful" for the honesty. So Crossman gave his friend one short piece of advice: "Look, Bob, whatever you do, when you get in there, lie low for six months."

The first day of the new Parliament was a historic moment. Amid pomp and ceremony, the Queen, as was customary, declared that a new Parliament was in session and read the new government's legislative program from the throne in the House of Lords. After she left, MPs filed back from the Lords into their own chamber. After thirteen years of Conservative rule, the House of Commons was filled with tense and excited politicians. Former Conservative ministers, suddenly shorn of the power and prestige of ministerial office, sat grimly in their new positions on the Opposition benches. Across the floor sat the nation's new masters, brimming with anticipation of exercising power. After a few courtesies, at precisely two minutes past five on that very first day of the new Parliament, Robert Maxwell stood up to make his maiden speech, the first maiden speech of all the new entrants and the first backbencher's speech of the new Parliament. The whole ministerial bench writhed in outrage. Sitting on the front bench, next to the new Prime Minister, Richard Crossman felt positively embarrassed: "It was absolutely disastrous. There he was trying to bash his way to fame in the first twenty-four hours." Wilson's fury was worsened by the smiles of Rab Butler and Alec Douglas-Home. Throughout the Labour benches there was dismay at Maxwell's impetuousness. After a full twenty minutes he resumed his seat. Harold Thompson quipped to Dalyell that night, "Let's just be thankful that Bob waited until the Queen sat down."

Maxwell's solecism was not just that it was an inopportune moment for a maiden speech but that it had lasted three times too long. He boasted openly of having "got in first" and was oblivious to the notion that he had "left a bad taste in everyone's mouth." It would take Maxwell many years before he recognized his folly and admitted, "I thought I was the cleverest thing on two legs there."

In content, Maxwell's speech was sound. After appealing on behalf of his constituency for improved civic amenities, help for the railway workshops, improved conditions in the brickworks (which were "shocking") and a plea to keep a local railway line open, he introduced himself as the nation's foremost scientific publisher and launched into a critique of the failure of applying science in Britain. His financial success, he believed, gave him a special status among politicians to pontificate about the nation's salvation. British industry, he complained, was failing to apply the "results of research faster" and the country's future productivity and profitability depended upon improvements. Attitudes had to be changed, he said, and wasteful government research contracts for defense and civil industry needed to be terminated. Concorde, especially, he insisted, should be cancelled because there was no "real social or economic demand." Having made the point, he then continued in the same vein despite the growing restlessness of those around him. The relief when he sat down was temporary. Over the next few days, he repeatedly stood up, interrupted speeches and shouted jibes to score political points until the Conservative Member Edward Du Cann castigated him bluntly: "I have never heard anybody make so many speeches as he has in the last two days." According to Crossman, "I don't suppose there's anybody who is less aware of the impression he's created when he tries to create a good impression and it's no good trying to warn him. He wanted to shine."

Disraeli also made an appalling debut in the Commons, but the similarity between the two men goes no further. Parliament is a reservoir and generator of every human imperfection, especially jealous rivalries exaggerated by the importance which its Members attribute to themselves. The businessman in Parliament is never a happy animal, especially a maverick who is accustomed to respect from his employees and shareholders. For a boardroom dictator willingly to accept the lowly status of a junior politician requires substantial self-awareness, and the humility which Maxwell described when he won the seat had already disappeared. The new Member was impatient to change the world and even more impatient with Parliament's time-wasting traditions. There was a conviction which ran through all his speeches that, if only one hundred other Maxwells could be marshalled, the nation would be saved. He exuded an ambition for power but no one was certain how he would use it. Some even wondered whether Maxwell knew himself.

Soon after his victory, Harold Wilson told the nation that it faced a grave economic crisis. His drastic cure included import surcharges, a range of new taxes and heavy borrowing from the International Monetary Fund. The remedy provoked hectic speculation against sterling, a crisis which preoccupied Parliament and the media. During those tense weeks, Maxwell was bursting to speak—and he succeeded, but his reward was the evaporation of his ministerial dreams.

First, he suggested that Labour MPs should contribute 10 per cent of their salaries to Transport House, an idea which was not welcomed by the nonmillionaires in the party's ranks. Then he loudly accused the previous Tory administration of "cooking the books" on the use of an obscure technical term that described an army unit. He was accurate but it was an irrelevance. Then he complained that printing of the Commons voting lists which were provided 24 hours after the vote was too slow. Again he was right but his manner grated. Finally, he attacked Parliament's traditions and his own ministers for conspiring with the Opposition to approve the annual cost of Britain's embassies without a debate. The vote to approve the costs was to have been a formality to clear the way for a major parliamentary debate, but Maxwell protested amid shouts and insults, mainly from Labour Members, "I did not realize, until I came into the House, how much of a rubber-stamping organization the House of Commons had become." He continued to speak for nineteen minutes while the crammed and agitated front benches waited to start the debate.

During his many forays abroad, he complained, he had been irritated by the condescending and dismissive attitudes of the public-school and Oxbridge types who then dominated the Foreign Office. Britain's diplomats were not helping to promote exports at a time when exports were falling "alarmingly." For them, trade was grubby, and Maxwell, like so many businessmen, was given short shrift in those citadels of class prejudice. "What worries me considerably," shouted Maxwell above a rising clamor of complaints and abuse, "is the extraordinary complacency and smugness." Unfortunately for the messenger, the same blindness afflicted his audience who in unison shouted "Nonsense" when he claimed that Britain was finding it harder to export its manufactures and the Foreign Office's attitude was destructive. When he finally sat down he was praised by the Tories and derided from the Labour benches. Maxwell was unaware that the Tory support arose out of glee over the government's embarrassment.

The price he paid was severe. "Crossbencher" in the *Sunday Express* dubbed him "the biggest gasbag in the Commons. . . . This handsome, debonair 41-year-old made the first maiden speech of the new Parliament, and he has scarcely sat down since." Crossbencher advised the newcomer "with a touch of old-world courtesy" to "Belt up." In the Commons, he was snubbed and mocked by his colleagues. "I am ambitious to get things done," he said, but few were listening.

At the end of his first year, he presented his local party with an annual report of his activities. He had spent 3,260 hours working on constituency business, including 1,580 inside Westminster. There had been 92 contributions or interventions in debates and 65 questions; he had written 215 letters to ministers and had led 20 deputations to ministries; he had written 4,000 letters on behalf of constituents and met 780 constituents on personal matters; he had attended 115 public meetings, made 6,000 telephone calls and traveled 15,000 miles. Few politicians would expect to be judged on statistics but the daily reports of the Commons proceedings in Hansard reveal his unconventional approach. Regularly he walked into the chamber, bowed to the Speaker, strode to his bench and either shouted a remark or rose to speak without knowing what had just been said. Repeatedly, he was rebuked: "If the honorable Gentleman had listened to the debate" or "That is a point which is not in dispute" or "The hon. Gentleman cannot walk into the Chamber at about a quarter to nine and expect to be allowed to interrupt. He is always doing it; I have watched him frequently."

This was the period when Maxwell won his reputation with the wider public by actively seeking media coverage. At the Commons bar, drinks were always on Maxwell. If his guest asked for a single, a double was ordered. Desmond Wilcox, then the executive editor of BBC television's *Man Alive* program, recalls that "Maxwell would always, at that time, make himself readily available for a TV appearance." He wanted recognition for himself and his theme which was that Britain's businessmen should follow his own example and export more, curb their accumulation of capital and increase their investments. As will be seen later, throughout his parliamentary career, he vigorously expanded his own business interests. The media publicity was not confined to his political pronouncements but was mixed with his commercial coups, negotiated either from Fitzroy Square or from his office in Parliament.

No business opportunity was ever missed, including those offered in his constituency. At the beginning of 1966, after buying a large factory at Fenny Stratford and the site of Bletchley Printers, he bought a 50,000-square-foot building at Olney with surrounding land. It was sited adjacent to the Wolverton railway workshops, where his promise to create 1,200 jobs was still unfulfilled. His plans were frustrated, he explained, because he could not obtain road access to the site. This latest acquisition was completed just after he spoke in a Commons debate where he had praised the proposed Land Commission. "For too long we have seen marketeers and land speculators holding the community to ransom," he said. That speech echoed a previous attack during a constituency meeting in April 1964 against "land speculators [who] have already cashed in on a gigantic scale."

Land was an issue which found Maxwell confused. Since the early 1960s Whitehall had mooted a new town for North Bucks which would be built on 27,000 acres of agricultural land and be called Milton Keynes. Initially Maxwell opposed the compulsory purchase of the land, the denial of compensation to tenant farmers and indeed the whole scheme, arguing that the expansion of existing towns would be preferable. But at the beginning of 1966 he changed his views and clashed in particular with the railway workers in Wolverton. "He told them frankly that they were old-fashioned and uninspired," recalls Barnard, his agent, "and began telling them how they should run their local council to take advantage of the new town. They didn't like his interference very much." It was a slight hiccup which was temporarily forgotten in the excitement of a new general election.

Harold Wilson prided himself on his sense of timing and the announcement of the election in March 1966 coincided perfectly with graphic newspaper accounts of disarray in the Conservative ranks. Few departing Members of Parliament doubted that a Labour government would be returned with a working majority and that a ministerial reshuffle would follow. Maxwell left Westminster hoping that Wilson, having paid off his political debts, would finally recognize his talents and invite him to assist in the rescue of the economy. On the eve of his own departure, Maxwell re-entered the chamber of the Commons and waited until just before the last formalities were completed to jump up and say farewell. Two days later he proudly told his local newspaper that the chance of speaking the first and last words of a Parliament "must be millions to one."

The confident Labour candidate fought the election with a new agent, Jim Lyons, since Barnard was himself standing as a candidate. Lyons inherited a highly tuned election machine and was presented with the campaign slogan, "Let Harold and Bob finish the job." Maxwell rushed around the constituency, extolling his record and his achievements, which included raising the money for a hospital and keeping a local railway line open. He was rewarded with an increased majority of 2,254 which, as Lyons said, was due to "an outstanding Member of Parliament, the enthusiasm of our members and their will to win."

For Maxwell, the victory was a personal triumph but his return to Westminster was an anticlimax. He was not invited to join the government and it seemed unlikely that he would be given the opportunity in the lifetime of that Parliament. "You're neither a trade unionist nor an intellectual socialist," Crossman told Maxwell. "So Harold won't have you." Tam Dalyell, reflecting a common view, says that "The problem was what job Harold could have given him. It would have to be important and that was too difficult." According to Merlyn Rees, "He had been too rude to people but one had to feel sorry for him." Maxwell accepted that he would remain a backbencher for the next five years and launched himself in every direction. "He was like the charge of the heavy cavalry," says one of his party colleagues. "He whooshed past with enormous speed and strength but one had absolutely no idea where he was going." Restless and ambitious he seized every opportunity regardless of the effect on his credibility.

In 1966, the publishers Calder and Boyars were prosecuted for publishing Hubert Selby's *Last Exit to Brooklyn* on the grounds that its description of a homosexual affair was obscene. Bernard Levin described it as "a dreadful, savage and shockingly moralistic book about a corner of New York where, to quote the British publishers, 'nothing matters except the precarious dollar and the pleasure of inflicting violence on someone weaker than oneself.' " Most of London's legal and cultural elite opposed the prosecution and hoped that it would meet the same fate as the case against D. H. Lawrence's *Lady Chatterley's Lover* in 1960. Their overwhelming opposition made the prosecution's task of finding expert witnesses who could evaluate the book's literary merit particularly difficult and it was therefore relieved when Maxwell was prepared to testify in what everyone accepted was a watershed case. Described as a publisher, politician and family man, Maxwell appeared at Marlborough Street Magistrates' Court and condemned the book as "brutal and filthy" and added that he was "horrified to be a member of the same association" as the publishers, who "disseminate this muck for profit."

Maxwell's appearance as an expert on literature was puzzling. He had never previously shown an interest in novels and it was reliably rumored that some of his shelves in Headington contained purely decorative book facias. Maxwell's condemnation of profits was also peculiar since he boasted about the pursuit of money, and his own bookshops had been selling the very book whose ban he demanded. The prosecution was successful but the conviction was later overturned on appeal. Maxwell's reward was to attract the added dislike of publishers who had not experienced the Simpkins crash. Two years later he admitted to the *Daily Express,* "I'm probably the most unpopular publisher among publishers. But I pay no attention to these matters. It's largely sour grapes. Remember, publishing is a trade for gentlemen. It's supposed to take three generations and 150 years to succeed." The same article quoted an "acquaintance" about Maxwell: "He's really incredibly complicated—megalomaniac, naive and sensitive at the same time. On the whole I admire him. He's nearly all hot air." Fifteen years later Maxwell made a bid to buy *Mayfair,* the sex magazine. "With consistency a great soul has simply nothing to do," said Ralph Emerson, but Maxwell's inconsistency was driven by self-promotion, to cement his self-esteem.

Like so many entrepreneurs, Maxwell had watched in frustration as Britain's industrial performance slid uncontrollably, and he blamed both the managers and the unions. Before the election of 1964, Wilson had often spoken about the need for technology and dynamism but the promised revolution had still not materialized. "If only the nation would follow my example," Maxwell was often heard to say, "so many problems would be cured." All that talent was at the nation's disposal but was rejected by the Labour Party, which was still steeped in the emotion, mythology and philosophy of state control. Maxwell was not in tune with much of the party. In particular, he could not understand the Labour stalwarts from the north who had graduated from the coal villages or the industrial slums. Their single-minded sentiment and political credo, which was ingrained with the bitterness of their local communities' fight against a pernicious class system, was alien to him. His own worldwide travel had exposed him to industrial and technical revolutions which were unknown to most workers from Bradford and Birmingham, but to his irritation they relished their ignorance and spurned his experience. They regarded Maxwell as an arrogant millionaire; after all, when charged with dangerous driving for shaving while driving at 90 m.p.h. in his Rolls-Royce, he failed four times to appear in court to answer the charge. The dialogue never began. "His success and wealth annoyed people," recalls Richard Marsh, who had been appointed Minister for Power and who would invite Maxwell to ministerial parties.

Marsh regularly hosted receptions for foreign delegations at Lancaster House and because budgets for interpreters were limited was grateful if Maxwell agreed to attend. On one occasion, as Maxwell strolled from one group to another changing languages to crack jokes, he arrived in front of Marsh and Sir Robert Marshall, who was then the Deputy Permanent Secretary at the Ministry.

"I hear that you speak German," began Maxwell.

"Yes," replied Marshall.

"Any other languages?"

"French."

"It is extraordinary," replied Maxwell, "how you educated people can only speak two foreign languages. I speak eleven."

Forlornly, Maxwell waited for an appointment, although his politics seemed too varied for him to be identified with a group within the party who needed to be rewarded. For example, at the ceremony in 1966 to receive on Pergamon's behalf the Queen's Award to Industry, he told his audience that the pound would never be devalued because it would cause a 1929-type "calamity." When the pound was devalued one year later, he hailed it as "the greatest opportunity for British exporters." In autumn 1966, he urged import quotas and a freeze on wages but when the government imposed draconian tax increases to rescue the free-falling economy, he lectured Wilson from the backbenches on his own survival plan which contradicted those policies. The government, he said, needed to produce a plan to increase productivity, to scrap its prices and incomes policy and to join the Common Market. Nothing he said had much effect, not even a sane 117-page report which recommended that the state should use its discretion in procurement to improve industry's efficiency, remove restrictive practices, encourage productivity agreements, retrain labor and boost exports. Crossman sympathized with his predicament and produced what he genuinely hoped would be a helpful solution. He asked Maxwell to become the chairman of the House of Commons Catering Committee.

The annual deficit of the Commons' kitchen had increased from £10,000 in 1966 to £33,000 in 1969, creating a combined deficit of £53,000. The Catering Committee blamed the losses on paying too much for food, on the abundance of waste, and on a complete lack of control over the movement of food and money through the kitchens. In summary, there was gross inefficiency and wholesale theft. Chairing the Commons Catering Committee was not a prestigious task and, as Marsh reflects, "No one was queuing for the job and I was surprised when Bob took it."

Maxwell's solution was radical. He negotiated a grant from the Treasury, fired a large number of the staff, reduced the quality of the meals and, at the price of eternal opprobrium, sold the entire cellar of vintage wines. At the end of the financial year, he claimed that his entrepreneurial skills had turned the huge deficit into profit.

His success, instead of enhancing his reputation, aroused the very antagonism he might have hoped to assuage. Question-time in the Commons was peppered with exchanges which were cannon-fodder to both wags and journalists anxious to poke fun at the millionaire socialist. He was asked about the substitution of powdered milk for fresh milk, the introduction of processed chips instead of fresh potatoes and the total weight of sausages consumed during one year (6,800 lb.). Regularly, MPs used the occasion to deliver embarrassing blows by asking why *oeuf en gêlée* was no longer on the menu or why the tea room no longer served "decent plain biscuits, only nasty cheap sugary ones." It was demeaning, and although he claimed that the £33,000 loss had been reversed to an annual £20,000 profit, critics, inside and outside the House of Commons, would later claim that his achievement owed much to accounting. If the Treasury grant and exceptional items were deducted, the annual losses had actually increased from £33,000 in 1968 to £57,000 in 1969. Crossman was nevertheless very pleased with Maxwell's performance.

Maxwell retired from the committee after two years, which coincided with the post-devaluation crisis, a wave of strikes, Cabinet splits and by-election defeats at home and the bitter wars in Vietnam and Nigeria. It was the nadir of the Labour government and, according to Cecil

King, Maxwell was among those who wanted to be counted among the dissidents. "Maxwell," he wrote in his diary, "has been pestering Hugh Cudlipp [the editor of the *Daily Mirror*] with phone calls and letters. He really will have to be given the brush-off." In public, Maxwell spoke about "leading the nation away from the British sickness" but he lacked any following. So when Wilson appealed for the "Dunkirk spirit" as the cornerstone in the fight for Britain's economic survival, Maxwell, driven by instinct and patriotism, was among the first to rally to the slogan. "Once their energy and talent is liberated [*sic*]," said Maxwell about the British workers, "nothing will stop this country regaining its place in the world." His sentiment was genuine. It was only a short step from there to his association with a new campaign which won him national recognition.

On New Year's Day 1968, five typists at a heating factory in Surbiton, Surrey, pledged themselves to work an extra half-hour every day for no pay as a real contribution to rectifying the country's perilous economy. On January 3, *The Times* carried a full-page advertisement from an advertising agency thanking the girls for the idea of an "I'm Backing Britain" campaign. For a nation shivering in anticipation of economic decline, the typists' gesture was seized upon by the newspapers as a "sunrise" issue for their readers. Editors and journalists were delighted to have a new and positive story in contrast to the daily diet of economic gloom. But eight days after the campaign had started, Maxwell decided that it was in danger of faltering because there was nothing new to report and because its new government-appointed sponsors, the Industrial Society, had adopted a moderate and unflamboyant style. Maxwell stepped in with a competing campaign and later told the Society's director, "The trouble with you is you're all trying to be virgins—whiter than white. I've succeeded in raping you all along." He would also tell the journalist Nicholas Tomalin that he had thought of the idea at the same time as the Surbiton girls: "That's the thing about me. I'm quick off the mark."

In the House of Commons, Maxwell launched the "Think British—Buy British" campaign. The launch guaranteed him appearances on that night's television and brought an invitation to meet David Frost, who was then basking in glory as the nation's pre-eminent satirist. Accompanied by a few trade unionists and employers, Maxwell breakfasted two days later with Frost and was invited with his supporters to present their views to the nation that weekend. Over the next few days the publicity was terrific and the names he collected seemed to covet public association with the campaign. Among them were the businessmen Joe Hyman, Sir Max Aitken, Sir Billy Butlin, Bernard Delfont, Lord Thomson and Arnold Weinstock, and the trade unionist Frank Cousins, an admirer of Maxwell's, who withstood the complaints of others in the Labour movement that it was a "pure gimmick." That Saturday night, Maxwell earnestly explained to the nation that everyone should "think before buying. Buy the home product or service first whenever you can even if it means buying less for a time." Minutes after he finished, his associate Joe Hyman, the chairman of the textile manufacturer Viyella, exploded that he could not approve of anything "so stupid which would provoke a trade war." Maxwell was undaunted by the evident split. "I move fast," he told Tomalin. "It is both efficient and politic. When there's an object in my way I smash it down, or race around it. And I move so fast that when people put bombs on my road I'm a hundred yards before they explode [*sic*]."

Maxwell now wanted to amalgamate with the Industrial Society, but the latter refused since he seemed to want to entrust them with the work while he took the credit. So Maxwell, with the help of an advertising agency, launched his own campaign with a poster headed "Sell British—Help Britain—Help Yourself." Using the names of his famous supporters, the newspaper advertisements listed "100 uncranky ways you can help Britain." It included the suggestion that children should not drink their free school milk. When it appeared on February 7, the campaign fell apart. None of the famous had been consulted by Maxwell and they had not given their approval. Weinstock called the advertisement "incredibly silly" and Delfont said, "I'm amazed. It shows what happens when you let people run amok." Delfont wanted his name taken off: "It's a pity such a good idea has started off so badly." Overnight, Maxwell became a target for ridicule, especially when he justified printing Pergamon's books and journals in eastern Europe because "it's cheaper." He did not understand his inconsistency but blamed "Britain's 'professional knockers'" who just turned their attention from Britain and directed it against me." When he wrapped up the campaign in March he sat alone, but he claimed nonetheless that the response had been "phenomenal." The campaign had amounted to a recorded telephone message urging support for Britain; the collection of signatures for a petition; the establishment of community baby-sitting groups; and the creation of a "clearing house" for complaints about shoddy British products and services. "Much has been achieved," said Maxwell. "It needed just one more heave"—but unfortunately he would not be able to take the campaign through to its completion because of pressure of other work.

The campaign's only discernible achievement was to turn Maxwell, courtesy of television, into a nationally recognized personality. Since there is little Fleet Street enjoys more than a Labour politician who can be lampooned, a bevy of defamatory tales began circulating. His stock fell. When a newspaper reported that amid the strikes and chaos the socialist supporter of the "I'm Backing Britain" campaign had, despite all the government's currency controls, spent a holiday on the luxury yacht *Shemara,* owned by Sir Bernard Docker, his stock sank still further: one week's charter cost more than the average Briton's annual wage. So, by the time Maxwell returned from his luxury cruise, his political career had passed its peak.

The sapping of his political life in Britain had not been noticed in Moscow. On the contrary, having awarded Maxwell such privileged status in Russia, the communists ignored any suggestion that their trading partner's importance could diminish.

Maxwell was always ebullient on his journeys to the Soviet Union. He felt important in a country which he liked. As he set off on yet another business trip to Russia during the last week of May 1968, there was every reason for him to believe that it would follow the normal course. But on that occasion, his visa application in London had been specially noted by the KGB, triggering a succession of consultations and conspiracies. What follows is an account given by Soviet intelligence officers.

In retrospect, it is obvious that planning the operation must have started months before but the first indication beyond the KGB's headquarters in the Lubyanka occurred on May 15, 1968.

The KGB's emissary was called Colonel Alexandre Yevgenovich Koinkov. His approach was to Zaloman Levitsky,* an officer of the GRU, the Soviet military intelligence service which is a parallel organization of the KGB. The two agencies enjoyed an uneasy relationship and co-operation between them was unusual but as Koinkov explained, Levitsky possessed special qualities which the KGB had sought in vain among its own ranks. Firstly, Levitsky was Jewish and the KGB had purged its own ranks of all Jews other than in the research department; secondly, he spoke fluent English; and thirdly, Levitsky had operated undercover in the west and understood a capitalist's mentality.

When the two met, Koinkov extracted an oath of silence from Levitsky. The GRU officer was not to reveal to his own service that he had been in contact with the KGB. That formality completed, Koinkov

---

* Pseudonym, although real name is known to author.

explained that their target was a British businessman and politician. No name was mentioned. In Berlin after the war, Koinkov continued, the Briton had signed an undertaking to help the KGB if required and the agency now needed his services. "We believe that he is planning to visit Russia," Koinkov continued. "We will contact you just before he arrives." The second meeting occurred on May 21. In a detailed conversation, Koinkov revealed that the target was Robert Maxwell who was expected to arrive later that week. He would be flying from Moscow to Minsk and Levitsky was to travel on the same airplane. "In the plane, you are to attract his attention," said Koinkov, "but nothing more."

On arrival, continued Koinkov, Maxwell would be met by a delegation who would take him to Minsk's Intourist hotel. Levitsky would be booked into the same hotel. The point of contact was to be the following morning. "Maxwell eats breakfast in the dining room," said Koinkov. "You will come in after he has started eating. We will ensure that all the tables are full and only the one next to Maxwell is free. Since your face should be familiar, he is certain to ask you to sit with him."

On May 28, Levitsky was seated on Aeroflot flight number 607 which departed Moscow's Sheremetevo airport at 8 a.m. Two rows behind the intelligence officer sat Maxwell reading English newspapers. Twenty minutes after take-off, Levitsky got up and approached Maxwell, speaking fluent English with a slight American accent: "Could I borrow one of your papers?"

Maxwell: "Are you English or American?"

Levitsky: "Neither."

Maxwell: "But you speak perfect English."

Levitsky: "I teach English."

Ten minutes before landing, Levitsky returned the newspapers to Maxwell. They smiled and parted. Levitsky, who lost sight of Maxwell inside the airport building, was met by three KGB officers from the Minsk headquarters who drove him to the hotel.

The following morning, Levitsky arrived in the dining room. As predicted, Maxwell was seated alone and seeing his traveling companion at the entrance waved. Feigning to ignore him, Levitsky began his forlorn search for a table. From the corner of his eye he could see Maxwell getting up and walking toward him. "Good morning," greeted Maxwell, "what a surprise. Why don't you join me?" Levitsky played coy but agreed.

Their conversation ranged across a wide span of topics until Maxwell asked, "Are you Jewish?" Their relationship warmed. Toward the end, Levitsky said: "Look you've been very kind, can I invite you for dinner tonight?" They agreed to meet at 5 p.m.

They ate in a small annex that night. It was just after they had toasted each other with the first vodka that Levitsky introduced himself: "I want you to know that I am a colonel of the KGB." Maxwell, according to Levitsky, showed no visible reaction. "You once agreed to help us and the moment has come where we would like your assistance." According to Levitsky, Maxwell replied, "With pleasure." Levitsky continued, "When you return to Moscow, you will receive a phone call. We would like you to meet chairman Andropov."

Yuri Andropov, appointed chairman of the KGB the previous year, would lead the organization until he became the country's leader in 1982. In the West he is regarded as probably the most intelligent and perceptive chairman in the KGB's history and was one who eventually understood the need for reform. Levitsky's statement provoked only a nod from Maxwell and the two continued their meal speaking about other topics. Levitsky flew back to Moscow the following day. Maxwell followed two days later.

The phone call was made by Koinkov on the morning of June 3. Koinkov collected Maxwell and introduced the British businessman and politician to one of Andropov's aides. Maxwell was escorted to meet Andropov. The only other person present was a male interpreter.

After that meeting, Maxwell was driven to the Hotel Sovietskaya, off Gorky street, where he ate lunch with Koinkov and Levitsky. The GRU officer recalls Koinkov saying, "Don't worry, we won't ask you to do anything trivial. It will be important." Maxwell seemed unruffled and subsequently returned to Britain.

The results of that approach are contained in Maxwell's KGB file to which only three officials have the automatic right of access: the Soviet president Mikhail Gorbachev; the KGB's chairman; and the head of the first directorate, the KGB's foreign intelligence section which is the equivalent of M.I.6 or the CIA.

Maxwell, it must be said, has never been accused or even suspected of any disloyalty to Britain. On the contrary, his passion for his adopted nation was occasionally embarrassing in its unequivocal intensity. There is no evidence that his expressions of patriotism were not genuine. But Maxwell was the archetypal opportunist and would have seen the advantages of performing a service which was not illegal. Nevertheless, at this stage, one can only speculate about the services which Andropov requested.

A year of extreme turbulence was 1968. The aftermath of the Six Day war in the Middle East, the war in Vietnam and the open struggle between the two ideologies in Africa generated waves of uncertainty and conspiracy theories in both Moscow and Washington. No group was more influenced by that turbulence than the postwar generation of students whose demonstrations and advocacy of revolution were unsettling and even threatening to all governments. The constant fear of a superpower confrontation which might escalate to nuclear war was only contained by an understanding called detente—an agreement between Washington and Moscow that the Yalta agreement which had firmly established the demarcation line of influence and control by the two powers in Europe in 1945 should not be challenged.

It was in the midst of that extraordinary year, that some members of the Czech communist party, supported by anticommunist nationalists, began successfully to liberalize the Stalinist legacy which had been imposed upon their country. In Moscow, the "Prague Spring" aroused fears that Soviet control might be effectively undermined. An article in *Pravda* in July blamed the CIA for inspiring the "ideological sabotage" of Czechoslovakia.

By then, Leonid Brezhnev had already decided to intervene but properly anticipated the consequences upon the Soviet Union's relations with Western countries. The danger was that the West might not remain a passive spectator as occurred when the Soviets crushed the Hungarian revolt in 1956. Russia needed friends in the West who would advocate the need to preserve peace despite the aggression.

On the night of August 20–21, the Warsaw Pact armies invaded Czechoslovakia. The outcry in the West was vociferous and the clamor for a military response to save the Czechs was deafening. In Britain, Harold Wilson, the prime minister, bowed to demands that Parliament should be recalled from the summer break for a special debate.

On August 26, MPs returned from all over the world to discuss the "rape of Czechoslovakia," one of those benchmark events by which history is recounted. Maxwell flew back from his luxury cruise in the Mediterranean to speak in that debate. His political career, as previously noted, was by then uncertain. Yet his contribution to that debate was noteworthy. It was the single moment when he finally held the attention of all politicians in the Commons chamber.

Over the previous four years, the sight of Maxwell rising to speak in the intimate atmosphere had increasingly provoked sniggers and sighs, but on this day everyone was quiet. "As is well known," he began, "I was born in Czechoslovakia. . . . I remember well the betrayal that I, though very young, and the whole nation of Czechoslovakia felt at being let down by Great Britain and France at Munich. . . ." To rapt attention, he outlined his escape and his decision to come to Britain, because "when the chips were down, Britain was willing to stand against Hitler alone." His advice was measured and moderate, and surprised the Tories. The government should take no reprisals which would disturb detente but should leave it to individuals to cancel their contacts with the Soviets to show their disapproval. It was a speech which moved the House. Advocating detente, despite the shocking events, seemed at the time a mature and reasoned argument. The question is what motivated him to propose a policy which accorded with Moscow's? Maxwell, it can be assumed, was not an agent seeking secrets, but he had become an agent of influence, a role that would intensify in later years when Mikhail Gorbachev became the Soviet leader.

By 1968, Maxwell had certainly made an indelible mark in the Commons, but not in quite the way he had intended. His weaknesses and strengths were tellingly revealed in a sympathetic profile written by David Wood, the respected political editor of *The Times,* which perfectly encompassed the vices and virtues of the man. Wood had been invited to meet Maxwell and his family at the mansion in Oxford and was impressed by the strong bonds which united the large clan. Surrounded by affection and respect, Wood had difficulty in equating the brave refugee with the much maligned public persona.

During the course of their interview, Wood asked Maxwell about his early years and faithfully reported the anomalous answer: "His own account of his christening as Ian Robert Maxwell is typical of the man. At the end of the war the army wanted to send him to Berlin on a mission and the officer who briefed him said that he had better find a respectable name to go with. Maxwell had no suggestions to offer. 'Then you'll be a Scotsman with my family name,' said the officer." This was an example of Maxwell's romanticizing which Wood recorded faithfully. Maxwell's secondment to the Control Commission was not "a mission" but a regular transfer; in any case, when he received his MC in January 1944 he was already called Maxwell. Exaggeration is one of Maxwell's vices and Wood identified the others which had by then sabotaged his political ambitions.

Robert Maxwell swept into the House . . . and gave every impression to the old hands that he was mounting a take-over bid for the place, lock, stock and barrel. He was loud and thrusting and probably no M.P. came new to Westminster was so little overawed by the surroundings. So far as there was a takeover bid intended Mr. Maxwell has failed. In the House he is still regarded as a maverick, a millionaire of unusual antecedents who obviously knows how to be a business tycoon but who will never understand the art of winning men.

Probably Maxwell did not, even in private, acknowledge the accuracy of Wood's summary, but in the midst of his next commercial sortie he effectively admitted its implications. While his bid for power in Parliament was failing, he was simultaneously undertaking a substantial expansion of his business empire. In October 1968, he thought that he had finally secured a power base in Fleet Street. He announced a bid for the *News of the World* and told inquirers that, if he was successful, he would resign his parliamentary seat. "The first we knew about that," said Frank Atter, the party official in Buckinghamshire, "was when we read it in the papers." Maxwell the aspiring tycoon, rather than Maxwell the politician, dominates the remainder of this story.

6

There was never any secret why Maxwell wanted to own a newspaper. The barons of Fleet Street were automatically granted influence and prestige, and Maxwell's bids for the left-wing *Daily Herald* and four years later for the right-wing *News of the World* indicated a consistency not of principle but of ambition. His disappointment at not winning office, contrasted with his enormous and accumulating wealth, laid the ground for a condition which the American politician Adlai Stevenson had aptly described five years earlier: "Power corrupts, but the lack of power corrupts absolutely."

In 1968, Pergamon seemed, according to the audited and published accounts, to be booming. Trading profits had risen from £145,000 in 1962 to £1.3 million in 1966, and in 1967 they increased again by 35 per cent. Pergamon's assets had, in four years, tripled in value to £6.9 million and the price of its shares had doubled over two years. Regardless of the setbacks in Parliament, Maxwell appreciated that his new wealth unveiled golden horizons.

The company's phenomenal expansion had not been effected without some difficulties. In France, Maxwell's second attempt to establish himself as a scientific publisher had just ended in acrimony and bankruptcy. The vehicle for his latest bid for imperial expansion had been the prestigious scientific publisher Gauthier Villars. The French publisher had been founded in 1864 and became a venerable institution entrusted with publishing the works of the École Polytechnique and many of France's most notable scientists. Fittingly, Gauthier Villars was housed in the ancient heart of the capital, in a huge and picturesque terrace built on the foundations of a fourteenth-century monastery overlooking the River Seine and Notre Dame. When, in 1959, Maxwell arrived by invitation for the first time at the Quai des Grands Augustins, he was inevitably enthralled by its history and tempted by the offer from its manager to become a major shareholder.

Paulette Gauthier Villars had been the publisher's managing director since 1951 when the professional manager who had guided the firm since her father's death in 1918 had himself died. While she owned 25 per cent of the shares, the remainder were spread between five nephews and nieces who did not share her sentimental passion to preserve the family business for a fourth generation. Rather than allow such a renowned publisher to pass into alien ownership, Paulette assumed the managing directorship but maintained her profession as professor of anatomical pathology. Her daily routine was to teach in the morning, to arrive at the Quai in time for lunch and a nap, and then to devote three hours in the afternoon to publishing. By 1959 she recognized that her part-time and unpaid stewardship had been flawed. During those eight years of unparalleled scientific activity, Gauthier Villars had failed to attract any new authors, its stocks of old books had accumulated in a leaky warehouse and had become unsaleable, costs had soared, income had fallen and the overmanned printing presses had become outdated. Her family business was on the verge of bankruptcy and needed new cash. Its only assets were the building and its name but Paulette was determined to prevent any of her French competitors from taking a share of the family business. With those limitations, she directed Louis Varenne, the company's manager, whom many would blame for the company's parlous financial state, to search for a savior.

On July 17, 1959, Varenne introduced Paulette to Maxwell whom he had met during the previous three years at the annual Frankfurt Book Fair. There is little doubt that Paulette's prejudices, xenophobia and possibly anti-Semitism, were dissolved by Maxwell's charm and good looks. Within four days she had written a long letter to the other family shareholders that she had found their benefactor, whom she described as "Monsieur X," whose expertise and enthusiasm would revitalize Gauthier Villars. The principal advantage of selling a 44 per cent stake for Frs 500,000 to this mysterious publisher, wrote Paulette, was his British nationality since he could market translated versions of Gauthier Villars's books throughout the world providing a huge new market for their authors which was important, she stressed, in the new era of the Common Market. In addition, she wrote, "youth would be injected into the company (I think that he is thirty-five years old) and significant financial expertise."

Paulette initially feared that the other four family shareholders would not give the unanimous approval which was necessary according to Gauthier Villars's articles of association. Her fears were unfounded. None were prepared to inject money into the business since they had never received a dividend and were relieved by the prospect of a genuine businessman taking control. Their enthusiasm seemed to be justified after their first formal meeting with Maxwell in November 1960 when the British publisher urged the board to agree to a massive increase in capacity which, he was convinced by his great experience, would treble the turnover within five years. Both Paulette and Varenne were overwhelmed by Maxwell's optimism that their debts and antediluvian attitudes could be overcome.

Soon after the deal was finalized, Maxwell appointed Paddy O'Hanlon, an experienced editor, to work at Gauthier Villars. "The initial reaction when I arrived," she recalls, "was 'Oh God, we're being invaded by the Brits' and that hostility never disappeared. Other French publishers disliked Maxwell for the same reason." In fact the disdain increased as Maxwell insisted that the worthless stock be thrown out, manuscripts be edited before publication and directed that they buy the magazine *Sciences et Avenir* which absorbed nearly his total investment. But he did little more. Considering the hostility toward the British, Maxwell, who in those days rarely mentioned his French wife or his love of France, was pleasing Paulette by his absence although their relationship was genuinely warm. To Paulette's satisfaction, Maxwell infrequently came to the building, even for the annual meetings, and gave little advice on reforming the company's finances except significantly when he remarked that the draft of the 1963 annual report was too "detailed" and that they should remove negative words like "difficulty" and "regrettable." The offending words were omitted, so conveying the impression of success which the increased turnover suggested.

Nineteen-sixty-four was Gauthier Villars's centenary and was marked by a special celebratory champagne party at the Sorbonne. At an early point during the festivities, Maxwell seized the opportunity to corner Gilles Gauthier Villars, then a student, and propose a deal. According to Gilles, Captain Maxwell, as he insisted on being called in France, "insisted that I regard him as a surrogate father, wanted me to sell to the company my share of the valuable building at the Quai des Grands Augustins." Unable to escape Maxwell's physical presence to reach the bar, Gilles became preoccupied signaling to his wife for a glass of champagne and a taste of the delicacies rather than listening to Maxwell's advice. Only twelve months later it became clear why Maxwell, who Gilles thought was supposed to improve the publishing business, was interested in the property.

In May 1965, Paulette was told that the company was once again heading irretrievably toward bankruptcy. The Maxwell-inspired rush for expansion had only multiplied the debts and brought none of the benefits which he had promised. An attempt in 1964, agreed by Maxwell, to revalue the old stock and increase the company's apparent worth by the equivalent of Frs 2 million had been rejected by the auditors as "creative accountancy." The books were worthless and the ruse was condemned. For all the family and especially Gilles, the news came as "a shock because I had believed that Maxwell was meant to save us and he had failed. But I didn't understand why." Paulette asked the shareholders including Maxwell whether they were prepared to invest any money. In unison the family refused. Maxwell however agreed but on one condition—that he was given more shares and therefore outright control of the publisher. Reluctantly, the family envisaged no alternative.

During the summer and autumn the Gauthier Villarses became increasingly irritated by Maxwell. Gilles in particular was annoyed after noticing a large number of packages of back issues at the entrance to the building addressed to Pergamon in Britain. Varenne had explained that Maxwell was buying a large amount of stock for resale. "I thought that we were selling our flesh," recalls Gilles, "because if Maxwell could sell it for himself, why could he not sell it for us? I was suspicious." According to Varenne, it was a ploy by Maxwell to inject money into the ailing company but the money was never received.

When therefore in early December, Gilles received a call from M. Pierre Bleton who asked whether he could call and outline a proposal for Gauthier's future, Gilles was receptive. Bleton, a journalist-cum-banker, explained that the Finacor bank wanted to form a new consortium of French scientific publishers and was prepared to pay the family Frs 220 per share on condition that each member of the family agreed and that no one told Maxwell. The temptation of Bleton's offer, according to Gilles, was overwhelming: "We were all interested because Bleton was offering us money for our shares while Maxwell intended to get our company for nothing. Under his scheme our shares would have been worthless and he would have control." Maxwell had failed to fulfill his grandiose promises and there was the added aggravation that, confident of success, he had already filed a request with the government for permission as a foreigner to own a French company.

Bleton exploited those grievances and also the family's mutual hostility which inhibited its members consulting each other. Individually, Bleton collected their signatures for the sale of their shares and asked them not to reveal their intention, especially to Maxwell. They needed little persuasion. "Bleton knew," says Gilles, "that we wouldn't ask Maxwell to make an offer for the shares because he could have bought one person's shares and cut the remainder out." One technicality remained. The company rules needed to be amended to allow the sale of shares to a non-shareholder. Since unanimity was crucial, Maxwell's own approval had to be obtained. Accordingly, Maxwell was told by Paulette and Varenne, orally and not in writing, that the family approved of his proposed investment but that as a formality they needed to amend the rules. Maxwell readily agreed. The stage was set for an extraordinary general meeting which was much more unusual than so many of the others Maxwell had attended.

Just before 11:30 on December 31, Gauthier Villars's shareholders began gathering on the second floor at the Quai des Grands Augustins. Unlike Maxwell who traveled from the rue des Écoles, the other participants lived in apartments at the Quai itself and as they individually closed their doors and walked down the stairs they were united by a conspiracy to outwit Maxwell and finally profit from the family business.

Everyone noticed that the unsuspecting Maxwell was exuberant as he arrived, insensitive to the stony silence. Paulette, chairing the meeting, was noticeably more efficient than usual, methodically working through the procedures and recording the votes. A mere fifteen minutes later, Paulette declared the meeting over. Maxwell was beaming, unconcerned that everyone filed expressionless and silently out of the room to return upstairs: "We didn't say a word," recalls Gilles, "because we knew that to be legally binding everything needed first to be properly registered."

Precisely two weeks later, Maxwell discovered that he had been outwitted. At first Paulette denied the conspiracy but after persistent phone calls from London she conceded that Maxwell had been deceived. "If this kind of trickery had been perpetuated by me on you, how would you feel about it?" protested Maxwell whose outrage stemmed alternately from being the artless victim of a perfidy to fury that he had been denied his prize. Simultaneously, Maxwell announced that he would be "pleased to pay the family Frs 350 per share" and instructed his lawyers to sue Paulette for fraud. The family felt no pity for their accuser because according to one member, "he was both a socialist and a shark. He wanted to use the asset because it existed but did not want to pay for it."

Inevitably Maxwell's interpretation was different, especially since his own investment was suddenly endangered. Unknown to the family, Finacor had been acting for Georges Dunod, Gauthier Villars's arch rival to whom Paulette had forsworn ever selling the business. Dunod took control without reckoning that Maxwell would exact his revenge; for the following four years he harassed and tried to sabotage Georges Dunod's attempts to save the company, investing more time and effort every month to his vendetta than he had expended in total on Gauthier Villars throughout the previous six years. Eventually after Paulette died (some would say that she was pushed to the grave also by Maxwell's vendetta in the courts) he conceded defeat and, complaining that as a foreigner he was too handicapped to operate in France, switched to solve his problems in America which was more important for his ambitions for building an empire.

A five-year agreement with the Macmillan Company of New York for the exclusive distribution of Pergamon books had been terminated in August 1964 amid acrimony, two years before its expiry. Macmillan had bought £3.7 million worth of Pergamon books (which added enormously to Pergamon's profits) but had sold only 57 per cent of the stock. Macmillan claimed that "the quality and saleability of the books which we were expected to buy fell below our expectations" and blamed Pergamon for selling its own translated versions of books earlier than previously agreed. Maxwell was naturally disappointed because Pergamon's success depended upon exports (40 per cent of its sales were in America) and blamed Macmillan's sales force.

Maxwell's privately owned American company, Maxwell Scientific International Inc. (MSI Inc.), bought the outstanding stock of books from Macmillan for £1.6 million so that Pergamon suffered no losses. When Maxwell was questioned in January 1966 about this apparent setback by Oliver Marriott of the *Sunday Times* he dismissed any suggestion that Pergamon's sales might suffer and boasted about the "quite abnormal profitability of Pergamon" which had been 130 per cent and 116 per cent pre-tax on the net capital employed over the previous two years. "These are the sort of returns," wrote Marriott, "which all industrialists dream about." Despite Maxwell's assurances, Marriott queried whether Pergamon could continue to perform so brilliantly.

Ebullient as ever, Maxwell dismissed the cautionary note and waved aside any doubts. He was set on a buying spree to build an empire, and to raise the money to finance his expansion 1.1 million Pergamon shares which were owned by his family trusts had been sold on the stock market after the flotation at a much higher price than that at which they had been issued, although some were immediately repurchased by nominee companies to ensure that Maxwell and his family retained absolute control of the company. His targets for purchasing were companies with printing and educational interests. The first was a venture into a field where he had absolutely no experience whatsoever.

On December 1, 1965, Maxwell paid £1 million in cash for the subscription-books division of George Newnes, which published two well-known encyclopedias, Chambers and Pictorial Knowledge. Encyclopedias, as a by-product of the expanding educational revolution, were in vogue in the 1960s, especially among the aspiring working and lower-middle classes, who had been convinced that knowledge was the key to improving their children's prospects. Chambers encyclopedias were well written, but the technique of marketing the fifteen volumes had aroused widespread controversy.

Since the traditional method of selling through shops was unsuitable, encyclopedia publishers had recruited freelance salesmen who, provided with lists of potential customers (usually parents of young children), arrived unannounced on the doorstep of the unsuspecting client. Doggedly and emotively, the salesmen sought to cross the threshold as the first step to persuade the client to sign a contract whose huge expense was partially concealed because the monthly repayments over three years promoted the illusion that the total investment was substantially less. Since the salesmen were paid purely on commission—no sale, no pay—the pressure exerted on the potential customer was sufficiently strong to provoke demands that Parliament should enact legislation to protect the weak and the gullible. By the time that Robert Maxwell, then a Labour Member of Parliament, made his first investment in the business, encyclopedia salesmen enjoyed dubious reputations. Cecil King, IPC's chairman, who had sold Newnes to Maxwell, said subsequently that he did not think that selling encyclopedias could be profitable unless methods were used which were not "ethical." Maxwell had a different view, although his own advisers cautioned him against the purchase on commercial grounds.

Chalmers Impey, Pergamon's auditor, had advised that the business contained a "higher speculative element" than Pergamon's traditional interests and pointed out that Newnes's profits over the past five years had substantially declined and it was now making a loss. Chalmers's opposition was supported by Ansbachers, Pergamon's merchant bankers. Maxwell ignored them both because he believed it would be a very profitable venture.

When Maxwell bought Newnes, the fourth edition of Chambers had already been printed but it took a further twelve months before sufficient volumes had been bound for Maxwell's newly recruited team to begin a concerted sales drive. Newnes's direct competitor was the New Caxton encyclopedia, a twenty-volume work owned by Caxton Holdings which, under the management of Hedley Le Bas, had pioneered the foot-in-the-door selling technique which had earned the business such a notorious reputation. To maximize its profits, Caxton also sold the same encyclopedia in parts to the British Printing Corporation (BPC), which marketed its version under the title Purnells New English encyclopedia. Consequently, in 1966 Maxwell was in competition with both Caxton and BPC in completely alien territory. He had never handled a similar product before and he had never been involved in direct selling.

Whatever criticism might be voiced about Maxwell's commercial behavior, it is indisputable that he never hesitated to mount a challenge in the market. More than most businessmen, he instinctively sought to defeat his competitors. Chambers was such a venture. Maxwell felt that he had "bought a bargain" and was optimistic that he could transform Chambers's recent losses into profits. "The encyclopedia business," he later explained, "was 97 per cent in U.S. hands. British encyclopedias were just as good but weren't being properly sold." Accordingly, Maxwell reported in a circular to shareholders that his huge investment would show a "satisfactory return" and set out to fulfill his promise by increasing his share of sales throughout the world, naturally at Caxton's expense.

On January 8, 1967, in an atmosphere of intentional melodrama, Maxwell called a press conference to announce that he was about to set off on a 50,000-mile world tour to promote the sales of the new edition of Chambers. After stating that he had already sold 3,500 sets in Britain, he explained that exports were his dream. "There is a tremendous thirst for knowledge all over the world," he told the assembled journalists, "and we have the right people and product to cash in." In every respect, it was a highly unusual event. First, most businessmen would never speak publicly before embarking on a speculative tour but would wait for the results. Secondly, it would be unusual even for a Conservative MP to summon the press to promote his business interests but it was rare for a socialist to do so. Yet Maxwell was abundantly confident of proving to Britain how he could win exports. It never occurred to him that what generated interest was the incongruity of a socialist peddling a disparaged product.

The first stop on the world tour was India, where he was greeted by Jawaharlal Nehru, the Prime Minister, an honor which set the pattern for the whole tour. In each country which he was to visit—Thailand, Japan, Hong Kong, Indonesia, Malaysia, Australia, New Zealand, Mexico, the United States and Canada—he had arranged to meet either the Prime Minister or the President, who would be given, in the presence of a photographer, a specially bound set of the encyclopedias. In each of those countries he had also arranged to meet leading bookdealers to conclude sales contracts and had set up an unlimited number of "media opportunities" for interviews.

As he toured the world, Maxwell reported back daily to his headquarters in England a succession of record sales. Philip Harris, the vicechairman of Buckingham Press, the Pergamon subsidiary which had bought Newnes, followed his success with amazement. Without consulting Maxwell, he took the initiative and began to plan a new print of the encyclopedias, reasoning that even the available stocks of 13,000 sets were grossly insufficient to satisfy the huge upsurge of demand which the tour was generating.

For Philip Okill, who was traveling with Maxwell, a different picture was emerging. Okill had just been promoted to head Newnes's international sales force when Pergamon had bought the company. Okill had taken a different route around the world from Maxwell's, but they had arranged that they would meet in predetermined capitals to compare results.

As a quiet-spoken, slightly built, methodical man who enjoys stroking cats, Okill would be the first to admit that he had little in common with his new employer. The first six months of operating under Pergamon had passed uneventfully, but the changes which Maxwell introduced immediately afterward were, Okill believed, drastic and dangerous: "I was expected to jump or dance when the maestro called the tunes, the maestro of course being Mr. Maxwell. And Mr. Maxwell's ideas of running a subscription-book division were quite different from anything I had experienced in twenty-odd years."

Okill was a cautious salesman with limited horizons. When Maxwell told him that his objective was to make Buckingham Press "the largest bookselling operators in the world" he was startled because he believed that his employer did not understand how to manage the operation: "He seemed to be fired with ambition but he had no experience." Okill's fears were confirmed during the tour. His task was to follow Maxwell and to complete the legal formalities for the sales which Maxwell had won. Yet in Calcutta where Maxwell had claimed sales of five hundred sets, Okill heard from a Mr. Pripittia: "No, we haven't placed an order. Mr. Maxwell offered us some sets of Chambers encyclopedia and told us we didn't have to worry about paying for them. That could be dealt with at a later date." Okill left without an order and discovered that India would never place an order because the encyclopedia's map showed the disputed territory of Kashmir as belonging to Pakistan.

Maxwell returned to Britain on February 23, before Okill. Promptly, he called another press conference at the Dorchester Hotel to announce the sale of seven thousand sets of Chambers worth £1 million. It was, he told the summoned journalists, a momentous achievement which was "a lesson for the rest of the British business community." His 5 per cent target, he declared, was "easily achievable." The headlines were fulsome and amusingly included his own quip that Maxwell, "when broken down into Chinese, means Mr. Ma, a man of great thoughts." Another of his philosophical comments, that he had realized the secret of the Japanese economic miracle when he had seen a newspaper delivery boy running, rebounded upon him. Cynical wags wondered whether the wretched fellow had not simply got out of bed late. But gratifyingly to Maxwell, the numerous newspaper accounts contained the impressive statistics he had compiled: "In seven weeks I traveled 70,000 miles, I visited 11 countries, 22 cities, held some 400 meetings and was interviewed on radio, television and by newspapers about 140 times. I obtained £1 million worth of orders for British books with some £3 million worth to follow and on my return received a telegram of congratulations from the President of the Board of Trade."

He then went back to his office and summoned Harris, who expected some praise for his percipient planning for a reprint. The contrary, according to Harris, occurred. He was told by Maxwell to cancel all plans because his claim of seven thousand sales was just for publicity. Okill was stunned when Harris relayed the news. Soon after, he was sitting with Maxwell in Fitzroy Square when Maxwell said, "Okill, you don't seem to like me, you don't seem to trust me. Why don't you?" Okill replied, "Because, Mr. Maxwell, you're the sincerest liar I've ever met." According to Okill, Maxwell laughed, "because, I genuinely think, he took that as one of the nicest compliments I could have paid him." Okill claims that the world tour resulted in no sales other than to a Pergamon subsidiary in New York. Maxwell denied the allegation and insisted that, with the exception of the Calcutta order, the sales which he announced were all genuine and were delivered. Okill's version was later supported by the government's investigation into Pergamon's affairs.

Maxwell was unconcerned by their disagreements since he was impatient to increase sales of Chambers and challenge his competitor, Caxton. Over previous years, Caxton had successfully established a strong sales team and was earning enticingly high profits in South Africa which contributed a quarter of the company's total income. Maxwell immediately began to search for ways to capture that money for himself. What followed was certainly controversial but definitely not illegal. On November 13, 1966, Maxwell recruited L. C. Schilling, who for the previous six years had been Caxton's secretary, to be the credit controller of Buckingham Press. Events then moved very swiftly. Just before Maxwell had left for his world tour, the head of Caxton's South African sales team had flown to London and had likewise agreed to work for Maxwell. Two months later, in February 1967, days after Maxwell returned to London, Maxwell sent Philip Harris to South Africa to recruit a new sales team. Harris returned to Britain forty-eight hours later, having accomplished his mission. The major casualty of Harris's spectacular success was Caxton, whose complete sales team had deserted their old employer. Harris was quite candid about the instructions Maxwell had given him on the eve of his departure. He was to "knock off the Caxton sales force." But Harris went even further and also alleged that Maxwell's true ulterior motive was to "bankrupt Caxton so that he would buy it cheaply." Maxwell strongly denied that claim.

By the time Harris came to make his allegations in 1970, he had become a disenchanted critic of Maxwell, but there is no doubt that Caxton was terminally crippled by the collapse of its sales in South Africa. The following month, in March, Maxwell made his first approach to Caxton's chairman, Hedley Le Bas, with an offer to buy his family's business. Not surprisingly, Le Bas was furious to find himself so quickly outclassed by his new competitor, and sought help from his partners, the British Printing Corporation (BPC).

BPC was Caxton's natural savior for three reasons: Caxton's encyclopedia was printed by Hazell, Watson and Viney, a BPC subsidiary; BPC sold part-issues of Caxton encyclopedias; and Caxton owed BPC a substantial sum of money. Yet at that precise moment, BPC, which would feature so massively throughout Maxwell's career, was jolting through a major management crisis.

BPC's turmoil had started the previous year. The company was an unhappy marriage created in 1964 of two printing conglomerates, Purnell & Sons and Hazell Sun. Just months after Purnell's chairman Wilfred Harvey, a swashbuckling individualist, had become chairman of the new company, he was overthrown in a public and very bloody boardroom coup after the discovery that he had illegally profited from earlier mergers and that he had arranged to pay himself the astronomical salary of £270,000 per year plus £600,000 in commissions. In 1966 BPC's managers were still reeling, and they left Le Bas in no doubt that they could not offer him any help.

Consequently, in April 1967, Le Bas began negotiating with Maxwell. On May 3, 1967, Bruce Ormrod, the joint managing director of Henry Ansbacher, announced that Maxwell had bought Caxton Holdings for £1.1 million. In a jubilant public statement, Maxwell estimated that there was a £200 million world market for encyclopedias of which he aimed to capture 5 per cent. Considering the enormous sales he claimed to have won during his recent world tour, his optimistic prediction was accepted as forecast.

Eight days after the merger announcement, Maxwell formally approached Sir Charles Hardie, the chairman of BPC, and Victor Bishop, the managing director, and suggested that BPC should join forces with the new Pergamon/Caxton company to sell encyclopedias together. The negotiations and the agreement which followed were crucial to the dramatic and very public collapse of Pergamon's own merger with the American company Leasco two years later.

BPC was keen to stay in the encyclopedia business since the company printed both the Chambers and Caxton encyclopedias, and Maxwell succeeded in persuading the BPC directors to unite and fight. On August 17, 1967, they signed a memorandum of intent which anticipated that the two companies would merge their interests into a new company called International Learning Systems Corporation Limited, a very grand name for an encyclopedia-selling operation. Their agreement contained one very important proviso: Pergamon guaranteed BPC that the new company's combined pre-tax profits would not be less than £500,000. Maxwell agreed that if the profits fell below that amount at the end of the first year, Pergamon would make up the shortfall in cash. Similarly, BPC guaranteed that the profits of its subsidiary Purnell until June 30, 1968 would be at least £98,000. The board of management reflected the merger. Hedley Le Bas was appointed ILSC's managing director, Maxwell was to be the chairman and chief executive and three BPC men were also appointed to the new board—Michael Pickard and Victor Bishop, who were both deputy chairmen of BPC, and Ralph Pollock, who was a BPC director.

From the outset, ILSC inherited from its three procreators the major problem which was endemic to the encyclopedia business: the head office was always uncertain whether the sales reported by its freelance teams were accurate and whether the customers would honor their contracts and make regular monthly payments. To compound the uncertainty of the new company's financial position, the salesmen were paid their full commission promptly on receipt by ILSC of the signed contract and they bore no responsibility if their quickly forgotten clients defaulted in their monthly payments. Since some salesmen earned as much as 40 per cent commission on a contract which would be paid over three years, ILSC's potential bad debts were ominously large. Okill claims that at Newnes the cancellation rate was on average 9 per cent, yet at Caxton under Le Bas it amounted to 40 per cent. The marriage of the two companies was beset from the outset by a clash of personalities and practices.

ILSC's board met for the first time on September 19, 1967. Le Bas gave an assurance that on balance the new company's forecast profits would be "very nearly met." Even on the basis of the information then available, Le Bas's assertion was inaccurate because the ILSC's accounts and book-keeping were in a "deplorable state," their overseas branches having failed to keep proper records. Maxwell endorsed those accounts, although it was only one year later that he was officially informed by ILSC's auditors about the true state of affairs. But by then he had publicly exploited Le Bas's assurances of ILSC's future profitability.

During the summer of 1967, Maxwell was planning his next acquisition. With Pergamon earning huge profits from its scientific journals and assured a big dividend if the forecast profits of ILSC materialized, Maxwell could afford to finance his next bid by offering Pergamon shares instead of cash. It was a much cheaper way to fund take-overs but depended upon the price of Pergamon shares remaining at their high level, which in turn was determined by Pergamon's high profits.

On October 11, 1967, Pergamon announced a bid for Butterworths, the venerable publisher with which Springer had twenty years earlier unsuccessfully attempted to begin a joint venture. Since that failure, Butterworths had steadily expanded its own prestigious scientific, medical and legal publications, but its profits had, on its own admission, increased only "marginally." Over the previous five years under a new chairman, Richard Millett, diverse attempts had been made to restructure and galvanize the old-fashioned publisher, but with only limited success. Millett was particularly anxious to avoid the clutches of unwelcome American predators able to recognize the real value of Butterworths's assets. To protect the company, Millett repeatedly but unsuccessfully sought possible mergers with other British publishers until on October 10, 1967 a letter was delivered by hand from Bruce Ormrod of Ansbachers announcing Maxwell's bid. Ormrod's letter did not come as a complete surprise. Commercially, the merger had positive merits since Pergamon's and Butterworths's publishing activities had much in common, and over the previous three years Maxwell had made repeated gestures toward Millett, suggesting friendly negotiations.

Millett was appalled. He harbored a deep suspicion of Maxwell which was on the verge of obsessional and stemmed from the days of Simpkin Marshall. After reading Ansbachers's letter, he spontaneously wrote to Maxwell telling him, according to Butterworths's official history, "to get lost." To *The Times* Millett said, "I would want to know a lot more about Pergamon before any merger and would be very reluctant to accept Pergamon paper under any circumstances." For the first time in Maxwell's career, a take-over battle became ferociously personal. Millett hired private detectives to scour the world for any details about Pergamon's activities, which Maxwell answered by a High Court writ. But within one month it was all over. Millett had also launched a frantic and wide-flung search for an alternative bidder and Cecil King offered substantially more for Butterworths than Maxwell, who reluctantly conceded defeat. Ormrod recalls that Maxwell accepted he had been beaten by a bigger fish but felt that at bottom it had been determined by prejudice: "He couldn't sit at the top table, as Macmillan would say." Maxwell had suffered a loss of face which would soon have been forgotten if the offer document issued by Pergamon for Butterworths had not contained statements about ILSC's finances which later proved to be seriously inaccurate.

The problem of consolidating ILSC into a coherent company was a difficult one. Unifying the production and printing of three organizations made commercial sense but arranging the financial operation required time and skilled management. At the outset, none of ILSC's directors knew much about the financial health of their company. Four weeks after Maxwell had made the bid for Butterworths, Cooper Brothers, the management consultancy firm, wrote personally to Maxwell pointing out the absence of reliable information about ILSC's finances. Both Pickard and Bishop, BPC's deputy chairmen who were ILSC directors, later admitted that the information they received about ILSC's finances, especially its bad debts, was until spring 1969 both "irregular and insufficient." Yet the formal offer presented by Ansbachers on Maxwell's behalf for the Butterworths bid contained a very reassuring statement about ILSC's finances. After explaining Pergamon's guarantee that ILSC's combined pre-tax profits for the first year would be "at least £500,000," the offer document stated that the target would be met: "The Board of ILSC has informed Pergamon that sales and profits for the first three months of operations are running at the level forecast when the arrangements were negotiated." This statement was crucial to fixing an estimate of Pergamon's profits and therefore to establishing the value of the shares it offered in exchange for Butterworths.

Bruce Ormrod, the Ansbachers banker handling the bid, admits that he never saw the relevant letter from the ILSC board to Pergamon containing that important assurance. "I was entirely at fault in not getting that as a copy for my own records," he later admitted. In the rush to make the bid, Ormrod said, he had relied entirely on Maxwell's promise that the letter did exist: "I was informed by Maxwell that he had obtained it." The BPC directors later claimed that they had not signed such a letter nor had they ever seen or approved the assurance which Maxwell gave Ormrod. In contradiction, Maxwell insisted that all three BPC directors had visited him at Fitzroy Square and had approved the whole document including the forecast about the profits. Whatever the truth, the profits forecast was wrong. It was a reflection of the style of operations at ILSC.

In December 1967, in response to Cooper Brothers's warning to Maxwell that ILSC's accounting system was unsatisfactory, Harold Moppel was appointed the company's financial director. On arrival, Moppel received optimistic assurances from both Maxwell and Le Bas that ILSC was "running at enormous profits" because of the high sales. Moppel however judged that ILSC was in a state of chaos and that in reality no one knew what profits would be earned. "No accounts had been produced of any nature," he said three years later.

During 1968, as Moppel and another accountant, George Hazard, grappled to organize the accounts, both became disenchanted with Maxwell's style and especially with his interference in their work. As in the affairs of Pergamon, Maxwell was reluctant to allow his employees to dictate to him how the financial position of a company which he owned should be presented.

At that time, no accountant was more aware of Maxwell's interest in his professional decisions than Peter Bennett, Pergamon's financial director. On September 2, 1966, Bennett wrote to Maxwell two memoranda about the purchase of Newnes. Although the binding of the

Chambers encyclopedias was still not completed and few sets had been sold, Bennett reported in the first memorandum that the "net profits" amounted to £105,000 and in the second that they would reach £222,000. How Bennett arrived at those unrealistic figures is subject to dispute, although their effect on the overall image of Pergamon's profits was extremely favorable. When asked about the second memorandum in 1970, Maxwell recalled that he had "honestly believed" that the profits were "properly made" and emphasized that "Mr. Bennett took the initiative in these matters" supported by Chalmers Impey, Pergamon's auditor. Bennett admitted that his views were "an error of judgment on my part," but he added, "my recollection is that these views were heavily influenced by Mr. Maxwell." Maxwell also believed, according to Bennett, that the £1 million he had paid for Chambers was £200,000 less than it was truly worth. He wanted that money reflected in the accounts. Bennett claims that he "thumped the table and said: 'Tell me where the £200,000 profit is.' "

It also fell to Bennett to prepare Pergamon's annual report for 1968. This stated that both Pergamon and BPC had been paid two dividends by ILSC. In December 1967, each had been paid £112,000 and in June 1968 each was to receive £187,000. Although both parent companies immediately returned the dividends to ILSC in the form of loans, the payments as presented in official reports effectively concealed the chaos at ILSC. Moppel and the accounts department did not know whether ILSC was even earning any profits on which to pay a dividend; although by April 1968 they realized that whatever the profits these were considerably lower than officially anticipated.

By mid-1968, Maxwell suspected that ILSC was in serious difficulties and that the bad reputation earned by the encyclopedia salesmen was reflecting upon him. In one attempt to stem the criticism, Maxwell appeared on BBC Television's *Braden's Week,* but when surprised by the concrete examples of abuse, agreed to investigate the complaints. Maxwell blamed in particular Le Bas and his Australian manager, Rod Jenman. In Australia, it was said, the list of new customers could be read off the tombstones in the Sydney cemeteries. The situation, recalled Maxwell, "was absolutely disastrous" and in the summer of 1968 he fired both men and three other senior officials for alleged incompetence (although the report of the Department of Trade and Industry inquiry would state that Maxwell's allegations were erroneous). Maxwell took over ILSC's daily management, which—combined with his many other interests—placed a huge burden upon him but did not stop his repeated public recommendations about how Britain's sluggish econ-

omy could be improved nor his boasts about his own qualifications for
the task.

One example that year followed the collapse of Craven Insurance,
a company which sold motor-car policies. A winding-up petition was
presented in the High Court by the Board of Trade but to the government's embarrassment Maxwell counter-petitioned the Court and insisted that the company was in fact solvent. Amid great publicity, he
pledged that he would save the insurance policies of 65,000 motorists
and promised to inject £200,000 into the company; he would also become the chairman. Few outsiders could understand the motives of a
scientific publisher and encyclopedia salesman who was also a Labour
politician, a public figure at the forefront of the "I'm Backing Britain"
campaign, becoming involved in motor insurance. Two months later,
Maxwell admitted that Craven was indeed bankrupt and blamed his
original intervention on "grossly misleading facts." Having lost all his
money, he admitted to being "very angry and very upset for myself,
my associates, the policy-holders and the staff. This is certainly my
worst disaster ever." Board of Trade officials were not amused.

When Maxwell presented himself on June 7 to the Pergamon shareholders for their annual general meeting, his "worst disaster" was already forgotten. The company's profits, said the chairman, were "a
new record," having increased by 33 per cent after tax during that year.
Twenty-one new journals had been published and Pergamon's book list
contained six thousand titles, a figure which would increase by six
hundred over the following twelve months.

In the company report, Maxwell stated that ILSC "is already making
a contribution to the profits of your Company." The source of those
profits, reported Maxwell, was the outright sale of 15,000 sets of Chambers encyclopedias in one year and the anticipated sale of another 15,000
sets in the following year: "This rate of annual sale is approximately
400 per cent higher than that achieved by the previous proprietors."
The £100,000 paid as a dividend by ILSC and immediately returned
was counted as a profit.

Maxwell also sent shareholders a separate circular which asserted
that "The Board of ILSC has informed Pergamon that sales and profits
. . . are running at the level forecast. . . ." Since the ILSC board had
not given Pergamon that information and since there was, at the time,
only a vague notion about ILSC's actual profits, Maxwell was characteristically optimistic. But his assurance had been supported in writing
by his financial director, Harold Moppel, who, like the chairman, believed that the recent devaluation of the pound would produce an

enormous windfall. The price of Pergamon shares increased accordingly, encouraging the strategy of paying for any acquisitions by offering valuable Pergamon shares. His next major opportunity presented itself in the summer of 1968.

Jacob Rothschild, then a partner of the merchant bank N. M. Rothschild, was seeking a purchaser for 25 per cent of the shares of the mass-circulation Sunday newspaper, the *News of the World*. Maxwell, who as we have seen had already made an attempt to take over the *Daily Herald*, did not conceal his enthusiasm when he telephoned the banker. Tantalizingly, it was an opportunity to launch a take-over bid which, if successful, would transform him in one swoop into a press baron with six million readers. The doors to the Establishment's citadel would open in a manner that mere membership in the House of Commons could never achieve.

Rothschild was acting for Professor Derek Jackson, an eccentric cousin of the incumbent chairman of the *News of the World,* fifty-six-year-old Sir William Carr. Jackson, who was enjoying his sixth marriage, divided his time between France and Switzerland and had little affection for the Carr family. Initially, he had offered the shares to his cousin but Carr's price of 28s which Hambros the merchant banker described as generous was, he felt, derisory and he was not averse to the idea that the family should therefore be discomfited by a take-over bid. Maxwell's agreement to pay 37s 6d for each share (they were trading at 29s 3d on the Stock Exchange) was welcomed as providing a good profit—and an ideal weapon in the family feud.

Sir William's family had edited the paper since 1891 and controlled 27 per cent of the shares. The remaining 48 per cent were mostly owned by twenty-eight individuals. The City institutions owned a negligible interest. Considering the dismal financial performance of the company under Carr's management during the previous years, Maxwell was confident of persuading an extra 26 per cent of the shareholders to sell to him at the higher price. With his new merchant bank adviser, Robert Clark of Hill Samuel, Maxwell calculated an offer which crucially depended upon the new peaked price of Pergamon shares, since the bid would be based on a swap of Pergamon shares for *News of the World* shares with a cash alternative.

By 1968, Carr had been chairman of the group for sixteen years, using the public company to provide the luxuries to which he had become accustomed. His opulent lifestyle, his personal golf courses and his horseracing were all paid out of the company's meager profits. The *News of the World,* under his dictatorial control, had continued to publish a consistent cocktail of rape, marital infidelity and saucy scandal but its circulation had fallen during his tenure by two million copies a week. Similarly, the group's other interests such as Eric Bemrose, a Liverpool subsidiary equipped with the latest gravure machinery for color printing, and thirty local newspapers had also suffered from his persistent neglect. Carr was unperturbed by his declining fortunes, if only because he was invariably drunk by half-past ten every morning, a habit which had earned him the popular alias "Pissing Billy."

On the morning of October 16, Robert Clark arrived at the offices of Hambros, which acted as adviser to the Carr family, and purposefully slapped an envelope down on Harry Sporborg's desk. The Hambros director found inside Maxwell's offer of 37s 6d for each share, a £26 million bid. "It came as a total surprise," recalls an eyewitness. When the news reached Carr, in bed at the time stricken with a serious heart ailment, he was unavailable for any discussions throughout the remainder of that day. On the Stock Exchange, the excitement of the unexpected bid pushed the price of *News of the World* shares immediately up from 29s 3d to a dizzy 40s 3d with expectations that the rise would continue. Few insiders had believed that the Labour MP could mount such an expensive bid.

While they gathered their thoughts, the Carr family issued a terse announcement that shareholders should do nothing until the board had properly considered the offer with Hambros. For his part, Maxwell told the press that he was confident of success because he believed that some members of the Carr family would desert to his camp; and, to the great surprise of his constituency, he announced that because of the extra commitments he would not seek to be renominated for the next general election. Informally he told newsmen that his aim was to be the "Arnold Weinstock of the printing and publishing world—a tough business man who can squeeze more profits out of assets than anyone else." The public comparison did not endear him to the cool, analytical industrialist but it was an adroit one for that "modernizing" era. His real motives were easy to guess: having failed that year to buy Butterworths and having been personally denied the opportunity to purchase a stake in BPC by Max Rayne, this was just his latest attempt to build an empire. But the publisher who had within recent memory supported the prosecution of the publisher of *Last Exit to Brooklyn* announced that he would not interfere with the paper's salacious editorial policy.

Nothing Maxwell promised could ever placate Sir William Carr and his long-serving editor, Stafford Somerfield. While Harry Sporborg began to consider the formal defense against the bid, the chairman and the editor published their own considered reply four days after Maxwell's bid was announced. That Sunday, millions read Somerfield's emotional and xenophobic riposte on the *News of the World*'s front page. Headed "We are having a little local difficulty," Somerfield's piece continued, "Why do I think it would not be a good thing for Mr. Maxwell, formerly Jan Ludwig [*sic*] Hoch to gain control of this newspaper which, I know, has your respect, loyalty and affection—a newspaper which I know is as British as roast beef and Yorkshire pudding?" Somerfield answered his own question by describing the paper's editorial policy, maintained by just six editors since 1891, as independent but right-wing. Unlike the Carr family, he wrote, Maxwell had no newspaper experience and was a socialist. There was, Somerfield claimed, no chance that Maxwell's promise of impartiality could be maintained. "I believe that Mr. Maxwell is interested in power and money. There is nothing wrong with that, but it is not everything." But the possibility of socialist interference was nothing compared to the peril of a foreigner taking control: "This is a British paper, run by British people. Let's keep it that way."

By any standards, Carr had gone beyond the pale. Even his supporters were shocked by this uninhibited display of anti-Semitism, especially against a man who had fought so bravely for Britain and was a Member of Parliament. Unfortunately for Maxwell, the tone set by the newspaper reflected the defensive tactics which were to be adopted by Carr's professional advisers in the City.

By 1968, Maxwell was by no means a stranger in the Square Mile, but this was the first time he had played in the First Division. It was ironic that opposing him was Hambros, the merchant bank which had financed his breakthrough twenty years earlier. But as Sporborg himself had taken the initiative in persuading Charles Hambro to break with Maxwell, any lingering sentiment between the two sides had disappeared by the end of the first day. "It was," admits one of the bankers advising Carr, "a thoroughly dirty battle where everyone played as hard as they could." As far as Maxwell was concerned, however, the players on the other side did not stick to the rules and the City Establishment tilted firmly in Carr's favor.

In the 1960s the City's reputation still basked under the reassuring slogan "My word is my bond." Although its inhabitants' nepotistic hegemony was already under strain, most of those employed in banking and brokering were still self-styled patrician gentlemen whose families had known each other for generations. Insider dealing and tax-evasion schemes flourished behind the comforting myth that the City's self-policing mechanisms were preventing any dubious profiteering.

At the time Maxwell made his bid, the City had experienced two years of unprecedented mergers and take-overs. No less than 70 per cent of Britain's hundred biggest companies had been involved in bids concerning nearly one-quarter of all British firms. British financial and commercial experts, as in other western capitals, were gripped by the fashionable nostrum that only giants, especially the newly termed multinational corporations, could hope to survive the coming technological revolution. The merger-mania had transformed the normally sober clientele of the Pall Mall clubs into replicas of the gun-slingers in a Wild West saloon. In their desperate urge to win individual take-over battles, prominent companies, having placed their bid at one price, were rigging the share market, crucially changing the nature of their businesses in the midst of a bid, and giving favored treatment to the more important shareholders, so destroying the cardinal rule that after a bid is launched all shareholders must be treated honestly and equally. By the end of 1967, any pretence of self-policing had been destroyed as evidence of deception by industrialists and their advisers provoked howls of outrage, yet never any suggestion of punishment.

To avoid government intervention, the Bank of England finally commissioned four experts to recommend a new code of practice which would guarantee fair play. Among those four draftsmen was Robert Clark, one of Maxwell's advisers in the *News of the World* bid. In March 1968, a new code was introduced, with a supervisory panel under the chairmanship of Sir Humphrey Mynors, a former deputy governor of the Bank of England. Maxwell's bid was among the first to be governed by the new code, and Mynors, as referee, had to prove that the City was capable of policing a fair fight.

As a mild-mannered rather uninspired former Bank official, Mynors was "charming, weak and too much of an insider to be effective." He was the natural choice of those who hoped that cosmetics would dispose of the political pressure for change. But in the course of two major take-over battles which occurred in the first months of his tenure, Mynors proved incapable of implementing the rules because the new code lacked any penalties which could be used against transgressors. Mynors could only rely upon his own personality, which was no match for the City giants who deigned to sit before him. Maxwell's success would therefore depend upon how ruthlessly both he and his advisers decided to fight Carr's resistance and especially whether they decided to adhere voluntarily to the unenforceable code.

By the first weekend, despite Somerfield's editorial, the omens were favorable. No rival bid seemed to have materialized and Maxwell announced that he was prepared to raise the value of his bid at a later date. For someone who had for the past three years been the butt of an avalanche of vituperative publicity, there was a pleasant surprise. Most press comment was inclined to see the advantages of the marriage. The *Sunday Times*'s cautiously favorable comment was typical: "There is no doubt that anyone with Maxwell's seemingly bottomless energy and flair can have a remarkably energizing effect on the largest of organizations."

Among the rash of sympathetic profiles, the *Financial Times* described Maxwell's charm, individual talent and care for ordinary workers. Anthony Harris sympathetically quoted Maxwell's own description of his earlier purchase of C. & E. Layton, a loss-making printer: " 'Nobody believed in the business any more. I talked to the workers individually and in groups, about their craft, the quality they had to offer. And I did something I believe that no other take-over bidder has ever done before. I gave a year's guarantee of employment to every man on the books. Then we got down to it.' By the end of the year Layton was making profits again."

There was also a lengthy, endearing interview in *The Times* which suggested that Maxwell, with his "Frankie Vaughan and Victor Mature" looks, had become a humbled parliamentarian who admitted he had been "a bit brash" and "impatient" in the House and had suffered a "boycott" by other Members. Despite the public image of a "boastful dictator and a megalomaniac," the profile concluded, he was "surprisingly mild." If nothing else, the hefty £200,000 which the bid would cost Maxwell had at least bought him an improved image.

But at the end of Monday, October 21, just five days after the bid had been announced, Maxwell's fortunes abruptly changed. Sporborg's tactics had taken a new, slightly sordid and definitely terminal twist. Soon after the bid was announced, the banker had placed £750,000 of Hambros's money at the disposal of its stockbrokers with instructions to buy every *News of the World* share on the market. Sporborg knew that his tactics were a clear breach of the "spirit" of the new code, which forbade companies to buy their own shares to frustrate a take-over bid, "but everyone seemed to be making it up as we went along." By the end of the week, Hambros owned 10 per cent of its client's shares, which Sporborg unconvincingly claimed was an independent stake. The banker had also cleverly secured contractual pledges of support from other shareholders for a payment of 10s each which guaranteed that the Carrs controlled a formidable 48 per cent of the votes. Robert Clark and Maxwell's other advisers were nonplussed. As one of the code's architects, Clark could only advise his own client to obey the rules. Maxwell raised his bid to £34 million, while Clark appealed to Mynors for help. In turn, Mynors summoned Hambros. Sporborg's attitude was simply that "one could drive a coach and horses through the rule book. He'd pop into Mynors and ask whether he could do something. Mynors would just reply: 'Why not?' It was a free-for-all." So at the beginning of the second week Maxwell could expect no help from the City Establishment, but on the Monday that was not of such paramount importance. More fateful was the secret arrival of a man whom Maxwell had recently met for the first time in Australia.

Rupert Murdoch had landed at Heathrow the previous day for the first round of what since became a regular if unequal bout between two ambitious individuals. Murdoch, then thirty-seven years old, started the competition with advantages which were denied to the forty-eight-year-old Maxwell. The Oxford-educated Australian had inherited from his father money, privileged social status and a small newspaper which he had successfully used to build a sizeable business in Australia. Murdoch was ready to expand into Britain. When he heard that Maxwell's bid was opposed by the Carrs, he dashed to London to propose a deal to Sporborg. In return for Murdoch's purchasing sufficient shares to tip the balance in Carr's favor, Sporborg should convince his client to merge his interests with Murdoch who, as a reliable and junior partner, would sympathize with his interests. The two would be joint managing directors while Carr would remain chairman. Since the investment was well protected and the possible rewards were enormous, Murdoch had everything to gain.

Knowing that after ten-thirty in the morning Carr would be incapable of making any decision, Sporborg and Murdoch drove on October 22 to Cliveden Place for breakfast in Carr's apartment. Winning his approval was unproblematical. The young Australian and Carr shared friends and acquaintances and both were committed newspapermen. Indeed, with the exception of his new *Australian,* all of Murdoch's own newspapers survived on a diet similar to the *News of the World*'s—sex and scandal. By the following day, Murdoch owned 3½ per cent of the shares. The news that Murdoch was a redeemer leaked quickly, provoking more banner headlines and placing Maxwell back in the center of the news. Following new complaints from Maxwell to the Panel, dealings in the shares were suspended, but Carr, with Murdoch's help, had already won majority control.

The Cliveden agreement stipulated that Murdoch would obtain a 40 per cent interest in the *News of the World* by purchasing a new issue of shares. In exchange for owning the biggest stake in the newspaper, Murdoch would invest into it "certain" of his own News Limited interests. Since Murdoch had no intention of investing anywhere near the same amount as the £34 million which Maxwell had bid, Carr was selling his newspaper for considerably less merely to satisfy his prejudice. But as a consequence the other shareholders were being denied the chance of receiving the 50s per share that Maxwell was now offering. Sporborg had masterminded another breach of the code, although in his combined defense with Murdoch's bankers, Morgan Grenfell, he justifiably insisted that Mynors had initially approved his tactics. The spirit, he conceded, might have been broken, but not the letter. Both bankers had just "popped in" to Mynors and won his agreement, but once the furor broke, Mynors quickly retreated. By then, of course, it was too late for Maxwell, who commented, "This is a disgraceful affair and it is up to the Takeover Panel to do its proper job." As a pointed supplementary, Maxwell wondered aloud how embracing an Australian protected the paper's uniquely "British" ownership. Others waited to see whether Anthony Crosland, the Labour Minister at the Board of Trade, would intervene to help his parliamentary comrade.

At the end of October, the final resolution of the battle depended on the extraordinary shareholders' meeting which was to be called to approve the issue of extra shares to complete the Cliveden agreement. The public outcry was too fierce for the City to allow events to take their course unimpeded. While Carr's advisers pleaded for time to negotiate their deal with Murdoch, Clark, after persuading Maxwell to fulminate in uncharacteristic silence on the sidelines, negotiated a major concession. Mynors, following a meeting summoned by Crosland, secured an agreement from the three merchant banks that they would not use at the decisive shareholders' meeting the 15 per cent of the shares which they had bought after Maxwell's bid. It was a belated attempt to save the Panel's reputation which presented Maxwell with new hope. Of the outstanding 85 per cent of shares, approximately 20 per cent were nominally uncommitted. Maxwell needed the bulk to win control. Overnight, the contest slumped to a new level.

Murdoch had suddenly seen the prize slip just beyond his immediate grasp. A series of stories began appearing in his own Sydney *Daily Mirror* about the tactics of ILSC's encyclopedia salesmen. Wounded, Maxwell issued the first of scores of writs which, over the next twenty years, he would hurl at newspapers to protect his reputation and, more important, to hide the truth. In London, Sporborg read Murdoch's files about his rival but was advised that they were too defamatory for publication. That hardly satisfied Carr, who, when approached during the day drinking dry Martinis at the Savoy, only asked his banker, "What are you doing to keep the foreigner out?" According to one of those present, "It was an appalling time. Carr insisted on personalizing the battle and our lawyers constantly crossed out paragraphs of our publicity as scurrilous." For Carr, defeating Maxwell was all that counted and even Murdoch's unilateral decision, conveyed in a letter, that Carr could not after all be joint managing director was quietly conceded to secure the Australian's continued support.

Maxwell fought with the same passion but not the same methods. With superhuman energy, his personal publicity machine ceaselessly pushed the advantages of his own bid while he sought from the courts injunctions and damages against every banker, adviser and director connected to the Carr family under every conceivable heading ranging from breach of fiduciary duty to conspiracy. He also sought the support of the trade unions and traveled to Southsea to discuss his plans with Bill Keyes and other SOGAT leaders. His scenario did not appeal to them. "He didn't understand deadlines," recalls Keyes, "he thought it was like a scientific magazine. He wanted to walk in and take over and just cut manning levels among the printers and the journalists. It was a naive bid for power. We told him that he didn't understand newspapers. He packed up his papers and walked out."

Maxwell felt the pressure tightening. The forecast of ILSC's profits was critical to the price of Pergamon shares, and keeping the price of those shares high was in turn crucial to his bid for the *News of the World*. Between June 4 and November 1, 1968, Pergamon's shares had risen from 34s 6d to 46s 10d, having peaked at 48s. As the take-over battle approached its climax, scattered and unsubstantiated rumors began circulating in the City that ILSC's profits would not be as high as Maxwell had suggested in his circular sent to shareholders on May 15. In a meeting with Maxwell on September 18 (which was confirmed in writing), Cooper Brothers, ILSC's consultants, who knew the rumors to be true, warned the chairman that ILSC's accounts were "unreliable."

That warning was discussed at an ILSC board meeting held on October 15, the day before the *News of the World* bid was announced. Maxwell and all his fellow directors acknowledged that their company's accounts were in such chaos that they would be unable to comply with their original objective of presenting the normal annual accounts for the year ending June 30, 1968 and would instead organize accounts for the eighteen months ending December 31, 1968. As the weeks passed and the take-over battle progressed, even that target seemed increasingly impossible to meet, fueling rumors about Pergamon's profits which were naturally encouraged by those acting for Carr.

Since maintaining the price of Pergamon's shares was vital, during the three weeks following Maxwell's bid announcement, one of his private companies, Maxwell Scientific International (Distribution Services) Ltd (MSI(DS)), bought 245,500 Pergamon shares in three transactions through Michael Richardson, who worked at Pergamon's stockbrokers, Panmure Gordon. The purchases, which cost £1,100,000, were properly announced by Panmure and complied with the take-over code. Those purchases clearly had an effect on keeping the share prices at their very high level although Maxwell later explained that it was done as a "longterm investment" on the advice of his bankers and brokers because "I was convinced that the bid would go through and that the price would rise very substantially."

As the battle dragged on, Maxwell was told by his bankers, Hill Samuel and Robert Fleming, that Pergamon's price was weakening. With his agreement and again with proper notifications, the two banks purchased a further 215,500 Pergamon shares in November and December. Maxwell gave undertakings to both banks that he would repurchase the shares at any time up to January 31, 1969.

Even as his chances were waning, Maxwell, unwilling to accept defeat, launched a frantic counter-attack. Michael Richardson was sent to Australia with the brief to launch a bid for Murdoch's own group. The half-hearted attempt, which was dubiously reported as having the support of Roy Thomson, quickly collapsed. Meanwhile in England, Maxwell personally telephoned dozens of shareholders to win their support. His calls revealed that most were antagonistic toward him, despite the press comment running in his favor. In desperation, he sent two thousand telegrams and even personally promised to pay for taxis to bring pensioners to the meeting. Yet on the eve of the final showdown, Maxwell's bid was certainly doomed. To the very last, Sporborg pulled the strings to engineer Maxwell's defeat.

The public venue for the decisive vote was the Connaught Rooms near Covent Garden. On Thursday January 2, 1969, dressed as always in a bright blue suit, Maxwell arrived just before ten-thirty to discover that the hall was packed with hundreds of Carr employees who had arrived in a fleet of company buses. In the front row sat the Carr family dressed in black, but united. Depressingly for Maxwell, that day's newspapers had led with Sporborg's late-night claim that he had collected sufficient proxies to guarantee victory. Visibly nervous in the hostile atmosphere, the outsider watched as Murdoch, smiling and confident, entered the room accompanied by his attractive wife. At a long table in the front sat Carr who, from his right side, would be supplied by Sporborg with an endless stream of prompt cards to answer the pre-arranged questions from the shareholders. "Unfortunately, he could not even read what was written," recalls one banker. Maxwell, by contrast, knew exactly what he wanted to say—that his bid promised shareholders unquestionably a lot more money. Unfortunately for him, the cold logic of the market place was not in issue. The vote was about Maxwell himself.

Others in that predicament, where the glare of television spotlights was certain to seize upon and record every glance of personal antagonism, might at that moment have chosen gracefully to accept the inevitable verdict and treat those who had denigrated him with dignified contempt. Yet it was the very nature of Maxwell to ignore defeat until every possible avenue had been exhausted and then, if possible, to start the fight again. Like a tireless salesman, he would never take no for an answer.

Cheers greeted Carr as he rose to open the meeting, the loudest from his own specially selected employees. Scathingly, he condemned Pergamon's lack of experience in newspapers and was skeptical about Pergamon itself, whose shares had been falling in value despite huge purchases by Maxwell and his friends to support the price. No one mentioned that the price of *News of the World* shares was also tumbling as Carr spoke. Murdoch followed with a succinct statement and was followed in turn by Maxwell. Amid jeers and catcalls, Maxwell launched an unrestrained but fumbling attack on Carr which was punctuated by shouts of "Go home" and "Rubbish" before finally ending in uproar. Many of those heckling were identified as "small men in mackintoshes," the traditional and loyal *News of the World* readers who were delighted to have an opportunity to vent their personal dislike of the publicity-seeking, foreign, socialist millionaire. Sitting just feet away, Murdoch ill-concealed his smile. The outburst of emotion only delayed the inevitable. Once the vote was taken, the hall emptied and only a few waited for the counting to be completed. Untrusting to the end, Maxwell strode into the scrutineers' room, only to be forcefully ejected by Carr. The result was a massive victory for Murdoch.

The final scene as the curtain fell was poignant. The victor embraced his wife. Carr looked on smiling, enjoying his moment, albeit briefly, because shortly afterward he would be unceremoniously ousted from power by his chosen redeemer. On the side, alone, stood Maxwell, a wet sheen glistening over his eyes, fixedly staring into the distance—an expression which always indicated that Maxwell either felt wounded or understood he had suffered public humiliation. Sportingly, he shook Murdoch's hand and congratulated him on catching "a big fish with a very small hook." To a journalist, inquiring about reaction to the City's conduct, he quipped, "I'm on the side of the angels; it's amazing." It was the first but also the last time over the next decade.

7

Days after the defeat, still suffering from the vilification and the abuse, Maxwell flew to New York. "I felt that the British would never let me succeed," he told a friend shortly afterward in a rare display of despair. The events in the Connaught Rooms had been the climax of a disastrous year. His new operation depended upon a constant stream of acquisitions, especially of companies like the *News of the World* whose valuable assets could be exploited more profitably, and throughout 1968 all his major bids had failed. Maintaining the high value of Pergamon's shares depended upon repeatedly improving his profits. In Oxford, his staff were compiling the 1968 accounts but he already knew that it would be impossible to beat the previous year's record. That presented a serious predicament. During the *News of the World* take-over battle, he had issued a forecast that Pergamon would earn around £2 million profit in 1968. If that forecast did not materialize, his future credibility would be harmed.

Whether by the time his plane landed in New York he had actually planned a detailed personal survival plan has always been unclear. But he had already anticipated that there was a fortune to be earned from developing a scientific information retrieval system based on computers and that, because of his poor reputation in Britain, he needed an American partner.

Three years earlier, in Pergamon's annual report, Maxwell had written about the "decisive importance" of a computer-based retrieval system. Although nowadays that statement seems unexceptional, it was in 1966 a percipient prediction because computer technology was still crude and very few people had even imagined the possibility of personal, desk-top computers. Maxwell had tried to obtain government funding for his ideas and approached Sir Frank Kearton, the chairman of the

Labour government's new investment bank, the Industrial Reorgani-sation Corporation. Kearton says that he had been "very impressed" by Maxwell's "vision and energy" but had rejected his application be-cause "the technology was simply not yet sufficiently developed." Nevertheless, Pergamon's 1966 report stated, "Pergamon is the only company in Europe in information retrieval."

In January 1969, Maxwell hoped that he would find a partner in America. He had approached several people before telephoning Saul Steinberg, a twenty-nine-year-old American multi-millionaire whose record was by any standards quite phenomenal.

Steinberg was a Jew from Brooklyn, New York who had graduated from the University of Pennsylvania. In the course of writing a pre-cocious thesis entitled "The Decline and Fall of IBM," he had recog-nized that IBM was losing potential customers for its computers either because they could not afford the price or because they were reluctant to invest in technology which would soon be redundant. Steinberg's coup was to create an arrangement whereby his company, Leasco, bought IBM computers with finance provided by banks and leased time on the computers to customers.

At the end of 1967, Leasco was worth about $75 million and was earning $1.4 million in profits, which gave it a rating, according to *Fortune* magazine, as one of the fastest-growing companies in the west. In 1968, Leasco's profits rocketed to $27 million and its assets soared to $1 billion. Steinberg had orchestrated a dazzling display of per-petual corporate restructures amid a blitz of take-overs and mergers. Within one year Leasco had expanded into management consultancy, shipping containers, and engineering and computer service groups in North America and western Europe. His biggest coup was a successful bid for the respectable Reliance Insurance Group worth a massive $740 million. For most of the year, Steinberg's star shone brightly and Leas-co's share price trebled but in late summer his ambitions were crushingly halted. He had let slip that he was planning a bid for the prestigious Chemical Bank. Wall Street was aghast and turned with a vengeance to punish the arrogance of a Brooklyn youngster. Leasco's shares plum-meted and many of Steinberg's sponsors cringed. Wounded, Steinberg retreated to ponder the predicament of the outsider. "I always knew there was an Establishment," he subsequently mused, "I just used to think I was part of it."

When destiny brought Maxwell and Steinberg together, the pride of both had therefore recently been shaken by public ostracism. Both were irreverent but wanted to be revered. Inured to criticism, their fantasies continued to flourish inside the bubbles of their own self-promotion. Both were enigmas since they shared an ambition for power but gave no intelligible explanation about how they would exercise it. Both shared another ambition, to become richer and yet more richer. As footballers are rated by the number of goals they have scored and pilots by the number of hours they have flown, businessmen are evaluated by the number of millions and billions at their disposal. In 1969, as today, Steinberg was much wealthier and therefore in their own terms a more successful man than Maxwell, which must have affected the forty-five-year-old's perception of the American *Wunderkind*.

There are three versions of how Robert Maxwell first met Steinberg. Two are apocryphal (but they are naturally the most attractive despite their lack of authenticity). Maxwell, it is said, was so keen to meet the man who was even more successful than himself that, from New York, he telephoned his personal secretary Jean Baddeley and asked her to find out which hotel the chubby-faced tycoon would next be breakfasting in. Reliable as always, Baddeley delivered the correct location and reserved the neighboring table for her boss. In the midst of his meal, Maxwell rose and addressed his neighbor: "Oi vey, have I got a deal for you," whereupon, it is said, Maxwell presented Pergamon's latest annual report to the surprised American and suggested that they discuss their joint future.

The second apocryphal version places Steinberg in the Connaught Hotel in London during Maxwell's battle to buy the *News of the World*. A loud conversation at a neighboring table distracts the American who after a thoughtful stare turns to his guest and whispers, "Gee, that's the famous Robert Maxwell," and introduces himself to the great man.

A variation of this version is that Steinberg indeed overheard the conversation about the newspaper battle in the dining room but was more impressed by the protagonist's beautiful blonde escort. He assumed that it was Maxwell but it was in fact Murdoch.

The truth is more prosaic, but only at the very outset. The relationship between the two rags-to-riches Jewish entrepreneurs would progress at a dizzy pace from reality to utter fantasy, in its path bruising the most protected egos, shredding carefully cultivated reputations and culminating in the apparent commercial ruin of Maxwell himself.

The first contact was made on January 14. Steinberg was working in his office in Great Neck, Long Island when Maxwell telephoned. Steinberg had heard about Maxwell during his recent visit to London and took the call to hear the Briton explain that he was at Kennedy airport and wanted to discuss a proposition. Within an hour the two met for the first time. Maxwell's proposal was simple but very attractive. Pergamon had a vast amount of scientific knowledge at its disposal while Leasco possessed enormous expertise in computers. The two should embark on a joint venture, he suggested, initially to compile a world patent index on computer which they would later expand into a scientific library with terminals throughout the world. A small Leasco subsidiary in Washington DC was already transferring some material from Pergamon journals on to computers and Maxwell believed there was scope for considerable expansion. Steinberg was gripped by the idea. Maxwell displayed impressive technical understanding about computers and information-retrieval. Recently, American newspapers had carried a brief report that Maxwell had made a take-over bid for Document Inc., a company which placed NASA's material on computers, but the bid had been thwarted by the federal government because of security implications. Maxwell clearly understood the scientific world and was also, by all accounts, a highly successful businessman. His *News of the World* bid had been accompanied by favorable publicity in the British financial press. This seemed to be confirmed as Steinberg glanced through the brochure of Pergamon's 1967 annual accounts which Maxwell had, with a slightly theatrical gesture, passed across the desk. After a limited amount of small talk which ended with Maxwell announcing that he would have to dash back to London to attend a debate in the House of Commons, the two parted on the understanding that there might be further exploratory discussions in the future.

But Steinberg quickly lost interest in the patent index because, as he explained in 1973, "it was unprofitable. I told Maxwell it was premature to discuss any joint venture and I wasn't sure that we needed his particular expertise." Over the following weeks, Steinberg noticed that Maxwell's name was frequently mentioned in the financial press, in connection either with Craven Insurance or with rumors that he would bid for McCorquodale, a specialized printing company. Maxwell was certainly worth closer attention. In early April, Steinberg was planning a trip to Britain and he telephoned Maxwell to suggest a meeting. Maxwell was on the verge of departing for another world tour but he proposed to delay his trip by one day because, as he told Steinberg, "I've been studying Leasco and there are many areas where we have a joint interest." He added, "Perhaps we can even discuss a merger." Steinberg was surprised but keen to explore the possibility. On April 25 he arrived in London with his wife and Robert Hodes, his lawyer, "for a preliminary discussion to see whether it made sense for us to acquire Pergamon."

In the turbulent and vituperative world of Wall Street corporate lawyers, Hodes was acknowledged as among the most honest and able. Throughout the turmoil of accusations and emotions that would characterize relations between the two tycoons over the following years, Hodes retained an accurate and relatively objective account of the events as they unfolded. In later statements, Hodes would say that there was confusion when the two sides met at Fitzroy Square. At the outset, their conversation was constantly interrupted by phone calls and visits: "It's Evelyn de Rothschild," said Maxwell, "he's come to see me about a political matter. I'll be right back." Minutes later, Maxwell was once again seated in the room but was again interrupted. Just after he had left the room, Tom Clark arrived and declared, "I'm just back from South Africa and the sales of encyclopedias are fantastic." Maxwell returned and the telephone calls began: "It's Moscow; it's Berlin; it's a government matter . . ." Awed, the two Americans watched Maxwell's simultaneous management of his political and business affairs. When it was over, Maxwell dropped his first bombshell: he wanted to buy Leasco's international operations. Steinberg was flummoxed. Comparatively, Leasco was a giant and Pergamon a mere minnow. Leasco's international section, worth over $200 million and growing rapidly, alone dwarfed Pergamon. Laughingly Steinberg replied that it was not for sale, but how did Maxwell even intend to pay? "I haven't worked it out yet," Maxwell replied, "but I'm prepared to give Pergamon stock."

There was a moment's silence broken by Steinberg. The only topic for discussion, he insisted, was whether Leasco would buy Pergamon. Maxwell reflected and then agreed. In principle, Maxwell had undertaken to sell his company for cash and accept a subordinate position under Steinberg within Leasco. His only stipulation was that the preliminary negotiations should be carried out in New York where his associate, Ladislaus Majthenyi, commonly known as "Martini," could supply all the relevant information about Pergamon's affairs. Steinberg and Maxwell stood up and solemnly shook hands; the visitors left soon afterward. Outside, Steinberg was visibly excited. Another profitable take-over was under way. Apparently he did not hesitate for a moment to ponder why Maxwell wanted to sell his business. For Steinberg it seemed understandable that even the British politician would want to be hitched to his star. Yet over the following two weeks Steinberg's excitement waxed and then waned. Some mornings, often before 6 a.m., as he traveled around the world, Maxwell called with ideas and even suggested names for their new venture, but Steinberg's staff reported that they had made no progress whatsoever with Majthenyi. At the end of the month, during a call from Maxwell who was by then in Australia, Steinberg sounded distinctly cooler. If there was to be a deal, he told Maxwell, he needed to have a lot of detailed information about Pergamon's business and Majthenyi was being distinctly unhelpful. Maxwell promised immediate action.

Two days later, Leasco's director of corporate planning, Michael Gibbs, who had been delegated to handle the discussions with Majthenyi, arrived at Pergamon's New York headquarters at the Book Center. Majthenyi, a Hungarian-born accountant, was effusive. Pergamon, he explained, was "very profitable" and its sales in the Americas through the privately owned company Maxwell Scientific International Inc. (MSI Inc.) had topped $2.5 million in the past year. But when Gibbs stepped out again into the Manhattan street his briefcase was strangely empty. Normally, in similar deals, he would leave the corporate headquarters with masses of documents over which he would pore in the days ahead to deliver a detailed report to Steinberg. But Majthenyi had pleaded that he was not authorized to pass on confidential papers. He had muttered something about the privileges of the private and public companies but Gibbs had not completely understood. Indeed, when he returned to Great Neck he was little wiser, beyond realizing that the take-over of Pergamon might be more complicated than he had imagined.

Steinberg was again uneasy and the following day when Maxwell called he complained about the lack of progress. Breezily casting aside the doubts, Maxwell reassured Steinberg that his trip was enhancing both ILSC's and Pergamon's profits and that he would immediately fly to New York. The two met in early May at the Del Monico Hotel. Maxwell was relaxed, charming and confident. Pergamon's sales for 1969, he told Steinberg, would be approximately $25 million with profits of £2 million. ILSC's profits would be about £1 million. "Pergamon's performance," he promised, was "right on target." Steinberg was somewhat reassured, and Maxwell was delighted that a deal, albeit still undefined, was under way. Steinberg's remaining doubts disappeared that evening.

Steinberg had arranged to attend a Democratic Party fundraising dinner and he apologized to Maxwell that he would be unable to entertain him since a dinner jacket was obligatory. "Don't worry," said Maxwell, "I'll get one." By the time they had arrived at the Waldorf Hotel, Steinberg was pleased that Maxwell was present because he would have an opportunity to impress the British politician by displaying the scope of his own contacts, especially with the party's leaders, Teddy Kennedy and Hubert Humphrey. No sooner had they walked into the ballroom than Steinberg's vanity was shaken. In his deep resonant voice, Maxwell yelled, "Hubert!" and Hubert Humphrey turned round in the middle of the crowded room and shouted, "Bob, what are you doing here?" According to Steinberg, "Maxwell knew more people there than I did." Any lingering doubts momentarily vanished.

In the course of the following two weeks, Maxwell sent Steinberg letters, telexes and reports from London with information about Pergamon. But on May 17 the mood abruptly changed. Maxwell telephoned Steinberg and announced that the deal would have to be completed before Pergamon's next annual meeting, which was scheduled for June 19, just four weeks later. "Speed is important," he said. Maxwell explained that he wanted to buy BPC's share of the "profitable" ILSC but it would be much easier if Pergamon were already a Leasco subsidiary. All the information he needed, Maxwell assured Steinberg, was contained in a letter to Bernard Schwartz, Leasco's president.

Maxwell's letter to Schwartz was unambiguous. After an informative résumé of Pergamon's recent take-overs and its future plans, Maxwell disclosed an eye-opening example of how Pergamon earned its profits: twenty thousand copies of the Pergamon *World Atlas* had been sold at £20 each while the cost of production to Pergamon was a mere £1 10s. But it was ILSC and Maxwell's relationship with BPC which dominated the letter. The joint company, he conceded, had not been as profitable as he had at first imagined. BPC, he wrote, "is afraid of me and desire to sever the partnership and acquire ILSC." He added that he wanted to do the reverse and acquire BPC, "whose sales and profits I know I could double within two years."

ILSC, he admitted, had run into some trouble and as a result Hedley Le Bas had been fired because, Maxwell alleged, "he was too fond of liquor," while Jenman was fired "because of dishonesty." Both men strongly denied the allegations. Although both dismissals were in May and June 1968, and Pergamon had issued public statements praising ILSC's profits since then, Maxwell nevertheless wrote to Schwartz to say that "It was not until after the battle for *News of the World,* toward the end of last year, that I realized the inadequacy of the then management." Harold Moppel, ILSC's financial director, he wrote, had also been fired and he, Maxwell, had taken on the day-to-day management.

Maxwell's compression of the chronology confused the issue, since the *News of the World* battle had only ended in January of that year, 1969, but his assurances about ILSC's current profits were exceptionally explicit: "I enclose . . . a copy of the first quarter's management accounts and profit forecast prepared on a most conservative basis. These accounts were presented to and accepted by the ILSC board last Thursday; you will see that the company is running well, margins have already improved substantially and will continue to do so as we reduce our administration costs."

The paragraph which followed was equally unambiguous: "ILSC made a substantial profit for its first 18 months' trading." But Maxwell added a critical qualification: "If the accounts were judged by American standards, the profits for that period would be £800,000, but if British accounting practices were used, then we shall end up making neither a profit nor a loss" although there would be "enhanced" profits from 1969 onward. The estimates Maxwell quoted were annual sales of $20 million "and rising very fast," especially in America.

Steinberg and Schwartz were reassured by Maxwell's letter and, although they realized that ILSC needed further examination, they still could not understand Maxwell's reasons for wanting to complete the deal at breakneck speed. But any doubts were cast aside the following week when Richard Fleming, the chairman of Robert Fleming, Pergamon's merchant bank, arrived in New York.

Fleming's role in the imbroglio which developed over the following months would unintentionally accord with the bank's own description of itself as "a rather remarkable merchant bank." The bank had been founded in 1932 and had deliberately retained a rather discreet image, unlike the family's two authors, Ian and Peter Fleming. Until the mid-1960s it had exclusively managed client funds which amounted to an impressive £1,200 million. But when the merger-mania began, Richard Fleming had decided that his bank should expand into corporate affairs and reap the enormous profits available. Richard Fleming's personal misfortune was that he understood little about corporations or their accounts.

Maxwell had approached Fleming in March 1968 (before the *News of the World* bid), to inquire whether the bank would act for Pergamon. Knowing of Maxwell's reputation, Fleming was hesitant but, keen to attract new corporate clients, he sought two guarantees. With Maxwell's agreement, Fleming commissioned the accountants Whinney Murray, who were closely connected to Fleming, to report on Pergamon. Fleming also wrote to Isidore Kerman, Maxwell's solicitor and a Pergamon director, asking for an "unprejudiced view" of the company. In a personal conversation, he explained to Kerman that the bank would rely on the lawyer's professional assessment. Kerman's written reply stated: "Mr. Maxwell is a man of undoubted integrity and Pergamon Press Ltd is well run." Pergamon's only problem, added Kerman, was that Maxwell "took on too much."

Whinney's report, which was presented on June 13, had also been reassuring. The adverse rumors in the City, wrote the accountants, were untrue: "The company has an undoubtedly impressive growth record. . . . None of this can have been achieved without good management." Maxwell was given great credit for his "drive and guidance." Regarding the state of the accounts, Whinney Murray had also been satisfied, reporting that all the budgets, expenses and sales forecasts "have been prepared in a proper manner." There was slight criticism of the "undoubted difficulties within the accountancy function" but this was to be expected of a company which "had to struggle in order to keep pace" with its growth. Their only caveat concerned ILSC's accounts, which Whinney had been "unable" to check, although "We have however been assured by Pergamon that all indications show ILSC's trading results to be ahead of budget." Fleming, at that time, possibly did not realize how crucial the encyclopedia profits were to Pergamon's fortunes.

On the basis of Whinney's report and Kerman's testimonial, Fleming's formal appointment as Pergamon's adviser was confirmed on June 21, 1968. But, less than four weeks later, Fleming told Maxwell that he had had second thoughts and would not be offended if they quietly dissolved their new relationship. Maxwell was disquieted and tried to persuade Fleming to reconsider. Within a few days, the banker told Maxwell that he would after all advise Pergamon but strictly on the condition that, to deflect the Establishment's prejudice, Maxwell should appoint both an independent chairman and a new financial director. Maxwell accepted the conditions but the appointments were not made. As will be seen later, a new group chief accountant, Edward Garside, had recently been hired, and that, Maxwell felt, was sufficient. But Fleming was uneasy during the next year before his departure to New York.

All of Fleming's discussions with Leasco executives were conducted on the basis of what Pergamon's accounts for 1968 would disclose. The New Yorkers, confident that their instincts were finely tuned, remained nevertheless unaware of the tension and drama which had preceded the publication of the twenty-page, purple-covered brochure containing Pergamon's 1968 accounts. Maxwell's business reputation centers on how those accounts were prepared, and what they revealed.

The schedule for preparing Pergamon's 1968 report was tight. The company's annual meeting was set for June 19, 1969, and, to meet the deadline, the printing and circulation of the report had to be completed by May 22. A company report is generally divided into three parts. The first contains a statement by the chairman describing key events over the past year and setting out his predictions for the future. The second part is the balance sheet as compiled by the company's own accountants to satisfy all the legal requirements. The third part, and probably the most important, is the verification by a reputable firm of accountants who, while paid by the company, are quite independent. Called the auditors, they state that having read the chairman's statement and having scrutinized the balance sheet, they are satisfied of its total veracity. The auditors' report, although normally brief, is the crucial guarantee both to the public and more importantly to all the City and government agencies that the company's officials have produced an honest and accurate statement concerning the company's health. For Maxwell, intent on demonstrating that Pergamon's pattern of growth was unceasing, the 1968 report was more important than ever.

For even the most successful and untroubled company, the compilation of the report produces a hectic period of intense discussion between the directors, accountants, bankers and auditors about how the company's affairs can and should be presented. As Maxwell was rightly fond of saying, accountancy is not a science but an art. With total honesty and strict adherence to the law, it is quite possible for the same accountants to draw up a balance sheet which, using identical basic facts, portrays the same company as highly profitable or as in debt. Simply by deciding whether income should be described as profit, or placed in the reserves column, or carried forward to the following year, or set off against an earlier loss, the image desired may be achieved. There are similar variations in valuing a company's assets—its property, stock and goodwill. But there are three major caveats to what might otherwise suggest controlled chaos. There must be consistency from one year to another; the accounts must comply with the law; and the accounts must also comply with the practices and standards which are agreed by the accountancy profession. There is no dispute that in 1969 the standards and practices of British accountancy were at best variable and at worst wildly misleading.

Maxwell would argue in the years ahead that during those first three weeks of May 1969 while Pergamon's annual report was being discussed and agreed he was the victim of the accountancy profession's lax and outdated habits. His accusers would claim with equal passion that, on the contrary, he exploited those weaknesses to their fullest extent. Both sides, however, agree that those weeks sealed his fate forever.

The heart of the matter was the size of Pergamon's profits: Maxwell wanted them, as usual, to be as high as possible. To achieve that objective depended upon triangular negotiations and agreements between Pergamon's in-house accountants, the company's auditor Chalmers Impey, and Pergamon's banker Robert Fleming. With the anticipated sale to Leasco, more depended upon that year's audited profit than previously and there were also more uncertainties to overcome.

In the course of the previous year, some of Pergamon's trading relationships had significantly shifted. The crux of that new pattern was a group of companies, some privately owned by Maxwell and his family trusts and some based in America. To understand the crisis and the accusations which would dominate Maxwell's life in the aftermath of his negotiations with Steinberg, it is necessary to penetrate this constellation of companies established by Maxwell around the publicly owned company Pergamon.

On March 24, 1959, Maxwell's original company, Low-Bell, and Maxwell Limited formally changed its name to Maxwell Scientific International (Distribution Services) Ltd—MSI(DS)—and simultaneously changed the objects clause in its memorandum of association, describing its future activities as general finance and investment. MSI(DS) was owned by Maxwell, his wife and Tom Clark. Maxwell was also associated with two other companies which bore very similar names but whose ownership and legal status were substantially different.

On July 1, 1964, just prior to the public flotation of Pergamon, MSI (1964) Ltd was created as a wholly owned Pergamon subsidiary whose function was to collect Pergamon's debts, a task which had previously been undertaken by MSI(DS).

The third company with a similar name was Maxwell Scientific International Inc. (MSI Inc.), which was a private company, incorporated and based in New York, and owned by two Liechtenstein-based trusts for the benefit of Maxwell's sister, Mrs. Brana Natkin, and her children. In law, Maxwell had absolutely no control over MSI Inc. or the Liechtenstein family trusts which owned MSI Inc. The company's main business was the purchase of books and journals from Pergamon in Britain for sale throughout America. MSI Inc. had one noteworthy subsidiary called MSI Publishers Inc. which Maxwell would later claim concentrated exclusively on trading in books rather than journals.

In addition, there were two other companies privately owned by Maxwell which from time to time featured in Pergamon's normal business. The first was Robert Maxwell & Co. Ltd, known as R.M. & Co., which was originally Lange, Maxwell and Springer. In 1955 the company had changed its name to I.R. Maxwell & Co. and in 1963 had changed it again to its current name. R.M. & Co. was granted the sole distribution rights to all Pergamon's publications in Britain and was the company which Maxwell used to establish his bookshops.

The second private company was Pergamon Press Incorporated (PPI), which was also founded in New York in 1952 and was owned by the same family trusts as owned MSI Inc. Indeed, both were housed in two premises, the brownstone at 122 East 55th Street which Maxwell had bought with the British Book Center, and Maxwell House in Elmsford, New York. Both companies were also managed by the same people: Maxwell, Majthenyi, Tom Clark and Laszlo Straka. Since 1958, PPI had enjoyed the exclusive rights to sell Pergamon's journals and reprints in the western hemisphere. PPI became even more important in Pergamon's overall activities just six weeks after Pergamon was established as a public company in Britain in 1964.

When in August 1964 Maxwell and Macmillan of New York terminated their five-year agreement, PPI had initially bought back Macmillan's stock. Maxwell explained later that he had ended the agreement with Macmillan because, firstly, "In all the three years that Macmillan purchased books from us, MSI was their biggest customer"; and secondly, the directors of PPI had said that they could earn better profits from the concession: "They made a good case out to me and I was very happy. . . ." PPI's shareholders at that stage were Majthenyi and R.M. & Co., of which Maxwell was also the principal shareholder. The termination had occurred just six weeks after the publication in London of Pergamon's prospectus for its flotation, but the prospectus did not mention the possibility that the profitable agreement with Macmillan would end prematurely or that Pergamon would sign a new agreement with PPI because, as Maxwell explained, "I certainly had no knowledge about terminating it."

Four months later, on December 2, 1964, Pergamon in Britain bought PPI from Maxwell's family trusts in exchange for 276,154 Pergamon shares. The new public shareholders of Pergamon were told about the arrangements in a circular on January 18, 1965. On Pergamon's behalf, Maxwell wrote that he was convinced that an agreement with PPI would be more efficient and more profitable. Then, as another stage of this convoluted series of agreements, on the very same day that Pergamon bought PPI, two further contracts were signed. First, MSI Inc. agreed with PPI to purchase the complete inventory of Pergamon books which PPI had just bought from Macmillan. Secondly, by another agreement signed on that same day, PPI agreed to distribute the same books in the western hemisphere on MSI Inc.'s behalf.

There are two interpretations of that series of agreements. Maxwell's critics claim that the agreement between MSI Inc. and PPI was an important maneuver to maintain Pergamon's high profits. If PPI, as a new Pergamon subsidiary, had just taken Macmillan's unsold stock and put it into a warehouse, the original sales to Macmillan could no longer have been counted as profits in Pergamon's accounts. By selling the Macmillan stock to the "independent" company, MSI Inc., Pergamon's profits were unaffected. Maxwell claimed that MSI Inc. possessed the "marketing ability" to sell the books while PPI had "no machinery, no ability and no experience and no know-how in this area." His justification seemed to contradict Pergamon's circular of January 1969, in which he had praised PPI's organization as having the capacity to "effectively . . . handle the sales." Significantly, exactly the same people were managing all these companies and none of these details was fully revealed by Pergamon in Britain during the take-over battles of 1968.

In a Pergamon circular sent by Maxwell in May 1968, he had stated that "no director had any interest in any asset acquired or disposed of by Pergamon since October 1967." The following year, the Take-over Panel would accept that the statement was legally true, but others were unhappy because the transactions were conducted by the Maxwell family trusts. Significantly, throughout this year, no one would ever actually read the legal documents which established the trusts or speak to the trustees who administered them. Consequently, there was no possibility of independently scrutinizing Maxwell's claim that he had absolutely no control over the trusts or of checking who were the beneficiaries. Nor apparently was Maxwell ever asked to prove his claims.

On August 15, 1968, Pergamon floated PPI as a public company on the New York Stock Exchange. Thirty per cent of its shares were offered for sale. At the time, the flotation seemed a prudent step to establish a firm American base for Pergamon in the future. The £400,000 which was raised was used to improve warehouse facilities and to reduce PPI's debt to Pergamon in Britain. Legally, PPI's relationship with MSI Inc. remained unaffected, yet within one year these otherwise unsensational arrangements exploded the Pergamon empire.

In Britain, the whole pattern of the agreements between Pergamon and the private companies was described in quite general and unrevealing terms by Maxwell before he began the serious negotiations with Leasco. Interested British shareholders and the City would have been hard pressed to glean from Pergamon's annual reports or circulars that PPI, prior to 1964, was a privately owned Maxwell company which had earned approximately $450,000 in each of the previous two years as commission from Pergamon for its sales and services to Macmillan. Shareholders also did not know about the intimate commercial relationship which developed between PPI and MSI Inc. after the break with Macmillan. They were not told that Majthenyi was the managing director of Maxwell's privately owned American company and of the subsidiary of the British public company. Nor were they told that the private and public companies shared common offices, warehouses and personnel for which MSI Inc. paid $600 per month.

Overall, most investors in Britain would have been unaware that Maxwell, in managing the public company of Pergamon, faced a potential conflict of interests. If there was a responsibility for publicizing those details, it rested not only on Maxwell but more importantly, as he later pointed out, on his advisers—the lawyers, bankers, accountants and brokers who joined together every year to formulate Pergamon's annual report and upon whose professionalism and independence the public depended.

The first check on any possible irregularities was Pergamon's independent auditor, Chalmers Impey, which was at the time Britain's foremost accountancy expert for the publishing industry. Chalmers Impey understood better than others how to value the various stocks of books and how to assess the profits of an industry whose terms of trade include the unpredictable "sale or return" agreements. The partner who had been responsible for Pergamon's accounts for nearly fifteen years was John Briggs, a sullen man who much admired Maxwell. Briggs suffered two major disabilities—a paralyzing stutter and alcoholism. While his speech impediment was instantly recognizable, he successfully concealed his drinking. The relationship between the very articulate Maxwell and the handicapped Briggs was very relevant to the intense discussions which began at the beginning of 1969 about Pergamon's profits for the previous year.

As early as February 1966, Briggs had written to Pergamon's directors expressing concern about the possible conflict of interests: "In our view it is undesirable that there should be a trading relationship between a public company and another company which, while not a subsidiary, is subject to any measure of common control, so as to leave room for the suggestion that the profits of the public company might be inflated or deflated as a result of such relationship." The advice had no effect.

The preparation of Pergamon's 1968 accounts had started in earnest soon after the Christmas holidays. At Headington Hall, three people were directly involved: Edward Garside, the chief accountant, Peter Bennett, the company secretary and financial director, and Tom Clark, an accountant who was also Pergamon's deputy chairman. Garside had been appointed in April 1968 after Chalmers Impey had complained that Bennett was unable to cope with the enormous workload. Like all new arrivals in the stable block adjacent to the Hall, he would be struck by the revelation that although Bennett was employed by Pergamon he also managed Maxwell's private companies' accounts from the same office. Instead of different accountants located in separate offices handling the potentially conflicting responsibilities, the cash books, wages and invoices for all Maxwell's interests passed across the same desk. Yet under the system of compartmentalization, only Maxwell really understood the affairs of each of the public and private companies, and that caused further complications.

Chalmers Impey was auditor for Pergamon but not for the private companies. Until 1969, it had accepted without question the terms of any transaction which Pergamon directors stated had been settled with Maxwell's private companies although, as a complicating factor, Pergamon's financial year ended on December 31 while the private companies' financial year ended on June 30. Briggs's subordinate who personally did all the leg-work to audit Pergamon accounts was Anthony Payne, an accountant with nineteen years' experience. Payne would later describe the reconciliation of Pergamon's accounts with those of the private companies as "basically impossible," because all the accounts were chaotic.

As he prepared the accounts in consultation with Maxwell and Clark, Bennett endeavored to meet Maxwell's prevailing commandment—profits were to be maximized to meet Maxwell's publicly announced forecast of over £2 million. There was absolutely nothing illegal or even unethical in that practice, especially since the Companies Act of 1967, by opening new loopholes, had left excessive discretion to the accountants.

At some stage during late 1968, Bennett was told by Maxwell that

MSI Inc. and R.M. & Co. had placed orders with Pergamon for two sales of back-issue journals which were worth £708,000. Bennett was also told that in anticipation of a further "firm" order from MSI Inc., other old journals which were also stored in Pergamon's warehouse in Olney should be recorded as profits to Pergamon. The back issues, which in previous years had been valued by Pergamon itself as nil, were written up as a £266,416 profit. Altogether, the new orders from the private companies added a total of £974,000 (of which approximately £700,000 was profit) to Pergamon's income. Effectively, one-third of Pergamon's total profits in 1968 would be derived from those two sales. Without them, Pergamon's profits would have been approximately £1.4 million, which was £100,000 less than the profits in 1967. Bennett, who claimed that he could never discover the exact terms of credit between Pergamon and MSI Inc., accepted the orders at face value. He insisted that he never saw a written invoice and had acted on Maxwell's oral assurance.

The draft accounts which Bennett therefore sent to Briggs and Payne at Chalmers Impey in March 1969 contained those profits. On the negative side, Bennett had also made two provisions. First, the dividend due from ILSC would be only half the amount expected (£180,000 instead of £350,000) and, disappointingly, could not be counted as profits; therefore there was no dividend from ILSC. Secondly, PPI's profits were lower than expected. In total, however, Pergamon's profits would be over £2 million, a new record which met Maxwell's public forecast.

Payne, a big, bluff Londoner, read the accounts and began his audit. In the normal course of his work, he would expect substantial horse-trading with every client, which would be governed by the law, the interpretation of the 1967 Companies Act by other accountants (which he could copy), and by his professional principles. It was the interpretation of the law which some in the accountancy profession in retrospect criticized at Chalmers Impey. Maxwell, however, was entitled to rely upon the agreement of his accountants and auditors.

By the end of March, Payne had approved the bulk of the accounts. His only concerns were three items: first, a payment of $800,000 from MSI Inc. to Pergamon; secondly, the sale by Pergamon for £100,000 of the Spanish translation rights of its books; and thirdly, MSI Inc.'s order for back issues which Pergamon had recorded as £266,416 profits.

Solving the $800,000 payment proved relatively easy—it had been erroneously entered by a clerk as a credit to Pergamon. It was the opposite. Payne corrected the mistake, so reducing Pergamon's profits, only to be surprised at Maxwell's reaction: Maxwell stated that it had been on his authority that MSI Inc. had been debited with that large amount. Relations between the two did not improve further when Payne requested proof of the sale of the translation rights.

On October 21, 1968, Maxwell had written to Payne to say that he had agreed to establish a joint publishing company with Spanish and Argentinian partners which would be legally watertight "before the end of the year." Maxwell estimated that the agreement would produce revenue "in excess of £100,000" but he was advised to allow only £100,000 to be part of the official profits forecast which at the time was being compiled for the *News of the World* bid. In March 1969, Payne wanted to see the formal agreement with proof of the £100,000 profits which Pergamon had earned the previous year. Payne also told the Pergamon accountants that he wanted to see the evidence of the MSI Inc. purchase worth £266,416.

By the end of the month, the written evidence for neither had been provided and suddenly the Pergamon board meeting which would approve the audited accounts for submission to the Stock Exchange was brought forward by two weeks, to April 2. Payne immediately reported to Briggs that two outstanding obstacles stood in the way of approval of the accounts. Briggs consulted Maxwell, who promised immediate action to meet his self-imposed deadline.

On March 31 a telex arrived from Dr. Edward Gray, MSI Inc.'s president in New York, which confirmed the profitable MSI Inc. order. But the telex ended with a puzzling sentence: "Our purchases as always in the past are subject to right of exchange if issues still in stock or reprint on a royalty basis if issues no longer available." Payne did not understand what Gray meant and Bennett would also later claim ignorance. Nevertheless the order seemed "firm" (although the interpretation would be later disputed). On the following day, two more telexes arrived. The first was also from Gray stating that MSI Inc. had assumed responsibility for the Spanish translation rights' contract, and the second was a confirmatory telex from MSI Inc.'s auditors. Any qualms Payne might have felt about the fate of the Spanish and Argentinian partners disappeared in the frantic rush to complete the accounts for the vital board meeting which was scheduled for 2 p.m. the following day.

During the night, Payne and Briggs discussed how the accounts should reflect the new value placed on the back issues of journals which were reserved for MSI Inc. One possibility was for a formal "Note," an explanation that would be included with the published accounts, but whether Briggs supported that course before April 2 is unknown; it seems unlikely. Briggs supported Maxwell's interpretation of how MSI Inc.'s order made the previously "valueless" journals valuable since he was satisfied by Maxwell's assurances that Pergamon had received a "firm" order. Payne struggled to complete the work and drove at break-neck speed from Oxford to Fitzroy Square—"I've never driven so fast in my life," he recalled—to arrive at what would be "the shortest board meeting I have ever attended."

Maxwell had barely entered the room before he announced, "I've got to take the President of Nigeria around the House of Commons. I hope everything is satisfactory." Whether Briggs had intended to mention his subordinate's concern and was prevented by his stammer from speaking is unknown. But certainly the board approved the accounts without any caveat or agreement for a "Note," just in time to authorize the Stock Exchange to make its preliminary announcement of "Pergamon's record profits." Maxwell swiftly left the meeting. In early May, the accounts were sent to Fleming and Whinney Murray. For both, the status of Maxwell's private companies had assumed great importance.

Fleming had already heard about the high values which Pergamon's accountants wanted to place on the company's stocks and about Pergamon's valuable sales to MSI Inc. Accordingly, in December 1968, he had asked Sir William Carrington of Whinney Murray to undertake a close watching brief on Pergamon's financial management, especially because there had been several resignations from the accounts department. Whinney already had considerable knowledge of Pergamon's affairs because it had written its wide-ranging and reassuring report the previous year. On December 9 Carrington met Maxwell and insisted that he would only accept the new responsibility if Maxwell agreed to allow Whinney's staff full access to Pergamon's employees and if he personally had the right to vet all major schemes. To preclude any misunderstandings, Carrington stipulated that these unusually strict conditions of employment had to be agreed to by all of Pergamon's directors and recorded in the company minutes. Carrington's proposals were never put to the Pergamon board. There are conflicting versions of what followed.

There can be no doubt that it is difficult for a merchant bank to establish an intimate relationship with its client while at the same time being totally frank with outsiders. In the course of his work, the banker will inevitably discover adverse facts regarding his client which, if publicized, would often create unnecessary short-term damage. Yet the banker's own interests and those of his other clients demand that on occasion a higher interest must be served which could well harm a client. This, at its most charitable, was Richard Fleming's predicament in early 1969. His relationship with Maxwell was akin to a good step-mother: while he had affection and respect for his "son," he also recognized his deficiencies, but found it difficult to break the relationship.

During March 1969, Fleming realized that the buoyant profit forecasts for ILSC which Pergamon had announced during the *News of the World* bid were unlikely to materialize. In the course of a lunch in mid-April, Maxwell confessed to Fleming that because of BPC's interference ILSC's profits would be lower than expected. Both men recognized that Pergamon's image as a booming company was endangered. Without evidence of perpetual growth, Pergamon would have difficulty in launching future bids and in raising capital. Maxwell then turned to the approach from Leasco which he had originally mentioned to Fleming in January, soon after his first meeting with Steinberg. He explained that, while he would prefer a joint company with Leasco in Britain, the best solution would be an association with a company like Xerox. When they parted, Fleming was still optimistic about Pergamon's future although he accepted that, in tune with merger-mania, it needed to be part of a bigger group. Hence, when at the end of the month Xerox rejected his feelers, Fleming gave his blessing to Maxwell's talks with Steinberg.

It was at that stage, in early May, that Maxwell flew to New York and met Steinberg at the Hotel Del Monico to allay the American's concerns. Meanwhile, in London, the preliminary accounts for 1968 had been sent to Fleming and his questions had become quite pertinent. Several important new factors had been introduced into the estimate of Pergamon's results for that year.

Fleming felt that the draft was comprehensive but complained that, in the light of their recent conversations, it was too optimistic and lacked precise figures. Carrington, however, was dissatisfied outright and insisted that Maxwell should explain in his chairman's statement the full details of both the unusual relationship between Pergamon and MSI Inc. and the new valuation of the stocks. He told Fleming that although he accepted that MSI Inc. was not a dummy company, it should be sold to avoid any doubts about its independence. In anticipation of his imminent trip to America, Fleming on about May 15 delegated the detailed negotiations to his associate, Burnet Stewart.

According to Fleming's account, by May 16 Stewart had returned to Pergamon a proof copy of the accounts. Enclosed was a list of questions prepared by Whinney Murray which were to be discussed at a meeting arranged for three days later. The most important item was the MSI Inc. contract and the need for what would become known as "Note 8," an explanation about the valuation of Pergamon's stocks. In the course of those three days, a bitter argument erupted between Maxwell and Briggs on the one side and Fleming and Whinney Murray on the other about that Note. The climax was a telephone call from Stewart, in the course of which the meeting scheduled for May 19 was canceled and Stewart announced that Flemings was forthwith withdrawing its services. For Maxwell, the row threatened a major crisis with unpalatable consequences. The slightest whisper in the City that his merchant bankers were resigning would threaten calamity. It was in the midst of this row that on May 17 Maxwell telephoned Steinberg and set the deadline for their negotiations—Leasco's take-over would have to be announced prior to Pergamon's annual meeting, which was scheduled just four weeks later.

By May 19, relations between Maxwell and his advisers had been generally repaired, although George Hazard, ILSC's financial director, had resigned, allegedly because he had disagreed with Maxwell's views of how the accounts should be prepared. On the same or the following day, all the parties met to discuss the Note. Carrington told both Maxwell and Briggs that a full and accurate description of Pergamon's relationship with MSI Inc. and its new methods of valuing its stock should be included as Note 8. Carrington claims that he left under the impression that Maxwell and his adviser had agreed. What remains unclear is whether Carrington also stipulated that there was to be explicit mention that there had been a "change of practice" in the valuation of stocks. Inclusion of that phrase would have drawn immediate attention to the major source of Pergamon's record "profits." On the same day Fleming flew to New York and on May 22 Pergamon's accounts were finally approved by everyone.

When Fleming met Bernard Schwartz, Leasco's president, on May 26, any disquiet he might have felt was well concealed behind the effete and rather charming self-assurance which at that time so characterized the traditional City gent. Like Steinberg, Schwartz was born in Brooklyn and displayed sophisticated acumen in finance; and like Steinberg, Schwartz had never been exposed to the unaccountable City institutions. Both Americans shared a naive but understandable trust in the supervision of financial affairs in London which dulled their instinctive streetwariness.

Inevitably the accounts of such an important conversation vary. Schwartz reported that Richard Fleming was reassuring about Pergamon and proved his confidence by explaining that his own bank held 13 per cent of Pergamon's stock on behalf of its clients: "Pergamon is worth more than its share price," said Fleming, "and I won't let you steal it." Fleming later denied saying those words and insisted that the meeting was no more than a chance encounter which covered merely general issues. He specifically recalled warning Schwartz to satisfy himself about Pergamon's financial situation. In view of what followed, Fleming's recollection is unlikely to be accurate since on the same day, over lunch at the fashionable Links Club, he repeated his glowing account to Leasco's lawyer, Robert Hodes. Fleming's account is that he described Maxwell as "a difficult person to control," but expressed his belief that Pergamon's business was "sound" although there was "some" dispute about the balance sheet. Hodes remembers Fleming being much less cautious and can specifically recall that Fleming made no mention of the heated disputes which he had left behind in London.

Indeed, Fleming had been so reassuring that three days later, on May 29, Steinberg, Schwartz and Leasco's director of corporate planning Michael Gibbs flew to London, more anxious than ever not to let the deal slip out of their grasp. What would later be dubbed "the SWAT team," referring to an elite American police unit, was well aware that Maxwell had imposed a deadline which expired in less than three weeks. But there was still mystery surrounding the company they were about to buy. Their strategy was single-minded. A list of questions had been drawn up before their departure from New York which needed to be answered if the $60 million deal was to succeed.

Maxwell, the generous host, had prepared a warm reception in Oxford, although Steinberg was not present as his two experts began the detailed discussions. Over drinks and lunch, the Leasco team was introduced to Kerman and Clark; and, while Kerman listened, Maxwell repeated how Pergamon's back-issue business was profitable and expanding. Specifically, the Leasco team claimed that over lunch Maxwell produced a balance sheet which stated that Pergamon would earn $8.4 million profits in 1969 and which included a forecast of $1.4 million profit if Pergamon owned ILSC completely. Afterward the two were given a tour of Pergamon's headquarters.

Gibbs then disappeared for nearly one week into Pergamon's offices. When he emerged, he had obtained some answers but also had accumulated considerably more questions. Pergamon's profits, he discovered, were falling and Whinney's complaint about the absence of proper internal accounts and inventory control was more serious than he imagined. Once again everyone assured him that ILSC's profits were high, although the final accounts were not yet available. (An earlier assurance that he would be given the accounts for the first eighteen months was not fulfilled.)

But what particularly puzzled Gibbs was the trading relationship between Pergamon and MSI Inc. in New York. Majthenyi had told Gibbs that MSI Inc. was an independent trading company which bought and sold Pergamon's publications. At the time it seemed quite insignificant but his investigation revealed that in the past year no less than $1.1 million of Pergamon's profits had been earned by sales to MSI Inc. To his surprise, Gibbs then discovered that the vast bulk of MSI Inc.'s purchases were still stored, unsold, in Pergamon's warehouse. Gibbs's anxiety was assuaged by Tom Clark. MSI Inc., Clark explained, was in fact owned by Isthmus Trust Inc., which in turn was owned by a secret Maxwell family trust. It was all part of a scheme to avoid Britain's draconian tax laws. The American could only smile at the contortions performed by a socialist politician.

Schwartz had in the meantime become impressed by Maxwell. Despite the warnings, Maxwell seemed always ready to co-operate and proved to be a very important person. Every day, Maxwell invited his guests to a social whirlwind of visits to the House of Commons, Woburn Abbey and the opera while the evenings were filled by sparkling and memorable dinners with the leaders of British society, including the Duke of Bedford, and concluded with dancing at Annabel's night club. According to Peter Stevens, who managed Steinberg's interests in Britain, "The SWAT team didn't have any time to swat." Schwartz disagreed, although he was irritated by Maxwell's insistence on the snap deadline. But even that was explicable. Maxwell, he realized, was a "quick" man who wanted to get things done and he seemed genuinely fearful that BPC would purchase his share of ILSC. Whenever Schwartz pointed out that Leasco needed hard facts, Maxwell promised his personal warranty which could be satisfied by the detailed investigation which would follow the public announcement of the bid. Schwartz left Oxford reassured, and agreed that they would be in contact again within a matter of days.

Traveling back across the Atlantic, the Leasco executives accepted that, although their original questions had been answered, there were many new ones which were equally pressing "We couldn't understand," recalled Gibbs, "all the different company names that kept cropping up. One of our concerns was that Maxwell was undisciplined and had bought a lot of small, unprofitable businesses. There seemed to be no rationale for his buying a lot of this crap." Schwartz could still not quite understand Maxwell's family trusts which in law were not controlled by Maxwell. They played an important role in both the ownership of Pergamon shares and the ownership of the companies which traded with Pergamon. But Schwartz believed that Maxwell had assured him that he could speak on behalf of the trusts in negotiating the deal. Consequently, their report to Steinberg was positive. The proposed merger was advantageous to Leasco since, although Maxwell had exaggerated Pergamon's computer expertise, he did possess substantial material which could be exploited by Leasco's new data-bank equipment while the books and encyclopedias had, in Maxwell's phrase, "synergistic opportunities" for the Americans. However, Gibbs cautioned that everything depended upon Maxwell's complete co-operation after the purchase. Only at the end of the first week of June had the Leasco team recognized the very sharp difference between Leasco's and Pergamon's style of management.

While both Maxwell and Steinberg were ambitious entrepreneurs with an enviably refined ability to exploit the fast-changing and complicated science of accountancy and corporate finance, there were few other similarities. In 1969, Maxwell was an impulsive juggler who disdained the type of cautious financial controls which less flamboyant corporate managers espoused. Many of Maxwell's commercial interests in printing and publishing were gathered as passing targets of opportunity since everything was secondary to his overriding ambition for growth and influence. The notion that Maxwell possessed a master plan was an image cultivated by his public relations. Pergamon *was* Maxwell, and he managed it single-handed. Nothing could be decided without reference to him. Although he spent the week in London and returned to the Oxford headquarters only on Friday afternoons, his staff spent many hours daily on the telephone to Fitzroy Square and were often summoned down to London for consultations which were invariably delayed for hours while Maxwell pursued other business. Throughout the negotiations with Leasco, Maxwell rarely allowed even his outside advisers—the lawyers, bankers and auditors—to discuss Pergamon's affairs if he was not present. If Maxwell was motivated by a commercial strategy during the early part of June 1969, it was definitely not clear then, and it remains bewildering over twenty years later. Maxwell himself has never been satisfactorily forthcoming. Some felt that he was bored by Pergamon and wanted the cash to buy the ailing *Sun* newspaper and launch a second career as a newspaper tycoon. Others later arrived at more complicated explanations.

Steinberg's intentions are somewhat clearer. Pergamon was a solid publisher with potential. Leasco, which was then valued at $530 million, could afford to buy Pergamon. Steinberg was and remains a shrewd and thoughtful strategist. "Every step which Saul takes," said his lawyer, "is part of a plan and he has very high standards." Pergamon, as presented in the accounts, fitted into his strategy, but the chance of a successful working relationship with Maxwell was slight. Steinberg believed in delegation. Having hired like-minded and talented staff from similar backgrounds, he relied on their work and judgment. Although his own authority was never questioned, there was a style of rigorous reporting, especially on financial matters, which Maxwell never contemplated. Steinberg, apparently excited by the deal itself, ignored their personality differences.

On June 4, after he had digested his executives' report, Steinberg called Jacob Rothschild in London. Normally merchant bankers are consulted much earlier than two weeks before a deal is announced and are asked for their advice at every stage. But Rothschild was merely told that a deal was probable and was asked if he would act on Leasco's behalf. He agreed but warned his client that he had grave doubts whether Maxwell was the type who could work as a subordinate. Steinberg's enthusiasm remained undented.

Unbeknown to Steinberg, Sir William Carrington wrote to Maxwell the following day (June 5), acknowledging receipt of Pergamon's accounts, which had been officially signed on May 22. Carrington stated that he was "perturbed to find" on reading the report that Note 8 was "considerably less informative than we had agreed in outline at our meeting." In the glossy publication, Maxwell had diluted and scattered the information about the relationship and new valuation. Under the heading "Acquisitions," on page six, the chairman reported that PPI would buy MSI Inc. from his family trust, while on page fifteen Note 8 baldly stated, "Stocks are valued at the lower of cost and net realizable value and include £266,416 of costs incurred in the year in respect of additional printing and reprinting of journals to meet firm orders." Carrington believed that the unaware would remain uninformed. He concluded his letter with the news that since Maxwell seemed "upset" about the questions which Briggs had been asked by Whinney, he had decided it was best that their proposed relationship be "abandoned."

On the same day, Fleming also wrote to Maxwell to point out that he shared Carrington's dismay about the accounts, and added that the confidence of the bank's investment staff had been "shaken" by Pergamon's profits and its prospects even if the new stock valuation was correct. He concluded that the bank should therefore resign its advisory role after the annual meeting two weeks later, but he nevertheless offered to give Maxwell further help if required in his discussions with Leasco. Again Maxwell placated his banker and obtained an assurance that no announcement would be made before the annual meeting, due two weeks later. His attention now switched to Leasco.

Over the following week, Maxwell and Steinberg were in constant communication. Any doubts Steinberg might have felt were swept aside by Maxwell's guarantees and references to the recently audited accounts which had been approved by his independent bankers. By June 10, Steinberg was satisfied that he should begin detailed negotiations and suggested that Maxwell fly immediately to New York. Maxwell agreed but, just before leaving, dictated letters to both Fleming and Carrington. Maxwell was wounded by their imputations and ultimatums and, after justifying the new and in his view fair valuation of the stocks, he asked them to reconsider their positions, especially their comments about Pergamon's profits.

The very next day Maxwell arrived in New York accompanied by Paul DiBiase, representing Kerman, and Lawrence Banks, representing Fleming. Over the following seven days the teams from both sides met daily. Throughout the weary, continuous negotiations, the major issue was Pergamon's accounts. The queries were always answered by production of the now completed 1968 report, which, as the Pergamon team emphasized, had been officially certified by Chalmers Impey. Two other obstacles were also removed. Since Maxwell's private companies were such an integral part of Pergamon's operations, he agreed to sell an option for their sale on generous terms; and on Schwartz's insistence Maxwell agreed to sign a warranty that "Maxwell has no knowledge that [Pergamon's] financial statements are inaccurate, taken as a whole."

Under the agreement, Leasco would bid 37s for each Pergamon share (at the time they were trading at approximately 27s). Maxwell would get a mixture of cash and Leasco stock in return for his own 34 per cent of Pergamon shares. He was to be deputy chairman of the main Leasco company and chairman of Leasco World Trade Company. In total, the bid valued Pergamon at £25.4 million, of which Maxwell and his family would receive over £8 million.

In New York on June 17, amid considerable excitement, Maxwell and Steinberg signed the agreement that Leasco could launch a formal bid for Pergamon, subject to Maxwell allowing a team of accountants appointed by Leasco to have complete access to every Pergamon file, bank statement, inventory and employee so that all their remaining questions would be satisfactorily answered. Several bottles of champagne were opened and everyone in the room laughed with relief. The impression of those who witnessed the two outsiders clink glasses was that a happy marriage would not easily be achieved but the two protagonists genuinely exuded a desire for a relationship.

The celebration was cut short. Maxwell insisted that they fly immediately to London to announce the deal the following day, just twenty-four hours before his deadline expired. As they dashed to Kennedy airport, phone calls were made to Jacob Rothschild and Richard Fleming asking them to arrange a press conference.

The following morning, instead of driving directly from Heathrow airport to the Rothschild bank, Steinberg first called to see Peter Stevens, his manager in Leasco's Knightsbridge office. "Baby, do I have a deal for you," cooed the beaming Steinberg as he walked through the door. Stevens was appalled when he heard the details. "I live in Britain," he told Steinberg, "and I hear the grass growing here. What I hear about this guy isn't good." Steinberg was unimpressed, least of all by Stevens's criticism that publishing and computers didn't mix because data banks were a gimmick. Nothing would sway Steinberg. He believed in Maxwell and in Pergamon. There was brilliance and energy which he could harness.

8

The reception at Rothschilds was warmer. Steinberg was excited by the number of journalists who had crowded into the conference room: "I was amazed that it was so significant." The two smiling businessmen sat flanked by their two sullen-faced bankers in a packed room of bemused journalists. Maxwell did most of the talking, which provoked the impression that it was he who was taking over Leasco. As the champion of the "I'm Backing Britain" campaign, he had to explain the apparent contradiction. Britain, he answered, did not have the finance or knowhow to develop a computer-based information-retrieval system. The deal would also benefit Britain's precarious balance of payments. Nearly everyone seemed satisfied.

There was only one slight blot on an otherwise ideal marriage announcement. It was a question from Robert Jones, an authoritative writer on business affairs for *The Times*. "What is Pergamon's overdraft?" he asked. Maxwell replied, "£500,000." Jones immediately countered that Pergamon's report coming out the following day showed £1.9 million. Politely but firmly Maxwell insisted that the position had much improved in the previous six months. For Steinberg, sitting nearby, the exchange was "curious. I didn't understand the significance at the time." As the journalists left he asked Maxwell for an explanation. "That man," replied his jubilant partner, "has been persecuting me for years." There was a germ of truth in Maxwell's exaggeration. Jones had for long been skeptical about Pergamon's affairs and had some months earlier been contacted by Richard Millett, Butterworths' former chairman, who had not ceased to investigate ILSC's finances. Jones would make only brief mention of his exchange with Maxwell in the following day's newspaper, but Steinberg would seek him out a few weeks later.

The newspaper headlines on June 19 reflected the infectious enthusiasm and hope portrayed in the photographs, placed alongside the articles, of the two laughing tycoons at their press conference. Everything seemed perfect. The next stage was, in theory, a pure formality. Leasco's bankers, lawyers and accountants would write the document which would spell out the formal offer to Pergamon's shareholders. Heading the task force was Rothschilds, who would co-operate with Leasco's accountants Touche Ross to undertake a detailed investigation in London and Oxford.

On that same day, Maxwell was deeply immersed in plans for his next venture, the purchase of the *Sun* newspaper from IPC. He had announced his interest two weeks earlier, in the midst of his negotiations with Steinberg, and had pledged that the paper would be "loyal to the Labour movement." He harbored high hopes that his third attempt to win control of a newspaper, financed by the sale of his Pergamon shares, would prove successful. At noon, his negotiations were to be temporarily interrupted as he presented Pergamon's 1968 annual report. The brochure's purple front cover encapsulated his achievement. Under a bold headline "Profit Growth," the profits for 1967 were shown as £1,541,000 and those for 1968 as £2,182,000. In his personal statement, he credited the "substantial increase in profits" to "internal growth," and reaffirmed his confidence in ILSC's "bright and profitable future." But when he arrived at the AGM in Belgrave Square he was already troubled.

Just before the meeting, halting and stuttering as always, John Briggs had told Maxwell that he had just been visited by Colin Simpson, a reporter from the *Sunday Times,* who had intimated that he possessed information that the auditing procedures adopted by Chalmers Impey for Pergamon's accounts were questionable. Maxwell was outraged. A few telephone calls confirmed that several other *Sunday Times* reporters had spoken to former Pergamon employees within the last twenty-four hours. After trying unsuccessfully to contact the *Sunday Times* editor, Harold Evans, Maxwell wrote directly to the proprietor of the paper, Lord Thomson. His letter's subheading showed that he feared the worst: "Maxwell, Crook or Paranoiac. An Insight exposé for publication in the next edition of the *Sunday Times*. . . ." The contents were equally sensational. Reporters on Thomson papers, Maxwell claimed, were intending to "rely on and repeat" information "from disgruntled ex-employees" which was "not only completely false but grossly defamatory." The information, he continued, was being offered "at the instigation of Rupert Murdoch" and he called on Thomson to terminate the "scurrilous attack on me." Within hours two more letters were hand-delivered to Evans—one from Maxwell and the other from Isidore Kerman. The politician's language in the letter to Evans seemed particularly intemperate: "I am reliably told that the team is burning the midnight oil so they can complete their dirty work in time." In a further letter the following day, he described the Insight team as "poison weed scribes." Both the journalists of the Insight team and Evans were stunned. "Quite honestly, we couldn't understand what he was on about," recalls Godfrey Hodgson, then editor of Insight.

In 1969, the *Sunday Times* was, in the judgment of many professionals, the best weekly newspaper in the world. Under Evans, the paper consistently set new and original standards in journalism and presentation. Insight was a concept, created by Evans, which would later be dubbed "investigative journalism." Essentially, a team of prominent *Sunday Times* journalists and "stringers" in Britain and throughout the world would, at the request of the Insight editors, either search for original and formerly unpublished information or try to establish the truth behind a major public event. As the individual journalists submitted their stories to London, the editors analyzed the combined information and wrote the story which appeared in the newspaper. Expense was rarely an obstacle to a scoop and it was quite normal for a dozen or more highly qualified journalists to contribute to a single story. By 1969, Insight had firmly established itself as the nation's agent to reveal serious scandals in the City, in industry, in government and generally wherever the powerbrokers of society had hitherto trod without fear of exposure. Its successes had already earned its editors quasi-legendary status among their peers. Revelations about the insurance scandals perpetuated by Emil Savundra and the Vehicle and General company, investigations into John Profumo and Kim Philby, and exposés of frauds in the wine and antiques world had all earned the Insight label sterling credibility. The mere mention that an Insight investigation was under way was often sufficient to imply that the subject had committed a wrong and had cause for concern. The corollary, which would be fiercely denied by members of the Insight team themselves, was that they behaved like self-appointed avenging angels whose conceit and arrogance blinded them to any facts, even the truth, if those facts did not suit their preconceived prejudices. This was undoubtedly Maxwell's reaction when he heard that Insight was preparing a profile.

Hodgson, who initiated the idea in the paper, insists that their early inquiries were completely innocent and devoid of any ulterior motives. Hodgson, then thirty-five years old, had been educated at Winchester and Oxford, and had only recently returned to London from Washington where he had reported the 1968 Presidential elections. He had not particularly welcomed his assignment to Insight since he saw himself as a gentle, intellectual analyst rather than the merciless investigator. Yet his interest in Maxwell was not entirely a passing whim.

Millett had not confined his suspicions about ILSC encyclopedia sales to Jones. Like all professions, the literary world thrives on gossip, and anything new about Maxwell, whose unpopularity repeatedly touched new peaks, was particularly welcome. It was not long before one of London's more eminent literary agents passed on the gossip to Hodgson. With Maxwell so regularly in the news and the contradiction of the socialist millionaire so evident, Hodgson sent out messages to *Sunday Times* correspondents and stringers throughout the world asking them to check the authenticity of Maxwell's claim about his sales of Chambers encyclopedia during the world tour. By early June, a number of replies tended to support Millett's allegations and Hodgson tried to arrange an appointment with Maxwell. The approach was unsuccessful since Maxwell was immersed in the negotiations with Steinberg. But by coincidence, on June 4, Maxwell announced his bid for the *Sun* newspaper, which included details of a "survival plan" involving massive staff cuts and new methods to finance his proposed tabloid *Sun*. Since Fleet Street has always shown an inexhaustible fascination in its own affairs, Hodgson suggested to Bruce Page, the *Sunday Times* managing editor for features, that a profile of the would-be newspaper proprietor was timely. Page, an intelligent and committed investigator, shared Hodgson's enthusiasm. Their instinct seemed doubly rewarded when, two weeks later, on a Wednesday night, Rothschilds announced a press conference concerning Maxwell for the following day. Reporters were rapidly dispatched to collect information for a profile of Maxwell which would appear in that weekend's edition. Twenty-four hours later, Maxwell's aggrieved letters brought their plans to a sudden halt.

Maxwell's explanation in 1973 for his eccentric onslaught against the *Sunday Times* was: "it seems to be a fashion of journalists in this country that if somebody gets to the top or tries to get there, then it is fair game to try to bring them down." It is debatable whether Maxwell was "on top" in June 1969 but indisputably it was the most critical moment in his career. The failure of all his bids in 1968 and his tactless political gaffes had generated a steady stream of abuse from many quarters, much of it unfair and defamatory but nevertheless provoked by what many viewed as irritating self-promotion. His bottomless reservoir of energy and self-confidence had apparently protected him from the wrath of his critics but, if caught unawares, he would concede that the vituperation in the City and in Westminster had exacted its toll. Selling Pergamon and buying the *Sun* offered to him a new and exciting opportunity which he would not allow his enemies to destroy. The *Sunday Times,* he feared, was their new vehicle.

But during the early afternoon of Friday June 20, Maxwell had second thoughts about his tactics toward the newspaper. In the course of a telephone conversation, Evans reassured him there was not a Murdoch-inspired vendetta and accordingly Maxwell offered to come to the *Sunday Times* building to meet the Insight team for "some straight talking." "They have worked on it," he told Evans, "and it would only be fair for me to talk to them."

The exchange which occurred in Evans's office that afternoon would have a profound effect on what became known as the Pergamon/Leasco affair. Both Page and Hodgson claim to have been severely shaken by Maxwell's written onslaught and consequently approached the occasion both indignant and unbenign. In what the two journalists reported as a "rambling conversation," Maxwell described his conviction that Rupert Murdoch had inspired the *Sunday Times* and others to launch the attack. Indeed, he had sent a letter that day to Murdoch threatening a writ for defamation to prevent further publication of the "vicious smear material which you caused to be manufactured during the battle for the *News of the World.*" Maxwell explained that he was selling Pergamon because he found it impossible to succeed in Britain.

Turning to Hodgson, Maxwell said, "I've checked you out with David Astor [then proprietor of the *Observer*] and I'm surprised to discover that you're an honest man." Hodgson was unimpressed. "Mr. Maxwell," he retorted, "you remind me of a chef in the restaurant where I once ate dinner. I tasted the mayonnaise served with my lobster and sent it back because I suspected it wasn't fresh and even possibly from a Heinz bottle. It had barely arrived in the kitchen before the chef rushed into the dining room screaming, 'Who's accusing me of lying in here?' " Maxwell had failed to allay Insight's suspicions and the journalists remained hostile.

Nevertheless, Maxwell agreed with Evans that he would co-operate in a profile. Whether he genuinely felt that he had nothing to hide is to enter into an unanswerable psychological conundrum, for no one, even possibly his wife, ever discovered whether Maxwell actually believed his own lies. The reality was that Maxwell, in deciding how to deal with the challenge posed by the *Sunday Times,* was convinced that his abilities would eclipse those of his adversaries. His very co-operation, he believed, would enable him to control the journalists. In return, Evans guaranteed by letter that Maxwell would "see" the text of the profile before publication and, while denied any powers of veto, they would "discuss" any disagreements. It was a highly unusual concession for a newspaper and would inevitably hinder the *Sunday Times* time-table. On the other hand, Maxwell was a public figure who had suffered a series of wounding defamations and clearly feared that his critics would readily pour out their embittered distortions. Evans calculated that Maxwell's co-operation was worth the risk. On June 24, Page and Hodgson arrived in Fitzroy Square for their first interview with Maxwell. "The meeting began," recalls Hodgson, "with Maxwell offering me a copy of the *Great Soviet Encyclopaedia* and ended with him threatening to hang me from the dome of St. Paul's."

ILSC dominated their discussion. The journalists wanted to know, first, how many sets of Chambers encyclopedia Maxwell had sold during his world tour and, secondly, when ILSC's accounts would be published. After conceding that his claims for sales in India were possibly mistaken, Maxwell asserted that ILSC's accounts would be published "at the end of the month." Both Hodgson and Page knew from other sources the impossibility of meeting that target and pressed the politician to substantiate his optimism. Dismayed that his word was being challenged, Maxwell became agitated and shouted, "I don't owe you a fucking thing." The three men parted on a sour note. Hodgson felt particularly insulted: "From the outset, Maxwell tried to dehumanize and treat me as an object to be bribed and cajoled. I resented it terribly." The die was set for Insight to embark upon the newspaper's most expensive and time-consuming investigation.

Page and Hodgson were diligent researchers with huge resources at their disposal. Within four days they had obtained detailed and revealing statements from two key ILSC executives about the state of the business, with the reliable promise of more information in the future. Meanwhile, Maxwell again complained to Evans about the two journalists' "very impertinent questions" and voiced his concern about an affidavit which had been sworn by a former employee of Chalmers Impey who alleged "irregularities" in Pergamon's accounts. Insight, whose notebooks were being filled with innumerable allegations but few provable facts, began searching for reliable sources. Among its targets were the bankers, brokers, lawyers, government officials and businessmen who were deeply immersed in the Leasco bid.

The take-over process had already lurched into an unconventional pattern. Normally, Pergamon's shares would be purchased after all the investigations had been completed and the formal offer document issued. But on June 20, just two days after the announcement of the bid, Rothschilds began buying Pergamon shares, on Leasco's orders, on the Stock Exchange. The reason for Steinberg's precipitate action before his accountants had even arrived in Oxford is disputed. Maxwell claims that the first he heard about the purchases was from Rothschilds. Steinberg claims that it was Maxwell who suggested the strategy during a phone call in which Maxwell reported the real possibility of a counterbid for Pergamon. Leasco, Maxwell is alleged to have urged, should act with haste. In contrast, Steinberg insists, "I didn't even realize shares could be bought on the open market before the formal offer had been published. It's not allowed in New York. It was Maxwell who encouraged me." Maxwell vigorously denied that account. In the event, by July 11, Rothschilds had bought just over 600,000 shares worth over £1 million in the name of nominees at an average price of just over 35s per share. Steinberg was pleased because the price was considerably less than their true worth as estimated by Fleming in New York just six weeks earlier, and it was also less than the bid price of 37s. The American was wholeheartedly committing Leasco to the take-over before he had satisfied himself about Pergamon's accounts.

The investigation of Pergamon's accounts was led by Jack Anderson of Leasco, Paul Thibodeaux of Touche Ross and two bankers from Rothschilds, Rodney Leach and Ivor Kennington. Together they intended to obtain an accurate description of Pergamon's activities and accounts. Full of optimism, Anderson had arrived in Britain on June 27 but Maxwell was too busy to meet him until six days later. Over the following forty-eight hours, Anderson says, "I put a lot of questions but only got fuzzy answers and even blank copies of bank statements." Maxwell seemed "reluctant to divulge hard facts and figures" and when asked about Note 8 in the accounts he gave "a twenty-minute dissertation in good clear English which I did not understand." Then for the following two days Maxwell took Anderson on a tour of Pergamon's printing plants, well away from the documents the American wanted to see.

On July 8, Anderson's patience expired. Puzzled and frustrated, he telephoned Schwartz in New York and revealed that Maxwell had shown him nothing "in terms of real numbers" and was treating him in an unpleasant way. "The delivery of information," recalled Steinberg, "was sluggish. Maxwell was used to bullying people which our people didn't like." Shortly afterward, Schwartz telephoned Maxwell and urged him to co-operate. Although Maxwell agreed, Anderson had already decided that he was "fed up" and would take a short holiday while Thibodeaux "filled in the blanks." Ostensibly, at the end of that afternoon in England, there was still no concern about the deal. A letter was sent to Bradford University proposing the establishment of a joint Leasco-Pergamon professorship, and Rothschilds dispatched a telex to New York confirming that Richard Fleming had sold Leasco 2.1 million Pergamon shares worth £3.8 million on behalf of his clients. Some would later criticize the deal as based upon insider information. By the end of that week, Leasco had accumulated a total of four million shares at a price of $17.5 million and had barely started its investigation.

At the end of the same day in New York, midnight in London, Rodney Leach, the Rothschilds banker, telephoned Schwartz. Leach, who had enjoyed a reputation as the cleverest undergraduate of his year in Oxford, had been visited during the day by his old college friend Godfrey Hodgson of the Insight team. The *Sunday Times* investigation had made very limited progress and needed some inside help. As a bait, Hodgson told Leach that they had unearthed a certain Kurt Wallersteiner who was trading in the South of France under the name Rothschild Trust. Leach was grateful for the tip. He was even more interested to hear the gossip about ILSC's finances and the controversial encyclopedia sales in Australia. It was these rumors which Leach passed on to Schwartz.

In New York the following day, July 9, Leach's cautionary report was discounted. The Leasco executives still placed great value on the official certification of Pergamon's accounts. Erroneously, they also believed that the same certification included ILSC's sales. By all accounts, everyone realized that the deal had hit some unusual problems but they were overridden by Steinberg's sense of personal commitment to Maxwell. He expected all the queries to be answered on his forthcoming visit to Britain.

Steinberg arrived on or around July 10, and stayed with Maxwell in Oxford. It was a whirlwind visit during which Steinberg's doubts were repeatedly raised only to be quashed by the succession of glittering social occasions which Maxwell had arranged. Steinberg, the twenty-nine-year-old from Brooklyn, was introduced by his host to an unending procession of Britain's elite from Prime Minister Harold Wilson and other Cabinet ministers including Anthony Crosland and Tony Benn to Isiah Berlin, the Duke of Bedford and Lord Hartwell. Steinberg admitted that he was stunned: "His scope of relations was incredible to me. I knew that the deal was important for Pergamon and Leasco, but it was amazing that everyone else thought it was so significant to the world." Their business discussions were affected by the constant introductions: "Whenever we had a doubt concerning his credibility, he would lay on these marvelous people and his credibility would be restored; and you would say to yourself, 'Really, how could I have thought such a thing about this man?'"

Leasco's lawyer Robert Hodes was also persuaded, though not in quite the same way: "We saw that the British Establishment were snobs and they thought Maxwell was a wog. We felt nothing against him because they condemned him as a noisy upstart—in fact we felt the opposite."

Others in Leasco were not so easily swayed. Peter Stevens, who managed Leasco's international affairs from London, had told Maxwell just two days after the deal was announced that he was leaving because he did not have confidence in his proposed superior. "Maxwell said to me," remembers Stevens, "'Peter, this is a made-in-heaven situation for you. We'll work together tremendously well.'" Stevens refused and cleared this desk, although he felt a grudging respect for Maxwell's achievements: "He came from the wrong side of the track without anything and made it." But, unknown to Maxwell, Stevens was also a Czech-born Jew who was cynical about his fellow countrymen. "Czechs," he is fond of saying, "can never find the easiest way to accomplish anything. They're unable to go in a straight line. The English Establishment never understood what was behind Maxwell's elegant front. He had to cut corners when he could have got to the same destination by the proper route."

For the remainder of July, Steinberg's sense of affinity and self-confidence assuaged any doubts. Rothschilds had bought on his behalf a total of 5.2 million shares which represented 38 per cent of Pergamon. Leasco owned a 4 per cent bigger stake in Pergamon than Maxwell. But on July 28, six weeks after the engagement was announced, the suitor felt major, irrepressible and bewildering pangs of doubt. In agonizing slow motion, the process for divorce began even before the marriage was properly legalized.

The first source of qualms was a succession of unsolicited telephone calls from disgruntled former Pergamon employees to Rodney Leach at Rothschilds. The callers were only rarely specific, but all hinted that the bank might find "something interesting" about the rapid turnover of staff in Pergamon's finance department. "Rothschilds realized that there was something fishy," says one of those involved, "but no one could put their finger on what was wrong. All we knew was that we were still denied unimpeded access to Pergamon's files." The telephone calls did, however, partly corroborate what Leach had heard from the Insight team. By mid-July, no less than six *Sunday Times* journalists in London were devoting their time exclusively to researching Maxwell's life. Their long conversations with Briggs, Wallersteiner, William Curtis (who had managed the Book Center in New York), Alan Back (of MSI Inc.), Hedley Le Bas and Philip Okill had provided them with a hitherto unimagined portrait of the socialist politician and would-be newspaper owner, albeit from Maxwell's arch-critics. Galvanizing their interest was the breathtaking speed with which Maxwell seemed always to know whom they had spoken with; he would even anticipate their next call. Regularly, there were heated and acrimonious exchanges between Maxwell and the journalists. These conversations were taped.

Late on July 19, for example, Maxwell had telephoned the home of John Fielding, who was in the delicate throes of persuading Wallersteiner to co-operate. In the course of a long attack on Fielding, Maxwell said, "The impression you created in his [Wallersteiner's] mind was that if he did not co-operate to help you to destroy me, then you will destroy Wallersteiner." Fielding's vigorous denials were eventually accepted by Maxwell but two days later a long letter from Kerman to Evans complained that the *Sunday Times* was still pursuing its "shameful vendetta of slander and innuendo in search of a 'story.' " Accompanying the letter was a writ for defamation, the first of many which would be exchanged between the protagonists.

Maxwell was worried. In the course of his career he had, not unusually, made many enemies and the *Sunday Times* seemed intent on seeking them out. Publicizing what he claimed was their distorted versions would, he rightly feared, cause irreparable damage. Others would read the *Sunday Times*'s account as the truth. But while his unique blend of charm and bullying had in the past been a key ingredient to his success, his aggression was now counterproductive. However unjust it might be, there were those who found it difficult to believe that his aggressive protests were simply the cry of an innocent victim. Inevitably, accounts of his exceptional behavior reached the bankers at Rothschilds.

Leach and his associate Ivor Kennington never revealed in their meetings with Maxwell their awareness of the *Sunday Times* research or of the denunciatory telephone calls, but by the third week of July they were convinced that Pergamon's accounts department and Pergamon's contracts with Maxwell's private companies were the key to the still indefinable mystery. Maxwell sensed their unease and asked the reason. When Leach revealed their concern, the businessman "exploded." Maxwell's familiar technique for handling hostile questions now came into play: the employment, first, of a charming, and distracting, story; then anger; and then, if the questioner persisted for a third time, abrasiveness and sarcasm. He continually misinterpreted his questioners' pliant demeanor as proof of his powers of persuasion. It did not seem to occur to him that his own personality might be generating more suspicions and revealing his own vulnerability.

By the last week of July a new element was added. Leach was puzzled that there was apparently an unstoppable flow of Pergamon shares for sale. The very lynchpin of the June 17 agreement in New York, that Leasco would bid only after the investigation was completed, had been eroded. While maintaining his bland and friendly approach toward Maxwell—even including a late-night game of chess which ended in disarray when both Maxwell's bishops were found to be on white squares—Leach asked for discreet inquiries to reveal who was actually selling the shares.

Schwartz in New York was also uneasy and on July 28 he decided to fly to London with Anderson. At their meeting with Maxwell the following day, Schwartz made a determined effort to persuade Pergamon's chairman to produce key documents: "We were always very polite with him—it was a bit like a parlor game—but we told him that he would have to deliver the information about MSI Inc. and ILSC in the end. In particular, we wanted to see the contract between Pergamon and MSI Inc."

Maxwell countered that he could not understand why the Americans were not satisfied: "This has all been looked into by my accountants." Schwartz replied. "We won't put in a formal offer until we get all the facts." Maxwell prevaricated and still refused to allow Anderson and Thibodeaux complete access to Pergamon's files. "It was nearly the end of the line for us," recalls a former Leasco executive. In New York, Steinberg acknowledged that something was seriously amiss but was as perplexed as everyone else about Maxwell's reluctance to give the accountants access.

On August 1, Touche Ross sent Tom Clark a list of questions, with an ultimatum requiring an answer within four days. Five days later, the information had still not been delivered and Rothschilds had by then received an astonishing response from the Stock Exchange. Among the Pergamon shares which Rothschilds had bought were 197,000 which had been secretly sold by a Maxwell family trust. The sale had been discovered by Robert Jones of *The Times,* who had dreamed the previous night that he should check Pergamon's register. When he had telephoned Maxwell with his discoveries, the Pergamon chairman had denied all knowledge of the transaction.

By Saturday August 9, Maxwell realized that Leasco's bid was seriously endangered. The *Financial Times* had reported that ILSC's profits would not be as high as forecast and City pundits were asking why the formal offer document was still not published. Equally worrying, Insight had spread its net throughout the world. Former encyclopedia sales managers had been approached in the Far East and Australia and some had sworn lengthy affidavits or had recorded conversations with Maxwell at the instigation of journalists. Charles Berger had even been interviewed in New Zealand about the sale of paint to German railways. None of the material, however, produced more than a hint of wrongdoing. For Steinberg, Insight was even losing some of its credibility. "They told us," he recalled, "that Maxwell didn't win the MC. But then Maxwell showed us the photo." Everyone's patience had been exhausted. In a long telephone call, Steinberg told Maxwell that he would call off the deal unless Thibodeaux and Anderson were allowed immediate access to the files in Oxford. Maxwell finally relented.

On August 10, the following day, the two were finally admitted to the Headington Hall offices. Acting on Schwartz's instructions, they began sifting through files to trace the detailed relationship of the family companies with Pergamon. On each sale to MSI Inc., Anderson wanted to establish exactly when the stock was shipped and to follow the money trail back. Yet, strangely, the two investigators could find very few MSI Inc. orders and those few were for large amounts. Among the invoices was one in particular which struck Anderson as odd. It was for one hundred sets of the *Journal of Inorganic Nuclear Chemistry,* volumes one to twenty-nine, worth $133,000. Anderson wondered whether there were one hundred potential customers for that set in America. Anderson, who had been suspicious on arrival, concluded that it was "arbitrary ordering, because they were the most expensive and the most unsaleable." Thibodeaux had in the meantime discovered in another file twelve blanked-out MSI Inc. invoices. Neither he nor Anderson quite appreciated the implications. Nevertheless, three of the blanked-out invoices were discreetly pocketed to show Schwartz. By the end of the day, both understood that MSI Inc. owed Pergamon no less than £800,000 for Pergamon journals and books. This was a huge proportion of Pergamon's £2.1 million profits. They now wanted to see Pergamon's warehouse at Olney.

On Monday August 11, the two accountants met Tadeusz Kamienski, the Polish warehouseman at Olney. Kamienski, who could barely speak

English, showed the visitors Pergamon's valuable assets—the piles of old journals and books stacked on shelves. He had few records, yet it was not difficult to discover that, within the warehouse, no distinction was made in the ownership of the stock between Pergamon, MSI Inc. and Robert Maxwell & Co. Under one roof was the physical evidence of the complete intermingling of the assets of the public and private companies.

Perusing the available records, Anderson saw that Pergamon's major customers for back journals were the two private family companies, yet none of MSI Inc.'s recent orders had even been shipped to America. "No one is buying the books at the other end," Anderson realized. That night he reported back to Schwartz: "Bernie, the situation is worse than we expected."

Anderson's discoveries, however, were not bad enough to interfere with the big party held at Steinberg's home at Hewlett Bay Park two days later to celebrate the multi-millionaire's thirtieth birthday. Maxwell arrived with his wife and two daughters to enjoy what everyone agrees was "an amazing and happy party." If the two fiancés were contemplating estrangement, it was not evident. One memorable comment that the British businessman evoked was that he seemed uninterested in women—"He just looked straight through them"—a noticeable contrast to his host, whose success with women was, among his friends, legendary.

That same night Jacob Rothschild and Leach arrived in New York. They did not go to the party but traveled direct to Leasco's offices in Manhattan. They had brought the proof that, despite Maxwell's assurances, ILSC's profits would probably be no more than one-tenth of the £500,000 which Maxwell had forecast just four weeks earlier. It had been agreed with Steinberg that, after the party, he would invite Maxwell to meet the bankers the following afternoon.

The meeting in Manhattan turned rapidly into a confrontation, but before he was allowed to return to London Maxwell agreed to a radical and major change in the June 17 agreement. Since the Pergamon profits were now in dispute, a complicated formula was introduced under which the price Leasco paid for Maxwell's shares would be reduced proportionately in accordance with the final independently audited profits. This latest term would be included in the new, fourteenth draft of the offer document. Maxwell agreed this orally and rushed to Kennedy airport to catch a plane for London. The following day, he telephoned Rothschild and canceled his agreement.

But later the same day Maxwell did agree to see Kennington. Once again the Rothschilds banker pressed him for evidence of the Pergamon/ MSI Inc. agreement. To the banker's relief, it was handed over. During that Friday night Kennington studied the contents and, as he said in a midnight phone call, "It has closed the circle in my mind."

Until that moment, Leasco's investigators had been searching, as is normal, for evidence that money was being siphoned out of Pergamon. Yet Kennington's search had revealed the exact opposite. The private companies were actually pumping money into Pergamon. But the money did not stay in the company. Kennington had also been handed a crucial document by a Pergamon employee which completely undermined Pergamon's audited 1968 accounts—a twenty-year agreement dated August 30, 1967, under which MSI Inc. had the right to return all the stock it had bought from Pergamon and demand repayment in full. Quite simply, more than one-third of Pergamon's profits could quite legally disappear.

At noon the following day, Saturday August 16, Steinberg was sitting next to his pool at Hewlett Bay Park watching his children splashing in the water. "I had the feeling that everything was right in the world. I was rich and my family was wonderful, when Robert, my valet, came with a vodka-martini and said George Bello, my finance director, was on the phone from London." Steinberg put the handset to his ear, looking forward to a brief conversation.

"Saul," said Bello, "we've discovered a major problem . . ."

Steinberg's memory of what followed is clear: "I put Bello on hold, shouted for another vodka-martini, drank it in one, and screamed, 'Whaaaat . . . ?' " Steinberg made five phone calls in rapid succession. The first to Hodes, the second to Jacob Rothschild, the third to Maxwell and the fourth to the travel agent for an immediate flight to London. The fifth was to Richard Fleming, to vent his spleen, but the banker was unobtainable—he was grouse-shooting in the Scottish Highlands.

Maxwell's immediate reaction to the allegation of foul play made by Steinberg is not easy to discern. With the exception of the accusation made subsequently to newspapers and television interviewers that "I was foolish to trust Mr. Steinberg and check that he had enough money to complete the deal," he has been resolutely unwilling to explain his behavior between June 17 and August 16. It is possible that he was agreeable to Steinberg's suggestion on the fateful day that they maneuver a quiet separation. Steinberg explained that it was in both their interests—"no noise, no loss of face, just let's slide out." There were no secrets about Steinberg's motives. Once Wall Street realized that he had spent $18 million on a possible hype, his rating would nosedive and the price of Leasco shares would tumble. Steinberg was well acquainted with the financial world's caste system and feared ostracism if the highly publicized deal collapsed, revealing that he had made a mistake and perhaps provoking a public brawl. Even worse, he would be liable to a stockholders' suit for failing to exercise due diligence and causing the corporation financial losses. He wanted a cover-up and he had every reason to believe that Maxwell had agreed. But by the time Steinberg landed in London on Sunday morning, Maxwell's attitude had again changed. "Under British rules," he told the American, "once a bid has been announced, it must be carried through." Technically, he was correct, but Rothschilds had already embarked on an operation to unravel the deal.

Leasco's bid was subject to scrutiny by the Take-over Panel which, in the wake of the *News of the World* debacle, had again been radically changed. Not only were some of the more glaring loopholes sealed, but three months earlier Sir Humphrey Mynors had been demoted and replaced by men whose credentials, the Bank of England believed, would guarantee that the Panel was authoritative, impartial and respected. Its new director was Ian Fraser, who had been recruited from the merchant bank Warburgs. During the previous week, Fraser had heard that the proposed bid was in trouble but he was unaware of the details. He was therefore not completely surprised when Jacob Rothschild telephoned on Sunday morning, soon after Steinberg had landed, and asked for an urgent meeting. The venue that afternoon was Fraser's house in Putney. Present were the banker, Steinberg and Thibodeaux.

Fraser's task was to judge whether or not Leasco had good grounds for withdrawing its bid and how, in either case, the ordinary shareholders' interests could be protected. Fraser had long been acquainted with Maxwell. In 1947, he had been a Reuters correspondent in Berlin and had hazy memories of the boisterous Maxwell enjoying his rank in the officers' bar, surrounded by bizarre rumors about a deal concerning a German scientific publisher. Fraser also knew that Warburgs had declined an approach to act as Maxwell's banker. But his attitude was nearly balanced by an equal lack of sympathy toward Steinberg who, most City gentlemen agreed, was a brash young man in far too much of a hurry. So with fair distaste for both sides, Fraser could judge the case on its merits. On that Sunday, Rothschilds' case—that Pergamon had announced inflated profits for the past three years—seemed irrefutable. When Steinberg reached his hotel that night he called Fleming.

"We've discovered that Pergamon isn't worth what you told us," said the American.

"How terrible," replied the banker in a monotone voice.

"We think you owe it to us to buy back all the stock you sold us."

"That's not possible," said the banker, replacing the receiver.

Flemings' clients' funds had received £3.8 million for their Pergamon shares, which five days later would become unsaleable and effectively worthless.

Maxwell's predicament was no less awkward when he met Fraser the following day.

"You are accused," said Fraser, "of inflating the profits."

"It's outrageous that you accuse me of lying," retorted Maxwell calmly, and he insisted that the deal should go through. That, of course, was just what Steinberg did not want, but having bought 38 per cent of Pergamon shares, insufficient for total control, he had become more anxious than ever to convince Maxwell that they should seek a private settlement.

The events and chronology of Monday August 18 are too blurred and contentious to permit accurate reconstruction. Leasco was certainly hoping to persuade the Panel to allow the bid to be withdrawn and there is evidence that Maxwell at one stage was also in favor, because late on the Monday afternoon Fleming drafted a press statement announcing the end of the bid. The draft was withdrawn when Maxwell suggested that they seek the help of someone in London who could be relied upon to act as a mutually trustworthy arbitrator—the solicitor Lord Goodman.

Harold Wilson introduced many unusual personalities into the mainstream of British political life during his terms of office and few of them seemed to wield as much influence as his personal lawyer Arnold Goodman. Not many observers outside or even inside Whitehall could understand why the Prime Minister should delegate negotiations with the white rebel regime in Rhodesia to the solicitor. The Leasco team would be similarly bemused when their request for his immediate mediation was rebuffed with the excuse, "I'm just trying to settle the Ulster problem at the moment. Could we meet later tonight?"

So, just after midnight on August 19, the two millionaires gathered at Lord Goodman's flat in Portland Place in central London. Poignantly, while Steinberg arrived with Leach and other Leasco executives, Maxwell was alone.

The Leasco team wanted to negotiate a price for Maxwell's shareholding which was dependent upon Pergamon's proven profits. If Maxwell agreed, then the trustees for the family trusts, who owned more than two million shares, would have to sign the agreement. But identifying who actually controlled the trusts was proving frustratingly difficult. When Ian Fraser had asked Maxwell about the sale of the 197,000 Pergamon shares sold by Bahamas Trustee & Executor, one of the family trusts, the businessman had pleaded that he had absolutely no control over the trusts. When a second tranche of 400,000 was sold by another family trust to the unsuspecting Rothschilds, Maxwell again insisted that he was powerless. But ten weeks earlier, on May 30, when Schwartz had asked about the trusts, Maxwell had said, according to Schwartz, that he could negotiate on their behalf. Yet when the two sides gathered that night at Goodman's flat, Maxwell flatly insisted, "I cannot speak on behalf of the trustees." When asked whether they could not be brought to London, Maxwell replied that one was in the Middle East while another was in Majorca and did not have a telephone.

As dawn broke over the London skyline, Steinberg made a final offer and Maxwell suddenly accepted. Steinberg announced that he would hire a private plane to bring the trustees to London to consider the same offer. "Oh that won't be necessary," said Maxwell, pulling out some papers from his jacket pocket, "they gave me signed proxies to negotiate on their behalf." Everyone was silent until Goodman said, "There you are. He's quite incorrigible." Maxwell's last words to the Leasco team as he left would for long ring in their ears: "I've done nothing wrong. We're all over twenty-one now."

Throughout Tuesday and again on Wednesday morning, Jacob Rothschild and Richard Fleming continued to negotiate the sale of Maxwell's shares on the basis that the Pergamon accounts were grossly inaccurate. Rothschild was offering 18s 6d per share instead of 37s unless Pergamon's profits exceeded £2.27 million. Relations remained brittle until Wednesday midday, at which point they broke.

The rupture was caused by a draft letter which Maxwell had just sent to Rothschild for inclusion in the formal offer document. It stated that "The internal management accounts show that ILSC is now trading profitably." Ostensibly it was an important verification of Pergamon's profits. Rothschild decided to investigate the letter's provenance and discovered that Maxwell was basing it on a statement signed on August 13 by Chalmers Impey and Cooper Brothers which affirmed that ILSC would make a trading profit of just £40,000 at the end of the first eighteen months. But Maxwell had not revealed that, as Pergamon's chairman, he had signed three agreements the day before with ILSC, of which he was also chairman. The first was to buy some of ILSC's stock of outdated encyclopedias for £200,000, the second was to buy some of ILSC's old debts for £114,895, and the third was to give ILSC £42,000 credit for services it had been charged for the use of the offices at Fitzroy Square. (The transactions only came to light some months later.) Certainly it was not illegal to move £356,895 from one company to another, but it was not what was usually understood by the phrase "trading profitably." This was the last straw for Steinberg.

On late Thursday afternoon, Jacob Rothschild issued a terse announcement that the Leasco bid was withdrawn, giving as the reason just the briefest reference to Pergamon's forecast earnings. It was an unprecedented situation involving such a public figure. Since it was August—the "silly season," when there is normally a dearth of news —and the Labour government's status had fallen to a new low in unpopularity, the politician's crisis was sensational news.

The public's sympathy at first leaned toward Maxwell. While Steinberg, acting under strict orders, was unable even to explain that it was not a sudden decision, Maxwell and Richard Fleming issued a statement expressing "regret" about the collapse, especially since only the previous Tuesday the two sides had met and had "reached full agreement on all outstanding points." The statement continued that Leasco's reasons for withdrawal "had previously been discussed with full information available and the points were not at issue." As he stepped out of his maroon Rolls-Royce in Fitzroy Square later that evening, Maxwell beamed at the television cameras. For the ordinary viewer, Maxwell was clearly the innocent victim of an unwelcome American predator. It was an untainted image, which Maxwell felt he deserved.

Among Maxwell's key defenses during the ensuing probes into his business activities has been his insistence that he had always relied upon his professional advisers and that they had always endorsed his conduct. A meeting held at Flemings on Friday August 22, the day after Leasco's public withdrawal, exemplified his justification. Among those gathered to discuss the state of ILSC were representatives of BPC, Hill Samuel, Chalmers Impey, Cooper Brothers and Whinney Murray and Maxwell's solicitor, Isidore Kerman. All of those in Flemings' conference room would have wished to be acknowledged as reputable and skilled professionals. At the end of the meeting, they unanimously agreed to a statement, to be circulated to all Pergamon shareholders the following day, which declared that "The management accounts of ILSC show that it is now trading profitably." The amount specified was just £40,000. There was no mention of their previous forecasts (the most recent had been four weeks earlier) that ILSC would earn "pre-tax profits of

£500,000 per annum" or of Pergamon's recent purchases from ILSC worth £356,895. Many of those present would later claim that they left that meeting with qualms; but that was only in retrospect, once the accounts were proven to be in shambles.

On Friday morning, in the wake of Rothschild's announcement, dealings in Pergamon shares were suspended. Maxwell, Briggs and David Pearson of Flemings were interviewed on the same day by Ian Fraser. The Panel's director left his audience in no doubt where his sympathies lay. In his view, the 1968 accounts were inaccurate. Maxwell was outraged and excited, claiming that Fraser was raising "unjust and unfair allegations." As Pearson attempted to soothe his client, Fraser went through Leasco's allegations until he reached Pergamon's sales to MSI Inc. "That's a reputable company," said Maxwell. "Who is the owner?" asked Fraser. "A trust," replied Maxwell. "Who is the beneficiary of the trust?" "I don't know." "I can tell you," interjected Fraser, "your sister." Both Briggs and Pearson claimed to have been surprised by the revelation. What probably shocked them more was the realization that their conduct was being questioned by their peers. The following day, Fraser announced that he was prepared to allow Leasco to withdraw its bid; Maxwell immediately appealed.

During that Saturday, Maxwell gave several interviews. There was nothing wrong with Pergamon, he insisted. The bid had collapsed, he said, "because Leasco did not have the cash to complete the deal." Both the *Sunday Times* and the *Sunday Telegraph* were assured by Maxwell personally that "I and my financial advisers are completely at a loss to understand why Leasco acted the way it did." When Richard Fleming read the newspapers on Sunday morning he instantly resigned as Maxwell's adviser, claiming that the statement had been made "without [my] knowledge or consent." Both Fleming and Rothschild disputed Maxwell's claim that Leasco lacked the funds. Nevertheless, Maxwell perpetuated that claim relentlessly. For it would be his style in the months ahead to solemnly issue statements which, possibly because of self-deception, he believed to be true but which others involved rightly condemned as wholly incorrect. Such a statement was Maxwell's explanation that Richard Fleming had resigned to avoid involvement in the legal proceedings which he, Maxwell, was threatening to launch against Leasco. Maxwell's bravado was impressive. "I shall ask the Panel," he told BBC radio news at Sunday lunchtime, "to investigate the real reasons as to why Leasco was unable go to through with the offer."

But even if the press that day reported Maxwell's comments in full, there was unanimity that his commercial fortunes were waning by the hour, possibly beyond the point of recovery. In fact, quoting his comments verbatim confirmed the gravity of his plight. He had been too arrogant in the past for most commentators not to reflect the prevailing sentiment in both the City and Parliament that Britain was witnessing his approach to the first station on the Via Dolorosa. Naturally, drawing on the information collected over the previous two months, the *Sunday Times* published the best analysis about the real cause of the collapse —ILSC and MSI Inc.

Maxwell was convinced that the newspaper and Rothschilds were conspiring to hasten his crucifixion. In a public statement, he attacked the "highly inaccurate and grossly defamatory article" which among many mistakes wrongly suggested that "Leasco and its advisers were [not] freely given all information required on ILSC, MSI Inc. and Robert Maxwell & Co." His comments were sufficient for his broker Panmure Gordon also to resign and even Chalmers Impey sent a long letter containing twenty-five questions and qualifications to its previous statement on Pergamon's accounts. Within two days, Maxwell found himself practically alone, firmly on the outside as he faced the first of the series of bruising investigations into his business conduct.

At 11 a.m. on Monday morning he arrived at the Bank of England's office in New Change, near St. Paul's Cathedral, to attend a meeting of the full Take-over Panel, which had to adjudicate on whether Leasco was entitled to withdraw the bid. Presiding over the ten panelists (all of them heads of City institutions) was Lord Shawcross, who had hurriedly returned during the weekend from his summer holiday in Yugoslavia. The former Labour Attorney-General enjoyed a reputation as one of Britain's most skilled courtroom interrogators who, with a minimum of words, could demolish the most reluctant witnesses. His appointment as chairman of the Panel in the wake of the *News of the World* bid was interpreted as the City's last chance to prove that it was able to regulate itself. The Pergamon bid was the new Panel's first major opportunity to prove its mettle—"to show we weren't going to pull our punches"—and it would not be an exaggeration to suggest that the City especially relished the prospect because of the subject himself.

Shawcross's ostensible style was to introduce a measure of informality into the proceedings. When Maxwell suggested that he wanted to be represented by John Silkin, his fellow Labour MP and friend, Shawcross looked through his half-moon glasses and said gently, "Come, Mr. Maxwell, you are perfectly eloquent to argue your own case." The first day was to be gentle. While the Leasco team waited in an adjoining room, Fraser put the case for the prosecution, displaying, it was noted by some, great confidence. Maxwell followed, speaking without notes and at great length. "I know nothing about accountancy and relied entirely upon Chalmers Impey," he pleaded, and everyone noticed that Briggs was absent, uncontactable on a fishing holiday in Scotland. Then, while Maxwell waited, Shawcross heard the Leasco case. "At that stage it was felt that the Americans had gone into it with their eyes wide open," recalls a panelist. "As far as we were concerned, both sides were mavericks who deserved each other. Later it became a joke that, for the first time in his life, Steinberg was the 'good guy.' "

It was on the second day that Shawcross applied the pressure. Probing and reasonable, but never aggressive, the lawyer cut through Maxwell's defense, forcing him first to admit that Leasco was not short of funds and then to concede that Leasco had not intended to depress the price of Pergamon shares to buy the company at a discount. "Everyone was impressed how Shawcross just pulled Maxwell's contradictions apart," remarked Ian Fraser at the time. Others were critical. "He was too aloof. You don't get the best out of professionals by treating them like Hermann Goering at Nuremberg." Nevertheless, by the end of the second day Shawcross's rapier questioning had exposed the questionable profits of the Spanish translation rights, the MSI sales and the ILSC profit forecasts. The ground was cleared, while the Panel adjourned, for some hard negotiations between Maxwell and Leasco.

Jacob Rothschild had been severely mauled by Shawcross and, although some believed that it was just for "form," Rothschild himself realized that the affair had not embellished his bank's reputation despite his initial cautionary advice to Steinberg. Whatever the Panel's decision, it was in the interests of Pergamon, in which Steinberg had invested £9 million, that a settlement should be reached. Late on Tuesday night, Leach had secretly asked Michael Richardson, Maxwell's friend and broker at Panmure Gordon, to act as an intermediary and persuade Maxwell of the advantages of urgent talks about a settlement. Richardson, who has always been faithful to Maxwell's interests, succeeded.

At Wednesday lunchtime, Maxwell, Kerman, Leach, Hodes and Fraser sat down for lunch at Rothschilds' headquarters to hammer out an agreement. By the end, Hodes believed that he had successfully extracted from Maxwell his near-complete surrender in a seven-point plan. Maxwell agreed that five Leasco nominees and two directors nominated by Rothschild would sit on Pergamon's board; that he would relinquish his own proposed position in Leasco and, while remaining chairman, would cease to be the managing director of Pergamon; and that, when Leasco's bid was relaunched, the amount paid for the outstanding shares would be proportional to the true profits, which would be determined by independent accountants. Maxwell's only victory was that his family trusts would keep the proceeds of the sale of their shares—effectively over £1 million. Those funds would be a vital ingredient in his eventual recovery.

On Thursday, the Panel reconvened. The first business was the previous day's agreement, which deprived Maxwell of any control over Pergamon. Shawcross approved the deal. Hodes asked that the agreement be properly signed and witnessed. Shawcross gave him an icy stare and in a most judicial voice replied, "The City, Mr. Hodes, operates on trust." Hodes had no chance to protest that it was precisely the collapse of that trust which had brought them all together. Shawcross had started to deliver the Panel's verdict, which according to Fraser was "expressed in the most memorable, beautiful English:" "The Panel is satisfied that Leasco's decision to withdraw from the proposed offer was the result . . . of a series of difficulties and doubts which eventually destroyed their confidence. . . . In all the circumstances, the Panel accepts Leasco's explanation for its withdrawal from the proposed offer." Couched in the most prudent form, Shawcross then listed the Panel's concern about ILSC and Pergamon's failure to disclose the trading links with the family companies.

When Maxwell and Silkin read the proposed statement, they became alarmed and urged its modification. Officially and unofficially, the Panel was concerned only with the take-over and it had never been suggested that there would be any mention about the internal affairs of Pergamon. Maxwell felt that he had not been given a proper opportunity to defend himself. The Panel's bias, he argued, was plain. Their statement was exclusively about Maxwell. There was no mention of Flemings, Chalmers Impey, Whinney Murray or Cooper Brothers, upon whom he had expressly relied. Even Flemings' hugely profitable sale of Pergamon shares was only referred to as requiring the Panel "to contemplate studying the general principles which should apply in circumstances where possible conflicts of interest may be. . . ." But, worst of all, the Panel called for a full Board of Trade inquiry. This was totally unprecedented as regards a profitable company. Maxwell demanded that Shawcross modify his statement.

Once again, Maxwell saw that the City would protect its own kind and damn the foreigner. It was the second station on the Via Dolorosa. But he had no intention of either playing the game or keeping a stiff upper lip. He demanded changes and then additions. As the night developed, everyone became hungry and thirsty. The only source of drinks was a vending machine and, appropriately, only the Rothschilds had the correct coins. Just three packets of biscuits were divided between twenty-nine men. By 2 a.m. Maxwell had secured the inclusion of an important caveat which would both precede and follow the criticism: "Nothing in the information before it casts doubt on the standing or future prospects of Pergamon, a company which under the energetic leadership of Mr. Maxwell has made notable progress. Nor is there any suggestion at all of personal misconduct on Mr. Maxwell's part." But Maxwell could not prevent the Panel recommending a full Board of Trade inquiry. His only course was for an appeal on the grounds that the Panel had gone beyond its terms of reference.

The public reaction to the report satisfied the Panel. "There can be no possible doubt that we now have a watchdog with teeth," commented *The Times* under the headline "Discipline Arrives in the Take-over World." Publicly, Maxwell did not dissent from the overwhelming praise. "A much better Panel than before," he declared on BBC television that night and pledged full co-operation with the Board of Trade inquiry. There was no suggestion from his side that he had been censured after four days inside a Star Chamber, that he had been abandoned by his advisers or that he would lose control of Pergamon. Instead, he acted as the champion. He naturally endorsed *The Times* editorial: "It has to be said that Mr. Maxwell has shown himself to be a man of quite remarkable energy and initiative and has conducted himself with courage throughout the proceedings."

The following day Maxwell posed, smiling, outside Rothschilds bank, shaking Steinberg's hand. The American had flown overnight from New York to approve the details which would incorporate Pergamon within Leasco, without Maxwell.

9

Steinberg's takeover of Pergamon was timed for Tuesday September 2. At 9:35 a.m., two Leasco executives arrived at Fitzroy Square. Peter Stevens had been designated managing director and George Bello finance director. Neither was enthusiastic about his task. Stevens had always been critical of the venture and had since become depressed by the particularly widespread *Schadenfreude* which the row had sparked in London. Too many had sniggered, "Let the two Jews fight it out." The Czech-born American had no illusions that managing Pergamon with Maxwell as chairman would be easy, but the heads of agreement as approved by Shawcross and the Panel seemed cast-iron.

As the Americans walked into the building, they were told that the Pergamon directors were meeting in the board room. Stevens asked for an office to make a brief telephone call. While he was speaking, Jean Baddeley told him that Maxwell was waiting. Stevens intimated that he would just finish his call. Two minutes later another telephone on the desk rang. "If you don't come immediately," snapped an unmistakable voice, "you can pack up and go home."

Stevens and Bello rushed into the board room. "He was furious," recalls Stevens, "almost incoherent, stabbing at that day's copy of *The Times,* which had my photograph and a caption describing me as the new managing director. He said that there was too much publicity, too many new directors and too many leaks to the press. It took me some time to calm him down."

Stevens suggested that Maxwell might introduce him to the directors. When this had been done, Stevens asked everyone to submit by the end of the morning a description "on one side of paper" of their duties and the relevant financial data in the individual departments. As he spoke, Maxwell became noticeably agitated: "We're not having all this

stuff. It's too early. Your appointment hasn't been made official yet."
Stevens had expected some tension and possibly some aggravation, but
no one had anticipated what Maxwell said next: "You know, Peter,
there's no agreement in writing about your appointment and no special
board meeting is planned, so I suggest that both you and George return
on the next flight to New York." After a brief pause, there was a roar:
"Get out!" Startled, George Bello looked at Stevens as, sweeping some
papers into his briefcase, the former declared, "I've got four kids and
I'm leaving."

Just before noon, the Americans were back in Knightsbridge reporting the latest twist in the saga to bankers, lawyers and Leasco
executives on both sides of the Atlantic. By mid-afternoon, many highly
paid and supposedly shrewd professionals were exasperated. Once
more, they had been smartly outwitted. The "seven heads of agreement" which had been negotiated at Rothschilds six days earlier, and
then approved by the Panel, had not, because of Shawcross's insistence
that in the City it was customary to abide by oral undertakings, been
formally recorded and signed.

Everyone knew, of course, that the cliché "My word is my bond"
was a sanctimonious bromide contrived for public relations. The Panel's
recent history was littered with examples of broken promises and avoidance of the rules which had passed unpunished, and none more so than
during the battle for the *News of the World*. Twelve months earlier,
the City herd had not been overly troubled by the anguish which the
outsider had suffered yet they still expected him to obey their club
rules. But since the children of peasants do not become multi-million-
aires unless they challenge those rules, it was not surprising that Maxwell saw no advantage in meekly complying.

In Maxwell's view, the City and Leasco were either intentionally or
by default destroying his company. The so-called "well-informed" stories over the weekend in the *Sunday Times* and *The Times* were undermining both his own and Pergamon's credibility. He blamed the
Leasco side for inspiring speculation that Pergamon's bank overdraft
had risen from £1.9 million to £4 million while he knew that it had
actually been reduced. Pergamon was his business and only he understood scientific journals. Respectable City institutions had endorsed all
his accounts but they, protected by their own kind, had seemingly
escaped blame. Yet he was expected to lose everything without a mur-
mur. For Maxwell that was unacceptable. He would not be taken to
the next station on the Via Dolorosa without a fight. His counter-attack
started with a detailed letter to *The Times* which ignored the Rothschilds

agreement and raised a raft of new and complicated demands. He had left the corner and was back in the center of the ring.

Subconsciously, Rodney Leach had anticipated that Maxwell would not go quietly. During the Panel's last, late-night session, he had thrust a letter of resignation drafted by a Rothschilds lawyer in front of Maxwell for signature, but it was deemed to be legally valueless. Soon after Stevens had telephoned him and reported his ejection from Fitzroy Square, Leach had appealed to Fraser, requesting that the "unconditional" agreement should be implemented. Fraser was naturally sympathetic but urged patience while Shawcross was again recalled from his holiday. Fraser also telephoned Maxwell.

Brazenly, Maxwell disputed Leach's and Fraser's interpretation of the agreement and insisted that Shawcross would support his version. The impasse was complete and he might have waited. Instead, a few days later, he issued a hazardous challenge. In a press release, he announced that because "Leasco and Pergamon cannot work together," and because the Pergamon directors would not surrender the company's management until Leasco had secured a majority of the shares, he was calling an extraordinary general meeting (EGM) of all shareholders on October 9 to decide whether Leasco was entitled to sole management. Maxwell the gambler had pushed aside the businessman and bargain-hunter. The player had committed his future to be determined at a public meeting.

After the sales by his family trusts, Maxwell controlled only 28 per cent of the shares against Steinberg's 38 per cent. His future depended upon the City institutions, who held 17 per cent of the stock. For Maxwell to have expected their support was to take an uneven risk. Regardless of the flattering newspaper comments in the previous week, the City was abuzz with rumors and defamatory allegations which made those circulating in the past seem tame by comparison. But Maxwell, who was always genuinely surprised that others did not share his high self-esteem, had spoken to the fund managers and calculated that he could count on their support because they agreed that, without him, Pergamon would collapse. There was also another motive. By then, one of the reasons for selling Pergamon had disappeared and his major ambition had again been thwarted.

Soon after he had expelled the Americans from Fitzroy Square, SOGAT had announced its "loss of confidence in Mr. Maxwell" as a possible proprietor of the *Sun*. Preoccupied by the fight to save Pergamon and deprived of the anticipated finance from the sale of his shares, Maxwell unemotionally conceded victory to Rupert Murdoch for the second time within twelve months. Thrice he had played by the rules and had pledged to support a Labour newspaper and each time he had failed. Maxwell did not ponder for long about the paradox that Murdoch without any social status in Britain could succeed while he, a Member of Parliament with a fine wartime record, should constantly fall flat on his face. His explanation was simply that he was the victim of the Establishment's prejudice. His own style was not a factor worth contemplating. He simply ignored criticism of his financial activities. This time, Fleet Street wrote off his ambitions forever. "This is obviously the end of Mr. Maxwell's dream of being the proprietor of a national newspaper," pronounced Hugh Cudlipp, the chairman of IPC, which owned the *Sun*. Many now predicted the same fate in the world of business.

Leasco placed a great deal of faith in Shawcross and in the City's much vaunted self-regulation to enforce the agreement made on August 28. Steinberg and Hodes flew from New York to be present when Shawcross returned from Yugoslavia. Maxwell had consented, in the event of any disagreements, to be bound by any new ruling which Shawcross might make. Maxwell was summoned to attend on September 9 at the Panel's office to explain why he had not relinquished management control.

Accompanied by his new merchant banker William Brandt, Maxwell told Shawcross that the lawyers' interpretation of the agreement was "wrong" and later denied that he had ever agreed to abide by any further rulings. His icy, impenetrable sense of righteousness disconcerted Shawcross but endowed Maxwell with increased courage. The next to arrive in Shawcross's room was Hodes, who asked what decisive remedy the Panel now proposed. He was answered by a deafening silence. Maxwell had not obeyed the ritual and had paralyzed his accusers. Despite his status, Shawcross was powerless and even humiliated.

Outside in the City streets Hodes and Steinberg assessed Leasco's dilemma. In New York, the Securities and Exchange Commission would have wiped Maxwell off the floor. But in London, while the City patricians smugly pretended that their behavior was impeccable, they condoned any malpractice so long as it was invisible; and when it burst out, they ignored their impotence. They were standing in the middle of a market which was nourished on a cracked ethic and managed, in Leasco's view, by amateurs who were not equipped with the technical expertise to understand a balance sheet. They heaped the blame upon Maxwell to protect themselves. There was no alternative but to remain and fight to recover their $18 million. "We shall gain control of Pergamon whatever happens," said Steinberg before flying back to New York.

Steinberg left a disaster and returned to an earthquake. Since the debacle, the price of Leasco shares had collapsed from $33 to $10 and there was serious unrest among his staff, who were uncertain about his company's very survival. His stake in Pergamon was also in doubt. If he completely eliminated any connection with Maxwell, the publisher might set up a competitive business or interfere with customers. He could cause unlimited damage especially if there were more unknown agreements with the family companies. Steinberg was frankly incredulous about the mistakes he had made. The only glimmer of hope was the announcement that Anthony Crosland had appointed a Board of Trade inquiry into Pergamon. The two inspectors, Owen Stable QC and Sir Ronald Leach, an accountant, were expected to deliver an interim report within three months. Their activities might persuade the City institutions to favor Leasco's bid.

For Maxwell, Crosland's decision was calamitous. Despite welcoming the announcement in public, he had lobbied his fellow politicians intensively to support him against the appointment of an inquiry, pleading that he was the victim of a vendetta. But pressure from the City, especially from Shawcross, and the oblique references to Simpkin Marshall, compelled Crosland to approve the investigation. When Maxwell heard that he had lost, he told David Pearson of Fleming that he would fight "tooth and nail."

Perhaps it was the realization that, unlike so many other setbacks, this one could not be lightly shrugged off that caused the first crack in Maxwell's hitherto resolute image. The occasion was his appeal against the Panel's decision. Hearing his case was a senior judge, Lord Pearce, who sat with three representatives of the City. The grounds of the appeal were restricted to procedure; the facts could not be re-argued. Maxwell claimed that he had been denied natural justice at the original hearing because Shawcross, without notice, had considered and commented on Pergamon's internal affairs, which were beyond the issue of the bid. Paying no heed to the restrictions of the appeal, Maxwell began to re-argue his case. Pearce continuously interrupted. Eventually, when Maxwell still persisted, Pearce said firmly, "I really can't understand your defense, Mr. Maxwell."

Large tears began to roll down Maxwell's cheeks; he blew his nose several times and in a cracking voice said, "I was born poor in a tiny village in a part of eastern Czechoslovakia which you have never heard of—" Pearce interrupted, "Oh yes I do, Mr. Maxwell. It's called 'Klein Russland.' I traveled there before the war." Maxwell continued, "All my family was lost in concentration camps. I fled the Nazis and joined and fought with the British army because I believed in Britain's justice and law and fair play, but I am now being denied it. . . ." Pearce was moved but unsympathetic to his plea. The appeal was rejected on September 18.

There were no lingering doubts that Maxwell was fighting for his very survival. The next arena was the EGM on Friday October 10 (it had been postponed by one day). Except for a brief lull when he disappeared on a brief trip to America, Maxwell maintained a barrage of publicity to secure the institutions' support, arguing that Pergamon's past success was synonymous with his personal management and that, until Leasco made an outright bid, it should be denied "ownership on the cheap." His only concession was that Leasco would be allowed to nominate three directors. During the early days, he was reasonably sure of success, especially after Norman Freeman, the manager of the ICI pension fund, intimated that he might offer his full support.

Steinberg, in contrast, had never enjoyed much support in the City and few believed that the unknown American could successfully manage a specialized publishing company based in Oxford. After Maxwell's refusal to implement the Rothschilds agreement, Steinberg had insisted on his complete removal. The Leasco package which was to be put to the shareholders would be to elect a new board of directors comprising independents and Leasco executives under an independent chairman. It was not an attractive package for the City fund managers who had lost money and disliked any interference with their quiet life. Leasco's refusal to bid for the remaining shares until the completion of an independent audit was considered to be irksome and its detailed explanations were too difficult to read and understand.

During the days before the EGM, the national newspapers, radio and television overflowed with pronouncements by commentators. None would have a more profound effect than the first part of the *Sunday Times*'s "intimate profile" published four days before the EGM, analyzing the "astonishing businessman" whose record "shows an uncanny capacity for rising from the ashes." Maxwell fought hard to prevent the article appearing.

Harold Evans had promised Maxwell in June that he could read and comment on the profile before publication. The draft of part one had been delivered at the end of August. Maxwell was appalled, since it confirmed his original fears that the *Sunday Times,* having interviewed disgruntled ex-employees, was going so far as to suggest that he was not an honest businessman. The journalists had been unwilling to accept his word and were, he believed, unenlightened about normal practices in the world of commerce. Evans believed that both he and his staff were trying to be fair while Maxwell was, to say the least, being disingenuous. On September 11, Evans wrote to Maxwell regarding a series of "corrections" the publisher had provided about the Book Center in New York, the "special exchange rate" in post-war Germany and Simpkin Marshall. After exhaustively re-researching their facts, Evans wrote, none of Maxwell's "corrections" had been substantiated: "I am certainly still very willing to consider carefully any comments you make, but on this experience I am also somewhat discouraged from taking assertions as fact." Maxwell's reply was the delivery of a writ, the second since June, seeking to prohibit publication. The tension increased.

Maxwell had heard that denunciatory affidavits from many of his enemies had been obtained by the *Sunday Times*. Documents which they supplied had been forensically tested, and they were deliberately telephoning him to tape conversations. Frantically, he cross-checked from country to country to unearth what was being said. In one instance, he heard that Paul Hövel of Springer had been tracked down to his holiday hotel in the Black Forest by the intrepid Anthony Terry in the hope that he would reveal some skullduggery about Maxwell's original 1947 deal. Hövel insisted that their agreement had been perfectly legal but Maxwell was convinced that the German had said the contrary. Yet remarkably, amid all the chasing and the checking, Page and Hodgson still visited Maxwell at Fitzroy Square to obtain material for the profile, albeit in fraught circumstances, while Maxwell and Evans regularly discussed the content on the telephone—on one occasion, nine times in a single day. "It was an exhausting psychological battle," recalls Hodgson.

On October 1, after Maxwell had read a newly revised version of the profile, he issued a fourth writ against the *Sunday Times* for defamation and, late at night, telephoned Evans at home. "This is worse, much worse than the first [draft]," he complained. "Let's meet." They met, but Evans insisted on publication, despite the objections, on October 5.

The profile began by stressing "the boldness of his courage and the poverty of his beginnings" and traced the foundations of Maxwell's fortunes as a turbulent and controversial entrepreneur whose business ethics were questionable. Few subjects on the eve of a fateful public meeting would have enjoyed a profile which, after mentioning the award of the Military Cross, concluded, "The boy from Slatinske Doly had definitely arrived," or, concerning his optimism about his recovery after the Simpkins crash, alluded to his nickname as "the bouncing Czech." But for once Maxwell was practically defenseless, and the topicality guaranteed a very wide readership. His only riposte was a long circular sent to all Pergamon shareholders denouncing the paper's allegations and its violation of Evans's original undertaking. Later he condemned the *Sunday Times* journalists to their face as "the forces of evil."

The opposition to Maxwell, undoubtedly influenced by the article, solidified over that last weekend. The institutions, on the advice of their newly appointed merchant bankers, Schroeder Wagg, decided unanimously on Maxwell's removal. Maxwell tried, on Tuesday October 7, to win a reprieve during a heated meeting with Schroeders' representatives. But he failed, and news began to trickle out during the next day of an unforeseen twist in his tactics.

Small batches of Pergamon shares were being issued to over one hundred Pergamon employees, which would enable them to attend and vote at the EGM. Leasco's lawyers scrambled to scrutinize Pergamon's rules and saw that on a mere show of hands Maxwell would have sufficient support to adjourn the meeting, delay his removal and remain in control of the company. Suspecting the worst, Leasco attempted to transfer some of its shares to one hundred supporters but, late in the afternoon on October 9, their request was refused by the company secretary.

The only solution, said Peter Curry, Leasco's lawyer in England, was an injunction from the High Court to prevent Maxwell adjourning the meeting. Three Rolls-Royces filled with bankers, lawyers and their clients from New York roared from the City toward the Strand. Impatiently they waited outside a courtroom for a judge to become available. At five o'clock, as the building closed, they were told that they had come to the wrong court. The bankers and the businessmen were struck with horror. "Don't worry," said Curry, "I know a judge who will help." In the early evening, the retinue crammed into the small chambers of the much needed friend, Mr. Justice Shaw. "Hello, Peter, how's your wife?" asked the judge, who then warned, "I've got a train to catch and you've got a few minutes to convince me. It won't be easy." Speaking in very blunt terms, the lawyers described Maxwell's alleged sins. The judge raised his eyebrows and Curry wrote on lined paper in longhand the required order. Mr. Justice Shaw signed, and there was a collective sigh. The injunction was formally served on

Maxwell at ten o'clock the following morning, two hours before the meeting was due to start.

The Connaught Rooms had few happy memories for Maxwell but they were nevertheless the venue for the EGM. Dressed as usual in his bright blue suit, he arrived with Betty, understandably tense. There had been no respite over the past weeks from the unrelenting pincer movement which would so unjustly destroy his own creation. "I and my family have been through hell," he would later reveal to the meeting. Some chairs on the podium were noticeably empty. Briggs and Payne from Chalmers Impey had refused to sit alongside their client. The remainder were occupied by Pergamon's directors shifting uneasily in anticipation of the embarrassments to come. A few had urged Maxwell to make the meeting as short as possible but they knew that their advice had been ignored. Earlier that morning, Maxwell had overridden their wishes by instructing Kerman to appeal for the injunctions to be set aside. He would fight to the last even if the outcome was a foregone conclusion. Just as Sir William Carr had packed the hall nine months earlier with his employees, now among the five hundred who had crowded into the hall were many Pergamon employees and sympathetic small shareholders who had cheered him when he entered. In the back stood Steinberg, relaxed and smiling, obviously enjoying life in London. The American had arrived arm-in-arm with two glamorous young women, both dressed in white, wearing large Ascot-type hats. Strangely, Maxwell felt no hostility toward his estranged partner and respected his business acumen. Overwhelmingly, his venom was directed at Jacob Rothschild.

The meeting began at noon. Maxwell spoke first into the microphone: "My Lord, ladies and gentlemen, at ten o'clock this morning I was served with an injunction by Messrs. Rothschild, without any notice," and a tirade against the bankers ensued. "This arrogant and stupid action by Rothschild is but the final chapter in the sorry way in which they have conducted the affairs of Leasco in this long-drawn-out battle." Maxwell thereupon did exactly what he was forbidden to do and adjourned the meeting, "because of this incredible and unbelievable behavior of Rothschild's," claiming that he wanted to await the outcome of his own appeal against the injunction.

Uproar and bedlam followed his words. Amid shouts of "Sit down!," "Stand up!," "This meeting is commenced and should proceed!," and "Shut up!," the directors slowly filed down from the platform. Curry made a dash for the microphone and had just begun to speak when Maxwell's hand snatched it from him: "This is a meeting of Pergamon representatives, not Leasco. Would you mind leaving this floor." Curry grabbed the microphone back, began speaking and was suddenly mute. The power had been switched off and his voice was drowned by slow handclapping. Maxwell beamed and after reconnecting the microphone announced that the meeting was not adjourned but "delayed" and would remain so. The chaos rose to a new crescendo as dozens of soberly suited men stood waving their arms in the air, sat down in frustration, only to rise again, their crouched bodies suspended in the air, their faces contorted in fury, their shouts inaudible.

Maxwell returned to the microphone and, pointing at Curry and Jacob Rothschild, said, "These men are obviously proposing to wreck this meeting. Maybe they are providing good entertainment . . . I propose to withdraw from the meeting and I invite you to deal with these gentlemen as you deem fit." Again there was uproar and again the microphone was switched off after Maxwell had threatened to call guards to remove those who gave "stupid advice" to their clients.

Inside the hall, Lord Aldington, formerly Toby Low, a Conservative Member of Parliament, watched in discomfort. His bank, William Brandt, had agreed to represent Pergamon, and he now feared that his reputation might suffer by association with the turmoil he was witnessing. During a five-minute discussion with his client he insisted that the meeting must continue and be "conducted according to the Queensberry Rules." Maxwell agreed and returned to the podium holding the microphone. "Ladies and gentlemen," he said, "let us forget all about that, shall we? I hope none of us will get unruly and disorderly. Particularly that is directed toward Rothschild lawyers." The meeting started.

Uninterrupted, Maxwell now launched a bid to reconvert the converted, namely the institutions: "Who are the brains that will run this business . . . ? a leading educational institution . . . cannot be run by experts only in financial affairs." After twenty minutes, he stopped and then started again. No one doubted that he was delaying the inevitable. Perhaps he was waiting for a divine spirit miraculously to sweep away the hostile faces before him and deliver Pergamon firmly back into his control. There were more attacks on Rothschilds—"I received many impertinent letters from Rothschild"—followed by several mournful appeals to Rothschilds to "withdraw their hostile, harmful and most damaging resolution to the company." Jacob Rothschild rose to give his reply. Perhaps Maxwell hoped against hope that this was the deliverance. "I propose," announced the tall banker, "that Mr. E.J. Buckley be and he is hereby removed as a director of the Pergamon Press

Limited." There was a cry of "Shame!" and it was nearly all over. Each vote would take ten embarrassing minutes as Maxwell sought to prevaricate and appeal to the institutions to reconsider. When Rothschild stood to propose Maxwell's own removal, the chairman uttered what seemed like his last words before the executioner's axe fell: "My record in peace or war is open and published in spite of the slander and innuendo in the story by the *Sunday Times*." But despite being deposed, Maxwell remained firmly in the chair to continue the proceedings.

Once the board had been dismissed, Maxwell momentarily relaxed and even cracked a joke. But as the elections for the new board progressed—and on Maxwell's recommendation Steinberg and Hodes would be elected unopposed—the deposed chairman once again began imploring the institutions to reconsider. When his pleas were answered by stony stares, his anger returned: "It is well known in the Square Mile of the City that the arrogance of Rothschild knows no bounds."

After four hours, Leasco was declared the victor with 61 per cent of the vote. No one claimed to emerge from the bear garden with any credit, although Maxwell delivered one final surprise. Ever anxious to retain the initiative, he announced that, with the Take-over Panel's agreement, he would make a cash offer of 25s for all non-Leasco shares. Everyone, including his own bankers, was stunned but too exhausted to ask where Maxwell could hope to raise £5 million. Maxwell refused to be drawn, although he believed that Leasco had only won a Pyrrhic victory. "I wish to thank you all for coming and God speed to you on your way out." After a burst of applause, it was all over. Standing alone in the emptying hall, humiliated and defeated, he admitted, "You can't expect me to be other than very, very sad." The men from Leasco looked at their tormentor. "Somehow," recalls Stevens, "Bob looked a lot more lovable in defeat."

The new managers of Pergamon did not open any champagne bottles when they met later that night at Rothschilds for a board meeting to consider their strategy. No one was sufficiently tactless to speculate about just why they found themselves managing a company which employed over 2,500 people, which had just lost its key personnel, and whose financial status was in dispute, although it definitely had no money in the bank. As Hodes silently mused, "We've been through the engagement and the divorce. Now it's the marriage." Briskly, they agreed that their priority was to establish exactly what they had purchased for £9 million and to invite Buckley, Gilbert Richards, who managed Pergamon's journals, and Anthony Wheaton, who managed a printing company, to rejoin the board. Then Steinberg, Hodes and

Schwartz formally resigned from the Pergamon board to which they had been elected just two hours earlier. For the moment they were replaced by just one new director and chairman, Sir Henry d'Avigdor-Goldsmid. The need for an independent chairman had surprised Leasco but it was the price which the institutions exacted in return for their support. "The institutions were terribly stuffy," recalls one of the bankers, "and decided that they wouldn't trust the Americans."

Finding a suitable nominee had not been easy. After two other men had refused, Sir Henry, a Conservative Member of Parliament, a banker and a leader of British Jewry, was approached. When Rothschild rang, Sir Henry was out hunting, which at least provided reassurance that the candidate was still active. Lady d'Avigdor-Goldsmid had answered and Rothschild explained why Sir Henry was needed. "He should accept," implored the banker, "for England." It was an appeal which Sir Henry eventually could not resist. Stevens wished later that his reluctance had been backed by stronger will-power: "He was so senile that he couldn't negotiate his way out of a paper bag."

The following day, Stevens drove with d'Avigdor-Goldsmid to Oxford. The politician's joints were stiff and heavily bandaged following falls from his horse. Stevens's concern about Sir Henry's capabilities had been placated by the bankers. "You'll really like him," he had been assured. "He'll never come to meetings." During the journey, Stevens started to discuss his objectives and tactics they might adopt when they arrived at Headington Hall. D'Avigdor-Goldsmid hearteningly replied that he too had priorities. Thereupon, to Stevens's dismay, he produced a list of recommended restaurants in the Oxford area. As Stevens swallowed his reaction, d'Avigdor-Goldsmid turned knowingly and said, "I've been appointed to make sure that neither side fouls the pavement."

Their entry into Pergamon's offices was an anticlimax. Sir Henry asked the secretary who welcomed them for "the papers." When she queried, "From which file?," he replied, "No, no, the newspapers." Stevens was dumbfounded: "I gawked and said nothing." Over a three-hour lunch, d'Avigdor-Goldsmid expounded his view: "I'm not allowing you to dig a tunnel into the company." As he spoke, the American was reassessing his plans. Leasco had no choice but to withdraw from any direct management and rely on the long-serving employees. Approaches were already under way to three of the deposed directors. Within four weeks, with Maxwell's encouragement, they would return to the company.

But the hands-off strategy was fraught with difficulty: Pergamon's editorial offices were built in the same grounds, approximately fifty yards distant from the house where the Maxwell family lived. Although the Hall was owned by Pergamon, it had been leased to Maxwell and he curtly refused even to consider leaving his low-rent "council house," which also served as the offices of his private companies. His constant physical presence, he told inquirers, was "my guarantee that I know the status of my shareholding." The extent of his supervision quickly became apparent.

Soon after the American take-over, Maxwell was seen at night prowling through the editorial offices. D'Avigdor-Goldsmid ordered guards to be posted around the building but, considering the enormous loyalty which so many Pergamon employees felt toward Maxwell, especially after the reappointment of the three directors, the guards were token symbols. The tension between the two sides—they were divided by a finely manicured lawn—broke into open warfare, often manifested in childish spite. The two buildings shared light and heating. Whenever their disputes intensified, Maxwell turned off their common boiler. In retaliation, d'Avigdor-Goldsmid ordered the Hall's electricity to be disconnected. "We froze and they sat in darkness," recalls Stevens. That the hiatus would continue was predictable, but no one had anticipated that the crisis would arise so quickly.

Leasco was intent on quickly establishing control over the Pergamon subsidiary in America, Pergamon Press Inc. (PPI), since 50 per cent of Pergamon's sales were exported to America and all the American journals were supervised from PPI's premises. PPI was the generator of Pergamon's future profits and growth. Pergamon in Britain owned 70 per cent of PPI, which was a public company. The remaining 30 per cent was owned by the American public. Under American law, Maxwell was president and chairman of PPI's board of directors. Prominent among those directors were his old friends—Laszlo Straka, Sigmund Wahrsager and Ladislaus "Martini" Majthenyi. Two days after removing Maxwell in London, Leasco's lawyers wrote to the secretary of PPI in New York requesting a special shareholders' meeting. They intended to remove Maxwell and his friends and appoint a new board of directors. Simultaneously, d'Avigdor-Goldsmid wrote to Maxwell asking for his resignation. Maxwell's rejection was carried by hand across the lawn. After criticizing d'Avigdor-Goldsmid's "crude attempt to go behind my back," Maxwell "deplored" the new chairman's lack of "courtesy and consideration" because "good manners cost nothing." The crux was that he refused to resign and "as the second-largest shareholder" defiantly insisted that he could not be ignored. By October 20, Pergamon's new management realized just how smartly they had been outwitted by Maxwell. Stevens admits his amazement: "We hadn't focused on the subsidiary and our own vulnerability until after Max had covered his arse." In fact, Maxwell had protected his position during the same week in June that he was in New York negotiating the original sale with Steinberg.

Unknown to the Pergamon directors other than Tom Clark, Maxwell had on June 12, 1969, approved a resolution at PPI's annual general meeting which stipulated that PPI's secretary was not obliged to call a special meeting at the request of a majority of the shareholders. In effect, under the new rules, Pergamon in Britain was deprived of its powers over its own company except at the annual meeting and the next meeting was not due until June 1970. The new rule was approved while Maxwell was in New York negotiating to sell Pergamon to Leasco. He would later produce affidavits to prove that the initiative for the change had been taken by his American lawyers, who believed that the previous rules were outdated, and it is possible that under any circumstances Leasco would have had difficulty in establishing control over PPI. Whatever the reason, Maxwell had cause to be confident at the end of the day in the Connaught Rooms that, because he retained total control over PPI, Leasco's victory was hollow.

In the second half of October, Leasco's accountants began sifting through the files in Oxford looking for the section concerning PPI. The revelation that MSI Inc. owed Pergamon $1.6 million and enjoyed a favorable "sale or return" contract with Pergamon suggested the real possibility of other unknown agreements. Yet the accountants found that Pergamon's files contained practically nothing relevant to PPI. There were no copies of bank statements, hardly any copies of correspondence or other contracts with MSI Inc., no list of assets and only sparse details of PPI's contracts with authors and customers. It was a textbook example of Maxwell's compartmentalization.

At Maxwell's disposal in New York was Detlev Raymond, who had worked for Pergamon since 1950. Maxwell could expect, with Raymond's loyalty and his long experience at PPI, to establish a rival company which would be a direct competitor with Pergamon in Britain. The risk was the more pertinent because the files in Oxford did not reveal whether Pergamon even owned the copyright of the articles in its own journals. Steinberg agreed that it was imperative to end Maxwell's control of PPI. The fight, which began in the last week of October, was ferocious and unrelenting.

Under PPI's new rules, a director of the company did have the power to call a special shareholders' meeting, and Leasco discovered that James B. Ross, a vice-president responsible for commissioning publications, was sympathetic toward their cause. Leasco's misfortune was that they contacted Ross two weeks after he had submitted his resignation although it had still not been formally accepted by Maxwell. At Leasco's behest, Ross withdrew his resignation.

Ross's next move was to reinstate himself in his office. It was an attempt which was forcibly opposed. Guards from the Burns security agency cut off his telephone, destroyed his mail and eventually manhandled him off the premises. Maxwell had by then accepted his resignation. To confirm Ross's impotence, PPI's rules were again amended on October 30, to empower only the president, that is, Maxwell, to call a special shareholders' meeting. By then, Ross had appealed to the courts. What followed was a succession of Keystone Kops-type contests between Leasco and Maxwell through the courts of New York, as Ross, financed by Leasco, attempted to call a special shareholders' meeting.

Throughout the contests which followed in New York's courts, Maxwell was represented by Maurice Nessen, a small, charming but brutally aggressive lawyer who had defended Clifford Irving, the "biographer" of the recluse Howard Hughes, against criminal charges. Nessen's tactic on Maxwell's behalf was to exploit every legitimate device in the lawyers' arsenal to delay and obfuscate Leasco's claims. Nessen's first riposte to Ross was to plead that Maxwell could not attend any court hearing due to a series of "mandatory votes" in the House of Commons over the following six weeks which needed his constant attendance. This excuse was dismissed by Quintin Hogg MP, QC (later Lord Hailsham) as "incredible" because "pairing" allowed MPs to travel. Nessen's next ploy was to deliver an affidavit in which Maxwell swore that d'Avigdor-Goldsmid had requested that he stay as chairman of PPI. Nessen was successfully frustrating Leasco's plans.

In the meantime, Ross formally announced a shareholders' meeting for the end of November. In reply, Maxwell, claiming to be the protector of PPI, sent the same shareholders a letter condemning the "reckless" Ross for his "unauthorized and illegal" action. Within three weeks the contest had sped through the judicial process up to the New York Supreme Court, and there Maxwell won. Leasco had no option but to wait until June 1970. For Maxwell, the victory was fundamental to his recovery. He gained a vital break which he would use to persuade d'Avigdor-Goldsmid to recognize his indispensability in the management and survival of Pergamon, while psychologically it boosted his will to fight against the avalanche of writs and investigations which, by the beginning of November, had enveloped him.

The first writs were delivered in New York on November 2 by Leasco alleging conspiracy for "fraud and deceit" and a claim for damages of $22 million. Those receiving the writs were Maxwell, Isidore Kerman, Robert Fleming, Chalmers Impey and the Maxwell family trusts. The writs alleged that Maxwell and his advisers had conspired to mislead Leasco about Pergamon's real financial status. Initially, Hodes had expected to sue Maxwell in Britain, but was advised that under British law the chances of success were extremely slim because neither Flemings nor Chalmers Impey owed a special duty of care to Leasco and so could not be liable even if they negligently endorsed false statements in the annual report. There was also, the British lawyers told Hodes, no claim whatsoever against Maxwell since his assurances had always been oral and therefore difficult to prove. He had not signed any documents which showed more than possible irresponsibility and anything else was based upon the certified accounts. Maxwell's only commitment in writing had been his letter to Schwartz on May 17, but that was ambiguous. Because American financial laws were much stricter and because, according to Leasco, the take-over agreement was negotiated and signed in New York at Maxwell's request, the writs were issued in New York.

Maxwell's defense and counter-claim was that Leasco had deliberately sought to depress the value of Pergamon shares in order to buy the company cheap, that he had never encouraged Leasco to buy Pergamon shares before the formal offer was accepted, that Leasco misrepresented its own financial position, and that, as a result of Leasco's mismanagement of Pergamon, the value of Maxwell's own shares had fallen.

John Briggs's defense was that he had acted in good faith and that, since he did not even know about Maxwell's negotiations with Leasco, he could not have been party to any conspiracy. Richard Fleming filed a defense claiming that he was only on the periphery of the deal, that he had not made any detailed representations and that he was present during the New York negotiations not as a representative of Maxwell but to protect the interests of the bank's unit trusts. Leasco's case against Kerman was eventually dropped.

But the first argument which Nessen deployed, and which would keep the dispute simmering for the following four years, was that the American courts had no jurisdiction because the dispute involved a British company and all the pertinent documents and witnesses were in Britain. That argument would be finally heard in the state Supreme Court.

Meanwhile, Maxwell was under investigation by two inquiries in Britain, both of which had begun formal hearings in late September. The first was mounted by the Board of Trade and the second was the independent audit by Price Waterhouse which would determine Pergamon's 1968 accounts. His attitudes to the two were sharply different.

Still suffering from the injustice he felt Shawcross had meted out at the Take-over Panel hearings, Maxwell feared that the Board of Trade inquiry might similarly maul his reputation without allowing him the opportunity to defend himself adequately. Therefore, before agreeing to appear, he asked the two inspectors to explain the procedures they would adopt and to assure him that he would enjoy the normal protections of a British court of law. Owen Stable QC and Ronald Leach were unwilling to give those guarantees. They argued that the efficient conduct of the inquiry depended upon informality and flexibility, which would be suffocated if they were to be "bound hand and foot" by legalisms and procedures. On September 22, Maxwell arrived for the first session. He gave his name and address, stated that he was the holder of the Military Cross and a Member of Parliament. Then he refused to answer any further questions. Instead, he applied to the High Court for an order requiring the inspectors to adopt a more formal procedure.

Since the Court would not hear the case for some months, the inspectors started their inquiry. Their first witness was Ian Fraser, followed in succession by Godfrey Hodgson, Jacob Rothschild, Rupert Murdoch and Richard Millett. Maxwell's fear that the inspectors were giving a platform to his enemies seemed to him to be fully justified. Others would say that the inspectors were merely calling witnesses who would deliver truthful evidence.

Maxwell's attitude toward the Price Waterhouse inquiry was quite different. If he was to retain his credibility, both commercial and moral, he had no choice but to co-operate since he had staked his reputation upon his company's profitability. Moreover, Steinberg had agreed to bid for the remaining shares within two months of the accountants' report and, as Maxwell had announced that he would make a counterbid, it was vital for Maxwell to persuade Price Waterhouse to accept his version of the 1968 accounts.

Martin Harris, a mild-mannered senior partner of Price Waterhouse, led the investigation, which the firm had initially been reluctant to carry out on account of the fear of endless litigation. Only after Maxwell sent written confirmation that both he and his family trusts would unconditionally co-operate, including the provision of any necessary documents, had Price Waterhouse committed itself. Within weeks that undertaking would be thwarted. MSI Inc. claimed that, on legal advice, it could not disclose any documents which would prejudice its defense against Leasco's suits. For the moment, the legal distinction between the trusts and Maxwell defeated the accountants.

Price Waterhouse adopted a textbook approach to its investigation. Maxwell, accompanied by Nessen, answered the accountant's questions for more than forty full days. Eight accountants divided into four teams worked through the files in Oxford. By the end of November, they had prepared a thick "summary of the facts" which was presented for comment to everyone who had been involved in preparing Pergamon's accounts. Over the following three weeks, daily from 9 a.m. until 7 p.m. in Price Waterhouse's Cheapside offices, there were four simultaneous interviewing sessions where the Pergamon directors and their auditors were invited to "indicate our errors." Questions were asked and answers written down in long hand. Voices were never raised and suspicions were never mentioned. But every night, when the team gathered for debriefing sessions which often continued until the early hours, the day's revelations swept aside their professional taciturnity. "Accountants are professional cynics," recalls one of the investigators, "and there was pure joy in unraveling the complex paper trail."

The questioning of Maxwell personally was "a poker game. We had to treat him gently to make sure that he stayed." It was characteristic of Maxwell when difficult questions were posed that he rambled into tangential areas. Whether it was intended to confuse the questioners or just, as Peter Stevens surmised, the common Czech inability to stay on a straight line, is debatable. The result was that Maxwell spoke at great length, giving an uninterrupted explanation, filled with facts and figures, which was all faithfully recorded. A couple of days later, the same question would be posed. Very often, Maxwell could not recall the identical facts and figures which he had so authoritatively cited just forty-eight hours earlier. "We quoted back to him what he had said earlier and it unnerved him," recalls one of the accountants.

At the end of the year, Harris handed Maxwell his preliminary conclusions. As he read through the thick folder, Maxwell recognized that it consisted of remorseless censure. Price Waterhouse had decided that Pergamon's audited 1968 profits of £2.1 million should be reduced by £1.6 million and that the remaining half million pounds would be swallowed up by the ILSC losses. According to Price Waterhouse, Pergamon had actually made a loss in 1968. "Maxwell was furious when he read our interim report," says a witness of the occasion, "so we offered him a cup of tea and spoke about the weather." To the accountants it seemed that Maxwell had placed himself inside a straitjacket.

Among the papers which they had discovered in Oxford was a contract, signed by Maxwell, for the resale of the Spanish translation rights from MSI Inc. back to PPI. The contract was dated October 6, 1969, just four days before the EGM. Maxwell had little choice but to agree that Pergamon could not claim the £104,000 as profit. Similarly, R.M. & Co. had in August returned to Pergamon books worth £149,000 from its warehouse in Wolverton. Finally, Pergamon's massive £1,250,000 "sale or return" deal for back issues signed on August 30, 1967, with MSI Inc. was clearly revocable and therefore had to be removed from Pergamon's income. In effect, the accountants had discovered that in the weeks before Maxwell's removal from Pergamon, Pergamon's profits had been depressed.

The beleaguered executive could count on few sympathetic ears for his explanations. In the era of Emil Savundra, Bernie Cornfeld's IOS and the sudden demise of the washing-machine salesman John Bloom, a certain seediness had infected the image of British business. Maxwell was afraid that he was being tarnished by the same brush, especially since his reputation had been severely damaged by newspaper and television coverage of Pergamon's tribulations. Again, none was more wounding than the accounts which appeared in Lord Thomson's newspapers.

The second part of the *Sunday Times* profile had appeared on October 12, two days after his epic defeat at the Connaught Rooms. According to the newspaper's heading, "Robert Maxwell Has Lost His Empire." In the center of the article was a photograph of Maxwell and Gaitskell laughing together in 1962, the caption stating that the Labour leader had been a "friend since the fifties," the era which was associated with Simpkin Marshall and so on. Maxwell was still a Member of Parliament and, with a general election due within two years, the article questioned his suitability.

By 1969, Maxwell's parliamentary career had barely progressed. His appearances and interventions in the chamber had sharply declined in number compared to earlier years and only his management of the House of Commons Catering Committee had been rated a success. The *Sunday Times* suspected that even that success was a mirage and approached Richard Crossman, who had originally nominated Maxwell. Crossman praised Maxwell's "staggering success." He continued, "He took over a department totally demoralized, whose staff included a number of prostitutes and thieves, all of whom he sacked without a strike. . . . He purged the gross abuse and pilfering; legs of mutton and rounds of beef were being regularly removed under their raincoats by members of the staff. All that is now stopped. . . . He took over a restaurant which was incurring gigantic losses in order to provide excellent food and drink. . . ." The published article ignored Crossman's favorable comment and dwelt on the accounts, which the journalists believed were controversial. Described as the "ballet of Robert Maxwell, caterer extraordinary," it lampooned his management technique and questioned his accountancy methods: "It displays all the classic movements in the Maxwell repertoire—the Amazing Leap from the wings with Loud Promises of Modern Efficiency; the Masterly Treatment of Accounts; and the Rapid Disappearance, just before the audience starts to throw things."

That cameo, in Maxwell's view, proved that the *Sunday Times* was determined to destroy his career, and he complained to the House of Commons Committee of Privileges. After thirteen meetings, his complaint was rejected, although the committee stated that there was no evidence that his conduct was "in any way improper or departed from normal procedures in compiling the accounts." The issue, and Maxwell's reputation, were left dangling.

Political life irked Maxwell. He was perplexed and frustrated that despite his ideas, energy and abilities, he had not won the Prime Minister's admiration. Equally, he was disillusioned by the government's policies. Despite the noble promises, British science and industry had not fared well; the government's tax policies and especially the Selective Employment Tax had been disastrous; the perpetual lurch through a succession of apparently insoluble financial crises had opened the door to the International Monetary Fund to act as sole arbiter of Britain's financial management; while the Labour movement lamentably persisted with a wave of suicidal strikes in the face of an unenforceable prices and incomes policy. Even Maxwell's own efforts to reform the inept management of the party headquarters at Transport House had been spurned. Within the Labour Party and inside the House, Maxwell was an awkward misfit who, though pleading for enterprise and for the rapid dismantling of Britain's pretensions to world-power status, had not managed to create an identifiable political cause for himself. His only success was to pilot through the Commons with the flamboyant Conservative Member, Sir Gerald Nabarro, an extension of the Clean Air Acts.

Yet in his constituency his efficient organization and his apparent relish for looking after his constituents' interests had earned him considerable popularity—not an easy achievement for a Labour MP representing a Home Counties constituency. Much of his success was owed to his political secretary, Judith Ennals, who managed and executed the bulk of the parliamentarian's routine and time-consuming chores. Constituents were encouraged to write with their problems, which Ennals researched and settled before obtaining Maxwell's endorsement and signature. Although this was an unusual arrangement for a Labour MP, the arrangement was common practice in the Conservative ranks. Under Ennals, Maxwell's political office scoured the announcements columns in the local newspapers and automatically sent congratulations or condolences to those advertising births, marriages or deaths. Even the victims of road accidents would receive a "get well" card from their MP. His motives were realistic. Every vote in the next election would count.

To describe his approach as squirarchical is not to be critical but merely acknowledges that, in the context of a hunting and shooting constituency, the Labour Member of Parliament's unorthodox lifestyle was not incongruous. Receptions, tea parties and meetings in his large mansion endeared him and his wife to most of his party workers. His constituency never suffered from a common Labour Party malaise of poor organization. On the contrary, his machine was so well oiled that it aroused, among the traditionalists, irritation and eventually outright anger.

Soon after his re-election in 1966, Maxwell had revamped the party organization. At the grass roots, so-called Polling District Committees were established in every village where no party group had previously existed. Like the branches, these "committees," even if they represented no more than two people, had the right according to the constituency's recently revised rules to send delegates to the all-powerful General Management Committee meetings, the constituency's governing body, to which Maxwell was answerable. Within a short time, Maxwell's support on the GMC was overwhelming and had aroused resentment among the working-class members who lived in the railway town of Wolverton.

Frank Atter, who had been a Labour Party supporter effectively since birth, was one of those who had become uneasy about the effects of the MP's organizational reforms. Atter, who had sat on the original selection committee in 1959 and was impressed by Maxwell, had gradually become disillusioned: "We began to get the feeling that unless you were a one hundred per cent Maxwell man, you were side-stepped. Ordinary party members were losing control to his own staff and that wasn't healthy." Maxwell, complained Atter, was not sympathetic to the democracy which was natural to the Labour Party. It was said that he just did not like opponents or critics. Party meetings rarely debated the government's performance or policies and never questioned their own Member's opinions.

Jim Lyons, Maxwell's agent in the constituency, suffered more than others his MP's reluctance to consult but he suffered in silence, even when he was severely embarrassed. One such case was Maxwell's announcement that he would resign if his bid for the *News of the World* was successful. Lyons had been neither forewarned nor consulted. He concealed his surprise and spoke for many in saying that he hoped his bid would fail because "We would not like to lose him." But, by election time, Maxwell was uneasy about his agent. Lyons was not as attentive to the party organization as Barnard had been and had not maintained the vital canvass of all the electorate. Although he had been warned by the regional agent, Geoff Foster, about his performance, Lyons had not worked as hard as Maxwell expected. Irritated, he had excluded Lyons from most decision-making and had reduced his responsibilities. Headington Hall had gradually become the *de facto* party headquarters where important meetings, often summoned without Lyons's knowledge, were held, and where official papers were stored. Even the constituency's budget was beyond Lyons's control. Most Labour members agree with Bryan Barnard that in the approach to the election the constituency was not "as well organized as before."

By spring 1970, the tide had turned for the Labour government. The appalling succession of economic crises which had cost the government its popularity suddenly seemed to have been overcome. Exports were rising and Britain was for the moment no longer the sick man of Europe. In mid-May, the opinion polls swung in Labour's favor. The Conservatives seemed vulnerable to Wilson's derision as heartless and incompetent politicians who could be mercilessly lampooned as "Yesterday's Men" or the "Selsdon Man." The Prime Minister decided to make a dash for victory and announced a general election for June 18. The party's slogan, "Now Britain's strong—let's make it great to live in," was not to every candidate's taste, but it satisfied Maxwell.

Maxwell might have expected his task to have been made more difficult by the adverse publicity about Pergamon. Yet party workers reported that his troubles in the City were barely mentioned during the three-week campaign. Voters were impressed by his constituency record and were not influenced by his apparent failure to win promotion. That he could cite as parliamentary achievements only his membership of

"UK parliamentary delegation to the Council of Europe" and the vice-chairmanship of its Committee on Science and Technology was irrelevant. His management of the Catering Committee was not mentioned. Some did notice that no senior government minister was prepared to speak on his behalf in the constituency, a surprising omission for a marginal.

The campaign, organized by Betty, his sons and his secretaries, did not differ from those of previous years. Charging around the constituency, his head sticking out of the top of a bright red Land Rover like a commander leading the assault, Maxwell's energy, oratory and charm won him warm ovations. The highlight of his speeches was his condemnation of the Conservatives' proposed legislation to prevent wildcat strikes. "This is not the way to run a country," he said about Tory leader Edward Heath's ideas. "This is one of the stupidest things anyone has tried to foist on this country." Fifteen years later, he would praise Mrs. Thatcher's anti-union legislation as a godsend and admit that it was the basis of his revived fortunes.

But after the first week of the campaign he recognized his difficulties. His new Conservative opponent, William Benyon, was superior to his predecessor, and the Conservative Party machine had been successfully overhauled. In comparison, Lyons had, he felt, failed dismally.

In the light of the unexpected national swing toward the Conservatives, Maxwell had perhaps only an even chance of holding his seat. Benyon won by 2,521 votes but the swing was less than half the national average. Although that was some consolation, the result was nevertheless a bitter blow for Maxwell. The television pictures showed a fallen face and glistening eyes, but he was gracious in defeat.

Away from the cameras, both Maxwell and his wife were, like most defeated politicians, desolate that their mammoth efforts and unswerving dedication could so easily and so ungratefully be disposed of. In all of Maxwell's other defeats, it had been possible to launch an immediate counter-attack. The democratic vote could not, however, be challenged. Instead, the Maxwells sought a scapegoat. On July 4, three weeks after the election, the GMC set in motion the censure of Jim Lyons. In ten days, no less than six resolutions expressing no confidence in the agent were passed. Lyons says that he was not notified that any of the branch meetings were discussing his conduct and was not even invited to attend his own branch meeting. Frank Atter is rueful: "If they win, they say it was a marvelous candidate; if they lose, they blame the agent. Maxwell just went too far."

10

With members of the legal profession Maxwell maintained an uneasy, bitter-sweet relationship. Lawyers thrive on interpreting, redefining and bending rules to suit their cause, but will always resort, when in doubt, to the law's preference for certainty. In contrast, if aspiring tycoons diligently obeyed every rule, their ambitions would be stymied. They normally choose to avoid the courts as unmanageable, unpredictable and therefore dangerous. Maxwell was the exception. By 1970, he had earned a contrary reputation as a breathless challenger of rules, but also as a most litigious person who would readily appeal to the courts to assert his rights. Paradoxically, he found the intellectual frisson of the lawyer's craft exciting, but he was also frustrated since his very reliance upon their expertise denied him total mastery of his fate. Nevertheless, until 1970, his combination of energetic determination and unique bravado usually cowed many defendants into reluctant submission. To the interested observer, Maxwell seemed positively to enjoy his appearances in the witness box and when sitting with his lawyers in the well of the courtroom. That changed during the Board of Trade inquiry.

Until 1970, Maxwell normally relied upon his confidant and business partner Isidore Kerman for legal advice. But once the inquiries into Pergamon began, Kerman was precluded from acting because, as a director, he was required by the inspectors to be a witness. The exposure of Maxwell's relationship with other lawyers therefore coincided with his intensive recourse to the courts to defend himself. Maxwell first consulted the solicitor David Freeman, a Labour supporter who had built a successful commercial practice in London's West End. Freeman selected as their advocate Morris Finer QC, who had earned a glowing reputation among his profession as the master of reducing the most complicated facts to a digestible and persuasive argument. Finer's supreme credential for arguing Maxwell's case was that he had recently investigated on behalf of the Board of Trade the collapse of John Bloom's washing-machine company, Rolls Razor. Freeman believed that Maxwell's greatest obstacle would be to secure a fair hearing, and there was no one better suited to argue that Leach and Stable were bound by what are known as the "rules of natural justice" than a former inspector himself. Maxwell was fortunate that his representatives were skilled and sympathetic and had also grown up in humble circumstances, but he was unable to desist from interference. Many of the conferences at the Temple became tetchy debates between Maxwell and the eminent barrister who, with grisly foreboding, could anticipate a judge's unsympathetic reaction. "Maxwell was always barking orders," recalls one of those present. "He was very clever, very intelligent, very hard-working, but utterly impossible."

The two inspectors, Owen Stable QC and Ronald Leach, both enjoyed redoubtable reputations. Stable was rated a high-flyer at the commercial Bar who had a good chance of appointment as a High Court judge once the inquiry was completed. As the lawyer, it was Stable's duty to ensure that the proper legal procedures were observed. Leach was an accountant and a senior partner of Peat Marwick Mitchell. Although he was considered to be among the nation's most senior practitioners, his appointment was not without its critics. As president of the Institute of Chartered Accountants, he was open to the charge that he might seek to deflect the widespread disillusion with his profession which the Pergamon affair had provoked. Yet these were common and inevitable vulnerabilities which would not ordinarily have affected his impartiality. Notionally, their appointment and the rules of procedure they would follow were no different from those of any previous departmental inquiry: the hearings would be in private and, while each person would receive a transcript of his own evidence, Maxwell would not have access to the transcripts of other witnesses. The inspectors' report would be confidential except for the portion which the government decided to publish. The core of their task was to undertake an investigation into Pergamon and to report on whether the shareholders "had been given all the information they might have expected." They were not adjudicating as in a trial.

Maxwell, however, believed that his circumstances were exceptional: Pergamon was still trading apparently profitably; the Leasco bid had provoked enormous controversial publicity; the past eighteen months had convincingly proven the City's and Fleet Street's antagonism toward him; an interim inspectors' report could be used by Leasco in pursuit of its claims in New York; and the inquiry would hamper any bid for Pergamon once the Price Waterhouse report was published. Among his unpublicized concerns was the inspectors' determination to investigate his private companies. That, he felt, was a sensitive area which should be barred to a government inquiry ostensibly concerned with a public company. He therefore sought, as a condition of his co-operation with the inquiry, guarantees that he would have the customary protection of natural justice afforded by a court of law—namely, that he could be accompanied by his lawyers, that his lawyers could cross-examine all the witnesses and that they would have full access to all the evidence which the inspectors were considering and make submissions about all that evidence. Lastly, he demanded that, if the inspectors came to any conclusions unfavorable to himself, they would be bound to offer him a chance to answer those criticisms.

The inspectors disagreed. On December 1 they wrote to Maxwell to explain that while they were "most anxious that no one affected by our inquiries should feel that he has been unjustly treated at our hands" they could not agree to unrestricted access to the transcripts of what were quite intentionally private meetings. The negotiations made no further progress and Maxwell threw down the gauntlet: he would only answer questions if ordered to do so by a court.

In early April 1970, the inspectors appealed to the High Court to order the Labour politician to answer their questions without further guarantees. On Maxwell's behalf, Finer appeared before Mr. Justice Plowman and argued that, as Maxwell was "under suspicion," he had the right to demand that the "freedoms and safeguards woven into the fabric of life in this country" as in a judicial inquiry would be observed.

In reply, the inspectors made a concession. They were not bound, they argued, by the rules of natural justice because they were undertaking an investigation and submitting a report whose publication was by no means a foregone conclusion. However, they assured the Court that they would not submit a critical report without giving Maxwell an opportunity to answer any points which they raised, although they would provide only a broad description of their complaints. Plowman supported the inspectors' argument and ordered that Maxwell answer their questions. Maxwell appealed.

Maxwell's strategy now led to his first break with a legal adviser, his solicitor David Freeman. There was a clash of personalities and a sharp disagreement about whether they could refuse to co-operate with the inspectors. Since Maxwell was committed to fight the inquiry "tooth and nail," he rejected any hint of concession and transferred to his friend John Silkin, the Labour Member of Parliament.

In July, Morris Finer re-argued his case in the Court of Appeal. Lord Denning agreed that the inspectors had to be fair and abide by the rules of natural justice because reputations and careers could be affected by their findings. Quite explicitly, Denning said that the inspectors had to give Maxwell an outline of any charge against him, so allowing a fair opportunity for correction or contradiction. But he rejected Finer's argument that the inspectors were bound to allow Maxwell the opportunity to rebut any adverse evidence and to cross-examine witnesses. The crux, according to Denning, was that the inspectors were investigators and needed flexibility. In the public interest, speed was essential and Maxwell was bound to help. If he refused, he would be in contempt of court and he could "expect no further mercy."

On September 4, 1970, Maxwell appeared for the first session of questioning at 11 Ironmonger Lane in the City. Displaying no apprehension, Maxwell treated the inquiry over the following months as a regrettably unavoidable chore to be slotted into his increasingly hectic schedule. He was energetically relaunching his business activities, a relaunch neatly coinciding with Denning's judgment.

In a four-page circular to shareholders, he announced that, supported by a major publisher who was still undecided, he would announce a bid for Pergamon once the Price Waterhouse report was published. Were he to win control, Maxwell also promised that he would assume the management for "up to two years . . . until the company was on its feet again," and then hand over to a younger man. He postulated that he would offer 25s per share for a further 23 per cent of the shares which, combined with his own 28 per cent holding, would leave Leasco stranded.

Maxwell prided himself on the timing of the announcement. Steinberg was once again fighting for survival as Leasco's fortunes tottered. Its share price, after slumping from $33 to $10, had dropped another $5. As a consequence, under a complicated series of warranties which had financed its purchase of the Reliance Insurance Group, the fall of its share price had triggered demands for Leasco to repay loans worth $31.9 million, an enormous burden. For the Americans, arranging the rescheduling of those loans in New York was infinitely more important than the time-consuming management of Pergamon.

The board meetings in Oxford, Schwartz and Stevens had discovered, were taken up by interminable discussions about finances and accounts and rarely about the business itself. The Americans decided that their attendance was a waste of time and selected Dr. Felix Kalinski to replace Bello on the board as a full-time appointment. Kalinski, who had been recruited from the CBS television network in New York by a firm of headhunters, was a former West Point graduate and a decorated combat pilot who demanded and received the then enormous annual salary of $80,000. Leasco hoped that Kalinski, as a full-time director, would monitor Pergamon's recovery pending delivery of the Price Waterhouse report and would protect their interests from the ever-ubiquitous presence of Maxwell.

On several occasions during the year, Maxwell had attempted to effect a reconciliation, either by approaching intermediaries or on one notable occasion by booking every available trans-Atlantic flight in order to be on the same plane as Steinberg. Having finally trapped the American in the first-class cabin at 39,000 feet, he unsuccessfully attempted to discuss a settlement of their differences. "I think he just took the next flight out of Kennedy back to London," recalled Steinberg.

In June more sober negotiations had started between Maxwell and d'Avigdor-Goldsmid under the chairmanship of Lord Aldington. Maxwell offered, in return for his reappointment as a Pergamon director and the cessation of the litigation against PPI in New York, to merge his family companies and PPI into Pergamon while both Leasco's and his own shareholdings would be committed to a trust pledged to support the board. Pressured by the Americans, who vetoed any proposal which included Maxwell's return, d'Avigdor-Goldsmid initially rejected the peace offer but after the middle of 1970 had become resentful of the New Yorkers' antagonism. Quite simply, d'Avigdor-Goldsmid disliked disagreements and was insulted by the Americans' dismissive criticisms of his role as an independent intermediary.

The Americans could not hide their disdain for the Colonel Blimp who lived in a huge, depressing house in Tonbridge where they had to wait until precisely twelve noon before they were offered a drink. "The house was so cold," recalled Steinberg, "that we had to go outside to warm up." Steinberg commuted regularly to London to persuade d'Avigdor-Goldsmid to break Maxwell's grip over Pergamon while Stevens shuttled across the Atlantic, sometimes three times weekly, to report on the problems which d'Avigdor-Goldsmid's stubbornness was causing. Their personal dislike of d'Avigdor-Goldsmid mirrored their contempt for the decayed British financial system but their undisguised irritation reinforced the chairman's obstinate refusal to manage Pergamon as they wished.

Maxwell in contrast had by the autumn charmed Sir Henry into believing that the two could work quite well together. Consequently d'Avigdor-Goldsmid had become unwilling, on Pergamon's behalf and at Steinberg's behest, to pursue Maxwell aggressively in the courts. In June 1970, Maxwell knew that he was safe in refusing outright to call the statutory PPI annual meeting in New York because d'Avigdor-Goldsmid would not enforce Pergamon's rights. Effectively, nine months after his humiliation at the Connaught Rooms, he still retained control of PPI and, negatively, of Pergamon.

In August, the Price Waterhouse report was finally published. The accountants explained that they had adopted "material changes" in preparing the 1968 accounts and accordingly had reduced the pre-tax profits from £2.1 million to £140,000, which did not take into account ILSC's accumulated losses of £2.1 million.

The report confirmed, in Leasco's view, that it was the innocent victim. Maxwell robustly argued that it proved the whimsy of accountants and absolved him from any blame. "I note," he wrote in a circular, "that hindsight has been employed," and blamed the new board for causing all the losses. The transactions with his family companies which had amounted to £2.5 million had, he claimed, "been fully disclosed and have been beneficial to your company." To those aware of the truth, Maxwell's excuse was unconvincing, not least because he did not explain why he had ordered the cancellation of those very transactions just before his removal from the board. In the same manner, he sought to explain the dramatic alteration in profits: "Shareholders need not be perturbed. The suggested scaling down of profits is well within the margins when reporting accountants apply different accounting principles."

Price Waterhouse had also prepared Pergamon's accounts for the first nine months of 1969. In the heyday of the negotiations with Leasco, Maxwell had forecast that Pergamon's profits would be £2.5 million. In New York in August 1969, he had agreed that they should be revised downward to £2 million. Price Waterhouse, however, calculated that Pergamon had actually made a profit of just £29,000 which was turned into a gigantic loss of nearly £2 million if the ILSC's losses and the revocation of MSI Inc.'s contract were also taken into account. It was an indictment, not least of the accountancy profession. Their report contained no outright blame for the discrepancies but Chalmers Impey was replaced by Cooper Brothers as the company's auditor.

Pergamon's annual report published in September 1970 reflected the gloom. "Ghastly" was the epithet which d'Avigdor-Goldsmid voiced to journalists. All the board's efforts, he said, "were concentrated on keeping [the] Company going." His admission was not an understatement. Investigation of Pergamon's files was continually revealing more unforeseen and costly anomalies. There was, for example, the European Printing Corporation (EPC), a firm of specialist printers in Dublin. EPC had been bought by Maxwell from Lord Thomson in 1967 and had never earned a profit. By 1970, EPC's total losses amounted to the substantial sum of £214,000. Pergamon's new managers were perplexed because EPC was owned by R.M. & Co. but Maxwell insisted that Pergamon had agreed to underwrite its massive debts. In pursuit of that money, Maxwell had written to d'Avigdor-Goldsmid on June 23, 1970, claiming that there existed a binding obligation upon Pergamon to buy EPC from R.M. & Co. which would cause R.M. & Co. to bear "neither profit nor loss." A search through the Pergamon files revealed unsatisfactory evidence of that liability, but in his annual report d'Avigdor-Goldsmid conceded that Pergamon would bear those losses.

D'Avigdor-Goldsmid also reported that Maxwell's continued control over PPI was proving costly. The British company was not receiving any funds from America, and Maxwell had actually sold two subsidiaries of PPI without any consultation. D'Avigdor-Goldsmid's summary was doom-laden. The threat of litigation, he said, "hangs over the company like the mushroom cloud at Hiroshima."

Maxwell, whose omnipresence also hovered like a cloud, was ebullient despite the unqualified censure of his company. Price Waterhouse, he felt, had been determined to paint the worst picture. Accounting, he commented cryptically, "is not the exact science which some of us thought it was." He blamed Price Waterhouse for denigrating the "substantial" profits which he claimed Pergamon earned from its trade with his private companies and attacked their "tortuous" compilation of unrecoverable debts which he could have collected. "In all things and at all times," he concluded, "I have acted in good faith and tried to serve both sides with fairness and equity." Maxwell's stout defense of himself and Chalmers Impey was par for the course—damning but unconvincing—but the principles of accountancy in Britain and in the profession's textbooks were quietly and substantially overhauled to prevent similar mistakes.

The delivery of the Price Waterhouse report set a two-month deadline for Leasco to publish details of its bid for the remaining 62 per cent of the shares. In New York, there was little enthusiasm for any further connection with Britain. Pergamon was plagued by uncertainties and owed more than £3 million, including £2.3 million to the National Westminster Bank. There seemed little reason to bid for a near-bankrupt company. Leasco had written down its $22 million investment to just one dollar in a rescue package which included writing off $44 million of its debts. But Rothschilds, who now valued Pergamon at just £3.6 million, urged their clients to make a bid of 3s 6d per share. The bankers feared that their reputation would suffer if Leasco withdrew, but sentiment and status were at a discount in the equation. On November 3, Leasco announced that "we do not wish to shoulder the burden of owning Pergamon," and both Schwartz and Stevens resigned from the board. Maxwell was jubilant. Keeping PPI had paid rich dividends and he was now poised for his comeback. "I could hardly have dealt the cards better myself," he told the *Daily Telegraph* after he returned from a negotiating session with d'Avigdor-Goldsmid. But speculation of a bid soon petered out. There were doubts whether he possessed enough money and whether the institutions approved of his conduct regarding PPI. But there was already a hint of victory.

During that winter, Maxwell executed another masterstroke. After winning the sympathy of d'Avigdor-Goldsmid, he also secured the allegiance of Leasco's appointee, Felix Kalinski, who abruptly deserted his patrons. Steinberg was incensed but powerless. The balance now depended upon a newcomer to the board, Sir Walter Coutts, a former governor of Uganda and later an assistant vice-chancellor for administration at Warwick University. "We were all fed up with the arguing," recalls Coutts, "but I was particularly antagonistic toward Maxwell." That would change, as Maxwell continued to exercise his charm, albeit from a distance. He took a six-month Kennedy fellowship at Harvard University to study a favorite theme: how to encourage industry to apply the results of scientific research and how governments could shape industry through their purchasing power. The fellowship was financed by an anonymous fund whose source the university was unwilling to reveal, although it was clear that it was in fact Maxwell himself. From afar Maxwell watched as Pergamon's fortunes stumbled and sank. Then he seized his opportunity.

In April 1971, d'Avigdor-Goldsmid was receptive to Maxwell's appeal that their differences should be buried. Pergamon's losses in 1970 had risen to £2.3 million (due mainly to reducing the valuation of the stock of journals and books) and the value of its assets had been reduced by a further £1.2 million to £6.1 million. D'Avigdor-Goldsmid was exhausted by the fight and he was convinced that the company needed calm and its founder's expertise if it were to survive. Unanimously Pergamon's directors, including Kalinski, agreed to forgive and forget everything. Effectively, all the disputes about the loans and all the litigation between Pergamon and Maxwell's private companies were to be dropped; MSI Inc. was to pay $1.5 million to Pergamon for all the rights in the back issues; and PPI was to be placed again under British control. In return, d'Avigdor-Goldsmid supported Maxwell's re-election to the board as a non-executive director. As a gesture of good-will, Pergamon also granted Maxwell a lease on the Hall until 1999 for an annual rent of £1,100 exclusive of overheads. In return, Maxwell offered d'Avigdor-Goldsmid some PPI shares for his personal owner-ship. After remonstration from Coutts, who complained that it was inappropriate, d'Avigdor-Goldsmid tore up the offer. "D'Avigdor-Goldsmid's conduct was sometimes difficult to understand," says Coutts. The DTI inspectors concluded that Maxwell had negotiated a very favorable settlement.

D'Avigdor-Goldsmid, who flew to New York to finalize the deal with the American board of PPI, was honest about his capitulation. Schwartz was outraged: "It was astonishing that Harry surrendered his only le-verage against Maxwell." Both Schwartz and Steinberg flew to Britain to persuade the pension funds to block Maxwell's formal election to the board at the annual meeting in July. Their arguments were greeted with the same stony looks which had glared at Maxwell when he had pleaded to the institutions in the Connaught Rooms 18 months earlier. Maxwell was on the verge of a victorious return. Just one final blemish needed to be cleared: his writs alleging defamation against the *Sunday Times*.

No publicity had been so permanently wounding to Maxwell as the Insight profiles. On the eve of his return to the board, Maxwell needed to prove publicly that the *Sunday Times* had retracted its allegations. To wait for a trial in court was unsatisfactory since it would not start for at least three years and would be both expensive and unpleasant. There were, he believed, more efficacious methods. On January 2, 1970, he had met Roy Thomson to propose that the Canadian become a partner in Maxwell's future bid for the outstanding Pergamon shares. Thomson had rejected the idea but Maxwell took the opportunity to discuss the possibility of settling the libel writs, although the newspa-per's proprietor had a reputation for not interfering with his editorial staff. What Thomson told Maxwell is uncertain but Thomson did ask his lawyers to "examine the idea from all angles, although I am not urging any kind of climb-down by the *Sunday Times.*" Two weeks later, Maxwell wrote to Thomson's son Kenneth, suggesting that since his father had agreed to a settlement it was surprising that the *Sunday*

Times lawyers had not yet submitted their proposals. Was there, he wondered, "some slip-up?" The executives of the Thomson organization were puzzled. Their firm understanding was that the initiative had been taken by Maxwell and that his solicitors would send their proposals. No, said Maxwell, Lord Thomson had personally said that he would initiate the apology. On reference back, Kenneth Thomson denied Maxwell's interpretation. There was again stalemate, although the official announcement that ILSC (which had been sold by d'Avigdor-Goldsmid to BPC in February 1970) had lost £3 million was gratifying confirmation for the Insight team that their initial allegations seemed well founded and that they would be totally vindicated in court. But, unknown to them, by July their editor Harold Evans was prepared to compromise. In return for Maxwell withdrawing the writs, he was ready to publish a long "question and answer" interview in which Maxwell would be permitted a free hand to make his case. Evans, it seems, had lost both belief and interest in the investigation. For the next nine months, Maxwell insisted that he wanted the article also to contain an official withdrawal and an apology, but that was refused. Nothing changed until on December 1, Maxwell telephoned Evans and urged a settlement "because I want to get my company back. Let's settle it. No money, no crawling." Evans recorded in a minute that Maxwell "went on for some time about how important it was for him to get an early settlement and couldn't I as a reasonable man work something out, etc."

Evans suggested again an interview to put the record straight but by the beginning of February their agreement was stumbling on Maxwell's insistence that the *Sunday Times* make a contribution to his costs. "He wants £5,000," minuted the *Sunday Times* lawyer, James Evans, "as the *sine qua non* of settlement." Both the lawyer and the editor rejected the condition because they feared the interpretation which Maxwell might publicly place upon any payment. On the eve of his return to the Pergamon board Maxwell compromised, because timing had become important.

At the end of April 1971, the journalists Hodgson and Page were both on holiday. Unknown to them, on May 2, their newspaper published an appeasing interview with Maxwell. The headline was bold: "The Week Robert Maxwell Bounced Back." The introduction explained that Maxwell, who had just rejoined the Pergamon board, had withdrawn his writs and in return the newspaper "has offered this remarkably resilient businessman the opportunity to express his point of view and describe his plans for Pergamon in the future."

Maxwell recounted that Pergamon had suffered without the benefit of his intimate relations with the journals' editors. Concerning his bid for the company, he was quoted as saying that, although he had sufficient personal finance, he would wait until the annual profits were at least £1 million: "I am not prepared to risk the accusation that I am trying to buy Pergamon back on the cheap." His immediate task, he said, was to relaunch the company's sales and reinvigorate its one thousand editorial advisers around the world. "Now I am back," he said, "we are out of the period of crisis . . . we are a force to be reckoned with." Besides the ebullience, there was also a dose of contrition. Maxwell conceded the validity of the criticism that Pergamon was "largely a one-man band . . . and the one man was spread pretty thin." He also admitted the mistake of selling encyclopedias, although only partially, with a familiar hint that others were really to blame: "I.L.S.C. was a real whopper—the one element in Pergamon that I really regret. I trusted people and I was let down. But as chairman I must and do accept full responsibility."

The article then permitted Maxwell to "correct" four allegations which he described as "of crucial importance, on which I am deeply concerned to set the record straight." In an answer which must reflect some confusion within the newspaper at the time, Maxwell said this about the relationship between Pergamon and MSI Inc.:

> These [relationships] were investigated in great detail by Price Waterhouse & Co., the leading accountants, and although their report described certain parts of the agreements between Pergamon and MSI Inc. as "contradictory to some extent" and ambiguous to a degree where their "precise legal effect is uncertain," it concluded by affirming that "in all the circumstances we consider that the accounting treatment adopted by the Group accounts at September 30, 1969, is fair." In the light of this, the business relationships between the Maxwell family companies and Pergamon have continued during the split, and will continue in the future, virtually as before.

This was an unusual interpretation of the Price Waterhouse report. The accountants in reporting that the treatment of the 1969 accounts was "fair" were referring to their *own* treatment, since they, Price Waterhouse, had compiled the 1969 accounts. The accountants were *not* referring to the trading relationship which Maxwell had cultivated between Pergamon and his own companies. On that issue, they had criticized and substantially changed the 1968 accounts because of the hitherto undisclosed agreements between Pergamon and MSI Inc.

The article ended with Maxwell buoyantly demanding the restoration of the Stock Exchange quotation since there was by then no chance of new revelations. "The [DTI] inspectors," he said, "would have been impelled to take action immediately if they found any evidence of serious offenses." If Maxwell was hoping that the article would aid his rehabilitation, he was not disappointed. It was so effective that the DTI deliberately timed the release of its first report to coincide with his anticipated return to Pergamon's board.

During the previous ten months, Maxwell had appeared before the inspectors, accompanied by John Silkin and occasionally by Morris Finer. Maxwell and his lawyers claim that the procedure adopted by the inspectors disarmed them completely. Questions would be asked, documents were either requested or proffered, but there were no allegations, criticisms or direct accusations. According to one of those at the hearings, "The inspectors never showed that they believed his critics or disbelieved Maxwell." The inspectors prided themselves on the fact that they never sprang any surprises upon him but gave clear notice of the areas of questioning. Regularly, he left the sessions content that the inspectors had accepted his explanations: "It was terribly chatty and chummy. The worst might be Stable saying, 'Oh, come, come, Mr. Maxwell,' but nothing more." Stable had after all said in the Court of Appeal that he would recall any individual if he was to be criticized and "ask them if there is an explanation. I think that natural justice requires that." In Maxwell's view, Stable's smokescreen was so effective that at one point, which they would quote in the report as an example of the "casual and unbusinesslike manner" in which ILSC was managed, Maxwell was even seduced to reply, "I can see the value of these enquiries."

On June 4, 1971, Maxwell was traveling by car with Silkin to the twelfth questioning session when he mentioned rumors that a first, interim report which concentrated exclusively upon ILSC had been completed. Maxwell suggested that Silkin should ask the two inspectors for confirmation. Silkin refused. At the end of the session, Maxwell, to Silkin's fury, asked Stable, "I have heard that the report is finished and it is damaging. I'm surprised because I thought that you were bound to requestion me if there was any criticism." Stable's reply, which was recorded in the official transcript, was to the effect that the report had not yet been submitted and that nothing critical would appear without first "fairly and squarely" informing Maxwell.

The report had in fact been completed and signed by the inspectors two days earlier although it was presented to the Conservative Minister, John Davies, only five days later. The decision whether to publish depended entirely upon Davies. Some time after the exchange between Maxwell and Stable, the inspector wrote to Silkin announcing that the report had been formally completed. On July 10 Davies, as required by law, had allowed the Pergamon board, including Maxwell, to read a copy of the report. Maxwell was appalled. Silkin, who knew that the courts had no power to prevent the government publishing, urged the DTI to desist because all the undertakings made by the inspectors had been broken.

Within days, the report's existence was widely known, and pressure intensified, especially from the City, for its immediate release. Lord Shawcross even allowed himself to be named as one of those lobbying the Minister. On July 13, the Minister agreed. The report was published, sweeping aside Maxwell's imminent re-election to the Pergamon board and changing his life forever.

Stable and Leach had adopted a style which would do credit to the author of a pot-boiling thriller. Under headings such as "A False Statement," "Another False Statement," "More Misleading Statements" and "Still More Misleading Statements" they wove a gripping narrative which persuasively suggested that ILSC was negligently and deceitfully managed. None of the revelations in their 209-page report would attract more attention than the chapter entitled "A Remarkable Sale."

The date of the "remarkable sale" was June 30, 1968, the day on which Pergamon, under certain circumstances, became liable to compensate BPC if ILSC's profits did not total £500,000. The sale was for no less than five thousand complete sets of New Caxton encyclopedias at $70 per set. ILSC's customer was Pergamon's own subsidiary, PPI in New York. At ILSC's board meeting the following day to review the company's profits, Maxwell, according to the inspectors, made no mention of that crucial sale. The inspectors also claimed that on that day ILSC neither had a written order for that sale nor even possessed that number of sets "in a deliverable state." The sale, they believed, was arranged in autumn 1968 and "deliberately ante-dated so that the profit on the so-called sale could be credited to ILSC in the warranty period which ended on the 30th June 1968." It amounted to a charge that Maxwell was guilty of deception. (Maxwell vigorously denied that the sale was ever credited to ILSC's profits and insisted that the inspectors ignored his evidence that ILSC did not make a profit on the transaction, and that he had notified the ILSC board. He repeatedly criticized the correctness of the inspectors' finding.)

The report's examination of Maxwell's management of the encyclopedia business was critical, especially of his dictatorial methods and his utterance of unsupported statements. The inspectors alleged that he had sent a crucial letter regarding the creation of ILSC which was "misleading and untrue"; that he allowed important documents to be destroyed; that proper records were not kept; that he must have known that the letter to Bernard Schwartz was not true; that his letter of August 23, 1969, that ILSC "is now trading profitably" was "calculated to mislead," and that "the history of ILSC, with regard to what was disclosed, is a series of suppressions of information and of optimism verging on recklessness with the occasional statement which was untrue and calculated to mislead."

According to the inspectors' account, Maxwell compounded his wrongdoing while giving his formal evidence on oath. They quote the example of the bid document for Butterworths which contained his reassuring statement that ILSC had "informed Pergamon that sales and profits for the first three months of operations are running at the level forecast." During the questioning Maxwell had insisted that the statement had been approved both by his advisers and by the BPC directors at a meeting in Fitzroy Square. In contradiction, Stable and Leach pointed out to Maxwell that not only did the BPC directors deny having seen the draft but they also denied there ever was a meeting in Fitzroy Square. Maxwell replied: "I am amazed. That is all I can say. It is incomprehensible to me," and he added that the circulars were given a wide distribution. Later he said, "I can recollect clearing the document with the BPC directors of ILSC." In their report, the inspectors state that they had requested searches in the files of eight separate principals and advisers—the merchant banks, solicitors, stockbrokers, at BPC and at Pergamon—and not a single original or carbon copy was found of the draft document. On a later occasion, the inspectors asked Maxwell if he himself had yet found a copy of a letter signed by an ILSC director which gave that memorable forecast. Maxwell replied, "Not yet." The inspectors therefore concluded, "Mr. Maxwell's assertion . . . is inaccurate." They also pointed out that neither Maxwell nor Kerman had ever, throughout the questioning, sought to "justify the statement."

Among several other deals questioned was the sale of Pictorial Knowledge for £200,000 from ILSC to Pergamon on August 12, 1969, which according to the inspectors betrayed "an element of desperation"

(Above) Maxwell as Private Du Maurier (back row, right), the keen footballer, with the Sixth Battalion of the North Staffs Regiment in Cliftonville in 1944.

(Left) Second Lieutenant Maxwell receiving the Military Cross from General Montgomery in March 1945.

(Below) Maxwell as an officer with the 1/5th Battalion of the Queen's Royal Regiment (West Surrey) before the crossing of the Rhine in late March 1945. Maxwell is in the back row, eighth from the left.

(Left) Maxwell and his wife, Elizabeth, in London in 1947.

(Below left) Maxwell with his eldest daughter, Anne. There were nine children in the Maxwell family.

(Below right) Peter Orton, Maxwell's partner at Lange, Maxwell & Springer, was an intellectual who did not always appreciate Maxwell's style of business.

(Left) Maxwell with Tönjes Lange, the Springer executive who taught him about the profitability of publishing scientific journals. Maxwell called him "Onkel."

(Below left) Gunther Heyden, recruited to LMS in Berlin, sitting on Maxwell's first Cadillac, in London in 1950. Ownership of foreign cars for British subjects was forbidden, so the car was not registered in Maxwell's name.

(Below right) Kurt Wallersteiner, Maxwell's partner in the hectic barter trade, an investor in Simpkin Marshall and later a convicted fraudster.

(III)

(Above left) Ambitious to become Britain's prime minister, Maxwell valued his friendship with Hugh Gaitskell; but his closeness to Labour leaders failed to win him the high office he felt he deserved.

(Above right) Maxwell's energetic election campaigns won him decisive votes in a marginal constituency, but by 1974 his style alienated some of his supporters and denied him the crucial support needed to win back his seat.

(Below) In 1968, Maxwell was prepared to give up politics to own the *News of the World,* but his bid was defeated by an alliance between Sir William "Pissing Billy" Carr, the newspaper's owner, and the then unknown Rupert Murdoch. Afterward, Maxwell was convinced that the Establishment would deny him the success he sought.

(Above) On June 18, 1969, Maxwell announced the sale of Pergamon to the American, Saul Steinberg, who described their agreement as "perfect."

(Below) At the press conference on June 18, Maxwell's banker Richard Fleming was less enthusiastic than his client, whom he had privately informed that he wanted to sever their relationship because he was dissatisfied with Pergamon's accounts.

(Below) The first investigation was conducted by Lord Shawcross, the chairman of the Takeover Panel. While some praised Shawcross's ability to destroy Maxwell's explanations, Maxwell complained that he had been unfairly victimized.

(Above) Even at the shareholders' meeting, on October 11, 1969, when he was deposed from the board of Pergamon, Maxwell's bitterness was interrupted by some good humor.

(Above) After more than a decade in the wilderness, Maxwell astonished his critics when in April 1981 he bought the British Printing Corporation and, with the support of Lord Kearton, saved the company from bankruptcy and earned himself new respectability in the City.

(Right) His most important ally in the resurrection was Sir Robert Clark, of the merchant bank Hill Samuel.

At 7pm on July 13, 1984, Leslie Carpenter *(above left)* and Sir Alex Jarratt *(above right)* of Reed International reluctantly agreed to sell Maxwell the Mirror Group of newspapers, transferring Northcliffe's former empire to the son of a Czech peasant.

(Above) Clive Thornton, the chairman of the Mirror Group, arrived at 7am on July 14 in his office. "I couldn't miss Mr. Maxwell," he told reporters later, "because he was sitting behind my desk."

(VII)

Cap'n Bob at the stern of his luxury yacht, the *Lady Ghislaine,*
from where he probably fell into the Atlantic on November 5, 1991.

Maxwell's "state" funeral in Jerusalem added the final mystery
to his life. "Now the circle closes," said Betty Maxwell.
"He has returned to his roots."

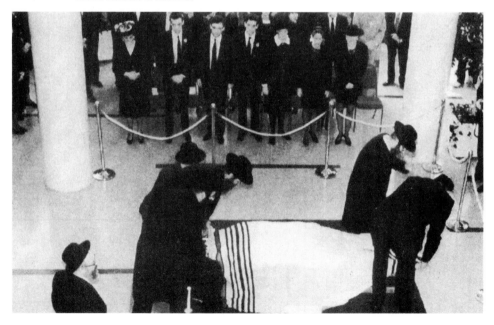

to boost ILSC's profits. Concerning that alleged contract, stated the report, "Not a single director of Pergamon [other than Mr. Maxwell] admitted ever having seen [the contract] or been aware that Pergamon had made this purchase." Altogether, the inspectors convincingly presented Maxwell as a liar and fraudster.

But the report was also, in some instances, unfairly biased against Maxwell. In the case of Hedley Le Bas and Rod Jenman, the two Caxton encyclopedia executives who bore tarnished reputations within the encyclopedia trade, the inspectors sided absolutely with Maxwell's critics although both had been dismissed for alleged dishonesty. Both Robert Fleming and Chalmers Impey were gently chided in the report but then seemingly excused by statements such as "Flemings too had lost faith in Mr. Maxwell and his integrity," or "Mr. Briggs, due to a severe impediment in his speech, is at a great disadvantage." Although other personalities involved, like Kerman, Ormrod and Clark, were criticized, the overwhelming preponderance of blame for the sins committed was placed on Maxwell. BPC's directors, who in many instances were also to blame, were censured but with considerably less emphasis. As Maxwell retorted, "I am constantly being amazed by the evidence from the BPC side." But whenever contradictions of evidence were cited, the inspectors invariably concluded that Maxwell's version was to be disbelieved.

Probably the inspectors best revealed their standpoint by their emotive explanation about how Maxwell recruited the Caxton sales team in South Africa. Describing what is normally called "headhunting," the inspectors stated, "Poaching is a polite [description]: sabotaging is a more robust description, but the complaint is sabotaging by poaching." The inspectors conceded that some might say that the poaching was "a perfectly standard commercial tug of war" but they felt that "such a standard leaves much to be desired." The inspectors were prim and naive about common business practices and demonstrated clear bias against Maxwell. Overall, the report revealed a lack of balance and a propensity to exaggerate where the bald facts appeared sufficiently discreditable.

The report's conclusions concentrated exclusively upon Maxwell. The catastrophic mismanagement of ILSC, the inspectors claimed, was principally due to Maxwell, of whom they said:

> He is a man of great energy, drive and imagination, but unfortunately an apparent fixation as to his own abilities causes him to ignore the views of others if these are not compatible. This is very

evident in the recurrent (and frequent) changes of personnel in ILSC which were one of the factors which contributed to the disaster. Neither his fellow directors, his professional advisers, nor his employees were able to sway his views and actions. The concept of a Board being responsible for policy was alien to him.

We are also convinced that Mr. Maxwell regarded his stewardship duties fulfilled by showing the maximum profits which any transaction could be devised to show. Furthermore, in reporting to shareholders and investors he had a reckless and unjustified optimism which enabled him on some occasions to disregard unpalatable facts and on others to state what he must have known to be untrue. . . .

We regret having to conclude that, notwithstanding Mr. Maxwell's acknowledged abilities and energy, he is not in our opinion a person who can be relied on to exercise proper stewardship of a publicly quoted company.

The publication of the last paragraph on July 13, 1971, was unprecedented, unmerciful and devastating. It amounted to nothing less, as a judge later said, than his "business murder." Maxwell had finally been crucified and, beyond his family and his closest advisers, there were few who expected or even willed a resurrection. At a press conference, Maxwell denounced the "so-called City Establishment" who had been let off very lightly. The report, he said, was "a smear and a witch-hunt." The inspectors had gone beyond their powers in what was a Star Chamber procedure and their unwarranted conclusion had virtually barred him from the possibility of making a living. Overnight, all Maxwell's hopes of election to the Pergamon board were utterly crushed. The inspectors' indictment, which was so warmly welcomed in the City, had intentionally made him a leper within the business community.

The publication was timed to coincide with Maxwell's return to the Pergamon board. That was no longer possible. Maxwell withdrew to Headington Hall. The Establishment, he felt, knew how to keep outsiders firmly beyond the pale.

If Maxwell had ever suffered a trauma, it was reflected on his face when he read for the first time the inspectors' report published in July 1971. Indelibly engraved on Maxwell's brow was the inspectors' damning judgment about his management of Pergamon. He always insisted that his fight through the courts to reverse their indictment was successful. That is not true, but understanding his persistent and erroneous insistence helps to explain both the inner dilemmas of Maxwell and the environment in Britain in which he desperately sought to succeed. Whether he would ever have been satisfied by any inspectors' report is most unlikely, but his initial apprehension about the inspectors' conduct of that inquiry, the realization of those suspicions and the attitude of Britain's judges toward both Maxwell and the inspectors confirmed for Maxwell the Establishment's prejudice, dishonesty and vindictiveness.

On the day of publication, Silkin issued a writ seeking a court declaration that the inspectors had failed in their obligation to be fair and accurate as required by the rules of natural justice. At the court hearing in September, Silkin asked Mr. Justice Forbes to prevent two further reports being published—the first on Pergamon itself and the second on MSI Inc.—until the trial concerning the inspectors had been completed.

Mr. Justice Forbes was sympathetic. In his view, Maxwell should have been given the opportunity to defend himself: "Surely, before they started making their swinging criticisms they should have said to Mr. Maxwell, 'Now look, we are minded to say this. You tell us why we should not.' " Counsel for the DTI insisted that the inspectors had said those words but Maxwell had failed to grasp the opportunities to defend himself. Forbes was unconvinced, especially after the inspectors admitted that they had not repeated every tentative accusation to Maxwell because it would be "unnecessarily burdensome." All they needed to do, they claimed, was to make sure that Maxwell realized that his "conduct was open to question." Forbes disagreed. The inspectors' failure, he judged, to allow Maxwell a proper opportunity to rebut their criticisms amounted to a denial of natural justice. He cited what Lord Denning had said in 1970: "Before they condemn or criticize a man they must give him a fair opportunity for correcting or contradicting what is said against him." That requirement, said Forbes, had not been followed and he criticized the inspectors for intentionally adopting a standard substantially below that set by Denning and very different to the procedure which they had originally pledged themselves to observe.

Although Forbes had given valuable ammunition to Maxwell, he emphasized that the inspectors had not been unfair but had simply not followed the correct procedure. On a technicality he refused to grant Maxwell's application for an injunction but urged a speedy trial on the substantial issue, which, he speculated, Maxwell would probably win and as a consequence there would have to be a new inquiry. This was welcome but nevertheless cold comfort. A single judge could not eradicate the damnation inflicted by the inspectors' concluding paragraph.

Maxwell did not appeal against the Forbes judgment but instead waited months for the trial to be heard. John Silkin was allowed to represent his interests on the Pergamon board while he remained as an unpaid consultant and still controlled PPI. But his opportunities of management were strictly limited.

On April 11, 1972, the DTI published the inspectors' second report, which concentrated upon his original entry into the encyclopedia business in 1965 with the purchase of Newnes and upon his subsequent highly publicized world tour to sell Chambers encyclopedias. In some respects, the report was more mellow, which suggested that the Forbes judgment might have caused the inspectors some concern. Greater allowances were made for the possibility of genuine accounting errors, but the overall effect, based on the evidence, was a severe criticism of Maxwell's management and his deliberate overstating of profits.

Quoting Maxwell's own oral evidence, the inspectors showed that while Maxwell had claimed that he had relied upon his experts, Briggs and Bennett, the accountants had testified that Maxwell bullied them into recording profits which they disputed. "I think," Bennett told the inspectors, "there is a limit how far one can argue when one is an employee." The inspectors accepted Bennett's evidence that Maxwell had forced him to record unrealistic profits but at times also accepted that Maxwell had support for his creative accounting from Chalmers Impey. The inspectors also suggested that Maxwell had submitted to them as evidence phony documents and had used "bogus" invoices to justify his claims of record profits. Concerning the press conference at the Dorchester on his return from the world tour, the inspectors stated, "We are firmly of the opinion that the claims which Mr. Maxwell made were exaggerated and that he knew that they were." His management, they reported, fell below the standards one should expect of the director of a public company.

At the end of this report, the two inspectors sought to defend themselves against the charges that they had breached the rules of natural justice, but by default they partially demonstrated the truth of Maxwell's complaints. "When we came to write this report," they stated, "and following our normal practice of checking we realized that we had not put to Mr. Maxwell the effect of the evidence which we had heard on the question of his world tour and the press conference which he is alleged to have held shortly after his return to the U.K. In order to remedy this oversight on our part Mr. Stable wrote to Mr. Maxwell's solicitor, Mr. Silkin, a letter dated July 14, 1971. . . ."

The coincidence that the letter should arrive the day following the publication of the first report was unfortunate. Stable had suggested that Maxwell give his answers within fourteen days but Silkin replied that they needed time for research, and suggested a session after August 18. Amid quibbling over dates and a refusal by the inspectors to guarantee that Maxwell's answer would be included in their final report, the dispute escalated. Silkin insisted that Maxwell's only recourse was to reapply to the courts. This the inspectors interpreted as a deliberate tactic to delay the completion of their reports. "Our own conviction," they stated, "is that Mr. Maxwell was given by us a fair and reasonable opportunity to deal with and comment on the matters raised. . . ."

The report's publication passed virtually unnoticed. For most, Maxwell was already commercially "dead" and the inspectors' findings served only to place another layer of cement over his grave. Maxwell, however, had become determined to avenge the injustice and was spending many hours every week with John Silkin and his assistant, John Levy, to prepare their arguments for the initial court case; namely a declaration that the inspectors were bound by the rules of natural justice which they had ignored.

The task for his lawyers was arduous. Only the publication of the first report, they would later explain, had caused Maxwell fully to understand the gravity of the charges against him and had spurred him to produce the documentary evidence which rebutted the inspectors' report. Even so, their endless consultations in his office would be repeatedly interrupted by his telephone calls to brokers, bankers, lawyers or editors occupied in producing Pergamon's scientific journals. His ability to glide apparently without a moment's pause from one complicated subject to another, often switching languages between simultaneous telephone conversations, was impressive. But, above all, they appreciated that as they worked amid a shower of curses and loud exhortations, his resilience was impenetrable. In one particularly difficult all-night session where two lawyers and three secretaries were editing one hundred pages of a closely argued legal submission, Maxwell was urged: "Do us a favor, Bob. Just go away and let us get on with it." To the lawyers' surprise, their client for once obeyed. At 6:00 a.m. he returned. Everyone assumed he had been asleep but he was dressed in the same clothes. "I didn't go to bed," he roared, "I've been earning your fees." Maxwell had been to the Les Ambassadeurs gaming club and had won over five thousand pounds. His visit to the casino was not unusual. Maxwell, an instinctive and natural gambler in business, was for years a familiar visitor in some London clubs and was known as a winner rather than a loser. Winning the case against the government inspectors before Mr. Justice Wien which started on November 20, 1972, was not as easy.

Sam Silkin QC MP, John's older brother, appeared for Maxwell and ran into difficulties immediately. Speaking in slow and measured terms which invited interruption, Silkin opened his argument by suggesting that, had the inspectors properly heard Maxwell's case, they would have written a different report. Even before lunch on that first day, Wien seemed to be fidgeting. By the end of the afternoon, he displayed unmistakable signs of impatience and interjected that he would not hear any arguments about facts or about the quality of the evidence. It was, he said, a case about procedure. An unedifying skirmishing started as Silkin persisted and Wien reprimanded him.

As they looked up at the judge, Maxwell's lawyers did not need the powers of clairvoyance to realize that there was no sympathy for the client or his cause on the bench above. Despondently they accepted that the odds were irrecoverably against them. The bias, they believed, was not only against their case but directed against them personally. The prejudice was unpleasant to mention but was, in their view, a reality. Like their client, all the barristers and solicitors were Jewish. "Before that day," recalls one of those lawyers, "I disbelieved the possibility of anti-semitism, but I realized the truth at the end." The sentiment was unanimous among Maxwell's lawyers, who had after all appeared before so many other judges, so one may conclude that their suspicions must have had some validity despite one circumstance which could also explain so much—namely, that Sir Phillip Wien was a Welsh Jew. (A less emotional view would be that Wien simply did not believe Maxwell's case.) That night, Maxwell refused to be infected by their despondency and belligerently urged them to fight on regardless.

For three days Silkin sought to weave the arguments about the merits of Maxwell's unargued case into the constraints that Wien had established. At the end of the third day, Maxwell demanded a change of tactics. Sitting cramped with his four lawyers in Silkin's room in the House of Commons, Maxwell was aggressive. "I must have my third leg," he shouted, implying that his lawyer should attack the inspectors themselves. Quietly, Silkin refused because Wien had emphatically forbidden that argument. Eventually, Maxwell seemed persuaded, climbed into his Rolls-Royce and drove off. Early the following morning, Maxwell telephoned his friend and said, "You're fired. I'll argue the case myself." His lawyers were amazed. "You're like a Christian going into the arena," said one but he was ignored. Silkin made his apologies to Wien and departed.

Dismissing the barristers was a doubly perilous act for a man who had defended himself in front of the DTI inspectors as a hapless innocent who relied in matters of accountancy and finance upon his experts. How would Wien interpret Maxwell's impetuosity other than as confirming the inspectors' conclusions about Maxwell "ignoring the views of others if these are not compatible." It was also a perfect example of Maxwell's inability to understand the impression he was creating. Anxious not to suffer the same accusations as the inspectors, Wien allowed Maxwell four days to prepare his case.

Working with his solicitor through the night in a suite at the Savoy Hotel, Maxwell prepared his presentation. On Monday morning, he rose with solemnity from the silk's bench in the courtroom. The result was an embarrassing shambles. Unable spontaneously to fashion a speech to build an argument, he presented a woolly monologue which ignored his prepared brief. In cross-examination of witnesses, he could not ask questions to support his case. At every stage, Wien was indignant about the submissions which Maxwell thrust toward him. With jarring repetition, Wien interjected: "What is the point of this, Mr. Maxwell?" Had Wien sat in Maxwell's board room with as limited an experience of finance as Maxwell displayed in the art of advocacy, Maxwell would have been equally impatient. After six days, Maxwell finally conceded that even he could not override the will of a British judge and selected a new barrister to represent him. Michael Ogden QC, an Establishment figure with a fruity voice, was deemed the most suitable. It was naturally to no avail.

In his judgment, Wien pulverized the plaintiff. The inspectors, he said, had acted "eminently fairly" despite Maxwell's deliberate obstruction, by giving him "chapter and verse" of the case he was expected to answer. They did not have to show Maxwell their draft conclusions before publication. It was sufficient, he judged, that they gave him "a fair opportunity of replying to what is said against him." Clearly irritated by Maxwell, Wien ended by echoing the inspectors' own conclusions: "He regarded professional advisers as tools to achieve his own ends and if they gave him advice not to his own liking he simply brushed it aside." Maxwell was not in court on December 20 to hear the judgment although the costs were estimated at £50,000. He announced that he would appeal. With absolute certainty, he would again be judged by Lord Denning.

One of Maxwell's great weaknesses and a source of irritation to others was his unwillingness to believe or even care that his behavior had left a bad taste in someone's mouth. His insensitivity was of course also a source of strength; but while that doggedness might have provided the finance to open the doors to the Court of Appeal, it did not help much further. In January 1974, Lord Denning might have surmised that he was in a slight quandary. After all, he had set the guidelines for the observance of natural justice in 1970 and both Forbes and Wien, in contradiction of each other, had claimed to implement them. It would be, however, to underestimate the potent virtue of the common law not to accept that each judge fashions the law to suit the case. If Lord Denning were to accept that the inspectors had not followed his requirements as rigorously enunciated four years earlier, they would have been obliged to reopen the whole inquiry. Maxwell, it was commonly agreed, had committed too many sins to be granted that victory. Hence a not unusual ritual was performed.

In his judgment, Lord Denning emphatically rejected Maxwell's appeal, citing from the original inquiry's transcript that in the case of each criticism the inspectors had indisputably put the facts "fairly and squarely to Mr. Maxwell." Wien was right, said Denning: "This is nothing more or less than an attempt by Mr. Maxwell to appeal from the findings of the inspectors to the courts. But Parliament has given no appeal. So Mr. Maxwell has tried to get round it by attacking the conduct of the inspectors themselves. In this he has failed utterly."

But Maxwell had not completely failed. Just as the accountancy profession changed their practices in the wake of the Pergamon revelations, so were the procedures for future DTI inquiries changed. Quietly, a procedural order was introduced spelling out how the rules of natural justice had to be followed; it included a provision that those who would be criticized in a report had to be given the opportunity to comment before publication. It was, some felt, an implicit criticism of Owen Stable's management of the inquiry.

Maxwell was naturally determined to have the last word. In November 1973, the third and final DTI report, concentrating upon the private companies, was published. It was a voluminous and once again damning indictment with accusations of phoney and back-dated invoices and of rewritten board minutes; examples of Maxwell presenting documents allegedly to support his case which failed completely to live up to their promise; and repeated examples of how Maxwell sowed unusual confusion between his private companies and Pergamon. The inspectors encapsulated that confusion perfectly in paragraph 916: "On the 30th

June 1969, the debt of £104,166 was paid by MSI(DS) on behalf of MSI Inc. to MSI (1964) on behalf of Pergamon with money received from R.M. & Co. as trustee of MSI Inc. out of the proceeds of sale of the warehouse property at Wolverton, which is . . .''

An example of Maxwell's compartmentalization suggesting the intentional injection of a conflict of interests into his commercial affairs which caused the inspectors to be so distrustful was cited in another exchange. Leach asked Maxwell why, in June 1966, there had been a sudden need for an agreement between Pergamon and MSI Inc. Maxwell replied: "Because MSI Inc. continuously feared the competition of R.M. & Co. . . . and R.M. & Co. refused to be bound by this arrangement." Both private companies were owned and effectively managed by Maxwell, yet he was suggesting that he was in genuine competition with himself.

The third report was tarnished by the inspectors' admission at the beginning that the next contained an error. Although it was not serious, and only affected 9 out of 1,254 paragraphs in the report, their embarrassment was perfect ammunition for Maxwell's counter-attack. Contemporaneous to the publication of the third DTI report, he issued a thick press release entitled "They Must Be Fair," which charged the inspectors with damaging his reputation and going out of their way "to whitewash everyone else."

Maxwell's document succinctly reflected the problem which the inspectors themselves found difficult to overcome. Every explanation provoked more questions and confusion. His own defense document proves that, even at the risk of possible unfairness, he was criticized on a balance of probabilities. Yet Maxwell's publication and the inspectors' own mistake sowed real seeds of doubt.

The publication of the third report in November 1973 coincided with another attempt by Maxwell to return to the Pergamon board. Few could believe it possible that after all the revelations he still possessed the sheer energy and courage to attempt a comeback. The inspectors did not hide their own dismay that despite their massive indictments he gave no appearance of being crippled. In their final report they stated: "to outward appearances, [the criticisms have not] abashed him or affected his fixation as to his own abilities." After more than three years' hard toil, they had failed to suppress the businessman. At last, Maxwell was on the verge of resurrecting himself.

11

The national newspaper headlines were succinct: "Maxwell Rides Again," "The Second Coming of Mr. Maxwell." He shared the belief that he was about to stage a triumphant return from the wilderness to become once again the chairman of Pergamon and a Member of Parliament. Just as he had never relinquished complete control of Pergamon, he had similarly struggled to retain his position in his Bucks constituency, although in the aftermath of his election defeat his relations with some important party members had soured. Even from his entrenched position, his bid to return was fraught.

Soon after the 1970 election, the Maxwells had organized votes of censure in several branches in the constituency against Jim Lyons, the election agent, whom they blamed for allowing the party organization to deteriorate to the extent that crucial votes had been lost. As the emotional accusations and critical reports materialized, Lyons requested that the party's National Executive Committee undertake a proper investigation. Reg Underhill, the assistant national agent, arrived in the constituency on a Friday morning in early January 1971 expecting to leave at the end of the day. Instead, the inquiry lasted until 2:45 on Sunday morning. The drama in the New Bradwell Labour Hall as both Maxwells set out the indictment against Lyons epitomized all the circumstances which had frustrated his political ambitions. On one side of the room was Underhill, formerly a junior insurance clerk, born in Leyton, east London, whose life's credo was steeped in the traditional strengths and weaknesses of the British working class— loyal, decent but for some too blinkered. Underhill was dedicated to the party and Transport House, whose inefficiency and petty politics were criticized even by Harold Wilson. On the other side of the room were two millionaires born in Czechoslovakia and France who had joined the party a mere eleven years earlier, and they were telling Underhill over and over again how the British working class should be organized. "I didn't want to crush him," sighed Underhill sixteen years later, "but he kept on repeating himself. He did go on." The rightness of the Maxwells' pleas was irrelevant. The Labour Party's representative was not in the mood to take lessons from their ilk.

Paradoxically, in view of Maxwell's complaints against the DTI inspectors, Lyons was not told beforehand what charges he was expected to answer, but he was not slow to argue that there had been no complaints, only praise, until the election defeat. That was not quite true but the official report issued by Transport House was prepared to accept Lyons's defense and condemned the Maxwells for having distorted the evidence and "exaggerated [the complaints] beyond limits that could be substantiated." Underhill's report illuminated a distasteful relationship between the family and the agent and criticized the manipulations of Maxwell's supporters to increase their representation in party meetings. Officially, Transport House "severely censured" Maxwell, his wife and "others associated with him" for interfering with Lyons's work and for denying the agent absolute control over the election funds. Further, it ordered the constituency's rules to be amended to prevent the packing of the General Management Committee. Maxwell was personally "warned as to his future conduct." There was little precedent for such a sweeping condemnation of a former MP and his wife. "I told the constituency," recalls Underhill, "to look for a new candidate."

Maxwell was in America when the report was publicized. If either he or Betty were embarrassed, it never showed. Both let it be known that they were still attached to the constituency and expected to fight the next election. In most parts of Buckinghamshire, there was little overt reaction to the prospect but in the working-class area of Wolverton there was positive dismay.

The Bucks Labour Party had been founded in Wolverton in 1917 and dedicated activists like Frank Atter, a party member for twenty-one years, saw themselves as the rock of socialism. To those members, loyalty to the party is as precious as loyalty to a school or a cricket club for those of another class. The Transport House inquiry and the censure were personally hurtful. During the summer, following the publication of the first DTI report, Atter and others in his branch were struck by the similarity in criticisms expressed by the inspectors and Transport House. From their limited and narrowly focused experiences, they had not realized that Maxwell's treatment of Lyons and his cavalier treatment of themselves as councillors reflected his behavior in business.

They were angry that Maxwell's oft repeated promises of future employment on the land he had bought from British Rail in Wolverton had failed to materialize and they more than ever resented his critical lectures about their allegedly parochial attitudes toward the new town in Milton Keynes. Compared to Maxwell they were inarticulate and even mute. To his face, they were unable adequately to express their disenchantment about his stranglehold over the party organization which prevented them openly debating with him their views about political events. He interpreted their passivity as acquiescence and prided himself on his qualities of leadership especially of the workers. Unfortunately, he failed to make the distinction that these were not his employees. "He just didn't think that the common man had any common sense," according to Geoff Foster, the regional organizer. The first to protest against the grip of pro-Maxwellites over the constituency had been Ray Bellchambers in 1960.

Bellchambers, who was employed at the Wolverton railway works and had been a member of the party since the age of fifteen, criticized Maxwell at a ward meeting. Without his knowledge, weeks later, Bellchambers was formally suspended from the party as the first step toward expulsion. "The first I heard was when a friend telephoned," he recalls. Bellchambers appealed to the party's National Executive at Transport House who ordered the pro-Maxwellites to reinstate the member because their act was unconstitutional. Reluctantly, the constituency complied but it did not hide its irritation.

The working-class unease about Maxwell after the 1970 election defeat was articulated by new members who had recently taken jobs at the Open University at Milton Keynes. Young men like Geoffrey Edge, a lecturer, did not believe that Maxwell was a natural socialist. They were ambitious, irreverent newcomers who expressed, in Maxwell's opinion, a lack of respect for the status quo. Like Atter and Bellchambers, Edge and the other lecturers joined and worked for the Labour Party not because of the candidate, but for the cause. In their minds, the party exists to change society, and the evenings spent in political debate were important to their lives. Edge says that they joined the party with the best intentions but gradually resented the stifling of opportunities for their brand of political debate, although it was unlikely that university socialism would find many converts in the old rural constituency. "If you didn't agree with him," says Edge, "you had to go. When the government inspectors said the same about him, we realized that our feelings weren't misplaced. We just didn't like the lack of freedom of speech in the constituency." Maxwell's belief that he would continue as their candidate provoked their ire. In the autumn of 1971, although there was no liaison between the two dissenting groups (the workers had little in common with the lecturers), they felt individually predisposed to demand a new candidate.

At the end of October, the Wolverton branch passed and publicized a motion of "no confidence" in Maxwell and warned that they would not work for him in future campaigns. The resolution, proposed by Frank Atter, stated that Maxwell's candidature "would result in a humiliating defeat at the next election, with a corresponding and lasting erosion of Labour morale and support." Within twenty-four hours the constituency Labour Party was deeply split. Wolverton's refusal to work for a candidate would be a serious impediment to any campaign. The question was whether the candidate was more important than party unity. Maxwell had no doubt about the answer. Confident that he still retained the support of the majority, he responded forcefully. Atter, he claimed, was unrepresentative, undemocratic and irresponsible. It was, he announced, "an unprovoked personal attack which was made without notice and without giving me the courtesy of an opportunity to reply." Atter's comment was harsh: "What notice did he give Jim Lyons or Ray Bellchambers?"

Throughout 1972 the local party was plunged into a frustrating, fratricidal conflict. Public rows are not uncommon in the Labour Party, but the effect on a marginal constituency is more damaging than most. At the end of the year, Lyons retired and Transport House refused to sanction the appointment of a new agent. The party's organization in the constituency began quickly to disintegrate as Geoff Foster paid repeated visits to "make sure we had no more shenanigans about membership." Fifteen years later, the scars had still not disappeared. "It was rugged and unpleasant," according to Atter, and "Absolutely unremitting," according to Edge. The pro-Maxwellites led by Jim Cassidy, the constituency's president, were equally hurt: "It was ugly." Although outsiders would attempt to characterize the battle as ideological, the issues of left and right were not strictly relevant. Cassidy and Atter never disagreed that the floating voter ruled in Bucks and only a centrist candidate could win the seat for Labour. The issue was Maxwell himself and for the majority like Cassidy, who described himself as a Gaitskellite, their former candidate was ideal: "He succeeded from nothing. The other side could never dream of the poverties and personal tragedies which Bob suffered. Yet he's a giver, not a taker."

By 1973, what had previously been confined to arguments hardened into an outright struggle for power. Under Betty Maxwell's chairmanship, a meeting approved a motion proposed by Robert Maxwell that Edge was "guilty of anti-party activities" and voted to expel him. Other anti-Maxwellites were not voted on to committees, and councillors who were critics of Maxwell lost their party's sponsorship for the local elections. Transport House was powerless other than to forbid the constituency to begin the process for selecting a parliamentary candidate. London's hope that another candidate would somehow appear to heal the divisions ignored the reality that the executive committee was firmly pro-Maxwell. In summer, the probability of a general election meant that a decision could no longer be delayed. Maxwell was summoned to Transport House for a private conversation about Underhill's report, while Cassidy was allowed to call a selection conference for September 29. Maxwell now tried to mend his relations with Wolverton.

On July 9 he politely wrote to Atter outlining their joint achievements since 1959 and asking that he be allowed to address the Wolverton party to win their support for the nomination as the candidate. By return, Atter curtly rejected the peace-feeler and Maxwell's request. Their feud was reopened and Maxwell replied that Atter's letter demonstrated "the latest shocking example of your continued unfairness to me and dictatorial behavior in matters concerning the Wolverton Local Labour Party which is so harmful to Party unity." There were, said Maxwell, many in Wolverton, and they represented the majority, who had pledged their support for him. Instead of leaving Wolverton to its fate, Betty Maxwell organized a petition to overrule the ward's decision. Unfortunately, she chose as her envoy someone who neither lived in Wolverton nor was a member of the Labour Party. Worse still, four days after launching the petition, the representative was tried in a local court for theft. The names on the final petition were a motley collection of non-Labour Party members, non-residents and people who eventually denied that they had signed. When Maxwell failed to win the nomination, he launched a public attack on Atter and the ward, who had nominated a left-wing academic, Stuart Holland, as their candidate.

Gratifyingly, the selection committee under Cassidy did not choose any other well-known centrist candidates for consideration. Holland, Maxwell's only other opponent, would hold little attraction for Buckinghamshire's voters. On the day of the selection conference, puffing a large cigar outside the Labour Hall in Bletchley, Maxwell showed some nervousness as he waited for the outcome. Inside, carefully supervised by Foster, who checked every delegate's credentials, Cassidy ran meticulously through the procedures, knowing that the result was a foregone conclusion. In the weeks before, Maxwell had successfully obtained sufficient nominations to guarantee the result—82 votes in his favor and 33 against. Maxwell and Betty were thrilled. It was proof, said Maxwell, of the strength of his support. Some leaving the hall claimed that the vote showed the strength of the opposition. In an appeal for unity, Foster asked the majority not to "hammer the dissidents" and told the latter, "Although I do not expect everyone to retract their attitudes towards the candidate, we must work to return a Labour MP from this constituency." Cassidy was confident: "With Bob, we've got a winner." Delighted, Maxwell boarded a chartered plane to fly to Blackpool for the party conference, certain of his return to Parliament. Hours after his arrival, he stepped ahead of dozens of other applicants on to the rostrum to address his comrades. On that occasion it was to advise the party organizers not to pay the rental fees for the hall unless the wages of its employees were improved. "Bob," it was muttered, "was true to form. He never makes the right speech. For him, just to have spoken is counted as a success." In retrospect, Maxwell would admit that, in the glow of reselection, he had been foolishly shortsighted.

Atter and Edge were simmering about their defeat but Maxwell made little attempt to placate his enemies. In Wolverton, eight weeks later, Atter seized upon the third DTI report as justification for the criticisms. The report disclosed that the fifteen acres of railway land at Wolverton which Maxwell had purchased in 1966 for £355,000 had been resold three years later for over £1 million. For the workers in the locality, his enormous profits seemed incompatible with socialism. Disgruntled, they predicted that Maxwell could now definitely not count upon their help and consequently he would never win the seat. He dismissed the dissenters as irrelevant. They had been defeated and now there was more good news. His triumph in politics coincided with his return to the board of Pergamon. After a hard year, his other enemies, in the City, had also been trounced.

During 1972, Pergamon, whose staff had shrunk to just over eight hundred, struggled to survive on the core of its scientific journals. Its profits of just £315,000 were dwarfed by debts of nearly £5 million. Sir Henry d'Avigdor-Goldsmid had resigned at the end of 1971 because he was unwilling to mediate in the continuing feud between Maxwell and Steinberg. He was replaced by Walter Coutts, who had inherited a board of directors which was, with one exception, totally pro-Maxwell. As a former colonial officer in East Africa with no commercial experience, Coutts had been appointed by his friend Toby Aldington to fill up the necessary quota of independent directors. If anything, Coutts was less suited to the task than d'Avigdor-Goldsmid, and he was equally uncomfortable in the chair. "I didn't like Maxwell," says Coutts, "and I had no time for Steinberg." His discomfort with both men was probably aggravated because during the year he needed to understand Pergamon's business, he became reluctantly convinced that Pergamon's survival depended upon its founder.

Soon after his appointment, Maxwell sought to impress Coutts with the support he enjoyed among the journals' editors, especially in America, and to explain how Pergamon's viability was endangered by their growing dissatisfaction. Coutts agreed to visit New York, Boston, Chicago and Los Angeles to meet groups of editors who had been preselected by Maxwell. He set out intending to explain that until the DTI's reports were all published and the government had signaled that there would be no criminal charges, Maxwell's reinstatement as Pergamon's manager was untenable. But by Chicago, the third stop, Coutts felt the noose tightening. "The strong undercurrent was that if Maxwell wasn't put back, we would lose their services," says Coutts. In Chicago, the discussion degenerated into a brawl: "I was violently attacked as an interloper and I was furious. I told them that the City would never let him return but they just abused me. I spat blood at Maxwell for that."

Nevertheless, after meeting thirty-one editors, Coutts returned impressed by Maxwell's indispensability, although those he had met represented only a minority of Pergamon's 128 editors. He was anxious to break the impasse. Steinberg was showing only negative interest in the company—"All he wanted was to keep Maxwell out," says Coutts; the Stock Exchange still blocked any chance of trading Pergamon shares; and the DTI inspectors, whom Coutts labelled "dodderers," had still not completed their reports, which until then had, in his view, resulted in "Nothing firm or positive." A shadow lay across the company which the authorities were deliberately unwilling to lift.

Stalemate is not a condition which Maxwell can endure for long. At the end of April 1973, he forced the issue by threatening to refuse to renew his consultancy contract in October unless he was voted on to the board. Coutts, fearing the prospect of Maxwell establishing a rival publishing house, summoned an extraordinary meeting for June 18. Pro-Maxwell editors were flown from America and introduced by Coutts to Norman Freeman, the ICI pension fund manager who coordinated the institutions' policy, to urge Maxwell's election. Freeman, who represented the balance of power, was unimpressed. Reluctantly, Coutts adjourned the extraordinary meeting and Maxwell's bravado seemed doomed. But Maxwell was unwilling to succumb. During July, when he realized that publication of the final report was imminent and could possibly again delay his return to the board, he gave Coutts another ultimatum. The chairman, whose several abilities did not include a willingness to stand between Maxwell and his opponents, felt vulnerable to Maxwell's renewed threat of resignation and agreed to reconvene the extraordinary meeting in November. Maxwell set about marshaling his supporters and telephoned Brian Spalding, a professor of heat transfer at Imperial College in London. Spalding, more than any other editor, tipped the balance firmly in Maxwell's favor.

The two had met in the mid-1960s at one of the multitude of scientific conferences which Maxwell attended, seeking new ideas. Among those new ventures was a journal on heat transfer under Spalding's editorship. Like most of Maxwell's editors, Spalding was sincerely grateful for the opportunity of controlling a journal and, like most of his colleagues, he had been frankly uninterested in the City squabbles and the DTI's criticism of Maxwell. But Spalding was particularly grateful to Maxwell because the publisher had offered to assist his campaign for a Soviet academician, Ben Levitch, to be allowed to emigrate to the west. "Maxwell said that he was going to Moscow and would speak with Brezhnev," recalls Spalding. Once in Russia, Maxwell visited Levitch's home and the Russian was eventually released. Spalding was touched that Maxwell had "gone out of his way to help."

In early 1973, Spalding was on the Yugoslav Adriatic, chairing the annual meeting of his journal's editorial board, to which scientists had traveled from Japan, Russia and France. He was surprised when Maxwell telephoned to say that he would be joining them. Maxwell was charming and generous, hosting two fine dinners, and made no bones that he wanted in return their support. Spalding was receptive and warmed to Maxwell's comparison of his plight with Levitch's. "Both had suffered from an unfair system," explains Spalding, "of faceless men in a Star Chamber court allowing no opportunity for a defense." Spalding admits that he has never read the DTI report and is quite candid that Maxwell's initial approach was "very subtle. He correctly assessed me that I felt this was something I wanted to do."

On his return to London, Spalding met Coutts who in turn confided to the professor that Pergamon had not a penny in the bank and was possibly bankrupt. "Coutts," says Spalding, "gave the impression that he was out of his depth and uncomfortable." By the end of the second meeting with Coutts, after many calls from Maxwell and visits to Oxford, Spalding was convinced that he was important to the company's survival: "I hadn't realized before that we had so much power, but I decided to use it."

Coutts, at Maxwell's suggestion, arranged a series of meetings between the scientist and Freeman. Their undisguised hope was that the institutions would bow to the pressure and switch their vote at the November extraordinary general meeting. As an afterthought, it was decided that Spalding should also meet Steinberg. The American had been aware of Maxwell's tactics and had organized a number of testimonials from American scientists to be delivered to Freeman pledging that there would not be mass defections from Pergamon if Maxwell was not on the board. Among them was Professor Bruce Chalmers of Harvard who wrote, "I specifically refute the implication that my continuing as editor of materials published by Pergamon Press is conditional on the reinstatement of Robert Maxwell." The battle for the hearts and minds of the editors and their influence upon Freeman was to be resolved in a conference room on the seventh floor of Imperial College, starting at 9 a.m. at the end of October.

Spalding was visibly surprised by the number of "City men" who had appeared, outnumbering the delegation of scientists. Maxwell, an uninvited guest, sat one floor below in Spalding's office. Steinberg meanwhile was 27,000 feet above London, stuck in a jumbo circling the capital and waiting for the weather to clear before his plane could land. Spalding, accompanied by Maxwell's faithful ally Professor Harold Thompson, used the time to tell Freeman that the scientists' loyalty was to Maxwell, "the devil that we know," and that they would withdraw if Maxwell were not put back in control. "Maxwell is indispensable," said Spalding, "because only he understands and encourages us while we have never heard a squeak from the Americans." Freeman interjected that Maxwell might face criminal charges, so forcing the editors to accept a change. Spalding was unmoved. Freeman's evident antagonism toward Maxwell had an adverse effect upon Spalding. "It's not our task," said the editor, to the fund manager's ill-concealed irritation, "to judge guilt. We are scientists who base our actions on what we know, not on value judgments which masquerade as statements of fact." There was little answer to such pious oratory, which ignored nearly one thousand pages of evidence to support the condemnation of Maxwell, as Steinberg discovered when he finally arrived in the afternoon. The American's offer of more money, new editors and a bid for the institutions' shares pleased Freeman but not Spalding, who announced that, after hearing the arguments, he would definitely speak on Maxwell's behalf at the extraordinary general meeting. "We want

Maxwell back," he said as he offered his guests a glass of whiskey before they left. He would never be rewarded for his support and would be surprised that Maxwell's promise to "rationalize" the journals, to reduce the costs for libraries, was not completely fulfilled. But he is pleased that Maxwell, despite its unprofitability, has protected Levitch's own journal on chemical-hydrodynamics.

Steinberg left Imperial College resolved to renew his campaign against Maxwell and now also against Coutts. "I am fed up with your confusion of our position," he told Coutts after he had read the chairman's letter to shareholders which condemned "eternal squabbles between contesting parties." Once again, the independent chairman with no financial stake in the company was siding with Maxwell. He had little choice. Four years after the debacle, Maxwell still controlled PPI and his family companies were still deeply intermingled in Pergamon's business because they had retained the exclusive worldwide rights to sell the journals. Pergamon's meager trading profits were still falling and there was the suggestion that, according to a secret agreement, in the event of Pergamon's bankruptcy the ownership of the journals reverted immediately to MSI Inc. More than ever, Maxwell had successfully frozen Steinberg on the sidelines.

In a pre-meeting circular, Coutts resolutely told shareholders that Maxwell would be brought on to the board regardless of any condemnation by the DTI. "The company," Coutts explained, "needs his entrepreneurial flair for recognizing the publishing opportunities in the international scientific world and I am unaware that the DTI inspectors have criticized that part of his work." Naively he asked Steinberg to abstain in the vote because "Maxwell has promised" not to interfere in the company's financial management. Steinberg thought the idea was preposterous but Coutts, urged on by Maxwell and the board, was set on the strategy. Notice was given that the extraordinary general meeting would be reconvened at the Connaught Rooms on November 20. When Steinberg protested, Coutts threatened that the board would just ignore the majority of shareholders and co-opt Maxwell.

Steinberg might fume, but other than making a bid and taking over Pergamon, or forcing the company into receivership, he was powerless. On Rothschilds' and his lawyers' advice, he had deliberately adopted a low profile and had not even given evidence to the DTI inspectors. Pergamon's problems had been ignored as he guided Reliance toward a remarkable recovery. His company was now rated by *Fortune* magazine as America's twenty-fourth largest with annual revenues of over $700 million and it was growing fast. But the American's strength could not neutralize Maxwell's single-minded strategy. Maxwell had skillfully convinced Freeman and the institutions about his own indispensability, and the City's disinclination to involve themselves directly in Pergamon's management by an alliance with Leasco had grown. Steinberg was therefore unable to extract anything from Coutts and could only threaten to vote against Maxwell's return. During the day before the meeting, Peter Stevens telephoned Coutts several times but he did not sense that a coup had been planned.

On the day itself, at precisely 8 a.m., the DTI released the third report describing the relationship between Pergamon and the private companies. Its timing was interpreted as an attempt to sabotage Maxwell's return. At 11:05, once again in the Connaught Rooms, the meeting was formally opened. Coutts announced that, since the report had just been released, the meeting would have to be adjourned until the board had given it proper consideration. Coutts and the board including Maxwell had been given copies four days earlier and some inspired leaks had already appeared in the newspapers about the inspectors' "blunder" of admitting a mistake although the error did only affect 9 out of the report's 1,254 paragraphs. But Coutts realized that the publication removed any hope that the institutions would support his proposal for Maxwell's return. But, just as the vote for the adjournment was to be taken, Spalding rose and urged the chairman, on behalf of the editors, to co-opt Maxwell on to the board. Coutts nodded and called for the vote which, on a show of hands, was approved. Puzzled, Stevens neither voted nor protested. It was just after the adjournment that Coutts delivered the bombshell. The board, he announced, had decided, considering the views which were expressed at the meeting, that Maxwell should be invited to return as a temporary measure until a proper extraordinary general meeting could be reconvened in January. The artifice, despite the failure to obtain approval, was engineered in Coutts's words by the generous agreement of John Silkin, who, "at his own risk," would allow Maxwell to sit as an "alternate director" in his place on the board.

In the afternoon, Stevens telephoned Coutts and demanded an explanation for his "outrageous capitulation." Coutts was unapologetic. There had just been "no time" to inform Stevens about the change of plan. "I had given Stevens nothing more than an undertaking that we would not co-opt Maxwell without further consultation," says Coutts. "If we were to continue to govern Pergamon, and keep the editors with us, we had to act immediately. Maxwell threatened the night before to vote against the adjournment because he would resign his consultancy if he wasn't allowed back on to the board. I had no alternative but to allow him back. There was no time to ask for Leasco's opinion. The question was whether Leasco would make a bid for the company or shut up."

Maxwell had no doubt that Steinberg was outwitted. In March he had strengthened his control over PPI by changing its certificate of incorporation. The British company would no longer be able to prevent Maxwell stripping PPI of its assets and could not even force PPI to repay its debts of nearly £1 million. To prove his point, Maxwell had sold Vieweg, a printing company in Brunswick, West Germany, which was wholly owned by PPI, for £400,000. The transaction perfectly symbolized Maxwell's control.

Throughout December and early January, all the actors in the drama frantically and wearily negotiated the terms of possible bids. In the background was Coutts's reminder that the whole board would resign and Pergamon be made bankrupt if the Americans did not make a final decision by the end of January. Six months earlier, Leasco had valued the company at 10p a share. Maxwell therefore lowered his bid to 11p a share and promised that, if successful, he would commit all the shares to an independent voting trust for two years. Cynics noted that four years earlier Maxwell and his advisers had suggested that Pergamon shares were worth 185p each. By January 20, Steinberg conceded that he would not take the risk. Maxwell had won back his company. Steinberg sold his 38 per cent holding for 12p a share to Maxwell, receiving just over £600,000 in return for his original £9 million investment. Freeman, for the institutions, negotiated the same deal. Maxwell was jubilant. For under £1 million, his new American company, Microforms International Marketing Corporation, owned 90 per cent of Pergamon. The sum was considerably less than his family trusts had received when they secretly sold their 600,000 shares in 1969. "Even with your huge fees," he laughingly told a lawyer, "I've come out of this with a big profit." Not quite.

In New York, in February 1974, the Supreme Court considered Leasco's suits against Maxwell and Flemings for violations of the antifraud provisions of the securities and exchange legislation. The judges ruled that the New York courts did have jurisdiction over the case. The trial was set to start in July 1974. In May, Flemings intimated its willingness to settle and its lawyers began negotiating. Maurice Nessen, on Maxwell's behalf, made his approach soon after. Their joint capitulation was announced in the *New York Times* on July 29 under the headline "Reliance Group Collect $6,250,000 from Robert Fleming Co. Ltd. and

Maxwell Family in Pergamon Fraud Settlement." The details were never revealed but it is believed that Maxwell paid $5 million and the bank paid $1.5 million in installments. By then, Maxwell had purchased the remaining 10 per cent of Pergamon shares and was set to rebuild the company's fortunes beyond the public's gaze and the City's control. Three years later, the Director of Public Prosecutions announced that criminal charges were no longer under consideration. The DPP's decision would pass unnoticed. By 1974, many other British politicians had been exposed for their murky dealings with the world of secondary banks, building corporations and company perks. Duncan Sandys, John Stonehouse, Reginald Maudling, Jeremy Thorpe and Edward Du Cann were all former ministers or privy councillors who were involved in business controversies. Even Edward Heath and one of his own ministers had enjoyed a close connection with a famous falling star called Jim Slater. None of them had attracted the opprobrium attached to Maxwell's complex affair and, among his colleagues in the parliamentary Labour Party, many had become very dubious about the provenance of the stigma which he had attracted.

Labour politicians are unique in criticizing capitalism while not really understanding the sophisticated banking, broking and market mechanisms upon which the system relies. Those furthest to the left, whose distrust of capitalism is greatest, know the least about business and finance. In the Commons, Maxwell's millions had lost him a lot of sympathy but he had won grudging respect, possibly even envy, for understanding the system. Amid that mixture of ignorance and jealousy, the overwhelming view in the Labour ranks about the DTI reports was that "they" had come down deliberately hard on a Labour supporter. "He was set up by the Tories," was a common sentiment among the party's hierarchy who vaguely recalled the report's damning conclusion and believed that the treatment of Maxwell had been exceptionally harsh whatever the reasons. Merlyn Rees, who does not believe that Maxwell was more than a man "who tried to cut corners," probably represents the views of most. "The DTI reports," he says, "did not convince me that he was dishonest." Michael Foot, the left-winger, agrees: "I was suspicious of the reports." For his friends like Tam Dalyell, "It was all very complicated." None, it must be said, had actually read the three volumes or probably even cared to understand the details. By January 1974, it had also become totally unimportant.

Maxwell's resumption of control over Pergamon was as dramatic as his removal, although there were few eyewitnesses. Three weeks after his bid had been accepted, Coutts was chairing a regular board meeting in Oxford. Suddenly the board-room doors burst open and Maxwell marched in with Elisabeth Maxwell, Tom Clark and other supporters running close behind. "Right, we're taking over now," said Maxwell with a grin. "You can all go." Coutts was startled: "I quickly picked up a few personal things and left. I didn't remember him saying thank-you or even goodbye. I was just glad to go."

After recovering his business, the next goal was to return to Parliament. Edward Heath's government had been flawed by U-turns in policy, an economic boom fuelled by property speculation and major industrial bankruptcies. In the midst of the 1973/4 winter, Heath and the miners declared war against each other and Britain became gradually paralyzed when the government restricted industry to a three-day week. In February, the Prime Minister appealed to the electorate for support against the unions, confident of success. But after the first week of the election campaign, the government's support began drifting away. In a marginal constituency, Maxwell had grounds for optimism.

Election to Parliament and ministerial office had always been foremost in Maxwell's ambitions but in 1974 his bid was especially important. The repeated defeats he had suffered in the courts about the DTI reports would become so much history if his fifth appeal to the electorate were successful. Buckinghamshire's positive verdict would embarrass the Establishment and give him an impregnable platform from which to wreak his revenge. The realization of his hopes depended much upon Bryan Barnard, his former agent and admirer who had returned to organize Labour's dispirited supporters. "It was worse than in 1959. There were no records, no canvass returns and we had the troubles in Wolverton," Barnard recalls. "But Bob was very optimistic and I thought in the circumstances of Heath's disasters that we had a good chance."

In normal circumstances, Maxwell would have expected support for his campaign from the party leadership. His constituency was, as always, an obvious target if Labour was to win a majority and even fleeting visits of national politicians would at least arouse enthusiasm among the party workers. In the event, only James Callaghan passed through. Others are still too wily to explain their absence. Maxwell therefore fought a solitary campaign, ignored even by the national media, which, had he been a lesser man not engulfed by passion and energy, he might have noticed.

Glimpses of the red Land Rover charging through Buckinghamshire's villages preceded by the familiar booming voice were soon reported in the local press. Maxwell on the campaign trail, appealing for support from the fold, was as always an impressive sight. The reception he won was polite, but also mixed. In the rural areas, the sensational rows and inquiries of the past five years had made slight impact on farmhands and villagers. Maxwell had been a warm friend to them and he quickly recovered any lost ground. "The reception was," says Barnard, "Poor old Bob, he's had a rough deal." They couldn't understand what the fuss was all about." But in the towns he encountered a different reception. The rows had left an irreconcilable gulf. "We were let down by Wolverton," recalls Barnard, "where some people just refused to work for us." In Milton Keynes and Newport Pagnell it was worse. Not only did the anti-Maxwell faction withhold their help, but in the absence of a party organization the undecided voters, especially among the newcomers, had not been pinpointed. As Barnard ruefully admits, "Bob's troubles didn't help us among those people and the Tories were well organized." But Maxwell enjoyed two major advantages. In the reorganization of the electoral boundaries, a solid Tory ward had been relocated to a neighboring constituency, and in the election itself there was an 0.8 per cent swing to Labour which allowed Harold Wilson to form a minority government. Labour won fourteen new seats, but Maxwell's was not among them.

The Tory candidate in Buckinghamshire did not so much win the election with his 3,123 majority, the biggest since 1945; rather it was lost against the national trend by Labour. The votes which Maxwell could have expected were won by the Liberals. The recriminations were inevitable and predictable. A certain Labour gain was lost, said many party stalwarts, because of the candidate. There was the familiar sheen over Maxwell's eyes as the accusations were made in the streets but he had no intention of surrendering. There were no comforts other than the expectation of another election within months to capitalize on the disarray in the Tory ranks. With a little time, his organization would improve and he would benefit from any national swing to Labour. Barnard and Cassidy were urged to hold the selection conference rapidly. In April, one hundred delegates crowded into the Labour club for an acrimonious four-hour meeting. They emerged with the same candidate, who had little chance and showed less willingness to heal the divisions. Instead, Maxwell publicly attacked Atter and his working-class critics, making it harder to persuade them to work for his re-election.

By the second election in October 1974, Barnard's hopes were limited. His candidate had become lackluster and the historic trend of the Home Counties in turning away from Labour had already begun. The second defeat was particularly painful because, while Maxwell's personal vote barely improved, the Labour Party won an overall majority. Barnard watched his candidate "collapse emotionally" when he was declared a loser for the fourth time. "He'd done his best and failed. He was ill for days afterwards." In their post-mortem, Maxwell finally admitted to his agent that Pergamon and the rows with his opponents had cost him the election. "He looked like a beaten man," recalls Barnard. When Maxwell emerged six days later from the shock, he announced that he would not stand for election in the constituency again. But his appetite for power and influence had not diminished.

After twenty years in the power game, his opportunities seemed exhausted. (Two later attempts to win nominations for Labour seats in fact failed.) Politically he was discredited and his commercial obituary was, it seemed, already written. As his friend the financial journalist William Davis said, "You don't get many second chances from the City. In order to succeed on the scale that he did before, you need millions. And you need the goodwill of the big institutions, and somehow I doubt if he'll ever get there again." Philip Okill, the encyclopedia salesman, knew differently. In 1973 he said, "I think that Mr. Maxwell will attempt to climb up the slippery pole as long as he's alive. Because he's that type of man. For tenacity of purpose, for determination, one can only admire him. It's the methods he uses that a lot of us don't like." Okill's perception was correct. Maxwell was set on a permanent resurrection which would, if successful, rank with Lazarus's. At that time his only concession to any fault was: "I was a bit too sure of myself and accused of trying a bit too hard, which is a characteristic the British Establishment didn't like. I should have been less brash and more tolerant of others than I have been. I have undoubtedly made many mistakes and certainly accept part of the blame for the difficulties that the company got into." But, he added, "I was not guilty of any misdemeanor. I had done nothing to be ashamed of." Few believed him when he claimed that his future was "very bright": no one could imagine a route out of the wilderness.

12

An unsolicited telephone call in April 1975 offered Maxwell the serious opportunity he sought for his rehabilitation. Two Scottish newspaper printers, Nathan Goldberg and Charlie Armstrong, were trawling through the rich of London to find a savior for their jobs in Glasgow. Both were former employees of the *Scottish Daily Express,* which Beaverbrook Newspapers had closed a year earlier to stem the company's financial hemorrhage. The two printers explained to Maxwell that about five hundred of the laid-off workers had established an Action Committee which hoped to buy from Beaverbrook the site on Albion Street where the *Express* had been printed and establish a workers' co-operative to produce a new newspaper called the *Scottish Daily News.* To their surprise, Maxwell, with the best of intentions, invited them to come immediately to Fitzroy Square.

Maxwell in the flesh is always impressive but for the two Scotsmen, who were unemployed and desperate, he personified a divine omen. In their presence he telephoned Sir Hugh Fraser, the owner of Glasgow's competitor newspaper, and spoke jocularly in the shorthand most mortals only witness on glossy television dramas: "Let's take it away from this boy-scout outfit and give it a bit of credibility, give the boys a break." After a few calculations, Maxwell told his incredulous visitors that he would contribute fifty pence for every pound invested by the workers up to a limit of £100,000. Maxwell did not disguise his motives as pure philanthropy. Under Tony Benn's aegis, workers' co-operatives had become synonymous with the socialist cause and the regeneration of British industry, and Maxwell could hope to win prestige in the party by aiding the venture.

The two printers returned to Glasgow euphoric. To have found someone who pledged support for a cause which invariably attracted cynical disdain was a success. To have ensnared Maxwell seemed particularly fortunate since he was a socialist. Others would see his offer as a characteristically flamboyant gesture which could be withdrawn later, similar to his abortive bid to save Aston Martin. But this venture had a particular attraction—it was a newspaper which he had twice failed to buy. The imponderable is whether he understood that a co-operative was a transient political opportunity and not a business proposition.

In its heyday, the *Scottish Daily Express* had become synonymous with the most outrageous excesses of Fleet Street—an extravagant style of tabloid journalism which thrived upon exorbitant expense claims and incredible overmanning among both the printers and the journalists. Beaverbrook's willing indulgence was reflected in the wildly misconceived redundancy program which had encouraged the most productive employees to leave at the highest rates only to require others to be hired as replacements. It was a madhouse with inevitable consequences. By 1974, Albion Street represented a legend with a falling circulation, an awesome reputation for industrial strife and a series of unsuccessful editors. The employees were nevertheless shocked when Beaverbrook finally declared that the salad days were over. Amid scenes of emotion, on March 28, 1974, the last edition appeared and 1,800 employees were unemployed. By then a caucus had formed who were committed to the political ideal of a newspaper owned and managed by the employees. With the support of Beaverbrook and Benn, the workers had one year in which to find £2.5 million to purchase the site on Albion Street and have sufficient working capital.

The inspiration and leader of the Action Committee was Allister Mackie, a forty-four-year-old compositor who enjoyed a reputation in his local community as a responsible politician, wily trade unionist and justice of the peace. Those who supported Mackie and awaited the realization of the *Scottish Daily News* were not the best and the brightest of the old *Express*. Generally, they were a mixture of idealists and those who had been unable to find alternative jobs. Among the best were the printers whose talents were becoming redundant with the introduction of new technology, while the least able were the journalists who lacked either the talent or the initiative to move elsewhere.

Maxwell recognized all those weaknesses and especially their ignorance of financial management. Soon after his introduction, he advised Mackie that he should seek the services of a professor of accountancy, Richard Briston. In September 1973, Briston, on his own initiative, had written an article in *Accountancy* magazine suggesting that Maxwell had been unfairly victimized by the DTI inspectors. The two later met for a pleasant and non-committal encounter which was followed by an urgent summons by Maxwell for the academic to undertake a critical analysis of the second DTI report. After an exhaustive session—"It was a lot of work and he wanted it yesterday," says Briston—the accountant delivered his critique personally to Maxwell at the Blackpool party conference. "After reading it," recalls Briston, "his mood changed completely. He started shouting, "This isn't what I wanted!" and became very rude. He had expected me to defend him on every count and that wasn't possible." Briston's fee of one thousand pounds remained, despite repeated reminders, unpaid and was effectively written off when Maxwell telephoned from Glasgow and suggested that Briston come immediately to Glasgow to advise the Action Committee, which was "financially naive," about negotiations with the government and Beaverbrook Newspapers. Briston undertook the task "because I thought it was worthwhile, but not for Maxwell."

Professor Briston quickly achieved results. Beaverbrook reduced the price for Albion Street from £2.4 million to £1.6 million and also agreed to a £725,000 loan to the co-operative. The source of most of the money, £1.2 million, was to be the DTI's Industrial Development Unit, which under Tony Benn's initiative was championing workers' co-operatives throughout the country. But Briston discovered that, despite the political directive, Benn's civil servants were reluctant to hand over the money. "They didn't hide their skepticism about Benn's policies or about the newspaper's chances of success," says Briston, who was handicapped by a pessimistic feasibility survey produced by a team of management consultants. "The civil servants," he says, "set impossible terms which they hoped the workers couldn't meet." Those "impossible terms" included the stipulation that part of the finance had to be raised from other sources besides Beaverbrook Newspapers. The casualty of that condition, Briston claims, was a secret agreement he negotiated with Jocelyn Stevens, Beaverbrook's managing director, that the latter would loan to the co-operative whatever amount was still outstanding after they had tried every other source. "Our deal meant," says Briston, "that the workers would never have needed Maxwell. Unfortunately, the DTI was tipped off about our arrangement." The alternative sources of finance were limited.

A deadline, March 28, 1975, had been set for the workers to raise the £475,000 needed to qualify for the government loan. By that date, the Action Committee had collected £350,000 in addition to Maxwell's £100,000. Just hours before the cut-off, Mackie and the committee were collected inside a stuffy hut, adjacent to Albion Street, awaiting Maxwell's arrival from London desperate for £25,000 to meet their target. They all, including Mackie, who was inimicably suspicious of Maxwell, acknowledged that he was their only hope if their dream were to be realized. Exuding confidence and wealth in his camelhair coat, Maxwell quickly removed their qualms and promised the extra money but only if some new conditions were accepted. He wanted a twenty-four-hour paper, a commitment by the workforce to unlimited overtime and an assurance that he would be appointed publisher of the newspaper and co-chairman of the co-operative. With expert brinkmanship, he eventually won the committee's acceptance although a last-minute contribution from two journalists reduced Maxwell's extra payment to £14,000. In unison, the Action Committee and Maxwell marched to the City Hall where the workers gave their savior a thunderous reception. When the cheering died down, Maxwell repeated the three conditions on which he was giving his money. "For 5 per cent of the finance," says Briston, "Maxwell won disproportionate influence. The DTI pushed the workers into Maxwell's arms."

Neither then nor in the aftermath would anyone take responsibility for the irony that, within just one year, the same government department which had published the unprecedented condemnation of the businessman had also officially committed taxpayers' money to a venture whose very birth was dependent upon his participation. Some suspected the DTI officials of a devious plot to use Maxwell's presence to destroy future co-operative schemes. But Tony Benn, who harbored serious misgivings that his officials were sabotaging his socialistic policies, was more intent on realizing his political ambitions than listening to any conspiracy theories. By all accounts, Benn could also be counted among those in the Labour Party who were skeptical of the inspectors' conclusions about his colleague. The Minister publicly told the members of the co-operative that they were fortunate to have Maxwell's help.

Once the Action Committee had bought Albion Street, tremendous efforts were made to organize the newspaper's launch, commercially and editorially. Maxwell volunteered his help and, without formally consulting the co-operative, negotiated during the first days for telephones, newsprint, the supply of news agency wire services and the hire of an advertising executive. Briston, Mackie and the renamed Workers' Council were irate. Maxwell, they felt, did not understand that he was not the boss but just one member of a team. Among his negotiations was a reduced rate for the use of the Press Association's wire services. But when he informed the council of his coup, it was instantly disavowed. The council wanted to pay an additional £16,000, nearly double Maxwell's deal, to prove that the workers would pay the "going commercial rate."

To outsiders it seemed to be a question of ethics. They were viewed as intent on ridding themselves of employers, profiteers and the purveyors of capitalist abuses, although some members of the Action Committee believed that they were commercially minded. Consequently, two weeks after his welcome, Mackie sensed that he could count on substantial support for a coup against Maxwell.

On April 17, at a meeting of the works council, Mackie proposed that Maxwell should lose his executive powers. In a heated session, Maxwell recited his commercial achievements on the co-operative's behalf. Briston, who by then half-regretted his original defense of Maxwell, had become strongly critical and cited a deal for newsprint negotiated by Maxwell which he described as excessively expensive. Maxwell fumed while Briston read out the damning conclusions of the DTI's report before commending Mackie's motion for the removal of a self-styled boss. "There'll be a writ in the post!" shouted Maxwell as his erstwhile defender left the hall and the workers voted on his removal from the council. Ostensibly, Maxwell accepted his demise in good heart and returned to Oxford, sharing the doubts of others who were not politically committed that a newspaper whose *raison d'être* was not to make profits but to keep five hundred people at work was doomed.

By definition, in a co-operative no single person becomes a leader to inspire the remainder. In a collective, there is either communal inspiration or nothing at all. But many would regard that idealism as incompatible with the realities of establishing the firm editorial leadership which a newspaper requires. The *News*'s editor was Fred Sillitto, a sixty-year-old former deputy editor of the defunct *Express* who was a compromise choice. Under his guidance, the paper lurched toward its unveiling without agreeing its strategy, its political point of view, its editorial style, how to attract sufficient advertising or even a purpose. Neither Sillitto nor the council had targeted who would buy the paper nor had they decided what type of stories they would want to read. A similar malaise affected the advertising and circulation departments who were organizing a launch during the traditionally lean summer months in the depths of an economic recession without an adequate brief to present to potential customers. Only the production section was well manned, and the printers were already anticipating the journalists' failures.

But there was only a passing hint of those shortcomings when the first edition of the newspaper came off the presses at midnight on

Sunday May 4. On the production floor, there was genuine euphoria as television cameras, journalists from other newspapers and well-wishers jostled Tony Benn and Maxwell, who stood reading the lead story about a successful model who, after "dying" in a car crash, had been resuscitated. If the headline, "It's Great to be Alive" was pedestrian or clichéd, that was not reflected in the first week's sales, which zoomed from 260,000 to 330,000 copies. As the novelty disappeared, a partial decline was inevitable. Every new newspaper suffers a jolting curve of expectation and sales at its birth but professionals can distinguish between the struggle for life and the inexorable decline to extinction. In the case of the *Scottish Daily News,* the circulation, in the second week, began to free-fall down toward 200,000 copies and the awful reality dawned. Even the most favorably prejudiced agreed that the newspaper was confused and dull. There was still a chance of survival if the Workers' Council would take swift remedial action but, to one outsider, it seemed fixated and paralyzed.

On May 19, Maxwell struck. In a telex to Mackie, Maxwell appealed to him to "sink our differences and work together" by lifting the ban on Maxwell selling advertising as the only way to "save the *Scottish Daily News.*" Mackie did not reply and the following day Maxwell sent another much longer telex to the council predicting that the *News* would collapse by October 31 if its editorial and commercial policies were not changed. The paper, he reminded his readers, had started its life with £950,000 cash in the bank. Sixteen days after its first publication, £500,000 remained and the losses, assuming circulation fell no further, were accumulating at £30,000 per week. On the existing pattern, there was, he said, no chance of redemption. "I know that your immediate reaction will be to accuse me of panic-mongering. The accusation would be as untrue as it is undeserved. . . . In view of the grave danger which our enterprise finds itself in, I hope that you will cease your stubborn refusal to comply with the letter and spirit of the workforce [sic] . . . and save 500 jobs." Considering the criticism which he would later attract for his role in the newspaper, his message is a model of moderation and sanity.

> Over a long period I gave you a considerable amount of my time free and unstintingly and many of my suggestions which the Action Committee followed were certainly instrumental as you yourself have admitted in getting the project off the ground. I was therefore surprised, to say the least, by your attempting to remove me from the co-chairmanship so soon after I had been instrumental in help-

ing you raise the necessary money to get the project launched.

However, I decided that this was your show and that you should be allowed to run things the way you liked. Several times I pointed out that without me or somebody like me you would find it difficult to launch the paper successfully, to maintain its high circulation and get quickly the necessary advertising. You insisted that you could do all this by yourself and "in any case you should be allowed to make your own mistakes." As unanimously desired by our workforce I agreed to keep my peace and not rock the boat and I have adhered to this decision.

Maxwell then pointed out that, with falling circulation and low advertising, "our workers co-operative is literally heading for the rocks." The political and human cost, he warned, would be "ghastly" and offered the council some "concrete proposals which may just save the situation"; these involved "improving the journalism, increasing circulation and selling more advertising."

The following day, the Workers' Council rebutted Maxwell's accounts and seemed to Maxwell, albeit erroneously, to be shrugging off its responsibility. Instead of losing £30,000 per week, the meeting agreed, the paper was at worst breaking even, but that was optimistic. When the riposte reached Maxwell, he was outraged. Albion Street suddenly represented everything he hated most: inefficiency, blinkered trade unionism and, worst of all, insubordination. The philanthropist launched a bid to take control of the newspaper's commercial transactions. The annual elections to the Workers' Council were due on June 4. By then, according to Maxwell, the circulation had fallen to 80,000, but according to some others 120,000, and the paper was attracting less than half the required advertising. Maxwell was proposed as a candidate by the journalists and, in an emotional speech which prophesied imminent ruin, he recommended himself, the socialist entrepreneur, as the redeemer. Mackie opposed his election but nevertheless, by seven votes, Maxwell was elected to the council which by then had become disillusioned and divided. His return brought a new, if controversial spirit.

Maxwell pledged himself to work exclusively for the *News* for three months and appealed to everyone not to be "cavalier . . . when dealing with public funds . . . and save our paper from extinction." But he did not hide his frustration that he controlled only the advertising and circulation departments. He wanted to be the newspaper's publisher, manager and editor and to thrust himself boisterously forward as the incomparable savior of the whole enterprise. In anticipation of victory, a Glasgow public relations company, Donald and Partner Ltd., was asked to conceive a campaign which would identify the newspapers under Maxwell's command. Their proposal was revealing of his intentions: "Since Maxwell is pivotal to all the changes taking place, he must unequivocally be seen to be taking the helm and setting the pace." Again Mackie opposed Maxwell's bid but on July 30, as the newspaper veered toward total collapse, Maxwell was granted full executive powers, although his control was subject to the votes of the council and the workforce. The collective had a boss.

In classic style, as "chief executive," Maxwell moved a bed into an office, fried his food in the canteen and walked around the building exhorting everyone to work harder. The next stage was a survival plan. Most were by then agreed that the paper should be relaunched as a tabloid, but Maxwell also argued that the cover price should be reduced by one penny. Mackie disputed the economics and asked him to prove that the newspaper's circulation would increase sufficiently to cover the fall in revenue. Maxwell brushed the detractor aside as someone ignorant about business and with a mixture of ultimatums and exhortations won the committee's support. The relaunched tabloid, published on August 17, was an immense improvement and sales soared. Had Maxwell patiently allowed his creation to develop gradually and not insisted on the counter-productive price cut, he might have reaped enormous praise. Instead, unwilling to suffer further the chaos of democracy, he sought to remove those who challenged his decisions, especially Allister Mackie, and he adopted controversial methods.

Mackie was anathema to Maxwell. His idealism had fertilized the concept of the *News* but he wanted to prove a principle and in Maxwell's view, not to make a profit. For Mackie, Maxwell represented the archetypal press baron and everything which was wrong in the industry. Mackie believed that he did understand commercial priorities but they were clearly different from Maxwell's. The new tabloid even contained a daily column written by Maxwell containing his thoughts, which Mackie noted was not blessed by sparkling prose or pithy insight. A showdown was inevitable and came in late August. It centered on a demand from Beaverbrook for a final payment of £59,000.

Maxwell had astutely discovered that Beaverbrook's negotiators had carelessly omitted to define the price for Albion Street as "exclusive of VAT." Accordingly, the price was inclusive and Beaverbrook would be expected to pay the £59,000 tax from the money already received. For Maxwell it was natural that Beaverbrook should suffer its own folly but for Mackie the notion was outrageous. Integrity was important to him, and on legal advice he signed a check and sent it to London. To Maxwell, who believed that survival in business depends upon extolling virtues, even those which are non-existent, and concealing glaring inadequacies, Mackie's behavior was inexplicable. Only a fool, he felt, would be charitable on his way to oblivion, and he ordered the bank to stop payment.

That confrontation confirmed Mackie's sentiment that the co-operative was dead. His view was shared by William Wolfe, the chairman of the Scottish Nationalist Party who was also the *News*'s company secretary. On about September 1, Wolfe handed the DTI a summary of the accounts which were compiled as if the paper were going into liquidation. "It was bankrupt, so what else could I do?" says Wolfe. Maxwell was irate and condemned both men as "irresponsible elements." To Wolfe in particular, he wrote describing his "disgust at your unprofessional conduct" because the company, he said, was definitely solvent. Hitherto, their dispute had been contained within the Workers' Council, but Maxwell decided to gather support among the workforce and began regularly using the loudspeaker system to denounce Mackie and his supporters as "fools," "knaves," "the enemy in our midst" and "terrible people." Ironically, it was the type of language which, when used by critics to describe Maxwell, would be answered with an avalanche of writs.

On September 3, just after 6 p.m., Maxwell's message over the loudspeaker presaged the climax: "Attention. This is Robert Maxwell speaking. We have doubled our circulation. What a time to pick by these terrible people, the enemy in our midst, to destroy our courage and reputation. I want you to reflect carefully on what I have said. Now is the time when you have got to stand up and make up your mind—either you want the management and leadership I have provided, or else you can take the situation which Mackie and Russell and their ilk have brought about." After outlining their disagreement about the check and suggesting that Mackie and Wolfe wanted to call in the liquidators, Maxwell delivered his ultimatum: "Now is the time to let your feelings be known . . . I want to hear from your chapel representatives what you want to do to save your jobs. Thank you and goodnight." The following week, he apologized. But the demoralization had spread rapidly and, after more confrontations, Maxwell appealed again to the workers.

On September 14 at a mass meeting, Maxwell promised to arrange new finance to stave off bankruptcy if a vote of no confidence was passed on Mackie and Wolfe. In Mackie's absence, Maxwell won, and both Wolfe and Mackie resigned the following day to be joined by the company's lawyers and accountants, including Briston. The newspaper's future now depended entirely upon Maxwell. At a press conference called soon after, which was filmed by BBC Television, Maxwell impatiently but authoritatively asserted, "We are very solvent; we have no financial problems . . . if every business in the United Kingdom was as well off for cash and paid its bills as promptly as this company, there would be no crisis." It is the very enigma of Maxwell: whether he believed that assurance to be accurate or whether, unwilling to accept defeat, he was putting on a brave face to buy time for a rescue.

The same week, on September 19, Maxwell informed the council that the newspaper would be bankrupt within one week but he showed no signs of panic. With a circulation of 150,000 and a revaluation of the assets by a new firm of accountants, he was optimistic that he could raise more loans from the major banks. Goldberg and Sillitto supported Maxwell and got down to improving the paper in a period of calm. Six days later their hopes were completely dashed. Mackie's departure had aroused curiosity in Fleet Street. The industry's trade paper, *Campaign,* quoted him as saying that the *News* was "finished" and then the *Sunday Times* decided to investigate Mr. Maxwell's latest enterprise.

The mastermind of the *Sunday Times*'s new venture was Bruce Page, who six years earlier had been one of the executive editors responsible for the Insight profiles. In the intervening years, he had observed that the DTI's reports had exposed Maxwell's commercial reputation as worse than the paper had imagined. Yet by 1975 the DTI's investigation had been practically forgotten and Maxwell had emerged apparently unscathed. The news of Mackie's resignation and the troubles in Glasgow were therefore a good "peg" to summarize the DTI's devastating reports and query just why the same department had committed taxpayers' money to that individual. Prior to embarking upon the story, Page naturally consulted Harold Evans, the editor, and won the assurance that under no circumstances would the *Sunday Times* capitulate to Maxwell's inevitable barrage of writs as on the previous encounter. Two journalists were dispatched to Scotland while Page remained in London. The result was a major article which appeared on September 21 under the sensational headline "How Maxwell Sabotaged the Workers' Dream." Breathless and blistering, it opened by alleging that Maxwell, "having cut a unique swathe through British capitalism, has now succeeded in turning the latest manifestation of British socialism—the workers' control movement—into an instrument of his own ambitions." The article's style lacked any pretence of neutrality in its summary of

Maxwell's past. But in putting all the blame for the *News*'s collapse upon Maxwell's stewardship, its bias was evident: "Without Maxwell, the socio-economic experiment would have been carried through to the end, the results observed, the lessons learned . . . For the lack of the last £114,000 that dream of the co-operative was sacrificed." The newspaper's editorial blamed the collapse on Maxwell's "insatiable appetite for control" although he had wielded complete power for a mere week and it omitted even to hint at the contribution made to the collapse by any additional factors. If the condemnation was harsh, it nevertheless reflected the feeling that Maxwell's past and personality made him an unacceptable recipient of public funds.

Maxwell was too vulnerable to withstand the onslaught. On October 1 he resigned despite the workforce's resolution that "We wish to put on record that our co-operative has benefited from Maxwell's consultation and his administration to further our project," and despite their overwhelming vote, 248 to 18, urging him to stay. He blamed Page for pursuing a vendetta and issued writs for defamation. The workforce was similarly outraged.

Kenneth Grant, a union official in Albion Street, protested to Page about his description of Maxwell: "Like everyone else he has his blemishes. Yet even his antagonists must concede that he is a courageous and brilliant entrepreneur. He can be aggressive but he can also be wounded to the moist-eyed stage by unmerited calumny . . . His unorthodoxy can be very upsetting to the conventional mentality. And his few aberrations appear to be his impulsive generosity and his desire to publish another newspaper." The Workers' Council also protested to Harold Evans that the allegations about the paper were "unfounded, cruel and irresponsible" and that he had endangered five hundred jobs. Evans printed their complaint but the *News* perished by the end of the month, precisely as Maxwell had predicted.

The wilderness neither intimidated nor frightened Maxwell. It was the natural habitat for someone who in the 1960s had confessed to being "a jungle man." The Teflon coating upon those who had passed through the school of Slatinske Doly and survived frontline warfare could easily shrug off the brick-bats aimed by men who were deemed to be vindictive and prejudiced. Maxwell retreated to his family, his reservoir of strength and support which few who have spent so much time away from home can possess. His relationship with Betty and his seven children galvanized his single-minded search for yet another opportunity to stage a recovery. At that moment the only testament to his record and ambitions were a series of huge, leather-bound scrapbooks which

Betty had meticulously collated. Every newspaper article and every significant piece of memorabilia had been diligently stuck on to the thick pages awaiting the needs of the future biographer. He could also rely upon his personal secretary, the auburn-haired, attractive Jean Baddeley, who, since joining him in 1962, had become his devoted servant: "What I felt for Robert Maxwell," the hitherto ultra-discreet secretary explained shortly after his death, "was love but for all the right reasons. My love for him was based on huge respect and deep affection for someone who was very important to me." Their relationship, she added, "started as a kind of hero-worship for a man who was incredibly kind. He had heart." Baddeley would never marry because the suitors "did not pass the Maxwell test." With Baddeley's help after 1975, Maxwell tried to emerge from the bunker but it was more than ever made difficult by his past. Only money could liberate him. The sole available source was Pergamon. Maxwell devoted his entire energies to rebuilding its fortunes.

Sir Walter Coutts had relinquished his chairmanship in 1974 when Maxwell had bought all the outstanding Pergamon shares. Three years later, under Maxwell's tight control, Pergamon's traditional business had been rebuilt. In 1977, the company employed a record three thousand personnel and was publishing 360 scientific journals and one thousand books a year. Its sales had increased from £7 million to £20 million and its net annual profits zoomed from £27,000 to £3.3 million. Organizing Pergamon's recovery required Maxwell to travel repeatedly to Moscow to rebuild interrupted contacts. He discovered two important changes. In 1973, the Soviet government had signed the International Copyright Convention and established VAAP, an agency which represented the commercial rights of Soviet writers, which was closely connected to the KGB. Money, said Yuri Gradov with whom Maxwell had written his first agreement in 1955, was now important. Pergamon, said Gradov, would have to pay commercial rates for the rights to publish Soviet journals and books in the west.

The second change was the disappearance of Pergamon's monopoly. Plenum, an American publisher, had become the Soviet's favored customer. Using charm and guile Maxwell sought to undermine his new competitor. Gradov resisted the pressure quite easily. Pergamon, the Russians had discovered, had not paid even the pittance due under the original agreement. "I've got authors at my throat demanding their money," Gradov told Maxwell who delivered a shocked response: "It's my accounting department's fault. I always tell them to pay. I'll get on to them immediately." Fifteen years later Gradov lamented, "We received so little from Maxwell and he earned so much from us." Neither the payment problem nor Maxwell's failure to account properly for the number of journals which had been printed damaged his favored status. On the contrary, Gradov's tough stance was undermined by orders from above: "We were told to give him all the book rights and some journals." The orders, Gradov believed, came from the Kremlin, but that is only part of the truth.

When Maxwell returned to Moscow in 1974, he naturally concealed from the Soviet publishers that he was discredited and politically impotent in Britain. The KGB was naturally aware of his circumstances. Maxwell's publishing contacts were resumed and his privileged status was both restored and augmented. With the help of many officials, including Boris Pankin, then a junior functionary at VAAP but later to become the foreign minister, Maxwell resumed his contacts with an enormous range of Russians. VAAP officials like Vladimir Tverdovsky, who worked with Maxwell, recognized that, "he had enormous political power" in Russia. Tverdovsky, like others, complained that Maxwell received many contracts to publish books but the books either failed to materialize or Maxwell did not remit the royalties he earned. In either case, Tverdovsky voiced a common complaint that Maxwell was not a profitable trading partner. Yet by 1977, Maxwell's commercial relationship with the Russian publishing agencies had become quite curious.

In that year, Maxwell arrived in Moscow with a new assistant, Richard Newnham, who had formerly worked for the British Council. Newnham was delighted to reintroduce Maxwell to a friend, a VAAP official. Amid their mutually warm greetings, Newnham discovered that the friend had known Maxwell in Berlin after the war. "It looked as if they were old friends. It was a very warm reunion," recalls Newnham.

But behind the great *bonhomie* which Maxwell exchanged with all the Russians, Newnham observed the "fear among the Russians when they negotiated with him because, knowing his connections, they didn't dare talk hard commercial language." The reason, Newnham discovered, was an inexplicable contradiction about the nature of Maxwell's commercial operations in Moscow which ran counter to all his other publishing deals.

While Gradov, Tverdovsky and others complained that Maxwell was not reimbursing them, which Newnham found very embarrassing, everyone concerned realized that Maxwell was actually losing money on the sale of the Russian scientists' books in the west. "The books were an albatross," recalls Newnham, "because, after paying for the translations and printing, we couldn't sell them." The losses provoked Pergamon's division chiefs in Britain to fury. "They were having to bear losses which counted against them," says Newnham who protested to Maxwell: "Face the facts. The books are valueless."

Maxwell's reply was short: "Stop showing me negative reports. Just do it."

Newnham's embarrassment in Moscow was therefore not that Pergamon owed the Russians money, but that Maxwell seemed to be actually subsidizing Soviet propaganda. If Newnham suspected a hidden agenda, he never discovered any evidence. But according to Viktor Shishkin, who bought Pergamon books for Soyuzkniga, VAAP, the KGB agency, and the Central Committee all paid Maxwell in hard currency. Unknown to Newnham, Maxwell was being reimbursed for his expenditure through indirect payments from Moscow to the Pergamon office in France. (One channel for the money was exposed in 1991 when confidential papers belonging to the Soviet Communist Party were published in Moscow revealing that Pergamon was listed as a "friendly firm" which was owed 500,000 roubles—about £500,000 at the official exchange rate. A spokesman at the Pergamon headquarters in Britain could not find any record of being paid that sum.)

Even for an individual of Maxwell's character, his confident approach toward Russia was remarkable. In early 1978, Maxwell heard that Progress Publishers, a Soviet organization, had compiled Brezhnev's biography. "Stop everything," Maxwell shouted at Newnham. "Forget about going home. Get the book, translate it and publish it within twelve days." Newnham was surprised that his employer should be so keen to sell "the worst sort of political clap trap. Junk." The reason became apparent a few weeks later.

The two had returned once again to Moscow to meet the Committee for Science and Technology. The meeting was interrupted by a summons for Maxwell. Driven at speed through the city, he was taken to the Kremlin. Newnham sat outside while Maxwell enjoyed a half an hour with Brezhnev. Maxwell emerged from the meeting beaming, most excited by the sight of the small telephone exchange on Brezhnev's desk. By the flick of any of the thirteen levers, the party chairman was in instant communication with each of the republics' first secretary. The power of communication was a notion which Maxwell admired.

The substance of Maxwell's conversation with Brezhnev has never been revealed, nor has the reason why he was received, although informed apparatchiks suggest that Yuri Andropov, chairman of the KGB, was influential. A photo of the two men was published in *Pravda*.

Among the visible results of that meeting was the "state" visit by Maxwell and his wife in September 1978 to his birthplace, situated in a border area which was normally closed to foreigners.

Every account of that five-day journey, including that of Irina Bodnya, their interpreter, suggests that the Maxwells were treated like royalty. Along the route, every top party functionary was present to pay his respects; ambassadors were summoned from all of the bordering countries to pay homage; the food and accommodation were the finest the Republic could provide; and Bodnya watched Maxwell's emotions as he walked through the streets where he had last seen his parents and family, to be greeted by the specially corralled crowds. Each evening there was a huge candlelit dinner followed by speeches of welcome. Newnham was waiting when the couple returned to Moscow: "They were exhausted. Even Maxwell, whose energy was phenomenal, just collapsed in bed."

On his return to Britain, Maxwell launched the "World Leaders" series which were biographies of the communist dictators. In the preface of the 1983 Pergamon biography of Nicolae Ceauşescu, subtitled "Builder of Modern Rumania and International Statesman," Maxwell praised the tyrant for his "constant, tireless activity for the good of the country." Maxwell had heaped similar flattery upon Gustav Husak ("this impressive man") and Todor Zhivkov, who in 1983 awarded Maxwell the Order of Stara Planina, first class, the communists' highest honor, was credited by Maxwell for building a "prosperous and happy nation."

The financial arrangements for that series remains unclear. Konstantin Dolgov, a past chairman of VAAP, believes, like many others, that Maxwell never fulfilled his promise to the leaders to publish and sell at least 10,000 of each volume. But Dolgov is certain that the communists were grateful that Maxwell courageously published the books when the communists were unpopular. Yegor Yakovlev, now the head of Soviet broadcasting, claims that the communists paid Maxwell through the Novosti news agency for printing 50,000 copies of the book but doubts whether even a fraction were produced. Others claim that embassy officials in London reported that the books were never seen to be on sale and therefore the communists lost the money they had invested in Maxwell. It was undoubtedly a contribution to Maxwell's growing funds which coincided with his careful reconstruction of his businesses.

Out of the public glare, the legal ownership had been transferred to Pergamon Holding Corporation, registered in the United States. The move was consistent with Maxwell's policy of minimizing his liability for taxes and cloaking his activities in as much secrecy as legally possible.

But since Pergamon was a private company and Maxwell was for most a forgotten and discredited figure, the recovery passed unnoticed by those whose profession involves an interest in corporate affairs. There were no City reports that for three consecutive years Pergamon had paid as a dividend its single shareholder, Maxwell and the family trusts in New York, £1.3 million. Even in January 1978, when fire destroyed most of the Oxford head office, the dividend was maintained.

By 1979, Pergamon had hit the same suffocating plateau which ten years earlier had provoked Maxwell's bid for the *News of the World* and the deal with Leasco. The sale of Pergamon journals was static and the printing subsidiaries were losing money. Once again Maxwell was frustrated and anxious to find new horizons. Over the previous five years the company had paid off its debts and amassed more than £5 million in its reserves. But since Maxwell could not expect financial support in the City, he needed more cash if he was to launch a bid. In 1979, Maxwell sought a new and potentially major source of income —dealings in shares. In the previous two years, he had speculated annually about £2 million in gilts in London and bonds in New York. The profits had been modest. In 1979, his speculation spiralled to £60 million but went sour in New York. He lost £1.5 million in that year's deals, which halved Pergamon's annual profits.

In 1980, his fifty-seventh year, an age when most men think about their retirement, Maxwell was sure that he had found an escape from oblivion. In preparation, the figures on Pergamon's balance sheet dramatically increased. The turnover in share deals expanded to £79.9 million and produced profits of £1 million. Pergamon's subscription income doubled, pouring no less than £11 million into the company. On paper, Pergamon's assets had increased fourfold in five years to £24 million. His personal fortune in the same period, from accumulated dividend payments and profits from the sale in the USA of scientific journals, can be conservatively estimated at a further £10 million. Maxwell was flush with money at the moment of his nemesis.

During 1980, Maxwell quietly began buying shares in the British Printing Corporation. By July, he had accumulated a stake just below the limit where he would be required to reveal his interest. There was at least £15 million of his own money to finance a gamble which he hoped would transform him from an outcast into a welcome visitor at places which were previously out of bounds.

Jonathan "Johnny" Bevan is a big man in stature, ambition and lifestyle—a prototype Yuppie long before any slick observer had imagined that those making money in the City could enjoy the glamour and power normally associated with a Hollywood studio boss. In Bevan's life, a "dawn raid" could be a breakneck race down the Cresta Run or the highly publicized seduction of a society belle. But Bevan has rarely been as thrilled as when he dispatched his dealers to the center of the Stock Exchange floor at precisely 9:30 a.m. on Friday July 18, 1980, to hold up their arms and offer to buy eleven and a half million shares of British Printing Corporation for 25p each, 7p more than their market price. Ten minutes later, as the waves of excitement still reverberated around the hall, Bevan was certain that his first dawn raid would earn a mention in history. His client had paid £2.9 million for 29.5 per cent of his estranged, erstwhile partner. By any yardstick—timing, price and strategy—it was an innovative coup which, on Maxwell's part, reflected the accumulation of thirty-five aggravated years of experience. That day, the Maxwell presented to the world was unbellicose, mellow and thoughtful. His public comments were unusually guarded; he suggested that BPC's management had nothing to fear from their new "constructive shareholder." The opposite, of course, was the truth. For Maxwell, his dawn raid was akin to the Normandy landings in June 1944: a bridgehead had been established and the ultimate goal was Berlin—to take the City by storm. After the smoke had cleared and the initial euphoria had waned, the real battle commenced.

No one was more surprised by the raid than Peter Robinson, BPC's chairman and managing director. As in a Hollywood "B" movie, the news had been delivered melodramatically, by Maxwell himself. At 9:30 in the morning, as Bevan's dealers stood on the floor of the Stock Exchange, Robinson's secretary had announced that Maxwell was on the telephone. The chief executive of Europe's largest printers assumed that it was just another of the regular business calls which he was compelled to take from a man for whom no one in BPC had any affection. Relations with Maxwell had been strained ever since the collapse of ILSC, and their conversations were never amicable. But, on this occasion, the announcement by the voice on the telephone that he had just become a major shareholder foretold disaster.

"I want a meeting," said Maxwell.

"I'm busy," replied Robinson, who feared that Maxwell would demand a seat on the board.

"What about over the weekend?"

"I'll be in Sevenoaks."

"I'll come down."

"Sorry, it will have to wait until Monday."

When he replaced the receiver, Robinson was disturbed and furious. The call was totally unexpected. Maxwell's timing had been impeccable. BPC, despite annual sales of £200 million, was losing a lot of money; its board of management was in disarray, grappling to steer their company away from bankruptcy. If Maxwell was set on realizing his ambition to control BPC, Robinson would fight back, not just for the company, but also on his own behalf. For a decade he had worked so hard to rescue the monster, and he was not about to open the door to the likes of Maxwell.

Robinson's promotion to manage BPC in 1970 had represented an acknowledgment that his technical abilities in the packaging division might heal the wounds which had bedeviled the company since its creation four years earlier. BPC had never fully recovered from the revelation that its megalomaniac founder, Wilfred Harvey, had perpetuated a succession of costly frauds. In the wake of his resignation, the new management had grappled with a disparate collection of printing companies and a legacy of massive debts which were augmented by the £5 million losses from ILSC and the publication of unsalable encyclopedias. BPC's debts had accumulated just as a succession of new disasters hit its core activity, printing.

During the 1950s, Britain's three major printers—Sun, Odhams and Bemrose—had individually expanded to capitalize on the boom in color women's magazines. Flush with orders and money, the managements bowed to most trade union demands for higher wages and more restrictive practices. By the late 1960s the boom was history. Television had cut deeply into magazine circulations but the print unions refused to acknowledge the new reality and accept any layoffs. At BPC's Sun Printers in Watford, as in Fleet Street, the weak management recoiled from confronting their nightmare until 1969. The resulting strike cost Sun Printers its most lucrative magazine contracts and cost BPC its total annual profits.

Throughout the 1970s, buffeted by postal strikes, power cuts and a gyrating economy, Robinson struggled to save the company although he was handicapped by his limited understanding of finance and by persistent industrial disputes. Although Robinson had reduced BPC's workforce by nearly 50 per cent, and restored the company to profitability until 1979 amid bitter confrontation with the union leaders, both Tony Dubbins and Joe Wade, the obdurate leaders of the NGA—the print union concerned—say they were not intimidated by his personality or character. According to Robinson, neither man was willing to discuss the company's survival or agree on productivity deals. As Robinson's stance alternated between politeness and desperation, the union leaders gained the impression that, despite his tough language, even accusing them to their faces of blackmail, he would often bow before their intransigence. Ironically, they blame Robinson for "never moving into our century."

To stem the losses, Robinson sold some printing plants and closed others, but lucrative customers, among them the *Economist* and *Newsweek,* were lost forever. The tilt toward bankruptcy was delivered in October 1978 at the Savoy Grill by Marmaduke Hussey, then the managing director of Thomson Newspapers. Robinson had been relieved that Thomson's contract to print the *Sunday Times* color magazine had been renewed. But, during the meal, to his consternation, the "Duke" briefed him that Thomson newspapers were going to "discipline" the Fleet Street workers by closing down their newspapers. "In one month," the "Duke" told the incredulous BPC chairman, "we'll have them in retreat." In humiliating circumstances, Hussey failed, but for Robinson the cancellation of the magazine's contract for one year caused a ruinous £2 million loss which was aggravated by more NGA strikes and the loss of more customers to foreign printers. As the abyss loomed, Robinson thought that he had snatched a lifeline by winning a seven-year contract to print the *TV Times*. Although BPC would lose £12 million that year and there was no money to pay for the new printing machinery which he had just ordered, Robinson was dreaming about deliverance by a miracle when Robert Maxwell telephoned.

The two came face to face on Monday morning, July 21, 1980, in Robinson's office. Maxwell's initial charm was offset by Robinson's frostiness. As Maxwell spoke about placing his talents at BPC's disposal to save the company from bankruptcy, Robinson reminded him of the DTI's conclusion that he could not be relied upon to be a steward of a publicly quoted company; an opinion which, over the weekend, all of BPC's bankers, brokers and major customers had repeated to each other.

"I want a position on the board," said Maxwell.

"I haven't decided," replied Robinson as the acrimony intensified.

"I demand it," hissed Maxwell as he left the room, "and I will expect the appointment by the time I return from Moscow."

Robinson was coldly non-committal, thinking that the origins of BPC's financial plight lay in Maxwell's own stewardship of ILSC twelve years earlier. After so many years struggling to manage BPC, he could barely perceive his own weaknesses but consoled himself with the reflection that his pleas about the very unsuitability of the predator would be heard sympathetically in the City and Whitehall. He ordered that BPC's defense should rest entirely on regurgitating Maxwell's record.

Compiling the indictment was assigned to a fellow director, Montague "Monty" Alfred, who set about plundering the DTI reports and newspaper cuttings. The character of Maxwell which Alfred chose to draw for submission to the Office of Fair Trading was of an evil genius who had been so persuasive that decent men would do and say things which they knew were wrong. But after three weeks Alfred acknowledged that for the board to rely uniquely upon such a negative argument was demoralizing and he decided as an afterthought to telephone a former colleague, Lord Kearton, with whom he had worked at Courtaulds, to seek his advice and help.

Kearton's career had won him prestige as a skilled and independent industrialist who was critical of what some called the City's traditions but which he condemned as incompetence. He had just retired as manager of the Labor government's agency which controlled North Sea oil but he was still a non-executive director of BPC's merchant bankers, Hill Samuel. To Alfred's relief, Kearton agreed to help the beleaguered board despite the company's tense relations with their bank who, it was inevitably but wrongly suspected, had "failed" to anticipate the dawn raid because of the close relationship between Maxwell and Hill Samuel's director, Sir Robert Clark.

Acting as the honest broker, Kearton called first on Henry Benson, who had a special responsibility for Britain's "sick industries" at the Bank of England. Kearton was surprised by his old friend's attitude. "His view was simply that BPC should be liquidated as quickly and quietly as possible," says Kearton, "and without a public row about Maxwell." At the DTI, Kearton found that Peter Carey, the permanent secretary, was similarly uninterested in BPC's fate. "Peter believed that it was beyond redemption and he wasn't keen on Maxwell." Kearton concluded that BPC, which was losing £1 million every month, was not only heading toward the rocks but was also friendless. By November, Robinson had discovered the same unpalatable truth but was desperate to deny Maxwell the prize he anxiously sought.

Robinson's relations with Hill Samuel had by then deteriorated and he sought the help of Hambros, who had enjoyed such a mixed relationship with Maxwell. Antony Beevor's brief was to produce any rescue package which was predicated first to exclude Maxwell and only secondly to save BPC. In the meantime, Robinson appealed to BPC's major creditor, the National Westminster Bank, with a formula which included the appointment of a new chairman. The response of Peter Dodds, the manager of NatWest's London District, was decidedly unsympathetic. He told Robinson that the only appointment he would consider was of a receiver and said further, "We are not neutral and we don't want a battle." The bank stood to lose £17 million if BPC collapsed and as far as Dodds was concerned, "We'd looked at so many of Robinson's schemes and none of them were attractive. Mr. Maxwell's ideas were the best to save our money and the company." Dodds insisted that Maxwell be given a seat on the board because he was offering to invest £10 million in the company. When Robinson queried whether Maxwell had that sort of money, Dodds was surprisingly well informed. Unknown to Robinson, Dodds was also Maxwell's banker. In fact, Maxwell was a very special client who had opened an account in Fitzroy Square in the early 1950s: "He had an excellent track record with us," recalls Dodds, "and had always fulfilled his undertakings. We never had any reason to doubt him. That counts for a lot with bankers." In lengthy sessions after the July raid, Maxwell had persuaded Dodds that the bank could depend upon Maxwell to recover its money and it should therefore grant him exceptionally favorable terms for the huge loans which he still required. The DTI reports, says Dodds, were "irrelevant." "A far-seeing man," is Kearton's judgment about Dodds.

By Christmas, Kearton's role had changed: he became the mediator between Maxwell, BPC and the City. "Maxwell had bombarded me with ideas on how to save the company," recalls Kearton, "and no one else was interested. I thought his survival plan might work, despite the unions and board saying it was 'impossible.' " Kearton had also shrugged off the many warnings from those who had been employed or had negotiated with Maxwell. Kearton could not understand their antagonism although he had never occupied either position. "He's just a hard taskmaster," says Kearton, later adding, "I'll concede that the one way to cease having any influence over him is to work for him." Kearton had also no sympathy with Robinson's references to the DTI reports: "I read them carefully and decided that Maxwell was the victim of his own exuberance, verbosity and optimism, but he wasn't wicked. I felt that his wrongdoings were small change compared to a lot of happenings in the City and the inspectors had been unfair on him." Kearton's conclusion stunned Robinson and Alfred: "I told them that they had no choice but to let Maxwell see the accounts and decide if he wanted to invest his money." Robinson resisted until Dodds issued a firm veto on a public battle with Maxwell, and Hambros's overly complicated rescue had to be jettisoned along with the bank. BPC's survival depended on Maxwell. In trepidation, Robinson returned to Hill Samuel and the unpalatable cure of Maxwell's "survival plan."

In Maxwell's life, it was a historic moment, similar to the award of the Military Cross, and on this occasion there could be no suggestion of reckless bravado. Deserted by all his bankers, Robinson had no choice by the end of January but to agree that Maxwell should effectively take over the company, which was on the verge of bankruptcy. "I feel pretty sick," Robinson told a friend.

Formally, on February 17, 1981, Maxwell was voted on to the board as deputy chairman and chief executive. Kearton was appointed chairman with Robinson as managing director. The next stage was for Maxwell to convince the print unions to dismantle their restrictive work practices since his personal investment and the National Westminster Bank's funds were available to save BPC only if the unions made enormous concessions. Maxwell was now on public trial not only to save a major British company but also to prove that he was a reformed man. Kearton sat as the judge.

Under Kearton's scrutiny, for sixteen hours seven days a week, Maxwell negotiated with the unions about the details of his "survival plan." Although it would cause 2,500 layoffs (one-quarter of the workforce), the closure of five printing plants, the wholesale removal of restrictive practices and the effective reduction of wages, Maxwell called it a "rebuilding exercise." Five years before Rupert Murdoch sabotaged trade union power in his British empire by a midnight flight to Wapping, Maxwell sought to unclasp the union's stranglehold at BPC by releasing an irresistible series of demands.

Representatives from each BPC factory were brought daily to the Queen Street headquarters in London where Maxwell had installed a bed in an office. With a rigid deadline of six weeks, the trade unionists were "locked" in a room to negotiate a survival plan. Fresh from their triumph over Thomson Newspapers, and after a decade of unparalleled union aggrandisement, they greeted Maxwell's unique brand of haggling with truculent disdain. "I watched with fascination," recalls Kearton, "how, moving from room to room, he gradually played off the rivalries between the chapels, and then between the chapels and the national organizations. They abused him but he never lost his temper, he never gave the impression of being under pressure and he was always the master of his facts. Above all, he left no one in any doubt that, without him, they'd all be unemployed." The recollections of the union representatives are less generous. Dumbfounded by the long hours and the unprecedented *diktat* of a deadline, they gradually retreated, deflated and perplexed to be dealing with a workaholic whose first offer had been the best. In one tense moment, as they argued to recover lost ground, Bill Miles, a SOGAT official, blurted out to the menacing publisher, "You've got so many balls in the air, Mr. Maxwell, but don't forget, two of them are mine." Maxwell roared with laughter, satisfied that his tactics were being rewarded.

But his growing success was also due to a consistent display of charm. For someone who is so notoriously impatient with lesser men, his performance over those six weeks was of a compassionate man anxious to understand the most mundane objection from the most inarticulate machine-minder. Forever darting in and out of those twenty rooms, Maxwell identified which local officials were presenting the obstacles. Either late that night or early the next morning, the intransigent union member would receive a phone call: "Hello, Robert Maxwell here. I just want to say . . ." and then would follow a conversation which was "a secret between the two of us. Not even the general secretary must know about this. But you and I can settle this because you are so important to our plans. . . ." At their next meeting, Maxwell's giant arms were wrapped around the printer. "My friend and I," Maxwell said to the bewilderment of the other negotiators, "have settled this problem." Bill Keyes was repeatedly amazed: "The greatest wheeler-dealer we'd ever met. He wasn't out to destroy the unions, but just to promote Bob, and also to be loved." Those very contradictions unnerved the blinkered union negotiators. The charisma, the complexity and the charm of a man who spoke their language so fluently was baffling. "He always had to prove himself," says Keyes, recalling how the "nice-guy act" was selective and rarely genuine, especially toward the BPC board: "They were treated with contempt."

The apparent cause of that contempt was Maxwell's anger about the abuses and profligacy which had been cultivated under Robinson's regime. At the Park Royal plant, which printed the *Radio Times,* the average pay was £15,000 a year for four days' work per week, and the car park, says Kearton, "was packed with Mercedes cars earned from second jobs." Inside Park Royal, six men instead of one were "minding" machines and if one of those six was absent through illness, the management were compelled to hire a temporary replacement with enormous penalty costs. Even seventy-year-olds were still on the payroll, although they were not working. Maxwell seized on these symbols to undermine the unions and humiliate Robinson's record. Although Robinson had inherited the anarchic conditions at Park Royal, he had deliberately not interfered to avoid endangering BPC's profitable contract with the BBC. That would change, Maxwell told Kearton. There would be no frills. Executives would follow his example and fly economy class. Expenses would be slashed. He had even noticed, he commented to Kearton, that excessive bottles of milk were ordered at several warehouses. Robinson was excluded from these sessions but Kearton was impressed. Any man who promised to eradicate the obesity and caprice of executive life appealed to Kearton, although there were not many who today would recognize the image of the self-denying millionaire which Maxwell portrayed for the *Bookseller* in August 1980: "I come from a farm-laboring family," he said, "and I don't go in for owning yachts or going to big parties."

Kearton had also paved the way in the City for Maxwell's return. "I assured everyone that, having seen Maxwell at close quarters, he was a genius. I even insured him for £15 million because of his importance." If in retrospect it seems that in BPC Maxwell had shrewdly chosen the firmest foundations for his latest relaunch, that was not the common opinion at the time. Maxwell, it was felt, was taking a major risk to buy his way back to respectability and his chances were slim. He would have agreed that his initial investment was a gamble, but it was of a different complexion from what others imagined. In all his years, other than the barter trade, he rarely invested in a business without anticipating or inventing a profitable exit. In BPC's case, his initial £2.9 million investment was certainly a risk, but it was also carefully calculated to lead to the next stage. For £10 million, Pergamon would own assets worth £70 million, a huge tax loss and a guaranteed income in the future because, even before committing his money to BPC, Maxwell had secured support and new orders from his future customers, among them the Thomson Organisation.

Despite their differences over the years, Roy's son Kenneth Thomson had sympathy for the irascible Maxwell. The impulsive, unpredictable salesman and trader possessed qualities which might destroy the same trade unions who had recently driven Thomson from Fleet Street. Like other customers for BPC's color magazines, Thomson saw no advantage if the choice of possible suppliers diminished. In Thomson's view, Maxwell was BPC's only hope, but was being harmed by carping criticisms which suggested that BPC's customers, including Thomson, would refuse to deal with Maxwell. In an unusual gesture of support, Gordon Brunton, Thomson's managing director in Britain, therefore issued a letter for circulation to both the unions and the City which promised that his group would place as many orders as possible with BPC if Maxwell were successful. The pledge would be honored for one year but ended when Maxwell tried, slyly in Thomson's view, to renegotiate the contracts.

Maxwell's potential losses were accordingly less than those extracted from BPC's employees, since his money was committed only when every chapel had succumbed and signed a binding and publishable agreement. Bill Keyes was present when the last chapel signed the agreement and as Maxwell theatrically wrote out the check for £10 million. "Do you want to come with me to the bank?" he asked the union leader. "You must be joking," Keyes replied, "I've just lost a lot of members." Among the assets which Pergamon now owned was ILSC and Caxton encyclopedias. The wheel of fortune had turned full circle.

A special shareholders' meeting was summoned for April 24 to approve the reconstruction of the company. The alternative, spelled out in bold, dark type on the memorandum, was that BPC would be placed in liquidation. Overwhelmingly, the proposals were supported, and Maxwell was rehabilitated. Appropriately, the meeting (held in the Connaught Rooms, the venue of so many past humiliations) was followed by a champagne celebration at BPC's headquarters. The star was jubilant, applauded and feted by men who six months earlier would have looked askance at him. This was a perfect moment to judge his character for, as Kearton would write on Maxwell's sixtieth birthday, "The best is still to come." Until then, in Maxwell's business life, the trait most frequently perceived was his indomitable will to recover from defeat. Repeatedly, Maxwell could be heard appealing for fairness and justice. Without precedent for a businessman who had so often tumbled and fallen, he had miraculously won another chance.

Peter Robinson did not arrive at the champagne celebration. During the shareholders' meeting he had collapsed from pneumonia caused by a suspected gallstone in his kidney. Maxwell had said little as the former chairman staggered from the hall. Understandably, Robinson had no future in BPC but nothing had prepared either Robinson or others for the scathing contempt felt for him by his successor. As Robinson lay sick in hospital, Maxwell showed that those who had no power to exert over him, whether employees or competitors, could expect neither respect nor their due. Robinson's office was occupied by Maxwell, his name was removed from the door, his papers sealed, and he was told of Maxwell's decision that, despite years of service, his performance at BPC disqualified him from receiving a pension. It was a telling omen which Kearton, with effort, rectified. Others, over the following years, would often fail to find a similar agent of mercy to give them protection. Few outside Maxwell's immediate employment, which until then had been so limited, had realized that a man who had personally suffered such scorn would himself seek to humiliate others. But Robinson's misery was long forgotten in the frantic schedule which Maxwell undertook in the weeks after the takeover.

Traveling incessantly by helicopter to BPC factories around the country, Maxwell appeared before all the BPC employees in the role he would come to adore. "Gentlemen," the giant would say, often standing astride a table in the canteen, "I am Robert Maxwell and this company has been grossly mismanaged. I am going to put it right. We must make more money. I am looking for job cuts, but I'll save the rest." As patches of hostility appeared, the voice rose slightly: "Gentlemen, you must remember that I am now the proprietor of this business." Few would be more impressed than his new employees at Taylous, near Maidenhead. So roused was his audience by the performance and by the promise of a bright future that they clapped and cheered, oblivious of the fact that their new hero had just announced that, to create the new Jerusalem, the majority were about to lose their jobs.

But in Queen Street, soon to be renamed Maxwell House, few observed that charm. Instead, his new staff experienced unprecedented scrutiny, especially of every penny's expenditure. Only Maxwell could sanction the purchase of a new car or the hire of a temporary secretary, or sign a check for over £500. On one memorable occasion, an assistant pushed a chit in front of him.

"What's this?" growled the great man.

"Approval for a new car for a rep," replied the humbled employee.

"Why does he need a new car?" asked the employer as his voice rose to a roar. "Why do we need this man? Fire him."

But not only reps were dismissed. In the first five years of Maxwell's reign, very few of the company's directors, even those whom he appointed, survived for more than one year. Few could satisfy his demands or cope with the stress. "It was annoying and mentally tiring," recalls David Perry, a former English rugby captain and the manager of BPC's factory at Taylous, "that he acted without consulting anyone."

Daily, after seven every morning, Perry and all the managers rang Maxwell for instructions. "Take this down," said the chairman, dictating the orders of the day before banging down the receiver. What emerged was not always pursued and indeed was often contradicted by Maxwell himself. Behind the bluster and the bullying there was a drastic strategy to reduce costs. The strategy was successful but the qualities of leadership and vision demanded by some were lacking. Overheads tumbled as the closures and redundancies were implemented. After one year the monthly £1 million loss was transformed into a £1 million profit. But those whom he admitted that he needed most—managers like Perry, the financial director David Harbut and the innovators like Peter Hassell—had decided to leave. They were weary and wary of an instant decision-maker, "shooting from the hip," who rejected the conventional organization of management and who seemed to thrive on creating rather than settling uncertainty. Perry calls it "motivation by fear" and, among other reasons, left because "I couldn't stand wondering when the stab would come." Monty Alfred was among the many who were embarrassed in front of other employees before leaving the corporation. It was a settling of scores.

By the end of 1981, BPC's survival was described even by Maxwell's most bitter critics as a miracle. Despite a major recession, the company's profits could finance a £100 million investment plan for new machinery. Yet, as his visibility grew, the apparent patience and understanding shown toward trade unionists, which won Kearton's blessing during those six weeks of negotiations, disappeared.

Throughout the 1960s, Maxwell had combined the role of buccaneer businessman with his pledge to socialism. In the House of Commons, he had been an outspoken if ineffectual critic of the suicidal Luddism which imbued both British management and unions. In the 1970s, he had observed his predictions come true and had eagerly awaited the opportunity to effect his draconian solutions. The BPC agreement which sliced trade union power was just a foretaste of "Maxwell's law." He realized that challenging trade unions where previous, supine managements had failed was a profitable strategy and one which, for him, was politically acceptable. Although the cause was also popular among the Conservatives, in his own ranks, where he became renowned as antitrade unionist, he provoked bitter opposition.

The first to protest were the unions at Pergamon's headquarters in Oxford. Maxwell's attitude toward his own employees had hardened since the days in Neal Street and Maxwell House in Marylebone. There were, he felt, to be no free meal tickets and he had ordered the installation of an electronic recording system which monitored the hours each employee worked. Maxwell still enjoyed using a loudspeaker system to address his workers, always prefacing his monologue, "Attention, attention, this is your chairman speaking. . . ." Some found the atmosphere unpalatable.

In a memorandum dated September 14, 1979, Maxwell had acknowledged that labor relations in his own publishing house were bad and cited as evidence the awkward fact that "during the past few months there has been a turnover of more than 50% within the Department. This high staff turnover is harmful. . . ." Feelings about working for Maxwell were mixed. Some were content, but a minority criticized the atmosphere as reminiscent of school. Throughout the 1970s, Maxwell had only reluctantly improved wages, which by 1980 ranked fifty-fourth in the NUJ's list of fifty-seven publishers. Similarly, fringe conditions such as maternity benefits had not improved since 1972 despite the company's new profitability. Patrick Tickell, who was employed as joint managing director for eight months in 1977, was among those who disliked the atmosphere and was deemed unable to cope with the exacting demands. "The reason for the level of turnover," says Tickell, "was simply that people did not like the conditions of work. They were expected to work extremely hard and never make mistakes. Yet their duties were never really explained to them. Instant dismissal without substantial justification was common, but I recall people being hastily reinstated after having been summarily fired by Mr. Maxwell."

After 1979, serious disagreements erupted between Maxwell and the unions concerning the further employment of two probationers. On reasonable grounds, Pergamon had not renewed their contracts, but the manner of their treatment prompted the NUJ in March 1981 to call for an official strike because, after two years, Maxwell had refused to negotiate a new wage settlement. Nine employees were summarily dismissed two days after they went on strike. Maxwell described the strikers as having "sacked themselves" and defamed them as "politically motivated musketeers" and even as "Trotskyites." Since the strikers were poorly supported, the dispute would not have escalated into a test of Maxwell's principles had a feeling not spread among many socialists that, although he was a member of both the Labour Party and the Association of Scientific, Technical and Managerial Staffs, he was bullying the union. Maxwell, who was operating in a goldfish bowl where every gesture was scrutinized, was sensitive to any coverage of his troubles, especially when it appeared on June 6, 1981, in the *Bookseller*. "I took a call from Maxwell," recalls David Whitaker, the publisher of the magazine, "and he demanded a retraction of the report. He said it was a libel. I told him we had just reported facts. He threatened a writ for defamation if I didn't apologize." The conversation ended dramatically.

"Rubbish," said Whitaker.

"Are you calling me a liar?" said Maxwell.

"No, I just think that you are very mistaken."

"I want a retraction."

"Balls," shouted Whitaker.

"I beg your pardon?"

"Balls," repeated Whitaker as the phone went dead.

In reply, Maxwell issued a writ and spent the following two years engaged in all ill-tempered struggle.

The magazine had reported that Maxwell's terms of employment and style of labor relations were not quite perfect. For more than one year, during the Pergamon dispute, Maxwell had either refused to meet union officials or canceled meetings. Often, he uttered exaggerated allegations about union officials and then, when national union officers answered his claims by substantiated and detailed rebuttals, he not only ignored their refutation but repeated the same unfounded allegations. For those with memories about Maxwell's speeches on the loudspeaker at the *Scottish Daily News,* the pattern was familiar: namely, any opponent or critic was deemed to be a subversive. By 1981, Maxwell was becoming estranged from his political allies. As Jonathan Hammond of the National Union of Journalists said, "Mr. Maxwell frequently boasts about his commitment to trade unionism and socialism . . . [but] is Mr. Maxwell's behavior at Pergamon consistent with the standards recognized by membership of those organizations?"

Hammond and the NUJ leaders were particularly irritated that Maxwell excused his refusal to negotiate by pleading travel abroad on business. On subsequent occasions, similar excuses were proven to be untrue. Twice in March 1982, Maxwell's lawyers had told industrial tribunals that their client was traveling in South Africa and Japan, while in fact he was in London and Oxford. Maxwell claimed that those trips were canceled "at the last moment" and blamed his subordinates for failing to remind him of his appointment in court. The unions threatened to escalate the anti-Maxwell campaign just as he was anxious for rehabilitation. Their ability to cause damage was undoubted and persuaded him to reinstate the Pergamon strikers and improve their conditions of employment. He also withdrew his writ against the *Bookseller* and paid a record £30,000 toward the publisher's costs.

The Pergamon dispute, literally on his own doorstep, was mild compared to his struggle with the typesetters and machine-minders at BPC's presses at Park Royal where the *Radio Times* was set and printed. Despite their written undertaking, the local union leaders, who were members of the NGA, had reneged on their agreement and, ignoring the orders of their national leaders, began two years of vituperative and disruptive strikes. Production was sabotaged by interfering with machinery, paper runs and the electricity supply, while the printers extracted agreements for double manning levels and pay increases which were three times higher than those of other BPC employees. It was a trial of strength which Maxwell could not afford to lose, either commercially or, more importantly, personally after the militants had doused him in oil and insulted him to his face.

If the original purchase of the BPC shares in the dawn raid three years earlier had been his Normandy landings, Park Royal was his Battle for Berlin. The ground had been carefully prepared. BPC workers at East Kilbride in Scotland and Leeds had been promised a glowing future if they agreed to print the *Radio Times,* and the national union leaders had been carefully maneuvered into dissociating themselves from their rebellious membership. On November 14, 1983, after sixteen million copies of the magazine had been lost, a group of large men with 14-lb. sledge hammers entered the premises and smashed the fifty-year-old presses to pieces. The printers watched with amazement as their sword of Damocles disintegrated before their eyes. Their reaction was unprintable. "Jungle man" was victorious. "If Britain had six more Maxwells," commented Lord Kearton, "the country would have no more worries." Maxwell beamed. This was a talent which he could capitalize on. After all the years in the wilderness, the emerging chrysalis was very confident: "If I can run BPC, then I can do so much more."

At the end of 1982, Maxwell admitted that he felt "slightly bored" and needed new challenges. That year, BPC boasted £20 million profits, "the highest in its history," and although the accounts played down its enormous debts which were published in the annual report, no one doubted that its salvation was secure. Maxwell's ambitions were signaled by the change of name to the British Printing and Communications Corporation, which encompassed his target of spreading into cable and satellite television, into computers and data banks, into electronic printing and every communications technology that was invented. Like a revolving door, "experts" passed through BPCC to satisfy the chairman's restless urge to develop his company to "rank among the world's ten largest communications corporations." The vision he extolled to Saul Steinberg in January 1969 would finally come to fruition. No one else in Britain could boast his foresight, which had been fed by an insatiable appetite to learn during his traveling. But he was sixty years old with at best a decade to achieve the everlasting fame which had for three decades so unfairly eluded him. BPCC needed more money and he wanted more activities to occupy himself. The solution was to return to what he could do so well, the mixed recipe of juggling and trading which had earned his fortune in Maxwell House on the Marylebone Road.

In rapid succession in 1983, Maxwell sought to rescue Oxford United football club from bankruptcy for £120,000, bought a 13.8 per cent stake in Central Television, and purchased a rash of companies with terminal financial problems. Most of the investments earned him headlines but only limited profits. At the end of 1981 Oxford United was in the Football League's Third Division losing £2,000 a week, when a Pergamon employee approached Maxwell and asked whether he would be interested in saving his local club from bankruptcy. During the 1960s Oxford United had enjoyed a mercurial revival but in the mid-1970s its fortunes began declining. According to Bill Reeves, then club chairman, "There was a crisis in football generally because the gate figures were dropping. There just wasn't any commercial input in the game." In Maxwell's view, the game was suffering the same malaise as BPC and so much else of British industry. It was managed by parochial, short-sighted and sometimes uncommercial men who had allowed their industry to degenerate in filthy stadiums plagued by hooliganism. In America, by contrast, the sport was beginning to thrive. Here was another chance for Maxwell the reformer to change another British institution. Despite his accountants' advice that the club was a bad investment, Maxwell agreed, on January 6, 1982, to pay off the club's debts of £128,000 in return for taking control. Since there were no evident business reasons for the investment (which was in any event a relatively insignificant amount), there can be no doubt that, despite the incredulity of the football world, he was solely motivated by philanthropy. "I'm doing it as a service to the community," he would say later about becoming involved in a new sphere. Two days after the acquisition he began looking for a new manager, and demanded that the local council should agree to moving the club to a new and larger stadium while granting permission for its old ground to be redeveloped. The council instantly rejected his demand and was rewarded by the traditional bombardment of criticisms and epithets. "When I became chairman," he later said, "I was promised by the City Council that we would get the Marston site for a new ground. Then they changed their minds." The Council denied his claims. As his row with football's establishment intensified, in April 1983 he proposed a radical new solution—to merge Oxford United with Reading FC. The idea collapsed one month later. But by then, his survival plan and the appointment of Jim Smith as manager had transformed the club's finances from debt into profit. More spectators were watching a winning side, yet his presence had caused endless controversy. The sport was perplexed by an overweight club owner running across the pitch, appearing on the terraces and basking in the applause of the fans demanding his autograph. The high profile earned him opprobrium and death threats as he waded into the terraces to stop fighting and threatened to close the club unless the Council cooperated with his efforts.

Three years later, when the club had won its way into the First Division, the Council agreed to invest in the club. Jim Smith, the star manager, however, resigned, claiming that he could no longer work with Maxwell. Smith had been surprised that his employer, who was involved in so many other businesses, still required to be regularly consulted about the weekly selection of the team, transfers of players and every aspect of the business. Maxwell easily shrugged off Smith's departure; but his difficulties in business were not so easily ignored.

In June 1983, he embarked upon a takeover bid which rebounded upon him and revealed, to his discomfort, that his past was still an albatross.

His new target was John Waddington, a small but important firm of printers and packagers whose expertise fitted in well with BPCC's aspirations. They were also the manufacturers of "Monopoly," the world's most famous game for aspiring capitalists. The bid started at 7:30 a.m. on June 17. Victor Watson, Waddington's impish chairman, had been at his desk for fifteen minutes when Maxwell telephoned. Later that morning, said the caller from London, he would be making a bid for the company. Watson was already fighting off another bid and Maxwell presented himself as a "white knight" who would save the beleaguered damsel.

"Waddington is not for sale," replied Watson, "and I won't meet you."

"I always win," snapped Maxwell. "So there's no point in fighting."

"We will fight you every inch of the way," said Watson.

But Maxwell's timing was perfect. Waddington had barely recovered from huge losses on video games and was vulnerable to a bid. "He was like a shark, who smells blood and chases the prey," says Watson.

In the three years since he had bought BPC, Maxwell had assumed that rejection was something of the past. He had after all become the printing industry's self-styled great hope. Over the following six weeks, as the two men engaged in a hectic battle to secure the support of Waddington's institutional shareholders, Maxwell was convinced of victory because he had secured acceptance in the City. But according to

Watson, "I was going to use any tactics to give him a nasty shock." Maxwell, however, possessed the initiative and his tactics were unnerving. There were regular telephone calls to both Watson and his managing director David Perry, who had recently resigned from BPC, to persuade them to surrender. Perry recalls particularly the calls early on Sunday mornings:

"Bob Maxwell here. I just want you to understand that we can work together."

"The business is not for sale," replied Perry.

"You know that I'm going to win. It's inevitable," concluded Maxwell with intimidating certainty.

Maxwell also persistently telephoned Watson in attempts to arrange a meeting. "I always refused," recalls Watson, "because I feared giving the wrong impression." Finally, on Maxwell's promise that he would never reveal the encounter, the two met to discuss Maxwell's offer of a better price for the company and a seat for Watson on BPCC's main board as the vice-chairman. This, Watson realized, was Maxwell's classic ploy which had so often evaporated. The story of Donald Davies, who had been offered the post as BPCC's managing director by Maxwell in 1982, was already legendary. At lunchtime, Davies had excitedly confided the offer to two friends in a pub, only to hear that they had received identical approaches. Watson thought of the Yorkshire maxim, "He talks as he warms." All Maxwell's offers were refused and Watson returned to Wakefield. The next day's newspapers carried reports that the two men had met. Watson was shocked and called in experts to check Waddington's offices for bugs. "He established an atmosphere of paranoia," recalls Perry, "and it seemed to be successful."

Toward the end of August, Maxwell was heading toward a slender majority. Watson was as desperate as Robinson had been three years earlier: "I wasn't going to let him win." His defenses included the use of private detectives. One of their tasks was to check the truth of a claim by BPCC that it had sold a large property in Watford for £20 million with planning permission for development as a shopping center. If true, BPCC's profits would be higher than predicted, so enhancing the value of the BPCC shares which were offered in the bid for Waddington. The detective reported to Watson that planning permission had not yet been granted since the local council was still hostile. BPCC's announcement had been premature.

Watson seized upon that mistake as an example of the "optimism" which characterized Maxwell's past transgressions. His targets for the message were Waddington's shareholders, among them the Norwich

Union, whose holding was 5 per cent. Their stake had already been pledged to Maxwell. "I appealed to the fund manager to change his allegiance," says Watson. "I told him it was his duty to see me on a moral issue." Take-over bids have rarely been perceived as moral issues but Watson transformed the bid for his small company into a test of Maxwell's character.

Unaccustomed in his recent past to such resistance, Maxwell was distressed by the unusual blitz of antagonistic propaganda which Watson had inspired. "I have had several Waddington shareholders complaining they had up to eight telephone calls urging them to withdraw their acceptances," he complained. "This borders on harassment." Maxwell had clearly forgotten his own tactics during his bid for the *News of the World*. But when the Norwich Union switched sides, Maxwell tersely conceded defeat: "Mr. Watson threw a googly at me." "When he said that," Watson remarks, "he betrayed himself as a foreigner because every Englishman knows you 'bowl' a googly." When prejudice and prospective profits compete in a contested bid, Maxwell would always be the loser. His opportunities lay only where the unique talents of the "jungle man" could be applied.

In 1982, Sir Alexander Jarratt, the chairman of Reed International, was seeking an opportunity to save the conglomerate from the legacy of merger mania and bankruptcy. Among its loss-makers was Odhams Press in Watford, an inheritance from the International Publishing Corporation, which was sited near BPC's Sun Printers. Odhams, which printed *Woman* and *Woman's Realm* magazines, would lose £5.5 million that year and had accumulated losses over the previous ten years of £30 million. Odham's plight could only worsen. Magazine circulations were still declining, there was chronic overmanning and there was no money to buy new printing machinery. Both Jarratt and the chairman of IPC, Leslie Carpenter, identified the only potential customer for their liability in Robert Maxwell. "Although Maxwell was helped by the change of environment introduced by the Thatcher government," says Jarratt, "he had also changed the environment. But also, we lacked Maxwell's temperament and style to confront the unions." Jarratt was soon to discover that he was a less effective negotiator than Maxwell.

"Negotiating with Bob," testify both Reed executives, "is not a pleasure. We agreed to the terms of the sale within ninety minutes and then he began haggling and spent days and weeks renegotiating and rewriting the deal we thought had been settled. He's a born haggler." When they finally did sign, Maxwell had obtained for a mere £1.5 million the Odhams factory, its twenty-three acres of land, a print order worth

£30 million for IPC magazines plus a £7.5 million interest-free loan from Reeds for two years. It was a brilliant deal if he could cow the unions into agreeing to mass layoffs. His scheme was to sack 1,500 Odhams employees and transfer the printing to BPC plants. He would then sell the Odhams estate. If the unions protested, he would threaten to close not only Odhams but also BPC's own Sun Printers on the grounds that only one factory could be profitable. As always, there would be a deadline. "Maxwell can say and do things," says Carpenter, "which would stick in the gullet of traditional British owners. He is hard, skillful and persuasive." All those qualities were exploited on the day the deal was signed. It ended, Jarratt recalls with amazement, "in true Maxwellian style."

Carpenter had traveled to Southend to brief SOGAT about the deal. Meanwhile in London, Jarratt, surrounded by lawyers, was signing the raft of documents which such agreements entail. Maxwell sat impatiently until he announced that he was flying by helicopter to Watford. Jarratt was still signing when one hour later Maxwell telephoned:

"I addressed all the workers in the canteen and told them that at least half of them would be made redundant but I would save the rest of their jobs."

"Yes," replied Jarratt in trepidation.

"And do you know, they cheered me . . ."

"Well done," interrupted Jarratt with relief.

"Yes, I'm rather good at that sort of thing," swooned the man in Watford with pride.

After financing the 1,400 layoffs, the remaining profits of the Odhams site saved BPC from losses in 1984. Without that property sale, and the purchase and asset-stripping of the Bishopsgate Trust in the same year, BPCC's spectacular growth of profits, which played such a vital role in Maxwell's self-promotion, would not have occurred. Combined with Pergamon's record profits from sales of journals and his share deals, Maxwell started 1984 with substantial funds.

In contrast, Carpenter and Jarratt were still pondering how they would rid themselves of their last commitment to Reed's printing legacy—the *Daily Mirror* group.

13

"I only want to be of service to my fellow man" is a phrase which Maxwell fondly professed whenever asked to justify the apparent contradictions of his politics, lifestyle and business career. To many listeners, it struck the same chord as the superlatives which peppered his companies' annual reports. Invariably, they contained a surfeit of phrases such as "excellent results," "valuable source," "record level," "outstanding contribution," "significant profit increase," "very substantial," "world leader," "dramatic profit growth," etc. Throughout Maxwell's life, his chosen words conveyed meanings to his audience very different from those he intended. Accordingly, while the phrase "service to my fellow man" implies the performance of a charitable or beneficial act, used by Maxwell in 1984 it meant, besides much else, his intention to purchase the *Daily Mirror*.

Soon after Odhams was sold, Alex Jarratt and the Reed board agreed that they also wanted to be rid of the *Daily Mirror* and the grinding struggle with Fleet Street's print unions which was sapping managerial energy in return for paltry profits—just £1 million on a turnover of £200 million. Jarratt is a former civil servant but with a distinctly non-Whitehall ability to take initiatives. He harbored no sentimental reservations about selling the *Mirror,* and had no wish to play the power game as the chairman of Britain's largest newspaper group whose six titles (*Daily Mirror, Sunday Mirror, Sunday People, Daily Record, Sunday Mail* and *Sporting Life*) sold thirty-one million copies every week. Jarratt was nevertheless mindful of the *Mirror*'s historic traditions.

Formerly owned by Lords Rothermere and Northcliffe, it had in recent memory been controlled by similar giants, Cecil King and Hugh Cudlipp. The paper's radical editor, Guy Bartholomew, who in fifteen years had pushed the newspaper's circulation from 720,000 to 4½ million, had secured for the *Mirror* a mention in history as the western world's largest-selling daily newspaper. Its soaring popularity was based upon a mixture of sensationalism, original journalism and easily digested but intelligent reporting. The newspaper's heady success bolstered its executives' image of themselves as godlike figures who could stride the world without care about censorship or cost. The first major casualty was Cecil King in 1968, after he wrote and published a signed editorial "Enough is Enough," demanding the removal of Harold Wilson, the Labor Prime Minister. Two years after his well-publicized dismissal, IPC merged with the Reed group, its glamour and prestige still intact, but its profitability declining fast.

Reed placed most of the blame for its losses on the thirteen trade unions in the Mirror Group. The machine room in the *Mirror* building had by 1970 become an unendearing model of anarchy and villainy. During the nights, especially Saturdays, large numbers of highly paid but unneeded printers sat in the basement of the ugly red-topped building watching blue movies or playing high-stake poker. Depending upon their seniority and muscle, many had even clocked in under two names and were receiving double wages for no work. Others had registered but were working or sleeping elsewhere. It was not unknown at the end of a shift for wage packets to remain unclaimed because the printers were too drunk to recall which phony names they had registered under on arrival. By any standards, their wages were phenomenally high, ample to provide luxurious homes, several foreign holidays every year and even funds to set up private businesses. It was an abuse whose roots could be traced back four centuries to the introduction of Gutenberg's presses. Although after 1970 technology had rendered their ancient crafts long redundant, the printers' jobs and privileges were protected by their mere threat to stop production if management dared to interfere.

At the *Mirror,* in common with all Fleet Street newspapers, the printers were paid not only to perform their task but also extra sums as "compensation" if work was contracted to outsiders. Whenever the management attempted to interfere with this notorious catalogue of "old Spanish customs," the consequences were predictable. A flick of a knife on a paper run or an inspired malfunction of a machine would sabotage that night's production, causing irrecoverable losses. Anxious to keep their papers on the street, the *Mirror*'s management paid their printers' demands and suffered in as much silence as their self-interest determined.

The management's tolerance of those abuses would have been surprising had they not enjoyed similar privileges. In the floors above the printing presses, the Mirror Group's executives and journalists enjoyed a lush all-expenses-paid lifestyle which their talents would not have earned in pastures outside journalism. Both Tony Miles, the chairman of the Mirror Group, and Douglas Long, the deputy chairman, were grateful that Reed's granting of total editorial independence allowed them considerable freedom over expenditure. New arrivals at the newspapers were always pleasantly astonished by gargantuan meals, constant high-cost celebrations on the smallest pretext and profligate foreign travel in the style which few could defend as vital for journalism. There was constant ribaldry that the Mirror management's introduction of new technology had actually increased costs while similar machinery installed in Lagos, Nigeria, was functioning perfectly and saving money.

Throughout the 1970s, Jarratt and Carpenter hardly interfered with the abuses in High Holborn and did not even appoint a representative to the Mirror board. Deliberately, they made High Holborn into a no-go area. The sole overt sign of their control was a monthly dinner which Jarratt hosted at the Savoy for the senior editors. Jarratt rarely complained that the *Mirror*'s circulation of 3.3 million had fallen behind the *Sun*'s or that the newspaper's profits were declining despite his editors' down-market chase in the nipple stakes. But by 1983 the excesses were infecting expectations of other employees throughout the group and Reed's share price was suffering by association with its unwholesome subsidiary. Nearly all the traditional newspaper families had been driven out of Fleet Street because of the abuses and Reed wanted to join the exodus, especially since its shares in the Reuters news agency had become unexpectedly valuable and boosted the price it might expect.

During the summer of 1983, Jarratt and Leslie Carpenter put out what are known as "discreet feelers" intimating that the newspaper group might be for sale. To their disappointment, there was absolutely no interest. "The papers' profits had fallen badly and the reputation for excesses was so bad that no one would risk their money," says Carpenter. Even Maxwell declined the offer, because, it was believed, he did not have the £100 million in cash which Carpenter mentioned as the price. Reed's problem was how to dispose of its costly asset. After brainstorming with its advisers, an unusual formula emerged which would make a virtue of their failure to find one individual who was prepared to buy the whole group.

In October 1983, Jarratt announced that Mirror Group newspapers would be floated as a separate company on the Stock Exchange and there would be a special provision in the conditions of the sale to prevent one individual winning total control. Ironically, since no one knew that he had privately rejected the chance to purchase the group, Jarratt's public announcement was interpreted as a deliberate snub to Maxwell's known ambitions. Jarratt mentioned two further conditions which would be included in the prospectus for the sale. The first was the tradition that the Mirror Group's editors had enjoyed unfettered freedom from the newspaper's owners. The second was the support for the Labour Party which the paper had espoused for decades. Reed's announcement was therefore greeted by the *Mirror*'s staff with some regret but no foreboding. It fell to Leslie Carpenter to supervise this unusual transaction.

Carpenter, who was educated at Hackney Technical College, had worked in the print industry all his life and was well acquainted with its problems and personalities. Unlike Jarratt, he was a technician but he shared the lack of sentiment about the proprietorship and power of newspapers. His first task was to select the chairman of the new company. Significantly, his ideal candidate was not expected to know anything about the newspaper industry; instead he was to be an expert in management and finance, since his function was to present a glowing prospectus of the independent Mirror Group to City institutions and persuade them to buy shares prior to the flotation. Since Jarratt's announcement had stressed that Reed intended that the paper should retain its pro-Labour bias, Carpenter's candidate needed also, for the sake of credibility, to be at least not an obvious Conservative, who might also keep the unions quiet "for the duration." Consistent with Reed's benevolence, Carpenter asked Tony Miles and the Mirror board to suggest their ideal candidate.

Their choice was Clive Thornton, the stocky, fifty-four-year-old chairman of the Abbey National Building Society. Over the previous four years, Thornton had become nationally recognized for transforming the dowdy savings and loan agency into an active cartel-buster, pushing the number of depositors up from four to nearly ten million in four years. Thornton, a solicitor, had enjoyed the glow of media attention which his success as a "people's maverick" had attracted and he responded swiftly and positively to Carpenter's approach. When, at their short introductory meeting, Carpenter suggested that Thornton might remain at the Abbey and take the Mirror chairmanship part-time, Thornton replied that he envisaged the chairmanship as a full-time job. Carpenter shrugged, pleased at least that there was someone who would take the responsibility. "Everyone thought that we had a credible and popular man who might become a super-hero," recalls one of Reed's advisers. "He had successfully turned an old-fashioned business around and we thought he would just run the business successfully until the float." A press release was issued which stated that, under Thornton's management, shares in the new Mirror company would be offered during 1984. The secret target date was January. The new chairman threw himself into the job with relish. "We thought that very unusual," says Jarratt.

Thornton is candid: "I am ambitious and I'm not everyone's cup of tea." Within weeks, relations between Carpenter and Thornton became uneasy. There were reports that Thornton was dictatorial and difficult toward the Mirror's executives, who had known their business for years. The cause was the new chairman's discovery of Fleet Street's debauched style of life. "It was the expenses of the executives which really hit me," recalls Thornton. "Everyone was spending thousands of pounds taking each other out for entertainment." He had heard about the Street of Shame but these antics were beyond his imagination, and on top of that were the intransigent print unions. As Thornton raged, Jarratt advised him to "ride your troops a little more gently." Thornton ignored the suggestion and in October handed Carpenter a poison pill: the flotation was impossible unless the union problems were resolved. "I told Carpenter and Jarratt that we needed a package agreement with the unions of no-strikes and non-automatic replacement of printers." At first the Reed executives were bemused. Thornton's aspiration had eluded the managers of Fleet Street for generations. Ennobled families like the Thomsons, Berrys and Beaverbrooks had been humbled to near ruin, unable to persuade the unions to agree to that simple formula. Thornton, the Reed executives signaled to each other, was naive. "Just float it first and worry about the union negotiations later," advised Jarratt. Thornton disagreed. He would not accept that trade unionists could behave so insanely and for the next months he intensively sought to reorganize the Mirror Group's industrial relations. The unions were decidedly unsympathetic. According to Bill Miles, the SOGAT representative in Fleet Street, "Thornton thought industrial relations was having cups of tea with the workers in the canteen." Bill Keyes was equally sceptical: "He spoke visions and not nuts and bolts. We couldn't lock into his proposals." Consequently, the flotation was repeatedly postponed.

By April 1984, Jarratt and Carpenter were seriously worried. Thornton had adopted a very high profile, eagerly giving press interviews about worker participation and the need for massive investments where he outlined his undiscussed plans to build a new printing plant costing £20 million in Manchester and to launch a range of new daily and evening newspapers once the *Mirror* was independent. Thornton, it was clear to the two Reed executives, was no longer just floating the company but apparently launching himself as a nascent newspaper baron. Of equal concern was Thornton's speculation in the interviews about worker participation and the need for massive investments by the unions and the Labour Party in the new group to protect it from capitalist predators, especially Maxwell. Carpenter feared that if reports of Thornton's arguments with the unions and the Mirror managers did not dissuade potential investors' interest, then his populism would certainly deter the conservative elements in the City. In Thornton's view, if he did not find a formula for industrial peace and a reduction of expenses, there would never be a float. "It was my open-mouth policy," he says, "because I was the ham in the sandwich between Reed, the unions and the potential investors."

By June 1984, Reed and its advisers had become decidedly unsympathetic toward their nominee, who they believed was becoming an unwelcome liability: "We wanted a sale, not a lot of socialist rubbish which was damaging the chances of the sale." In the third week of June, they set July 19 as the irrevocable date for the float. For the countdown, Thornton's office in the Mirror building was turned into a battle headquarters, housing up to twenty advisers to write the prospectus for potential investors. Among those advisers was Derek Higgs of Warburgs, Reed's merchant bankers, who had unexpectedly delivered some very gloomy news.

Twelve months earlier, Higgs had estimated the Mirror Group to be worth £100 million and had hailed Thornton's appointment as "a masterstroke," but he was fast revising his opinion. Price Waterhouse, the accountants, had been asked to undertake an independent survey to produce the "short form" report for the prospectus which would give investors an informed idea about the company's true value. Unknown to the unions or many managers, the accountants had surreptitiously visited the Mirror building at sensitive moments and noted the excesses. Among their revelations was that "James Bond" and "Mickey Mouse" had signed on as printers, and the discovery of horrendous facts about the petty cash, the car pool, drinks and women. The group was more out of control than anyone had realized. Everyone's fears seemed confirmed by a short SOGAT strike in the spring. Considering that there was also a possible liability for large layoff payments, the bankers told Reed on June 27 that they would be lucky to receive £60 million and it might fall as low as £40 million. Thornton was furious: "They completely undervalued their assets and the pension fund," he says, but Warburgs insist that their assessment was fair.

Jarratt and Carpenter were also shaken by the sudden diminution of their potential prize. Their options suddenly seemed to be quite limited because of their public assurance that no dominant shareholder would be permitted to buy control and because employees were to be encouraged to buy shares. However, they decided that there was no alternative other than to proceed and, after much discussion, the mechanism to implement that assurance was agreed at the end of June. The articles of the new company would forbid the registration of one person's share ownership if it exceeded 15 per cent. Just four days after agreeing that clause, the very person whom it was intended to obstruct made an anticipatory move. Maxwell once again fulfilled his notable reputation as a master of timing.

How Maxwell discovered about the 15 per cent rule and that the flotation was becoming stymied by disarray among the personalities involved has been a matter of conjecture ever since. Thornton is certain that Maxwell had an informant among his own staff on the ninth floor: "How else would he have known?" Jarratt implies the same: "Mr. Maxwell was certainly well informed." Traces of paranoia often afflict Maxwell's victims since it is an element of his tactics. Part of the explanation may well be that, metaphorically and physically, Maxwell was always awake when others were asleep and he undoubtedly did have good contacts among the senior *Sunday Mirror* executives. Alternatively, he might have read about the Mirror Group's problems in the *Financial Times*.

Maxwell's lust to own a national newspaper had been an unfulfilled ambition for fifteen years. In the previous three years there had been two other opportunities. The first was the *Times* group which Thomson offered for sale in October 1980. Maxwell was the first to show an interest but since he was still in the midst of battling to win control of BPC he was dismissed as having neither the money nor the reputation as a candidate for the Top People's newspaper. His second and more serious bid was launched in April 1984 for the *Observer*. Tiny Rowland, the newspaper's owner, was in the midst of a public row with the newspaper's editor, Donald Trelford. Their disagreement concerned a story, written by Trelford about atrocities allegedly commited in Zimbabwe, which greatly embarrassed Rowland, who prides himself on affectionate relations with Africa's leaders. Rowland, like many tycoons, was unaccustomed to being defied by his employees, especially those who were not earning any profits. But Rowland's arsenal of threats was limited since Trelford had won the decisive support of the independent directors whose authority had been guaranteed by Rowland as a condition of his original purchase. Rowland's only course was either to accept defeat or to sell the newspaper. He hinted that he was "fed up" and considering the latter option and released the news the day before the independent directors and their editor were due to meet. Trelford, who was already concerned because Britain's oldest newspaper had barely recovered from a succession of ownerships, became alarmed when Rowland also leaked that the new owner could be Maxwell, whom he described as a "super leader" for the paper. That was of course exactly what Trelford was resisting. "I'd want the same guarantees of independence," he said, thinking aloud about Maxwell's condemnation of his recent report that Mark Thatcher, the Prime Minister's son, had been engaged in doubtful business exploits in Oman.

The *Observer*'s directors were due to meet at midday on April 23 and Maxwell was the bogeyman whom Rowland had introduced to upset their discussions. Normally, Rowland is the most discreet of businessmen who eschews personal publicity and deals only with a few trusted journalists who can be gently controlled. Yet on this occasion every newsroom was informed that, at 9 a.m. on the day the directors were meeting, Rowland had invited Maxwell to breakfast at Claridge's Hotel in Mayfair. Not surprisingly a large crowd of journalists and cameras were waiting on the pavement as the German and Czech multimillionaires, who both delight in speaking with impeccable English accents, stepped on to the street. Rowland stood slightly back smiling as Maxwell went to the cameras. The talks, Maxwell said, were "productive, positive and pleasurable," and "I am keen to buy" the paper, although there were still a few obstacles. Everything could be settled within a day. Rowland then stepped forward: "We had a good long chat and Bob tells me that he is very keen to buy." It seemed to confirm that morning's *Daily Mirror* headline, "Maxwell set to buy *Observer*." Still smiling, Rowland stepped into his Rolls and sped off to meet the independent directors. Maxwell went back inside the hotel, his temporary headquarters since striking printers were in the second week of occupying Maxwell House in protest against his policies. By the following day, it was all over. Rowland had accepted a reprimand from the *Observer*'s independent directors for his attempt to censure Trelford, and talk about selling the newspaper fizzled out as fast as it had arisen. Using Maxwell as a threat had been unproductive and he was soon forgotten by Rowland. If Maxwell felt exploited, it barely showed. Players in the big league expect to be treated in the same way as they treat others.

Yet Maxwell's fortunes had rocketed during that year. The price of BPCC shares had risen from 12p to 160p since his take-over and Pergamon was reporting "record" profits. Maxwell had both money and a reputation and now he wanted the power and influence which he believed came automatically with ownership of a newspaper. In May, Maxwell had telephoned Carpenter about the sale of the *Daily Mirror:* "I'm about to invest in the *Express,"* he confided to a man whom he had known since the 1950s, "but I won't if there's a chance that I can buy the *Mirror.* Can you give me any encouragement that I might?" Carpenter replied that he could not. On June 22 Maxwell paid approximately £16 million for 10 per cent of Fleet, the owners of the *Express,* who were known to be unhappy owners of the fading Beaverbrook empire. It was, Maxwell said, "a stake for the future." Over the following week, everything changed. Maxwell heard from a senior Mirror executive that there was strife among those planning the group's flotation, especially between the Reed executives and Thornton. The suspected presence of Maxwell's mole inside the Mirror camp would become part of the saga's folklore.

On the ninth floor of the Mirror building, Thornton was disputing Warburgs' low assessment of the group's potential value and insisted that the company be sold for £100 million. Higgs advised Jarratt and Carpenter that both the high price and the 15 per cent limit would endanger a flotation, and with the additional union problems they could not expect any serious investment. "Warburgs told us to pull back. We were going to flop," recalls one of the Reed executives. Maxwell heard about that terminal warning and on Sunday morning, July 1, telephoned Carpenter at home: "I am going to make a bid for the *Mirror.* Can we meet?" To stall Maxwell, Carpenter resorted to a well-used excuse: "I'm sorry, I don't discuss business on Sundays." Early on Monday morning, Maxwell telephoned again. Carpenter told Maxwell that the group was not for sale to a single bidder and that they could not meet. Just to be in his presence, Carpenter knew, would start the slide into his clutches. But the rejection was too polite to have any effect. The following day, Tuesday, Maxwell sent a letter to Jarratt outlining his offer and ending with the assurance that Jarratt had ample time for consideration. There was, however, no advantage for Maxwell in uncharacteristically restraining himself. The very next day, July 4, he called a press conference and issued a public statement that Pergamon had made "a formal offer of not less than £80 million cash for Mirror Group Newspapers. If justified by the financial and other information on the group, Pergamon will increase its offer to a sum not exceeding £100 million." After adding that he had given assurances about the papers' future "prosperity and . . . political line," Maxwell concluded:

> Some people may call me a predator but it is the proposed public flotation which will expose the group to the laws of the jungle. I regard myself as the savior of the group against the heavy commercial advantages of its rivals. Mr. Molloy, Editor of the *Daily Mirror,* has said in a recent article in the *Guardian* that "The Mirror Group has lacked the kind of autocratic player who can take his seat in the Fleet Street poker game." If Pergamon succeeds, then, as Mr. Molloy and all his colleagues must wish, power will once again truly return to the ninth floor at Holborn Circus.

Jarratt and Carpenter were not surprised, but Thornton was afraid and arranged to meet Carpenter that night. Thornton had always suspected Maxwell as a potential buyer and, on his second meeting with Carpenter a year earlier, had asked why Reed did not sell the *Mirror* to the publisher. Carpenter had explained that Maxwell had shown no interest. Three times during that last year, Maxwell had contacted Thornton with offers to print the *Mirror* but had been brusquely rejected. An element of paranoia had entered Thornton's feelings after Charles Williams, the chairman of Ansbachers, who were Maxwell's original merchant bankers, had visited Thornton to discuss the flotation. Williams had claimed he was representing the Labour Party's interests, but Thornton feared otherwise, though Williams denies that those fears had any justification. But on July 4 the threat of Maxwell had become a reality and Thornton was afraid that Carpenter would be attracted by a guarantee of £80 million instead of risking the flotation. The only obstacle to taking the money immediately was Jarratt's public pledge not to sell to a single bidder. "I was sure that Carpenter wanted to sell to Maxwell immediately," says Thornton, "but Jarratt felt bound by his honor."

Over the next four days, while Thornton labored under intense pressure to finalize the prospectus, Maxwell bombarded the Reed board with phone calls, letters and telexes demanding meetings and issuing ultimatums. He was met by silence. "We refused to take any of his phone calls," says one Reed executive, "but you could feel his presence everywhere." As connoisseurs of Maxwell's style, Jarratt and Carpenter knew that it was precisely the effect which he intended. On July 8, Maxwell sent Jarratt another telex, except that on this occasion Jarratt had already read the message on a news agency tape. The £80 million cash offer, said Maxwell, was completely unconditional and could be increased to £100 million. More phone calls and telexes with deadlines followed—"It felt like a bombardment"—but Jarratt and Carpenter refused to be drawn. Two days later, Jarratt read on the agency tapes the contents of another letter which Maxwell had sent. The offer had been raised to an unconditional £100 million cash with another £20 million available. Jarratt once again rejected the offer, but Maxwell refused to take no for an answer. "They've not turned down my offer; they can't turn down my offer," he told Channel 4 News. Inside Reed House in Piccadilly, Jarratt was perplexed: "He just won't go away."

Thornton felt more intimidated than most. His *Daily Mirror* horoscope for July 9 read: "Unless you have written guarantees and solid promises, then leave financial matters alone for a while. Others may seems plausible and reliable, but the chances are that you are being manipulated in some way or worse." Clearly the ninth-floor mole, he felt, was telling him something.

To exert more pressure, Maxwell had revealed as an aside in his letter to Jarratt, which was released to the press, that Derek Higgs of Warburgs had spoken to Maxwell's banker at Hill Samuel. He went so far as to accuse Warburgs of failing in its duty to represent Reed in a proper fashion. To the casual reader that mention would be unimportant but on the City grapevine everyone knew the significance. Warburgs had never hidden its distaste for Maxwell, whom it dubbed a despot, and would have preferred to have no dealings with him whatsoever. Even if his accusation were untrue, everyone inside Reed's barricade realized that it was a valid ploy to compel them talk to Maxwell; once the discussions began, it would be difficult to withdraw. Thornton became alarmed about his employers' growing instability. "Both of them looked nervous but again assured me that they would never sell to Maxwell. What could I do other than believe them?"

Warburgs's doubts were influencing the two Reed executives. They were worried about Thornton's failure to control the unions, whom the City universally regarded as gangsters and a risk to their investment. To counter that sentiment, Thornton summoned the unions on Wednesday July 11. For three hours he explained that he needed a no-strike guarantee or else Maxwell would be their new employer. Both Bill Miles and Keyes suddenly forgot their disdain for Thornton and agreed. Only the NGA withheld their support, because ironically they could not believe that Jarratt would break his pledge. Without a unanimous guarantee, Thornton had nothing new to offer when he telephoned Carpenter late that afternoon and was told that Maxwell was tightening the screws.

In their Piccadilly headquarters, the two Reed executives had just heard that they had a new neighbor. Across the street, in the Ritz Hotel, Maxwell had rented a suite, "so that I can be closer to be of assistance to you," he told them. Both men felt the noose tightening and had reluctantly agreed that Warburgs could send Maxwell some draft agreements but strictly "without commitment." Like a Don Juan seducing a woman, Maxwell knew, as the first resistance disappeared, that it was just a matter of delicate tactics before all the defenses began to crumble. He was on the verge of becoming a press baron. Only Jarratt and his conscience blocked his way.

Neil Kinnock, the Labour Party's leader, was delighted by Jarratt's conscience. The Mirror Group's traditionally pro-left position is considered crucial to the party's very survival, since its millions of readers are the bedrock of its electoral support. During every election, the *Mirror*'s coverage is scrutinized for the slightest hint of criticism. Kinnock was convinced that Thornton's plan was the best guarantee for the continuation of that heritage and that Maxwell's bid was not in the party's interests. Convincing the Labour Party that they could trust him was vital for Maxwell if he was to persuade Jarratt to break his undertaking.

On Wednesday July 11, Maxwell drove to Hampstead in northwest London. He had telephoned Michael Foot, the former Labour Party leader, and invited himself to lunch at the left-winger's home. Maxwell was politically estranged from Foot and the two had spoken only rarely over the past twenty-five years. But Foot was grateful to Maxwell for contributing £38,000 in 1983 toward the legal fees for a High Court action against the Boundary Commission's recommendations for the redrawing of constituency borders which would deprive the party of thirty seats in the House of Commons. More recently, Foot had hosted a lunch for Maxwell at the Gay Hussar restaurant in Soho to discuss the possibility of a new left-wing paper. Maxwell, whose mind in such matters resembled a ledger—"I owe you, you owe me"—wanted Foot's support for his bid.

Foot was sympathetic. By the Wednesday, the newspaper reports suggested that the flotation was endangered and Foot feared that if Maxwell did not secure the *Mirror,* it might fall into the hands of the Conservatives. "Maxwell had been a Labor MP and a long-serving member of the party," recalls Foot. "He promised that the papers would continue to support the party and I felt that we could trust him. The *Mirror* would be in safe hands." Maxwell left satisfied and communicated Foot's approval to others.

On Thursday morning, July 12, Jarratt was painfully facing his dilemma. Infuriatingly Maxwell had interfered in the flotation and his public negotiations with Reed through the media had irritated the former civil servant. One could not deny Maxwell's financial astuteness —his success at Odhams had been awesome, and with hindsight Jarratt realized that they had sold it far too cheaply. He feared the man. Would the country thank Reed for allowing Maxwell to become a press baron who might one day even bid for Reed itself? By the end of the morning, closeted with Carpenter and Higgs, Jarratt accepted that he owed a higher duty to his shareholders. Maxwell's offer was too good to reject.

One mile away in Holborn, the *Mirror* journalists were waking up to the possibility of Reed's capitulation. Hitherto, they had been remarkably docile, relying on information about their fate from newspaper coverage which repeated Reed's assurances. Some wags would later carp that the alcohol level was so high in their favorite hostelry, the Wig and Pen, that those who heard the rumors were too drunk to understand. The truth was nevertheless harsh. The *Mirror*'s own management had lost its way and could offer no leadership. Miles and Long had allowed the newspaper to go down-market to compete with the *Sun,* and every night their staff nervously anticipated what new angle the *Sun* would invent on the same regurgitated stories. The group's managers lacked innovative vision and their disagreements with Thornton did not suggest that the flotation would greatly improve the company's management.

On the Thursday morning, however, rumors were flying around the Mirror building and the fourth floor became the location of a continuous meeting. No fiction writer could ever conjure up a more pitiful image. Dozens of highly paid men and women who prided themselves on their ability to embarrass the powerful and to fashion the views of millions were flapping to find an answer to a plight which they had so often witnessed others suffering. Initially, their feelings about Maxwell were evenly divided. Many felt that he might give the paper a new sense of direction, even self-respect, especially since tabloids seemed to flourish better under the shadow of a giant than under that of an anonymous conglomerate. Among those supporting Maxwell were Bob Edwards, editor of the *Sunday Mirror,* and Terence Lancaster, the *Mirror*'s political editor.

But the mood changed markedly once Joe Haines, the *Mirror*'s esteemed columnist, began speaking. Haines, a small, spiky figure born in Rotherhithe, south-east London, had been Harold Wilson's press secretary between 1969 and 1976 and knew both the Labour Party and its leading luminaries intimately. Inside 10 Downing Street, Haines had been renowned for what some of Wilson's kitchen cabinet called the "Bermondsey Dockers' Syndrome"—an antagonism toward the elite, especially the educated, the wealthy and the City. Firmly etched in the memory of those close to Wilson was Haines's advice to the Prime Minister whenever Maxwell's name surfaced: "Don't touch that man with a bargepole." Most of the *Mirror* staff had come to share Wilson's appreciation for Haines's flair with words.

At the meeting on the fourth floor, Haines rose to a pitch of eloquence well suited to the heated occasion. Standing next to Haines as he spoke was Geoffrey Goodman, the *Mirror*'s respected industrial editor. He and others heard Haines say, using the most graphic words, that Maxwell could not be trusted and should be opposed. Most of his audience, who knew very little about the details of Maxwell's past, were impressed with Haines's vehement denunciation of Maxwell's character and personality. The meeting voted in favor of a motion condemning Maxwell and urging Reed to stand by its assurances. For professional cynics, especially self-proclaimed critics of capitalism, they were surprisingly trusting that Reed would place its honor above profits.

At about 10 a.m. on Friday, Roy Hattersley, the Labour Party's deputy leader, received a call at his home from his friend Charles Williams. "Don't let anyone know I've phoned you," said Maxwell's banker, "but Bob will be buying the *Mirror* today. Jarratt cannot afford to keep his promise." Hattersley, despite rumors to the contrary, had little affection for Maxwell, but as a shrewd political animal he understood the implications for the party. Immediately after Williams's call, Maxwell had also phoned and asked Hattersley to tell Kinnock. Thirty minutes later, Hattersley walked into Kinnock's office in the House of Commons to find the leader drafting a public statement supporting the flotation and criticizing any proposal which allowed Maxwell or a single proprietor to take control.

"He's going to buy the *Mirror* whatever you write," said Hattersley.

"What do you think about that?" asked Kinnock.

"In my opinion, any man who can afford to buy a newspaper should not be allowed to own one. But there's nothing we can do."

Kinnock's proposed statement, advised Hattersley, would be injudicious, since Reed's decision would not be influenced by the party's attitude, and if Maxwell won, the relationship between the party and the newspaper would be imperilled: "It's a risk we cannot afford." Unlike his predecessors as leader, Kinnock was neither cosmopolitan nor impressed by self-made businessmen. Maxwell had provided the party with a lot of financial support which would probably increase in the future. He therefore accepted Hattersley's warning that an outright condemnation would be folly. A mild statement would be issued instead.

By lunchtime in Piccadilly, no one dared look out across the street to the Ritz in case they glimpsed Maxwell standing by the window staring back. Carpenter had finished outlining his final opinion to Jarratt. The advice about the flotation upon which they had relied, he said, was flawed. Reed might raise no more than £45 million, perhaps even less, and that was indefensible to the shareholders. Thornton had been the Mirror executives' own choice and they would have to bear the consequences of their error. Maxwell's offer was too good to refuse. When the board arrived at 2 p.m., they would recommend acceptance. Jarratt's conscience was overridden by his legal duty to the shareholders. By 4 p.m., the board had agreed that Carpenter should negotiate and return with an outline of Maxwell's best offer. The meeting was adjourned while Carpenter walked across the street to meet Maxwell in his suite. Tea and cucumber sandwiches were already prepared. Maxwell could not hide his excitement as the cups were filled.

Carpenter had one goal—if there was a deal, Maxwell would not be given an opportunity to haggle. Maxwell's style was always to make an agreement and then start wearing everyone down by renegotiating everything. That was why the Odhams sale had been so painful. To avoid a repetition, Warburgs, before allowing Carpenter to cross the street, had extracted an agreement that Maxwell not only would pay cash, but would pay every penny the same day. It was a very unusual demand. Maxwell was to be held to his word that his £100 million offer was unconditional and he would pay on the spot.

The £100 million, however, contained provision for £23 million which Reed owed to the Mirror Group. Therefore, when Carpenter arrived, Maxwell's offer stood at £77 million. Carpenter believed that Maxwell was buying blind since they had forbidden him sight of the Mirror accounts but he nevertheless insisted that the Reed board wanted more. After some discussion, Maxwell slowly raised his offer to £84 million —"That's it, my final offer." Compared with the £45 million which the float would raise, Carpenter had every reason to feel pleased, but instead he said, "I want ninety."

"No," said Maxwell.

Carpenter rose and walked toward the door: "It's ninety or nothing."

"I just don't have that last £6 million," Maxwell said.

Carpenter pondered: "I'll lend it to you for six months at the bank's rate of interest."

Maxwell sighed and agreed. "It's a deal."

At 5:30, they shook hands. Carpenter felt elated. He had extracted blood from a stone. The board would approve. Maxwell was doubly pleased. On his sixth attempt, he was on the verge of becoming a press baron, and the price was low. Fortunately, he thought, Reed had been unwise. The value of the Mirror building had been underestimated and they had not realized that there was a surplus in the pension fund. Probably neither knew that the Reuters shares would become even more valuable. But both sides accepted there was a premium on Maxwell's inimitable style with the unions. His threats would carry conviction. "The assets," Maxwell later boasted, "are equal to what I paid. The newspapers are in for free." His grandfather, Yaacov Schlomovitch, would have been proud of his strategy.

As he recrossed Piccadilly, Carpenter's private telephone was ringing. It was Thornton to report that all the union leaders who had rushed to his office that morning had now agreed to a no-strike deal. A secretary took a note of the details. "Has anything happened with Maxwell?" he asked. "No, nothing," was the reply. "The board is still meeting."

Carpenter was reporting to the board the £90 million cash offer. By 6:30 p.m., they were agreed. The sale should proceed. Outside, the telephone was ringing again. It was Thornton. Carpenter took the call.

"Has there been a deal?" asked Thornton.

"No," replied Carpenter, which was technically still correct.

"You know about the unions' undertaking?"

"Yes."

"Does Jarratt's pledge still stand?"

"Yes," said Carpenter.

As he spoke, dark-suited lawyers and bankers began filing into the board room to complete the mammoth legal transaction. Dozens of thick documents whose contents had been unofficially discussed over the previous days appeared from briefcases and were passed around. An exuberant Maxwell arrived at 7 p.m., and was greeted with polite resignation by Jarratt and Carpenter. "I haven't sold the *Mirror* to Maxwell," mused Jarratt as he watched the huge man lumber around his board room. "He's bought it off me." Around the polished table, their experts were scrutinizing phrases and figures, and feeding an endless stream of amendments into a battery of word processors to produce a contract which would transfer Northcliffe's former empire to the son of a peasant.

Maxwell and Carpenter began talking about why Reed had sold the papers. "Our share price will substantially improve," said Carpenter.

"I doubt it," said Maxwell.

"A £10 bet?"

"Done," said Maxwell. Carpenter would win the bet.

Outside, Carpenter's phone was again ringing. It was Thornton again. He was told that the board was still meeting. There was no news.

Inside, as the rewriting and signings continued, Higgs asked Leslie Goodman of Hill Samuel whether he had the money. Goodman showed the banker a document which guaranteed that Hill Samuel would pay the entire £90 million if Maxwell's check did not arrive the following day. Higgs, who feared anarchy at the *Mirror* when the news finally leaked out, folded it carefully.

There were no celebrations as the signing ended at midnight. Higgs turned to Maxwell: "Are you going home now?"

"Yes, off to bed," he replied.

Carpenter intervened: "Bob, do me a favor. Don't go to the *Mirror* tonight. Let's be tactful and break it in the morning, or else you'll have a stoppage."

"Yes, you're quite right," said Maxwell.

Maxwell walked out into Piccadilly and got into his Rolls. "To the Mirror building," he told Les Williams, his long-suffering chauffeur.

The journey from Piccadilly to Holborn lasted just five minutes. As the Rolls raced toward his latest acquisition, Maxwell was preoccupied, an informed guess suggests, by his image as the new Beaverbrook. He would become a great newspaper tycoon, leading from the front, inspiring great feats of reportage. The *Mirror* would once again become a great newspaper with unbridled influence. He, Robert Maxwell, would be the modern colossus, bestriding Fleet Street, Westminster and the City. Like the "Beaver," his counsel would be sought by politicians, financiers and even trade unionists. All would seek his advice and help, and eagerly await his judicious opinions on solving Britain's major problems. Daily, his newspapers would disseminate his views to the world in what he would publicly describe as "a small contribution." Then, preferably sooner rather than later, as his influence increased, governments would entrust him, as the Beaver had been entrusted, with the tasks which only the recognized talents of a tycoon could accomplish; and then the honors would follow. As the limousine silently drew up outside the grotesque glass tower, a monument to modern philistinism, there might, as he stepped out, have been a subconscious, transient flash: "The *Daily Maxwell.*"

Daydreams are normal. Actually realizing them is a joy denied to most, even to the rich. Aged sixty-one years, this was a new climax to his career and who would deny any man the pleasure at that joyous moment as he walked through the glass door and replied to an innocent inquirer about his business in the building: "I've just bought it. I'm the new proprietor." But as he traveled up to the ninth floor in the leather-lined executive's lift ("inside Cecil King's wallet" was the old joke), there were no thoughts about telephoning his cronies to come for a celebration as Beaverbrook would have done. Maxwell had no cronies in London to summon at that time, only employees and contacts. That was his lifestyle and it had never troubled him. As he walked into the chairman's empty office, he had fulfilled his dreams to avenge Murdoch, and that was sufficient. But his pride in his self-education had deluded him about the subtle difference between image and substance. His only similarities with Beaverbrook were the ownership of newspapers and a burning ambition to influence history. Their major difference was that, unlike Maxwell, Beaverbrook understood both newspapers and history.

The Beaver had understood that those who desire to make history must also be students of their predecessors. Beaverbrook may have been a tyrant, but he was highly educated and could hold his own in discussion with H.G. Wells and Arnold Bennett. For him, making his millions was a means to an end, and the end was managing newspapers. Finance and industrial management occupied only minutes of his day. He was an intellectual who boorishly injected his prejudice into his daily newspapers but also knew how to cultivate an atmosphere for great stars to develop within his firmament. This, above all, won him recognition, even by his political opponents. To his most distinguished employees like the *Daily Express* editor Arthur Christiansen, the *Evening Standard* editor Michael Foot and the historian A.J.P. Taylor, he was a great journalist who possessed both that instinctive genius for identifying "news" and the art of reporting.

Since Maxwell read few books and had forgotten long ago the art of instinctive learning, the delicate relationship between dictator and creator was elusive. Fixed in his mind was a confused impression of the pre-war newspaper giants and television image of Murdoch supervising the smallest details of his own newspapers just as Arno Scholz had done forty years earlier in Berlin. Maxwell's moment had finally arrived: now he was to perform the same task. Without any self-doubts, he would control everything because he knew best how to defeat Murdoch and rank alongside Beaverbrook. In his view, the quality of a leader depended upon a display of despotism. Exactly twenty years earlier he had entered the Commons because he wanted power; in Richard Crossman's words, "he wanted to shine." But those closest to him also say that he wanted to be loved. The paradox of a bulldozer seeking affection is not an unusual one. Ownership of the *Mirror* would be a passport to all of that and more. Maxwell truly believed that the world revolved around himself. His being was the news and his thoughts would sell newspapers. And if it didn't, so what? The newspapers belonged to him and he was intent on enjoying the rewards of his exceptional struggle. If ever an aspiring Citizen Kane was incarnated in London, it was on July 13, 1984.

Seated behind the desk in the chairman's office, looking out at the dark and sleeping capital, this was the *Mirror*'s new proprietor. He would seek fulfillment and pleasure but not confrontation. The arguments came naturally as a condition of leadership. During that night, the first article of Lex Maxwelliana was imposed on the fallen citadel: Who works for Maxwell, jumps to his command. "When Maxwell shouts 'jump!,' " a long-forgotten employee had explained years earlier, "my only response is, 'How high?' " So, members of the Mirror Group board were woken and told that they were expected to attend an immediate meeting with their new proprietor. The executives emerged from their introductory meeting as daylight broke, nervous but reassured. Maxwell had been firm but charming, and a courtship had been established. Only a few believed that the future was rosy. "Maxwell's assurances are nice," someone later told the *Daily Mail*. "But I went to bed last night on a long-standing assurance that the paper would never belong to one man."

Thornton was not invited to that meeting. He had heard the news finally from Carpenter just after midnight and arrived at his office at 7:30 that morning. "I couldn't miss Mr. Maxwell because he was sitting behind my desk," he said as he left the building. "I congratulated him and packed my things."

The new captain of a faltering ship can choose between two methods of introducing himself to those for whom he is newly responsible. Roy Thomson chose the gentle approach when he bought the *Sunday Times* in 1959. Walking around the machine room, he was introduced to a printer. "How do you do," he said, "I'm Roy Thomson, the new owner of this paper." "You may own it," replied the man, "but I run it." That unrectified truism cost the Thomson family approximately £70 million.

Maxwell chose a different style. At midday, on July 13, he summoned the *Mirror*'s union leaders, the Fathers of the Chapel, to a meeting in the Rotunda, on the third floor. His speech started jovially. After explaining that he wanted to restore the *Mirror* to "its former glory," he admitted that his ambition was to topple Murdoch's *Sun* as Britain's "Number One Paper" and earn the same high profits which News International, owner of the *Sun,* was reaping—£23 million as opposed to the *Daily Mirror*'s £1.6 million. It need an extra million sales, and while there would be no compulsory layoffs he would be negotiating a reduction of printers with the unions. He added that he would also be launching a London evening newspaper "in the autumn" and would want to introduce color.

The atmosphere began to turn sour soon after his introduction. Referring to the rumors that some printers had considered stopping the previous night's production in protest at his takeover, he said in a soft but deliberately menacing tone: "If you would have stopped the paper, it would have stayed shut and if you don't believe me, ask the people at Park Royal." As the audience became sullen, Maxwell began using swear words, but, after protests, apologized. "Do you think that I am on an ego-trip?"

"Yes," shouted the audience in near-unison.

"I have invested £90 million in this business and I don't belong to the Salvation Army. . . . I am the proprietor. I am the boss. And I want that to be understood very clearly. There can only be one boss and that is me." It was an honest riposte. For £90 million, he was entitled to create a profit-making business by removing those managers who had so badly failed and simultaneously to indulge himself, if he cared to do so.

Only four people applauded as he sat down. Many were too fearful to move. Later that day, the same four provided the only votes against a motion condemning Reed for breaking its promise and insisting that Maxwell adhere to his guarantees of non-interference in editorial content. Maxwell had in the meantime dictated the following day's front page, a bold statement to the readers. "The Mirror Group newspapers have changed ownership," it read. "Their policies will not change. I am proud to be the proprietor of this group of publications." (One week later, after urgent calls from his lawyers, he angrily denied his own statement that he was the proprietor of the group, and insisted that he was only the publisher. In his exuberance, he had forgotten his carefully constructed facade to avoid paying British taxes.)

That afternoon, Maxwell held a press conference. His carefully phrased statement was a pledge of intent, repeating the very assurances which he had given to both Jarratt and Foot and, more importantly, to his senior editors and staff:

> I am very proud to be associated with Mirror Group Newspapers. . . . It is my intention to restore the *Daily Mirror* to its rightful place as Britain's biggest-circulation popular newspaper without sacrificing any of its influence or tone. . . . I shall ensure that the Mirror Group becomes more efficient and more competitive and more attractive and exciting so that it can attract readers from other tabloids which seem to me to pursue policies which are against the best interest of many, many millions of our citizens in these islands. Under my management, editors in the group will be free to produce their newspapers without interference, with their journalistic skills and judgment.
>
> I shall place only two strictures on those who have editorial responsibility for newspapers that are members of the Mirror Group. One, the papers must retain their broadly sympathetic approach to the labor movement. . . . Two, the papers must and will have a "Britain first" policy. I want them to inform Britain, entertain Britain and boost Britain. Morale in Britain is low at present, but there is much in our country that is good and I want that to find a voice in the Mirror Group papers, on an even better and larger scale than is the case at present. We can and must revive our fortunes for our own sake and for our young people, so many of whom are being thrown on the scrapheap before they've even begun to live their lives.

His critics readily noted his promises in order to compare them with his performance over the following twelve months. The comparison would, they felt, reveal a lot about Maxwell's attitudes, his character and above all his veracity. Although he had successfully compartmentalized his activities, his behavior at the *Daily Mirror* would determine whether the allegations and criticisms about his business career were valid or whether he had, as he claimed, been unfairly maligned. The commercial world is complicated and shadowy, and Maxwell, like all other entrepreneurs, operated within a ghetto. Whatever had been revealed was a mere glimpse compared to what remained hidden behind the walls. In sharp contrast, at the *Mirror,* all his performances would be witnessed by professionals whose only motive when something of interest occurs is to publicize the deed as quickly as possible. Inside the Mirror building, Maxwell had established his own ground rules by which he could be judged. Intentionally, he exposed himself more than any other present-day publisher. He had forsaken the ghetto for a goldfish bowl and could be held to account by his critics without redress against accusations of distortion.

On Sunday morning, Joe Haines arrived at his desk to begin collecting his belongings. Like most *Mirror* staff, he had heard the news of the take-over on Friday's early-morning news. His forceful speech against Maxwell at the union meeting had undoubtedly been reported to the new proprietor. He had meant every word he had uttered. Maxwell was unfit to own the newspaper and much worse. The day previously, he had told a friend, "I'll be cashing in my railcard on Monday morning." Minutes later his telephone rang. It was Maxwell. "Joe, come up please." Haines expected to be dismissed and told his trusting colleagues later, "I didn't want to work for Maxwell." But Maxwell had decided that he needed Haines. He had not calculated how long he needed his talents, but it was wise to juggle the options and forestall any headline about hacks leaving the sinking ship. Pinpointing an enemy's price and winning his sympathy lay at the heart of Maxwell's technique, and to Haines's surprise, he was offered promotion and a glowing future. If Haines was torn, his dilemma was soon resolved; he agreed to stay on two conditions: a guarantee of non-interference with his work and a promise that the *Mirror* would continue to support the Labour Party. "What could I do?" he asked his colleagues dejectedly when he explained his acceptance, but it did not stop one observer rattling some coins as he walked past. Another of the *Mirror*'s star columnists who expected dismissal was the investigative reporter Paul Foot. To his surprise, after he had insisted that he would stay only if he could write without interference, Maxwell agreed to his terms.

A third who was offered similar conditions was Geoffrey Goodman. Maxwell asked him to "help me revive the *Mirror* and join my Politburo to steer the paper," and promised that there would be "no interference in your writing."

For Haines, Foot and Goodman, those guarantees were vital to their self-respect. All three also believed that the *Mirror*'s readers, to whom they felt a responsibility, would cease buying the paper if, instead of proper reporting, they read the proprietor's opinionated articles. But they were the exceptions. Few of their senior colleagues stipulated similar conditions for remaining.

The day following the take-over, Maxwell wrote a front-page article re-explaining his policies and aspirations. It was forceful and pungent. Within two weeks it was clear that, as many suspected, his self-introduction was not an isolated appearance.

July was the fourth month of the miners' strike, which many already suspected was no longer an industrial dispute but had evolved into a clear-cut political battle between the Prime Minister and the miners' leader, Arthur Scargill. Many Conservatives believed that Scargill was intent on repeating his 1974 victory over Edward Heath. In their view, the very survival of both the government and the nation was at stake and the compromises which were customarily engineered to settle strikes should be ignored. Their priority was finally and utterly to rout the miners and deal the trade unions' hegemony a mortal blow.

The *Mirror* was in an awkward predicament. Normally, it would be sympathetic to the miners but, like the Labour Party leadership, the newspapers' editors and senior staff were disturbed by Scargill's extremism, by the violence around the pits, and most of all by the union's refusal to ballot its members. Nevertheless, many socialists felt that the government had deliberately cut off any chances of negotiation and that the long-term damage caused to the Labor movement would be grave.

One of the *Mirror*'s voices on these issues was their well-informed and distinguished industrial editor Geoffrey Goodman. Goodman was politically left-wing and had often found himself, during more than 30 years on the staff, in opposition to the newspaper's editorials especially about the common market, unilateral disarmament and governments' economic policies. On several occasions, the disagreements had ended in emotional rows. On July 26, Goodman wrote a column about the strike entitled "Digging into a Vendetta." Writing in the *Mirror*'s colloquial style, Goodman alleged that during the miners' strike in 1974, Margaret Thatcher had been, with one other, a lone voice in the Heath Cabinet urging her Prime Minister to "Take on the miners, fight 'em to a finish and win. . . ." The present strike, claimed Goodman, was the delayed "vast political test of will and strength" which the present Prime Minister had urged one decade earlier. In the emotion generated by the strike it was a distinctly anti-government story.

That night, Goodman left his office believing that the article would work its way through the editorial machine and appear the following day. Instead, in his absence, Maxwell seized his piece, personally crossed out all references to a "vendetta" and headed the revised and now rather confused column, "The Enemy Within." As the rumors of Maxwell's interference, executed without consulting Goodman, spread through the Mirror building during the morning of July 27, the reality of Lex Maxwelliana dawned and questions began to be asked: Had Goodman protested? Had Joe Haines, promoted to assistant editor, raged? Had the editor Mike Molloy himself threatened to resign in defense of his staff? In fact, none of these had happened.

Goodman had been telephoned at 11 p.m. and told about Maxwell's changes. Minutes later he had threatened Molloy that he would resign if his own article were not resuscitated but he was persuaded to wait until the morning. When he met Maxwell at 10 a.m., the proprietor "put his arms around me and said, 'How can you ever forgive me for such a thing? I should never have done it.' " Goodman did forgive his employer, agreeing that in future he would send his articles in advance to Maxwell to read, and the proprietor insisted, "I promise that I won't interfere." The proprietor had struck and, despite the overwhelming might which the opposition could have brought to bear against him, he encountered only appeasement. "I fooled myself," says Goodman, "that he'd keep to his promise." Maxwell, many would discover, respected only those who resisted his cajolery.

That same morning, after settling the local difficulty, Maxwell summoned his senior staff and enthusiastically outlined his next foray. There would be a special issue three days later about the strike. Goodman was detailed to arrange a secret meeting between Maxwell and Scargill at the Hallam Tower Hotel outside Sheffield. When they met, Goodman observed, the two "got on very well together. They were practically interchangeable. Maxwell was very impressed by Scargill and especially by his complaints about police violence." Yet, as the special issue was being prepared, Maxwell's animosity toward the miners seemed to wax. An opinion piece was commissioned whose line was to be critical of the miners. Reluctantly, Goodman and Terry Lancaster wrote the article for Maxwell's approval but refused to allow their names to be printed above it. Since Maxwell demurred placing his own name as the byline, Molloy suggested that they use the alias "Charles Wilberforce," which had previously been used by Cudlipp. Maxwell was satisfied and particularly approved the splash headline: "The Pigheaded Identical Twins." The journalists left his office dejected. "We had become accomplices to his destruction of editorial independence," says Goodman. In the lift going down from Maxwell's office, he confessed his fears to Molloy. "There's no point going on, Mike," he said.

"Let's fight it out. Don't hand it over to him," replied Molloy, who was afraid that any opposition would be greeted by dismissal. "It's his paper."

Molloy's pragmatism was born of long experience. In his view the ritualistic worship of editorial independence was a myth, especially on the *Mirror,* because he could well recall how both King and Cudlipp would constantly interfere. If Goodman did not like the new owner, he had the simple but effective option of resigning.

Seated in his ninth-floor office, Maxwell warmed to the notion that he, using the *Mirror* as a platform, could solve the strike. Among those who were summoned to serve that purpose was David Seymour, the newspaper's second-ranking leader writer beneath Joe Haines. Seymour is a committed and professional journalist of the sort which newspapers need if they are to innovate and thrive. During his thirteen years with the *Mirror,* Seymour had earned a reputation for writing *"Mirror* Comment" pieces which evoked the spirit of both the newspaper and its readers. Seymour had been surprised when Maxwell, soon after his arrival, had asked to see his "Comment" pieces and had begun changing occasional words. Since none of his superiors objected, he was left with no alternative but to wait most days with crowds of other journalists in the ante-room to Maxwell's office to submit his articles.

"I want you to use all your Jewish chutzpah to write the following . . ." would often be the introduction to the proprietor's command. The editor Mike Molloy was rarely by Maxwell's side. Over the next weeks, Seymour regularly wrote the *"Mirror* Comment" about the strike, consciously distorting what he felt to be the truth to suit Maxwell's views. "The whole strike became a blur for me," he recalls, "because I was being battered the whole time by Maxwell, who was jumping up and down on my head telling me what was happening, which I knew was wrong." Regularly, Seymour sat in Maxwell's office, negotiating the following day's "Comment" amid constant telephone calls to the proprietor from stockbrokers, property dealers, the manager of Oxford United football club, other City tycoons and an endless stream of unidentifiable foreigners to whom Maxwell spoke in one of his eight languages. All these conversations about take-over deals, transfers of soccer players and currency movements, a testament to an unusually agile mind, took place while Seymour sat worrying about the advancing deadline, watching Jean Baddeley scurrying in and out of the office to feed the revised copy into the Wang computer, and pondering with others about the consequences for the newspaper's reputation.

For the *Mirror* men who had prided themselves on their accuracy about industrial matters, the opprobrium they were gradually receiving from their readers was disquieting. The process reached a zenith on September 10. The *Mirror*'s headline was dramatic: "Scargill to Ballot Members on Final Offer." The report explained that the miners would be allowed to vote on the coal board's final offer. Alongside the article was an anonymous "Comment" entitled "A Vote For Sanity." The story, which followed strenuous efforts by Maxwell to act as a peacemaker, was untrue. For the *Mirror* to publish an error on such a major issue further undermined the newspaper's credibility.

Maxwell was unperturbed. At both the TUC and Labour Party conferences, as the *Mirror*'s proprietor he had become the center of attention, wielding the political power which he had sought for so long. According to Seymour, "He just didn't seem to care that we were wrong." He was also unconcerned about contradicting the assurances he had given at the July 14 press conference when he was asked how he could achieve the editorial changes without interference. His reply had been, "(a) I haven't got the time and (b) if you've got the talent of the kind that we have on these newspapers, what the hell are you going to do—tell them how to do their job? Come off it." That statement was, he later said, a "guarantee of editorial integrity" because the editors were not "just a bunch of lackies and zombies [who] will do what I bid them."

Days after making that statement, Maxwell was filmed by BBC Television inside the Mirror building asking why a photographer was being sent to a James Bond set—why couldn't the film's producers provide a photograph free?; telling Peter Thompson, the *Sunday Mirror* editor, that he would not tolerate the newspaper following Liz Taylor to Richard Burton's grave, and later explaining, "I refused to allow any of our photographers or reporters to go and invade [her] privacy;" and declaring that he was "shocked" by the Press Council's condoning the *Sunday Times*'s exposure of suspicious transactions as evidenced by Denis Thatcher's bank accounts. There was, said Maxwell, to be no "checkbook journalism" and "no nipples." Gloom spread among the *Mirror*'s staff. Everything they feared about Maxwell seemed to be true, especially in the one area where his arrival might have promised improvements.

Maxwell brought two great strengths to Holborn. He understood printing and the print unions, which he could reorganize efficiently, and he claimed that he was a superb salesman. Once those talents were utilized, he said, the *Mirror* would be profitable. Since the Fleet Street chapels were more powerful than those he had confronted at BPC, their subjugation would take time. The salesman's promise of "One million extra readers within one year" could, he believed, be realized without delay. After waiting so many years, Maxwell was more impatient than usual to confront his arch-rival and overtake the *Sun*. In his first press conference on July 14 Maxwell had said, referring to the daily prize games which newspapers were using to attract readers, "I am not very keen on Bingo," because it was a considerable expense which the *Mirror* had been compelled to undertake to match Murdoch. He wanted it to end.

Three days later, Maxwell telephoned John Banks, the chairman and chief executive of the advertising agency Young and Rubicam, who had handled the Mirror Group account for many years. According to Banks, the instructions were "to invent the most sensational game for his group of newspapers." The brief was to produce a campaign within three days to "beat the Bingo sensation of the *Sun*" which would be "the most exciting game of the decade." This time Banks's agency could not automatically expect to launch the new campaign because Maxwell had asked other agencies also to offer presentations. So when Banks arrived at Headington Hall on the Sunday morning, he needed to present a concept which was even more audacious than his client could have imagined. Banks was unusually excited with his agency's idea. Called "Who Dares Wins," a play on the motto of the crack SAS regiment, Banks presented a campaign which he calculated would endear itself to the architect of a "Forward with Britain posture." The game itself was nothing more than a variation of bingo but Banks added two major innovations. The prize would be £1 million cash and Maxwell would appear on television in person to introduce the new game with the immortal phrase, "I'll make you a millionaire."

Banks pitched his presentation to appeal to his client's vanity: "You epitomize the new spirit and change in the *Mirror* and you have a vision for the paper. We think that your presence on screen would enhance the paper and yourself." Maxwell did not commit himself immediately. His reluctance was purely about his own appearance. He apparently had no qualms about the game, thus contradicting his earlier distaste for selling papers by means of bingo instead of journalism.

After reflection, he telephoned Banks and agreed to the package and to his appearance. It seems he did not take into account the fact that Murdoch had earned his fortune and phenomenal success without appearing on television and was in fact beginning to eschew publicity. Maxwell adopted the contrary view and warmed to Banks's notion that his appearance to promote bingo-fever could sell his newspaper. He explained his conversion later: "Since I arrived at Fleet Street and everybody is playing the game, I've decided to play the game for real." The justification for the game was that his newspaper, rather than making rash promises like its competitors, was actually paying a million pounds, proving "the integrity of the *Mirror*." If ever Maxwell exposed himself as a player and not as a strategist, this was the moment. The filming was to take place in his office in the Mirror building.

Maxwell was of course no stranger to television performances and he can be surprisingly patient with its tiresome demands, but on this occasion Banks was expecting him to behave like an actor whose words and movements had been carefully scripted. To begin with, when filming started at 2 p.m. in his office, everything looked easy:

When I bought Mirror Group Newspapers, I asked our people to come up with the most spectacular free game ever. They've done it. It's not bingo. It's the "Win a million game." I'm writing the check for a million pounds now. It's not made out to anyone, but for the first time in Britain I guarantee one of you will win it. So buy the *Daily Mirror, Sunday Mirror* or *Sunday People* and play the "Win a Million" game. I could be writing your name in here very soon. It's fun, instant and free. There are thousands of cash prizes to be won, and I'm waiting to make one of you a millionaire.

By the third attempt of filming the thirty-second speech, the proprietor was becoming weary. It was, he complained, too complicated. Not the words, but everything else. He was expected not only to speak, but also to sit at the desk, write the check, put the checkbook into a drawer and the signed check into his pocket, get up, and walk across to a logo saying, "Who Dares Wins." Meanwhile he would be smiling and speaking and being careful not to trip over anything.

There was a printing empire to manage, deals on the stock and currency exchanges to consider and there were constant telephone calls from all around the world to handle. His office was crowded with people and cumbersome equipment, and the lights were hot. Lines were fluffed, lights fused and, infuriatingly, he completed his walk and talk in either twenty-nine or thirty-one seconds whereas he was required to take precisely thirty seconds. Yet by 7 p.m. one take was judged suitable enough for transmission. Maxwell was thrilled with the results but by then the gimmick was no longer a secret. The *Mirror*'s competitors had heard the news and made hasty plans to launch an identical campaign. "There's no better form of flattery than copying," said Maxwell, basking in the success of his own "scoop," which was aired on ITV on August 17.

The following day, Maxwell's photograph and message covered the *Mirror*'s front page. The game was explained over three more pages and similar mass coverage reappeared in the newspaper on each of the following three days. The miners' strike, which days earlier had been described as "terribly damaging," was relegated while pages and pages of the *Mirror* were devoted to the game and its beaming proprietor who had warmed to Banks's pitch that he personally "epitomizes the new spirit." Joyfully, he felt that he was beating Murdoch. Not only had he launched the biggest bingo game in history but he had also resisted following the *Sun*'s price increase despite the higher cost of newsprint. "We have won hands down," he said to his editorial conference. "[Murdoch] spends most of his time in America. I think he'll seriously have to consider coming home." As always in his career, his optimism blinded him to so many awkward truths, not least of which was that Murdoch trusted his staff in Britain to handle the challenge. Delegation was a management style which Maxwell could not accept, despite his frequent assertion that "I am a very efficient manager of men and assets."

Just five days after the hugely expensive campaign to boost the *Mirror* was launched, it was scooped by its rival. On August 23, the *Sun* announced the first bingo millionaire. The television pictures showed Maxwell gritting his teeth. Murdoch had beaten him, again. Churlishly, he directed the paper to make the best of his defeat by proclaiming all over the *Mirror*'s front page, the "*Sun*'s millionaire can thank the *Mirror.*" But Banks had unwittingly released an irrepressible genie.

Maxwell enjoyed appearing on television. The day following his first appearance, he telephoned Banks: "John, I've arranged it all. Get your cameras round there immediately." Coutts Bank, at Maxwell's behest, had agreed to provide one million pounds in notes on a trolley for a new commercial in which he would star. In the meantime, he resorted to his other favorite to stimulate sales. The *Mirror*'s price was cut by one penny—a tactic he had unsuccessfully employed nine years earlier at the *Scottish Daily News*. Every day for three weeks, the *Mirror*'s front page was dominated by news of its price cut and the "million pound game." At the end, he gave away his million pounds and sur-reptitiously increased the price. The enormous impact which Banks had promised had rebounded. The readers had become unsettled. The gy-rations in price reflected the newspaper's variations in content. Molloy and his staff knew the cause. Their newspaper was less spicy and less fun to read. If they tried to intervene, Maxwell ignored them. He was enjoying the publicity and it was fun running newspapers. His contri-bution, he felt, was satisfying and should increase even if the *Mirror*'s circulation, after a slight increase, was beginning to fall. All that was needed, he believed, was a greater contribution from himself.

In October, Britain became aware of a dreadful famine in Ethiopia. The television news pictures were dramatic and Maxwell saw a chance to help the starving and the *Mirror*. In line with its great tradition, the *Mirror* would save the unfortunates with Maxwell in charge of the operation. He launched a public appeal for food and clothing which would be airfreighted to Africa.

At 6 p.m. one day in mid-October, Lord King, the chairman of British Airways, who had donated the aeroplane for no charge, was waiting at Heathrow to bid Maxwell farewell on that mercy voyage. Alongside his lordship was the mayor of Cardiff and a galaxy of helpers. They waited in vain. Maxwell was in Oxford watching his football team bat-tling against Arsenal in the Milk Cup. While King fumed and struggled against a dose of flu, Maxwell refused to leave the ground until the second half. "Well, he owned the team, didn't he?" recalls his aide Neil Bentley. "And he was damned if he'd miss the match." Maxwell arrived four hours late, ignored King's curses and rushed up the plane's steps. The negatives of the photos taken for the next day's *Mirror* of Maxwell waving farewell were destroyed to save Maxwell from em-barrassment. A large wet patch was evident around the crotch of his trousers.

Few journalists traveling with him on the specially chartered "mercy mission" to Addis Ababa were convinced that this was a normal ven-ture, since Maxwell featured so heavily in the *Mirror*'s coverage of the victims' plight. He and his retinue were omnipresent, a trait which few outside his organization had yet witnessed. The personal attendants, the battery of telephones, the huge consumption of food and his sheer need to place himself, rather than the victims, at the center of attention contrasted strangely with the images of famine. Back in London, David Seymour, Goodman and other *Mirror* staff were startled when the proprietor, having commandeered the Hilton Hotel in Addis, sent mes-sages dictating what action the newspaper should demand to solve the latest crisis in the miners' strike: "He was completely out of touch but still sending us his "action memos" as if we were a business not a newspaper and his judgments were contradicted by the facts." Like so many others, Seymour and Goodman would eventually leave in despair.

On Maxwell's return, the escapades increasingly promoted Maxwell rather than the newspaper. On March 4, *Mirror* readers were entertained by a flattering profile of the President of Bulgaria who was believed to have organized the murder in London of the dissident Georgi Markov with a poisoned umbrella and to have sanctioned the attempted murder of the Pope. At the end of the gushy eulogy about a country which few *Mirror* readers would appreciate, the article mentioned the President's "special guest across the table, Robert Maxwell," who apparently "had just struck a huge deal with the Bulgarian Government to help update the country's printing and packaging industries." Tucked away elsewhere, the paper reported that the miners' strike had ended on the previous day.

After the end of May, Maxwell was presented in the *Mirror* as a roving ambassador. Photographs would appear of Maxwell with Soviet and Chinese leaders exchanging views about the world situation. There was also a footnote mentioning that a lucrative business deal had been concluded. During a trip to Poland, Maxwell visited General Jaruzelski, the Polish military leader who had organized the first military coup against a civilian Communist government in the Soviet bloc but had failed to squash the Solidarity movement. In a radio interview recorded after his dinner with Jaruzelski, Maxwell said that the Solidarity problem was "solved" and that his newspapers would be "devoting less space" to the dissenters. The accurate reporting of his comments in London caused an outcry. He countered that he had been distorted, especially by a "mendacious" *Times* article. Nevertheless he found that he was defending himself against accusations that he was promoting not just himself but also his business interests.

The *Mirror,* it was said, had become a family photograph album which reflected the family business. No fewer than five of the seven children were now employed by their father's companies, which silenced any suggestion that on his death there would be no inheritance. His sons Kevin and Ian had become key executives in the management team. The three would meet at 8 a.m. for private discussions, before Maxwell encountered other executives. The *Mirror*'s front-page story on June 10, 1985, confirmed the trend. It reported that Maxwell would rescue Britain's technical wizard, Sir Clive Sinclair, whose company was tottering toward bankruptcy. Maxwell, according to the report,

328 · TOM BOWER

would launch of £12 million bid to save the company. Like his earlier bid to rescue Aston Martin, it was described as an act of patriotism. Production of that night's newspaper was delayed while the announcement was dispatched from Headington Hall to the Mirror building. Maxwell was subsequently asked why he had ordered the editor to carry the Sinclair story on the front page. He replied: "The fact that I was involved in it is incidental. . . . I'm certainly not aware [of holding up the front page]. The matter of the front page is a decision for the editor." Asked if a rescue bid mounted by someone else would have appeared so prominently, Maxwell replied, "I never answer hypothetical questions." In August with noticeably less publicity, he pulled out of the deal. Profits, he decided, were more important than patriotism.

After one year, despite spending £5 million in promotion, the *Mirror* had lost 350,000 sales. Six months later the circulation would fall to 2.9 million, a massive half a million less than when he bought it. It confounded the new proprietor's commitment to achieve daily sales of four million copies. The combined daily loss for the whole group was one million sales. It was an unprecedented collapse in the history of Fleet Street. *Marketing Week* commented, "It takes something close to genius to lose so much circulation so quickly." His target of overtaking the *Sun* within one year had withered.

Maxwell, understandably worried, consulted Molloy. Molloy's advice was to return to the old formula of checkbook journalism and heavy advertising. In April, Maxwell announced a £10 million promotion campaign, sanctioned the use of "dolly birds" and approved the invasion of privacy. *Mirror* executives were authorized to buy the titillating memoirs of Peter Bogdanovich, a film director whose beautiful girlfriend, a model called Dorothy Stratten, had been brutally murdered. Bogdanovich claimed that she had been the victim of sexual perverts associated with Hugh Hefner's Playboy empire. It was an averagely intrusive and voyeuristic sex saga.

In normal circumstances, the serialization would have passed off unnoticed but since it was Maxwell's latest stratagem against Murdoch, there was an opportunity for his competitors to lampoon the challenger. By that time, Maxwell's energetic self-promotion in his newspapers and on television chat shows was a major topic of conversation. While Maxwell assumed that all the requests for interviews and appearances were recognition of his importance, the invitations were in fact often motivated by the search for good entertainment, especially to expose any glaring inconsistencies. So, when Fleet Street heard that he had strayed into areas beyond his experience, the incentive to embarrass

"Cap'n Bob," as he had unaffectionately been dubbed, was irresistible. The *Sun* decided to run the identical story about the model's murder but culled from contemporaneous newspaper accounts. In the industry it is called "a spoiler" and can be deflected by time-honored methods. Maxwell naturally was ignorant of those devices and resorted once again to asking the courts for an injunction against the *Sun*. In the process, the owner of the *Mirror* was boosting his competitor's circulation.

Standing outside the High Court in the Strand, Maxwell condemned the *Sun* as a "lying, cheating, thieving paper" for regurgitating an old interview with the model and dressing it up as a scoop. There was even talk of demanding the imprisonment of the *Sun*'s editor. Inside the courtroom, the judge rejected Maxwell's case and ordered that he pay the £50,000 costs. Outside in the streets again, Maxwell said, "Spoiling may be legal, but it's not nice." Fleet Street, he said, needed to be "cleaned up." The cleansing would no longer concern the coverage of lurid sex scandals but would be designed to prevent competition. "Everything's got a moral, if you can only find it," as the Duchess said to Alice.

On the first anniversary of his purchase Maxwell was asked about his interference: "I don't think that has any effect on the sales of the paper except to improve the adrenalin throughout the building. . . . Whether I appear in the paper or not, that's a matter for them to decide, not for me." When pressed to explain whether those stories would have received such prominence or even coverage if Maxwell had not featured, he replied, "You'll have to ask the editor, not me. . . . It's the editors who interfere in the publisher's prerogative, not the other way round."

In August 1985, Maxwell was finally persuaded that his enjoyment was too expensive. His financial staff forecast that the group's paltry £1 million profit would be replaced during that year by a £6 million loss. His salesmanship had failed and he had made no progress in reducing the *Mirror*'s printing costs, which were approximately three times higher than the *Sun*'s. His flamboyance had disillusioned his editorial staff and, worse, had undermined his credibility with the unions. His warning, issued in April, that all the newspapers would close if there were not "massive cost reductions" had been ignored. Although he spoke about the "People inside Mirror newspapers [who] know that I do not bluff. I will close the newspapers if they are ever brought to a halt by the unions," the unions had not shifted their ground. Reasoned negotiations had failed and the papers' future was overshadowed by the threat posed by Eddie Shah's proposed *Today*. With the latest

German presses and free of all union restrictions, Shah promised to produce a national color tabloid, which at the time seemed to threaten all of Fleet Street's tabloids. In August, Maxwell launched a broadside against the unions using the anticipated appearance of *Today* to focus attention on the finite nature of their monopoly. As the Mirror Group losses mounted, Bill Miles noticed that the "air of compromise disappeared. He became much more aggressive." Maxwell's mixed blessing was that the appalling relations between SOGAT and the NGA, and between the national officials and the in-house shop stewards (FOCs), would enable him to play off one group of workers against the other. "We realized that when Maxwell bought the *Mirror,* the writing was on the wall," says Miles. "I always believed his threats, but others didn't."

At the beginning of August, Maxwell adopted the same tactics as at BPC. All the chapel leaders were summoned to the Mirror building and under the threat of a deadline began simultaneous negotiations to achieve voluntary redundancies. The crux of Maxwell's demands was that the *Sporting Life,* which was losing £3 million annually, should be printed by a subsidiary of Pergamon, which was not bound by Fleet Street's restrictions. At the end of two weeks, Maxwell struck a complicated deal with the NGA's general secretary Tony Dubbins, which allowed the printing of the *Sporting Life* to be moved. Hours later, the FOC of the NGA in the Mirror building refused to accept the agreement. To put pressure on Maxwell, NGA members, on August 21, disrupted the *Mirror*'s production. Maxwell retaliated the following day by stopping production of all the newspapers and warning that 6,500 employees faced dismissal. "The NGA were not like kamikaze pilots," says Bill Keyes, "because at least the kamikazes knew what they were doing." When Maxwell's threat failed to persuade the NGA to surrender, he announced on August 30 that the *Mirror* would no longer be printed in Fleet Street. "It is impossible to build success on anarchy," he said. "It seems equally impossible to be rid of that anarchy, so deeply entrenched has it become. . . . I believed I could change a floundering enterprise into a flourishing one. Regrettably, I must admit failure so far. . . . The choice facing Fleet Street and its unions is to change or perish. The unions, by refusing to allow me to publish except on their anarchical terms, have demonstrated their unwillingness to change." The *Sporting Life,* he announced, was for sale. The union leaders were divided about the credibility of Maxwell's threats.

Bill Keyes believed that Maxwell was serious. After their violent stand-up rows about the closure of Park Royal, which the union had lost, Keyes had won a notable victory over Maxwell in their last dispute in April 1984. Printers had occupied the computer floor at Maxwell House. In retaliation, Maxwell issued a writ claiming damages from the union under the 1982 Employment Act. Keyes had been appalled that a socialist should use Tory legislation and was even more so when the Court imposed a £75,000 fine. "I told Maxwell that we weren't going to pay," says Keyes, "and we'd never meet him again." Keyes was "shocked" that Maxwell could claim to be a member of the Labour Party. On a Sunday night, Maxwell phoned Keyes, Dubbins and Brenda Dean, the general secretary of SOGAT, and asked them to come to Oxford the following day to negotiate a settlement. All three arrived in adamant mood. "If you don't pay the fine," said Keyes, "we'll go for broke and close down everything." Maxwell refused. "It was the same old Maxwell," recalls Keyes, "He'd say one thing and then change his mind." All three walked out. The following day, Keyes traveled to Ayr in Scotland: "That day, he and his lawyers phoned me seventeen times. We finally agreed a settlement which included Maxwell paying our fine." They arranged to meet the following day at noon after the union's appearance in the High Court. At breakfast time Maxwell telephoned. "I'm not paying," he told Keyes.

"Then there's no deal," answered the union leader.

At 11:40, Maxwell, according to Keyes, "caved in."

"Why did you do it?" Keyes asked his old adversary when he later collected the check.

"Because I'm a good socialist," replied Maxwell smiling. "Everyone's entitled to second thoughts."

"It's like Russian roulette with you, Bob," said Keyes, delighted to have won. "You're an out-and-out bully."

Yet when Keyes faced Maxwell about the future of the *Mirror* in August, the conditions had changed: "Normally, his tactics were to never let us know where we stood. The sands were always shifting." This time, Keyes did not think Maxwell was bluffing. "We thought that he could recoup his investment by selling the Mirror building and do an Eddie Shah with the papers."

The confrontation and shut-down coincided with the TUC conference in Blackpool. The unions wanted to talk and Maxwell agreed. He booked a suite of rooms and began nonstop negotiations. The very future of the Mirror Group depended upon Maxwell's tactics and personality. Although he had failed to organize alternative printing in Manchester, he was, Bill Miles noticed, unconciliatory about the *Sporting Life:* "He said there was nothing to talk about. It was gone. Then he presented his 'survival plan' for the rest." For two days it was "constant aggression, constant attack. It was exhausting. He would have closed the papers down."

By September 3, Maxwell's energy and tactics had won an agreement embracing the sale of the *Sporting Life* and the removal of some "old Spanish customs," including the non-automatic replacement of the three hundred *Sporting Life* staff. The *Mirror* began publication the following day. Over the following eight weeks, there were isolated disputes and copies were lost. On November 1, Maxwell claimed that the September agreement for uninterrupted production had been broken and announced that unless the unions agreed to an immediate cut of 2,000 out of the 6,500 jobs, of whom 1,100 were over sixty years old, the *Mirror* would close. Every employee was issued a dismissal notice. To take advantage of the new Employment Act, Maxwell "awarded" the contract for the printing of the Mirror newspapers in Holborn after December 31 to a subsidiary of BPCC. Future disputes would therefore be hindered by the laws against secondary action. Combined with the constant reporting of the "Shah revolution," the union leaders began to cower.

Maxwell imposed a deadline of December 10 and again, after a series of tempestuous conversations with the union leaders, corralled all the negotiators into a number of rooms to discuss how they would achieve his demands. By the final day, he had achieved an overwhelming victory. Most of the overmanning and excesses would disappear; 2,100 employees were laid off and their payments would be largely funded from the surplus in their pension fund. The annual saving was £40 million. Maxwell's triumph was accompanied by the announcement that Mike Molloy was to be promoted and replaced by Richard Stott. Some *Mirror* staff believe that Stott made it a condition of his appointment that Maxwell would no longer interfere in the editorial process. Others believe it was Maxwell who proposed his own departure because he was bored with his toy. Although the center of his operations was now on the ninth floor, his new ambitions precluded any interest in the daily management of a mere newspaper because he was now determined that BPCC would become one of the world's ten largest communications organizations and the *Mirror* would be just a small part of the Maxwell empire.

Those successes, which realized the possibility of enormous opportunities, caused Maxwell to reflect upon his past, his relationship with his family and especially about his life in Britain. Like so many overt bullies, Maxwell's aggression concealed genuine tenderness and a propensity of offering charity toward those who were less fortunate. It was Maxwell's misfortune that his sentiment to help would so often provoke suspicion rather than gratitude among Britons. Partly, he was to blame. His desire to be a topic of public interest invariably caused him to make comments which were either ridiculed or misunderstood. Among the latter was his quip, "I never had the privilege of youth."

The mark of a true human being is one who, reflecting upon his material success, seeks at some stage an explanation and a focus for gratitude. Undoubtedly, the trigger for that search is the realization of mortality. In 1985, aged sixty-two, surrounded by the material wealth which, despite the prejudice of the British, he had finally amassed, Maxwell was wearied by his status as the outsider. Driven by an anxiety which he could never explain to himself, he decided to visit Israel, a country which he had ignored and which represented the religion which he had publicly abandoned.

Only the victim of persecution can understand that survival can provoke a trauma which continues until death. Most Jews who survived the Holocaust and prospered in their adopted refuges, clung on to their emotional memories of their homes and families which had been abandoned in central and eastern Europe. Reminiscing about those times with fellow sufferers was a unique anchor in the painful and rootless struggle to survive. Until 1985, Maxwell had denied himself that palliative. That changed when he arrived in Israel.

Among those whom he met was Yehuda Bauer who specialized in Holocaust studies. With Bauer, Maxwell visited for the first time the Yad Vashem memorial in Jerusalem which commemorates the Nazis' murder of six million Jews. As they walked through the darkened, austere rooms where the flickering memorial flame illuminated the names of the extermination camps and the towns from which their victims had been plucked, Bauer watched with surprise as this huge man began to weep. "He had never thought about the Holocaust before," observed Bauer, "because he was scared of it and couldn't understand it." As Maxwell's emotions uncoiled Bauer recognized the familiar signs of guilt. "He suddenly felt sorrow for his parents and guilty that he had not been beside them when it happened." Forty-seven years after he had bid his parents farewell, Maxwell had found their grave.

Israel arouses extreme emotions but for Jews it is the guarantee of their survival and rights of individuality. As Maxwell left the memorial and walked through Jerusalem, he suddenly recognized that, after forty-seven years of travel, having covered literally millions of miles, the wandering Jew had found a place which might be called home.

Over the following years, encouraged by his wife, Maxwell became a frequent visitor to Israel. Together, they financed Bauer's magazine, *Holocaust and Genocide Studies* and organized a week's seminar in Oxford on the same theme where Maxwell gave an emotional account of his own suffering. Maxwell had recognized that among his fellow Jews he was relieved of the pressures and discrimination which he otherwise suffered in Britain. Israel offered a path to rediscover his roots and a congenial environment where he was, like in Russia, not a stranger. In Israel the outsider could be an insider.

14

On a warm June night in 1985, the concentric spheres of Maxwell's life gathered at Headington Hall to celebrate his fortieth wedding anniversary. Inside the floodlit mansion, with the strains of the Salon Orchestra of the Royal Air Force playing in the background, Robert, Elisabeth and their seven children stood in a reception line to welcome five hundred guests to a gargantuan display of the family's wealth and happiness. Maxwell the celebrity was also a collector of celebrities and as he shook hands with dinner-jacketed politicians, bankers, businessmen, scientists, journalists, lawyers, trade union leaders, footballers and showbiz personalities, it was evident that their host had overcome his adversaries and fulfilled the ambitions which he had confided to Betty during their courtship in Paris. Clasping glasses of champagne, Harold Wilson, David Frost, Sir Robin Day, Ludovic Kennedy, Lord Rothermere, Lord Sieff, Hugh Scanlon, Ray Buckton and many other household names mingled to the beaming appreciation of their generous and good-humored host as they awaited the year's most expensive dinner party. "Many were his friends but the others came because they knew that everyone would be there," says Richard Marsh, the former Labour minister and currently the chairman of the Newspaper Publishers Association. Displays of wealth are often vulgar but the natural vulnerability of a close family celebrating an admirable anniversary tempered the ostentation.

Just before 8 p.m., as the laughter and conversation reached a crescendo, the multitude were invited to enter a vast marquee which covered the swimming pool and a dance floor, to seek their places at one of the forty-four tastefully decorated tables. Each guest had been provided with a table plan and among the silver cutlery they each found a present from "Bob and Betty"—an expensive leather toilet case. All agreed that it was a generous start to an unforgettable evening. As their hosts took their seats at the two main tables in the center of the marquee, Robert Maxwell was pleased to reflect that the seating sensitively accommodated his guests' common interests and the perfection of compartmentalization.

At a neighboring table on his right was Jean Baddeley, his faithful assistant who had recently been appointed a director of Pergamon Holdings, with Detlev Raymond and Laszlo Straka, his close lieutenants from New York. Together, these three knew more of his secrets than the remaining guests combined although even their knowledge was strictly limited. Close by on his left was one of his brokers, Jonathan Bevan, his lawyer John Silkin and his old banking friend Charles Williams. They had laid the foundations for his BPC coup five years earlier. At his own table sat Sir Robert Clark of Hill Samuel, and Lord Kearton, to whom he was equally grateful for his recent successes, and, for sentimental reasons, Charles Hambro. Scattered through the rest of the marquee, his children were hosting tables which appropriately reflected their personal interests. His son Kevin, at twenty-four already the heir apparent, entertained the chairman of Pergamon's first merchant bankers, Lord Spens of Ansbachers, and its current analyst, Henry Poole. Maxwell's youngest daughter Ghislaine, twenty-two, who had ambitions to manage the Mirror Group, sat with journalists; similarly, his twin daughters Christine and Isabel, thirty-three, and his son Ian, twenty-seven, who all worked for BPCC, hosted tables of media stars; his eldest daughter Anne, thirty-eight, who had been an actress and was now a teacher, sat with educationalists; while his eldest son Philip, thirty-four, who is interested in science, sat with editors of Pergamon journals. If ever the constellations could be momentarily fixed in place around their sun, that moment was Friday, June 7, 1985.

After four courses, there were the speeches. Elisabeth spoke movingly about her husband's achievements and of her suffering during the lonely years as he shuttled frenziedly across the world to build his fortune. All seven children stood, one on a table, as their own successes—"O" levels, "A" levels, university degrees—were recited for the guests to appreciate. Philip recounted his father's life story in a style which some thought faintly reminiscent of an impassive company report. (All the children, it was said, displayed an automaton loyalty to their father.) Harold Wilson, no longer in the best of health, praised the institution of marriage and his host, although he had personally denied his subject the prize he had most earnestly sought. Then Maxwell rose and spoke as a man who harbored no doubts that, after fighting a tough battle, he had won against all the odds. His words were un-memorable but the image was indelible. A huge man, in physique and personality, tinged with mystery, beaming in self-congratulation, but unable to conceal his impatience in the face of the elusiveness of the international status of Armand Hammer, Aristotle Onassis or William Hearst. His destiny—to become a national powerbroker and an inter-national star—remained on the distant horizon, and he was sixty-three years old. Aristotle Onassis had died aged sixty-nine. Time was limited if he was to be more than a footnote in history. His large family would ensure that he was not forgotten but he wanted to enjoy his success before it was inherited. Those who were close and loyal understood his vision but only he could realize his desires. He wanted the world to forget his defeats and admire his empire. It was all implicit in his speech that night. After polite applause, the toasts were made, the champagne was drunk and everyone could dance to the music of Joe Loss's Ambassadors.

His guests began drifting away after midnight. Few could deny, even those glitterati who attend innumerable functions, that this occasion was memorable. "A collector's item," says one. "Unbelievable," opines another. There were comparisons with F. Scott Fitzgerald's *The Great Gatsby,* especially that immortal phrase, "I was one of the few guests who had actually been invited. People were not invited—they went there." Everyone had of course been invited to Headington Hall but who, some wondered, had refused invitations?

Three years earlier, for Maxwell's sixtieth birthday, he had hosted another lavish party. In preparation, Betty had sent hundreds of letters asking for contributions to a *Festschrift,* a collection of individual rec-ollections about Maxwell's life collected in a book. The responses could be divided into four. Those who wrote a testimony and went to the party; those who wrote but declined the invitation to the party; or went to the party but did not want their name to appear in the *Festschrift*; and those who refused both to write and to attend the celebration. Two years later, many of those who had refused invitations to the birthday party were now quite prepared to be seen with Maxwell, since his aspirations and achievements had become impossible to ignore. The trappings of empire were being fast accumulated.

By this time, Maxwell had gathered close to him on the ninth floor of the Mirror building a diverse retinue reflecting his multifarious ac-tivities; they included several former Labour government luminaries whose past proximity to power appealed to him. Among them was Sir Thomas McCaffrey, an ex-Labour MP and formerly the press spokesman for James Callaghan at Downing Street, who had been appointed to perform the same function for Maxwell. There was Peter Jay, Callaghan's son-in-law and the last Labour government's ambassador in Washington, who was Maxwell's chief of staff. After a costly debacle at Ansbachers, Charles Williams, who had become a Labour peer, was employed as a financial adviser to the Mirror Group. And there was Joe Haines. Although others in the original politburo found their influence had waned, Haines had been elevated from lead writer and political editor to become one of Maxwell's most trusted lieutenants with a clutch of directorships of Mirror Group subsidiaries. Haines's friends explain the conversion from arch-critic to idolater as consistent with the character they recall working for Harold Wilson: "Joe needs to worship somebody and gratefully devotes himself to a powerbroker. He just convinced himself that Maxwell was right on every issue." When McCaffrey resigned in anger about Maxwell's treatment of employees, Haines arranged for another former Downing Street press officer, Janet Hewlett-Davies, to replace him. She too would resign after one year. The frequent turnover of staff was a clear sign of an unsatisfactory working environment. Everyone was expected to adhere to the publisher's eighteen-hour working day, although the demarcation between sleeping and waking hours was never established. At all times, they were on call through the omnipresent communications network which each senior staffer accepted as a condition of service. There was no management structure. Everything revolved around and depended upon the emperor. "It resembles more a communist rather than a capitalist bureaucracy," suggested one insider. In the outer office for the inner staff, his personal secretary Debbie Dynes had a list of those telephoners who could be connected to her boss irrespective of whether there was a meeting in progress. Telephone calls interrupted everything, including meals in his private dining room.

Eating had become one of Maxwell's preoccupations. There was a constant supply of lobster, salmon, caviar and other expensive dishes with the best wines and champagnes. His kitchen had a list of graduated menus, where the quality of the meal depended upon the importance of the guests. Those invited had no doubts about who ranked as the most important. Their host was always the first to be served by the liveried waiter, and he always received the biggest portion. At large parties, by the time the waiter had arrived to serve the guest on Maxwell's right, the host had already finished eating and was pushing his plate forward to demand attention for the discussion. Everyone thereafter ate in suspended animation. Maxwell's table talk varied between stimulating banter and heavy pontification. The latter predominated at the twice-monthly editors' lunches, at which policy was enunciated. Smoking was not allowed in Maxwell's presence, although he enjoyed Cuban cigars and, disconcertingly for some, habitually dipped the end into a glass of brandy. If the cigar plopped accidentally into his neighbor's glass, nothing would be said. Occasionally, as the meal ended, departing guests watched as the debris of salmon and champagne was swiftly removed to be replaced by beer and sandwiches, because a trade union delegation was about to be ushered in. The graduated menu was part of the performance.

Maxwell's diary was crowded with meals and meetings. Strand House, a neighboring building in Holborn, was bought to be partially converted into a home and the roof to be transformed into London's only private heliport. The two-floor flat, on which no expense was to be spared, was designed as a miniature Xanadu, filled with priceless objets d'art and garish, gold-plated, modern appliances. Visitors found that it was less a home than a testament of wealth, where taste was not allowed to interfere with the spectacle.

Yet one man who was never present at the parties but whose ghost had nevertheless hung over everything for the previous two decades of Maxwell's life was Rupert Murdoch. Maxwell had striven to catch up with the Australian and his ruby anniversary party marked the moment when he believed that his opportunity might finally come. Within five years he would, if not eclipse Murdoch's empire, at least rank as an equal. In 1985, News Corporation's annual turnover was £1.5 billion, four times the combined equivalent of BPCC and Pergamon. Maxwell's target was to become one of the world's ten largest "global information and communications" companies within five years. To realize that ambition would rank alongside Sir Edmund Hillary's ascent of Mount Everest.

Six days after the anniversary party, BPCC held its annual meeting. In his report, Maxwell unveiled how the company would be transformed from a traditional printing and publishing conglomerate into an integrated, technology-based corporation which offered newspapers, banks, brokers and packagers worldwide access through satellites to the most modern, computer-fed, color presses and a wide assortment of other technical services. Everything depended upon increasing the fortune in his kitty to finance a buying spree for expansion. To some it seemed that there was no strategy other than rushing helter-skelter to be the biggest. The 1984 annual report explained, in his familiar vocabulary, where the money was to come from. Under the heading,

"Another Outstanding Year," Maxwell described BPCC's "dramatic profit growth," which had risen before tax by 71.5 per cent to £37 million. But that huge increase was due, not to printing or publishing, but to property speculation. Although media companies do not usually depend upon property for their income, Maxwell said that property deals had become, and would continue to be, "a significant profit center for the Group." His aggressive crusade did not start auspiciously.

In October 1984, Maxwell made a new £44 million cash bid for John Waddington, which he still identified as ripe for asset-stripping and incorporation within BPCC. Over the previous twelve months, he had denied that he had bought extra shares or that he had any intention of buying the company. Victor Watson, Waddingtons' chairman, had been skeptical of those hand-on-heart denials and tried to discover the fate of Maxwell's shareholding. The trail passed through the hands of Tiny Rowland of Lonrho but disappeared in New York. New shares, he discovered, had been purchased and were secretly owned by Maxwell's private American company, Pergamon Press Inc. (PPI). Consequently, at the outset of his latest bid, Maxwell owned a 23 per cent stake in Waddingtons. Piqued by the guile, Watson says, "We decided to treat him to his own medicine and by God we wanted to hurt him."

The merchant banker at Kleinwort Benson detailed to fight Maxwell on Waddingtons' behalf was Christopher Eugster, a mild-mannered, upper-crust Englishman who, with his colleagues, had perfected a strategy for defending companies against unwelcome predators. Eugster was surprised that BPCC could afford to pay for its spate of recent acquisitions because its borrowings, although cleverly dressed up by the accountants, were high. Since Maxwell was offering to pay the £44 million in cash, Eugster set out to follow the money trail. BPCC was owned by Pergamon, which was a private company, but Pergamon, as revealed in BPCC's annual report, was ultimately owned by the Pergamon Holding Foundation which was a trust incorporated in one of the world's most secret sanctuaries, Liechtenstein.

Maxwell had used trusts as tax havens for thirty years but few had noticed in 1982 that the ownership of Pergamon had moved from New York to Liechtenstein. Among Maxwell's reasons was the reform of American banking laws which had undermined the original guarantee of secrecy and freedom from taxation. The state of Liechtenstein, in contrast, promised its clients total anonymity since its law did not require that a trust be registered and the state did not provide a public record which indicated that a trust even existed. Such is the perfection of the service to guarantee anonymity that Liechtenstein law does not require the creator of the trust to identify who are the intended beneficiaries and even allows the founder to sign in a nominee name. Accordingly, the Liechtenstein government can honestly state that it remains unaware who created the trust and to what end, although the law requires the founder to promise that his trust has no criminal purpose. Nevertheless, Liechtenstein is an ideal location for invisibly amassing and dispensing a fortune or even concealing the reality that there is no fortune whatsoever and there are only debts which are guaranteed by other assets. Liechtenstein was simply ideal to avoid answering awkward questions.

Maxwell's decision to cloak his activities in the secrecy of Liechtenstein was already public knowledge when Eugster began searching for ruses in Waddingtons' defense. The magazine *Private Eye* had four months earlier mentioned the transfer but such are the vagaries and weaknesses of British journalism that at the time the item passed without comment. Eugster consulted Anthony Cardew, a public relations expert retained by Waddingtons, about exploiting the Liechtenstein connection and received an ecstatic response: "This story has got legs. It's going to run and run." The fifty-six square miles of Liechtenstein represented the antithesis of everything Maxwell publicly claimed to espouse. Highlighting his use of a tax haven was the ideal weapon to embarrass a man who was a self-proclaimed socialist, whose newspapers thrived and survived upon exposing the intimate details of others' lives, and who campaigned on the slogan "Britain First." Eugster and Cardew dressed up the old as the new and hinted to friendly Fleet Street journalists that here was an area which was worthy of investigation. The first of a series of stories appeared at the beginning of December.

One week later, Dr. Walter Keicher, a plump, aging lawyer in Vaduz, the capital of Liechtenstein, was identified as the representative of the Pergamon *Stiftung*. When approached to reveal the trust's secrets, Keicher reacted with the embarrassment which might be expected of a young maiden tactlessly invited to lose her virginity. His doors were politely slammed and he grabbed for the telephone to call London. Maxwell could no longer ignore the intrusion but was furious that a take-over battle had once again degenerated into a smear about what he believed were his private affairs. In a statement, he condemned the "outrageous and irrelevant smokescreen" raised by Waddingtons, which "obscures the straightforward issues." Watson countered that the obfuscation was caused by the Liechtenstein ownership of Maxwell's companies. Since it was impossible to establish the ultimate ownership of Pergamon because of Liechtenstein's laws, claimed Watson, no one knew what hidden financial liabilities Pergamon had incurred. "If it was all as clear as Mr. Maxwell says, then why does he keep it so secret?" he asked.

At the beginning of the second week of December, Maxwell's bid was delicately poised. He had already attracted 15 per cent acceptances which, in addition to his own 23 per cent, placed him in a stronger position than one year earlier. He would win the prize and humiliate Watson if a 15 per cent stake owned by Warburg Investments and held on behalf of the Sainsbury Group's pension fund were sold to him. As so often in his dealings, Maxwell had set a deadline of December 13 for acceptances and was convinced that Warburgs were bound to sell to him as the highest bidder. There was only the matter of disposing of the Liechtenstein embarrassment.

On December 10, Ansbachers issued a statement on Maxwell's behalf about Liechtenstein. Keicher, it said, had represented Maxwell's interests for "over thirty years and it is well known that the persons ultimately entitled [to the trust] comprise a number of charities and relatives of the respective grandparents of Mr. and Mrs. Robert Maxwell not resident in the United Kingdom." The statement raised more questions than it answered. Although it was consistent with Maxwell's oft-proclaimed assurance that his children "would not inherit one penny," it was pointed out that since his children were all French citizens (because they were born in France), it was possible that under Liechtenstein law they could be deemed "not to be resident in the UK" and therefore inherit their father's business. Indeed, Liechtenstein law might not even apply because the secret trust document might contain a unique definition of "residence." The very reason for Maxwell's seeking the protection of Liechtenstein was to allow the trustees to enjoy the freedom of writing their own rules and it would be consistent with Liechtenstein's laws for Maxwell secretly to retain control over the trust. But the statement did explain why Maxwell had been anxious to correct his own front-page article in the *Daily Mirror* on July 14, 1983, which had declared that he was "proud to be the proprietor of this group of publications." A short time later, he had stated: "I am the publisher, not the proprietor." The legal difference was important for tax purposes in Britain since it was Pergamon Media Trust which owned the *Mirror*. But since no one had seen the Liechtenstein trust documents and therefore could not authoritatively contradict his assertion until after his death, his denials were not treated seriously. To Maxwell's irritation, the mystery began seriously to undermine his ambitions.

On December 12, however, Eugster's exposé only partially contributed to Maxwell's discomfiture. During that week, Maxwell had held a series of conversations with a senior member of the Sainsburys board about the sale of the pension fund's 15 per cent stake in Waddingtons. The tone of his remarks irritated the executive and triggered, just before the deadline expired, the sale of the shares to Waddingtons' bankers, Kleinworts. "Maxwell knew that he blew it," says a close adviser. Others blamed Ansbachers for failing to secure the stake. Maxwell conceded defeat but instead of consoling himself with the profit on his shares, his row with Watson rumbled on in public for some months under the heading in a circular, "Damn the Truth—a New Waddington Game." "His lectures about the responsibility which a director owes to his shareholders and employees could have been called 'Pot calls kettle black,' " recalls Watson, who embarked on a popular lecture tour explaining how he had fought off Maxwell's bids.

The publicity surrounding Maxwell's defeat combined with the loss in circulation of one million newspapers in the Mirror Group was not enhancing his image at the end of 1985. The reverses were reflected in the accounts. BPCC's profits had fallen from £37 million to £25 million because the property deals which one year earlier had been described as a "significant profit center" had actually lost the company £1.8 million and other anticipated profits in publishing had dived, because of industrial disputes, from £4.3 million to just one quarter of a million pounds. The annual report minimized those reverses and Maxwell optimistically predicted that the worst of the expensive closures and layoffs were over. The report also contained an extraordinarily ambitious prediction: "The aim of this reorganization is to accomplish, from a British and European base, our great objective of successfully becoming a multi-faceted worldwide information and communications enterprise with revenues of £3 to £5 billion by 1990 with profits to match." In 1985, BPCC's turnover was £265 million and gross profits were £79 million. Maxwell had forecast that there would be an eleven- to eighteen-fold multiplication of sales and profits within five years. Twenty years earlier, Oliver Marriott had said of Pergamon's huge profits: "These are the sort of returns which all industrialists dream about." The same could describe his new ambitions, which seemed to a few to harbor the presentiment of disaster.

The first stage of his expansion plan was BPCC's purchase of Pergamon's 361 scientific journals, which in 1985 had earned £19 million profits. Automatically, BPCC's profits in 1986 would increase by 70 per cent. Because Maxwell's public company was buying his private interests it was necessary to assuage those who might be suspicious of intercompany trading. Bankers Trust was commissioned to value the journals independently and it set the price at £238.65 million. To reconfirm that this was a fair assessment, Maxwell announced that there had been "stiff competition" from overseas buyers for Pergamon's journals "but BPCC had won." BPCC, of which Maxwell was chairman and chief executive, paid Pergamon, of which Maxwell was chairman, a new issue of 107.5 million BPCC shares. That meant that once more Maxwell personally owned over 70 per cent of the company and could embark on the next stage of his plan, which was to earn cash by quick deals.

In spring 1986, Maxwell was involved in so many bids that it was quipped, "Maxwell has more fingers in more pies than most people have fingers." By buying strategic stakes in companies which were in the midst of take-over bids, he hoped to profit by selling to the highest bidder. He was acting as an impromptu arbitrageur, when the term was still fashionable, posing as the "white knight." Ostensibly he would arrive to save a company from an unwelcome bid but the subjects of his warm embrace soon noticed that his bear-like arms had gradually tightened around their throat. The self-styled savior would become a predator. "There is no secret strategy," commented Maxwell as his frantic burst of bids and deals provoked questions about his idiosyncratic methods, "other than to make money." The first intervention concerned Britannia Arrow, a financial group, and the second was for Extel, which provided financial information and confidential printing services. In both cases, Maxwell placed himself in the middle of a take-over battle to exercise decisive power and derive substantial profit from the predicament of others; and in both events he became allied with David Stevens, the chairman of United Newspapers, which had recently bought the Express newspaper group.

Stevens, whose diminutive stature and cool personality contrasted with Maxwell's, nevertheless shared his occasional partner's ambitions and some of his characteristics. "Their combined aggression and rudeness is awesome," recalled Michael Newman, the chief executive of Britannia Arrow, who, through Geoffrey Rippon, the former Conservative minister, initially appealed to Maxwell for help but was eventually forced by Stevens to resign. "Maxwell was burned at the beginning," said Newman, "and appealed to Stevens for help. At the end, Stevens's profit was Maxwell's loss."

"There is no friendship between those men," according to Richard Marsh, who sees Maxwell, Stevens, Murdoch and Rothermere at the regular Reuters board meetings and the innumerable official functions which newspaper owners attend. "They are streetfighters who don't particularly care if they are liked or hated. They have a common interest in forming temporary alliances and, whenever it suits them, to engineer another's downfall."

Maxwell's bid for Extel started in his traditional manner. Extel was fighting off a bid from the Demerger Corporation and was hoping to attract the support of an Egyptian financier, Ashraf Marwan, who owned a decisive shareholding in Extel. Early in the morning of February 12, Alan Brooker, Extel's chairman and an employee of the company for twenty-eight years, received a phone call from Maxwell. "This is to inform you," said the voice, "that you are no longer dealing with Marwan but with me. I have bought his stake. I think we should meet. I would like everything to be friendly and conducted in a gentlemanly manner." Brooker is quite honest about his reaction. "I was frightened. We were an independent agency and Maxwell is an interventionist. We knew his presence would frighten away our clients, who expected independent advice. Maxwell was as much an anathema to them as to us." Brooker refused Maxwell's entreaties and expected a formal announcement of his bid. Instead, after the bid failed due to a breach of the Takeover Panel's regulations one month later, the Panel ordered Maxwell's bid to be frozen for one year.

"During that year, he harassed, chased and upset us," recalls Brooker. He sought advice. "Victor Watson was very helpful and we decided to use the 'Liechtenstein defense.' After all, the shareholders and employees were entitled to know who would own their company if Maxwell's bid was successful." Like Watson, Brooker spent a fortune on lawyers in an attempt to unravel the ownership, only to discover that Liechtenstein's reputation for secrecy is well deserved.

On March 13, 1987, Maxwell wrote to Brooker to let him know that he intended to launch a bid the following month. Brooker replied with an onslaught of actions under the Companies Act 1985 to establish who was controlling the Extel shares owned by BPCC and the Pergamon Holding Foundation Corporation. On March 31 Maxwell responded to what he interpreted as harassment: "I entirely fail to understand the pressure which Extel seeks to attribute to its demands [sic] . . . and reserve my right to draw this matter to the attention of shareholders of Extel and to the attention of the regulatory authorities including the Secretary of State." For Maxwell to threaten to appeal to the British government to protect a Liechtenstein trust seemed to Brooker richly ironic, but his bewilderment was compounded on April 5. Keicher, the Liechtenstein lawyer, wrote to say that the Pergamon Holding Foundation did not control the Extel shareholding. Control, he explained, was exercised by its subsidiary, the Pergamon Media Trust, but "neither our Foundation nor Pergamon Holding Corporation (which holds shares in PMT as our nominees) are so interested. This is because neither our Foundation nor PHC are entitled to exercise or control the exercise of one-third or more of the voting power of PMT." Keicher had added to the confusion and accordingly Brooker asked Maxwell to explain the contradiction between the Foundation lawyer's insistence that he did not control the Extel shares and Maxwell's claims. On the same day Maxwell replied, "There is no mystery," but he revealed nothing more. Instead he attacked Brooker's use of the Liechtenstein ploy, criticized him for not giving the Extel shareholders the chance "to choose to take a bona fide cash bid for their shares" (although Maxwell had still not made a bid), and finally announced that he would not after all bid for Extel. Clearly the exposure of the Liechtenstein connection was successful, thus exposing Maxwell's Achilles heel for those who wanted an easy defense in future bids.

Yet the fate and handling of Maxwell's stake in Extel displayed his rehabilitation in the City. He announced that the shares were to be auctioned and requested sealed bids. Acting on his behalf was his old contact Michael Richardson, who in 1969 at stockbrokers Panmure Gordon had represented Pergamon's interests but had resigned when Leasco's bid collapsed. In 1981 Richardson became a managing director at Rothschilds, the merchant bank which had fought on Leasco's behalf against Maxwell. Richardson's endorsement was a critical benchmark of Maxwell's rehabilitation which had developed gradually since Maxwell took control of BPCC in 1980. Richardson, a quintessential Englishman with a pukka accent and country house, had been BPCC's broker when Maxwell launched the dawn raid and was part of Maxwell's inheritance following the company's take-over. Similarly, Maxwell had inherited Hill Samuel, BPCC's reputable merchant bankers, and also its auditors, Coopers & Lybrand Deloitte—one of Britain's biggest and most prestigious partnerships.

Regardless of those bankers' and accountants' discomfort, they had little choice but to continue working for BPCC and its new chairman. Indeed, like the National Westminster Bank, they accepted that only the devil they knew might save their own investment. By 1985, their reluctance had evaporated. Thanks to Maxwell, not only BPCC was saved, but the Mirror Group was an additional client. Within those five years, Maxwell had displayed none of the sins condemned by the DTI inspectors. On the contrary, some in the City establishment—notably those who took his fees—had remarked how responsibly and respect-fully he had behaved. Moreover, as Maxwell increased his political activities around the world, those in the City involved with Maxwell could only be impressed by the endorsement he had won not only from the Labour party but also seemingly from Buckingham Palace and the prime minister, Margaret Thatcher. For those earning increasing fees from Maxwell, self-interest dictated that if the DTI inspectors' con-demnation had not been quite forgotten, the past had at least been forgiven. Some, like Michael Richardson, a friend of the prime minister, went further. The inspectors' report, he believed, had been "unfair" and "over the top." They were not only grateful that Maxwell had saved their investment in BPCC but positively basked in the enhance-ment of their own reputation as BPCC's fortunes rose while their client promoted himself as an international star.

But there was added symbolism when, in 1986, Richardson, on behalf of Rothschild, agreed to represent Maxwell in the Extel bid. Seventeen years earlier, Jacob Rothschild, representing Leasco, had uncovered the evidence of Maxwell's fraud. Since then, amid some acrimony, he had left the family bank and established his own investment house in St. James, central London. From there, he watched with "amazement" as his cousin Evelyn Rothschild ignored the family's experience in 1969 and consorted with Maxwell. Apparently, the events of 1969 were for-gotten. Maxwell was too important and was spending too much money for Rothschilds to spurn his business on an old matter of principle. But Rothschild was not alone in agreeing to serve Maxwell. Others in the City, discarding similar prejudices, would soon follow their lead. In the Extel case, Maxwell's shares were sold to David Stevens of United Newspapers at a profit, in theory, of £5 million.

In fact, it was impossible to ascertain what real profits were earned by Maxwell's interventions because, as will be seen shortly, despite his cultivated image of adroitly juggling a dozen balls which all produced profits, the truth was often different. While he dealt, a collection of highly paid executives waited permanently and forlornly outside his office for his decisions and approvals. Those delays caused incalculable losses. But it is a maxim of big business that one deal leads to another and that a high profile encourages a "player's credibility." Image is sometimes as important as substance and by August 1986 Maxwell had projected himself as a major and irresistible entrepreneur who led a corporation with surging profits. The key to that transformation was a "corporate restructure" which, although dull in layman's terms, turned a sow's skin into a silk purse. The editorial section of Mirror Group

Newspapers was legally separated from the printing presses, which had been transferred to a new subsidary of BPCC, the strike-free British Newspaper Printing Corporation (BNPC). Accordingly, Mirror Group Newspapers, which was owned by Pergamon (Maxwell's private company), contracted with BNPC to print its newspapers. The contract increased the flow of money and new profits into BPCC, so enhancing the public company's balance sheet. Similarly, the sale of Pergamon journals increased BPCC's turnover and profits. Consequently, in August 1986, Maxwell could confidently announce that BPCC's pre-tax profits in the first six months had no less than doubled and Maxwell's image and substance coincided to pave the way for an important coup.

In City jargon, having your "paper accepted" means that you are creditworthy. When Maxwell had tried to buy Waddingtons two years earlier, he had offered cash because no one would risk taking BPCC shares in exchange for Waddingtons' shares or "paper." After announcing BPCC's mid-1986 profits, Maxwell's credit rating changed. BPCC shares, which in 1981 had traded at 12p, were worth 298p, and Maxwell's promises of greater profits to come were taken at face value. In August, Maxwell heard on the City grapevine that there was dissatisfaction with the management of the Philip Hill Investment Trust and that the Trust was for sale. He offered £355 million but said that he would only pay in newly issued BPCC shares. The Trust's shareholders were City institutions who for fifteen years had looked askance at the bidder, but after skillful lobbying by mutually trusted City operators they were prepared to concede that he now possessed financial credibility and to accept his offer. Within twenty-four hours of the purchase, Maxwell had sold most of the Trust's investments for cash and used the money to buy two American printers, Webb Co. Inc. and Providence Gravure, enabling him to become the second-largest printer in America. Within the Square Mile it was hailed as a masterstroke. Overnight, BPCC was bigger and richer, and the blitz of media attention devoted to the constantly photographed and interviewed Maxwell increased his self-esteem. The Midas touch could clearly, he felt, be extended to any venture. At that moment he was presiding over the Commonwealth Games in Scotland, which he had himself saved from catastrophe.

Edinburgh had been awarded the Games in 1980 and, at the time, the organizers had been told by ministers that, since the event was expected to be self-financing, they should not expect any government aid. The estimated cost was £14 million, a pittance compared to the Los Angeles Olympics, which had raised £340 million and had actually ended with a surplus. But six years later, on the eve of the opening ceremony, the chairman of the Edinburgh Games organizing committee, Kenneth Borthwick, a wholesale confectioner and former Lord Provost of the city, privately acknowledged that he had failed to secure sufficient sponsorship contracts. Some blamed his amateurism, but excuses were irrelevant at the end of May. With just eight weeks left Borthwick was anticipating that the deficit might amount to £5 million. Without extra money the Games would not be able to start and the proud city would be embarrassed. In some panic, Borthwick secretly appealed to the government for help, but Malcolm Rifkind, the minister for Scottish Affairs, unhesitatingly refused and suggested that he might approach the nation's rich. Among Borthwick's thirty-seven pleading letters addressed to names culled from the *Financial Times* was one to Maxwell.

Maxwell and the Mirror Group had been approached for money more than one year earlier but, despite their profitable newspaper interests in Scotland, had refused their support. In the meantime, however, the Mirror Group in Scotland had been involved in a bruising battle with all its employees on the *Daily Record* and *Sunday Mail* to enforce an extension of the working week and obtain the unconditional acceptance of new technology. When the negotiations had failed, 1,050 printers and journalists were overnight deemed by Maxwell to have "dismissed themselves" and, in a familiar pattern, a deadline was imposed to negotiate a survival plan. As the dispute stretched into the third week, barbed wire appeared around the premises and emotions became inflamed. Memories of Maxwell's behavior at the *Scottish Daily News* were rekindled and he was castigated for resorting to Tory anti-trade union laws and for emulating Murdoch's methods at Fortress Wapping, despite his own gibe that the Australian's was "not the British way of doing things." Undeterred, Maxwell invited his "ex-employees" to reapply for their jobs on his terms. Finally, in April 1986, the unions conceded a 30 per cent cut in the labor force and agreed to abandon their traditional work practices. But Maxwell's overwhelming victory had scorched his image, so Borthwick's request to save the Games came as an attractive opportunity to repair the damage and, in a favored phrase, "to be of service to my fellow man."

On June 19 it was announced that Maxwell and a team from the Mirror Group would assume responsibility for the Games' finances. The *Mirror*'s front page blazed, "*Mirror* Saves the Games" and the *Record* trumpeted "*Record* Saves the Games," but both agreed that their owner would become chairman of the company managing the event, although the confusion over what his help implied was evident on the first day. For Borthwick, saving the Games meant that Maxwell would pour in a few of his many millions to remove the deficit. Suffice to say that this was neither Maxwell's understanding nor his intent.

Maxwell believed in self-help. In offering his money for the *Scottish Daily News* or for the Labour Party, he stipulated that he would match the amount raised by those seeking assistance. "If I just gave," he once said, "they would do nothing themselves." When he accepted Borthwick's offer, there was, in Maxwell's view, no commitment to contribute a penny.

"I guarantee unconditionally that the Games will go ahead," he told a press conference on his arrival on June 19, four weeks before the opening ceremony. "I hope you will agree that there is nothing more important than that." Attempts to extract from him an indication of whether he had promised to contribute any money were shrugged off. Instead he assured everyone that he would seek new sponsors so that the Games did not become a burden for the taxpayer. Under his command, he promised, "There will be no deficit at all." When pressed to reveal his secret plan, he smilingly acknowledged his financial acumen but urged his skeptical audience to understand that "Jerusalem was not built in a day. We have got quite a few weeks left." The skeptics remained unconvinced and suspected what he would repeatedly have to deny: "I hope that will put paid to any nonsense about my being in this business to hijack the Games for the benefit of the *Daily Mirror* or that the *Mirror* and *Record* are going to have any special privileges or that I or any of my family will be handing out medals."

For four weeks, Maxwell and his associates enjoyed a honeymoon period to produce the £4 million which had eluded the hapless Borthwick. On July 18, six days before the Games started, it seemed that he had indeed performed a miracle. Maxwell announced his success to a group of what he now unlovingly called "hacks": "When it comes to elbow-twisting on a major scale I am particularly good at it. . . . The Games are financially secure. The job is virtually done." In other words, he had found £4 million, and he even suggested that there would be a surplus. To prove how the money was pouring in, he pulled from his pocket a letter from a well-wisher in London which pledged the sum of two pounds. "It is unbelievable," he pronounced, alluding to the avalanche of donations.

During that penultimate week, the Games had become beset by a further albatross. In protest against Mrs. Thatcher's refusal to countenance sanctions against South Africa, the Afro-Asian members had resorted to the same protest which she had encouraged for the Moscow Olympics after the Soviet invasion of Afghanistan. Thirty-two nations declared that they would boycott the Edinburgh Games. If the Games were now not short of funds, there was a definite lack of competitors. Caught in the maelstrom of international politics, Maxwell was spokesman to the world about the sorry fate of the competition. Only his irrepressible energy and unfounded optimism could support his pronouncements that the Games would go ahead, be a success and not incur an enormous deficit. But four days before the Games started, on July 20, when the daunting repercussions of the boycott had registered, Maxwell suddenly acknowledged that there was again a deficit and that the Prime Minister would be expected to pick up the bill.

His contradiction inevitably provoked those whom he had labeled "hacks who normally ask silly questions." They could not tally the arithmetic and asked him to reconcile the statement he had made on July 16 that the £4 million deficit had been overcome with his latest claim that while the boycott would cost £1 million, the deficit was £2 million. Two Scottish journalists, Derek Bateman and Derek Douglas, persistently asked him for explanations since he had also earlier said that the Mirror Group "had contributed £1 million to the Games." Spotting an unequal equation did not require the skill of a City analyst, as Maxwell admitted when he rushed from their interrogation saying, "I certainly needed this job like a hole in the head." In all the newspapers other than those owned by the Mirror Group, Maxwell was attracting the blame for a disaster of others' making and was receiving neither sympathy nor gratitude for his efforts. Yet most would have acknowledged that without him the Games would have collapsed before their opening. But the goodwill was fast dissipating as the background to the bargain price became exposed.

During his many press statements before the Games, Maxwell had emphasized that the deficit had disappeared and he denied "hijacking the Games" for his personal prestige and his newspapers' profits. Yet every day during the competition, the nation's television, radio and newspapers were saturated by his image and words. Edinburgh, a growing chorus chanted, had become the venue of the "Maxwell Games." Maxwell hung a gold medal around the neck of the decathlon champion Daley Thompson, he stood next to the Queen and Prime Minister on the dais, and the Mirror Group's red and white colors dominated the stadium and its scoreboards. His presence became so pervasive that at one crucial moment during the last day's closing ceremonies when Maxwell drew the winning ticket for the "Save the Games" competition, the Queen had disappeared from the dais and BBC Television stopped broadcasting from the Games and returned to the studio. As Bateman and Douglas wrote, "Immediately after the tombola drum and the Maxwell entourage had departed, normal service was resumed."

Soon after the Games ended, Maxwell announced that the deficit was £4 million, which was exactly the sum when he had arrived. The company managing the Games had been bankrupt throughout the proceedings and it fell to Maxwell as its chairman to explain the discrepancies since Whitehall still refused to cover the deficit. "If Mr. Maxwell is really concerned about his creditors," a minister confided to the press, "he and his Mirror Group should make good the losses in recognition of the huge publicity he's got. It's a flea-bite to him." Maxwell was clearly under renewed pressure to reconcile all his conflicting statements and, in the wake of the enormous publicity he and his businesses had enjoyed, to quantify his personal contribution. Before the Games, BPCC's accountants, Coopers & Lybrand, had estimated that if Maxwell contributed £4.3 million (that is, the whole projected deficit), "it would produce a significant commercial advantage to yourself." Yet Maxwell apparently (since he declined to quantify his contribution) was unwilling to pay more than £250,000 and possibly as little as £100,000. Instead, he tried first to raise money from national corporations. Now that the Games were over, his efforts proved even less successful than before the event. Secondly, he tried to extract money from the British government and those nations which had boycotted the Games. That also proved fruitless. His third target, Ryoichi Sasakawa, surprised everyone. Sasakawa, an obscure eighty-seven-year-old Japanese, had, according to Maxwell, "devoted himself to world philanthropy" and claimed to control an $8.4 billion empire. Over the previous twenty years, Sasakawa had given away, said Maxwell, $12,000 million, a sum which reduced his own fortune to minuscule proportions and the £4 million deficit to a financial irrelevance. But considering the philanthropist's background, Maxwell's endorsement was decidedly odd. During the war, Sasakawa had commanded a sizable fascist army and in 1945 he had been interned by the Americans for three years as a suspected war criminal. But imprisonment had been his good fortune since among his fellow inmates were the architects of Japan's peacetime prosperity who, on the basis of their close friendship, afforded him lucrative opportunities. Forty years later, on October 13, Sasakawa authorized Maxwell to unveil their joint rescue package.

By unilaterally rejecting various accounts and charges from contractors, Maxwell claimed that the deficit had been reduced to £3.2 million.

To settle the remainder, he announced that Sasakawa was prepared to contribute £1.3 million and Maxwell would personally pay £700,000 on condition that the British government paid £1 million. To his delight, the ball was firmly placed in Whitehall's camp, but only for the briefest moment. The government reaffirmed its refusal to provide a subsidy. By 1988, the deficit had grown to £3.8 million and there was still no solution in sight, despite his claim that "all outstanding debts have been settled." Maxwell had moved on to many other ventures but he had enjoyed saving the Games.

The first casualty when Maxwell emerged from the morass in Edinburgh in September 1986 was a project which was very close to his heart—the proposed London evening newspaper. For years Maxwell had aspired to challenge the monopoly of the *Evening Standard,* which was owned by Lord Rothermere and which he had unsuccessfully sought to purchase. Although the sale of evening newspapers in London had declined from two million in 1960 to half a million in 1986, Maxwell believed that the capital was big and wealthy enough to support two newspapers. In April he had appointed Magnus Linklater as the paper's first editor and the projected launch date was set for October 1986. During those summer weeks while Maxwell was "saving the Games," Linklater had great difficulty in gaining access to the one person who could endorse a series of vital decisions and authorize critical expenditure. By the time Maxwell emerged from Edinburgh, Linklater feared that his creation might be stillborn unless the launch was postponed.

Linklater, then forty-four, is an Old Etonian who, with a successful career on the *Evening Standard, Sunday Times* and *Observer,* was naturally ambitious for an editorship; Maxwell's proposals seemed very attractive. Although the newspaper's editorial offices would be adjacent to the *Daily Mirror* in New Fetter Lane, the venture was to be on what Maxwell described as a "greenfield site" and would espouse his oft-vaunted ideals for printing a newspaper. The journalists would set the pages using computers while the traditional unions would be excluded by contracting out the printing to other national daily newspapers whose presses were idle during the daytime. Even distributing the paper from the five locations would be entrusted to a new organization, Newsflow, instead of the established wholesalers who used union labor. "We are breaking free of the *Mirror* and old Fleet Street attitudes," said Maxwell, but his absence in Scotland had delayed crucial negotiations to contract three essentials: the printing, the computers and the distribution. On his return, Linklater and Bill Gillespie, the chief executive, faced the unpleasant task of persuading their employer to delay publication and therefore reverse his public commitment. Their problem was symptomatic of his organization's weakness. "No one ever says to Maxwell, 'It's your fault,' " recalls one executive. "There's fear in confronting him with reality and equally there is fear of being caught concealing reality. Even the strongest hearts avoid those face-to-face sessions because when he voices his anger it lacerates and bruises." When the truth was unfolded, his explosion was predictable but he reluctantly agreed. Since it was close to Christmas, they recommended that the next optimum launch would be early February 1987. But in accepting their advice, Maxwell added an emollient which proved that there was a heavy price for his persistent juggling.

Among Maxwell's several reactions was to dispatch a team to the United States to investigate the feasibility of a twenty-four-hour newspaper. Eleven years earlier, one of the conditions he had set for his final contribution to the *Scottish Daily News* was acceptance by the unions of a twenty-four-hour newspaper, and his hankering for the concept had never dimmed. The commercial attraction was simply that, while the editorial content changed during the day, the advertisers were guaranteed readers in both the morning and the evening. The overriding disadvantage to the publisher was the increased labor costs. Maxwell's fact finders, who included Linklater, traveled to New York, Detroit and Florida to taste the American experience and returned convinced that the idea was unprofitable, if only because, despite the propaganda, there were no genuine and profitable twenty-four-hour newspapers in America. "Most of the newspapers we visited had abandoned or retained only a vestige of the concept," said Linklater. Maxwell dismissed the findings of their report.

On September 18, 1986, Maxwell summoned a press conference at the Rotunda in which he would announce the delay of the newspaper's publication. His approach on that day would not differ from the countless previous occasions when his press office had sent summonses for journalists to attend for his latest communication. Maxwell wants these encounters to excite and interest his audience: "He likes to believe their jaws have dropped and they're sitting up. He wants to be certain that he'll be the talking-point for the rest of the day." Since Maxwell was always a "good story," he normally achieved his object by calculating what would most surprise. That press conference was no exception.

"I have called you here today," he began, "to make an important and exciting announcement. The new London evening newspaper is to become Britain's first twenty-four-hour paper, which will provide the best possible service from breakfast to bedtime." After explaining how the twenty-four-hour concept would revolutionize Britain's newspaper industry, he allowed a pause for the drama. "This project has been so top secret that not even the editor knew about it until this morning." The assembled journalists gasped. Linklater looked embarrassed and interrupted: "That's a slight exaggeration, Bob." "Well, all right, all right," conceded his employer, unruffled. He added that accordingly the launch would be delayed to plan for "this exciting new development." Asked to reveal the anticipated circulation of the newspaper, Maxwell unhesitatingly replied, "One million." Again there was dismay on the dais, but this time it was felt by his other neighbor, Bill Gillespie, who was horrified. Advertisers' rates are calculated upon circulation and if the actual circulation falls below the amount guaranteed by the publisher the advertisers are automatically entitled to a refund. After heated whispering, Maxwell announced that the "guaranteed circulation will be half a million." Even that figure was higher than Gillespie had suggested. "It was an unnecessary hostage to fortune," said one of the team afterward. As usual, Maxwell's optimism had outpaced realism. He had not assessed the full implications, especially the cost. Linklater and Gillespie consoled themselves with the knowledge that they had at least won another four months' preparation. Maxwell meanwhile stepped up another gear into more frenzied activity. During the week of November 3, another of his ambitions was fulfilled. For seven days he dominated the news.

In the autumn, the buying spree to enlarge his fortune had recommenced, initially through Hollis, a small publicly quoted timber merchant and furniture manufacturer which Maxwell controlled but which was managed by his son Kevin. Hollis had recently bid for a diverse range of insolvent engineering companies, a crane manufacturer and an electronics specialist and had paid £30 million in an intercompany transaction for some Pergamon assets. But those deals were eclipsed on November 3 when Maxwell in the name of Hollis offered £265 million for AE, a well-known Rugby-based engineering group. AE was in the midst of an exhausting take-over battle and Maxwell presented himself once more in the guise of the "white knight." "Publisher Rescues Engineer" was not a convincing headline that week (the AE bid in fact later collapsed) but in another bitter and much publicized take-over battle between two printers, the management of McCorquodale and Norton Opax, he maximized his interventionist role. He had bought a strategic 19 per cent shareholding in McCorquodales and he encouraged both sides to bid against the other for his support. The Dutch auction for his favors had continued for several weeks, often late into the night as he coolly haggled for a better price between two increasingly exasperated bidders. During the week of November 3, as the climax of bid and counter-bid approached, Maxwell's name appeared daily in bold, large print in the news, financial and legal sections of every paper— "In the center of the stage," "The global player," "The big-league player who is no longer in it for the money," and "The incredible all-performing Robert Maxwell." It was also the week that a Chinook helicopter which was part of the fleet Maxwell had bought six months earlier from British Airways for approximately £14 million crashed in the North Sea killing forty-five people, the world's worst civil helicopter crash in history. Moreover when, at 2 a.m. on November 6, he finally came down on the side of Norton Opax, he was spending his daytime in the High Court fighting a libel action against *Private Eye*.

Among the several paradoxes reaffirmed about Maxwell during that epochal week was his sensitivity about his reputation. *Private Eye* had falsely alleged in July 1985 that Maxwell had paid for the travel expenses of Neil Kinnock to East Africa in the hope that he would, as the Labour leader's "paymaster," be recommended for a peerage. When the item had appeared, Maxwell had denied the story (and was subsequently vindicated by the jury), asked for a published apology and a payment of £10,000 for the *Mirror*'s Ethiopian famine fund. The *Eye*'s editor, Shrewsbury-educated Richard Ingrams, had spurned his protest and had unwisely repeated the allegation. For many years, Maxwell and his wife had been a standing butt of facetious comment in the magazine and Maxwell was also the subject of a regular, laconic strip cartoon. The stimulus, he believed, was Ingrams's xenophobia and anti-Semitism which sprang from the same "forces of evil" which had pursued him since 1969. For Ingrams, Maxwell represented the worst type of humbug—a man who perpetually cried "foul" but committed identical sins about which he vociferously complained. One of the *Eye*'s functions, which Ingrams had repeatedly expounded during his twenty-five-year editorship, was to expose what he thought to be the hypocrisy of the rich and powerful, who in turn were outraged that those beyond their employ did not display the respect which they desired. In 1985, Ingrams, who was contemplating retirement, viewed Maxwell as a prime candidate for that treatment and therefore ignored his complaint. Maxwell's lawyers served a writ alleging defamation. In reply, a member of the *Eye*'s staff swore an affidavit, which was presented to a judge, claiming that he would be able to prove the "peerage" story if the issue came to trial.

Maxwell's relationship with Kinnock was workmanlike despite the

Mirror's publisher occasionally posing as the alternative Opposition. With the exception of policies on trade union laws and defense, where his views had changed from two decades earlier (he was now opposed to unilateralism), Maxwell broadly supported the party leadership. His endorsement was welcomed by the Labour leader, who more than ever needed the *Mirror*'s support, although he was dismayed by the newspaper's rush downmarket, at the expense of political coverage, to chase the *Sun*. Maxwell, whose personal loyalty to the party was never in doubt, was clearly an important benefactor because there were few socialist millionaires who could afford to make large contributions, although excepting one donation of £34,000 in 1984, Maxwell would never give any more substantial amounts to his party. It was clearly within Kinnock's gift to recommend peerages and, after the elevation to the House of Lords of Maxwell's employees and fellow Labour Party supporters Charles Williams, Bernard Donoughue and Sam Silkin in 1984, the *Mirror*'s publisher might reasonably have expected the same recognition. Indeed, according to Maxwell, soon after the three appointments he was "asked" by Roy Hattersley whether he too would like a peerage but he had rejected the offer. Maxwell would cite this exchange in the High Court case against the *Eye* as the second occasion on which he had refused the offer of a peerage, and as proof that he had no need to bribe the Labour leader. Hattersley insists that the question he posed at a social event was an "obvious jest" and that Maxwell later privately apologized for mentioning the "offer" in court. Kinnock is equally emphatic that he would only recommend Labour supporters as peers who would solemnly undertake to appear regularly in the House of Lords and dedicate themselves to work for the Opposition. Since Maxwell would be unable to commit himself to those long hours, he was therefore automatically excluded.

Nevertheless, such was Maxwell's obvious interest in power and recognition that when Ingrams was handed the story he approved publication because, even if he could not produce a witness to the alleged transaction, "it seemed right." Newspaper barons in Britain were customarily created peers and there was every reason to imply that Maxwell might expect the same. A jury, Ingrams calculated, would sympathetically interpret and share his prejudices against power and wealth and, even if the case were lost, the free publicity of daily coverage in the national newspapers would be worth a fortune. Since Ingrams had entered "litigation" as one of his recreations in *Who's Who*, observers might have expected his familiarity with the law of defamation and the vagaries of the courts to make him hesitate to engage Maxwell in battle unless his case were stronger. It was a challenge to Maxwell, who readily accepted the chance to teach the public school establishment a lesson and to protect his standing in the Labour Party. By the end of the first day's hearing on November 2, it was obvious that the same British cult of amateurism which had enabled Maxwell to earn his fortune had blinded Ingrams and his legal advisers to the interpretation which a jury of common men would put on their criticisms. The opening speeches in Court 11 showed that the trial would not be about buying a peerage, because the *Eye* could not substantiate its allegations. Its "eyewitnesses" could not be named nor could they appear. Their case was a bluff. Maxwell *v*. Pressdam, alias School Bully *v*. School Sneak, became Nasty Outsider *v*. Nasty Insider.

The magazine attempted, within the limitations of the alleged defamation, to put Maxwell himself on trial by probing his quest for publicity, his own newspaper's mistakes and how he might expect his support for the Labour Party to be ultimately rewarded. Maxwell, who had spent a lifetime defending himself against more formidable advocates armed with more incriminating allegations, not only withstood the attack without demur but turned the spotlight upon his accusers. On the third day, when he was giving evidence, Maxwell performed a remarkable somersault. Maxwell the ogre and bully became Maxwell the underdog.

The issue was a regular "letter" purportedly sent by his wife to the magazine asking whether readers had noticed the similarity between two photographs. The personalities for comparison one week from "Ena B. Maxwell" were the Duke of Edinburgh and Colonel Adolf Eichmann, who had organized the Third Reich's "Final Solution" for the extermination of European Jewry. Eichmann had personally supervised the deportation of 400,000 Jews from Hungary for extermination at Auschwitz, and Maxwell's parents had been among those victims. The "Ena B. Maxwell" letter was an example of the magazine's regular lampooning of the millionaire and Maxwell would probably have known in advance which examples his counsel would have offered him for comment in the witness box. No one, however, anticipated his reaction.

As he looked at the page, tears began falling down his cheeks and, according to the following day's *Daily Mirror* report, Maxwell "shook with emotion and banged his hands on the witness box as he said, 'My family was destroyed by Eichmann.' . . . It was several minutes before he composed himself, wiped his eyes and took a sip of the glass of water handed to him. He then turned to the judge and said, 'I'm sorry.' " In the *Eye* camp, there was astonishment. "When I saw him blubber, I knew that we'd lost," confessed one of their heavier, hard-nosed investigators. Ingrams did not help his case by admitting in evidence his ignorance about Eichmann's role in the fate of Maxwell's family. The *Mirror*'s headline was the gravestone inscription over the *Eye*'s case: "Maxwell Weeps over Family Massacre—Publisher's Fury at *Eye*'s Fake Letters." As the case spun out from the expected one week into the third week, the champions of anti-privilege began massaging their brows: Maxwell was winning sympathy as the victim of gross insensitivity.

The jury's award against the *Eye* for the defamation was an unimpressive £5,000. But they awarded an extra £50,000 as punitive damages because the *Eye*'s journalist misleadingly swore an affidavit claiming that he would be able to prove his allegation. In addition there were an estimated £250,000 legal costs, which the *Eye* was ordered to pay. "Bloody hell . . . bloody hell" was the crisp reaction of the *Eye*'s managing director, the aptly named David Cash, as the jury recited the damages. In his own valediction, Ingrams, who was not in court to hear the verdict, advised potential litigants, "If your lawyers tell you that you have a very good case, you should settle immediately," and blamed the jury who "while good and true [are] immensely thick." Maxwell disagreed. "People, family and friends," his voice boomed across the courtroom, "have been recklessly attacked for years. We have exposed once and for all that they will publish anything for profit. They do not check their sources, they do not have the guts to apologize or withdraw. They are pedlars of lies and filth." Asked what he would do with the damages, he answered, "The money might go to AIDS research. After all it came from an infected organ and will go to help cure another."

In November 1982, Maxwell had reviewed a book which recounted the history of the *Eye* and he had asked, "Does it really make a valuable contribution to our society to destroy both in our own eyes and in those of the world at large our major national asset of incorruptibility in public life—to replace it with a belief that the instincts of the piggery motivate our public servants and successful entrepreneurs?" Four years later he went further and argued that the *Eye* should be closed down. The *Eye*'s readers did not agree. The alleged scandals surrounding the Guinness bid for Distillers (Maxwell had publicly supported Ernest Saunders for reneging on a solemn pledge about the composition of the new board), the endless corruption in local authorities, the chain of negligence which led to the sinking of the Townsend ferry at Zeebrugge and the admission of Britain's senior civil servant who gave evidence in the "Spycatcher" trial in Australia that he had been "economical with the truth" pointed to a need for the *Eye*. Britain, the *Eye*'s supporters argued, does not enjoy incorruptibility but suffers from a lack of formalized accountability. In the vacuum of parliamentary power, the press was Britain's last safeguard against "our public servants and successful entrepreneurs." But, for Maxwell, "The *Eye* has become the Joe McCarthy of British journalism [and it] cannot justify its continued existence." His desire for its eradication revealed a limited understanding about newspapers. The *Eye* enjoyed sustained credibility, something which Maxwell's own newspaper could not boast.

"Watching Maxwell play with newspapers is like a child with a Meccano set," said Keith Waterhouse, who resigned as a columnist on the *Mirror* in disgruntlement. "When he's fed up with one toy, he looks for another." By the end of 1986, Maxwell had successfully maximized the Mirror Group's profits. Having slashed its overheads in London, Manchester and Glasgow, BPCC entered 1987 aiming to fulfill his objective of becoming an "enterprise with earnings of £3–5 billion with earnings per share to match." The focus in early 1987 returned to his newspapers, although the omens were not encouraging. A new sports magazine, *Sportsweek,* launched in September 1986, had collapsed three weeks after its launch; he publicly alternated his views about continuing to print in Holborn; despite his announcement that the *Mirror* would be printed with color pictures, no such pictures had appeared; and BPCC had lost the contracts for the color magazines of the *Observer* and the *Mail on Sunday*. Balancing achievements were securing the contract for the *Sunday Express* Magazine, for satelliting the *China Daily* from Beijing to distribute 20,000 copies throughout Europe, and the launch at last of the *London Daily News*.

The delay in launching the evening newspaper had probably improved morale among the newly hired journalists, who had wanted more time to prepare. Five weeks after the decision was announced, Maxwell organized a sumptuous weekend at Ettington Park where, to the delight of the 180 staff, the famed chef Michael Quinn served a gourmet's dinner which was eaten off an enormous refectory table. The highlight on Sunday was the arrival by helicopter of Maxwell himself with Betty and his after-lunch speech. "You are the staff I have hired," he averred, "and I am going to stick with you through thick and thin. There will be no blood-letting. I am not the kind of proprietor who will close you down. You have my guarantee that you have two to three years to prove yourselves." There were cheers and Maxwell began to take his leave when a note was thrust into his hands. The chef wondered whether he might have a ride on the helicopter. Proudly the publisher agreed and the two artistes flew off over the Warwickshire countryside. On the ground, however, there was one man who was disturbed by Maxwell's whole approach—Bill Gillespie, the paper's publisher and the managing director of BNPC.

Until the spring of 1986, Gillespie had been working for Murdoch's News International. Maxwell had telephoned and offered him a high salary to manage the newly incorporated printing operation and oversee the creation of the London newspaper. Gillespie's credentials were impeccable. Under his supervision, all of Murdoch's newspapers had been moved overnight to Wapping, utterly routing the unions, and he had pioneered News International's own blueprint for a London evening newspaper. Since Maxwell prided himself on his ruthless and commercial unsentimentality toward newspapers, Gillespie was an astute choice. But by the summer Gillespie had become disconcerted by the contrast between working for Maxwell and working for Murdoch. Under the new regime, he was denied independence, initiative, information and access. While Murdoch had a deep understanding of newspapers, the foundation of a long-term strategy, Maxwell thought that creating a newspaper was similar to dealing on the Stock Exchange; he only needed to bark down a telephone "buy" or "sell" and the whole deed could be completed by his backroom "number crunchers." "He was so arrogant," complained one executive, "that he believed that if he just blew on the new paper, it would blossom." Gillespie's confidence had already been shaken when Maxwell, without his knowledge, personally negotiated on a Sunday night in Oxford an agreement with the print union leaders (which later collapsed), and his unease was aggravated by the circumstances surrounding the delayed launch. Three years earlier, the collapse in the *Mirror*'s sales had exposed Maxwell's weak understanding of consumer journalism. The two months after Ettington Park tarnished his image as an innovator.

Initially, Maxwell's brief was that the newspaper operation would be a "greenfield site," excluding not only the print unions but also the Mirror Group's management. His edict irritated the group's incumbents, especially his senior executives. "Their constant criticism of us poisoned relations," recalls one executive, "and it got worse." Gillespie became another casualty of compartmentalization and of the confusion which surrounds many of Maxwell's ventures. The *London Daily News* was owned by Mirror Group Newspapers (MGN), which ultimately is owned by Pergamon. Gillespie was the publisher of the new paper and was therefore employed by MGN. Its printing was entrusted by MGN to BNPC, of which Gillespie was chief executive. But although Gillespie was simultaneously employed by MGN and BNPC and both companies were housed in the same building and were ultimately owned by the same man, Gillespie discovered that the relationship between the public and private companies was obscure, especially regarding the terms of the contract between MGN and BNPC. His efforts to establish the price BNPC would charge MGN for printing were unsuccessful and his requests to Maxwell were never comprehensively answered. Their relationship became strained, especially as the precise problems of managing a twenty-four-hour newspaper became apparent.

Maxwell had embraced the notion of such a newspaper without understanding that the term was a misnomer. Its theoretical attraction was the guarantee that the newspaper would be on sale early in the morning, before the *Standard,* with a large section containing classified advertisements for cars, homes and jobs, and that the same advertisements but with different editorial copy would also be read in the evening. To achieve that required fast printing, efficient distribution throughout London, and a sales force to attract the advertising. Maxwell, in Gillespie's view, was impatient with the implementation of that detail. As the telephone calls about all his other interests cascaded into his office, he brusquely swept aside Gillespie's queries and explanations. To his irritated executives, it seemed that he liked the architect's colorful sketches but did not understand that to fit the complex jigsaw neatly together needed meticulous calculations. "The unseen foundations were left in the air because they bored him," says one of the newspaper's founders. "Since he refused to delegate and was rarely accessible, we never made decisions until it was too late." Anxiety, about the delays and about Maxwell's indecision, grew. "Gillespie was blamed for everything," recalls an eyewitness, "although it was Maxwell who was constantly changing his mind, possibly because he couldn't remember what he had previously decided. When he began to reverse his 'greenfield' policy by ordering Gillespie to consult Mirror executives ['We have all the expertise here,' said Maxwell], that threw everybody." Gillespie reluctantly agreed to the changes, but on one issue, the title of the newspaper, he was unyielding.

The market research agency had tested four possible titles: *The Londoner, London Newsday, Newsday London* and the *London Daily News.* Although the latter had been the working title, the researchers reported that *The Londoner* evoked the most favorable reaction. Linklater insisted upon the *London Daily News* and was supported by Maxwell. Their choice might have been less controversial if Gillespie had not heard that Rothermere's managers were informally asking the *Standard* delivery drivers how much extra they would require for handling a second newspaper. To Gillespie that could only mean that Rothermere was considering the relaunch of his defunct *Evening News,* which would be a perfect spoiler against Maxwell. "It was going to be a dirty war," said Bert Hardy, one of Rothermere's senior executives, "and we were going to meet Maxwell at every stage."

On Saturday, November 22, 1986, Maxwell had summoned yet another all-day conference at Headington Hall to discuss the newspaper's progress. Although all the editorial and commercial executives were summoned for 10 a.m., they expected to wait as usual for at least two hours before Maxwell appeared. True to form, he was delayed arriving from Heathrow airport but on this occasion, before entering his home, he encountered Gillespie waiting in the drive. The Irishman, whose attitude was by then quite jaded, issued an ultimatum that unless the proprietor reconsidered the newspaper's title, he would resign. Maxwell was unmoved and Gillespie departed.

Maxwell was unruffled when he greeted his remaining executives. "I'll take over Gillespie's job," he announced, and thereafter became more accessible. "My problem now is that I can't get away from him long enough to shape the paper," Linklater told his colleagues. Constant meetings were not a substitute for strategy and throughout those weeks what struck those incarcerated on the ninth floor was Maxwell's delight in his image as the skilled entrepreneur. "Maxwell believes in the art of brutal buying," observed one seasoned negotiator. "A deal struck at the last minute, he thought, was sure to be the most profitable." Deadline deals have their attractions for buying and selling, but they posed problems if hundreds of staff needed to be trained in the use of a computer system, if five editions of a newspaper were to be printed in five different locations every day and distributed throughout London, and if the paper needed a battle plan to fight for a place in a competitive and declining marketplace. Creating new consumer demand requires a peculiar intellectual skill which was not evident as the revised launch date of February 10, 1987, approached. Joe Haines probably understood Maxwell's nonchalance on such critical questions better than most: "He has a touching faith in the printed word. He's one of the last men in the world who really believes in the power of the press." Like many Haines misjudged Maxwell. The newspaper was just his latest toy.

By mid-January another of Maxwell's commercial innovations had been discarded. Experts were required to "paste up" the newspaper pages and Maxwell ordained that laid-off members of the NGA in the Mirror Group should be hired. His "greenfield site" ideal was further contaminated. But the potential advertisers liked the "dummies" of the new paper and for the journalists working a regular sixteen-hour day the omens still seemed promising.

Maureen Smith, one of London's more successful new band of hypists, was hired by Maxwell to organize a spectacular launch. Not unnaturally, since her new client thought big and regularly dispensed sums of money which resembled telephone numbers, she proposed a program to match his ambitions. By chance, Smith discovered that the Albert Hall, which is normally booked for at least two years in advance, was free on the day prior to the launch. She found little difficulty in convincing Maxwell that the building would be an ideal venue for an unforgettable twenty-four-hour party to mirror the newspaper's novelty. Oysters and Guinness would be served to the newspaper's vendors in the morning, followed by a fashion show for the glitterati at lunchtime, a children's party in the afternoon, *Tout Londres* would be invited for a gala celebration in the evening and the "young things" could dance through the night to receive the first edition in the morning. It would cost a quarter of a million pounds.

Everything had been prepared when quite by chance, ten days before the party, Smith heard that the launch had once more been canceled. The reason was that the NGA "pasters" had still not signed a contract, but cynics joked that Maxwell just wanted an excuse to avoid paying a fortune for a party. In reality, his newspaper was beset by an avalanche of problems. He had still not contracted for the printing, the distribution was still not settled and the new computer system for setting the pages was still troublesome. By the third and final launch date, February 24, little had improved and the essential launch party was quickly improvised.

The organizer was Harvey Goldsmith: "You want the biggest party London has ever seen? You've got it. You want VIPs? You've got them. You want a spectacular? Leave it to me." The venue was the circulation department on the Mirror building's first floor which was gutted and reconstructed to resemble a fashionable nightclub. The centerpiece was an ice sculpture resembling the *London Daily News* masthead. Beneath stood a vast cake with the chef ready to inscribe in icing a facsimile of the first front page when it was agreed. Once again *Tout Londres* was invited, but the handful of celebrities who did come left before the appearance of the first edition, which had missed its deadlines. Among those who remained was a delegation from the Telegraph group of newspapers. Over the previous five months, Maxwell had been negotiating to print his afternoon editions on the Telegraph's new computer-fed printing presses in the converted London docks, but each time a contract was near to signature Maxwell began renegotiating. "He always wanted more than his pound of flesh," says one of those angered by his brinkmanship. By the night of the launch, there was a real possibility that the following afternoon's edition would not be printed. At the party, Maxwell was located by the delegation in a booth occupied by a fortune-teller. "Not the right place to discuss business," he said jovially as he led his anxious guests to another part of the room where at last he signed. Most of the revelers around them were the worse for drink when, two hours after the deadline, the trumpets of four Life Guards heralded the birth. As the Guards slowly marched toward the center of the room, the proprietor, clearly impatient with their melodramatic progress, gruffly pushed them aside and made his way to the dais, followed by an embarrassed-looking editor. As he made his speech, the Telegraph team hurried away, concerned about the need to hire and train the operators who would print the newspaper the following day and in the months ahead.

No Londoner was unaware of the arrival. Maureen Smith's team had persuaded every television and radio producer that Maxwell's exclusive appearance on their show was a once-and-for-all privilege which only the foolhardy could forsake. Every chat show from breakfast time to the epilogue featured the smiling proprietor and occasionally his editor. Even to the casual viewer, they propounded different messages and cast different images. Those who did not watch or listen were not spared exposure to the announcement because every doubledecker bus was covered with the slogan "For the city which never sleeps, the paper that never stops." Every publicity gimmick was tried and exploited with the exception of an irreverent proposal from somewhere in the *Daily Mirror* to launch a "Win a Peerage" competition. The idea was understandably suffocated before it rose to the ninth floor for approval. Maxwell unveiled an unusual touch: "2,000 of the prettiest models will be walking around London looking for people holding the *Standard* and politely offer to exchange them for our paper. We'll then send them back to Bert Hardy." Rothermere's agent was unmoved by the parvenu's tactics: "No city in the world can support more than one evening paper and Maxwell will lose." Twenty-five million pounds had been spent for Londoners to have the choice they had gradually rejected for twenty years, and to Maxwell's exclusive surprise their choice was trebled. As Gillespie had predicted, Rothermere, with a delicate preparation which Maxwell could only envy, launched his spoiler on the same day. The *Evening News* was reborn amid massive publicity, at 10p as opposed to the *News*'s 20p, and the *Standard*'s street vendors loyally agreed not to handle Maxwell's product. Rothermere's *Standard,* which had been substantially improved in the previous months, launched a "Win a House" competition but majestically remained aloof. Those who could find the new *London Daily News* read a professional if rather worthy paper, which offered neither a substantial section of classified ads nor a good competition. In the streets, there was bemusement, but in the Mirror building there was panic.

Maxwell's much vaunted notion of contracting out the printing had proved to be disastrous. Deadlines which were missed in the editorial office meant that the papers were late off the presses and arrived in central London too late to beat the *Standard.* Some of the Newsflow van drivers had collected their loads and, after carefully locking their vehicles, had headed for breakfast. No one had explained to the newly recruited employees that speed of delivery was essential. Even those few street vendors who would accept the papers were, like the newsagents and the readers, confused by the idea of a twenty-four-hour newspaper. How could the reader in the evening know that he was not buying the morning edition? How could the casual buyer distinguish between the *London Daily News* and the *Evening News* when even Maxwell, in television interviews, said, "I am very proud to have launched the *Evening News.* " Rothermere's spoiler was causing havoc and piles of discarded copies of the *London Daily News* littered the streets and were piled high in the newsagents. The first day's circulation of 400,000 began plummeting.

"We need more WOBs," shouted Maxwell as he marched through the editorial offices one evening, suggesting remedies to improve sales. White headlines on black backgrounds was the latest advice he had heard from Mirror executives on how to improve the *News*'s design. On his return journey, he called them "BLOBs," but everyone knew that he meant "WOBs"—he just had a problem of enunciating names correctly. Later he wanted the masthead bigger and bigger still, and then smaller but the headlines increased. "We need more subheads," he boomed, when he meant crossheads, "to break up the pages." Then later he suggested changing the color of the paper to distinguish between editions and after discarding that idea warmed to the notion that the stories should be in "bite-size chunks." The "McNugget idea," as it was dubbed, was another ruse to relieve the paper's dense feel by shortening the articles and using more pictures. But nothing seemed to halt the inexorable decline in sales. The substance was of a middle-class newspaper which described itself as "independent" but urged its readers to vote Labour during the General Election trying to appeal to London's right-wing electorate without a sufficient dose of dazzling magic. During those first weeks, it was not necessarily a fatal condition but it needed careful corrective surgery. Linklater and his senior staff were soon immersed in constant meetings.

Editorial changes were relatively easy to accomplish but the accumulated commercial handicaps were unmanageable. Bad distribution and late printing were still unresolved nightmares. There was an increasing gap where classified ads should have appeared. The massive publicity machine had fallen silent because no one had conceived a second stage for the launch strategy. The paper was losing half a million pounds every week. To rectify all those misjudgments required thought, time and discussion. Impulsively, soon after the launch, Maxwell had banged the table. "I'm going to slash the price to 10p." The universal reaction had been amazement. Every sinew of the professionals tensed as the arguments against were recited. The *London Daily News* would be competing with the *Evening News* instead of the *Standard*; the advertisers favored an upmarket paper while the *Evening News* was so downmarket as to cause even the *Sun* editors to blush; the newsagents would not earn enough; and the loss of revenue would be excessive. Maxwell was unmoved. His grandfather's deals in Carpo-Ruthenia and his own deals in the late 1940s had all been won on undercutting the competitor. His chafing experience at the *Scottish Daily News* and the *Mirror* on the same issue had not altered his views. The price was cut, but in retaliation, the *Evening News* price was reduced to 5p and everyone was confused except Lord Rothermere. Sales of the *London Daily News* fell faster and further while the *Standard*'s increased. One further attempt to halt the hemorrhage by purchasing the *Today* newspaper and its presses from Tiny Rowland failed when Murdoch once again pipped his old competitor at the post. Maxwell's attempt to buy the loss-making tabloid confirmed that his repeated flourishes about BNPC's rosy future in supplying contract printing facilities for other national newspapers were illusory. By July, the economics were firmly against continuing the *London Daily News,* although the price was once again 20p. The newspaper was barely selling 100,000 copies and was firmly in a rut.

On July 18 Linklater presented to Maxwell his survival plan—a thick volume which had taken two weeks to compile. Linklater, who was admired by his staff, nervously awaited Maxwell's reaction. The wall-to-wall meetings had taken a heavy toll and some of those surrounding Maxwell had barely hidden their ill will. Five days later, he summoned Linklater for the denouement. Using his favored military analogies, Maxwell's opening remarks, spoken with unusual calm, were unequivocal: "I can't fight on two fronts, nor can I keep on pissing in the sand. The paper will have to close." Further discussion was pointless and there would be no post-mortems. He personally told the staff at 12:15 the following day, Friday, July 24. "No one thought it would go," said Linklater, affected by the emotion of the moment. "It was like a death in the family." But about Maxwell he had few harsh words: "He's an attractive man. A true human being." Rothermere presented each of his staff with a bottle of champagne.

There are not many who can lose £50 million and a similar amount of prestige without feeling some hurt. The successful launch of the *Independent* newspaper had proved that new papers were not a foolhardy venture. But none of those around Maxwell would dare to confront their master with the truth: that his dream had died because of its parentage, and the same pedigree had borne other disappointments that summer.

On May 24, Maxwell announced a $2 billion bid for Harcourt Brace Jovanovich, an American educational publisher which had diversified into theme-park entertainments in Florida. The offer, which was in cash, valued Harcourt's shares (which had been trading at below $30) at $44 each. If Maxwell were successful, he would at one stroke achieve the $3 billion status he so earnestly desired. Even if he failed, the financial community would be staggered that Rothschilds had been able to collect that huge amount of money in Maxwell's name. His credit seemed unassailable, except to William Jovanovich, Harcourt's sixty-seven-year-old chairman, whose response to the bid was of a style which Maxwell uncomfortably recognized. "The sudden, unsolicited and hostile offer," said the American, "is preposterous both as to intent and value." He continued in a vein which caused Maxwell to reflect on his failure to bury the old skeletons. "Mr. Maxwell's dealings since he emerged from the mists of Ruthenia after World War Two have not always favored shareholders—as Mr. Sol [*sic*] Steinberg can attest." A few days later, Jovanovich issued another vitriolic statement declaring that Maxwell was "unfit to control" America's largest textbook publisher because he was not only a socialist with good connections in eastern Europe but was also tainted by "hidden" sources of income. All the past vices had been resurrected. "Mr. Maxwell has money, but not enough. He has ambition but no standing. He ought to be sent packing to Liechtenstein." Money, even billions, was not enough, Maxwell realized, to remove the stains. On July 27, he backed off. It was the latest failure echoing another failed bid the previous year for *Scientific American,* whose owners favored a German bid, although Maxwell had offered more money, and repeated months later when Elsevier of Holland, the world's largest scientific publisher, also shunned his advances, albeit with less public malice.*

Credibility was Maxwell's problem. To deflect the weakness, he placed even more emphasis on personal appearances, especially alongside the great and the good. With his personal photographer in attendance as he ceaselessly flew around the world in a private jet, he arranged that after concluding contracts there would be a meeting and a photo opportunity with the country's prime minister or president. After television rights in France, Spain, Portugal and China had been secured, the photographer was present to record Maxwell shaking hands with President Mitterrand and the other national leaders. But the appearances were misinterpreted as designed to boost his ego rather than confirm his importance. In a supreme effort to overcome the doubters, his new brokers, Alexander, Laing & Cruickshank, published in September the first detailed analysis of BPCC. Its author was Henry Poole, who two months earlier had completed the issue of new BPCC shares worth £630 million which had powerfully enhanced Maxwell's kitty for another Harcourt Brace-type purchase.

Poole's report was called "Unraveling the Melmotte Skein." Melmotte was a character in Trollope's novel, *The Way We Live Now,* who though a tower of strength was thought by many to be built on sand. Like Melmotte, Poole suggested, Maxwell had suffered every wrongful accusation. The report, which Poole calculated took an average ninety minutes to read, reaffirmed its author's verdict at the company's June annual general meeting that Maxwell's empire was built upon secure foundations. To accept Poole's argument depended upon the reader's faith in Maxwell personally. No less than half of the anticipated pre-tax profits for 1990 were grouped in a column marked "Other." The understanding was that besides the profits to come from Pergamon's "Orbit InfoLine," the computerized patent index and scientific information service and acquisitions, BPCC would earn over £100 million in one year from speculation on the world's stock markets and currency exchanges. Seasoned Maxwell watchers looked askance and reflected that no less than half of the £630 million raised in what was claimed to

---

* Pergamon remained the third-largest scientific publisher after Springer.

be the second largest rights issue in the city was in fact contributed by Pergamon. Citing Melmotte rather gave a hostage to fortune, but the brokers were apparently content to risk their reputation on the claim that their major client would create a £3 to £5 billion corporation by 1990.

On September 25 the new vehicle for that spectacular growth was revealed. BPCC, it was announced, was changing its name to Maxwell Communications Corporation. The name BPCC, said Maxwell, was confusing for a company which engaged in so much more than just printing and was spread worldwide. He wanted to be shed of the image of "dark northern printing halls." Peter Jay, his chief of staff, told the *Financial Times*: "People said: We have read about you. We all know about you. For God's sake, even if it is personally embarrassing, you have got to get your name in the name of the company." So Maxwell agreed, explaining, "It's not an ego trip. I don't go in for ego trips. It's not my style. It was a decision reluctantly taken. I was forced into it by my colleagues." Four weeks later a new eight-page glossy color bulletin was published by Maxwell Communications to publicize the corporation's latest achievements. Maxwell's photograph appeared posing in nine different locations including one captioned, "Robert Maxwell discussing world affairs with Henry Kissinger in Tokyo."

Maxwell warmed to Henry Poole's suggestions that he enjoyed "an acute sense of vision." His detractors observe that Poole's "reality of the vision" was merely a rapacious appetite to buy and become "big." Most of the new assets were established printers and publishers. Some deals, such as the purchase of a compact-disc manufacturer, defy logic but could produce profits. Other deals, like the attempted purchase of Watford Football Club, would seem not only to have catered to his love of the sport, but also to have raised fears he might be interested in the potential land value; and Maxwell had an idea that when British soccer ceases to cater almost exclusively for the working classes and can attract the middle classes, as football does in America, it will be profitable. At Watford, his ambitions were stymied. The Football League in January 1988 blocked his take-over bid until he and his family interests divested themselves of their other interests in Oxford United, Derby County and Reading. Maxwell accepted their ruling with a minimum of complaint. His real businesses demanded attention and the City was again puzzled by the absence of any evident strategy. In late September 1987 he had announced the purchase of stock in an assortment of companies, banks and retail stores. A baffled inquirer on Thames Television's "City Programme" asked Maxwell on September

24 to explain his motives. "The rationale," he replied curtly, "could not be easier—to make money." The stock market crash three weeks later, on October 19, affected that ambition, although he was noticeably reluctant to admit his losses. Instead he told several newspapers that he had astutely avoided the crash by selling his equities and buying safe government bonds. He did not contradict *The Economist* [November 14, 1987], which therefore concluded that he still retained £500 million in cash, and boasted to the *Wall Street Journal*: "Now cash is king and I've got the cash." The truth, which was the *opposite,* would emerge later. His behavior was reminiscent of the past and the familiar pattern reappeared in a deal which was concluded at an extraordinary general meeting on December 31, 1987. It was one of the most peculiar in Maxwell's history. On December 14, MCC had circulated to its shareholders a proposal to buy from Pergamon three companies—Orbit InfoLine, Molecular Design, an American data system for chemical information, and Pergamon Books. (There was also a separate transaction to purchase some property in New York state.) The initial price for what were called the "Acquisition Groups" was £56 million in cash; but a further £15.3 million would be payable during 1988 if the companies' combined profits for 1987 exceeded £4 million, and an additional £28.7 million would be paid if 1988's profits exceeded £7.5 million. In all, the price could total £100 million. The proviso on profits was significant because in the first eight months of 1987 Orbit InfoLine and Molecular Design had earned a mere £579,000, although according to the prospectus this would increase substantially in the last quarter. (Pergamon Books had actually made a net loss.) Nevertheless, one stark fact was highlighted. Orbit's profits would have to increase substantially in just two years to produce the £100 million pre-tax profits forecast by his brokers three months earlier. Molecular Design had been purchased by Pergamon only three months earlier and few public corporations would hold special meetings on New Year's Eve or on the very last day of its accounting year to approve a take-over except for a special reason.

In the prospectus, MCC's board stressed that it "engaged Bankers Trust to provide an independent valuation" of the three companies and that the Trust had stated that they were worth "between £70 million and £107 million." The MCC board had decided to pay £100 million if the profits came in on forecast. Yet the valuation report supplied by Bankers Trust showed that their scope for independence was severely curtailed by Pergamon: "The estimates of sales and earnings for the years 1987 and 1988 have been prepared solely by Pergamon. No independent accountant has expressed an opinion on these estimates. Furthermore, we have not independently verified the financial results of the Acquisition Groups." In other words, the public company was buying assets from the private company on faith that the latter's valuation was accurate. Moreover, although most of the Acquisition Group's trade was based in America, the conversion rate to the pound adopted for the purchase was $1.83 while the conversion rate for the profits was $1.60. Yet the actual conversion rate at the end of 1987 was $1.86. Since MCC was paying in sterling, the deal seemed unsatisfactory to some in the City.

Shortly before 10 a.m. on New Year's Eve, a collection of journalists gathered at the Mirror building to witness the meeting. Since Maxwell was faced with a conflict of interest, he was automatically deemed ineligible to exercise his 51 per cent shareholding in MCC to approve the deal. Hence it fell to the remaining independent directors to recommend the purchase as "fair and reasonable . . . [and] in the best interests of the Company." Since the independent and non-executive directors—including Lord Rippon, a former Conservative minister, and Lord Silkin, a former Labour attorney general—had never knowingly opposed Maxwell, it was an opportunity for the minority shareholders to voice their opinion. The journalists, however, would not have witnessed that unprecedented revolt. To their surprise, they were barred by security guards from entering the conference room and asked to leave the building. Maxwell, the self-publicist, was not only shy but positively irate at the skepticism with which some had looked on his latest deal. The press, said Maxwell, were "ignorant and stupid" and were "unjustified" in spreading "misinformation." Inside, within five minutes, the deal was approved without dissent even from the few pension fund managers who had earlier intimated their dissatisfaction. All that remained was for Maxwell to announce his plans for the future—to relaunch a London newspaper to be called *The Londoner*; to launch a Europe-wide middle-market color newspaper; and the possible purchase of Murdoch's loss-making *New York Post*. None of these ventures would produce any profits in the foreseeable future and would just slightly add to MCC's size. The year 1987 closed with a cloud and a whimper rather than the bang he had anticipated.

15

Fury fueled by frustration galvanized Maxwell as he sped from the disagreeable press conference toward the sanctuary of his private quarters adjacent to the Mirror tower. While most Londoners were contemplating the New Year's Eve revelries and the drowsy aftermath, Maxwell barked orders to summon a meeting of advisers for early the following day, regardless that it was a holiday. The subject for discussion was to be Maxwell's television interests, or to be more precise, his setbacks to fulfill the aphorism immortalized by the Canadian press baron Lord Thomson that a stake in TV was "a license to print money."

Maxwell was irked that Rupert Murdoch had established, albeit at great cost, the Sky TV satellite channel and Fox TV, the network which spanned the USA as a rival to the Big Three. The Australian's achievement underlined the unreality of the new name—the Maxwell Communications Corporation. Inserting "Communications" was possibly a statement of future intentions but was certainly not yet a fact. MCC was an established printer and also a publisher of information, but only of small-circulation scientific tomes; MCC was not yet a mass media communicator. Even if MCC "bought" all the interests owned by his Liechtenstein-based Pergamon Holdings—Mirror Group Newspapers, a 20 per cent stake in Central Television, a 12.5 per cent stake in TF1, French TV's channel one, its shares in MTV Europe and Premiere (both loss-making music and film satellite channels), and an insignificant British cable TV network—MCC could still not stand among the ranks of "the ten global media" barons by the end of the decade. Consequently, on New Year's Eve 1987, Maxwell was searching for new acquisitions to fulfill his public pledge and triple the size of MCC within the following two years.

All four men who obeyed Maxwell's summons—his office manager

Peter Jay; Peter Laister, a non-executive director, who in 1985 had lost his chairmanship of EMI, the electronics conglomerate, because of a financial crisis for which he was blamed; Patrick Cox, recently hired to rationalize and manage all Maxwell's television interests; and Geoffrey Smith, formerly of Thames TV—sat expressionless as their employer speculated about where he should pounce for new prey. Unknown to them, Maxwell had already instructed Robert Pirie, the chief executive of Rothschild Inc. in New York, that Macmillan, the American publisher, should be prepared as a possible new target—the hitherto elusive "Big One." But those present on New Year's Day knew that Maxwell's bids to seek admittance into the common cage with other predators were often prone to rejection. They were summoned and paid to ponder one aspect of that predicament. On that day, the topic was Maxwell's cable franchises. In 1984, Maxwell had bought the small and defunct Rediffusion cable network which offered little more than the four standard "off-air" channels. Bereft of investment, the losses had escalated. The deal illustrated a familiar pattern. Swept up in the current vogue that television, through cable and satellite, would in the future serve a massive pan-European audience, Maxwell had snapped at that opportunity like several others to stake his claim as a major player. But the rewards after three years revealed a potpourri rather than a strategy and there were no profits. At the New Year's Day meeting, Maxwell's plans for increased expenditure were criticized because the minuscule cable industry in Britain would never be profitable. But as usual, Maxwell was hostile to adverse advice and, at the earliest opportunity, everyone left the building to snatch the last few hours of the holiday. Unruffled, Maxwell, who would soon fly to his yacht moored in the Caribbean, once again reassessed his opportunities for 1988. Besides the Big One in America, continental Europe offered some possibilities. His forays into Germany and Italy had stumbled against entrenched national giants, but France opened up opportunities.

In the wake of his drubbing at Gauthier Villars, Maxwell had ignored France. That changed in January 1985 when Jacques Pomonti telephoned Maxwell. Pomonti, who had been appointed president of the Institut National de l'Audiovisuel in Christmas 1984, was charged to seek foreign investors for TDF1, France's proposed Frs2 billion television satellite service. Pomonti had met Maxwell in Holborn only days earlier: "Maxwell was then unknown in France. I briefed him on the French government's new television policy and he just said, 'I'll take a 20 per cent stake.' " Pomonti returned to Paris particularly pleased by his success although Murdoch, despite his known prejudice against the non-English-speaking world, had also agreed to consider the project. Maxwell however had spoken some French and had even mentioned in passing that his family was French. To Pomonti, the commitment seemed serious. Back in London, Maxwell had mused about the prospect.

At that time, French television was renowned, even notorious, in the media world, for stodgy programs which were obedient to tight, centralized government control, excluding foreign programs in the cause of protecting French culture. But in 1982 fearing that France, like neighboring Italy, would be swamped by pirate TV stations unless there were liberal controls President Mitterrand had terminated the government's monopoly. By 1985, when the first commercial station was transmitting, the president feared that the socialists would lose the parliamentary elections in 1986. To forestall a right-wing monopoly, two more ground stations were sanctioned to start transmission within twelve months. La Cinq was awarded to the "left-wing" Italian Silvio Berlusconi and to Jérôme Seydoux, a friend of the president. It was in that atmosphere of politically motivated expansionism that Pomonti enticed Maxwell to buy a stake in France's satellite, TDF1, whose four channels, according to Mitterrand, would be divided equally between French and foreign companies.

As his relationship with Pomonti warmed during 1985, Maxwell's interest in France grew. He quickly grasped that, unlike in Britain and America, any success needed the goodwill of the head of state. Dealing with presidents and prime ministers had become a custom art for Maxwell. He prided himself on his catalogues of photographs which portrayed the business tycoon discussing world affairs with statesmen. When he therefore asked his new friend Jacques Pomonti to arrange a meeting with the president, he took it for granted that Pomonti, who had known Mitterrand for more than twenty years, could easily oblige. The most suitable date, August 6, just happened to coincide with Maxwell's anticipated return from the Soviet Union and China.

On the appointed day, Maxwell lost little time in letting slip to the president that, after meeting the Soviet and Chinese leaders, he had flown directly from Beijing to Paris and could therefore be counted among the best informed in the west. Mitterrand, who is attracted to extraordinary personalities, was, according to eyewitnesses, taken by the huge personality who rattled out, in what became his standard pitch, his local antecedents: his brilliant war, his French wife and children, and for the president, his lifelong devotion to socialism. "Mitterrand," recalls one of the aides, "sensed that there could be some benefits from

Maxwell. By then we feared annihilation at the polls. The political climate was against us. We were friendless, especially among the media barons, and here was a Francophile press magnate, a man who gave the impression that he was the biggest in the world, offering us, the socialists, his friendship. The opportunity was too good to miss. The mutuality of business interests—that the president wanted to privatize TV and Maxwell wanted a satellite—seemed at that moment purely coincidental."

Once outside Mitterrand's office, Maxwell conferred with Jean-Claude Colliard, the director of the president's Cabinet. His friendship, he expostulated, was unconditional. Colliard, who included among his duties caring for Mitterrand's personal finances, reflected his master's pleasure. Before he had even left the Elysée, Maxwell was already calculating the possible prizes: "I don't know if it's good for France," he half-joked to Pomonti, "but this has all been very good for Maxwell." Over the following weeks, with Pomonti's help, Maxwell was introduced to a range of French powerbrokers. In November, he hosted a dinner in London, arranged by Pomonti, to meet Berlusconi, who was negotiating to rent the satellite's second channel. "They didn't get on," recalls Pomonti. They were probably too similar. Nevertheless, by the end of summer 1985 Pomonti had secured their agreements.

Beaming, Maxwell announced on November 20, 1985, that he had rented one channel which "would reach 230 million viewers" and anticipated winning the competition for an audience against Murdoch. Berlusconi and Seydoux had signed an agreement for the second channel. Three weeks later the deal began to sour.

Government officials criticized the Frs60 million annual rent which Pomonti had charged Maxwell as insufficient and a political row erupted about government subsidies. The agreements were renegotiated and Maxwell found himself, somewhat disagreeably, as part of a consortium whose contracts were hastily ratified just days before the election. But the effort was wasted. As the socialists feared, Jacques Chirac became prime minister and repudiated the agreements. Financially, Maxwell suffered minimal losses but his exposure in France was profitable. For the first time he had been firmly associated in the media with the world of satellites and television. France, he realized, although still a sideshow in his erratic plans, offered an important route toward fulfilling the "Communications" sobriquet in his corporation's title. For family reasons, it was convenient that his efforts would be spearheaded formally by his son Ian, then thirty years old, who had a home in Paris. "Together they could create a new virginity for Maxwell," observed one cynic.

During the summer of 1986, Maxwell assiduously cultivated new relationships while bombarding François Léotard, the new minister of culture and communications, with demands to explain his repudiation of the satellite contract. At first Léotard ignored his protests but in November Maxwell's persistence was rewarded. The minister had invited the three friendly press groups, Hachette, Havas and Hersant, to consider applying for the same satellite channels and he leaked that Maxwell had also been invited to participate. It was a moment of success. Maxwell had established himself as the only English-speaking press magnate in France. By then, Ian had also cultivated Colliard in the Elysée and heard of a proposition which could help MCC's fortunes.

Gaston Defferre, the legendary resistance leader, former minister of interior, mayor of Marseilles and leading socialist, had died in May 1986. Among his estate was the Agence Centrale de Presse (ACP) which, although ranking as France's second largest wire service for newspapers, was dwarfed by the Agence France Presse (AFP). ACP had been losing approximately Frs1 million per month when, in October 1986, it had been transferred to a liquidator. The few who were interested in rescuing the agency presented survival plans based upon wholesale layoffs and ACP's absorption into their own agencies. That solution upset a few sentimentalists at the Elysée who were anxious to preserve any monument created by their old comrade and friend. Since Maxwell was the only socialist newspaper owner known to the Elysée, Jean-Claude Colliard raised the prospect of its purchase. At Frs20 million Maxwell judged that it was a cheap investment to win the president's gratitude and an established presence in France.

In January 1987, Ian Maxwell was officially presented as ACP's new chief executive and the savior of a French institution. The communiqué stressed that the new owner was "French by my mother, French by birth and French by choice." ACP's offices in the rue de Sentier, a narrow, pot-holed road in Paris's garment district, became Maxwell's French headquarters. It was an unglamorous location but among its staff was Michel Burton who would be Maxwell's eager and initial guide through the Elysée.

"I'm here to solve your problems," Maxwell told Mitterrand's beleaguered staff after rescuing ACP. Among the president's needs was money for the bicentenary celebration of the French Revolution. "We had no money," recalls a presidential aide, "and Maxwell just offered his wallet." "The Revolution's ideals are the most important in my life," proclaimed Maxwell with apparent sincerity and proclaimed that he would commission the storage on video discs of the one million original documents of the French Revolution stored at the National Library for worldwide distribution by Pergamon. It would feature as one of two thousand projects associated with the celebrations, mostly financed by discreet donations.

Naturally, the announcement, which also mentioned Maxwell's interest in France's satellite, raised little interest beyond the media world but it did register with Patrick Le Lay, the vice president of the giant Bouygues construction group. As head of diversification at Bouygues, Le Lay had developed Bouygues's interests in batteries, water and tourism. At that moment, Le Lay, a forty-five-year-old graduate of the École Supérieure de Travaux Publiques et Sciences-Politiques, whose metal-rimmed glasses accurately reflected the persona of a cold, efficient businessman, was planning his corporation's application to buy a stake in TF1, French television's Channel One, which the Chirac government had announced in May 1986 would be privatized. Although François Bouygues, the sixty-seven-year-old autocratic founder and chairman of the Frs8 billion group, was keen to diversify into the media, Le Lay thought that even "Mr. Cement" would flinch when the government announced on February 5, 1987, that the price was three billion francs for 50 per cent of the shares and there would be a 50 per cent premium on the price of shares bought by the winning consortium. The bid would cost one billion francs more than the Frs500 million Bouygues had expected to pay for a 25 per cent stake. "I asked François if he was still interested," recalls Le Lay, "and to my surprise he said we should stay in the race." Others in his consortium were less convinced that TF1 was still a profitable investment and withdrew. "We were alone and I needed new partners, fast," recalls Le Lay. Since "The Three H's" were already excluded as potential partners because they were forming their own consortia, Le Lay needed by default to look to foreigners for support. "I also needed someone with media experience. Two names sprang to mind—Murdoch and Maxwell. Of course I didn't know either of them."

In rapid succession on the morning of February 9, Le Lay personally phoned the rivals in London. The answer from News International was curt: Murdoch was unavailable to take the call. The second call produced the publisher himself on the line. His response was spontaneous: "Come to London immediately. Have you got a plane? Fly to Biggin Hill and my helicopter will bring you to my office in London." No executive in the world's largest construction corporation had ever matched the pace which the studious-looking Le Lay was set during the ensuing nine hours. "It was a marvelous sunny day and Maxwell's helicopter flew along the Thames, over the Tower of London and landed in the middle of the City, on the roof of Maxwell's headquarters. Of course I was impressed." Le Lay was met by Maxwell, Ian and two lawyers. The tentative fifteen-minute meeting was extended through lunch and, as a sign of its importance, was uninterrupted by any phone calls, except one. Maxwell had never heard of Bouygues and in front of Le Lay telephoned Sir Nigel Broakes, the chairman of Trafalgar House, a British construction company about one-third the size of Bouygues. "Maxwell asked for a reference. Then he told me to wait in a small office outside." Thirty minutes later Le Lay was summoned:

"I'll take twenty per cent."

"We're only offering you ten per cent," countered Le Lay who finally agreed to 15 per cent to secure the deal but knew that it would have to be reduced. "Come and meet François Bouygues," said Le Lay as they shook hands. "I'll come tomorrow," replied his new partner. "I understand he has a pretty daughter. Make sure she's there too."

The lunch in Paris the following day was clearly memorable for Maxwell. Whereas in London he was being assailed for his unsuitability as a would-be media mogul because the launch of the *London Daily News* had been postponed for the second time and the *Daily Mirror*'s circulation continued to plummet, in Paris he was regaled by "Mr. Cement" as a world star. Unhesitatingly, Maxwell emphasized to Bouygues his "considerable international media expertise," since he had already correctly assessed that Bouygues's unsolicited invitation was motivated not only by the Frenchman's need for extra cash but also because no one else in his consortium had any connection with either television or daily newspapers. Bouygues's application needed credibility and without Maxwell the prospects of success were reduced, not least because Bouygues's foremost rival was a consortium including the Hachette publishing company and *Le Monde*. At that moment, the Hachette consortium, led by Jean-Luc Lagardère, was the favorite. The conservative prime minister, Jacques Chirac, had even been overheard quipping to his friend: "So Jean-Luc, you must be a happy man." As the experts would later comment, it was Hachette's race to lose.

Whether Maxwell correctly assessed the personality and character of his partner-to-be at that lunch is unlikely. Although he would later say that "We have similar personalities—he is energetic and enterprising like me," Maxwell was unaccustomed to dealing with builders, was inevitably excited by his own self-importance, and was insensitive to the nuances of dealing with a man whose wily, aggressive reputation was second only to his own. That imperviousness was augmented because they spoke in French and Maxwell deluded himself that as a much-publicized polyglot he could sense the meaning in Bouygues's words. It was a flaw which would recur many times. Accordingly, Maxwell left the celebration convinced of receiving assurances that he, "as the expert," would wield significant responsibilities in the management of the TV station, if the Bouygues consortium won. Similarly, when Bouygues bade the foreigner farewell, he was satisfied that, having lured both money and status to his side, he would retain full management control, as was customary in all his investments. Bouygues's only concession had been to allow Maxwell a 12.5 per cent stake. Membership would cost Maxwell approximately Frs750 million in one lump sum. The potential for disagreements would always exist since both men boasted the reputation that their signature on a contract just excluded the competition but did not bar aggressive renegotiations. Yet, with the deadline for the public hearings on April 3 so close, it was not the moment for any misgivings.

Maxwell's role during the following seven weeks has been variously described as "crucial" and "negative." Le Lay insists: "Maxwell played no part in writing the proposal which I submitted to the Commission," the CNCL. His reasons are dismissive: "Maxwell is a foreigner and his past activities created suspicions." But the proposal was only one ingredient in the campaign to win the license. Lobbying the thirteen members of the CNCL was equally important. Hachette's success seemed a foregone conclusion if only because ten CNCL members were Chirac appointees, inevitably sympathetic to Lagardère. Yet during those last four weeks, as the Bouygues consortium systematically "marched through the CNCL's rue Jacob offices like an army," visiting each of the thirteen members at least twice, Bertrand Labrusse, one of the two socialist appointees, became convinced that Maxwell's presence was "decisive."

Maxwell's personal tactics to sway the pro-Hachette members were vintage and masterly. During his expeditions to France, Maxwell had rapidly absorbed the common complaint that, compared to Britain and America, the French media were primitive and as some insisted, "in the midst of a crisis." Its television service, cocooned from *l'invasion américaine,* was unsophisticated and unimaginative. The producers, encrusted by the traditions of government service, had failed to innovate. Maxwell therefore presented himself to the CNCL as the harbinger of the "best of British" and the "guarantee of media experience." Labrusse was not the only member of the CNCL to be swayed by Maxwell's pitch: "He told us about his interests in TV, cable and satellite and we were very impressed." No one, it seems, was sufficiently troubled to investigate the reality of those claims and to discover that Maxwell's television investments were either loss-makers or, like Central TV, were strictly financial stakes which explicitly denied him any participation in managing the TV station. In fact, none of the CNCL committee inquired whether Maxwell had ever commissioned or produced a television program, whether he had ever mastered the art of scheduling broadcasts or whether he actually understood the peculiarity of TV management where so much depends upon delegation to encourage originality—the very antithesis of all Maxwell's operations. Any doubts were swept aside by Maxwell's leviathan presence and his self-salesmanship.

His parallel platform, his personal antecedents, was also played, according to one recipient, "very astutely." He was, he told each of the commission members with charm and a fixed gaze, married to a French woman, the father of French children, had fought a glorious war and believed passionately in the European ideal. "The epicenter of European television," he ingratiatingly told those who wanted to believe fantasies, "lies in France." To Labrusse and Catherine Tasca, he confided, "I am a man of the left." To the right-wing members he hinted, "I'm neutral and sympathize with the Chirac government."

Maxwell's certainty of his own importance was not shared by Bouygues. In the builder's view, although Maxwell had some value, it was he who had constructed a coalition, including arbiters of culture and prominent freemasons, which delicately reflected approval from the hidden levers of influence. Bouygues even built bridges to the president by visiting his office to "inform us of his candidature. His brave gesture," recalls a presidential aide, "despite the adverse political climate at the time was appreciated." But above all, Bouygues, whose quintessential talent was in tendering for projects and lobbying for their approval, understood precisely the mechanics to organize the bid. "At six p.m., at the end of every working day," recalls Jacques Duquesnes, the editor of *Le Point* magazine, "we met at Bouygues's offices on the Champs Elysées to discuss progress and assign tasks for the next day." On the advice of Bernard Tapie, a wheeler-dealer who invested in bankrupt companies and was offering to buy a 1.66 per cent stake in TF1, all the consortium members except Maxwell were also coached for three days by "Newsplus" on the technique of public speaking. Maxwell never attended those meetings except the day he arrived with an army of lawyers and advisers to sign the agreement formally. "We were all overwhelmed," recalls one of those present. "He not only took over

Bouygues's offices, but a whole corridor at the Plaza-Athénée hotel. To our minds, any man who could afford all that was amazingly rich and very powerful." It was an impression which Maxwell would not want to ruffle. On the contrary, it was reinforced when, after signing, the former captain proclaimed with a theatrical flourish, "You are our major, Monsieur Bouygues. We will follow you." "François believed Maxwell," said Le Lay eight months later.

By the morning of April 3, when the CNCL opened its hearings, the odds against Bouygues had narrowed. The session, broadcast on television, was devoted to Lagardère who, despite losing partners in embarrassing circumstances, rested on his laurels. In a woolly address, Lagardère suggested a willingness to promise anything the commission required. Even his star, Christine Ockrent, an attractive and intelligent journalist—"the best anchorman in TV," according to admirers—displayed a weakness common to most television presenters: excessive self-confidence fed by fame.

In the afternoon session, crisp and businesslike, François Bouygues focused on promises of huge investments in future productions, the financing of independent producers and turning TF1 into an international production group based in specially constructed headquarters.

Bouygues's introduction of Maxwell was markedly hyped to emphasize that television was a multinational business which needed to be depoliticized and ideologically independent. Maxwell's scientific publishing group, he claimed, "is the largest in the world." In fact it ranked number three. The *Daily Mirror,* said Bouygues, "one of a dozen Maxwell newspapers," prints 3.5 million copies a day. In fact the Mirror Group embraces six newspapers and the *Mirror* was selling 2.9 million. Finally, Bouygues stated that Maxwell was "an important figure in British television" which by any definition was an exaggeration. But the overstatements confirmed Maxwell's importance to Bouygues's chances of success.

Maxwell's personal and noticeably short contribution, which had become his set piece for all future interviews, repeated that he was "the father of seven children, all born at Maisons-Laffitte," Pergamon's reproduction of one million pages of revolutionary documents marked his commitment to "human rights," and concluded with a tickle of France's vanity. With his participation, he claimed, French television would "play an important role in Europe and the world."

That night, Lagardère suspected defeat. Unlike Bouygues, he lamented, his team had not resorted to circus training: "That was a great pity," commented one council member.

The commission announced Bouygues's victory the following day—by eight votes to four. "The take-over of TF1 is my greatest professional joy," commented Bouygues with an unusual hint of modesty when he arrived that night with Le Lay at TF1's headquarters in the Cognac Jay. The announcement had been unexpectedly early and there was no time to summon Maxwell. "Anyway," recalls Le Lay, "it was a Bouygues victory." At that moment, Maxwell believed that he was on the verge of becoming a major player in France and did not lament his absence.

In October 1987, soon after Maxwell had begun negotiating to buy ACP, Michel Burton who was employed at ACP told his future employer that Anne-Marie Laffont-Leenhardt, a substantial but minority shareholder in the profitable Provençal newspaper group, had been anxious for three years to sell her shares.

The Provençal group had been taken over in 1945 by Gaston Defferre, a leader of the French resistance, under a liberation law which sequestrated newspapers from proprietors who had collaborated. Instead of retaining total control, Defferre, who became an important politician, had divided the shares among fifteen fellow resistance fighters. When he died in May 1986, control was in the hands of three women including his widow Edmonde Charles-Roux and Anne-Marie Laffont.

Unlike other French newspapers, the Provençal group had enjoyed exemplary management under Defferre. As early as 1974, with complete union agreement, the group's presses had been modernized, the latest computer technology installed and restrictive labor practices abandoned. The group still employed 8000 people who produced 350,000 papers a day and sales were expanding. But the cost had been enormous. Defferre's death had exposed the group's huge debts and the need for professional financial management.

Fresh from triumphantly reducing staff and costs at the *Daily Mirror* in London, Maxwell had already noticed that the French newspaper industry was also ripe for his methods of rationalization. Most French newspapers produced negligible profits and the proprietors, fragmented and old, were at the mercy of the print unions and an inefficient distribution network. Increasingly, the historic proprietors were obliged to sell. If Maxwell could secure the Provençal group as a first base, it would be an ideal jewel in his crown.

Laffont's search for a purchaser had been hampered by three factors. Firstly, under the company's articles, none of the shareholders could sell their shares without the approval of a majority of the managing board; secondly, while Defferre lived, no one on principle would be deemed acceptable; thirdly, after Defferre's death, the three women shareholders, although united by history, were irreconcilably divided by personality and character. "The only chemistry between them was hostile," said one of the newspaper's managers. "They simply never spoke to one another." Once Defferre died, the principal obstacle had been removed, especially since Christian de Barberin, the chairman of the board, business manager of the group and Defferre's stepson, told the three women that the group desperately needed new funds to survive. Neither Charles-Roux nor Antoine Cordesse paid any attention until Laffont proposed Maxwell as an acceptable purchaser. Maxwell had wooed Laffont. He extolled his socialism; he mentioned that their mutual friends at the Elysée had suggested his purchase of ACP and now "supported" his ownership of the Provençal group; and he produced the notable discovery that the Laffonts were distantly related to Betty Maxwell's family.

In November 1986, Laffont and de Barberin met Maxwell in Paris. Flaunting wealth might be antisocial in France but Maxwell had discovered that nevertheless it paid handsome dividends. Like so many other French men and women over the following months, Laffont and de Barberin were overwhelmed by the helicopters, private jets and apparently unlimited finances. "He is attractive and so rich. So very, very rich," de Barberin reported to the two other shareholders with the news that Laffont wanted their approval for the sale.

Defferre's widow, Edmonde Charles-Roux, the largest single shareholder, was Maxwell's next target and fortunately was inclined to support his bid. The daughter of a former ambassador to Czechoslovakia, Charles-Roux had spent seven years of her childhood in Prague and later returned to live for another seven years in the country which she affectionately describes as, "like my native land. I am very pro-Czech and very pro-Semitic." Charles-Roux boasts two prides: her pedigree as "one of the greatest left-wing families of France"; and secondly, as "a daughter of Marseilles—an old city, older than Paris; very democratic but also very touchy." Charles-Roux is also a professional journalist who edited the French edition of *Vogue* for ten years and won the Prix Goncourt which, while impressive for most mortals, would not have caused Maxwell to revise his initial hunch that winning her approval was a formality.

Maxwell adopted his classic style of seduction. A telephone call to Marseilles with an invitation to lunch. Then a very slight pause and, "I'll send my jet to pick you up." On landing at a small airfield near Oxford, even Charles-Roux was impressed by "a superb red Rolls

Royce which drove up to the stairs and whisked me away to lunch at Headington Hall." If Charles-Roux had expected an intimate, working meal, she was to be disappointed. Nearly thirty people sat around Maxwell's table in the ornate dining room. Maxwell was holding court to a collection of international businessmen, relating one of his set pieces. At that moment it was his wartime experiences. Nevertheless, Charles-Roux felt instinctively attracted to the former peasant boy from Carpo-Ruthenia—"where I had spent a lot of time"—and toward Betty because "I have strong bonds with the Protestant milieu in the south." The prize seemed Maxwell's for the asking.

But instead Charles-Roux became irritated. "I thought that he would talk to me about maintaining the newspapers' traditions, guaranteeing the workers' prospects, and of Marseilles. Instead he said nothing of substance." Charles-Roux's litmus test for judging Maxwell's acceptability would be his nominees to become the group's director. She had expected Maxwell to propose names of eminent *polytechniciens* or *normaliens*. However, Maxwell confirmed there was just one candidate: his son Ian. Charles-Roux's reaction was emphatic: "No twenty-four-year-old can manage that business." Ian was then nearly thirty-one.

Unanimously, all those who had met Ian in Paris agreed that he was intelligent and charming. Gracefully yet assiduously, he had cultivated those relationships in France which could benefit his father's business. Yet few in France believed that he was a leader of men, a view which is enhanced by those who can recall the image of the father's treatment of his sibling. While lobbying the CNCL, Ian's task was to respond promptly to his father's aside, "What's the word in French I'm looking for?" In the ACP office, the erstwhile chief executive became the barman when the father snapped as he walked in the door: "Open a bottle of champagne!" In London, he invariably became the messenger boy. "If Maxwell treats his senior representative in France as a boy, then we must assume the truth of what we see," was a common complaint from those who negotiated with Maxwell.

Whatever Charles-Roux's reservations when she left Oxford, she invited Ian to lunch in Paris on March 12, 1987. The purpose was to introduce Antoine Cordesse whose elderly mother owned the third stake in the newspaper group. Cordesse, an unremarkable inheritor of Defferre's creation, had joined the group in 1978 after an unsuccessful career as a government researcher. He epitomized an unforeseen problem. In some aspects, the Marseillais have more in common with Naples than Paris: their secrecy, suspicions and caution are difficult to overcome but that was Ian's task at Charles-Roux's lunch. Ian failed although Cordesse now claims that he arrived in Paris outrightly opposed to any sale to Maxwell. In theory, Cordesse's veto was not fatal since Charles-Roux and Laffont combined still wielded a majority but Charles-Roux's own doubts were increasing and Maxwell's offers had propelled her to accept de Barberin's argument that they needed to sell their shares. Maxwell's offer had succeeded only in galvanizing their search for rival buyers.

On April 15, unaware of the uncertainties, Maxwell was preparing for a glittering celebration. That evening, at Les Pyramides in Port-Marly, Hervé Bourges, the outgoing head of TF1, had organized a massive party which would combine a vulgar display of the victors' wealth with garish homage to his deposed regime. Watched by the guests, Maxwell arrived by helicopter and sat at the principal table with his friend François Bouygues. His neighbor was André Santini, a heavy Corsican who was then minister of communications. "It was," he recalls, "a club of elephants," referring to everyone's girth. Santini also noticed that Maxwell "knew everyone," an observation by a government minister which was useful for Maxwell since he was keen to be accepted as an insider in the tight circle which governs France. Santini would next see Maxwell at Edgar Faure's funeral in March 1988. To his surprise Maxwell was standing at the front of the congregation, in the midst of government ministers. Having worked through the celebrities at Les Pyramides, Maxwell lifted off, looking forward to the following day.

At 3 p.m., TF1's new board assembled for their first meeting in studio six at Cognac Jay. Bouygues was appointed president, Le Lay the vice president and Maxwell, director general. Immediately afterward, amid showbiz razzmatazz, Bouygues and Maxwell smilingly handed over their check for Frs3 billion to Édouard Balladur, the minister of finance, in his baroque office on the rue de Rivoli. After more self-congratulatory speeches, the victors dispersed. Just before the ceremony, Bouygues had ordered his bank to delay payment for one day—to earn extra interest. Four weeks later, the station was reeling amid rumor, crisis and resignations.

The cause of dissatisfaction was François Bouygues's decision to manage his new asset directly and fire some senior executives. Their noisy departure coincided with the resignation of a clutch of stars lured to a rival channel by inflated salaries who were suddenly dissatisfied by the new "dictatorial style" and "incoherent strategy" of an entrepreneur whose construction company glorified the cult of group loyalty, requiring its employees to wear orange "Ordre des Minoranges" labels which proclaimed "I belong to Bouygues." In Cognac Jay they wore "TF1" labels. Adopting the Japanese shogun mentality might appeal to builders but was hardly attractive to supposedly creative individuals. Fair-minded observers would characterize the troubles as the inevitable consequence of dramatic change. Others thought their fears were confirmed by Le Lay's flash confession when explaining the motives for his investment: "Bouygues became interested in television when he realized that it was just another service industry. We already install electric cables so why shouldn't we use the cable to transmit images. That's what they're made for." Le Lay's insensitivity did not trouble Maxwell but his apparent inability to influence the management incensed him.

Maxwell had found himself in a peculiar position. Whereas Bouygues's investment was financed with his own cash, Maxwell had borrowed most of the Frs750 million. To break even, he needed to earn annually about Frs100 million to repay the interest and earn another 15 per cent or Frs110 million to justify the investment. It required TF1's management to generate profits immediately: "Maxwell felt that his presence had won the bid so he was owed equal rights," recalls one of his aides. Soon after they had won the bid, Maxwell and Bouygues had agreed that they would speak daily at 6 p.m. regardless of where they found themselves in the world and meet every Friday in Paris for a "Council of War." Partly as a safeguard to protect his interest and partly because he believed that his expertise was invaluable, Maxwell also insisted, and Bouygues agreed, that Ian Maxwell should be appointed as head of the new "International Division," responsible for buying and selling programs. Ian's status remained a personal matter between the Maxwells until the son arrived at TF1's headquarters at Cognac Jay. Then his status became a reflection of his father. According to some board members, Robert Maxwell was furious about Ian's treatment by Le Lay: "He didn't have a proper office or an adequate car." Le Lay denies any knowledge of Ian's complaints: "I was desperately trying to reorganize and save the company. Ian was never there."

Even the most experienced television executive would have found the challenge daunting and, whatever his talents, Le Lay was a novice at TF1. Early projections suggested that there might be no earnings for at least one year. The cause was certainly not TF1's failure to attract an audience which was running at an impressive minimum 40 per cent. Capitalizing on that dominance depended upon charging the highest rates for advertising, reducing production and administrative costs and selling TF1's programs around the world. Among the obstacles were the restrictions on advertising; the limitation on the numbers of cinema films which could be broadcast; and the stipulation that 50 per cent of the programs be produced in Francophone nations. International sales and co-productions were vital for profits but Ian was handicapped. "The Maxwells knew nothing about television," says Jacques Pomonti. "They didn't understand how programs were commissioned, made or sold. They thought it's just like newspapers and that was their great mistake." Pomonti could accurately add that Robert Maxwell did not actually watch television, yet claimed with authority that universally "audiences are bored."

Le Lay was also an apprentice in television but he was unwilling to allow Ian the same privilege. To protect Bouygues's interests, he had appointed Christine Ockrent as an executive above Ian Maxwell. Both Le Lay and the star assumed that her expertise as a performer was a qualification to manage a business. Both were disillusioned and on July 8, amid great publicity, Ockrent resigned. Ian, subject to constant demands from his father, would fare little better. To Le Lay's irritation, Ian was his father's agent and constantly absent caring for the family's other French interests. Among them was his bid for Provençal.

Soon after TF1's hand-over party, Maxwell, irrepressibly self-confident, had flown to the MIP-TV trade fair at Cannes. Like an excited schoolboy on his birthday, he impatiently awaited sight of his newest toy, the *Lady Ghislaine,* a 155-foot, 430 tons, five-deck yacht which he had bought for about £15 million from Adnan Khashoggi's brother and named after Maxwell's youngest daughter. During the previous year, the yacht had undergone a lavish refit to incorporate the latest communications equipment and expensive furnishings. One alteration had been undertaken on his wife's particular insistence. The glass walls of the sunken swimming pool, through which the Khashoggi brothers had hoped to watch nubile nymphettes swim while drinking in the lounge, were replaced by solid paneling. Now, anchored alongside Cannes's sea wall, its new owner pouted at the symbol of his international mega-stardom.

Chattels only become status symbols after they are seen. Accordingly, on April 24, Maxwell hosted an enormous party on board to which Bouygues, Le Lay and the whole French TV world were invited. The symbol was the message: Maxwell's wealth was incalculable and his power was irresistible. Even Bouygues was impressed: "I'm a hardened businessman and I have a tough skin. But frankly, he is a mammoth . . ."

The following day, taking the stage in his new role as co-owner of

TF1, Maxwell felt the need to address the world's press about his empire's expansion, especially in Europe. "It was inevitable," he told the hordes who gathered, "that I would invest massively in France" as a springboard first for expansion into Spanish and Portuguese television and then into Latin America. As an initial investment, he was putting $200 million into a production company headed by TF1's former director, Hervé Bourges. Megadeals, proclaimed Maxwell, had already been signed and this was only the beginning. Clearly enjoying the chance to grab the headlines, Maxwell added some juicy and ridiculous comments about his competitors. Berlusconi he condemned as a man who "doesn't understand" France, while Murdoch "couldn't even find France or Spain on a map." And there was more to underscore his adoption of France, "a country which I love." Very shortly, he announced, he would launch France's first national daily newspaper printed in various locations; and in the meantime his son Ian "is negotiating to buy the Provençal."

"That was a bad mistake," insists one of Laffont's advisers. Charles-Roux's hesitation turned to anger when she heard about Maxwell's boasts that he had secured Laffont's signed pledge to sell the shares. "It was intimidation by a man who is like a locomotive. He thought we were imbeciles or amateurs." Her reaction to *Le Monde* was cautious: "He is as good a partner as any and we have no reason to slam the door in his face . . . but at the moment we are not selling." In fact, she confided her anger to Maître Paul Lombard, the family lawyer in Paris. Her brief was simple. She was now willing to consider any reasonable proposal for selling the newspaper other than from Maxwell. Within days, Lombard introduced a keen purchaser—Jean-Luc Lagardère who was still smarting from his loss of TF1.

In early May, having tactfully smoothed the way, Lombard introduced Charles-Roux, Antoine Cordesse and his mother to Lagardère in the Matra building overlooking the Étoile. After the discussions with Maxwell, it was reassuring to discuss the newspapers' future with a Frenchman, if only because there were no language barriers. Charles-Roux's initial reservations about selling to a non-socialist evaporated with the publisher's promise to adhere to the group's traditional policies: "It's only commercial sense. Marseilles already has a right-wing newspaper." By the end of the afternoon, the deal was practically sealed. All that remained was to draw up a contract and eventually inform the other shareholders.

In early June, de Barberin telephoned Maxwell whom he had recently met in Cannes. The situation since then had changed radically. A sale of the Provençal group to Lagardère, Barberin told Maxwell, had been agreed and the vendors held the majority on the board. "Bob and young Ian bombarded de Barberin's office with calls," remembers one observer, "urging him to intervene, but he was powerless." Charles-Roux's formal announcement on July 2 of the sale to Lagardère was greeted by Maxwell with a telex offering 20 per cent more than any sum the Frenchman had agreed to pay. "De Barberin told Maxwell that they had no chance but Maxwell would not listen." After a simple lunch for the family and Lagardère in the Provençal's dining room, the offer was formally considered. "It was a frosty meeting but Laffont knew that she could not block the sale," says one of those present. Litigation was always Maxwell's last resort and despite the vote, Laffont, with Maxwell's support, began legal proceedings alleging that the winners had conspired. Maxwell lost interest in the court battle soon after it began. His whirlwind had passed yet the three shareholders expected to be immersed in their strife until the 1990s.

Throughout the remainder of 1987, Maxwell felt uncertain about the direction of his French venture. The bullish mood which had driven him throughout that year to conclude a myriad of acquisitions world-wide had netted a few investments in France: a stake in the Sygma photo agency; the outright purchase of APEI, a small magazine publisher; Canal 4, a data information publisher; and he was on the verge of investing in the Channel Tunnel and announcing the launch of a new newspaper, the *European,* on January 1, 1989, for distribution across the Continent. But at the end of 1987, France was still a temporary, albeit amusing, diversion while he awaited the realization of his dream—the Big One. As so often in his career, Maxwell judged that a blaze of activity might produce some new opportunities. Having played the share-dealer in both London and New York, he would try his luck in Paris.

On January 4, 1988, Michel Vigier, a senior analyst at Maxwell's French brokers Cholet-Dupont flew to London to prepare the prospectus for the launch of MCC's shares on the Bourse, planned for the following month. Vigier was met by Richard Baker, MCC's deputy managing director, Reg Mogg, the finance director, and Henry Poole, the analyst at MCC's London broker, Alexander, Laing & Cruickshank, which had recently been bought by Maxwell's new bankers, Crédit Lyonnais. For Maxwell, the launch of MCC shares would certify further international respectability. Yet at the end of the day, Vigier returned to Paris little wiser about his new client. Both Baker and Poole had not fully answered his inquiries about the terms of trade between MCC and the private companies, especially the Liechtenstein-based Pergamon Holdings, and had firmly but politely resisted his attempts to extract detailed answers to his questions about MCC's 1987 results. Language difficulties between the two sides may have been to blame, but there was another possible explanation. The Britons might have been reluctant to reveal that MCC's growth was not as spectacular as Maxwell had predicted. Even with the last-minute "purchase" on New Year's Eve of the package of Pergamon companies from Liechtenstein, MCC had only achieved sales of £881 million, a long way from the £3 to £5 billion which Maxwell was pledged to achieve by 1990. But more pertinent, Poole's prediction just three months earlier that the company would earn £75 million in 1987 from speculation on shares, currency and property had proven to be optimistic. The preliminary accounts showed that MCC had actually lost nearly £50 million in speculation. Moreover, Maxwell's repeated claim that he was "cash rich" was no longer valid. The £630 million which he had raised just six months earlier had been spent on what one analyst would later dub "a hotchpotch"—nearly 50 per cent on purchases from his own Liechtenstein companies.

Inevitably, when the annual results would be published in June, MCC's share price would suffer. This in turn would seriously undermine Maxwell's plans for future acquisitions because he would neither be able to raise extra money by issuing more shares nor, in a take-over bid, would people be willing to accept MCC shares instead of cash. There was also a second problem. He had begun borrowing money from banks using his own MCC shares as a guarantee. If the price of MCC's shares fell, the banks would demand more shares to guarantee their loans or would demand further assets. The published results for 1986 of just two private companies, Pergamon Holdings Ltd. and Mirror Holdings Ltd., showed debts against his MCC shareholdings of nearly £285 million. In 1987, they would borrow a further £140 million. Other debts would be hidden behind nominee names which disguised the Liechtenstein connection. The combination of compartmentalization, unsupervisable trading between the private and public companies, different financial year endings of the companies and Liechtenstein itself encouraged suspicion that money was being churned uncontrollably through the system. Just as in the 1960s, fulfilling his ambitions depended upon keeping Pergamon's share price high, in 1988 so much would depend upon MCC's price.

Vigier heard none of this. Instead he was presented with Maxwell's standard formula to avoid unpleasant questions: gloss and hyperactivity.

A video, he was told, "a superb production," according to one of Maxwell's staff, would explain everything that the French audience needed to hear when Maxwell chaired the launch. And indeed they were right.

At a packed meeting held in the picturesque Pavillon Gabriel at the bottom of the Champs Elysées on January 29, 1988, Maxwell regaled the three hundred brokers with humor, platitudes, boasts and little information. *Le Quotidien de Paris* had described him that morning as the inheritor of the "crown of the oldest printer in the civilized world, after Gutenberg and a few others. He is a modern day emperor of the media. He has the stature, the charisma and the cash . . ." The only ripple in an otherwise flawless presentation was his snappy reply to a question about the Liechtenstein connection: "That's private. It's none of your business." Everyone laughed. Maxwell had made it into that type of occasion.

Maxwell found little to amuse himself however across the Seine at Cognac Jay. At board meetings the previous September and November, he had sniped at Le Lay's management. At the first, posturing as a socialist, he had complained about the treatment of employees. Then, at the second meeting, he had condemned the lack of profits and, in the opinion of some, had only just restrained himself from demanding mass layoffs.

Le Lay had watched Maxwell's gyrations with detached bemusement. The foreigner's forays were irrelevant to his daily task of turning TF1 into a profitable company. Less amusing in Le Lay's view was Ian's obedience to his father and his long absences. Even when Ian was at Cognac Jay, meetings would be interrupted to take phone calls from his jetting father voicing a frequent complaint: "Why are you letting them do this to us?" After eight months, the competing pressures were excessive—"Le Lay made his life difficult," said one observer—and Ian resigned complaining of illness.

His son's expulsion outraged Maxwell. Although he was unaware of the criticism, the Bouygues team had decided that their partner had been overestimated. "He is a one-man band. He has no one in France," Le Lay murmured to his chief. To remedy that impression, Maxwell dispatched in mid-January Patrick Cox as his new representative. Cox, whose father was a founder of Britain's independent television news, had built a career in broadcasting. Soon after Cox's arrival, Maxwell admitted his own impotence: "For the first time I found that I had responsibilities but no power. I can tell you that it won't happen again." Cox was to be his agent to regain control. But far from smoothing ruffled feelings, Cox articulated his boss's emphatic opinions and compounded the disagreements with Le Lay, provoking an unfortunate comparison with his predecessor: "Maxwell withdraws one small man and sends another." The bitchiness reflected the new tension between Maxwell and Bouygues. Board meetings at Cognac Jay had become bear fights. "Bouygues and Maxwell just shouted at each other," says one of the smaller shareholders. "They shouted slogans about knowledge banks, profits, satellites and TV jargon but they didn't seem to care about television. It seemed they cared less about television than about power. In fact they didn't seem to even listen to each other." Bouygues, who suffers slight deafness, would, on those occasions, seem "selectively deaf." By May, when Maxwell and Le Lay met at Cannes, Maxwell effectively conceded that he had been outwitted by Bouygues and was powerless to control his investment. Le Lay was granted total control and within weeks Cox was recalled to London and soon afterward resigned from MCC. It was not the only reverse Maxwell suffered.

The publication of MCC's annual report in May had not been received with the customary praise Maxwell desired. Unease had crept into City analysts' attitudes toward Maxwell's boasts of "nearly doubled sales and more than doubled profits" which he claimed took his company "well on the way to achieving the objective . . . by 1990 of a £3,000-to £5,000-million bracket a year [business] with profit growth to match." Their sentiments hardened after close reading of the small print in the report finally revealed some hard facts about Maxwell's track record in the October crash. On page 47, in footnote 14 headed "Fixed Asset Investments," the accountants revealed a loss of £49 million. Usually the heading "Fixed Asset Investments" is unimportant. The sum listed in the previous year under that heading was a mere £600,000. Now it had exploded to £332.6 million. The reason was simple. The accountants had agreed to place the shares which MCC had bought and not resold under "Fixed Asset Investments" because accountancy rules allowed any losses under that heading to be excluded from the corporation's annual profit and loss results. Accordingly, with the benefit of that creative albeit legal accountancy, Maxwell could still claim that MCC's profits had "more than doubled." When asked about this, Reg Mogg, MCC's finance director, claimed on Maxwell's behalf that the losses were not permanent but "just a hiccup in the market." Yet Mogg would soon know that the "hiccup" was permanent. In the first six months of 1988 Maxwell's profits from his much vaunted Treasury investments had already fallen from £32 million to £9 million. MCC's profits were static and there was a crashing 30 per cent drop in earnings per share.

Maxwell's ebullience, which seemed undiminished, puzzled the City. The price of MCC shares began to slip from their peak of 395p down to 250p—a decline which was exacerbated by a series of take-over failures.

At the end of March Maxwell had announced a "successful" A$800 million bid for David Syme and Co., an Australian publishing group which owns *The Age.* One month later, the deal collapsed. In May he had sold Hollis and admitted that his ambition to build an engineering company had failed. His only consolation was the purchase of a 30 per cent stake for $9 million in the Israeli newspaper, *Ma'ariv.*

The purchase of the *Ma'ariv* shares signaled Maxwell's commitment to Israel. Through a network of contacts supplied by his lawyer, Yakov Neman, an Orthodox Jew who is considered to be Israel's leading tax expert, Maxwell had established close relations with the country's chief political leaders. Skillfully he would avoid showing favor to either Yitzak Shamir or Shimon Peres, the opposing leaders of the two main parties, by giving each identical contributions. In August 1988, Ido Dissentchik, *Ma'ariv*'s editor, invited Maxwell to dinner to meet President Chaim Herzog. Within minutes the two men discovered that they had served in the same army corps in Normandy. Both were soon immersed in discussing their respective wars, a friendly old warriors' reunion. Israel had become Maxwell's sanctuary from controversy and venom.

Powerful by his mere physical presence, for the beleaguered Israelis, who felt themselves isolated, neglected and hated, Maxwell's enthusiasm was astonishing. "Here was a foreigner saying we were wonderful," commented Ehud Olmert, the minister of health who became a close friend, "and he could open doors for us anywhere." Stickers began appearing bearing the slogan "Maxwell buy me" as he invested $100 million, an unprecedented amount for any individual, in chemical, publishing and high-tech industries. Maxwell proved his commitment by appearing at conferences in Europe and America to encourage other Jews to invest in Israel. The proof of his advice was his $39 million investment in Scitex would be realized for $302 million. "I've made money in Israel," he preached, "so can you." Israelis applauded. "No one else had said such good things about Israel," was the common praise.

It was at the end of the business day that his associates witnessed the true reason for his investment in Israel. Opening the windows of his Jerusalem office, Tommy Lapid, his office manager, watched the man stare out over the city and tears roll from his eyes. "I feel close to my parents here," he whispered in a manner which no one in London could imagine. "I've tried all the world and I'm only happy here with you."

His success in Israel was matched by his glowing and growing confidence in France where, in the absence of any other activity, he decided to play his popularity to its fullest extent.

Over the previous months the Italian Carlo De Benedetti had been battling to seize the ownership of Belgium's biggest corporation, La Société Générale de Belgique. By June, the predator had been defeated but at great cost to the Compagnie Financière de Suez which had bought about half of the SGB shares accumulated by Benedetti. Keen to reduce the stockpile, Suez had offered Maxwell 10 per cent of the SGB shares. The reply was positive but on one condition: that Suez agree to sell to Maxwell SGB's 5 per cent stake in Havas, France's biggest advertising and communications conglomerate which was partly state owned. Havas's future was still uncertain until the new socialist government had clarified how it intended to dilute the corporation's strongly right-wing management. It was an ideal opportunity for Maxwell since, frustrated at TF1, he judged that Havas under his control would be an ideal vehicle to assert his major status in France; especially because Havas had already obtained access to two channels on the TDF satellite. After securing tentative agreement with Suez, Maxwell began secretly buying another 5 per cent of Havas's shares on the market. With 10 per cent he would be Havas's largest single shareholder after the government. A full bid, he understood, depended upon the Elysée's blessing.

Unlike in American and Britain, the French head of state wields decisive influence in commercial affairs without any protest from the tight circle of key personalities who manage and influence the economy. French businessmen's activities on the Bourse are not governed by strict laws as on Wall Street but by political arrangements which are themselves subject to what the insiders agree to be in the supreme interest of France. It is those impenetrable privileged relationships which had deterred Murdoch from attempting any major deals in France. In contrast, Maxwell, who in repeated interviews had reiterated his "Frenchness," believed by the end of June that he could count himself as one of those insiders. "My friend the president" had tripped off his lips during several interviews in France that year, displaying his remarkable confidence in the relationship and the consequence of his Henry Kissinger style shuttle-tycoonery.

Knowing the importance of the Elysée's attitude toward the Havas deal, Maxwell arranged to visit Mitterrand's assistant Jacques Attali in the palace on the morning of June 17. The topic for discussion was not Havas but Maxwell's intention to make a generous donation to the presidency.

Like his recent predecessors, Mitterrand's intent to bequeath an edifice of his reign to the City of Paris was widely known. In May 1987, two years before the Bicentenary celebrations, Edgar Faure had suggested that La Grande Arche, an office block then under construction by Bouygues, should be the symbol of the Bicentenary just as the Eiffel Tower commemorated the first centenary. The Arche is a radical cube building, measuring 110 by 106 meters, which is clearly visible when looking up along the Champs Elysées and through the Arc de Triomphe. Faure further suggested that the Arche should house a new Rights of Man organization to symbolize the revolution. On June 24 Mitterrand formally endorsed Faure's "good idea."

Over the following months, Faure sought rich donors to finance the Rights of Man organization. Among those willing to contribute was Maxwell who in return for his money was made Faure's deputy. On Faure's death, Maxwell assumed the presidency. His arrival at the meeting at the skyscraper Défense building to confirm his appointment was characteristic. "A helicopter arrived on the roof," recalls the Organization's secretary, "and Maxwell emerged followed by a blond secretary carrying a portable typewriter." After his appointment, he departed and was not seen again for the remainder of that year although the Organization's future was in grave doubt. In Britain, the appointment would be erroneously translated to suggest that Maxwell was the second-in-command of the whole celebration, a mistake which remained generally uncorrected.

By June 1988, the Arche's future use had become a potential political embarrassment. The entire basement area—16,000 square meters below ground without a single window—was unsold. Maxwell's visit to Attali in the Elysée was to offer a solution. He and the Caisse Dépôt would buy the white elephant through a joint company called SAGA. Maxwell's contribution for five-eighths of the shares would be approximately Frs175 million. A further Frs150 million would be needed to fit the interior despite its limited potential. As a further act of generosity, Maxwell dedicated the area to stage the Bicentenary events. Having received Attali's thanks, Maxwell prepared himself for an appearance that night on *Apostrophes,* France's widely watched literary chat show.

Maxwell had become a well-known personality in France by June 1988. Besides frequent references in the financial press to investments in printing plants, film production companies and reconfirmation that he would launch both the *European* and a popular daily, which in view of the socialist victory would be center-left rather than center-right, he had just published his authorized biography. His appearance was, by anyone's reckoning, polished and appealing except for one slight hitch.

While the other invited guests were discussing the Elysée's unseen but powerful influence in financial affairs, Maxwell, unwilling and unable to act the wallflower, interrupted to deny the thesis: "I don't agree at all."

He in turn was interrupted by a young and smiling financial journalist, Stephan Denis: "But even you, Mr. Maxwell, if you need something, you go to the Elysée."

Maxwell: "Not at all . . ."

Denis, rapier-like and with a laugh: "You were there this morning."

Without a visible blink, despite the loud scoffs of the other guests, Maxwell explained that he had visited the Elysée to make a donation. After the program, Maxwell approached Denis who was quite clearly well connected: "How did you know?"

"Because we passed each other in the corridor," replied Denis who agreed to meet Maxwell for lunch. There would only be one topic: the identities of France's powerbrokers. The Englishman's interest was not simply to promote his businesses but to feed his unsatisfied lust for political intrigue and influence. France, with its centralized powerhouse, was a marvelous playground for a frustrated would-be politician.

But it was time for celebration and two days later would be Maxwell's sixty-fifth birthday. As a devotee of parties, especially his own, his wife had organized no fewer than four parties over that weekend in Oxford for 3500 guests. The cost would be at least a quarter of a million pounds. The closest five hundred guests received invitations to "a Gala Dinner and Dance to celebrate the fortieth anniversary of Pergamon Press and the sixty-fifth birthday of its founder." As was customary, the marquees had been set up, the best wines ordered, the finest food prepared, the music arranged and the gifts organized. Instead of the previous year's fine leather toiletry case, Betty Maxwell had decided upon something more pragmatic. Each guest was to find a copy of the recently published authorized biography of their host by his faithful employee, Joe Haines. Since sales had been sluggish, the hosts could be forgiven for combining their natural generosity and instinctive self-promotion with commercial necessity. Disposing of surplus stock had always been an intriguing feature of the star's business career.

The book's publication had been promoted enthusiastically by Maxwell. Gleeful appearances on television and radio had been accompanied by the Maxwell stories about his unemployed father and his revelations about his Liechtenstein trust. Under the reassuring headline in the *Daily Mirror*, "The truth about the money in Liechtenstein: the answers will amaze you," Maxwell announced that he had amassed no less than £1 billion in the tax haven. How he had earned that fortune remained unexplained and did not apparently provoke the interest of the British Inland Revenue, but its eventual destiny was, he said, fixed—"My children will not get a penny"—because everything would go to charities. It was an interesting shift from his earlier assurance that the money would go both to charities and to "all my relatives not resident in Britain" which had not precluded his children. But there was some consistency that his children would have to make their own way in the world.

Frivolities aside, Maxwell's abrupt change of the ultimate beneficiaries of his supposed fortune raised a serious issue. If he could alter them so easily, then were the minority shareholders of his public company, MCC, not also vulnerable to his whim since, in theory, the Liechtenstein trustees could secretly transform MCC into a worthless shell? Curiously, Britain's fuzzy law-makers and indolent supervisory agencies tolerated the confusions without demur. Operating in unusually murky waters was second nature to Maxwell whose manipulative skills were now to be displayed in France in his attempted purchase of Havas.

On June 22, Maxwell announced that an agreement to create a joint £150 million international media company with SGB was "at an advanced stage." There was no mention that he had purchased 5 per cent of Havas. That news emerged only on July 7, provoking consternation in the Elysée: "He had done everything without telling us." For the first time, the French had observed Maxwell the predator, wheeler-dealer and juggler who did not feel himself answerable to anyone. He had intended to consult the Elysée but only after he had finalized the Suez/SGB deal. Instead, his random pot-shot triggered a series of unpredictable alliances which characterize the labyrinth of France's Byzantine politics. The hegemony of the network vaporized Maxwell's new patronage in the Elysée.

The campaign against Maxwell, the foreign *nouveau riche,* was initiated by Jérôme Monod, the president of the Lyonnaise d'Eaux, a pillar of the French establishment and a member of the boards of both the Compagnie Suez and Havas. Monod epitomized the inherent conflicts of interest which are endemic in French commercial life. He is a man who quite naturally flexes his muscles through the Elysée and his principal ally in this case would be André Rousselet, a former aide and friend of the president.

At the very moment that Maxwell's plot against Havas was exposed, Rousselet was himself negotiating with the president to buy a stake in the same company. The decision between Maxwell and Rousselet depended entirely upon the Elysée. Hence Maxwell had visited Jacques Attali on June 17, hoping that he could persuade the president that his own bid was fair and honest. Initially he was optimistic but he failed to take into account the realities of well-established relationships: namely, Monod's influence and that on Mondays the president usually played golf at the exclusive St. Cloud club with Rousselet. It was Colliard who telephoned Maxwell: "You'll have to pull out. You've lost."

Maxwell barely reflected on the motives for the defeat. He had long ago immunized himself to ostracism and failure. The Havas bid, he believed, proved his unmistakable presence in France. Yet its outcome also confirmed a trend. Throughout 1988, all his major projects had foundered. He was frustrated and furious. He needed new allies in France. His search would be led by Jean-Pierre Anselmini, a managing director at the Crédit Lyonnais—which, to the Frenchman's pride, had become Maxwell's lead bank—who was appointed as a vice president of MCC responsible for the group's strategy. Anselmini's task would be to create the opportunities in France and quietly remove the obstacles. In the meantime, there were just eighteen months to fulfill his prediction of creating a £3,000- to £5,000-million company. Since his expansion in France had been thwarted, he looked again toward America.

Maxwell's cultivated relationship with bankers had always been his specialty. Unlike other business people, they usually form a discreet fraternity around their customers' affairs and they are eager to encourage their clients to increasingly ambitious bids. Equally, Maxwell, understanding the bankers' individual ambition and vanity, sought to cultivate those whom he judged susceptible to his requirements. There would be requests that the young banker be allowed to travel with Maxwell to negotiate deals in foreign countries where the *Lady Ghislaine* would be moored, the helicopter stationed and entertainment provided suitable for a Hollywood mogul. "It was all like a James Bond movie," recounted an awed financier who recalled the huge bowl of caviar on the yacht's dining table. "A gift from Gorbachev," said his client, and there was no inclination to disbelieve the tale.

Several young bankers, especially in New York, would owe their promotion to an approach to their superiors by Maxwell: "I like dealing with this man, but it is fitting that he should be a director if our relationship is to develop." In return, the grateful banker would seek to satisfy Maxwell's increasing lending requirements. Among the gullible victims was Bankers Trust which, in the days before Maxwell died, advanced a £50 million loan against worthless security.

In 1988, the bankers encouraged gargantuan deals with the passion of zealots. In the wake of London's "Big Bang" they were flush with funds, keenly competing to lend money. Maxwell was among the beneficiaries, attracting interest not only from the British banks but increasingly from foreign banks, especially American, French, Swiss and Japanese. To all of those non-British banks, Maxwell recited a distorted account of the Pergamon/Leasco saga, emphasizing his victimization by the British Establishment, falsely claiming that he had been exonerated by the British courts, and preferring the latest glossy brochure of MCC's accounts which, he indicated, had been audited by the prestigious partnership of Coopers & Lybrand. His performance and self-pity elicited a warm response, especially in New York.

For some American bankers, anyone who clashed with Saul Steinberg could generate sympathy, especially if the prize was the territory of the British banks. For Bankers Trust, First Chicago, the Bank of Nova Scotia, Citibank and the others, the attraction of lending to Maxwell was the implicit promise that the lenders would be allowed to earn fees from his deals. The most privileged of the advisory banks was Rothschild Inc., a subsidiary of Rothschilds in London. By 1988, Maxwell had established a relationship with Bob Pirie, the president of Rothschild Inc. who had represented both Hanson and Goldsmith in previous bids. Pirie, who had advised Maxwell on his bid for Harcourt Brace, prided himself that he could represent both Maxwell and Murdoch: "Our clients have to trust me, trust my judgment and trust that I am looking out for their best interests." An atypical banker, Pirie put on a particular gracious act which appealed to Maxwell. His Cuban cigars, English-cut shirts and allusions to East Coast establishment were precisely the style which Maxwell believed would win him acceptance in New York. That was the reason that Pirie had won the beauty contest in 1986 at the Waldorf Astoria in New York. While his competitors queued outside to present their arguments for serving Maxwell, Pirie had promised "constant" availability and class. Pirie was constantly looking for new opportunities for Maxwell, and the fees for himself.

In July 1988, the American Macmillan publishing company was in the midst of a hostile take-over bid. The city was still mesmerized by the corporate raiders ruthlessly competing against each other to pay vast sums for every unsecured asset. On July 21 Maxwell joined the frenzy and formally announced that he would join the bidding. His adversary was Edward "Ned" Evans, a Rhode Islander with an earlier career in steel and cement who, since buying the ailing publisher in 1980, had transformed its fortunes. Macmillan, he would subsequently complain, did not need to be taken over to be improved. Macmillan was just another victim of the mad eighties. "Every company not nailed to the floor is up for grabs," he later lamented.

Maxwell's offer of $80 a share valued the company which had published Ernest Hemingway and Scott Fitzgerald at $2 billion. "This is the Big One," said Maxwell who, unlike his previous bid for Harcourt Brace, refrained from ensconcing himself in battle headquarters in a New York hotel. Instead, he gently stated that his offer was "conditional on the Macmillan board's endorsement." Initially, Edward Evans, chief executive of Macmillan's board, was noncommittal. Over the previous eight weeks, Macmillan had been fighting a hostile bid from the Bass group which had offered $64 per share against the quoted price of $50. The Bass offer had risen to $73 when Maxwell entered the fray at $80. His tactics had been astute. Macmillan was worth at most $70 a share. Bass's extra $3 was the expected premium in a hostile bid. The $80 bid would cut out Bass and allow Maxwell to pose as the "white knight," anxious to help a fellow publisher. To reinforce the unhostile tone, Maxwell had even provided his jet to fly selected journalists for a briefing on board the yacht anchored at Bastia, Corsica. Dressed in a bright pink shirt and surrounded by bright silver-blue decor he explained: "We wish this to be a friendly deal—the synergy is wonderful. We like Mr. Evans and we like his management. He has done extremely well—not quite as well as MCC—but nevertheless an impressive performance." He added that $80 was a "fair price. I will not pay a stupid price for it." After the smoke of the battle had cleared, the Americans would compliment Maxwell's initial and untrue statements as "cute."

Since nearly all the $2 billion offered was raised as loans from Crédit Lyonnais and Samuel Montagu, Maxwell had smartly launched the offer from an off-the-shelf company, Mills Acquisition, to avoid the huge debt affecting MCC's balance sheet. And to avoid Evans deploying the Liechtenstein defense, he had switched 21.9 per cent of the Foundation's 52 per cent holding to Headington Investments which was registered in Britain at a theoretical value of £297 million. Although MCC would still remain formally registered in the tax haven, his Rothschild bankers were allowed to meet Keicher and see what were presented as the trust documents. In turn, the Securities and Exchange Commission

(SEC) in New York had been persuaded that the majority shareholding in MCC was now held by British subjects. No one at the SEC demanded further proof that the transfer between Maxwell wearing two hats was not irrevocable. But unknown to the Americans, Headington was really owned by an off-shore secret trust registered in Gibraltar, which led back to Liechtenstein.

The initial reactions to the bid in Wall Street were uncomplimentary. "Maxwell is not very well regarded in the United States," said Bert Boksen, an analyst. "He's a little like Crazy Eddie," commented an American publisher. "You pay attention because he's screaming at you, not because you like him." Macmillan rejected his offer in early September.

On September 9, Maxwell raised his bid to $84 but there was already a hint of desperation. He wanted to know which managers were prepared to stay and the blunt reply was that if his bid succeeded they would depart *en masse*. The pundits, who had already all but written off Maxwell's chances, wrote the final chapter after Macmillan announced that it had hired Kohlberg Kravis Roberts, the inventors and doyens of leveraged buy-outs, to assemble a financial plan, raising huge loans, which would allow Macmillan executives to buy back all the company's shares. On September 13, KKR announced an offer of $85, including a "poison pill agreement" whereby KKR's hefty $23 million bill would be paid for by Maxwell and a $860 million core of the business would be excluded from the sale. In New York, KKR's riposte was hailed as "the knock-out blow." Three days later, to dispel those murky waters, Maxwell raised his offer to $86.50 and appealed to the court to dismantle the defense.

Hitherto the battle had followed a conventional pattern. But KKR's latest ploy threw Maxwell into a serious quandary. At $86.50, Maxwell would pay at least $300 million more than Macmillan was worth. His banks, especially Crédit Lyonnais which was itself ambitious to break into the international market, were willing to augment their loans but the cost was increasing. Interest rates were rising and, more worrying, the price of MCC shares had fallen heavily. They were down to 185p, less than half the 395p one year earlier, and a massive 30 per cent worse than the market average. That bare fact dashed any hope of Maxwell raising extra money by another share issue.

The City's skepticism was growing. Printing, which Maxwell repeatedly described as MCC's "core business" providing "a vertical strategy for long-term growth," would, according to the most optimistic forecast from Poole, earn relatively low profits by 1990. Worse still, there were definite signs that several major customers of MCC's new expensive printing plants had decided to move their business elsewhere when the contracts expired. Despite his earlier confidence, no other newspaper owner was prepared to contract his nightly print run to Maxwell's presses. Maxwell's much vaunted print strategy was souring. Simultaneously, Maxwell had also noticed that companies like Reed International, which had abandoned printing, were earning profits from publishing magazines and books. The pattern was worldwide. Publishing earned profits while printing was marginal. Maxwell began considering selling the print plants partly to pay for Macmillan and also to forestall the embarrassment when the print contracts were lost. His much vaunted strategy might be in shreds but he was not going to suffer another humiliating defeat in America. That sentiment was supported by Pirie: "If you want to be in the media business," advised the Rothschild banker, "you've got to be prepared to pay the price." Pirie did not add that he would earn higher fees if Maxwell won. Telling his client, "You're paying top dollar," Pirie did not discourage Maxwell's desire to go for broke.

On September 26, Maxwell raised his offer to $89. Two days later, KKR placed a counter-offer of $90.05 which Edward Evans accepted as final. It was the fatal mistake. According to the rules, Maxwell had to be given an opportunity to counter-offer. Evans had ignored that provision because at $90.05, KKR was paying $600 million more than the company was worth. Evans and KKR had reached their limit. Their only remaining weapon was to leak that as a three-time loser, Maxwell's ambitions could be written off. They had failed to reckon with Maxwell's determination.

On October 5, Maxwell's lawyers rushed to the Delaware Court to demand that Evans be forced to offer Maxwell another chance to bid, and to drop the "poison pill" defense concocted by KKR. Simultaneously they announced that Maxwell had raised his cash offer to $90.25 which meant that Evans had denied shareholders the better offer. "I'm in it to win," said Maxwell unconcerned by the extra $600 million he was committed to pay. The battle was not about commercial sense but over a man's place in history.

On that same day, October 5, as the lawyers had filed their complaints in the Delaware Court, Maxwell's frustration in America spilled over into a major row with François Bouygues in Paris. Since Cox's departure, Maxwell had lacked any direct influence over TF1's management. The meetings of the strategic committee had in the view of another participant become "contests between dinosaurs where Maxwell was angry that no one was treating him with the respect he believed that he deserved." Maxwell's anger with Bouygues for failing to turn TF1 into a profit-machine by effecting dismissals of the conservative staff and producing new programs equaled his contempt for the other board members. Unlike Maxwell and Bouygues, they were employees, unenterprising functionaries, even weirdos, who were simply thrilled to be part of the television world and were less concerned about profits. "We were prepared to be patient for the evolution of change," said one member. "For us it is a long-term investment and a service to the nation. Mr. Maxwell, of course, is not French and cares about profits and not about people or even the company."

During September, Le Lay had met Maxwell six times, including over a weekend in London, to explain TF1's problems and his future plans. Le Lay found Maxwell constructive, even admitting that he had "written off" his investment in TF1 because he realized that there would be no profits. At their penultimate meeting in September, Le Lay had raised the most sensitive issue. François Bouygues, he explained, would be retiring from the presidency at the next board meeting and intended proposing Le Lay as his successor. Maxwell voiced no opposition although he had neither forgiven nor forgotten Le Lay's treatment of Ian. But at the end of September, when there seemed to be no solution to MCC's low share price and the fate of the Macmillan bid remained uncertain, he began discussing a coup against Le Lay and Bouygues which would release his frustration.

Maxwell's ally was Bernard Tapie whose juggling, publicity-seeking business style vaguely mirrored Maxwell's own, but on a very minor scale. Tapie resented Bouygues's rejection of his claim for a place on the main board. Instead he was the jester on the strategic committee and the butt of others' humor. On one occasion, when Tapie attempted, by tapping on the table, to interrupt a row between Maxwell and Bouygues, he received short shrift. "To bang on the table," growled Maxwell at his would-be ally, "you've got to have a table to bang on and with your one per cent stake, you ain't gotta table." Everyone roared, especially Bouygues because in his opinion Maxwell's 12 per cent barely gave him a table either.

In business there are no friends, only temporary alliances. Toward mid-September both Maxwell and Tapie, for different motives, shared a dislike of François Bouygues. There had been rumors that Bouygues was ill and the company was vulnerable. After a fall in earnings, its shares were undervalued and whoever captured the main company would inherit control over the 25 per cent stake in TF1.

On September 28, Maxwell had arrived at Bouygues's home for breakfast. His visit was not to inquire about his adversary's health but because heavy trading in Bouygues's shares that week had raised the price and fueled speculation of a take-over bid. "Can I help you?" asked Maxwell with his familiar benign expression. "I'll buy some shares to support your position."

Bouygues grimaced. Since he controlled about 45 per cent of the voting stock, the offer seemed somewhat preposterous. His answer was accordingly cynical: "I don't need any help, but I'll buy shares in your company if you're in danger." Bouygues's riposte struck home. MCC shares at their four-year low suggested that Maxwell's credibility was under attack. As a tough street-fighter, Bouygues was uninhibited in declaring that Maxwell had a problem in Paris too. His guest departed with a bitter smile.

The following day, to prove his strength and Bouygues's vulnerability, the news was leaked that Maxwell had bought a 5 per cent stake in Bouygues. Tapie had bought a smaller interest. "When François discovered Maxwell's tactics," recalls Le Lay, "he phoned Maxwell and exploded." At the weekend, Maxwell, tongue-in-cheek, explained his purchase to the *Herald Tribune* as a ploy to ensure that no one could capture control of TF1 by buying Bouygues: "It looks like there may be a predator on the prowl for Bouygues. I don't want my friends pushed around." Bouygues would later claim that Maxwell's raid was inspired by disgruntled government officials.

The fourth meeting of TF1's main board was set for October 11. The tension, which was already noticeable following Maxwell's share raid, rose as the clock neared 3 p.m. François Bouygues is a purist for punctuality and Maxwell, his son and two other board members were absent. They would arrive fifteen minutes later and together. Maxwell had invited them to lunch and delayed their departure. Bouygues was intended to interpret their joint arrival as a conspiracy.

The screw tightened as the first item was discussed. "Why," asked Maxwell, "was the excellent profile of General de Gaulle screened after 10 p.m.? It should have been shown in prime time." The reply was direct. "Because audience research showed it was correct."

Next item: the move to new headquarters at Montparnasse. The contract for construction had been awarded by TF1 to Bouygues. It was the type of inter-company deal which Maxwell knew so well. "I oppose this until the contract goes to tender," said Maxwell who suggested that it was the first time the issue had been raised. "It was discussed in September," replied Bouygues pushing the past minutes to a shaking Maxwell. A patched compromise was agreed.

At 5 p.m. the board reached the last item: miscellaneous. Bouygues announced that he intended to resign and nominated Le Lay as his successor.

"Why was I not told about this before," exploded Maxwell. "It's not on the agenda."

"You can't say that," screamed Bouygues pounding on the table. "You can't say that you weren't told. You're a liar! I telephoned and told you."

"Rubbish," snarled the bear.

"But Mr. Maxwell," intervened Le Lay perplexed by the unprecedented twist, "Yesterday you congratulated me on the appointment and asked if I was happy."

Maxwell rose to leave. When cornered he usually changed tack or ran. On that night, there was no escape route: "I'm leaving, François. You're attacking my honor."

Bouygues had no intention of releasing his grip: "No. I notified you. You're lying."

"Retract that word or I'm leaving."

Bouygues could only win. "Let's say, I didn't call you a liar. But nonetheless, I did notify you . . ." The board voted for Le Lay's appointment. The two Maxwells abstained.

Eleven days later, on October 16, Maxwell held a press conference aboard his yacht in Cannes to declare war formally on Bouygues: "I'm not at all certain about the legitimacy of Le Lay's election." In Paris Le Lay fumed: "That's it. We'll get him." Eighteen months earlier, in happier times on board Maxwell's yacht in Cannes, Bouygues had described his partner as "a mammoth." Now was the moment to puncture the myth. Coolly, he set in motion discreet soundings with those who pull the levers of power. Maxwell, he suggested, should be removed from TF1.

Unconcerned about the antics of a mere organ grinder, Maxwell returned to Britain. It was time to consider the future. France had been an amusing diversion but of little consequence. The real action was in America. The Delaware Supreme Court would rule on November 2 and the omens were promising. Macmillan had been unable to prove that the auction for the company had not been rigged in KKR's favor. He had given more than usual thought to the consequences of a $2.6 billion debt incurred to buy a company whose assets were worth at best

$1.65 billion. He would announce "a new strategy" but would insist that it had been planned long ago.

It was late afternoon in London when the three Delaware judges handed out their unanimous decision in Maxwell's favor. The balance was decisively tipped but he kept his silence anticipating that KKR, whose reputation was at stake, might mount a new ruse. Less than twenty-four hours later, he knew that victory was his. Edward Evans, sad to be a victim of the eighties, recommended Maxwell's bid and sold his own shares at a hefty profit. Evans would later tell friends, "When he came to the headquarters, I showed him around, gave him the keys, and left."

On November 4, Maxwell appeared in New York to claim his victory. No reasonable man was inclined to begrudge him the pleasure of that hour. After all, only he had the task of finding the money. His solution confirmed every skeptic's suspicion: that Maxwell's strategy was just to win the next deal. "Maxwell Communications," he announced, "is placing all its printing plants up for sale." That included BPCC which prints magazines, BNPC which prints the Mirror Group newspapers and all the acquisitions in France, Belgium and the USA. The much vaunted "integrated core business" was no longer a core but a disposable: "I am a publisher and not a printer . . . I have been working on this strategy for years." His audience could only wonder why they had never been told. Their hurrah was brief. Precisely six days later, Maxwell issued another statement. MCC in fact intended to retain 40 per cent of its printing plants. Control of the companies would be sold to its management. The reversal confirmed the character of the strategy: confused.

16

Robert Pirie hosted a small party to celebrate Maxwell's success in winning the Macmillan battle. Maxwell shone in this firmament. In the relationship business, or the Big Man's club, Maxwell liked to mix with fellow kings and Pirie, the eccentric patrician, understood precisely Maxwell's weaknesses. "Plays him like a puppet," sniped one of those who watched the banker's sycophancy. Pirie knew that Maxwell would not tolerate advisers who contradicted his wishes and wisely stayed out of the way of the moving train. Like an amateur psychiatrist, Pirie knew what Maxwell wanted and gave it to him, which was the least he could do. After all, he had just pocketed a reputed $14 million in fees. That night, Maxwell wanted to be surrounded by New York's rich and powerful. Pirie obliged, delighted to encourage Maxwell's disdain for the pompous bankers in the City of London and feed his belief that his future was in America. He would encourage Maxwell to hire Hill & Knowlton, the public-relations consultants, and lobbyists like ex-senator John Tower and former vice-president Walter Mondale to serve the publisher's interests. Since 90 per cent of MCC were American businesses, Maxwell was tempted to make a final move.

On board his Gulfstream, call sign VR-BOB, flying back to London, Maxwell was unconcerned by two uncomfortable truths: that his company now owed bankers more than it was actually worth; and that his businesses were not producing enough money to pay off the loans. Every year, he would need to find $290 million to repay the interest on the $2.6 billion he had borrowed. Debts, Maxwell reasoned, were not problems but challenges to overcome. Long forgotten was his claim, uttered only months earlier, of his £1 billion stored in Liechtenstein. The *Daily Mirror* headline about that fortune—"It's all being given away"—seemed uncannily accurate although the recipients of the money were not the charities he mentioned. The notion of that El Dorado had evaporated when he borrowed the billions to buy Macmillan and later the *Official Airline Guide* for which he paid $750 million rather than use his own money.

The deadline to become a £3–£5 billion company was thirteen months away. Earnings were falling and he could no longer afford to buy companies to expand. His public credit was good enough to deny that he was short of money because banks were still willing to lend. Shareholders, of which he was by far the most important, would also not suffer. MCC's main attraction to investors was its unusually high dividends. But it was impossible to hide one truth. He had taken on too many other activities. Soon after he landed, he would publicly pledge: "I have taken on too much. I must get back to the core priorities of our business and ruthlessly prune back on peripherals." He would quote uncertainty about his health as the reason for his decision although, in reality, he excelled under pressure. As the helicopter landed on the Mirror building, the publisher's optimism was impregnable.

Although the public image was of a man singlehandedly running his business, Maxwell could rely on trusted, long-serving and faithful advisers to earn profits away from the public eye. The most important were the accountants who were nurtured to ensure their fidelity and permanence. Unlike his other employees, they were not "slaves" but colleagues who would and should never be dismissed.

On the ninth floor was Richard Baker, MCC's deputy managing director, who was a sophisticated currency and money dealer. Nearby was Albert Fuller who sorted out the paperwork of the hundreds of millions Maxwell would regularly invest by personal phone calls in shares and gilts. Fuller was helped by Debbie Maxwell, a lawyer. Others nearby were managing the £300 million property portfolio. Together they were producing more real profits than the combined earnings of the thousands in publishing whom he employed. How that was shifted between the public and private companies depended upon his instructions to Robert Bunn, the faithful accountant employed by Maxwell for 15 years who supervised his private companies. Of course Bunn's discretion was restricted. No one within the empire would ever be allowed to know more than a limited amount about Maxwell's operations and no one in headquarters could cross the boundary between the public and private interests except Kevin and himself. Kevin's importance inside MCC had grown since his appointment at 28 years of age as joint managing director in 1987, while his father devoted more time to politics and cultivating his international stardom. While Ian, also a joint managing director since 1987 when he was 31 years old, was tolerated and humiliated by his father, Kevin was humiliated but increasingly allowed to mastermind the financial intricacies of both the public and private companies, especially the negotiations with the banks for the loans. For those bankers admitted into the heart of the Maxwell empire, there was no doubt that "Kevin ran the shop" for he was as "bright" as any Harvard graduate, although unlike his father, he was a practitioner, not a creator.

Kevin's relations with Robert Maxwell, always conditioned by the beatings which he had suffered as a child, were nevertheless close, despite continued invasions of the son's life. In 1984 Robert had exercised his considerable powers of persuasion in a vain attempt to prevent Kevin from marrying Pandora Warnford-Davis. The cause of Robert Maxwell's antagonism was Pandora's personality and religion. She was a "goy," complained Maxwell, a non-Jew, which confused Kevin because he himself was not Jewish. They were also too young, complained the father. The legacy of that antagonism never disappeared. Pandora's ungraciousness toward her father-in-law and those involved in the family's business reflected Kevin's own sense that "he wasn't enjoying himself" but was prepared to accept his father's humiliation as the price for all the perks of executive life. Some would say that Kevin was in an impossible position since he, unlike his elder brother and twin sisters, had crossed the Rubicon and was employed by his father. Loyalty was expected and, regardless of the consequences, Kevin fulfilled his father's requirements.

The compensation was to relish the power of managing a billion pound business, which was quite unique for someone still under thirty years old. While his contemporaries, even the successful ones, might be engaged on the periphery of thirty sizable deals, Kevin was at the center, calling the shots and telling some of the world's principal bankers and lawyers what *he* wanted on one hundred deals worth billions of dollars. Few mortals would not be thrilled by a trip from London to New York, but how many would, like Kevin, travel from their corporate headquarters in central London to Heathrow airport by helicopter, land next to the Concorde, whose departure had been delayed to await the arrival of the young tycoon, and be waved through immigration by a specially assigned passport official? Kevin glowed in others' servility and, according to bankers who observed his behavior, grew to believe he was above the law. "He thought what he did was cute," explains one Wall Street banker, "and it made no difference so long as he wasn't caught." Naturally, Kevin exploited the compartmentalized system which his father had created.

In fact, physically he could not avoid it. To prevent the customary interaction among employees, Maxwell had imposed a tight security screen throughout the building, especially among executives. Access to each director's office was possible only through use of an individual electronic security card. Hence it was impossible, for example, for the finance director to stroll into the neighboring office unless admitted. All movement on the ninth floor was recorded by video cameras connected to television screens in Maxwell's office. Instinctively, Maxwell's directors were inhibited from discussion in each other's office. Maxwell's intention was not to prevent unauthorized enquiries but to reinforce the atmosphere of non-disclosure upon those admitted to his sanctum of secrecy. Outsiders would interpret the obsessive security as an indication of Maxwell's paranoia.

Robert Bunn, the finance director of the private companies, understood how compartmentalization denied him the ability to fulfill his task: "I am not saying that we are blameless, but Robert Maxwell isolated us in boxes and we did not know the extent of what was happening." Even in BPC, the publicly owned company, Maxwell had secured his dictatorial powers quite legally. On November 26, 1981, the BPC board had granted Maxwell total powers without need to refer to the board. Maxwell by himself could declare that he was a "committee of the board" and exercise the board's powers. Over the following years, not one of the directors disclosed their impotence.

Maxwell's empire was constructed on the identical principle as twenty years earlier. At the center was a publicly quoted company whose share price was the key to his operations. Surrounding that jewel was a constellation of private companies whose activities, like those of their predecessors in the sixties, were inextricably linked to MCC. But only Maxwell knew all the details, as the ownership of public and private assets was switched to cope with demands for cash. Knowledge was power and only his family could be trusted with more than a smidgen of the network of obligations which underpinned his operations. Among those who were not excluded from the private companies were the auditors of the public company, Coopers & Lybrand Deloitte, who in 1991 would earn approximately £4 million for auditing the public and private companies.

Maxwell's relationship with Coopers was conducted by Reg Mogg, MCC's finance director. Hired in 1982, Mogg had proved himself a trusted keeper of the secrets. Although he would later protest, "I wasn't Maxwell's patsy, I am a professional accountant who could sleep quite easily at night," Mogg read his master's mind perfectly. An ambitious, self-made man, Mogg understood how, quite legally, he could make the accounts of the debt-laden company seem profitable. Naturally, it was instinctive, creative work whose success depended upon his personal relationship with MCC's auditors, Coopers & Lybrand, and in particular Neil Taberner, the senior partner responsible for MCC. "Taberner was always at my shoulder," smiled Mogg knowing that, whatever the criticisms, the accounts had been formally approved by Coopers. "The annual report was a most important document. That's what people knew about us," says Mogg who agrees that Maxwell's credibility depended upon that glossy brochure.

When the accounts were approved by Coopers, the next step was to encourage investors to buy MCC shares, which depended upon convincing the stockbrokers to advise clients that MCC was a good investment. In 1988, among the most important salesmen preaching about Maxwell's successes was Henry Poole, the analyst from the brokers Laing & Cruickshank. But ever since the Macmillan purchase, Poole's doubts were growing.

Like all disciples who begin questioning their faith, Poole's reaction to his own concerns was violent. "Henry's turned," was the quip on the Laing trading floor. "He's even advising clients to sell Maxwell's shares." The news could not have pleased Maxwell. He was Laing's biggest client and his bankers, Crédit Lyonnais, had bought the brokers. Ian Hay Davison, Laing's chairman, was summoned to Holborn. The meeting was tense. Laing's client explained that he expected his shares to be puffed and Poole was doing the opposite. Hay Davison, who had been responsible for investigating fraud at Lloyds insurance, was an unlikely candidate for intimidation. "You've got bad ratings because of your accounts," an eyewitness heard Hay Davison explain.

The heart of the problem was to justify Maxwell's boast of 1985 that his corporation would generate sales of £3 billion to £5 billion by 1990. Every year since, he had aggressively reasserted his prediction and caustically damned those who queried his calculations. In 1987, Poole had publicly assured the City that MCC would earn pre-tax profits of £405 million by 1990. In March 1989, the profits were half that amount. Poole realized that, to achieve Maxwell's target, MCC would need to treble in size within nine months. Laing's directors agreed that producing optimistic forecasts was problematic. Poole stood down and Johnny Bevan, Maxwell's energetic broker, was hired to lead the charge. But even Bevan's talents could not repair the rot. Laing's salesmen were dispirited. "No one wants to listen to stories about the Maxwell magic," Bevan lamented. Investors in Maxwell had already lost too much money.

As the American deals were analyzed, the value of MCC's shares was falling. Within that year, they would drop from 395p to 167p. Ignoring the fall, Maxwell began raising loans by pledging his MCC shares as a security or collateral. Those loans were secured against 145 per cent of MCC's current share price. In other words, for each £100 that Maxwell borrowed, he had to provide £145 worth of shares. His agreement with the banks stipulated that if MCC's share price fell, Maxwell would be forced to give additional guarantees. As interest rates rose, Maxwell's fate became inextricably tied to the price of MCC's shares and compelled him to resort to a succession of stratagems to keep the price high.

Maxwell's task was not inexorably difficult. Britain's regulatory authorities in the Stock Exchange, the Department of Trade and Industry and Bank of England were, in his opinion, staffed by third-rate bureaucrats whose proven indolence and incompetence had contributed to his good fortune. Others might say that his propaganda and secrecy had stifled their enquiries.

The estimated forty banks with whom he dealt were also eager to part with their money. Bankers after all can make profits only if they lend the money which others have deposited. For all his faults, Maxwell had always repaid his loans and his relationship with the bankers, especially the National Westminster, was firmly established over the previous forty years. Bankers, however, are self-interested and notoriously gullible. Easily flattered by types like Maxwell, few had studied his history or his pattern of operations. Accordingly, they did not understand the significance of his decision to change MCC's financial year.

MCC, Maxwell announced, would not as usual present its accounts for the year ending December 1988, but would extend them to March 1989. Maxwell used the two American deals as justification although the two companies were yet not part of MCC. Significantly, his private companies continued to end their financial years in December. To some, it was reminiscent of similar tactics he had used in the sixties which the DTI inspectors had condemned because it had allowed him to switch money and contracts between the public and private companies during those three months, artificially inflating Pergamon's profits.

But at the end of the three-month delay, MCC did not, as promised, consolidate the two acquisitions into MCC's accounts. The auditors,

Coopers & Lybrand, made no comment about that failure. Instead, it was only in the March 1990 accounts (published in July) that the consolidation was set out. The result presented a confused report of MCC's finances. The most significant complication was the distinctive difference in the treatment of one-time profits and one-time losses which gave unjustified credibility to Maxwell's claim that MCC's results were "highly satisfactory." The huge debts which Maxwell had accumulated to pay for Macmillan and the *Official Airline Guide* had been concealed.

During March 1989, Mogg presented his preliminary assessment of MCC's accounts. The profits from publishing had fallen. Maxwell would need to include property sales, currency speculation and exceptional items to present a rosier picture, which would depend upon his personal arrangements with the private companies.

The annual report put a brave face on the results. The pre-tax profits in the special fifteen-month period were £192 million on sales of £1.39 billion. The graph of profits, benefiting from the exceptional fifteen-month period, seemed to soar to a new record high, yet Maxwell, under pressure from the board, bowed to one reality.

On April 6, 1989, the chairman announced that his hallowed sales target of "£3–£5 billion" by 1990 was "meaningless" because the purchase of Macmillan and OAG had put him among the top ten media companies. The logic was baffling, although his claim that profits from publishing were more "succulent" than those from printing was certainly correct. Naturally, Maxwell ignored those who carped that his decade's endeavors were not ending in glory but were souring. However on the television monitors in his office, he watched the consequence of their criticism: MCC's share price was falling as the first debt repayments became due.

Under pressure to explain his solution to the debt predicament, Maxwell revived the possibility that the Mirror Group would partly be sold to the public. But that course was hazardous. It might reveal his intercompany trading; the new public company would have to pay dividends, which was costly; and he would lose a source of easy loans. Flotation of the *Mirror,* he knew, was an option of last resort and therefore, having raised the possibility, he quietly dropped it.

The only solution was to sell parts of what he had just bought. Despite both his own and Kevin's repeated assurances that Macmillan would not be broken up, he announced amalgamations and sales of $1 billion of Macmillan's "peripheral" assets which included Macmillan's core educational publishing business. While former Macmillan executives were wondering why Maxwell had bought their company in the first place if it was now being sold off, Maxwell went in search of potential purchasers. His timing, uncharacteristically, was inopportune. The recession was beginning and, with one exception, customers were fast melting away. The exception was Maxwell himself.

In the course of 1989, the Mirror Group paid £270.3 million for MCC's printing presses. It was a generous price that Maxwell was privately paying for a publicly owned asset. Again, it was a familiar pattern of the sixties. Maxwell was pumping money into the public company to boost the share price. His dilemma was to find the finance to pay MCC.

Among the other jewels which MCC was selling was a 44 per cent share of Berlitz, the profitable American language school, which was part of the Macmillan empire. In August 1989, Maxwell invited Goldman Sachs to sell the Berlitz shares and they eagerly accepted his business.

The relationship between Maxwell and Goldman Sachs, which would become a sensitive factor in the controversy about Maxwell's survival as a businessman in the very hours before his death, had begun by accident in 1984. Robert Conway, sent from New York to establish Goldman's presence in London, rented office space in a Maxwell-owned property behind the *Mirror* building. Gradually the two men became acquainted.

During the booming eighties, Goldman Sachs watched with dismay as its rivals pocketed the large fees of the corporate raiders like Drexel and Milken while they remained firmly excluded from those profits. Irritated, in 1988, they smartly stepped into the market and agreed to sell an international gold flotation for Alan Bond which had been rejected by other houses. Goldman lost a fortune. Despite the setback, Goldman managers anxiously sought the fees paid by active entrepreneurs. In the wake of the Macmillan take-over, Don Opatrny, a corporate finance executive of Czech origin, welcomed Maxwell's offer to float Berlitz. Not everyone in Goldman Sachs was enthusiastic about representing Maxwell but the promise of fees overruled any doubts. Maxwell, eager to consolidate his position in New York, welcomed his endorsement by the prestigious firm.

Since Maxwell had decided that Kevin should run Macmillan, it was natural that both father and son should arrive at Goldman Sachs's Manhattan office for the first meetings. The disagreements began soon afterward.

Maxwell was concerned about two issues. First, that his French banking friends should have a slice of the business. "That's not on," he was told by Chuck Harris who was one of those assigned to manage the sale. Harris and the Maxwells would disagree continuously until the Goldman executive won the point.

Their second disagreement was over the price of the shares. Goldman Sachs wanted to offer the shares for $16; Maxwell wanted $4 more. Since Goldman would pay for any unsold shares, the Americans' interest was to ensure that the price was realistic. "You're just greedy, Bob," said Harris who began to fear that Maxwell was deliberately ignoring the interests of the minority shareholders. "Both Maxwells behaved appallingly," recalled one of the executives, "but Kevin behaved worst of all. We soon hated them."

"Harris's main problem," recalls another observer, "was Kevin."

Goldman executives suspected that the thirty-year-old son, in responding to his father's challenge, was keen to prove his prowess: "Kevin would ring Harris up at 4 a.m. and get him out of bed for nothing that couldn't wait," says one insider.

The father's games were more sophisticated. Summoned to London for a meeting, the bankers waited for an hour in the outer office before being called. Once admitted, the pattern was familiar. Their discussions were continuously interrupted by messages from government ministers delivered by Peter Jay, the office manager, or by the telephone: "Yes, thank the president for his endorsement," said Maxwell in a call which ostensibly came from the White House. "That was all set up to impress us," was the unanimous conclusion when the bankers emerged into Holborn.

Eventually Harris was assigned to other duties. The flotation nevertheless passed successfully on December 13, 1989. If Goldman Sachs in New York decided that Maxwell was a customer they might want to lose, that option was closed. By then, Goldman were inextricably linked to Maxwell through their London office and in particular by Eric Sheinberg.

Eric Sheinberg, a senior partner of Goldman Sachs in London, is an accomplished broker whose performance had won privileged access to Maxwell. "Eric's a trader's trader," they sang in Goldman's new Fleet Street headquarters, as Sheinberg huddled over the phone giving advice to Maxwell, reputed in the market to be among the biggest individual players. Eric, it was said, had once told a fellow employee that Goldman Sachs was his first love; his wife took second place. But contrary to the "Wall Street" image, Sheinberg's reputation was that of a distinctly quiet and honest practitioner. He successfully tempted Maxwell to practice his first love—trading—with Goldman Sachs. Even when he was losing, Maxwell did not complain, because he was paying gratuitously for the services of a prestigious first-division broker.

Informed estimates suggest that, communicating with each other throughout the day from mobile phones as they both criss-crossed the globe, Sheinberg was handling, at any time, $50 million of Maxwell's money. While at Goldman's headquarters in New York they might have worried about Maxwell as a customer, Sheinberg was delighted about his client's hyperactivity. Maxwell naturally expected something in return for the business which Sheinberg received. Namely, support for MCC shares.

In the anti-climax which followed the City of London's euphoric "Big Bang," those watching the monitors in the brokers' trading rooms across London say that they could see at a glance who was offering to buy Maxwell's shares. Goldman Sachs's price for MCC shares was marginally better, a suggestion which Goldman denies. Every day at rival brokers Phillips and Drew, Derek Terrington heard his market makers shaking their heads, "Goldman's on the bid again." The timing was always the same and sellers waited for the moment. Daily, at 2:30 p.m., just as the New York exchange opened, Goldman Sachs, according to Terrington, "hoovered up all the available MCC shares."

Sheinberg and Maxwell were aware of two salient facts. Despite Maxwell personally owning over 50 per cent of MCC (and his ownership would grow to 68 per cent and then secretly and illegally to nearly 80 per cent), the number of MCC shares which could be traded was still substantial, although in Sheinberg's defense it could also be added that the definition of creating a false market is less explicit in British law than in American. Secondly, Goldman, although not a mainstream British broker, was sufficiently formidable that its decision to buy or sell could influence a share's price. Sheinberg knew that it would be beneficial to Maxwell if Goldman actively traded in MCC's shares. That is what occurred in 1989. MCC's price steadied, which was welcome news to Maxwell. Sheinberg was admitted as one of Maxwell's intimates. Sheinberg was in the company of a man whose range of contacts was genuinely remarkable.

Driving one night in his red Rolls Royce along the Strand to a dinner at the Savoy, Maxwell was gratified to read a short personal note, starting "Dear Bob" and signed "George," from the American president thanking him for some advice he had volunteered after a journey to Moscow. His reading was interrupted by the car's telephone. On the line was President Mitterrand. More talk about the turmoil in Moscow and eastern Europe. Here was real evidence of his importance as a diplomatic broker. He was of an age and experience to play the international statesman, although to some it seemed that he seized upon any opportunity to jet to any location to be greeted by the head of state, regardless of the host.

On October 2, 1989, Maxwell flew to East Berlin. The communists' control was faltering as East Germans abandoned the socialist paradise traveling via Czechoslovakia to the west. Poland had already negotiated its freedom from Moscow and most East European experts were confidently predicting the end of Soviet control.

Maxwell's flight to the communist capital was, Berlin's officials would later say, at his own request. Erich Honecker was struggling for survival. To Honecker's staff, Maxwell seemed oblivious to the political swirl within the walled city. Maxwell's relationship with the embattled politician was close. In 1981, on the twentieth anniversary of the wall's construction, Maxwell had written in the preface of Honecker's autobiography which Pergamon had published: "I have the honor of presenting to the public . . . the life and work of Erich Honecker." One chapter was a self-congratulatory account of how the author had masterminded the wall's construction, which, he concluded, "fills me with satisfaction."

Maxwell had returned to Berlin to re-cement that relationship. Just one month before the wall would be breached, Maxwell, in a stage-managed ceremony, presented the German with two leather-bound Pergamon volumes of the *Encyclopaedia of the German Democratic Republic,* priced at £110 per set. As the cameras whirred in the Central Committee's headquarters, the dictator and the publisher, ignoring the political earthquake in the streets outside, greeted each other as old friends. Maxwell had afterward told reporters that Honecker had been "a reformer all his life" and was "in very good nick."

Maxwell's presence could be interpreted as a sign of *naïveté* or as an indication that he was not a fair-weather friend. He would later claim that he was interceding at the West German government's request to negotiate about the plight of East German refugees. But the reality was more mundane. Maxwell enjoyed the welcome accorded to statesmen at foreign airports—the waiving of passport formalities, the swift passage of government limousines through the town and the pomp of officialdom. Standing alongside the famous appealed to his vanity but also encouraged his conviction of being an agent of influence. But his visit to Berlin was spurred by commerce as well. Pergamon had invested heavily in producing vast quantities of the books which were stored in a Berlin warehouse and he hoped to recoup some of the money before it was too late.

Four months after the communist collapse, Maxwell would be asked to explain his relationships with the communists. Hinting at a secret agenda, he replied, "I indispensably contributed to saving eastern Europe." He added that the series of autobiographies by the communist tyrants always included disclaimers. They are hard to find. "Have you never made a mistake?" he asked rhetorically. "I regret not saying publicly how critical I was to their faces."

That apparent and unusual humility was tarnished when he then minimalized his profits in eastern Europe: "Over forty years I only sold a few books and journals." The notion, he asserted, that Pergamon's early fortune relied upon communist trade was "black propaganda." A few weeks later he would quantify those profits as, "0.001 per cent of my business . . . It was done at the request of the U.S. government. It was a five-year program which was loss making." Ignoring Pergamon's own 1962 annual report which boasted making £50,000 profits in trade with the USSR, Maxwell concluded "I did no business with eastern Europe before the Berlin Wall came down."

The opposite was the truth. Despite his claims to unique advantages, Maxwell did little business in eastern Europe *after* the wall came down. His energetic flights around the newly liberated nations resulted in remarkably limited investments: a half share in the Berliner Verlag; a minority stake in two Hungarian newspapers; a management school in Bulgaria; and a host of activities but not investments in the Soviet Union.

By common consent, Mikhail Gorbachev is the protégé of Yuri Andropov. The KGB chairman had analyzed that the stagnant Soviet economy needed reform. Gorbachev was groomed as the party's architect of the changes which would remove unnecessary controls, encourage innovation and introduce some limited capitalist ideas. But like all the members of the communist hierarchy, Gorbachev was ignorant about capitalism and sought friendly advice. In 1985, Maxwell, stepping into the shoes of Armand Hammer, offered to fulfill that requirement. But there was one difference between the two entrepreneurs. While Hammer brought real business to Russia, Maxwell brought promises which he hoped would engender political influence. Alternatively, Maxwell's role as an agent of influence, established twenty years earlier, had been resumed.

Soon after Gorbachev's appointment, Maxwell searched for profitable ventures in a country where his reputation and contacts were unique. At Moscow's Sheremetevo airport, he could not fail to impress the waiting Kremlin officials as he stepped off his personal jet surrounded by an entourage of subordinates. Soviet officials responded eagerly to Maxwell's promise of a "mountain of gold": management courses, offers to equip scientific institutions with computers, proposals for joint ventures to provide "online" technology via satellite, and speculation about a variety of newspapers.

Among the journalistic endeavors which he initiated was a business and cultural magazine, a television station and a "Heritage" agreement with Raisa Gorbachev and the Cultural Foundation. In his wake gasped a second generation of bewildered Russians. Maxwell's broken promises were partly due to his precarious finances but also his recognition that any money invested in Russia would be lost forever. His real interest was to influence Russia's fortunes by brokering on behalf of western political leaders.

Nothing stimulated Maxwell more, when in conversation with a cast list which included George Bush, Margaret Thatcher, John Major, François Mitterrand, Helmut Kohl and Gorbachev, than beginning a sentence by referring to his tête-à-tête, just hours earlier, with another member of that club.

It was to become a broker of influence in Moscow that in 1986 Maxwell invested in *Moscow News,* a pathfinder of perestroika, which was edited by Yegor Yakovlev, a friend of Gorbachev. Yakovlev claims that he accepted Maxwell's offer to print *Moscow News* because he believed that Maxwell had received payments laundered through a Soviet press agency for printing 50,000 of the leaders' books, although no one ever discovered how many had been produced. "Maxwell was trusted by the communists," says Yakovlev. Maxwell's commitment was naturally equivocal.

"Maxwell broke with us when we criticized Gorbachev for the suppression of Lithuanian nationalists in February 1990," recalls Yakovlev. The row was ferocious. "Maxwell tried to impose his views and we rejected them," says Yakovlev, who published a highly defamatory attack on Maxwell. Enforcing the laws of defamation in Russia, Maxwell knew, was difficult. Others hint that Maxwell was dissatisfied with the quality of the Russian staff whom he was subsidizing in London. The grounds for the row are irrelevant now although the rancor against Maxwell still lingers in Moscow.

Russia, for Maxwell, was a source of political not financial dividends and his American appearance alongside Gorbachev in Minneapolis in June 1990 to create the $100 million "Gorbachev Maxwell Institute" to unite the world's scientists proved that he was certainly reaping rich rewards for his scrapbook. Photographs and newspaper headlines about the two men were reproduced worldwide. When, following a toast-laden lunch, both men departed from Minneapolis, Maxwell forgot his promise to donate $50 million to the Institute.

In May 1990, Maxwell had never felt more confident of his future. The phrase "the Maxwell empire" tripped naturally off people's tongues. At times he even felt like an Emperor.

Regardless of the debts, his publishing business was prospering, especially the newspapers. For the first time, the *Daily Mirror* had dented the *Sun*'s supremacy and was earning one million pounds a week. The credit was due to Maxwell's cost cutting and anticipation that color printing would win readers—a judgment which Murdoch had originally spurned and was struggling to reverse.

Launching new activities was always Maxwell's palliative to pressure. A cheap diversion would be to hurtle out of London by helicopter or jet for a business meeting, a day on his yacht or, better still, consultations with a statesman. A more expensive diversion would be a take-over bid or the launch of a new newspaper.

Surrounded by his symbols of wealth and prestige, Maxwell announced a $362 million bid for the *National Enquirer,* America's biggest selling tabloid; a $100 million bid for a group of three other American tabloids; and an offer of £120 million for a stake in the remains of Alan Bond's Australian newspapers. All three bids failed.

The successful alternative was to create his own newspaper and on May 11 he hosted a glittering breakfast launch for the *European* in the New Connaught Rooms where thirty-one years earlier Rupert Murdoch had sabotaged his bid for the *News of the World.* Now, ten stone heavier and, on his reckoning, one thousand times richer, Maxwell addressed an assortment of diplomats, politicians, bankers and journalists about his latest venture, a newspaper which he described as "the triumph of vision over common sense."

Since the *London Daily News* had proved a costly humiliation, most anticipated that his boast, "I am the European," signaled a similar disaster. There was supporting evidence for that prejudice. It was nearly three years earlier that he had heralded a tabloid European daily. Subsequently, there had been so many failed attempts that just to have delivered a handsome weekly color broadsheet was judged a success, despite its limp content.

That morning, at the champagne breakfast launch, he adopted a Churchillian tone to transmit his philosophy. Europe, he declared, was about to regain the leadership of the world and, based on what his promo-video called "the ideals of the French Revolution," he intended to make "a small contribution" to that process. Although Maxwell's critics would find it occasionally difficult to credit the publisher with either unselfish principles or a steadfast philosophy, there was little evidence which disputed his commitment to forging a united and peaceful Europe in the summer of 1990. After all, he had urged the Labour Party forlornly twenty-five years earlier to abandon its ideological antagonism toward the European Community. If Maxwell thought that a newspaper could change history, the journalists who were now invited to interview the publisher were too self-interested to dispute the importance of their trade.

To Maxwell, the launch of a newspaper implied opportunities of personal publicity. His self-confidence, never restrained in the past, overwhelmed his interviewers. Visitors who were invited to his duplex adjacent to the *Mirror* building in Holborn were mesmerized by the sheer scale of gold and green marble, specially woven carpet, tapestries and seventeenth-century French paintings. Other interviewers, invited aboard his helicopter and/or jet, recorded, as Maxwell desired, that he possessed incalculable wealth and, at his own insistence, that he was an individual exercising "power." Less satisfying perhaps were the accompanying headlines: "The ego spreads his wings" and "The ego has landed." But the hidden agenda was successful.

Just as some City analysts were concluding that his company was "clearly dancing on the edge," Maxwell had positioned himself as a powerbroker of infinite wealth. Discarding his earlier platitudes about not interfering with his editors, he emphasized his role at the *European:* "I'm in charge. I'm the editor-in-chief." He had learned the lessons of the *London Daily News,* he explained, of "stupidly leaving it to the professionals." It was both Maxwell's strength and weakness that his perception of the truth, erroneous as it might be, remained unchallengeable. His treatment of subordinates, especially his editors, had crystallized: "When I fire someone it is like a thunderclap. My primary duty is to hire and fire editors. I treat them like a Field Marshal."

Many professional journalists greeted the *European* as economically unviable but the publisher was committed to spending £50 million. His editor, Ian Watson, a lean Scot who had formerly worked at the *Sunday Telegraph,* had redesigned the paper to allow Maxwell the pleasure of assuming responsibility for its fine looks. Aware of the fate of other Maxwell employees, the editor had wisely fixed to his wall the life-cycle of an important product: "1. Wild enthusiasm. 2. Disillusion. 3. Total confusion. 4. Search for the guilty. 5. Punishment of the innocent. 6. Promotion of the non-participants." After fourteen months, Watson would have gone through the whole cycle and be sidelined. By then sales were languishing at 250,000 instead of flourishing at the anticipated one million and the losses were estimated at £10 million annually.

But before his dismissal, Watson witnessed and related the legends of his proprietor. Like the night that Maxwell, impatient because no key was immediately available to open an office door, successfully crow-barred his entry; or the conversation which was overheard between Maxwell and a tardy supplier of computer terminals: "Have you ever been circumcized? Well, you soon will be unless you're here with those terminals by this afternoon. And what's more, I'll throw away the big bit." Two hours later, the terminals were being installed into the very floors where the ill-fated *London Daily News* was born and died. But on this occasion, despite the losses, Maxwell's commitment seemed solid. Unfortunately, the recession had just hit the natural market for his publication.

The noticeable casualties of the recession were the eighties' glamour boys whose empires, built on loans or manipulation, became victims of soaring interest rates. As the scandals—Guinness, Barlow Clowes, Polly Peck and Blue Arrow—were investigated and prosecuted, other flamboyant businessmen's activities were scrutinized—including Maxwell's. Suspicion was aroused by Maxwell's debts which he claimed in June 1990 were down to £1.9 billion. The first repayment of $415 million was due on October 23, 1990, and could only be raised by selling parts of the empire. The suspicions were fueled by doubts about the actual value of his empire which was directly linked to the value of MCC's shares.

As MCC's share price fell, Maxwell took an unusual risk. On August 14, he sold to Goldman Sachs in New York a "put-option" for 15.65 million MCC shares for November 30, 1990. In August, MCC shares were quoted at 170p, and Maxwell had effectively promised Goldman that, fourteen weeks later, he would buy from the brokers 15.65 million MCC shares at 185p. Maxwell's object was to encourage Goldman Sachs to buy 15.65 million MCC shares immediately—at the lower price then quoted—so forcing up demand for the shares. The incentive to Goldman Sachs was the guarantee that Maxwell was a certain buyer for those shares. Maxwell gambled that the "put-option" would influence the stock market and MCC's price would increase to at least 185p.

The gamble was particularly sensitive. Maxwell's maneuver covered the two months before MCC would announce its 1990 results. As a director, Maxwell was legally forbidden during that period to buy MCC shares either in his own name or anyone else's. But according to this plan, Maxwell was not technically purchasing shares but selling an option.

On October 17, 1990, £4.5 million was paid into Corry Stiftung and £4 million paid out on the same day to PH(US)Inc, a private Maxwell holding company registered in Delaware. The payer to Corry Stiftung was a London solicitor, Titmus, Sanier & Webb, who represented both Maxwell and MCC—a confusion which the partners, it would be claimed, did not seek to clarify. On October 29, Corry Stiftung paid £319,476 for MCC shares. A further £38,570 was drawn from the account on November 12 to buy MCC shares. It was a clever device which distorted the market.

Goldman Sachs however insists that the option was agreed before the closed period began, which is correct, and that it already owned the 15.65 million shares, although it has not produced the paperwork as proof. At best, the deal can be said to have encouraged Goldman Sachs not to sell MCC's shares which would have depressed the price.

By law, that deal should have been disclosed to the board of MCC but Jean-Pierre Anselmini, the deputy chairman, subsequently stated that he was not formally informed. Andy Smith, a junior press officer at MCC, registered the disclosure at the Stock Exchange's Companies' Announcement Office where it remained unseen by, among others, MCC's broker, Michael Richardson.

During that period, Goldman Sachs bought or continued to hold not only those 15.65 million MCC shares but bought a further 25 million in the market. By the second week of October 1990, Goldman Sachs was holding 47 million MCC shares which, since Goldman Sachs insists it was not buying on Maxwell's behalf, suggests that the brokers had great faith in MCC's fortunes.

October was not only the publication date of the 1990 annual report but also the deadline for the first repayment of the debt. Amid the uncongenial publicity, Maxwell could find no buyers for the companies he wanted to sell. Reluctantly, he resorted to a familiar solution. He announced that the privately owned Mirror Group would buy MCC's printing plants in Canada and America. The deals were notable.

Andrew Capitman, a divisional managing director of Bankers Trust in London, secured the business of valuing Quebecor Printing and Donohue for MCC. Capitman's task was made easier by the knowledge that Maxwell was eager to pay "book value" for the plants, which was generous because he wanted to inject money into MCC. Even if the banker had known that Maxwell was "taking a step too far," Capitman's primary interest was to earn the $700,000 in fees for one week's work to produce a "slam dunk opinion." He need not puzzle why Maxwell was paying money into MCC. Nor would he know that after the deal, Maxwell would borrow the purchase price back from MCC to cover the debt. Historians would pinpoint this moment as the beginning of the dramatic climax which ended Maxwell's ambitions.

Quebecor Printing was sold by MCC to the Mirror Group for £58 million, 70 per cent more than Maxwell might have received from a disinterested purchaser. (The 25.8 per cent stake in Quebecor was sold in January 1992 for £51 million despite its £66.4 million valuation in Mirror's accounts.) A second print plant, Donohue in the U.S.A., was sold by MCC to the Mirror Group for $19 per share, $8 more than Donohue's shares were selling on the stock exchange. Maxwell was injecting £135 million of his private money into the public company to keep MCC's share price high. The previous year, the private companies had bought £336.1 million of other MCC assets. In addition, MCC had bought Merrill's College Publishing, an educational publisher, for $200 million in cash. The purchase served Maxwell's gargantuan ambitions but placed an increased burden on his finances. Indeed, Kevin would later blame the Merrill purchase for triggering the empire's collapse. The critical factor was that Maxwell had to borrow all that money and that he used MCC shares as the guarantee for the loan. The price of MCC's shares had become an issue of more than passing interest.

Sensing that his critics were still dissatisfied, Maxwell announced two further deals: the sale of Pannini, an Italian manufacturer of stickers, for £60 million; and the sale of Collier, the American encyclopedia publishers, for a sum still to be negotiated. As the deals were publicized, Maxwell watched MCC's shares rise on his monitor. Gratified, he did not mention for some time that those two companies had not been sold.

Throughout that year, Maxwell's enthusiasm and boisterous self-confidence had grown in parallel with his debts. The 1990 report was written by Reg Mogg just before what Mogg calls his "career move" to Polly Peck, whose chairman and managing director, Asil Nadir, would soon after be charged with theft and deception and the company declared bankrupt. In the report, approved by Coopers & Lybrand, Maxwell praised "the remarkable and rapid transformation in the affairs and standing of our group." Heaping more praise, he added that the company had achieved "virtually all the principal targets which we set ourselves a year ago."

Indeed, according to the accounts, pre-tax profits in the last twelve months had reached a record £172.3 million and there had been record sales of £1.2 billion, although the growth rate was falling. But once again, the profits were not earned from publishing but from what were called "discontinued activities" (£34.6 million) and "other operating income" (£47.9 million). Moreover, according to the accounts, interest payments on the £1.9 billion debt were up from £17 million to £108 million, notably strange amounts on those huge sums.

But among the most significant items in that year's accounts was the value of the "intangibles": that is, the monetary values which the accountants decided they could place on the goodwill and publishing rights which MCC owned. Those values would then be entered in the MCC balance sheet which would show what MCC was worth. The critical importance of the "intangible" values was that they directly influenced Maxwell's business credibility. It was in Maxwell's interest to persuade the accountants to agree to value the "intangibles" as high as possible because his borrowing powers were boosted and the price of MCC's shares would rise—which was exactly what Maxwell desired.

When those 1990 accounts were being written, some believed that Maxwell had overpaid by about $1 billion for Macmillan. Reg Mogg disagreed. After conducting what Mogg describes as a "thorough valuation," Mogg entered MCC's "intangibles" at a hefty £2.2 billion. "It was a very professional operation," he says. "I think you need to take a twenty-year view on values." Mogg secured the agreement of Neil Taberner of Coopers & Lybrand to those valuations and accordingly had fulfilled his statutory duty. Other qualified accountants assessed MCC's "intangibles" at £1.5 billion. After subtracting all MCC's debts, those independent accountants claimed that MCC was only worth £300 million. Which figures were chosen was subjective but the choice was of singular influence on Maxwell's ability to raise more loans and to bid for more businesses. Once the "intangibles" were agreed at £2.2 billion, Maxwell needed only to find profits which would match that figure. Doubts were growing about what City jargon called "the quality of the profits."

By the time the 1990 report was published, Maxwell had parted with Laing & Cruickshank and moved to the City brokers Smith New Court. The magnet was Sir Michael Richardson, Smith's chairman, who had known Maxwell since he organized the flotation of Pergamon Press in 1964. Richardson, renowned in the City as one who marches toward the sound of gunfire, knew his advice would be needed during his friend's ups and downs: "I was perfectly happy to take over when Bob asked me." Hyperactive clients, Richardson knew, produce fees. As Maxwell's problems increased, Richardson would explain that the crisis was in Maxwell's private companies which were beyond his responsibility. Smith, like Goldman, began buying MCC shares and urging their clients to follow. But changing brokers could provide only a cosmetic, temporary respite.

Maxwell's "put-option" gamble with Goldman Sachs had failed. When it expired, MCC's shares were selling at 155p, 30p less than he had bet. The cost to Maxwell was £5 million. As newspaper reports speculated about the debt, MCC shares continued to fall to new lows around 140p. Maxwell admitted that support for the MCC share price had cost £75 million, although some suspected a higher amount. Maxwell needed money and his only immediate source was MCC's interim dividend due in December. The board meeting at the end of November was more heated than normal.

In November 1990, MCC reported its six-month profits (to September). As usual, Maxwell reported increased profits (up 6 per cent from £85.1 million to £90.1 million) but the good news was not due to publishing. Instead there was a £41 million increase in what were called "foreign exchange profits." Once again Maxwell declared himself "satisfied" and "confident," raised the dividend and watched as the shares rose 5p (149.5p to 154p). The debt was still £1.9 billion and he was pledged to reduce it by $750 million within four months. But not everyone on the board was satisfied. Jean-Pierre Anselmini, the deputy chairman, was, reportedly, still furious about the "put-option."

"Maxwell promised that he would tell Jean-Pierre if he took out another 'put-option,' " recalls one eyewitness. For Anselmini it was disturbing that he was not regularly consulted by Maxwell. He was concerned by the "confidence" which Maxwell always included in company statements. In November he was particularly worried about MCC's proposed interim dividend payments.

Until then, Maxwell had often taken shares instead of cash, but in November he wanted cash. Basil Brookes, the new finance director, opposed his employer. "We can't afford a high dividend and we can't afford you taking cash," he told Maxwell. Their argument was heated and there were suggestions that Brookes might threaten his resignation. Brookes was already concerned that Maxwell's attitude toward observing the Stock Exchange rules was cavalier. "They're a bunch of has-been, useless stockbrokers," scoffed Maxwell. "I'll decide what they can have and when." Nevertheless Brookes seemed to have won.

Maxwell even agreed that his assurance would be in writing. But the victory was shortlived. Maxwell needed cash, not shares, and he acted accordingly.

There was however some consoling news. The "poison pill," used by Harcourt Brace Jovanovich to block Maxwell's bid, had become a suicide pill: Harcourt was on the verge of bankruptcy. More good news was that Murdoch's debts (£10.5 billion) eclipsed even MCC's problems and News International's share price seemed to be in free fall. There was a notable difference, it was said, between Maxwell and Murdoch. The Australian owed the banks so much that banks could not afford to allow him to go broke without bankrupting themselves. Maxwell's business was too small for his and his banks' survival to be dependent upon each other.

Yet his dream of rivaling Murdoch had disappeared. In July he had been unable to bid for a share of BSB, the British satellite TV station, and in early October he pulled out of television altogether by selling his stake in Central TV for £24.6 million, half of what he would have got had he waited another six months. He also sold his stake in the French station, and all his cable interests including a 51 per cent interest in MTV, the pop station. His dream of becoming a satellite owner rivaling Sky had evaporated.

In the weeks before Christmas, Maxwell's pace had occasionally slowed. His business disappointments were mirrored by his worsening relationship with Betty. His matriarchal wife had increasingly withdrawn to Oxford while her husband remained in London or traveled constantly to avoid his solitary existence at home. On the rare occasions when they traveled together, they would sleep in different rooms and even on different floors in hotels. Betty's occasional journeys to London provoked a flurry of concern lest she find evidence of his increasing liaisons of a temporary nature with younger women. Although she had always suspected his relationships with his secretaries, Anne Dove and Jean Baddeley, Betty had ignored the evidence because of the reality of life with a large family. But with age, they had grown too distant to ease her toleration of his behavior. Possibly she was suspect for having tolerated him for so long. Gradually, their separate lives became permanent as she sought to develop her own activities and he sought the company of young women who were attracted to wealth and power.

His dalliances were just a symptom of how he had changed. His vanity had become oppressive. Twice monthly George Wheeler, a hairdresser, would be summoned—even onto the yacht—to apply L'Oreal Crescendo to dye Maxwell's white hair. He ate enormous amounts of food, which showed in his enormous girth. He had also become, Betty suspected, quite paranoid. Her husband was in continual contact with John Pole, the Mirror's security chief. Unbeknownst to anyone, Maxwell was receiving daily reports and transcripts of the telephone conversations made by his top executives and even his son Kevin. Pole was also responsible for supplying a constant stream of reports from private detectives hired to investigate Maxwell's "enemies." Paranoia had gripped a man who basked in self-idolatry. Increasingly, he would enjoy flying to his yacht, the *Lady Ghislaine,* to relax in a style which ranked him among the world's richest. In both the main stateroom, dominated by a 180-degree curved window above a silver sofa, and on the four decks Maxwell could entertain and impress dozens of visitors with comfort. All were asked to remove their shoes before boarding. The craft, with its normal complement of thirteen crew and two chefs, could be chartered for about £100,000 per week. Part of Christmas 1990 was spent in the Caribbean. Maxwell enjoyed speaking on one satellite phone while another line transmitted a fax.

The festivities did not dispel the problems. MCC's share price was at the same level as in 1985. Two directors resigned and Richard Baker, MCC's deputy managing director, left after twenty-three years' service. These were the first of a trickle of accountants who began resigning from Maxwell's employment. Most would complain of exhaustion but their grounds were said to be Maxwell's inexplicable demands. On January 4, Headington sold a five-week "put-option" of 30 million shares to Goldman Sachs. Anselmini would reportedly complain that, contrary to the agreement, he was not told by Maxwell. Maxwell would not lose any money on that gamble.

By early 1991, Maxwell owned just 68 per cent of MCC, 16 per cent more than nine months earlier. Buying shares legally and increasing his holding beyond the precluded 70 per cent threshold was no longer an option and Maxwell had run out of money. Worse—although this was a closely guarded secret, Maxwell knew that his collection of diverse private companies, aggravated by the recession, were unprofitable. The income from the MCC and MGN dividends could barely compensate for the private losses of £150 million in that year or reduce the accumulated debts, which were approaching £800 million. Since the private assets, valued at approximately £670 million, had been fully mortgaged against loans, Maxwell could no longer offer any more security.

The losses had accumulated because Maxwell, having completed two profitable deals—namely BPC in 1980 and the purchase of the Mirror Group in 1984—had otherwise traded and juggled a succession of losers. AGB International, a market-research conglomerate bought in 1988 for £138 million, was unprofitable and worth only about £70 million in 1991. Maxwell had also lost millions of pounds on a myriad of deals including Norton Opax, the Midland Bank, and French television, where he deluded himself that his intervention guaranteed profits. In addition, there was the cost of his lifestyle—alias "Bob's toys." The accumulated expenditure on the yacht, helicopters, executive jets, houses, staff and food was draining millions from the threadbare profits.

Paradoxically, at this moment, in the *Sunday Times*'s league of Britain's richest men, Maxwell was featured as eighth richest, owning an estimated £1.2 billion of assets; *Forbes* magazine also estimated his fortune at $1.9 billion. In truth, he was on the verge of insolvency. For the first time, pundits introduced the term, the "Max-Factor." For some the term meant that MCC was undervalued because of his presence. Others used it as a euphemism for their outright suspicion.

In February 1991, Maxwell flew to New York to seek a solution. Among those consulted was Robert Pirie. Over coffee on a Saturday morning, the American banker, who had been Maxwell's adviser when his client became so indebted, suggested that his client sell Pergamon Press. According to Pirie, "Maxwell said yes." The sale would be a watershed. The empire would lose its biggest cash producer. Maxwell also finally resolved to sell a minority share in the Mirror Group. The Macmillan legacy was the dismantlement of the jewels of his empire. Kevin's boast in 1988 that only three out of thirty-one Macmillan employees had left after their take-over was obsolete as about another dozen followed. Macmillan remained profitable but unsettled. David Shaffer, Macmillan's president, was among those who openly joked that Maxwell had paid too much for the company and it was his job to make the impossible profitable.

It was at this point that Maxwell ignored reality and compounded his plight by indulging in an ambitious fantasy. By profession, traders are natural gamblers, but their skill lies in limiting risk to realistic proportions. Maxwell had accumulated his fortune by a combination of brilliant foresight, original intuition and taking outrageous risks. Gambling with cards and especially roulette had long been part of Maxwell's life. Gossips in London related in awe how he visited the capital's casinos and simultaneously played high stakes on two tables where, by the laws of the game, he would eventually lose heavily. In contrast, Maxwell's gambles in stocks, bonds, gilts and currency would, for a time, earn impressive profits but, like any gamble, eventually, losses were inevitable.

Professional traders, recognizing that reality, carefully resist the temptation to load their wealth into one deal. Instead their risks are spread so that losses, while painful, can be contained. Over the years even Maxwell had operated in that manner, trading and juggling a wide range of deals in the belief that the losses would be offset by giant successes. But in early 1991, to reverse his plight, Maxwell decided that his salvation depended upon a succession of extraordinary risks.

Throughout his career, Maxwell's psychology could never be compared against normal standards. Accordingly, those who tried to understand and interpret Maxwell's motives and reasoning failed because Maxwell did not think or reason like others. Maxwell was not mad but simply unique, truly obsessed by the conviction that his abilities could overcome the natural consequences of any decision he cared to make.

For fifty years, Maxwell had yearned to be famous in America. That New York boasted thousands of similar hustlers was never a deterrent. Nor was he deterred by the certainty that if an American regulatory authority had passed upon him judgment similar to that of the DTI inspectors' his career would have been permanently terminated. His success since 1988 was irrefutable, and in March 1991 an opportunity arose which he could not resist. His target was the *New York Daily News,* owned by the Chicago Tribune Group, which for the previous two years had been racked by industrial strife.

The *Daily News* was suffering an illness which Maxwell believed he could cure: overmanning by a rebellious and corrupt labor force, crippling restrictive practices, uncontrolled expenditure, antiquated machinery and weak management. One of three tabloids in New York, the *News* in its heyday was the nation's largest daily with a circulation of two million. But, in March 1991, the employees who were members of trade unions had been on strike for nearly five months. Although published and sold throughout the dispute by non-unionists, the *News*'s circulation had collapsed to 300,000 and its advertising revenue had practically disappeared. According to the owners, the accumulated losses since 1980 were $250 million, half having been incurred in the previous fifteen months. Unable to cope with the violence and the daily losses of $700,000, the Tribune's management had threatened that unless the strike ended by March 14, the newspaper would be closed. But even closure would cost an estimated $100 million in pay-offs to the workers.

Such is the state of New York's politics that the Tribune's managers had received scant support from politicians. Governor Mario Cuomo spoke for many when he urged the strikers who were burning delivery trucks and intimidating non-strikers to: "Stay strong, you're fighting for all of us." Even the police had failed to protect the legitimate business.

Bestriding an irreconcilable dispute was honey to Maxwell. Not since he defeated the Mirror Group's unionists during the eighties had such an opportunity arisen and it was the same city where Murdoch had lost a fortune before abandoning his attempt to modernize another tabloid, the *Post.*

Over the previous years, Maxwell had stayed in contact with Jim Hoge, the *News*'s publisher and president. Either Maxwell or Sidney Gruson from Rothschild Inc. would discreetly telephone Hoge to ask if the paper was for sale. Regularly and politely Hoge would decline the offer.

Just before the strike, union leaders had phoned Maxwell to ask him to consider buying the paper. Maxwell had laughed when Hoge again declined the offer: "Only those who own the paper can sell it." That changed when the Tribune issued its ultimatum to the unions and looked for buyers. Maxwell declared his interest but told Hoge that he refused to become involved in a competition. He would only come in when the other bidders had left the arena. "He played it according to Hoyle, the whole way," commented Hoge, comparing Maxwell to the bridge master.

On March 5, the all-clear was given to Maxwell via Robert Pirie. At the same time, Hoge told the trade union leader George McDonald to telephone Maxwell in London. McDonald knew that it was a crucial call. Without any competing bidders, the newspaper's existence depended upon Maxwell's decision. Potentially, Maxwell's position was powerful and the unionist's was weak. Even McDonald, a seasoned fighter, was nervous when he made that nighttime call but his fears soon dissolved. Maxwell's response was surprisingly weak: "Do you think it's worth my while to come?" asked Maxwell.

"We'll give you concessions," answered McDonald. Ten minutes later, McDonald felt he had achieved more with Maxwell than in two years with the Tribune group. But he sensed that Maxwell was hooked. "You know," he smiled with a New York accent, "owning the *Daily News* is like a visiting card for sheiks, kings and queens. It opens the door for people and I guessed he wanted it that bad."

On March 6, Maxwell announced that he would negotiate with the unions to save the newspaper. Armed with the Tribune's offer of $60 million if he took over the liability no later than March 15, Maxwell imposed a tougher deadline. The unions were given just five days, until

March 11, to capitulate to his demands. While Maxwell was flying to New York, McDonald responded stridently and predictably: "Maxwell will not be granted 'management rights.' . . . We will of course consider any demands he makes." The hint of concessions was music to Maxwell.

True to form, when Maxwell met McDonald on March 7 on the tenth floor of Macmillan's Manhattan offices, their conversation was marked by Maxwell's particular charm and cordiality—precisely characteristic of Bill Keyes's epitaph: "He'll charm the birds off the trees and then shoot them." According to McDonald, "I called the unions in Britain and they'd told me what a scoundrel he was. They said that I had to get everything down on paper. And I did." Maxwell demanded that 800 of the 2,300 employees be dismissed and added, as recorded by the television cameras, "I'm not asking for 'management rights.' " McDonald noticed that sign of weakness. "When the cameras had gone he told me, 'I want the paper,' so I knew that we had a deal if I got all nine unions into line and gave a few concessions and redundancies which the Tribune was paying for."

The talks followed an established pattern. Each union was given its own office so that Maxwell could shuttle between the fiefs, playing upon old rivalries. "Maxwell was going backwards and forwards saying 'yes' and 'no' often to things he didn't understand," recalls Hoge who was also given a suite of offices and observed Maxwell's punishing schedule. "We told him what concessions he needed to make profits but I could see he would ignore us. He didn't analyze. He wanted the paper."

After the first day, McDonald emerged: "The progress made was terrific." By the second day, after a night's talks, Maxwell was reported to be demanding even bigger savings than the Tribune. "Fine," commented McDonald leaving the building with noticeable diminution of enthusiasm. The crisis hit at the weekend. Inevitably, Maxwell demanded exactly the opposite of his earlier promises. Namely the "management rights" which the unions had adamantly refused to accept from the Tribune. It was a good moment for Maxwell to play his ace. "I'm going back to London now," he told the startled negotiators on Saturday evening. It was his wife's birthday. His parting words were intentionally ominous: "I'm not so optimistic." To a passing journalist he added, "When I pass a belt, I can't resist hitting below it." This was vintage Maxwell.

Charles Wilson, the former editor of *The Times*, continued the negotiations. McDonald was not worried. On Sunday, the unions believed Maxwell's bluff had been called. "They rewrote what we didn't like," says McDonald who made the required phone call to London: "Come back. We're still talking." Maxwell returned and negotiated. "It was a walk-out that didn't work," thought Hoge bemused. Maxwell would, he realized, "do anything to get the paper. The unions knew that he wouldn't walk away."

One of the Tribune's bankers was less diplomatic: "He was so arrogant and unreceptive to advice. He could have got a much better deal if he had driven harder. He lost tens of millions." It was later admitted by the Tribune Group that Maxwell was paid an additional $7 million when the audit was completed.

Some of the blame is placed once again on Robert Pirie who, excitable in negotiations, failed to restrain Maxwell's own excitement which was fed by his regular walks through the Macmillan lobby. There, surrounded by eager journalists and waving television cameras, Maxwell became infected by his prominence and gradually lost the freedom to say the deal was off.

In Chicago, Charles Brumback, president of the Tribune Company, understood the difference between his own company and Maxwell's. "We were looking at a fifty-year investment. He was sixty-seven and wanted to enjoy a piece of his lifetime's ambition." It was a vanity purchase.

By March 13, Maxwell clinched a deal which supposedly saved $72 million a year on costs. "He's a tough negotiator who understands the problems fast," praised McDonald that night. Now he admits that "Maxwell could have got more concessions. We weren't hurt as much as we might have been." The immediate cost to Maxwell was paying $1 million every week for the newspaper's losses and to guarantee paying the remaining layoff costs which could amount to $50 million.

"We're in danger of soon making a profit," Maxwell smiled as he walked down to waiting newsmen in the lobby. His red bow-tie seemed incongruous below the plebeian blue *Daily News* baseball cap. In classic Maxwelliana, he announced a deal which was "historical and unprecedented." Watching from the side as Maxwell basked in the publicity, Hoge understood the new owner's motives.

"Cap'n Bob bites the Big Apple," screamed his newest acquisition. "Brit saves *Daily News*," blared a rival's headline as the Great Savior allowed himself to be sucked into a rapacious publicity machine which blitzed the white knight with memorable adulation. Maxwell, the star, was surrounded by genuine admirers.

Ten floors above, surrounded by a legion of lawyers, Hoge would spend two hours putting his signature on to more than a hundred documents concerning taxes, inventory, liabilities and the one for the sale itself. After Maxwell had signed a token document, Hoge suggested a party to introduce the new publisher to the city's powerbrokers.

New Yorkers are not easily impressed yet few remained unswayed by the Briton's style. Living on board the *Lady Ghislaine* which had hurriedly sailed across the Atlantic and was moored not far from the United Nations building, Maxwell was featured as he desired: the megatycoon, interrupted by phone calls, receiving a parade of shoeless guests in the splendid lounge bedecked with photographs of the publisher greeting world leaders. He was not averse to being compared with Randolph Hearst.

The return of the *Daily News* was a glorious moment for Maxwell. Every television and radio station beamed his voice across the city declaring his love for New York, just as on earlier occasions he had declared his love for Holland, Canada, Russia and Israel. Over the following six months, he pledged, he would remain as a "hands-on" publisher. Hoge duly appeared with the city's leaders who, shoeless, paid their respects to the new publisher. Maxwell's presence was felt and nowhere was it more prominent than on his own newspaper's front page where he solemnly declared himself to be "a peacemaker."

Once inside the *News*'s building, the returning strikers discovered that the jovialities were strictly confined to the streets outside. Telephone operators were cursed for failing to man the switchboard twenty-four hours a day. Others were cursed for failing to put down tools and greet their new employer. Among the first to be fired were 130 security men, spluttering bewilderment about who would protect the middle management from the ire of the returning strikers. Little did they realize that the managers were the next to be fired. Maxwell, they would now learn, understood only two relationships: that of customer and supplier, and master and slave. The peacemaker made his mark: "When I call, I require instant service." Somewhere from beyond a voice counseled, "When Maxwell shouts 'jump,' just ask, 'how high?' "

Meetings, orders, summonses and declarations poured forth from a man whose task was herculean. Restoring a newspaper's morale, motivation and style required energy and leadership which were Maxwell's forte. This was a rerun of the *Daily Mirror;* a challenge which only Maxwell was either sufficiently courageous or foolhardy to undertake. With time and money, he was sure of success.

In the first days the omens were not good. Important writers were still deserting; advertising remained poor; and the value of the Tribune's shares zoomed by $1 billion just for having paid Maxwell $60 million for getting rid of the problem. Only gradually would Maxwell realize that this was not Britain. That his ban on overtime would need to be revoked. That the replacements for the managers would need to be ex-union men. That unless he remained in New York, his revolution would dissipate. All that was ignored. For, as the representative of a new constituency, his real desire was recognition.

Throughout those negotiations, Maxwell knew that Hoge was invited at the end of that week to the celebrated "Gridiron" dinner at the Capital Hilton in Washington. The hosts were the nation's top satirists and their guests were the president, senators, judges, bankers and the Great and Good of America. Maxwell wanted to attend that dinner. Indeed, some in the Tribune camp believe that Maxwell's haste to sign the agreement with the unions was in order to qualify for the invitation.

The occasion required tails. Having just risked $100 million, which he did not have, Maxwell naturally showed no hesitation in requiring a courier to be dispatched by Concorde from London with his best suit.

Having enjoyed the most expensive meal of his life, Maxwell stayed in Washington overnight. The following day, Hoge was invited to a private lunch for about twenty-five where President Bush was guest of honor. The new owner of the *Daily News* ensured that he was seated next to the president. He gloried in the recognition. Never had he featured more in newspapers. The extravaganza bore the hallmarks of the Last Hurrah.

Intoxicated by the publicity, Maxwell returned to London where his fortunes reflected his dazzling New York success. Even in Maxwell's career, the frenzied succession of announcements as he unfolded his latest strategy was unprecedented. For Maxwell, turbulence was a palliative to his problems. The hyperactivity provoked relief while simultaneously producing a smokescreen to conceal the crisis from outsiders.

Yet paradoxically, it was at that moment that he needed an outsider to bestow credibility upon his empire. The first of his proclamations was therefore the most unexpected.

On March 24, Maxwell announced that he was resigning as chairman of MCC and would hand over the task to a "senior City figure" to whom his two sons would be answerable. The decision was presented as Maxwell's determination to pass on the inheritance while he expanded his newspaper interests, managing the Mirror Group, whose flotation was finally imminent, and saving the *Daily News*.

Five days later, the sale was announced of Pergamon for £440 million to his Dutch competitor, Elsevier. Since Pergamon was valued in MCC's "intangibles" at £260 million, its purchase price, Maxwell would thereafter quote that profit as proof that MCC's valuation was not exaggerated, although he would be asked to repay £45 million. "The proof of the pudding is in the eating," said Richardson to a skeptic. Richardson failed to disclose that Maxwell's sales, while ostensibly executed to repay MCC's loans, were in fact to keep the company afloat.

Selling a "core business" refueled speculation by critics who remained unaware that on March 27, Maxwell had pledged 26 million MCC shares to Goldman Sachs as a collateral for a £25 million loan. That loan was not disclosed and the circumstances seemed odd. The loan was made by Goldman Sachs in New York. Under American laws there was no need for disclosure. But under British laws, a loan by a foreign bank needed to be disclosed. So if the deal was arranged through New York to maintain secrecy it failed. When four months later Goldman in Britain recognized its mistake, the loan was immediately disclosed, but it added strength to a discreet demand first to the Stock Exchange and six months later to the Department of Trade and Industry from an irate shareholder that an inquiry be instituted into Goldman Sachs's manipulation of the market. Given the lax attitude by Britain's regulators which had always benefited Maxwell, neither the protest nor the subsequent inquiry had any effect upon Maxwell's operations. That disclosure revealed that for one brief moment, Goldman Sachs owned no less than 13 per cent of MCC worth £143 million and that £106 million of that amount was as collateral for the loans. The temporary secrecy served Maxwell well. His star seemed once again to be rising.

By the month's end, Michael Richardson had finally secured the agreement of Peter Walker, a fellow director in his brokerage house, to become chairman of MCC. Walker, who had recently announced his intention to retire from politics, was a self-made millionaire and former Conservative minister who had regained the City's respect despite his own controversial past. Having secured Walker's agreement, Richardson understandably had one more point to raise.

"Bob," purred Richardson, "Peter Walker has agreed to become chairman." Maxwell voiced delight. "But there is a slight embarrassment," continued Richardson. "Peter finds it difficult to accept the position while his own firm is still owed fees. As you know there have been repeated reminders. Could we remove that problem?"

Maxwell hit the phone. "Why are we still owing Smith New Court their fees?" he raged at a minion. "I've told you so often to pay." Richardson smiled at the familiar performance.

News of Walker's appointment was interpreted by some as the reason why MCC's share price began to rise. The *Sunday Telegraph*'s description of Maxwell as "one of Britain's most successful businessmen in the past decade . . . one of the most outstanding performers of the year" was precisely the puff which Maxwell desired. Some believed his repeated bluff, "I haven't got an appointment with my bankers until October 1992." They forgot his appointment with the bankers of his private companies. But in light of subsequent events, it is certain that by approving Walker's appointment, Maxwell could not at that stage have imagined that two months later he would begin plundering the pension funds. The more realistic interpretation is that Maxwell was genuinely tired, that he wanted to spend more time on the international stage, and that in March he did not believe that his financial position was fatal.

Yet ten days later, tucked inside a circular about the sale of Pergamon, was an admission that MCC's profits, for the first time, would fall because the sale of assets was proving difficult. Yet MCC's share price was still rising. Within two weeks the price shot up from 150p to 223p.

Although in real terms, the price was still only half the 1984 value, the sudden increase was not natural because Maxwell was the buyer. Between March and July 1991, Maxwell secretly bought about 10 per cent of MCC, mostly through Goldman Sachs and Shearson Lehman Brothers. Under British law, it is illegal for a company to *facilitate* the purchase of its own shares. It was not the first time Maxwell had secretly bought MCC's shares. The put option agreements with Goldman Sachs in 1990 indicated a support operation. But these latest purchases were on a different scale. The total amount which he spent after payments began in April was approximately £400 million. Half the money passed through his private companies and the remainder through over twenty off-shore nominee trusts. Among the sources of that money were loans which Maxwell drew from MCC and MGN and the sale of shares which belonged to the two public companies' pension funds.

In theory, the contracts made by the off-shore trusts—among them Corry Stiftung, Allandra, Bacando, Akim, Kiara, Servex, Yakosa Finanzierung and Jungo, which were based in the British Virgin Islands, Panama, Liechtenstein and Switzerland—were cloaked in sufficient secrecy for the brokers not to know the identity of the purchaser. But in practice, because payment for the shares was made by Maxwell's private companies, the truth was not hidden.

Among the first critical purchases was an order on April 26 by Yakosa Finanzierung, a Swiss-registered company, which bought from Goldman Sachs between 20 million and 25 million MCC shares worth £56 million. Payment for the shares was made by the Bishopsgate Investment Trust, a London company which was ultimately owned by Maxwell. There was correspondence between Sheinberg and a Swiss lawyer connected to Yakosa about the sale.

The subsequent issue would be whether Eric Sheinberg and Goldman Sachs's settlement staff knew that Yakosa and the other trusts were acting on Maxwell's behalf or were aware of BIT's owner.

In the first three weeks after Maxwell's death, before the frauds were discovered, spokesmen for Goldman Sachs denied that the brokers were the most aggressive buyers in the market—which was untrue—and then asserted that the brokers were unaware of the identity of the purchaser or purchasers since it was "too time consuming" to delve into the old contract notes.

But as the investigation got underway, some Goldman Sachs lawyers would claim that their officers had obtained a written undertaking from the off-shore trusts that they were not acting for Maxwell. That, however, suggested that either Sheinberg was immediately suspicious or, alternatively, that Goldman Sachs's officials were conspiring to prepare an excuse for the unforeseeable future.

The suggestion of "written undertakings" was soon replaced by suggestions that Goldman Sachs had received "oral assurances" that Maxwell was not the ultimate purchaser. The overt flaw in these excuses was the method of payment. Although many of the orders for the purchase of shares were coming from non-British trusts, some of the payments were being made by banks and companies in London that had known connections to Maxwell.

Other orders in April came from a small and unknown group of friends upon whose discretion Maxwell could rely: in particular, Ellis Freedman, an American lawyer, and Geoffre de la Pradelle, a French businessman. Both were directors of Swico, a Liechtenstein trust. The two directors bought about 10.01 million MCC shares, paying approximately £22 million.

Approximately 2 million additional shares were bought by Shelly Aboff, a New York accountant who had worked for Maxwell and Pergamon for nearly twenty years. Aboff had received £4.35 million from a London & Bishopsgate company and the Robert Maxwell Group to finance the purchase.

As the number of purchases increased, the money was routed from London in an increasingly complicated and frenetic fashion, occasionally to conceal the purpose and origin, but otherwise because Maxwell had ordered the shares but had failed to direct money to the proper bank account. In the melee to divert the money, some of the bank officials involved in the constant transfers must have become aware of the circumstances.

Maxwell was not managing the flow of money and constant borrowings alone. Indeed, often he did not take the lead, delegating the task to his son Kevin. As Ian Maxwell later confided, Kevin was "the person who did more than anybody to manage the borrowings." It was not a coincidence that the shares were bought just as the publication of the prospectus to float the Mirror Group was imminent.

Samuel Montagu was not Maxwell's first choice to mastermind the Mirror Group's flotation. At least two other City merchant banks had been approached and rejected. When Montagu accepted, Maxwell was grateful that someone was willing to take the estimated £4 million in fees. Heading the operation was Andrew Galloway, a director, who was appointed in December 1990—the past six months had not been easy.

Over the previous five years, Maxwell had regularly predicted the flotation only to announce a delay while he wrestled with the dilemma of whether he should allow teams of bankers and accountants to trawl through his private company, prying into the myriad of inter-company deals which had so usefully concealed his financial problems. But the debts of the Macmillan legacy had left no alternative. By the time the accountants from Coopers were allowed to see the books, Maxwell's staff had disentangled the private and public company deals and eliminated any traces of sweetheart deals.

Galloway and Montagu's deputy chief executive, Ian McIntosh, were summoned to Maxwell's office. McIntosh had met Maxwell twenty years earlier while an accountant at Coopers & Lybrand, so there could be no doubt about Maxwell's past methods of business. But like Sir Robert Clarke, a pillar of the City establishment and an old friend of Maxwell's who had agreed to become a non-executive director of MGN, McIntosh believed that Maxwell had been wronged by the DTI inspectors and that he had subsequently changed. "He's now prepared to take advice," McIntosh explained. McIntosh wanted to earn the fees for the flotation and compensate for the claims against his bank of £100 million in the wake of the collapse of the £1 billion British and Commonwealth Group. The normal long wait ensued before the two men were admitted. The bankers' timetable was not helped by their client's first words delivered in his uniquely sonorous tone: "The company is worth £1 billion." It was not. Both the recession and the "Max Factor" put its value at half that amount. Settling the disagreement would be acrimonious and time consuming. There were constant phone calls, day and night, as the owner tried to persuade the bankers to risk a higher price than they advised. To the bankers' advantage was Maxwell's financial plight. "Our biggest problem, Bob," said one of the more courageous of the team, "is you."

British fund managers, explained the banker, guided by their anti-Maxwell sentiment, would resist the offer's natural attractions: "They didn't like Maxwell retaining the majority of shares. And then they didn't like seeing how much of their money he would keep." Eventually Maxwell was bound to accept the banker's argument.

It fell to Tony Carlisle of Dewe Rogerson, the communications advisers, and Terry Connor, of the brokers Smith New Court, to overcome the "Max Factor." Their program was brief. Maxwell toured six Scottish institutions in one day and was presented to potential London investors at three dinners in Claridges. On one occasion, Maxwell appeared at the dinner by satellite from New York. Asked by one guest about his debt, the tycoon snarled, "I'm not answering stupid questions like that," and ordered the satellite to be disconnected.

"They weren't terribly successful," admits one of the advisers. Many of the conversations followed a similar pattern:

"Don't you think, Mr. Maxwell, that you've invested too much in the printing presses?"

"What the hell do you know about printing?" the master salesman asked the fund manager. Maxwell could no longer tolerate a challenge, even from a customer. But he remained confident because the fund managers, "men who are paid to have good manners," concealed their distrust.

Publicly Maxwell spoke about "giving Mirror Group workers a chance to share in the profits" but he knew it was exaggerated sales talk. In an interview with the *Sunday Times,* on April 14, 1991, repeated to analysts, Maxwell claimed that the *Mirror*'s Holborn headquarters, worth £100 million, would be included in the sale. It was untrue and sparked an unusual proliferation of newspaper comment about his "secrecy, deviousness and refusal to conform to expected behavior."

One aspect of the *Mirror* launch would remain unrevealed until four months after the flotation. Under the heading "Key information," the bankers had mentioned in the prospectus that the Mirror Group was owned by Robert Maxwell Holdings, "whose ultimate parent is Headington Investment." Headington was a company suitably registered in Britain but it was not the ultimate parent. The "ultimate" economic owner, as set out in the prospectus, was the Liechtenstein Trust which allegedly held "non-voting" shares in Headington. The bankers were suggesting that Maxwell controlled the votes of Headington, but since the bankers refused to reveal whether they had seen the Liechtenstein Trust deed, there remained an element of doubt. Moreover, it was later revealed that in between Headington Investments and the Liechtenstein Trust was yet another trust called the InterEuropean Trust which was registered in Gibraltar.

The bankers would tell inquirers that the Gibraltar link was known but not mentioned because "as long as Maxwell controlled Headington, it wasn't relevant." Everyone not employed by the bank in the flotation "could not recall" when the Gibraltar connection became apparent. Others believed it was omitted because it would seem suspicious. "We were not sorry that we did not buy the shares," says one fund manager.

One aspect of the prospectus which did not arouse public controversy at the time was the section describing the *Mirror*'s pension fund. In 1984, when Maxwell bought the *Mirror,* he had realized the potential value of the pension fund because it possessed more cash than was legally required. Accordingly, Maxwell had realized that as an employer, he would be excused paying contributions for some time, allowing the use of that money for other purposes. Another surplus of £149.3 million had also, according to the 1991 prospectus, built up by 1990, when the *Mirror*'s pension fund was worth £431 million. How that surplus arose is still not clear, because it depended upon the valuations of the investments bought by the fund managers. The prospectus's assessment of the pension fund's surplus was dated 1990 and not 1991—a significance which escaped public mention both at the time of the flotation and until after Maxwell's death. Both Kevin and his father had successfully persuaded Peter Walsh at Coopers & Lybrand that the fund's audit, due in April 1991, should be postponed until December on the grounds that an audit would interfere with arrangements for the flotation. Walsh also accepted that a December audit would bring the Mirror Group's financial year in line with the remainder of the group. Andrew Galloway, banker at Samuel Montagu, admits that he was not suspicious: "It didn't interest me frankly. I accepted what Coopers told me."

In previous months, lawyers and representatives of the 12,400-strong Association of *Mirror* Pensioners had been complaining to the pension fund's manager and its lawyers about discrepancies in the fund's management and especially about the trustee's refusal since 1985, despite the surplus in the fund, to increase the pensions.

The lawyer representing the Association of *Mirror* Pensioners was Giles Orton, a calm, thirty-two-year-old based in Derby, north England. Initially, Orton's complaints had been addressed to Trevor Cook, the manager of the pension fund who worked completely under Maxwell's influence. As Orton's complaints became more specific, and the threat of legal action increased, Maxwell withdrew responsibility for dealing with the issue from Cook and entrusted it to Ian Pittaway, a lawyer specializing in pensions, who was given verbal instructions to delay any reply and then refuse to divulge any information regardless of the pensioners' entitlement under the law. Pittaway's aggressive defense of Maxwell's management went beyond his professional duties, while his procrastination continued even in the days after Maxwell's death.

The *Mirror* pensioners had not realized until after the *Mirror* prospectus was published that Maxwell had removed all but one of the trade unionists from the board of trustees of the common investment fund. Their replacements were Kevin and Ian Maxwell. Accordingly, there were, in Orton's view, insufficient independent fund managers to balance Maxwell's personal and dominant control over the fund.

The pensioners were also concerned that 65 per cent of the pension fund had been taken over by a Maxwell company, Bishopsgate Investment Management Limited (BIM), which by November 1991 was officially managing £727 million of pension funds belonging to the Mirror Group and MCC. Together, the fund contained the life savings of 23,400 employees. BIM was ostensibly controlled by a Liechtenstein trust but was, in fact, owned by Maxwell.

A further 20 per cent of the pension fund was partly managed by another Maxwell-owned company. In their wisdom, the Maxwells had decided that about 10 per cent of the pension fund should be invested in Maxwell-owned companies, principally MCC. Forty per cent of the investments, it would later be discovered, were invested outside of Britain, which was an unusually high proportion. Even more unusual was the fund's investment in Israeli companies, which it was thought Maxwell had bought in his own name; in a French media conglomerate which Maxwell had targeted for a take-over bid; and in property which was bought from Maxwell personally without an independent valuation.

The pensioners' ability to complain was restricted because Maxwell had deliberately restricted the amount of information available about the fund's management. Although their complaints increased after the publication of the flotation prospectus for the *Mirror* revealed what they suspected was questionable management, Pittaway, who handled their protests, could quite justifiably reply that their complaints were "without substance."

But even on the limited knowledge available, Orton believed that the pension funds were at risk and he began lobbying Maxwell, as chairman of the trustees, for reassurance that the funds were not endangered. Simultaneously, he wrote to IMRO, the government's watchdog, alerting the regulators to his concern. Maxwell's response, received in mid-October, was intended to be reassuring. It was based on the advice of his lawyer Ian Pittaway, who had investigated the complaints and decided that "they were all unfounded." Pittaway's letter to Orton outlined the success and security of the fund's investments and condemned Orton's "very serious allegations" as "misleading."

IMRO seemingly also endorsed Maxwell's assurances. Under the complacent British laws governing pension-fund investments, the trustees were only required to "behave as ordinary men of business" investing the money with due prudence across a range of safe investments. In practice, as Maxwell knew, the exercise of his discretion was unchallengeable. Orton's complaints were effectively ignored while Maxwell, with the assistance of many newspapers, launched a campaign of self-congratulation about his achievements. Pittaway would subsequently comment, "I have no regrets about the advice I gave or my actions."

Maxwell's flourishes about transforming the unprofitable newspaper company and multiplying his £90 million purchase price five-fold within seven years were true. He had performed similar miracles upon the British Printing Corporation and Pergamon. Less flattering was the 19 per cent decline in the *Mirror*'s circulation since 1984 compared to the *Sun*'s 10 per cent.

Many continued to blame the owner's interference in the newspaper for that decline. In February 1990, Roy Greenslade, a senior editor at the *Sunday Times,* was appointed editor of the *Daily Mirror.* Like so many, Greenslade accepted Maxwell's offer with the conviction that, unlike his predecessors, he would be able to withstand the owner's demands. Reality arrived swiftly when, as usual, Maxwell inquired about Greenslade's intentions: "It was the day that the Russians invaded Lithuania. He rang from his yacht. I explained that there were some horrific pictures from Vilnius.

" 'So what?' he asked.

" 'Well, Bob, what appears to be happening is a virtual invasion of the country.' "

Before Greenslade could complete his sentence, Maxwell interrupted, "We must not abandon Gorbachev. I will decide."

"But news is news, Bob."

"You're talking nonsense. Don't you realize that Gorbachev wouldn't do anything without ringing me first?"

Greenslade credits himself with steadfastly refusing to publish fanciful stories supplied by Maxwell, such as his prediction that the Gulf war would end within forty-eight hours, whereas in fact it would continue for weeks; and his rejection of Maxwell's request not to mention the jailing of Gerald Ronson, a personal friend. Like most proprietors, Maxwell expected an editor to curtsy to his vanity and power. Editorial interference at the *Mirror* was not unusual. Greenslade's error, having accepted Maxwell's employment, was in failing to curb his professional pride.

Two months before the flotation, Greenslade joined the legions of Maxwell's "Field Marshals" and was sacked like a thunderclap for giving a pessimistic interview to the *UK Press Gazette,* a trade magazine. "It didn't help us," admits one of the flotation team. "We were impressed by Greenslade and his dismissal confirmed the suspicions about Maxwell among fund managers."

Unrepentant, Maxwell relished the prospect of launching the sale. Those who crammed into the *Mirror*'s headquarters on April 17 detected only glee as the proprietor presented his latest success of rising sales and zooming profits. The first question soured the occasion.

How, asked a young reporter, did Maxwell square his promises about the *Mirror* with the DTI Inspectors' damning conclusions in 1971 about his fitness to manage a public company? Maxwell could not disguise the pain. Twenty years had passed and he was still haunted by that calumny. "The bitchiness of British journalists continues," complained Maxwell, whose employees in the floors above were at that moment writing editorials and stories which would cause other individuals embarrassment and misery. "This is a country which hates success," continued Maxwell, forgetting that the sale of Mirror Group shares was forced by his own failure to manage MCC properly.

"I felt sick as a parrot," says one of those advisers, who had been sitting beside Maxwell, whose frozen, pained face could be seen on television that night. "A cheap shot," moaned an adviser. "It ruined the launch. I thought that was all forgotten, although I think it caused sympathy for him." No one mentioned the disaster after the conference had limped to its early conclusion. More significantly, none of the bankers or brokers employed by Maxwell believed the journalist's observations to be relevant.

The victim's furor was not concealed. Such open skepticism would have been unimaginable twelve months earlier and his rage intensified when Derek Terrington, a City analyst who had critically stalked Maxwell for some years, issued a circular entitled, "Can't Recommend A Purchase" because the shares were overpriced. "CRAP" provoked a succession of complaints and threats by Maxwell. Terrington's employer, Phillips and Drew, annoyed that its analyst was damaging the opportunity to recruit more corporate clients, issued a reprimand. Terrington's judgment had provoked Maxwell to utter an admission of near defeat: "It's the last straw."

"We've got difficulties," sighed a broker. Few major British institutions or major investors were prepared to buy the *Mirror*'s shares. Unusually, the refusal by the Prudential and Mercury Asset Management was publicized. Anxious to raise more money, Maxwell argued that the shares should be sold at better terms. The bankers refused. The crisis was solved in New York.

In New York it was so different. Bolstered by his image as savior of the *Daily News,* Maxwell was a king. John Gutfreund, the legendary emperor of Salomon Brothers, assured Maxwell, a fellow gambler with a high profile, of both respect and support. Where Samuel Montagu had barely succeeded in getting the flotation underwritten and Smith New Court had failed outright to attract sufficient interest, Salomon delivered buyers. Maxwell contrived a clamor of interest which generated rumors in London that British fund managers were scrambling for shares in New York. The publicists were working overtime, generating welcome comment in British newspapers about oversubscription. "Even a one-eyed Albanian can work out there is going to be a premium to the issue price," promised Maxwell in anticipation of a hefty profit for his admirers.

On May 17, the shares were launched at 125p. Just before 2:30 p.m. Maxwell arrived at Smith New Court to watch the trade begin. Standing with Richardson behind the dealers' screens he watched as the sellers outnumbered the buyers and the price fell: "He was surprised. He didn't believe there would be sellers. I don't think he understood the 'Max Factor.' He had the ability to blank that out of his mind." Smith's client, who had not been offered any champagne, wandered off to make phone calls.

Salomon Brothers later admitted losses of £5 million on the sale. Some suspected that Maxwell had an arrangement to buy any surplus shares privately. Two weeks later, on May 28, Maxwell quietly mortgaged 13 million Mirror Group shares to Midland Bank in return for more loans.

All those problems were forgotten on May 18, the night after the flotation. Traditionally, every institution involved in those money-making exercises hosts a lavish celebration to toast itself and discreetly seek more work. Maxwell, who hosted many generous champagne parties during his life, might well have thought, while dancing in the marquee at his home in Oxford, that once again his problems had been overcome. An outsider maybe, but equally a survivor. There would always be battles, but as he approached his sixty-eighth birthday, they seemed quite manageable. MCC would be safe under Peter Walker and Kevin. More companies would have to be sold off but that was not serious. For himself, he would indulge in his expanding newspaper empire, especially in New York where the *Daily News*'s losses were already reduced, albeit continuing at about $30 million a year but expected to be zero by Christmas. In three weeks, the *Daily News* would sponsor New York's tickertape parade to welcome home those who had fought in the Gulf. He would be the host standing alongside the mayor and General Norman Schwarzkopf as guest of honor. He had also struck an important posture among New York's Jewish community. Edgar Bronfman, president of the World Jewish Congress, hosted a dinner for Maxwell. Maxwell's after-dinner speech, concentrating upon his virtues and business achievements, was not well received. Bronfman had secured the Briton's promise of donating funds for the community. Naturally, it was not fulfilled.

But first he needed to settle MCC's annual accounts and the overriding issue was familiar. He wanted to present glowing results. As before, one snag was overwhelming. Nearly all the publishing profits had been wiped out by interest payments. Only £13 million remained as profits from publishing. But by the time he had finished, the accounts showed that MCC had earned pre-tax profits of £145.5 million. Half of those profits were apparently earned from currency speculation and most of the remainder from sales of the company itself. Other accountants, using other standards, would suggest that MCC earned at best a net profit of £6.3 million or, at worst, an actual loss of £6.35 million. Subsequent investigation would reveal that all the profits ascribed to property, foreign-exchange dealings and one-off sales were suspect. Coopers & Lybrand nevertheless approved MCC's interpretation. Similarly, Coopers approved the valuation of MCC's intangibles at £2.41 billion and its assets at £2.81 billion.

In May, the market price of MCC, according to the share price, was £1.2 billion. But the real value, after deducting debts, was barely £400 million. Others suggested that MCC was worth minus £1.3 billion. But on one fact all interpretations agreed: Maxwell's presence was vital to securing the continuation of the collateral on the loans. His presence alone, charming the bankers and brokers, juggling their pressing demands for repayment, maintained the impression of calm. Only he understood all the parts of the whole and how to keep the rickety edifice together. Maxwell understood the "Max Factor" to imply that he was the glue that kept the company from disintegration. Yet among his undisclosed ploys was to pledge shares owned by the Mirror Group pension fund as collateral for his loans. Maxwell's motives when he began selling assets belonging to the £765 million pension fund were not, in his mind, for personal enrichment. Nor was he minded to believe that his secret disposals would be more than a temporary measure. Initially it was not premeditated theft. Deluded by self-assessment of his abilities, Maxwell reasoned that he was suffering a short-term liquidity problem which would be rectified when his deals, gambles and sales restored his riches.

But while in the short term it could be argued that Maxwell was seeking temporary relief, as the weeks progressed and the sales continued, Maxwell knew that it was no longer a straightforward intercompany loan. He was seeking to avoid the collapse in the price of MCC shares which would eradicate his personal fortune. Once repayments became impossible because of the size of the debt, he had become too singlemindedly immersed in the task of survival to consider the criminality of his actions. The ends justified the means.

Dishonesty did not trouble Maxwell. Throughout his life, he had ignored the customary norms of morality. Indeed, his fortune had been constructed, lost and rebuilt by deliberately trespassing, outwitting and outrunning his opponents regardless of any infringement of laws. According to the ethics he had learned as a child, the goal was survival and profit, and the consequences to the losers were irrelevant.

Yet as he began a pattern which would shortly deprive widows, orphans and decent workers of their lives' savings, Maxwell would have been appalled if told that another had perpetuated that crime on innocents. A signed editorial in the *Daily Mirror* would certainly have demanded the severest punishment for the culprit. The same man who delivered assistance to the starving of Africa and AIDS sufferers and cried for the victims of the Holocaust was blind to the implications of his own behavior. Like so many who are fundamentally dishonest, his charity to others could at best be evidence of a schizoid personality or, at worst, coolly calculated mitigation money. In any case, in May 1991, Maxwell's need for money was so rapacious that the option of repayment had disappeared.

Maxwell needed £1 billion to pay the interest on his secret debts, to pay for his purchase of MCC's shares, and to pay for his failed gambles on the price of stocks, gilts and currency. The so-called "ring fence" which the bankers at Samuel Montagu claimed had been constructed around the *Mirror*'s funds specifically to protect against Maxwell had been effortlessly penetrated.

Maxwell's route over the ring fence was quite simple and identical to his attempted fraud in the 1968 Pergamon saga. There were a succession of deals between apparently independent companies, all of whom shared a common chairman, namely Robert Maxwell. Considering Maxwell's previous pattern of operations, the arrangements were not unusual. Maxwell's trading between the public and private companies on his own terms was customary, as was the movement of funds from public to private companies and vice versa. No director is known to have protested.

The diversion of the pension funds began in May, and it is pertinent that his initial moves were quite legal. The passage of the pension funds was simple. A board meeting of the Mirror Group pension fund in 1989 had authorized the chairman of the fund, namely Robert Maxwell, to transfer management of an unlimited amount of pension funds to Bishopsgate Investment Management, which was described as an expert in the management of stock and equities. By 1991 nearly 65 per cent of the funds had been handed over to BIM.

BIM was chaired by Maxwell, and its other directors were Ian and Kevin Maxwell, Trevor Çook, manager of the Mirror Group Pension scheme, and Ronald Woods, one of Maxwell's tax experts.

BIM's sixth director was Lawrence Trachtenberg, an American computer expert who had lectured briefly at the London School of Economics and whom Maxwell had met in 1987. The judgment about Trachtenberg is mixed. While Maxwell believed him to be a genius, others considered that he was simply a fine self-promoter who eventually became nothing more than Robert and Kevin Maxwell's bagman.

When they met, Trachtenberg was managing an investment consultancy company called Global Analysis Systems (GAS 100) with Andrew Smith, "a smooth New York computer jock" who had also attended the London School of Economics. Smith had masterminded a computer system which, in theory, monitored all the international economies and markets to prematurely identify, before mere mortals, the perfect investment opportunities.

Trachtenberg and Smith had a third partner, the British peer Lord Donoughue. Formerly known as Bernard Donoughue, he was a socialist academic who had served as a policy adviser in the 1970s to Harold Wilson, the Labour prime minister. In the 1980s, Donoughue had switched ideologies and pledged himself to serve capitalism and Maxwell.

In 1988, Maxwell's private company, Headington Investments, bought a 60 per cent stake in GAS, which was then renamed London & Bishopsgate International Investment Inc. (LBII). Smith, who would later insist that he was "squeaky clean," as well as "disturbed and pissed off" that anyone should question his probity when he was so closely involved with both Trachtenberg and Maxwell, was vice chairman of LBII, with connections to several of the very different "Bishopsgate" companies.

The similarity of the "Bishopsgate" company names, especially with the company managing the *Mirror* pension fund, Bishopsgate Investment Management (BIM), was not accidental. Maxwell's intention was to confuse outsiders, especially since all the companies bearing the name "Bishopsgate" played very different roles in the developing saga. For example, there was another company called London & Bishopsgate International NV, which was a mutual fund registered in the Dutch Antilles which handled foreign-exchange dealings, and London & Bishopsgate Traders. More important, there was another company called London and Bishopsgate International Investment Management (LBIIM), through which Maxwell would illegally dispose the pension funds.

Initially, Smith and Trachtenberg's LBII managed £20 million on behalf of Maxwell. By 1990, the amount had increased to £50 million. By the time of Maxwell's death, LBII was managing funds worth nearly $500 million, some of which had come originally from Bishopsgate Investment Management, the official managers of the pension fund. The sequence of events started in early 1991.

During spring 1991, three of BIM's directors signed several transfers allowing a portfolio of shares belonging to the pension fund, and worth £430 million, to be "loaned" to two private companies owned by Maxwell: namely, the Robert Maxwell Group and Headington Investments. The signatories were Robert, Kevin and Ian Maxwell. This was not illegal nor in theory unusual. "Stock lending" is a normal commercial practice but on the strict condition that the lender receives some collateral or a guarantee for that loan and that it is intended to last for a short period. Those shares were then loaned to L&B International Investment Management (L&BIIM), whose directors were Trachtenberg and Donoughue.

In late June 1991, Maxwell ordered Trachtenberg to transfer all the share certificates held by L&BIIM in their Shoe Lane office, which would be placed in his own private safe in nearby Maxwell House. Initially, Maxwell used those shares as collateral to raise loans.

At the end of June, as his need for money grew, he began selling those shares, which belonged to the pension fund. In some instances the banks, who believed that their original loan was secured against the shares, were not told.

Curiously, selling the shares was not illegal if the proceeds were returned to the pension fund, but that did not happen. Instead, Maxwell used the money to pay off his personal debts. Through L&BIIM, he had stolen £426 million from the pension fund.

Simultaneously, he also sold whatever collateral the two private companies, the Robert Maxwell Group and Headington Investments, had given to the Mirror Group pension fund for borrowing the shares.

One recipient of the money were Shearson Lehman nominee accounts which on June 26 bought 19.6 million MCC shares and two days later bought an additional 6.48 million MCC shares. At that stage Maxwell began a second circle: He pledged the MCC shares that he had bought using "stolen" money as collateral for additional loans from banks. He then used that "new" money to buy more MCC shares or to subsidize his loss-making companies. The circle was self-perpetuating so long as the price of MCC's shares remained stable.

Donoughue resigned from London & Bishopsgate in July 1991. He would subsequently claim that he had only stayed to ensure that the stock lending ceased, but others claim that he had stayed only to negotiate a high pay-off from Maxwell. In either version, he failed to stop the stock lending.

Bankers would later complain that the disappearance of the money was a "mystery," "extremely complicated" and a "construct which could only have been understood by a man with a brain like Mr. Maxwell's—the brain of an ex-army intelligence officer." In fact, Maxwell's theft was an extremely simple scheme, and the failure of bankers, lawyers and the fund managers to detect it was more a reflection on their intelligence than Maxwell's. Similarly culpable were all the directors of Maxwell's two public companies.

On July 4, the full board of MCC directors met to formally approve the company's annual accounts for 1991. By any measure the directors should have known that the financial outlook was precarious and that their options were narrowing. If all the directors had not been subservient to the Maxwells, they could have, at that moment, prevented the worst of the frauds from occurring. Instead, they performed as Maxwell expected.

Over the previous weeks, Basil Brookes, MCC's young finance director, had been diligently following his predecessor's pattern for completing the accounts. He recalls markedly few disagreements between himself and the two Maxwells about the treatment of profits. On one issue, however, Brookes was advised by Coopers to present a memorandum to the board.

The previous year, MCC had sold properties to Corry Stiftung and Hesto, both Liechtenstein trusts, but the payments were to come in stages. Neil Taberner, the auditor from Coopers, had agreed to Maxwell's request that MCC claim in 1990 and 1991 the total profits from the sales even though the payments would be staggered until 1997. Maxwell's purpose, and the subsequent effect, was to boost MCC's profits and allow Maxwell to proclaim to the public "record profits" from property deals—even though the money hadn't yet been received.

Another example was in 1990 when Maxwell claimed profits from the sale of his interest in the Paris "Arche," President Mitterrand's prestigious building, of £45 million. The buyer was Hesto, which agreed to pay £21.7 million in 1990 and £23.3 million in 1991.

Significantly, all those property deals were concluded in March, just before the end of the financial year. To the suspicious it might seem that the "profits" had opportunely been earned just in time to permit the chairman to claim "record profits."

But MCC's directors seemingly weren't suspicious. Indeed, they even took part in what investigators would later characterize as "a farce."

Basil Brookes had been told by Taberner of Coopers that, for legal reasons, it was necessary for MCC's directors to confirm that none of them had any financial interest in the property deals.

Letters were produced from lawyers representing the two Liechtenstein trusts, Corry Stiftung and Hesto, and from two other companies, Bantry Bay and Leparra, based in the Virgin Islands who were also involved in "profitable" property deals, categorically stating that there was no relationship between the trusts and the Maxwells.

The lawyer who had inquired into the status of the two Liechtenstein trusts was David Vogel of Titmus, Sainer & Webb. According to Peter Laister, Vogel enjoyed "a close professional relationship with Maxwell." Many lawyers were involved in Maxwell's affairs, but Vogel was, says Laister, "more in evidence than the others." Vogel prepared the letters from the two Liechtenstein trusts which stated that they had no relationship with Maxwell or his family. "We had no reason to disbelieve those letters," comments Laister, a non-executive director. "After all, Titmus had produced the same letters before and neither the directors nor Taberner of Coopers had questioned them." Laister adds, "Perhaps we were all over-innocent but it was all too blatant to be suspicious at that time. We relied on Vogel and Taberner." Among the other "innocents" was Jean-Pierre Anselmini, the deputy chairman, who rarely spoke.

At the board meeting on July 4, the letters were produced and each director present was formally asked whether he had a personal interest in the transactions which in 1991 would contribute £23 million to MCC's profits, an important amount considering that MCC's publishing profits were so low. Brookes watched as both Robert and Kevin Maxwell with "dead pan, poker faces" denied any connection with Corry, Hesto and the other trusts.

Brookes says he too was not suspicious. Identical procedures had been followed by his predecessor, Reg Mogg, and neither Coopers nor the other directors had ever commented upon the coincidence of a Liechtenstein trust having a relationship with the Maxwell family. Accordingly, recorded in the formal minutes was that the directors were not aware of any connection between the group, its directors, and the trusts. Yet the registered addresses in Liechtenstein of both Hesto and Corry Stiftung were identical to Maxwell's family trusts. Brookes and Laister say that they did not note the coincidence. Significantly, Lord Rippon, another MCC non-executive director, was not present.

Lord Rippon, a minister in the Conservative government of 1970–73, was directly connected to the Leparra trust because he was chairman of a small merchant bank, Robert Fraser, which was involved in property deals with the Maxwells totalling £102 million. Investigators would later pinpoint those property deals as significant in Maxwell's frauds.

Similarly at that same board meeting Brookes did not enquire about £80.7 million in profits from foreign exchange deals which MCC was announcing. That amount was in stark contrast to £23.4 million which MCC earned from publishing. Although Brookes was the company's finance director, he possessed neither knowledge nor control of how those profits were earned or calculated. "I was just given them by Albert Fuller, the Treasurer," explained Brookes. Unusual in a public company, Fuller, who worked both for the private and the public companies, reported directly to Maxwell, bypassing Brookes, who never complained which naturally satisfied Maxwell. Indeed, none of the directors ever commented on Maxwell's strange relationships and deals. On some accounts, the directors were supine, which was precisely their attraction to Maxwell.

In fact, during the previous year Maxwell had speculated on £750 million in currency deals. He had earned a staggering £37 million profit in just three deals. For the 1991 annual accounts, his gambles had seemingly saved MCC and his reputation.

Once the board had approved the accounts, Brookes, relieved that the annual chore was completed, returned to his normal duties. But on July 5, glancing through the company's current bank accounts, he was suddenly struck by huge withdrawals of money by Robert Maxwell from the MCC account. It soon became apparent that over the previous months, the chairman had been transferring millions of pounds from the publicly owned MCC into his private companies. These "inter-company loans" were arranged by Maxwell quite secretly. At the end of May, Maxwell had taken £180 million, but by early July the amount had risen to £276 million and would actually peak on one day at £305 million. In effect Maxwell was using the MCC's money for his private purposes, although his private companies were paying normal interest rates.

In principle, Brookes was not surprised by Maxwell's use of MCC's funds because over previous years, the passage of money between the public and private companies had become quite normal. On rare oc-casions in the past, the public companies had even been indebted to the private companies. But in early July, the young finance director was alarmed by the sheer size and substantial increase of the outstanding debt. He made an appointment to see both Maxwells.

Their reaction was friendly. "Don't worry, Basil," said Maxwell. "It's temporary." Within days, as Brookes scrutinized the bank accounts, he saw "money come slushing in" but became alarmed when huge sums, including one payment of £75 million, went out. Brookes's concern grew: "I couldn't understand where the money was coming from." It was the first income from the pension fund sales.

On the morning of July 8, Brookes walked into Kevin's office to raise the issue: Where was Maxwell finding the money to repay the loans? Kevin's reply was unexpected: "I'm under instructions from Bob not to talk about it." Brookes now sought a meeting with Maxwell but for the first time discovered that the chairman made himself unreachable. Maxwell's unavailability continued for two weeks, and in the mean time, huge amounts of unsourced money were going through the ac-counts. Among the sources of money during those critical weeks of

July was Kevin's "manipulation deals" totalling no less than £660 million. In jargon, he was "cross firing."

Throughout that month, Kevin was in effect selling currency to banks but delaying delivery of the money to obtain interest-free loans.

For example, he would begin the day by asking Goldman Sachs whether it would like to buy from him $10 million and deliver the equivalent in sterling. The bank agreed and within hours deposited the proper amount in a Maxwell account. But at the end of the day the bank had not received the $10 million from Kevin. Anxious phone calls would be made to Kevin who feigned forgetfulness, confusion, or offered apologies. Kevin's purpose was to delay delivery because the bank's deposit had become an interest-free loan.

By the time the $10 million was finally delivered to the original bank, Kevin had concluded a succession of similar deals with other banks, constantly switching and apologizing and being unavailable just to delay completion. By that method, during July, Kevin successfully "borrowed" £105 million—interest free.

In early August, the banks, tiring of his games, called a halt. By then Maxwell's new strategy had begun to collapse.

On July 15, Peter Walker announced that he would not be taking over Maxwell's chairmanship of MCC. In any other context, Walker's reasons would have seemed sensible. He explained that, after examination, it was clear that MCC, which he had told Richardson was a "terrific company," had become an American company. He recommended that it should be demerged and run from New York, but for personal reasons he did not want to leave Britain. Skeptics remained unconvinced.

As he pondered Walker's resignation and announced that he would continue as chairman while searching in New York for a bank that would mastermind the American flotation of MCC, Maxwell realized for the first time the dangers ahead.

Both MCC's and Mirror Group's share prices had begun falling. Since the flotation of the Mirror Group in May, the price of MCC shares had slipped from its peak of 241p and was heading toward 141p. Mirror Group shares were falling from 125p toward 80p. The headlines spoke of "Maxwell's nightmare" but no outsider knew the full details. As MCC's price fell, Maxwell was secretly buying more shares in the belief that the basic rule of market forces would compel the price to rise because of demand. But here Maxwell revealed a fundamental misunderstanding. The dealers were "roasting a Teddy." Knowing that there was no real demand for MCC shares, the dealers were selling shares which they did not possess—in technical jargon, "selling short." Then the dealers marked MCC's price *down,* hoping that as the price fell, other stockholders, fearing further losses, would sell their MCC shares. The dealers could then buy those shares to fulfill their original sale. In the meantime Maxwell, seeing MCC's price fall, began buying again to support the price, and the downward process continued. Dealers on the London market, sipping champagne as they profited from the antics of an amateur, could happily reflect on the traditional ditties quoted over past years in such identical circumstances:

"A deal without cash,
is like love without pash."

Or

"He who sells that which isn't his'ems
and can't deliver, goes to pris'ems."

Maxwell's ploy could only have worked if he had bought literally all of MCC's shares, forcing the market dealers to offer sky-high prices to fulfill their contracts. "Bob always thought he was bigger than the City," lamented Johnny Bevan, one of Maxwell's brokers. "But he never understood that they could be cleverer than him."

The cost of the share-support operation was about £400 million. In addition, during 1991 Maxwell would pay £80 million to the *New York Daily News* and *The European;* £150 million to the private companies; pay the interest on the private company debts; and pay the losses on speculative foreign-exchange gambles. (At the end of 1991, Goldman Sachs would still be owed $29 million and Salomon Brothers, $23.7 million.) Maxwell could only find that money and more by selling more of the pension fund's assets.

On July 26, wrestling with private debts which were estimated as high as £1 billion, Maxwell mortgaged another 27 million Mirror Group shares to Midland Bank, bringing the estimated total to 40 million. He also turned to Goldman Sachs, which had been holding 26.3 million MCC shares as collateral (whose value had temporarily risen), and on August 5 borrowed a further £20 million which was secured by 40 million Mirror Group shares as collateral. Goldman had lent Maxwell about £100 million. Many other loans were arranged, including one to finance a currency gamble with Citibank, America's leading bank. As always, the loan was secured against MCC shares. It was a sign of desperation.

Having wasted millions on interest charges and on his lifestyle, Maxwell was playing the markets to make up the shortfall. By then he had spent about £150 million to buy MCC shares. If he failed, the consequences were unthinkable.

One loan, however, remained undisclosed. Both public companies had "lent" Maxwell's private companies an estimated £300 million. At that moment, Brookes says that he became "very concerned" about Maxwell's increasing use of MCC's money. Appointed by Maxwell despite his relative inexperience and because Maxwell considered him pliable, Brookes was undoubtedly influenced by that week's newspaper headlines. The *Sunday Times* was explicit: "Doubts grow over Maxwell" was the headline in the influential business section over an account which mentioned that Maxwell had issued writs alleging defamation against other newspapers that had questioned his finances and reported that Walker's resignation indicated that MCC was possibly "heading toward the rocks."

Brookes was plainly scared that he might be associated with a crash or, worse still, be expected to bear some responsibility for the unforeseen. On July 25, he finally secured a meeting with Maxwell. The loans, soothed the chairman, were for "foreign-exchange deals and don't concern you." Dissatisfied, Brookes consulted Richard Baker, the retired director. Baker's advice, undoubtedly motivated by resentment, was blunt and accepted by Brookes.

On July 29, Brookes entered Kevin Maxwell's office and, after expressing his "unhappiness" about the withholding of information from him, claims that he tendered his resignation. "I don't think that Kevin understood the real implications," recalled Brookes, who believed that Kevin, recently appointed MCC's chief executive, was an ally against his own father. Urging patience, Kevin organized a telephone conversation between Brookes and Maxwell, who was then sailing on the *Lady Ghislaine*. Maxwell's persuasive charm tempted the finance director, who might not easily have found another similarly well-paying job, to step back from the brink pending further discussions.

Four days later, Brookes turned to Peter Laister, a non-executive director who was frequently in Maxwell House, for further advice. Like all those businessmen, journalists and lawyers who had "accepted the Captain's shilling," Laister had been recruited by Maxwell in the expectation of his compliant behavior. Although Laister had considerable experience in business, his reputation in the City was tarnished by a succession of financial failures. Laister was surprised by Brookes's information. "It was the first time the inter-company loans were a problem," says Laister. "After all, both the company's auditors and its outside lawyers had never complained about Maxwell's use of public money."

Laister called an informal meeting of directors, excluding the Maxwells: "It wasn't secret," says Laister, although the result was potentially threatening to the family. "We decided to consult outside lawyers because Bob was being cavalier with the shareholders," says Laister, who concedes that he was not "worried."

Unlike New York's lawyers, their British brethren are by instinct conservative and uncombative. The MacFarlanes lawyers consulted by the MCC directors were consistent traditionalists. Instead of urging the directors to launch an investigation, the two partners recommended silence. Since the loans were not "wrongful" there were no grounds for complaint, and publicizing concern would, said MacFarlanes, be prejudicial to the interests of MCC. Instead, the lawyers recommended that both Maxwells be asked to reply to a list of written questions. The most important was whether the private companies were buying MCC shares: "I didn't think he'd be so daft," says Laister, "but we needed to ask."

Maxwell's response was a confrontation. Outraged that the directors should resort to formalities, he accused his executives of "caballing against me." Maxwell's conviction of a conspiracy against him would grow as the web of his deceit spread and suspicions grew.

Yet Laister, like Brookes, remained unsuspicious: "Just angry that Bob was angry. We just wanted to protect him by making sure he played by the rules." Believing that Maxwell would obey the rules was clearly a self-delusion, since the rule book had been rewritten in 1981 to give Maxwell dictatorial powers. Laister ignored some realities, since his principal concern was that the price of the shares was "tender" and that the threat of resignations would "upset the apple cart." It was a brand of gentility which Maxwell encouraged.

On August 16 the Maxwells gave their fellow directors "full satisfaction." Within a tabulated folder was a note hand written by Robert Maxwell: "I confirm that the borrowings by Headington Investments from Maxwell Communications Corporation have not been used in any way which would mean that MCC has breached the Companies Act." Maxwell and Kevin were the signatories. Laister and Brookes believed that Maxwell had agreed to procedural reforms, especially compelling Fuller, the treasurer, to report to Brookes. Even better in Laister's view, the Maxwells gave assurances that the loans were covered by the private companies' assets—"at least three times the amount," said Maxwell. Moreover, Maxwell agreed to reduce the loans. "We were very pleased," says Laister.

Brookes had simultaneously taken separate advice from another firm of lawyers, called Lovell, White, Durrant. Their advice, Brookes was "pleased" to note, was to remain silent and not to consider resignation in order "to protect the shareholders and the interest of the company." But like MacFarlanes, Brookes's lawyers also advised that the shareholders should not be told anything. The lawyers recommended that the directors should not even consult the company's auditors, Coopers & Lybrand. "There was no need," Brookes was told. Without questioning that recommendation, the directors obeyed. "We were pleased with the advice," reaffirms Brookes. Their self-imposed silence, encouraged by the lawyers, could only assist Maxwell's continued plunder of the funds. Sufficient members of the British legal profession had taken fright of Maxwell.

August in Britain is traditionally the "silly season" when everyone disappears on vacation and only limited business is transacted. The departure of the MCC directors reduced the tension inside Maxwell House, but when Brookes returned in September he discovered that the "atmosphere was deteriorating."

Maxwell seemed, however, to be repaying the loans. The amount outstanding steadily dropped, from £276 million toward £73 million. Undoubtedly one of Maxwell's motives was the arrival of Neil Taberner and a team of accountants from Coopers & Lybrand to conduct the interim audit. Concerned by newspaper comments, Laister took the opportunity to ask Coopers for a presentation on the value of the intangibles. The ninety-minute illustrated lecture by Andrew Smith reassured Laister that MCC was secure.

In the meantime, on the other side of Maxwell's headquarters, Lawrence Guest, the finance director of the Mirror Group, was totally unaware of MCC's problems. He was also unaware that the company's pension fund was being plundered. Maxwell's compartmentalization was perfect. Despite their proximity, Guest and Brookes spoke to each other rarely and met even less.

Another loan carried a particular danger. Under an agreement, Maxwell would be in default of a £170 million loan if his stake in Mirror Group fell below 50 per cent, which would happen if Goldman Sachs ever sold its 40 million Mirror Group shares. Privately, Maxwell feared what Kevin Maxwell would later describe as "meltdown."

In the execution of his crime, Maxwell was aided by the City regulators. On October 18, Giles Orton, the solicitor representing the Mirror Group pensioners, was told by Ian Pittaway, the lawyer representing Maxwell, that the fund's trustee had found the "arrangements for making and monitoring its investments perfectly satisfactory." Moreover, the trustee added that the fund's investments were "appropriate for a pension fund." Considering that by that time Maxwell had cancelled most of the safe investments and liquidated a large proportion of the shares, it was a hollow assurance.

At noon on September 11, Maxwell attended in the *Mirror* building what would be his last annual general meeting. His multicolored tie was stained. Not even his two sons, both so humiliated in the past, had dared warn their father.

Despite protestations from shareholders about his debts, Maxwell reaffirmed that he was, as always, "confident" about the future. "Take the criticisms," he advised, "with a pinch of salt. Your company's future is secure." Sitting as far away from Maxwell as possible was Peter Walker, wishing he was somewhere else. Negotiations for the sale of at least eight assets, Maxwell continued, were underway. No one mentioned that, even if successful, those sales were insufficient to cover the debts. Asked about the permanency of his tenure, Maxwell replied, "At the age of sixty-eight I can give no such assurance." There was also a protest. The "Pergamon 23," employees who had been dismissed in a bid to win recognition of their trade union in Oxford, protested about a socialist's "conduct prejudicial to the Party." It was an old struggle which Maxwell had long ignored. The protesters were treated to a tirade accusing their union, the NUJ, of being led by Trotskyites.

It was vintage Maxwell. Those around could only marvel at his resilience and apparent lack of concern: "You could shoot bullets at Maxwell and they would just bounce off his broad, armor-plated bum," marveled an admirer. Two reports ruffled that ostensible calm.

A front-page article in the *Wall Street Journal* headed "Bloated Empire," describing what were his well-known problems in London, unsettled his New York bankers. The second report, a BBC television program called *The Max Factor* shown on *Panorama,* caused him greater worry.

Throughout the week prior to the September 23 transmission, Maxwell had bombarded BBC executives to prevent the program's transmission. When he failed, both his Sunday newspapers condemned the BBC executives as "jackals." Among his fears was that *Panorama* would be examining his management of the pension fund. To his relief he discovered that the topic had been dropped. In his attack against the BBC which was published in the *Sunday Mirror,* Maxwell wrote,

"I am concerned about needless anxiety which the program may cause to pensioners in our Group. For some months, a lawyer and a small group of pensioners have claimed their pensions should have been higher. They haven't a case. Long-term MGN pensioners are better treated than they would have been by their former employers." His statement was the classic Maxwell: the size of his lie could be judged by the force of his counter-attack. Nevertheless, the program's implications were worse than he had imagined. Nisha Pillai, the reporter, not only covered his debt and concealment activities, but also revealed that Maxwell had personally organized bogus bingo games for *Mirror* readers: "It was Mr. Maxwell himself," reported Pillai, "who decided to run a dishonest game and cheat his readers." The dishonesty charge, gleefully repeated by Maxwell's rival newspapers, provoked a cascade of threats by Maxwell but they failed to dent the BBC's official endorsement of the allegations.

The unease about Maxwell's management now erupted in MCC's boardroom. On October 4, Jean-Pierre Anselmini, his deputy chairman, resigned. Although it was later reported that the Frenchman was annoyed that Maxwell broke his promise not to take cash as a dividend payment, Anselmini was reportedly also provoked by the revelation of Goldman Sachs's second "put-option": "Jean-Pierre just did not like it anymore that Maxwell did not consult him as the deputy chairman felt was his due," observed an eyewitness in Maxwell's office. Three weeks later, Harry McQuillen, the president of Macmillan in America, already preceded by seven other senior executives, also resigned. "The resignations just encouraged more calls from bankers," confides an insider. On the ninth floor, Maxwell was struggling with a genuine crisis.

At that moment, not more than two hundred yards away, in the headquarters of the small, independent publisher Faber & Faber, Matthew Evans, its chairman, could barely contain his excitement. Amid secrecy over the previous weeks, Evans had been preparing the sale of an American book called *The Samson Option* which purported "stunning disclosures" about the politics and deployment of Israel's secret nuclear bomb. Written by Seymour Hersh, who was styled as an "award-winning American writer" and an "icon of America's army of investigative reporters," this book would clearly be an embarrassment to Maxwell.

To increase British sales, Evans had asked the author to include a special British angle. Hersh volunteered that he possessed proof that in 1986 Robert Maxwell had knowingly assisted Mossad, the Israeli intelligence agency. Hersh outlined Maxwell's responsibility for the plight of Mordechai Vanunu, an Israeli technician who in 1986 had sold information and photographs of Israel's secret bomb to the *Sunday Times*.

Vanunu's deal had become complicated because the same information had been offered to the *Sunday Mirror* but instead of accepting the scoop, Maxwell's newspaper had published an article ridiculing Vanunu's account as "a hoax, or even something more sinister—a plot to discredit Israel."

Before the *Sunday Times*'s publication, and despite precautions, Vanunu was lured out of his hiding place in London by a Mossad honeytrap, kidnapped in Rome, and flown to Israel where he was sentenced to eighteen years' imprisonment. Hersh claimed that the *Mirror*'s foreign editor Nick Davies, at the request of Maxwell, had intentionally revealed Vanunu's hideaway in London to Mossad and that the *Mirror*'s smear of Vanunu was dictated by Maxwell in cooperation with Mossad.

The source of Hersh's information was Ari Ben-Menasche, an Israeli, whose fraudulent claims to be a former Mossad officer were believed by Hersh. "I checked his story carefully," said Hersh.

Hersh believed Ben-Menasche's tale that after 1983 he and Davies had been secretly selling weapons to Iran with the full knowledge of George Bush, then the vice-president, and Yitzhak Shamir, the Israeli prime minister. The Israeli claimed that when he recruited Davies as an intelligence "asset," he was unaware that Davies was a journalist. Davies, known in the *Mirror* as a flash would-be entrepreneur, denied involvement in arms dealing. Maxwell's acceptance of Davies's denial was conditioned by his long-term friendship which had built up over the years traveling around the world, his use of Davies as a trouble shooter and, more important, by Maxwell's apparent infatuation with Davies's girlfriend, Andrea Martin, who was also one of Maxwell's secretaries.

The publication of Hersh's book on October 20, 1991 was greeted by writs for defamation by Maxwell and Davies. Hersh's defamatory allegations were legally unreportable.

Two days later, encouraged by Maxwell's critics, a Member of Parliament, protected by Parliamentary privilege, expressed concern in the House at the allegation that: "The *Daily Mirror* and its proprietor Robert Maxwell have maintained a close relationship with Mossad." Protected by the legal right to report Parliamentary statements, every newspaper repeated Hersh's allegations. "Maxwell man named as spy" was the headline which associated Maxwell with Davies. "Mirrorgate" was born and Maxwell was under renewed pressure.

At Faber, Matthew Evans could not believe his good fortune. Creating publicity is a publisher's nightmare but successfully provoking a controversy is a publisher's dream. Flown to London, Hersh was presented before a packed news conference. Although his hesitant performance was disappointing, even skeptics were well disposed to anyone providing ammunition against Maxwell who, in typically exaggerated language, had condemned the allegations as "ludicrous, a total invention." Maxwell had accepted Davies's denials, especially one critical allegation by Hersh suggesting that the journalist had come to Ohio in 1985 to buy arms from an American dealer. "Forgery," screamed a *Mirror* headline condemning a letter which apparently connected Davies with the Ohio negotiations. "I swear I've never been to Ohio in my life," pleaded Davies.

"You Liar," replied the *Sun* two days later. A photograph was published which proved Davies had visited Ohio. Davies apologized for his "lapse of memory" but on October 28 was fired. The *Mirror*'s credibility sank, closely followed by Maxwell's reputation, as his link to Mossad's kidnapping of Vanunu seemed proven. "Mirrorgate" had become a gripping scandal selling newspapers and books.

Despite the evidence having been unpublished originally because the legal proof was deemed to be insufficient, Hersh had persuaded Evans that the Vanunu case was a mere symbol of Maxwell's close involvement in Mossad operations. According to Hersh, Maxwell had, on Israel's behalf, dealt in weapons, laundered money and had even paid Ben-Menasche a commission for transferring Israel's weapons.

Although Evans would later admit that Ben-Menasche had not been completely proven as "24 carat," Evans had been assured by Hersh that there were "other unnamed sources" who confirmed his information. Evans discounted the credibility of Maxwell's unspecific denials. But to others it was clear that Maxwell was innocent for several reasons.

Firstly, in 1985 Maxwell had peripheral connections with Israel. Secondly, "Irangate" had proven Israel's ability to ship arms to Iran since 1982. There was no reason for Israel to seek Maxwell's assistance. Thirdly, Maxwell had just bought the *Mirror* and had absolutely no knowledge of the arms trade. Fourthly, Hersh's only source was Ari Ben-Menasche, who was a compulsive liar, who had never served in Mossad, and boasted a long history of selling gullible journalists fabricated stories. Ben-Menasche had possessed no proof of Maxwell's links to Mossad or arms deals. Nor was there simply any occasion for Maxwell to become involved.

Maxwell's displays of temper were not unusual but during those last days of October even those habitually around Maxwell in the *Mirror*'s headquarters remarked upon the vehemence of their employer's anger. Outside, there was no sympathy. Maxwell's complaints about unfair allegations—when his fortune and status had been earned by encouraging his own newspapers to turn a merciless spotlight on so many innocent individuals—provoked smears about hypocrisy. The intensity of "Mirrorgate" reflected the delight among his critics of turning the spotlight back on to a habitual accuser. Memories were still fresh about Maxwell's sermon in 1984 describing the importance he attached to the rights of privacy and the avoidance of prurience. He had soon forsaken those values. His newspapers had been happy to expose the visits by Major Ronald Ferguson to a London massage parlor but no word was allowed of Maxwell's own indiscretions. Maxwell had initially approved the publication of photographs in the *People* of Prince Harry urinating in a park but might have been differently minded had his own grandchild been photographed. The publisher had authorized the payment for a color spread of the nude Princess Stephanie of Monaco in her private pool with a boyfriend, but might well have objected if his daughters were similarly compromised.

Paradoxically, Maxwell, who had issued more writs for defamation than anyone else in Britain, was merciless when others complained about his newspapers' wrongdoings. Throughout his ownership, Mirror Group newspapers lost more libel cases than any other newspaper. Few forgot his punishment in 1988 for vehemently refusing to authorize an apology to Koo Stark, the former girlfriend of Prince Andrew. Miss Stark was awarded record damages. In the view of those who were pursuing "Mirrorgate," Maxwell was a sinner whose own pleas of innocence should be ignored. That pursuit, combined with the *Panorama* and *Wall Street Journal* reports, influenced sentiment in New York.

In previous weeks, senior executives of Goldman Sachs in America had reviewed their relationship with Maxwell and become uneasy. The MCC shares were losing value, down to approximately 145p, a 100p drop in six months; the press reports were negative; and Maxwell was not, despite repeated requests, repaying the two loans worth over £80 million which were outstanding. The prevailing sentiment was clear: "Maxwell isn't special to us. We should do what we feel we have to do." Goldman began selling its entire holding of MCC shares. By October 22, 25 million shares would be gone: "We had gotten rid of everything that we were holding." Insiders might reflect that Maxwell was losing one of his staunchest allies but Goldman later claimed that those sales were "not significant."

Goldman were still holding 26 million MCC shares and 40 million Mirror Group shares as collateral for the $60 million loans. During early October, Maxwell was repeatedly urged from New York to repay one loan of about £25 million: "We're not a bank but brokers. The money was lent on March 27 for seven days and now we want our money." Using his charm, Maxwell attempted to calm the anger but apparently had no ability to repay the money.

Other banks were also demanding repayment, and since he could no longer borrow money against MCC shares, Maxwell began taking money from MCC and MGN bank accounts. By October about £240 million had passed to the private companies without any security but not without the knowledge of Brookes and Guest, the respective finance directors.

Goldman was not the only creditor demanding repayment. Among the many European and American banks whose irritated voices he heard daily was Swiss Bank. This complaint, as Maxwell knew, was among the most serious. The loan was worth £57.5 million and the background to the deal was suspicious.

It had started in 1988 when a private company owned by Maxwell called London and Bishopsgate Holdings had bought a 24.9 per cent stake in an investment fund called New Tokyo Investment Trust. The Trust, managed in Edinburgh, invested in Japanese stocks. Maxwell's representative on the Trust board was Bernard Donoughue, a former socialist academic who, having served Harold Wilson as a policy adviser, had switched ideologies and pledged himself to serve both capitalism and Maxwell.

In January 1989, Donoughue argued that he could produce better profits for the Trust. The Scottish directors agreed that Donoughue and the Maxwell company should manage the Trust's investments for which a high fee would be paid.

Donoughue's confidence was misplaced. By September 1990, the Trust had lost nearly half its money: down from £80.4 million to £46.3 million. Moreover, Donoughue had personally failed to induce any major investor to trust his judgment and place funds under his management. Even Maxwell concluded that the former socialist was there for a free ride. As a solution, the Trust's board agreed that the stock could be "lent out" to speculators, a specialized and legal activity on which fees can be earned. According to Donoughue, but uncorroborated by anyone else, the L&BIIM directors began at that stage to quarrel among themselves about the stock-lending deals. Although Donoughue's signature appears on many of the contracts, he says that his arguments with Trachtenberg on that issue led to his eventual resignation. Others say that the arguments sprang purely from personality differences.

But in early 1991, the Scottish directors discovered that, unknown to them, the Maxwell company had been lending the stocks to other Maxwell companies. Maxwell had been using the stocks to cover his own debts. In the rows which followed, the Scots accused Maxwell of "theft." To placate the situation, in July 1991 Maxwell agreed to buy the Trust for £57.5 million, a generous price. Since he had no money to pay, Kevin Maxwell negotiated on July 3 to borrow £60 million from Swiss Bank. In the end, Maxwell drew only £55 million. The security offered to Swiss Bank for the loan was the Trust's shares.

Under the loan agreement, Maxwell agreed to deposit all the Trust's shares with Swiss Bank and agreed not to use the shares as a collateral for any other loan. On August 6, 1991, Maxwell received the money and the Swiss awaited delivery of the Trust's stock certificates. But just five days earlier, on August 1, Maxwell had begun to sell the shares which he had pledged to Swiss Bank. The first sale raised £16.4 million, which was deposited in a Maxwell private company. Simultaneously, Maxwell secretly used more shares from that portfolio worth £29.1 million as collateral for a loan from Credit Suisse, and another block of shares worth £4.6 million as collateral for a loan from Shearson Lehman Brothers. Both banks would soon after sell the shares when Maxwell failed to repay the loans. At the outset, neither Credit Suisse nor Shearson knew that those same shares had been pledged to Swiss Bank.

Swiss Bank meanwhile was demanding from Maxwell the certificates to the original portfolio of shares. Inevitably, Maxwell could not send the certificates. "We were always fobbed off," complained Swiss Bank. Instead, Maxwell offered to simply repay the loan. His offer was accepted, but he now faced another problem: he needed to procure the money to pay Swiss Bank.

By October, as the pressure from Goldman, Citibank and other financial institutions was intensifying, Swiss Bank began issuing threats. Just as in his reply to Goldman, Maxwell could only resort to charm and platitudes. Kevin Maxwell promised sufficient cash to make up any shortfall. Although apparently at one stage Kevin reportedly admitted that the shares had been sold, he later said he knew nothing about the deal. Equivocation seemed the best cover for embarrassment. Unimpressed, the Swiss threatened to call the Fraud Squad. Maxwell was in trouble and tried to withdraw his offer to repay the money. That option was firmly rejected by Swiss Bank.

There was additional pressure from within his organization. On October 2, Lawrence Guest, the MGN finance director, had raised a troubling issue: the disappearance of £47 million. "I saw Maxwell," recalls Guest, who complained to him about the Treasury policies. "I wasn't happy with the reply." Guest confided his fear to three other directors.

Guest returned to the issue at another meeting with Maxwell on October 15. "Until then I had believed Maxwell's promises," says Guest, who, following that discussion wrote a memorandum to three other directors: "I am now convinced that MGN resources have been used to support other parts of the group. But I have no proof. I think I have frightened the chairman, but my main concern must be to get the money back."

Like the other directors and Maxwell's other employees, Guest was nevertheless over-awed by Maxwell and the deification which he commanded. Shortly after that confrontation, Guest and the other Mirror Group directors had bowed to Maxwell's insistence that Mirror Group Newspapers should extend the lease of their headquarters with MCC. Although the Mirror Group directors would later say that they had protested, the increase was approved, although the agreement would sabotage the Mirror Group's plan, as promised in the flotation prospectus, to leave Central London for cheaper premises. Guest claims that he was not told about the crucial board meeting until it was too late for him to attend. But, like his fellow director Ernest Burrington, a former journalist, he did not formally protest.

Soon after, on Maxwell's telephoned instructions, the directors of MCC agreed to borrow £80 million more on the strength of the new Mirror Group lease. Such were the methods by which Maxwell manipulated his employees and, uncontrolled, exploited the funds of the public companies for his own purposes.

Directors like Guest and Burrington accepted that they had no power to stop Maxwell using the money. Their only option was resignation in protest. Self-sacrifice was not an option which they considered.

Nevertheless, on October 21 Guest did complain to Maxwell that £47 million of the Mirror's cash which he had borrowed had not been returned. "Don't worry. You are losing sleep and that's not right. I've put it into gilts and it's safe," said a smiling Maxwell. Guest consoled himself that the truth would eventually emerge in the annual audit, and he decided to return to the issue later. Unbeknownst to Guest, Basil Brookes, the finance director of MCC, was also waiting to see Maxwell about similar matters.

Clearly anxious about the possible danger, Maxwell demoted Guest by promoting Michael Stoney, a trusted employee, as deputy managing director (finance) above Guest. According to Guest, Stoney had in previous months blocked Guest's inquiries about the movement of money. By then Maxwell was reading of Guest's concern in transcripts of Guest's telephone conversations obtained from voice-activated bugs which had been installed some weeks previously. Critically, Guest received only limited support from the other executive directors and non-executive directors during the last days of October.

There was certainly no help from Stoney, who was a director of nearly 100 Maxwell private companies and Kevin Maxwell's "financial man." Stoney would authorize at least one transfer of Mirror Group money to a Maxwell private company. On that same day, October 21, Stoney was also the co-signatory on a £50 million loan to the Mirror Group which Maxwell had negotiated with Ralph MacDonald, a member of the management committee of Bankers Trust. The £50 million would disappear, and there was no security.

In the meantime, Maxwell was touring the City seeking more loans. The eyewitness was his chauffeur, John Featley. "I knew something was up," explained the Cockney driver. "Something was suspicious, when we started visiting places we would not normally go to. The boss was a bit subdued on the way to these bankers, but usually happy when we left."

At that moment in New York, the senior directors of Goldman Sachs decided that Maxwell was no longer a valued customer. They wanted repayment of £25 million. "Let's pull the plug" was reportedly the decision-making phrase. From London came a final plea: Goldman Sachs had successfully topped the league of advisers in Europe's explosion of cross-border deals and had been retained in some of Britain's most publicized take-over battles. The image of the "ugly American" undermining a British firm would be unhelpful. That was rejected. On October 30, in New York someone "at the highest level" issued an ultimatum: "Repay now or we'll sell some of the collateral." Across the city, the directors of Citibank had also decided to sell some MCC shares held as collateral because Maxwell had failed to repay his debts. In London, Guest made an appointment to again ask Maxwell to repay the missing £47 million to the *Mirror*. He was told to be in the chairman's office at 8:30 a.m. and expected to wait a long time. The appointment was canceled the previous night: "I was told that Maxwell would be unreachable."

Basil Brookes also had an appointment to see Maxwell that day to discuss the terms of his resignation. Since he was still prevaricating because "I didn't want to spark a share price collapse," he hoped for a quiet arrangement. After waiting in the outer office of the ninth floor, he was told that Maxwell was no longer available.

Throughout his career, Maxwell was accused of committing many sins but he had always honored the timely repayment of his bank loans. For the first time, he seemed unable or unwilling to fulfill his obligations.

On October 31, Goldman Sachs sold 2.2 million MCC shares: "We gave him a warning." The gravity of this transaction for Maxwell could not be overstated. Formal notification to MCC of that sale could be delayed for two business days. Deliberately, Goldman decided not to release the news: "We wanted to save the pain and hoped we could slip it out when no one noticed."

On Monday, November 4, Goldman Sachs officially informed MCC of the sale. After waiting twenty-four hours, MCC's company secretary told the Stock Exchange of the sale. Citibank also sold some MCC shares that morning. It was not announced as required by the regulations.

It was 1 p.m. on November 5 when a short announcement streamed across all brokers' monitors baldly stating that Goldman's percentage holding of MCC had declined. No comment was added. No other broker could have known immediately that Goldman had dropped the Sword of Damocles.

One hour later, at 2 p.m., a Goldman executive watching the monitor gasped. MCC's price "began to tank. Everyone was selling." Eric Sheinberg had started making his way toward the *Mirror* building. The rumors were already circulating that Maxwell was missing.

17

On the evening of Wednesday October 30, Angus Rankin, captain of the *Lady Ghislaine,* was telephoned by a secretary in the *Mirror* office in Holborn and was told that Maxwell would be flying down to Gibraltar the following day to board the yacht.

Maxwell was suffering a cold, "one of the filthiest colds he'd ever had," according to Michael Richardson. For ten years Maxwell had also suffered from pulmonary edema, a congestion of the lungs which causes asphyxia and can damage the heart. Considering his weight, 308 pounds, and the lack of one lung, Maxwell took advice to travel to the sun to recover: "I'm going for five days to the sunshine to get rid of this cold and then I'll be fine."

As day broke over London, at 6:30 a.m. on October 31, Maxwell left his Holborn apartment, went to the helipad on the roof of the *Mirror* building, and flew to Luton. Neither a secretary nor his valet was accompanying him. Traveling to the yacht without a secretary was not unusual. His suitcases, brought separately by car, had already been loaded. The Gulfstream was soon airborne for a two-hour flight to the British colony.

Rankin was waiting when the jet landed. The captain of the *Lady Ghislaine* had been employed by Maxwell for about one year. None of the ten remaining crew had served for more than six months. Some say that Maxwell was in a bad temper when he stepped into the sunshine. Others, including Rankin, report that he was his usual self.

Maxwell was certainly better tempered after a stewardess stepped ashore just before 4 p.m. when the yacht set sail for Madeira, 600 miles away. The voyage took two days. When the *Lady Ghislaine* docked in Funchal, Maxwell was driven into town. After unsuccessfully searching for a history of the island, he visited Reid's hotel, drank a beer at the bar, and then returned to the boat to be taken to the Desertas beach to swim. Maxwell enjoyed swimming in the nude and he enjoyed snorkel diving. That evening, he visited a casino with $3,000 drawn from his safe and after twenty-five minutes returned to the boat for the night.

The following day, Sunday, Maxwell was seen eating on the ship's stern, chatting to Rankin who would later say that Maxwell was in a "very good mood." Maxwell decided to stay on the boat for its next 250-mile hop to Tenerife. At one stage he decided to dispatch his Gulfstream jet to London to collect his sons. Ten minutes later, he countermanded his order and decided to stay alone on the yacht. It had not been a straightforward decision because he was committed to another eighteen hours at sea. He was due to give a speech to the Anglo-Israeli Association in London on Monday. Since his Gulfstream was flying on to Tenerife, he ordered that it fly low over his yacht, which, according to Rankin, seemed to "humor him."

At 10 a.m. on November 4, the *Lady Ghislaine* sailed into Darcena Pesquera, the fishing port two kilometers north of Santa Cruz. Maxwell's Gulfstream was waiting at the island's southern airport near Los Christianos for the return flight to London.

Just before lunch, the yacht sailed south to Poris de Abona, a secluded spot, where Maxwell swam. All the reported accounts of that day's telephone calls agree that Maxwell was in good humor despite his complaints to Ian that his cold made him feel unwell. Father and son were telephoning back and forth jointly compiling his speech for that evening. Ian had realized that his father would expect the son to deliver his speech.

In between calls, Maxwell had also been speaking to Samuel Pisar, a French lawyer and Auschwitz survivor, to whom he had become increasingly attached during his growing involvement in Israel. Their conversation included references to Maxwell's nomination to receive the Légion d'honneur, France's highest award, and an exchange of jokes which Maxwell had included in that evening's speech.

There were calls from Kevin about Goldman's decision to sell MCC shares from the collateral, about Swiss Bank's threats to call in the Fraud Squad; Kevin mentioned that Basil Brookes, the finance director of MCC, had discovered that Maxwell had exercised his legal powers to transfer £240 million from the company to himself. Brookes, said Kevin, had threatened his resignation but had been persuaded to desist. The resolution was to await Maxwell's return. There were calls from two French banks, the Paribas and the Crédit Lyonnais, both anxious about loan repayments; and a host of calls about deals on the Stock Exchange. Among the latter was Michael Richardson who, after discussing MCC's market price, set a date to meet the following day to discuss a forthcoming deal. By the end of those conversations, the *Ghislaine* had returned to Santa Cruz.

As Maxwell stepped ashore that night, Betty Maxwell was telling the organizers of the dinner in London that he was too unwell to attend. At 8 p.m., as Maxwell got into a taxi driven by Arturo Trujillo, Ian read his father's speech. It was a hawkish attack on President Bush's decision to freeze loans to Israel: "We Jews of the Diaspora and of Israel are willing to go into hock ourselves. . . . No one can understand the world today and no one can understand Israel and the Jewish people unless they can appreciate how close Hitler came to wiping us out."

Squashed into a Toyota Camry, Trujillo pushed the front seat back to allow more room for Maxwell's legs while they drove, at Maxwell's request, to the best hotel in town.

Wearing a beige blazer, check trousers and a blue baseball cap, Maxwell walked into the Hotel Mencey, an elegant turn-of-the-century building at the top of a steep hill in the town's center. It was 8:25 p.m. Trujillo escorted Maxwell to tip the staff that their customer was important and then waited outside.

The waiters could hardly fail to notice their latest guest in the empty restaurant. When Maxwell ordered a beer, the waiter immediately brought two "because he was so big." Maxwell chose a green salad followed by hake with clams in a parsley and mushroom sauce. While he waited, he ate an asparagus mousse dip. Some waiters would later comment that Maxwell seemed quite content although "agitated" when his portable telephone to the *Ghislaine* failed to function. He was not short of breath. After puffing on a Havana cigar, he paid his £24 bill and bid farewell. Seeing that he had forgotten his jacket, a waiter raced after him. "Maxwell," he later said, "seemed preoccupied."

As he squeezed back into Trujillo's waiting taxi, Maxwell mentioned that the meal was "very good" and asked for a cup of coffee. Trujillo drove to the El Olimpo, a well-known bar where Maxwell sat outside, drinking a cappuccino, while continuing to talk on the portable telephone. After fifteen minutes, Maxwell paid and asked Trujillo about flamenco shows. Since the nearest was thirty-three kilometers away, he abandoned the idea and ordered the taxi to return to the harbor.

At 10 p.m., Maxwell drove up to the *Lady Ghislaine*. Amid some laughter, needing an extra 1000 pesetas for the tip, he borrowed a note from the crew. It was the last debt which he would incur. It would not be repaid.

Not wanting to sleep alongside the bleak wharf overshadowed by bare rock, Maxwell ordered Rankin to set off to sea for the night. Although Maxwell occasionally suffered from seasickness, the water this night was calm. Rankin was given no instructions about the ship's course and made a random choice.

Once out of the harbor, Maxwell telephoned Pisar, held a conference call with Rabbi Feivish Vogel of the British Lubavitch to discuss the recovery of Jewish archives from the Lenin library in Moscow, spoke to the *Daily Mirror*'s editor, and later heard from Ian a report about the dinner. "He was in good form despite his cold," recalled Ian. The *Lady Ghislaine* was cruising slowly a few miles off land. Ian's last exchange with his father was confirmation that he would be back in London the following day. "See you tomorrow," ended Ian. "You bet," replied his father, the last words he is known to have spoken to his family.

It was around midnight at the beginning of November 5. The *Lady Ghislaine* was sailing, according to the captain, from Tenerife across to Gran Canaria and would then sail southward five miles off the island's east coast.

Two members of the crew were on watch, two engineers were on duty below and the captain was on the bridge. The surveillance video was not operating which was normal at sea. At 4:25 a.m., a member of the crew reported seeing Maxwell on the deck. He was wearing a three-quarter length, V-neck, buttoned nightgown. Twenty minutes later, Maxwell called up to the bridge. The air conditioning was too high, he complained. Some time after that call, Maxwell got out of bed, walked out of the cabin, locked the door, and walked on to the deck. The boards were moist and he was not wearing slippers.

One can only speculate about his thoughts. Paramount would have been the plight of his self-styled empire. In his mind there were problems but he did not harbor even a subconscious admission that his edifice was tottering toward collapse. Critics might suspect fraud and contrive to find the evidence but he relished a struggle for survival and possessed the strength which other mortals could neither comprehend nor command. So there would be a fight, but he was certain of victory.

According to the best reconstruction by Spanish police and the pathologists in Madrid, Maxwell walked to the rear of the yacht. While standing by the thin metal rail, possibly urinating, definitely vomiting, he suffered a heart attack, lost his balance and fell into the sea.

The cause of the attack was a chronic defect in his heart. As he struggled consciously or unconsciously for survival, his luxury craft unwittingly glided toward its rendezvous with his Gulfstream jet. On board the yacht was that month's *Playboy* magazine. A twelve-page interview recorded Maxwell's boasts about his achievements. Within the narrative, amid his name-dropping and descriptions of interrupting phone calls from presidents and prime ministers, Maxwell had suddenly anticipated his death: "I too have a contract that expires one day— with the good Lord."

Since no water was found in the lungs, the pathologists concluded that Maxwell's last moments were spent gasping above the water as the heart attack came to its ultimate conclusion. They could neither determine how long the attack continued nor how long the victim remained conscious. Ten weeks later in February 1992, an alternative verdict would be postulated by a British pathologist, Dr. Iain West.

According to Rankin, the *Ghislaine* dropped anchor at Los Christianos at the southern tip of Tenerife at 9:45 a.m. The craft had covered about sixty miles. Later an employee of the local jetfoil said he saw the boat on arriving for work at 7 a.m., but that was subsequently discounted.

In London, Kevin was being interviewed by Bronwen Maddox of the *Financial Times*. Maddox had completed a trawl through dozens of annual reports at Companies House filed by Maxwell's private companies and produced the most detailed scheme disentangling the web of Maxwell's empire. After a review, Kevin commented, "Yes there's a lot of it," but suggested there were fewer companies than before. Although the records suggested that the Maxwell companies owed about £2.2 billion, Kevin added, "For the first time in years it's really not much of a strain on us all."

Elsewhere in the building, there was a meeting with a group of financial advisers including Michael Richardson. Everyone present was aware that MCC's half yearly results due shortly would, for the first time, show a loss. Combined with the threats from Swiss Bank, Goldman Sachs and others.

In Moscow, President Gorbachev was complaining to Yegor Yakovlev of *Moscow News* that so many western businessmen had promised help but few delivered. Both laughed when Gorbachev called it the "Maxwell Syndrome." Elsewhere in that city, in the KGB's headquarters, General Alexander Karabainov, the agency's press chief, was discussing Maxwell's latest proposal that his organization might publish a magazine containing reports from the KGB's archives.

At 11:10 a.m., on board the yacht, seven hours after Maxwell was last seen, the telephone rang. It was a call from New York where it was 6 a.m. The call was put through to Maxwell's bedroom but there was no reply. Rankin went down to his cabin. The door was locked which was not unusual when Maxwell was asleep. A master key opened the door. The room was empty. Maxwell's nightgown was on the bed. Rankin ordered the ship's crew to search the boat. When Maxwell was not found, he ordered another search and then a third search. Maxwell had disappeared.

Rankin's first call was to London. It was just before 11:30. The call was eventually put through to Kevin. His shock can be imagined. After telling his family, Ian summoned Ernie Burrington, the Mirror Group's managing director. "Dad's missing, lost overboard," said one of the sons.

Their composure was remarkable. Their determination to take command was impressive. Their fear of the perils was concealed from Burrington. For the moment, that was confined within the family. During that hour they were overwhelmed by their emotions.

The time was 12:25. Fifty-five minutes after Kevin first heard the news, Gus Rankin dispatched a satellite distress signal that his employer was missing. There has been no explanation why nearly an hour elapsed between Rankin's call to London and his distress signal. Within that time, Betty Maxwell and her son Philip sought a plane to fly to Las Palmas. Surprisingly few private papers were found when the police boarded the yacht, leading to speculation as to whether they were destroyed after Maxwell's disappearance.But now, every minute, there were clear broadcast signals around the Canary islands alerting ships to search for Maxwell. He was mentioned by name. Fifty-five minutes of further agonized conversation continued in Maxwell's office—the emotional chaos successfully contained from seeping to the floors below and beyond—before a decision was made.

Kevin feared the effect on MCC's shares if the news leaked. It was lunchtime, an important moment in the City's day for intimate meetings. Desperately he sought Michael Richardson, but his father's trusted broker could not be found. Next, Kevin telephoned Samuel Montagu. Unable to reach Ian McIntosh, he contacted Clive Chalk, also employed in the corporate finance department, who was in the bank's dining room. The banker was urged to come to Holborn immediately.

It was 1:05. Five minutes earlier, a short announcement had streamed across the Stock Exchange monitors that Goldman Sachs had reduced its percentage holdings in MCC. It was lunchtime and there was no reaction.

At 1:45 Chalk walked into Maxwell's office. Both sons were distraught. Richardson could still not be found. Chalk recommended that he call the Stock Exchange and request that both MCC and Mirror Group shares be suspended. Kevin agreed.

At 1:55 p.m., two and a half hours after Rankin's first message, Chalk telephoned the Stock Exchange's Quotation Committee. The banker confided to an official that Maxwell was missing and asked for the shares' suspension.

It was an unusual request. If shares were suspended every time a company chairman died, especially of such an important company as MCC, the market would be thrown into perpetual confusion. In principle, the officials also disliked talking to a banker. They preferred brokers. The official demurred to consider the option with three colleagues.

By 2 p.m. Richardson had been contacted in his car. Twenty minutes later he walked into the distraught atmosphere to find the brothers, whom he had known as small children, white faced: "Dad's missing," said Kevin. Richardson was clearly shocked. Controlling their emotions, their conversation was terse. Everyone knew about MCC's precarious state and the significance of Goldman's announcement. At that moment, Richardson's experience counted: "They'll be a false market if trading continues."

Richardson telephoned the Stock Exchange but the reply was still prevaricating: "We have an obligation to all the investors," Richardson was told. "We need to undertake consultations." It was the makings of the very farce which always provoked Maxwell's contempt for the "has-beens" employed at the Exchange.

Within minutes of Chalk's first phone call, the news about Maxwell had leaked and shares were being sold. MCC's share price began falling toward a new low of 121p while the Mirror Group's fell to 77.5p. Within that hour, Kevin Maxwell had called his father's other important contacts. Among them was Eric Sheinberg.

At 2:58 p.m., the Exchange officially suspended trading of MCC and MGN shares. Those brokers who were not "insiders" on the information loop, and had not quickly taken their money, believed the reason was the company's financial plight. Ten minutes later, the first flash announcement stated "with deep regret" that Maxwell was missing at sea.

Maxwell's employees in Holborn had been already summoned. The news was given by Richard Stott, the *Mirror*'s editor. Clearly concerned about the image which would be conveyed to outsiders, departmental heads had already been warned to caution staff about their behavior. "He didn't want them all in the boozer that night telling Maxwell jokes," recalls one employee. That night, the British media, already in overdrive, would find difficulties obtaining sound bites and quotes from the staff.

At 4 p.m., to calm City fears, Ian and Kevin Maxwell were appointed by the respective boards as acting chairmen of Mirror Group and MCC. By then the Spanish air-sea rescue service had dispatched three helicopters and a light airplane to search the area. Ships also joined the search. At 5 p.m. a fishing boat reported sighting a body which was confirmed at 5:55 p.m. by Madrid Air-Sea Rescue. The position was given as about twenty-eight miles off the coast of Gran Canaria, about a hundred miles east of Tenerife. The coordinates, later confirmed, were 27 degrees 46.6 north, 16 degrees 0.6 west.

At 18:46, a Superpuma helicopter hovered over the recognizable corpse. "It was naked, stiff and floating face up, not face down which is normal," reported one of the rescuers. Guided by a searchlight, the crew struggled to winch the 300-pound remains onto their craft.

The news was flashed to London. MCC's board was meeting when news of the identification arrived. Kevin broke into tears, but soon after, at *Mirror* headquarters, both sons, remarkably composed, appeared before excited journalists to pledge that they would manage their father's "wonderful publishing business." "Love him or hate him," stated Kevin Maxwell, "he touched the lives of many millions of people." Observers later suggested that the sons' apparent lack of emotion was possibly unconscious relief that the burden of their father's omnipotence had been finally lifted. Kevin, aged thirty-three, would become acting chairman of MCC while Ian, thirty-six, became chief of the Mirror Group.

At that moment, Robert Maxwell was being transported by helicopter in the darkness to Gando military airport, on Gran Canaria. Wearing black, Betty and Philip Maxwell landed at the same airbase at 8:30 p.m. and were met by the British vice-consul Campbell Livingstone. Together they waited for José Fernandez, the duty judge, before going to identify the body which had been moved to the Salon de Juntas, a room in the airport building reserved for important meetings. "They were trying to do their best for somebody whom they knew was important," Livingstone recalls.

Betty's husband, whom she had met forty-seven years earlier as a poor, handsome, idealistic and courageous soldier, lay on the helicopter's stretcher on a table. At 9 p.m. the mother and son walked toward the corpse covered by a heavy, orange, plastic sheet.

There was silence in the room as the plastic was lifted and Betty nodded. No tears fell as she murmured, "He's a colossus lying there, as he'd been in life." Eyewitnesses say that she was "composed, calm and dignified." Tears fell from Philip. Betty was questioned by Dr. Carlos Lopez de Lamela, director of the local forensic institute where the autopsy would be conducted. Asked whether Maxwell could have committed suicide, she replied, "It is absolutely out of the question." Lamela asked about Maxwell's medical history and the drugs which he took. Betty Maxwell revealed that her husband had been taking drugs to counter his pulmonary edema. Other tablets were mentioned. Twenty minutes had passed. "As far as I'm concerned, we're done," announced Lamela.

The formality completed, a local judge ordered the helicopter to deliver Robert Maxwell to the morgue in Las Palmas. Betty spoke to her two sons in London and flew to Tenerife. She decided against sleeping in a hotel and opted for the *Lady Ghislaine*. Gus Rankin and some members of the crew would then be taken for questioning by the civil guard.

Throughout that night, Betty was on the telephone discussing the funeral arrangements. Earlier that year, on a journey to Jerusalem with her husband, they had stood on the Panorama promenade beneath Jerusalem's Intercontinental hotel overlooking the cemetery on the Mount of Olives, the holiest of Israel's burial grounds. Maxwell had mentioned that he had told his lawyer Yakov Neman two years earlier that this was the site where he wanted to be buried. "I want to be near my parents," he told Betty. He was referring to a plaque in the Yad Vashem memorial engraved with the name of his village, Slatinske Doly. The tragedy of the Holocaust had by then completely permeated his life. "I cannot ever forget it. I can't forgive it," he murmured about his parents' murder. "I was my mother's favorite." Within that tormented tyrant was a small boy wanting to return home.

Nothing had been arranged to implement Maxwell's wish to be buried in Israel. As a Christian, Betty naturally was ignorant of the requirements. That night, one of her children telephoned Yakov Neman, the lawyer, seeking help. "Under Orthodox law, the body must be here before Shabbat," Neman explained. There were less than sixty hours to complete the formalities in Tenerife and fly the body to Israel, a

Herculean undertaking since the pathologists wanted to keep the corpse until the tests were complete, three weeks later.

While the family marshaled their lawyers and advisers to dragoon the Spanish authorities into line, Neman began planning his movements for the following day, November 6. His first task would be to find a grave to bury Maxwell's body. No preparations had been made. At daybreak, Neman would contact Chananya Chachor, the cemetery's administrator. Then he would need to call in every political debt to produce a memorable funeral. It would be a pleasure to succeed.

In Tenerife at noon, three pathologists, Dr. Carlos Lopez de Lamela, Dr. Maria Ramos and Dr. Louisa Garcia Cohen began their initial autopsy, called an "opening of the cavities." As they proceeded, they recorded finding a little water in the lungs, a graze of the forehead, a fissure behind the ear. The corpse had suffered only three lesions, no broken nose, and only bruising which was consistent with the rescue. Taken together, the visual evidence disproved any suggestion of Maxwell's death by violence. They also took samples from the lung, kidney, pancreas, stomach and of the blood for further tests to be carried out in Madrid. Those tests would establish the presence of toxic substances, Maxwell's medical history and the presence of minuscule traces of algae which would have entered the bloodstream through the lungs to determine how long Maxwell spent in the water. As a routine procedure, scrapings were taken from beneath the nails to discover any fragments which would disclose whether Maxwell had clutched at an object or a person as he fell.

After three and a half hours, the pathologists reported to Judge Luis Gutierrez that their work was completed. Gutierrez told a local radio station that there was "no evidence of criminality. We are treating it as a simple accident." Suicide was clearly ruled out because there were no marks of how Maxwell would have killed himself. Death could not have been from drowning because there was no water in his lungs. "The initial forensic reports suggests a natural death before Mr. Maxwell fell into the sea," Gutierrez told Betty Maxwell, who by then was clutching a bible. When she emerged from his office, the widow said that she believed that death had been due to natural causes. Other doctors spoke of a "cardiac or cardiovascular attack."

By daybreak, Samuel Pisar had, with the help of friends in Madrid, appointed Julio Claverie as the family's lawyer on the island. Claverie had two tasks. Firstly, to persuade Isabel Oliva, the thirty-one-year-old investigating magistrate to complete the formalities to allow the body to be flown to Israel; and secondly, to oversee the pathologists' and magistrate's report.

Judge Gutierrez had originally said that Maxwell was dead before he fell into the water. The mystery was how he fell over the one-and-a-half-meter solid rail around the decks. The only place where a fall was possible was at the low, metal cord barriers at the rear of the yacht on the lower deck. Strung between the thin, three-foot chrome rails, were wires. It was a place where Maxwell often stood and from where he could easily have toppled over and slid into the sea. The crew, watching from the bridge, would have neither heard nor seen him.

Since that was the only place from which he could have fallen, there remained for the Spanish investigators one critical question: was he pushed or did he fall? If it was murder and he was pushed or thrown into the sea, then, since the boat was sailing on an unscheduled course, only members of the crew could be responsible. The yacht's course was not predetermined so a second boat could not have met the *Ghislaine* at sea. The crew, reported Livingstone, the British vice-consul, were "shocked and depressed" when they sailed back to Santa Cruz. They would be eliminated from the inquiry after one week.

If Maxwell had fallen, there were two options. Either he had suffered a heart attack on board the boat and had then fallen into the water; or he had fallen alive into the water and had suffered an attack while swimming in the sea, watching his boat sail away. Few in Britain had much confidence in the competence of the Spanish police to establish the truth.

Those were the questions which concerned a handful of individuals in the surreal setting off the African coast. But in the metropolis where Maxwell had sought to impose his writ, the deceased was subject to the attention he had devoted his lifetime seeking.

Momentarily, within minutes of publication of the news, the course of the world's events had changed. Broadcasts in every language mentioned Maxwell's death and began reciting his achievements. Like the assassination of John Kennedy and the resignation of Margaret Thatcher, many would remember forever where and how they heard the news. Tributes flowed from world leaders praising his character, wide-ranging interests and humanitarian activities. Douglas Hurd, the British foreign secretary, declared his death "robbed Britain of one of our most colorful and energetic figures."

The obituaries, not surprisingly, were mixed. The *Daily Mirror* published Maxwell's own assessment of his greatest achievement that he was the "man who saved the *Mirror*." The *Independent* called him a "liar, a cheat and a bully [who] did more than any other individual to pervert the British law of libel." In the *Daily Telegraph,* Max Hastings commented, "The nation's headlines will be much the poorer for his passing, and the length of his journey from the place and circumstances of his birth demand respect from all of us who have had to travel much less far, to rise much less high." But according to *The Times* he was "an egoist and a monstrously improbable socialist."

Elsewhere Matthew Evans, the chairman of Faber, was confidently asserting knowledge about the cause of death: "It was directly linked to fresh allegations which will be made in the next few weeks. Of course there is a link. A story is going to break which would have made his position untenable." Referring to Hersh's claims that Maxwell was a Mossad agent involved in gun running, money laundering and directly responsible for Mossad discovering Vanunu, Evans added that neither he nor Hersh "would be surprised if he had committed suicide. There is a lot more involved in this story than has come out." From Washington, Hersh claimed, "We are in possession of a considerable amount of evidence in relation to Mr. Maxwell and we are deciding what to do with it." Hersh then revealed the existence of a video. It showed, he claimed, Mossad agents discussing finding Vanunu and mentioning Maxwell. "I'm a predator," boasted the American, "and I'll milk the story for every last drop."

From Sydney, Ben-Menasche, also free from restraint of libel proceedings, added that he suspected that Mossad agents possibly had murdered Maxwell because the publisher was involved in massive arms deals. "Since 1985 I used to meet him in the *Mirror* building. . . . He was the one who opened the door for us [Israel] in the Eastern bloc." Both Hersh and Evans confirmed Ben-Menasche's claims. That was the substance of Evans's assertion of "a lot more to come."

While Hersh basked in the glow of media attention, the Maxwell family were discussing their father's funeral. Neman had secured a plot on the Mount of Olives. He had paid $5,000 to Chananya Chachor and was satisfied with the deal. His telephone calls to the offices of the president, prime minister, and other leading politicians had reassured him that Maxwell's parting from the world would be marked as an important event. His client would have been proud of his lawyer. "We must show how we value Jews who return to Israel," was the message which passed around Jerusalem's corridors of power.

In Liechtenstein, Dr. Werner Keicher seemed relaxed. Speaking for the first time, the Maxwell trust's lawyer told inquirers that he was not expecting any telephone call from London. Maxwell's bastion of secrecy seemed secure. The impression was that everything was working as arranged which seemed contradictory to Maxwell's pledge in 1988 that "my children will not inherit a penny. Everything will go to charity." Like so much else from that source, the truth was the opposite. In London, both sons spent the first day after their father's death locked in discussions with bankers negotiating to maintain their new inheritance said to amount to at least £2.5 billion in debts.

At some stage during the day, Kevin Maxwell, under pressure to produce more collateral for the loans which were still undisclosed, pledged as collateral for a private loan from Natwest Bank 25 million shares of the Israeli company Teva Pharmaceutical Industries, which belonged to the *Mirror* pension fund. The legality of the transaction was doubtful, which he certainly realized. But the family's financial predicament was worsening by the hour. Kevin's prime consideration was survival and not the consequences of his decisions. This was an imbroglio which Kevin, unlike his father, had never experienced. The telephone conversations which had been prefaced with expressions of grief and respect soon switched to veiled threats if loans were not repaid.

Among those many callers was a representative of Shearson Lehman Brothers. He threatened to seize installments of Berlitz shares which had been pledged as collateral for a loan to the private companies. The use of MCC's 56 per cent stake in Berlitz by Robert and Kevin Maxwell (which they controlled through Macmillan Inc.) would become a critical factor because in the aftermath of Robert Maxwell's death it would be realized that the Maxwells had used their stake fraudulently.

According to a document discovered in Maxwell's files, three directors, Robert, Kevin, and David Shaffer, president of Macmillan, had agreed at a special board meeting on November 5, 1990 to transfer 10.6 million Berlitz shares (the 56 per cent holding) under a nominee agreement to Bishopsgate Investment Management (BIM) via Bishopsgate Investment Trust (BIT)—both Maxwell private companies. Whether that meeting actually occurred is still uncertain and Shaeffer says he has no recollection of it, but the effect was that during 1991 when Maxwell needed to produce collateral for loans, he could assert to the banks that the Berlitz shares were controlled by his private companies.

Shearson Lehman Brothers would later claim that it had specifically asked for and obtained assurances that the shares did not belong to the public company. Kevin could only urge patience as he sought more collateral, while speculation fueled the wild gyrations in the public companies' share prices.

In London, the British banks, owed about £950 million, had seen their own share prices fall that morning because of the risks which they faced. The bankers were prepared to take any collateral, regardless of the true owners, to protect their money. Later, told that Kevin had acted illegally in handing over the various share certificates, they would refuse to return the securities despite the cost to the pension fund.

On Thursday morning, November 7, the suspension of share dealings in MCC and Mirror Group was lifted. With the juggler absent from the stage, everyone knew that the balls would crash while others suspected that some of the balls would be missing. MCC's price plunged from 121p to 74p, reducing its value by £150 million. Mirror Group's rose from 77.5p to 106p in the expectation that the family would have to sell its controlling interest and that without Maxwell the business would make better profits. Since the company's debt seemed the most pressing issue, MCC's new chairman announced the proposed sale of its 56 per cent stake in Berlitz to the Fukutake Publishing Company for £149 million ($265 million). It was a deal that Shaffer had negotiated under Kevin's supervision. As usual, the other directors simply accepted Kevin's statement although for the astute there were already grounds for suspicion.

Amid the chaos on the days following Maxwell's death, David Shaffer, Macmillan's president, had telephoned Basil Brookes. The subject was the payment for Que, a Macmillan subsidiary which published computer books. The sale had been agreed by the MCC board and signed the previous Sunday November 2. Shaffer was concerned that Kevin had asked that the purchasers make their payment into a Citibank account from which Maxwell's private companies had, quite unusually, the right to draw money.

Shaffer was concerned because Macmillan's lawyers had been reassured by a senior partner of the British lawyers Titmus, Sainer & Webb to use that account. The lawyers had believed that Titmus represented MCC. In fact, the British lawyers also represented Maxwell's private companies. It was a deliberate confusion which suited Maxwell and which Titmus, acting on Maxwell's instructions and anxious to earn fees, did not seek to clarify.

In the event, Shaffer's call to clarify the imbroglio was critical. "It was at the last minute," recalls Laister, who gave Kevin "an instruction." The money was to be paid into MCC's account at Natwest Bank. At that moment none of the directors suspected that MCC was in danger. "Kevin mumbled an excuse," says Laister, "saying that he wasn't responsible. He blamed confusion. I did not press it further."

By mid-morning in Tenerife, Claverie had fulfilled part of his task.

Contrary to the pathologists' requests and contrary to Jewish law, Maxwell's body was being embalmed. During the night the lawyer had asked the pathologists to reexamine their initial conclusion that death was by natural causes. In telephone calls, Claverie questioned the possibility of "accident" being included in the pathologists' report. Maxwell's life had been insured by the Maxwell companies for £20 million but only in the event of an accident.

The rush to clear formalities was being completed. At Los Rodeos airport, loaders were attempting to fit his empty coffin on to the Gulfstream jet for its flight to Israel. After several hours, they conceded that the owner's air-conditioned 200-kilo oak casket, with viewing window, sold by the island's undertaker, was too big for the plane. Hours would now be lost while a Challenger jet was chartered in Geneva. Special clearance would be given for its flight into Israeli airspace.

Forty-eight hours had now passed since the first report to Maxwell headquarters. The shock had been digested and the reports from Tenerife were now receiving closer scrutiny. British pathologists volunteered that the cause of death entered on the death certificate, "respiratory cardiac arrest," was "meaningless." It was a mode, not the cause, of death. Signs such as myocardial infarct or coronary thrombosis would be required to indicate a heart attack and that had not been mentioned.

Having deliberately praised the local authorities for their cooperation to remove any obstacle to the swift completion of formalities to move the corpse to Israel, the Maxwell family now cast doubt on the Spanish pathologists' conclusions about the cause of death.

After constant communications between the sons in London and Betty, Philip and his youngest daughter Ghislaine who had arrived on the island, the family claimed that the heart attack could have occurred after Robert Maxwell fell into the water and therefore his death was an accident. The time and cause of death were still unknown, confirmed Isabel Oliva: "As far as I'm concerned, the investigations carry on." To fuel the mystery, Maxwell's private doctor Dr. Joseph Joseph suggested that the death was "suspicious." Since Dr. Joseph made his judgment from Wimpole Street in London, he only succeeded in multiplying the unease about the conflicting medical and other expert evidence.

At 2 a.m. on Friday morning, November 8, the embalming was completed. The coffin was loaded onto the Challenger. At 3:30 a.m., Betty Maxwell boarded the airplane. Throughout her whole stay on the island, no one had seen her shed a tear.

At that moment, Kevin was arriving in New York. He drove to the *News* building, where the flags flew at half mast, to reassert the family's interest in the *Daily News*. After reassuring conversations with both the print unions and management, he posed at a newsstand outside the building for photographers, wearing a blue *Daily News* baseball hat, selling the *News*. For many, it seemed a peculiar pose to adopt in the midst of grief.

Yet Charles Brombach, the president of the Tribune Company which had sold Maxwell the newspaper, was particularly pleased that Kevin, whom he had never met, telephoned Chicago to reassure the president of the family's determination to save one of "Bob's great prides." Kevin's message was reassuring: "We'll just clarify our relationship with the banks and it should be business as normal within one week." The soothsayer then rushed to Kennedy airport for the Concorde trip to London, to fly the following day by private jet to Israel.

Maxwell's body arrived at Tel Aviv airport before noon and was driven to Jerusalem. "I was born Jewish and I shall die Jewish," Maxwell said in 1986 but few had believed him. On Saturday, Dr. Iain West, one of Britain's leading pathologists, arrived in Israel. Sent by the Lloyds syndicate of insurance companies, he was hired to complete another autopsy by Sunday morning. To claim the £20 million, the Maxwell family needed to prove that the deceased had not only left the boat alive but could also have been revived had he died on board the yacht. In such circumstances his death would have been "accidental." West worked with his wife, Dr. Vesna Djurovic, also a pathologist, and three Israeli pathologists. He worked under a handicap. Maxwell's heart was in Spain and the remaining organs were too damaged to permit any meaningful investigation. Yet West could not be unmindful of the interests of his employers. Unable to determine the precise cause of death from the corpse, he decided to search elsewhere.

Not far from the frustrated pathologist, a Palestinian gravedigger was confirming on his portable telephone his latest instructions that the grave should be wider and longer than normal.

There lay the owner of $250 million worth of Israeli assets which included a leading newspaper, Jerusalem's two football clubs, industrial investments and, most important of all, the private telephone number of President Gorbachev whose help he had sought to hasten the emigration of Soviet Jews to Israel.

At 2:30 in the afternoon, the first of four hundred mourners arrived in the hall to pass by the body and pay their respects to the family who stood in a half circle.

Neman could reflect that Maxwell would have smiled with pleasure at the spectacle. Unlike in England, he was remembered in Israel for his successes and his ability to overcome his failures. "Robert Maxwell was a folk hero in Israel. A Holocaust survivor who made good," said one mourner. Israel, he continued, "is the only solution for the Jews. Maxwell's return was the symbol to Diaspora Jews to return to your own people." Those sentiments would puzzle the British who had accepted his declarations of patriotism at face value. But for those standing around the shrouded corpse in Jerusalem there was no mystery. Maxwell, despite his efforts, had been rejected by the British because, despite his best efforts, he remained a Jew. Only in Israel did he find acceptance and peace.

The first to speak was President Chaim Herzog, first in Hebrew but then in English because none of the family understood. His eulogy was resounding: "He scaled the heights. Kings and barons besieged his doorstep. He was a figure of almost mythological stature. An actor of the world stage, bestriding the globe as Shakespeare says, like a colossus." Most people in Britain would be puzzled by Herzog's praise. Searching for a hidden connection, most would be convinced that Maxwell was being rewarded for his services to Mossad. None could believe or understand that the hidden agenda was simply Maxwell's uncompromised relationship with his fellow countrymen.

Herzog was followed by Maxwell's eldest son Philip, unable to disguise his emotions: "Dear Dad . . . soldier, publisher and patriot. Warrior and globe trotter. Father of nine children and grandfather of eight. We love you, we need you, we miss you . . . May you rest in peace."

Sam Pisar said Kaddish, the Jewish prayer; and then the mourners moved outside. Rabbi Shear-Yashuv Cohen of Haifa who, according to the laws of the Cohens, cannot enter a building containing a dead body because of the danger of impurity, gave the final blessing: "Robert Maxwell started his life as an Orthodox Jew and has now traveled the full circle and returns to his origins." United by the common bond of surviving two millennia of persecution, Cohen praised their brother who, having survived prejudice and malice, had returned home. The outsider had become an insider.

It was approaching sunset when the cavalcade drove through closed roads, passing the Damascus Gate, toward the Mount of Olives overlooking the traditional site of the Garden of Gethsemane. On the site most coveted by Jews, where it is said those buried will be the first to hear the call of the Messiah at the Day of Judgment, the mourners collected. Cynics would add, "Trust Cap'n Bob. Making sure that he would be first in the line."

A pink light from the horizon reflected on the Dome of the Rock as the Jewish ceremony began, mingled with Moslem laments from the Old City. Not so long before, Maxwell, overlooking the cemetery from the royal suite in the King David Hotel, was playing his power games. How he would have enjoyed seeing all the nation's most powerful— the president, the prime minister Yitzhak Shamir, Cabinet ministers Ariel Sharon, Moshe Arens and Ehoud Olmert and Shimon Peres— all gathered as if it were a state funeral—an honor which would be mocked in Britain. Hence his final rejection of that country.

Olmert, who months earlier had sat with Maxwell in Holborn watching the World Cup, delivered the graveside farewell:

"He once said to me, 'After all, I have not done so badly for a young Jewish boy from the *shtetl* [ghetto].' " Looking down at the grave, Olmert continued, "Indeed, Bob Maxwell, you have not done badly at all. May your soul rest in peace in this ancient ground which finally became yours." The sentiment was echoed by his widow: "Now the circle closes. He has returned to his roots."

There was no grace for the dead in England. The following day, Monday November 11, Kevin and Ian Maxwell were still struggling to keep their empire intact. There was no respite. MCC's shares continued to fall.

At 2 o'clock that afternoon, a press conference was called by Matthew Evans. Guarded by security men and watched by over one hundred journalists, Evans read a six-page statement written by his author, Seymour Hersh. In a convoluted narrative, Hersh stated that he had obtained solid evidence from a private detective which linked the *Daily Mirror* with Mossad's kidnap of Vanunu. Hersh's statement concluded that he had fulfilled his obligation "to tell the truth and all the truth." Within hours, British journalists had established that Hersh and Evans, who had paid the "detective" £1,290 in Amsterdam, were the victims of a hoaxer. All their allegations against Maxwell had collapsed within twenty-four hours of his burial. Hersh was totally discredited.

In Maxwell's honor, the print unions in New York had decided to finance the planting of trees in Israel; Jack Lang, the French Minister of Culture, had initiated arrangements for a memorial service in Paris which would be attended by senior government ministers; and in London, Lord Goodman had, after an approach from Betty Maxwell, arranged that a memorial service could be held in St. Paul's Cathedral, although the widow said that her preference was Westminster Abbey. But even as these and other benedictions were planned, Maxwell's reputation was being shredded in the City of London.

When the MCC directors met on Tuesday November 12, the first board meeting after Maxwell's funeral, there was common sentiment of sorrow for Ian and Kevin. The sale of Berlitz was discussed, although unbeknownst to the board other than the Maxwell brothers, the previous day Shearson Lehman had taken control of 1.9 million Berlitz shares worth $30 million. Kevin did not mention that seizure.

In the week since Maxwell's death, it had emerged that the private companies which, to everyone's surprise, were said to number four hundred, had borrowed £758 million from a number of banks in Britain, France, Switzerland, Japan, Canada and the United States. Most of the thirty banks had lent their millions amid the secrecy required by Maxwell. Over the previous days, each of those banks had watched in horror as the collateral which Maxwell had presented for those loans, the shares of the two public companies, collapsed in value.

On November 11, six days after Maxwell's death, Richard Stone, a corporate rescue specialist at Coopers & Lybrand, was asked by those banks to investigate the finances of the private companies and "get control" of the situation. Stone's problem in those early days was his understandable ignorance of the real questions which needed to be asked. To break through Maxwell's web of secrets, he sought first to rely upon Kevin and Ian. Even in retrospect, he believes that during those first days, both answered all his questions "honestly and gave us all the information we required."

Four days after Stone had begun his investigation, on November 15, Lawrence Guest received a report from a director of MIM, an independent pension fund management group, that some share certificates belonging to the *Mirror* fund could not be found. Their value was about £750,000. The MIM director believed their disappearance to be an administrative error. Guest knew about the stock lending program and was not worried, even after he discovered that the stock had actually been sold. Nevertheless, Guest telephoned Trevor Cook, who was responsible for the Mirror Group's pension fund money. Cook was already running a check through the share portfolio. "I think he knew that something might be wrong," recalls Guest, unintentionally revealing Maxwell's criteria for recruiting staff.

On November 19, MCC's shares fell to 46p and would fall another 10p the following day. In real terms, they were worth about 5 per cent of their value when he had boasted about his ambitions to become a £3–£5 billion corporation. The family's own paper fortune was sliced by £500 million.

There was talk of £1 billion of private debts and of £594 million to be repaid by the end of the year. The Fraud Squad's investigations had been leaked and the family's fortune was reportedly near to collapse. Alarmists were mentioning the possibility of bankruptcy as the shares fell further to 31p. Holding on by their fingertips, the family's only hope was that the forty-three banks could recover their money either if MCC was saved or if its assets were carefully sold off. That required calm and patience. That possibility disappeared at a meeting of the MCC board on the morning of November 19. With a show of concern which convinced his fellow directors, Kevin Maxwell announced that the sale of Berlitz had encountered a problem: "It seems that a share certificate representing 1.9 million Berlitz shares is missing." There was no explanation, although there had been a warning the previous day.

David Shaffer had called Laister from New York, reporting that an announcement had passed across the market dealers' screen announcing that "someone" had an interest in 1.9 million Berlitz shares. "Who is the owner?" asked Laister. Shaffer did not know. The two directors assumed that there must have been some "bad housekeeping" but "nothing serious."

"Kevin was very clever at that meeting," says Brookes. "He put the burden on me to find the missing certificate, but he knew that it had been pledged to Shearson Lehman Brothers. Kevin came across as wanting to be different than Bob, so we wanted to believe him."

Unbeknownst to the board, Ian Maxwell had six days earlier signed a second transfer of Berlitz shares as a guarantee of a £40 million loan to the Swiss Volksbank. That sale was agreed at a board meeting of the Robert Maxwell Group at which Ian and Trachtenberg were the only directors present. "Trachtenberg put the form in front of Ian and he signed," it was later reported. Swiss Bank would insist that it had received assurances that the shares were owned by Maxwell's private companies.

At 11 a.m. on November 20, Guest and Burrington arranged a meeting with Ian Maxwell. Also invited was Alan Clements, a non-executive director of the group. Trevor Cook was to brief the directors about the pension. He arrived "white faced and trembling." His message was unambiguous: "£100 million is missing and there might be more." It was the first hint about Maxwell's use of the pension funds. To those gathered, Ian seemed remarkably calm. According to Guest, "The atmosphere wasn't bad. I don't think Ian realized how serious it was. Ian relied upon his little brother." If pushed, even Guest admits that he and the other directors did not realize the full gravity of the situation. The picture was still very incomplete, but not only because of Robert Maxwell's deceit. "I don't think," says Guest, "that the directors should have known what was happening. It was not their responsibility."

A second hint of the abyss ahead was delivered on Sunday November 24 by the American law firm Wilkie, Farr & Gallagher. Acting on Shaffer's instructions, the lawyers had been searching for the owner of the 1.9 million Berlitz shares. Although the identity had not yet been established, the lawyers had discovered that the total number of Berlitz shares which others were claiming to possess had increased to 2.4 million. There were good grounds to believe that the amount would increase. Shaffer's news astonished Laister.

At 9 a.m. the following morning, Monday November 25, Laister barged into Kevin's office. "We've got a major problem," said Laister. As he described the problem, Kevin displayed apparent genuine astonishment. "We've got to find out who the owner is," agreed Kevin, who endorsed Laister's opinion that the certificate "must have been stolen." Kevin's act, Laister would lament some days later, was a fine replica of his father's familiar routine. Others would say that Kevin was never honest. Or, alternatively, that while fooling others, Kevin also fooled himself.

By any measure, that day was critical. While the frenzy of reports described a tottering empire, no one yet imagined the possibility of a collapse. The least suspicious seemed to be the ninety bankers who gathered on that Monday at the Chartered Insurance Institute in the City of London, a Gothic edifice whose wood paneling and red cushions evoked a fittingly somber atmosphere. Their purpose was to bring order to their competing bids for the remains of Maxwell's private companies. Colin Keer of Bankers Trust made the first presentation. Reading from blue-bound books bearing the inscription "Project Sage," Keer assured the bankers that the Maxwell family's assets, which they valued at between £1.1 billion and £1.4 billion, were worth nearly £200 million more than its debts, which were assessed at £850 million. Characteristic of the bank's judgment was that Keer valued *The European* at £27 million. Six weeks later, the newspaper would be sold for a pittance.

The second presentation was given by Richard Stone, the Coopers & Lybrand rescue specialist. Stone's assessment was cautious, surrounded by caveats, but nevertheless reassuring. Stone believed that Maxwell's private companies owed MCC and MGN £70 million and owed about £70 million to the pension fund. Stone advised that if the banks did not agree to a standstill the group would be insolvent, but there was a probability of salvation. He asked for one more week to complete his investigation, especially to resolve questions about the pension fund. Since he did not emphasize any importance about the pensions, his audience was not alarmed. Some of the bankers were skeptical, but even they were apparently willing to believe the good news that their loans would be repaid. After all, to admit at that stage that they had been mistaken in lending to Maxwell would be embarrassing. More embarrassing was their knowledge that millions had been lent without properly inquiring into the companies' accounts and without heeding the track record of the borrower.

Searching for self-justification, they allowed themselves to be encouraged by the assurance that the investigating committee of bankers and accountants had benefited from "long discussions" with both Kevin and Ian and had subsequently won firm pledges from the brothers that independent auditors would, for the first time, be allowed to scrutinize the internal accounts of the private companies.

On the advice of John Melbourn, the chief of credit control at NatWest Bank, the assembled bankers agreed to give Stone one more week. As Melbourn said, the alternative was "to lose everything." Nevertheless, the credibility of Robert Maxwell's glowing reports and expressions of confidence about the future had passed. After that meeting, there was an indisputable sense that the final rites had been delivered to the independence of the Maxwell empire.

On the basis of the Keer and Stone reports, Rothschild Inc. agreed to lend £2 million to the private businesses to ensure their immediate survival. Other banks promised approximately £8 million. They judged that there was a problem within the private companies but that it was surmountable. To some it seemed that the Maxwell brothers had achieved a victory. The unanswered question is whether Kevin believed that the full truth would not emerge. Probably he did not consider the question, because at about this time he borrowed $3.8 million from the account of the jointly owned Berlin newspaper company. On December 2, Bertelsman, the German partners, discovered the loan and demanded its repayment. It would be too late. Bertelsman became just another creditor.

After his presentation to the bankers on November 25, Stone and his team moved into Maxwell House and began an exhaustive examination of the papers to which hitherto only Maxwell and Kevin had complete access. They were joined by bankers from N.M. Rothschild led by Richard Davey, who specialized in corporate rescue, and officials from NatWest—a total of about forty experts. Together they began interviewing individual bankers and Maxwell's staff to establish the flow of money. Simultaneously, other accountants began a paper chase to reconstruct what had actually happened to the funds. Progress, recalls Davey, was slow: "Everything was coming out in dribbles." Maxwell's staff members were pressured to deliver information faster.

The omens worsened each day. On November 27, MCC postponed publication of its results. "Now that Bob has gone, we need to find out the truth," said one banker. Outsiders remained puzzled.

The secrets of Maxwell's 400 private companies began to unfold on Thursday, November 28. By following the paper trail, the investigators established that about £100 million was missing. There was still no major concern.

The following day, Friday, the investigators heard that Basil Brookes had compiled his own schedule of loans two days earlier but had not passed it on. It was not suspicious but simply the perpetuation of Maxwell's compartmentalization. By then, Michael Stoney had been recruited by the investigators as a link to Maxwell's staff. It was Stoney who arranged for Brooke's schedule to be faxed to the investigators. Its arrival on Friday afternoon fundamentally changed the nature of the investigation. Simultaneously, Stone discovered that the £47 million which Guest had been chasing had in fact been transferred from the Mirror Group to the private companies. The amount missing, it seemed, was £297 million (£250 million to MCC and £47 million to MGN). Critically, the money was not owed to banks but to the public companies. For the first time the investigators understood the nature and extent of Maxwell's operations: namely, the secret intercompany loans which opened up the web of Maxwell's fraud. "We suddenly realized," recalls Stone, "that a number of people must have known about those loans and that amount of money." Exactly four weeks after Maxwell had flown to the Canary Islands, his plunder of the pension fund was also about to be unraveled. "It was the moment we realized that we needed to open up the pension can of worms," said Davey. "It was a crucial moment," confirms Richard Stone.

Early on Saturday morning, Stone's investigators assembled at Maxwell House. Throughout the previous week they had sought information about the pension fund. Finally they possessed the key. Richard Stone knew precisely who could answer the investigators' questions: Trevor Cook and Larry Trachtenberg. It was the first time the investigators had access to Trachtenberg's files. Until then he, like Kevin, had accepted the advice of his lawyer, Lord Mishcon, not to answer any question about the pension fund. Although Cook refused both to return to his office or to speak to the investigators directly, he agreed that he would answer questions through Stoney. "He had known that something was wrong," says Richard Stone, "but it never occurred to him what the mechanics were leading up to or the size of the problem. He just gave the certificates to Trachtenberg and after June never realized what happened. It all happened so quickly. He had the shock of his life."

By telephone, Cook guided Stoney through his files to the papers which showed how the pension fund's shares had been pledged to the banks. Trachtenberg completed other details. "By the end of Saturday," says Stone, "we understood the rape of the funds." Blaming those individuals was not an issue. "They were all cut off from one another in different buildings. None of them knew the whole picture." Nevertheless, the investigators were convinced that both Cook and Trachtenberg "knew they were sitting on a bomb."

The total liabilities had by the end of the day risen from £300 million to over £1.8 billion (£1.5 billion of outright debt and £300 million in stock loans). Since the assets were worth at most £800 million, Maxwell's net debts totaled £1 billion. There was no longer any question of rescuing the private companies.

The total money taken by Maxwell from MCC was £244 million. MGN had lost £47 million. The total pension losses were estimated at £400 million and would later be revised to £467 million. The total debt of the private companies to the pension fund and public companies was estimated at £758 million and later revised to £808 million.

Investigators and bankers that night began to speculate on the possibility of a gigantic fraud. Although none doubted that Robert Maxwell had perpetuated a crime, there was still compassion for his sons. For some, that began to dissipate the following day.

On Sunday morning, Richard Stone was puzzling over one particular issue: how MCC's holding of 56 per cent of Berlitz shares had fallen into the possession of the Swiss Volksbank which claimed that it had lent money not to MCC but to a Maxwell private company.

Stone had discussed the Berlitz shares with Kevin three days earlier, when the pension funds problem first appeared. According to Kevin, "I went with Bob to the Volksbank for a loan and he pledged the Berlitz shares. Bob told the bankers that the shares were privately owned because they had been transferred from MCC to BIT [Bishopsgate Investment Trust]." Kevin added, "I had no reason to doubt my father." Similarly Stone believed that he had no reason on Thursday

November 28 to doubt Kevin, although it would later be discovered that other shares of Berlitz were also pledged as collateral to three other banks: the Swiss Bank Corporation, Advest of New York and Morgan Stanley. Kevin, it would be said, knew precisely when to look sheepish: "He was there to protect the family." Stone's doubts on Sunday morning concerned MCC. If Maxwell had been using MCC's pension and funds as he had the private companies', the consequences for the public company were severe. Until then the two public companies, whose shares on Friday were still traded on the stock exchange, had not been subject to any investigation.

Throughout Sunday, as bankers, accountants, lawyers and Maxwell's staff met in a hectic succession of committees, Andrew Galloway and Ian McIntosh, the directors of Samuel Montagu, embarrassed by their association with the *Mirror* flotation, queried their clients as the first details of the pension fraud emerged. "We're shattered," said Kevin. "It's terrible what Bob's been up to." No one, recalled the bankers, "was pointing a finger at the brothers." The bankers were still unaware of the full account.

That night, Stone and Davey visited John Melbourn at NatWest's headquarters in Lothbury to advise the banker that the private companies would need £500 million to survive. Despite Kevin's insistence that an Israeli investor was prepared to save the group, Melbourn was told that survival was unrealistic. Melbourn replied: "I'm unwilling to pull the rug. Let's give them time. They've still got a fifty-fifty chance of survival." His optimism was based on the same lack of reality which had lubricated Robert Maxwell's ability to continue borrowing money long after he was insolvent. Regardless of Melbourn, Richard Stone's report to the banks on Tuesday would advise that the standstill could achieve no purpose.

At the same time, the directors of both MCC and MGN were summoned to consider their future. Initially both brothers were calm, even defiant. At the MGN meeting, Ian told a fellow director about the bankers: "These gray suits are crazy. They want to suspend the share price, yet we've got an injection coming on Friday which will save us." To his fellow directors, Ian urged, "Don't rock the boat. Don't get in a flap." But as the complete details of the pension fraud were explained, Ian's demeanor changed. "He looked shattered; even uncomprehending." McIntosh, head in hands, stuttered, "This is awful." In less than one hour, Ian capitulated—there was no alternative but to once again suspend MGN's shares.

At the later meeting of MCC's directors, the revelations about the pension fund made Laister look as if "he had been hit by a club" while Kevin, still calm, recommended that Coopers & Lybrand be asked to conduct a speedy audit of the pension fund. But it was the revelations about the Berlitz shares which turned the board against Kevin.

During that Sunday, David Shaffer had called Laister from New York several times, but it was the call toward 8 p.m. which Laister most recalls. In some shock, Shaffer reported that at least 10.1 million Berlitz shares had been pledged as collateral. "Who are the owners?" asked Laister. Shaffer revealed that Shearson Lehman Brothers was listed among the certified owners. The signature on the transfer certificate was Kevin's. Another transfer certificate to the Swiss Volksbank, dated November 5 but signed November 13, bore Ian Maxwell's signature. The hapless son would later claim that Trachtenberg had pushed a form under his nose and he had just signed.

Shaffer's discovery provoked an immediate confrontation between Kevin and the directors. Shaffer took part on a telephone conference line.

Laister led the demand for Kevin's resignation. "Until then," recalls Laister, "his excuse for refusing to resign was fear of jeopardizing the rescue of the private companies." That excuse had disappeared. But MCC's articles required that the chairman could only be sacked if the directors were unanimous. Ian Maxwell could block the move. Unwilling to control his temper, Laister burst into Kevin's office that night and threatened public exposure if Kevin refused to go. Calmly, Kevin insisted on considering his position.

Confronted by Laister about his duplicity, Kevin replied: "I didn't sign the transfer in my capacity as an MCC director. I was under the impression that they were private holdings."

Outside, the only evidence of the weekend's convulsions were the tight faces which emerged into Holborn that night. Even the scantiest details were withheld. "I would love to help," uttered the unusually tight-lipped Michael Richardson, "but we have agreed to say absolutely nothing." The first public inkling of the disaster was the announcement at 8:30 on Monday morning that dealings in the shares of both MCC and the Mirror Group would be suspended—MCC at 35p and the Mirror Group at 125p. It was December 2.

During the course of the day the reasons began to emerge. The estimate of the private companies' debts had increased from £850 million to over £1 billion. To address that problem, the family announced sales of £50 million worth of assets.

On the morning of December 3, Kevin and Ian Maxwell arrived again at the Chartered Insurance Institute to hear Richard Stone's second report. Kevin confidently quipped: "We have put a case which we think is correct. It is now up to the bankers." To some it seemed that the unsubstantiated optimism bore a familiar echo. The reality was spelled out by Stone in the "Russet Report." The debts, Stone told the same bankers, were "far higher than expected on November 25." An audible gasp—some said of agony—rose from his audience. Maxwell's private companies owed MCC £244 million, MGN £94 million and BIM £311 million. Added to the total of £602 million was another £156 million from stock lending.

Moreover, because Maxwell had taken £758 million from the pension funds and public companies (of which £658 million had been taken between May and October 1991), Maxwell's private companies' total debts, according to Stone, were £1.864 billion: £970 million to the banks, £758 million to the private companies and pension fund and £136 million to others. The following day, December 4, an additional £50 million was discovered missing from MGN, bringing the total losses to over £800 million.

Maxwell had used the money to pay £80 million in interest payments; £150 million as collateral for the bank loans of his family private companies; £150 million to buy MCC shares; and £100 million to pay a debt due to BBPC printing company's depleted pension fund which he sold in a management buy-out two years previously.

In addition to the private companies' liabilities, MCC had debts of between £1.4 billion ($2.6 billion) and £1.6 billion, of which between £800 million and £900 million were owed to forty-three banks. The biggest potential losers among British banks included Midland, which had lent £130 million; Lloyds, which was owed £180 million; NatWest was owed £150 million and Barclays, £150 million. Among the foreign creditors were Credit Lyonnais, which was owed £150 million; Parisbas, £82.6 million; the Swiss Volksbank, £39.9 million; Swiss Bank Corporation was owed about £60 million; the Japanese Long Term Credit Bank was owed £12 million; the Sumitomo Bank and Trust was owed £12 million; and Bankers Trust was owed approximately £90 million. There were unspecified debts to the Credit Agricole, Banque National de Paris, First Chicago and Citibank.

Stone concluded that the private companies needed at least £400 million just to survive and a freeze on repayments of loans and interest. His conclusion: "Survival impossible."

"In all my career," he added as a private conclusion, "I've never seen anything like this but the symptoms are the same. It was a desperate man trying to shore up the crumbling pillars of his empire."

Kevin pleaded for time to find an investor to save the private companies. The bankers skeptically agreed to allow three more days. Anything was acceptable, since the bankers wanted only one panacea: their money back with as little embarrassment as possible. The amount which they needed had increased from £400 million to £700 million. Only one banker, the Japanese representative of the Long Term Credit Bank, was unable to contain his emotions: "You lied to us. Why?" Kevin remained silent. There was nothing more to say.

The unfolding of events now assumed the nature of a runaway train. Shock followed surprise as the unimaginable was overtaken by even more unexpected revelations. Stone's team revealed that a combination of three signatures had transferred the pension money to the private companies: those of Robert Maxwell and his two sons.

Just after noon, Kevin left that meeting and walked into a press conference in Maxwell House. Coolly—some would say icily—he announced his resignation as MCC's chairman, claiming that he wanted to avoid a conflict of interest because of his loyalty to his father and because of the impending investigation into the relationship between the public and private companies.

When asked if money was missing from the pension fund, Kevin replied, "I can't say," adding that he was satisfied that all the transactions between the private and public companies had been authorized and properly recorded: "My brother and I were board colleagues with my father for many years. But clearly we didn't know everything that was going on. My father had a style of business based on 'need to know' rather than a sharing of information all the time." Twenty-one years earlier, the two DTI inspectors had described Robert Maxwell's business methods more succinctly. Richardson was moved to comment that Kevin's performance was "brilliant."

Kevin's replacement was Peter Laister, whose salary, because he would be working full-time, was raised to £250,000, a five-fold increase. "A bit rich," fumed one banker when it was discovered four weeks later. David Shaffer, the president of Macmillan in America, became managing director.

Ian had meanwhile returned to Mirror Group headquarters to face questions from staff, particularly about their pensions. The majority of the directors advised that there was no alternative but resignation. Among the minority urging him to stay was Joe Haines, unrealistic to the last. Pathetically, Ian, whose understanding of business and newspapers was severely limited, appealed to Burrington to rally support.

"Ian, if your name was Smith, there wouldn't be a problem," said the former journalist who still failed to understand the reality of Ian's responsibility. "But your name is Maxwell and I don't see how you can stay." Burrington nevertheless promised to seek advice. Shortly after he returned to his office, Ian telephoned: "Don't worry, Ernie. I'll go." Ian was replaced as chairman by Burrington.

The unanswered question was whether Ian had sincerely believed his public utterance four weeks earlier that the Mirror Group was "sound, strong and successful and will continue to be so."

That night, the *Daily Mirror*'s headline about Ian's resignation revealed that its editor shared the opinion of his new chairman: "He had to go because his name was Maxwell."

Exactly one month since the brothers had assumed control, both had resigned as directors of both public companies. Ostensibly they pleaded a conflict of interest between their duties as directors of public companies and their need to protect their private companies. But their excuses were symbolic. Their father's prophecy that "my children won't inherit a penny" had been proven correct. They had inherited enormous debts. The front page of the "newspaper he saved" was plastered with four words, "Millions Missing from *Mirror*." The following day, the *Mirror*'s headline claimed that its owner had stolen £526 million—a slight exaggeration. Maxwell the savior and the larger-than-life personality had been transformed into a gigantic fraudster.

The Maxwells' personal battle for survival was lost. They entered into that twilight world of insolvency where enormous effort is expended in return for no profit and no gratitude. Every aspect of their father's empire was under scrutiny by teams of experienced and skeptical accountants, and there was every possibility of criminal charges once the investigations were completed.

As the Maxwell brothers resigned, John Talbot, the head of corporate recovery for Arthur Andersen, was awaiting the summons. With an appearance befitting a corporate undertaker, Talbot was officially asked by the banks on December 5 to take over as administrator to the Robert Maxwell Group and Headington Investments. Maxwell's insolvency was official. Leading 120 accountants, Talbot directed his staff to "get control of the companies while all hell was breaking loose." Talbot's task was to sell off as much of the remains of the private companies as possible for the benefit of the creditors. Winning control meant sending accountants to Hungary, Germany, Israel and the United States. In London, the Maxwell brothers "openly answered" the administrator's trading and operational questions. Kevin, says Talbot, was "very helpful," while Ian was "only specific." Among the items immediately for sale were Bob's toys: one luxury yacht, some helicopters, two executive jets, and a Rolls Royce. More substantially, there was *AGB*, *The European* and the *New York Daily News*.

Late that same night, Kevin flew by Concorde to New York. At Heathrow, he murmured expressions of sorrow for the plight of the pensioners and gave assurances that he would "cooperate to the fullest extent" with Talbot and the administrators to recover the money. Yet Kevin's hasty flight struck Talbot as peculiar. The *Daily News* was owned by the Robert Maxwell Group, which Talbot now controlled; yet Kevin's mother had spent £5,030 on an air ticket to save a newspaper over which, under British law, he exercised limited control. Was the son, thought Talbot, trying to imitate his father's performance twenty years earlier and rebuild the empire in America? There was a hint of conspiracy in the appointment of Ellis Freedman and Shelly Aboff as directors to the board of the *Daily News* shortly before the newspaper filed for bankruptcy. Both were old cronies of Maxwell and knew nothing about newspapers. If it was not a plot, then Kevin lacked any sense of reality.

Kevin was welcomed in New York. Earlier that day, the *Daily News* had filed for protection from its creditors under Chapter 11. Until then, the newspaper's editors had concealed their additional troubles from their readers by barely mentioning their publisher's plight. The revelations in London over the past days had come as a "great disappointment" to Charles Brombach, the *Tribune* president who had sold the newspaper to Maxwell, and "a shock" to Jim Hoge, the newspaper's previous publisher: "I didn't think he was milk and cookies," said Hoge, "but I didn't think he was a crook." Like so many others, they could only question their own judgment and then console themselves, albeit self-servingly, that no one had known about Maxwell's criminality.

Nevertheless, there was gratitude for Maxwell. Nine months earlier, he had been the newspaper's only possible savior, and no other candidate could have galvanized the dispirited workforce and reestablished the relationship with the advertisers. Kevin was the beneficiary of that lingering legacy. He had become the publisher, and he seemed determined to exercise his responsibility. In New York he faced no opposition, although James Willsey, the newspaper's editor, was "surprised about his sudden interest. After all, we were not the keystone of the crumbling empire." The sentiment in London had not yet percolated across the Atlantic, and it was an advantage which Kevin sought to exploit.

Instead of remaining withdrawn, Kevin imitated his father, believing that any publicity he generated was advantageous and would remain under his control.

Calling a press conference at *Daily News* headquarters, Kevin announced that the newspaper was not for sale since he had sufficient money to continue to cover its losses, which had already cost his family $25 million. Then he was challenged about the administrator's control in London. The icy self-control dissolved: "There's no conflict of interest. That's bullshit." The next question went even closer to the heart: "Was your father the crook of the century?" "Out of order!" someone shouted as Maxwell's son, amid chaos, bolted toward the door to return to London and face writs to secure the return of the missing millions and writs to disclose information. The *Daily News*'s executives began reconsidering the advantage of maintaining their connection with Kevin.

In London, Kevin's foundations were crumbling even faster than in New York. Early that morning, December 6, David Lee, a specialist investigator for the accountants, Price Waterhouse, arrived at Maxwell House. Lee, a thirty-nine-year-old partner of the accountancy firm, had recently completed a two year attachment at Scotland Yard's Serious Fraud Office where he had investigated most of London's more serious frauds. But none had involved such a public personality as Robert Maxwell nor such enormous sums of money.

Lee's welcome was not euphoric. "I'll need an office," he told the receptionist.

"Well, I'm sure we can find you a desk somewhere," replied the reluctant woman.

"There'll be thirty of us." A short silence followed before Lee's next demand, "Take me to Robert Maxwell's office."

"Oh, no one's allowed in there. Only R.M."

"I don't think you understand," said Lee, smiling as he walked toward the lift.

Once ensconced in Maxwell's black leather chair surrounded by oak paneled walls, Lee ordered new security filing cabinets and a guide to show him around the offices. "Take me to Kevin's office," he asked. Once again there was prevarication and discussion that entry was only possible by the holder of an individual electronic security card. The resistance continued even as Lee entered Kevin's sanctuary.

Inside were six lawyers. On Kevin's desk were huge piles of documents. In low voices, the lawyers were distributing Kevin's papers among themselves. Three from Herbert Smith, representing the public company, MCC, and three from Titmus Sainer & Webb, representing the private companies, were seeking to disentangle the physical evidence of the Maxwell empire's intercompany trading. This was the third day of their endeavors.

"I'd like to see those," said Lee concealing his innate zeal.

"Client confidentiality I'm afraid old chap," said the lawyers in their well-rehearsed choreography.

Lee retired gracefully. Two hours later eight officers of the Serious Fraud Squad arrived at Maxwell House to remove any documents which would aid in their investigation. Twenty-four hours earlier, the same squad had admitted their reluctance to become involved because of the cost and staff required by an investigation. It was as if a corpse with a knife implanted needed to be found on the Fraud Squad's doorstep to provoke a reaction. Four weeks later, there would be five separate Fraud Squad investigations.

As the police arrived, the oak panels in the ninth floor's "oak room" which had surrounded the most famous editors of the *Daily Mirror* were being ripped out to reveal the wires and signal booster of the bugging system which Maxwell had installed. Their existence was inadvertently revealed in a conversation with another employee by John Pole, a former Scotland Yard chief superintendent, who six years earlier had been appointed as Maxwell's security officer. The first evidence was the discovery of a bug in Guest's telephone. Eventually the eavesdropping equipment was traced to three other telephones, including Kevin's. Ernest Burrington, a former editor of *The People,* and a Mirror Group director, was not completely surprised: "We used to say, 'Bob must have a bug in here. He knows so much of what is going on.' And then I would say loudly, 'You haven't, have you, Bob, you miserable old bastard?' He probably even heard that."

The Fraud Squad immediately moved into Kevin's office. Inside sat the six lawyers, still diligently separating Kevin's papers. "I'll have those, thanks very much," said the policeman waving his warrant under the noses of those who started to chorus, "Client confidentiality."

Outside, Lee smiled. He was soon sitting in another room with the police discussing their mutual interests when the door burst open. "What are you doing in my office?" fumed Ian Maxwell. "Out," snapped a police officer, slamming the door in Ian's face.

Moments later, Lee was summoned to the boardroom. MCC's directors were white faced. "The Fraud Squad is here," came a mute mutter from what seemed to Lee a mass of jelly fish.

Fear and shock had spread throughout Maxwell's headquarters. Like an earthquake, the arrival of the police and the administrators had finally demolished the legacy of the Maxwellian aura which had survived exactly one month since his death.

Ernest Burrington, like so many other former acolytes, admirers and sycophants of Maxwell within the *Mirror* building, was shedding his allegiance. "The increasingly desperate actions of a desperate man" was Burrington's accurate judgment.

Joe Haines confessed to his readers that he'd suffered "an awful week, the worst I can remember." He continued, proving his naive and eager self-deception: "Bob Maxwell, the man who once genuinely saved the *Mirror,* has through his manipulations of that money, now delivered us into the hands of those whom he hated, the pinstripes of the City of London." Even at the end, Haines, the former spokesman of a discredited British prime minister, deluded himself that Maxwell hated the City. In truth, Maxwell desired above all to be accepted by the City establishment. Like all the other Mirror Group directors, Haines voiced no responsibility for failing to safeguard the shareholders' and pensioners' funds.

But that night, no one's self-delusion eclipsed that of the *Mirror*'s editor, Richard Stott. In an editorial titled "Where We Stand," Stott, who had servilely scrapped the floor at Maxwell's feet for six years, pronounced that any future owner of the newspaper must "*continue* the independence of the editors from an owner's interference." Apparently without appreciating the irony, he added, "We fight for the millions of people who have no other voice against public bullies and private cheats, against corrupt businessmen and incompetent politicians and against bigotry and racism." Considering that it was Stott who published a succession of articles and photographs of Maxwell regaling the communist tyrants and Stott who, by his acquiescence, endorsed Maxwell's bullying and cheating, the editorial was an eloquent testimonial to the morality of those who served Maxwell.

On December 12, John Talbot, the administrator investigating Maxwell's private companies, made an appointment to see Kevin. Over the previous two days, despite his public promise to help the administrators, Kevin had ceased to be unconditionally helpful, especially concerning the location of the companies' money. Convinced that Kevin was deliberately prevaricating, Talbot was not surprised that for the first time a lawyer was sitting in Kevin's office. Monty Raphael, who had defended some of the most notorious of the eighties fraudsters, had been hired to protect Kevin on "this sensitive issue." At the end of a difficult meeting, Talbot was certain of only one fact: Kevin was refusing to answer his questions about how the Maxwells pumped money through the off-shore trusts.

The administrator's powers under the Insolvency Act are quite draconian. Failure to answer his questions can be declared by a judge to be a contempt of law and punishable by imprisonment. The administrator applied for that order against Kevin and Ian. Kevin was represented by George Carman QC, whose diminutive stature is compensated by his quick wit and outstanding courtroom performance. Success in notable trials had pushed Carman's reputed fees into the stratosphere—£500 per hour. Since the Maxwell family were all suddenly pleading poverty, the source of the £1 million defense fund which was guaranteed to Carman before he accepted the case was naturally an important secret. Insiders, however, knew that the payor was Betty Maxwell, who, as the marriage disintegrated, had secured her own fortune from her late husband. Carman's advice to his client was succinct: Don't speak a word because it would undoubtedly be self-incriminatory and used in the eventual and inevitable criminal trial. The right to silence, said the lawyer, was inalienably protected by the constitution. But since Britain's constitution is unwritten, the administrators would have good grounds to challenge the lawyer's assertion. "You'll probably be sent to jail for six months," said a smiling Carman, "but there's no alternative."

In High Court, Carman argued that Kevin would not prejudice his chance of a fair trial. His pledge on Kevin's behalf to spend "every waking hour" to help trace the missing millions did not impress the judge, who ordered the brothers to answer the administrator's questions and ordered that their passports be surrendered.

In a midnight hearing, a judge restored the passports. Kevin, it was explained, wanted to save the empire in New York. The following day, December 10, he flew once again by Concorde across the Atlantic. The cost was once again borne by his mother, whose own alleged financial plight had just been reported on the front pages. Headington Hill Hall, it was claimed, was closed, the furniture was abandoned to the administrator, and Mrs. Maxwell had tearfully bid her staff farewell, pleading that she was broke. It was completely untrue.

Kevin's Concorde flight was not uneventful. Sitting in the adjacent seat was Harry Arnold, a veteran *Daily Mirror* reporter. Sliding beside his late employer's captive son, the reporter extracted a memorable reply to a much-pondered question: "What do you think of your father being labeled one of history's biggest crooks?" Kevin replied, "A lot of it is fair comment." But he resolutely refused to discuss his own involvement.

Kevin's position at the *Daily News* had worsened slightly. The newspaper's executives were struggling for survival within the framework of Chapter 11. Unlike their position the previous May, they possessed one major advantage: the unions had lost their power to blackmail. Their owner's bankruptcy meant that there was no money to pay any redundant employees. There were also no alternative employers in New York. The unions began discussing with management ideas to save costs.

As the publisher, Kevin Maxwell's role was in theory critical. Although he told reporters, "I have promised that if I become a liability, I will step down," no one had made that request. His efficacy depended, however, upon his constant presence in New York. Since that was impossible, he sought to prove his presence by appearing on national television. His chosen vehicle was ABC's "Prime Time." Faced with Sam Donaldson, one of America's more acerbic reporters, Kevin revealed that, while possibly an accomplished financial technician like his father, he was incompetent inside a fish bowl. Donaldson's question was why he wanted to keep the newspaper afloat.

"It's absolutely a way to make money," replied Kevin.

"Is that the main reason you're in it?" responded Donaldson.

"I don't think that anyone would ever describe me as being a member of the Salvation Army and I'm not in business just for the pleasure of it. I'm in business to make money."

For Jim Hoge and the other *Daily News* executives, the performance was a revelation. The son of a crook was pleading the Fifth Amendment; and while he lacked any money to invest in the newspaper, he declared that his exclusive interest in their beloved's survival was to become rich. Jim Willsey, the newspaper's editor, reconsidered his attitude: "Kevin's problems in London were influencing his credibility in the U.S." Willsey had already forced the resignation of Aboff and Freedman from the board when their names were mentioned as participants in Maxwell's share-support operation. Now Willsey moved against Kevin. "He wanted to stay but I persuaded him to go," admits Willsey, understating the pressure he exerted to overcome Kevin's reluctance. Kevin returned to London stripped of his last hope for salvaging the empire.

Since Ian had collapsed from the strain, it fell to Kevin to defend the family's honor, protect its hidden assets and lead the fight to stay out of prison. Among his first tasks was to establish his "poverty." Accordingly, Kevin invited the *Sunday Mirror* to photograph himself, his wife and three children traveling by public transport from his Chelsea home to Piccadilly. Looking suitably miserable, Kevin was asked to comment about allegations that his father had bugged his own son: "No reaction at all"—which might well have been true.

Only one piece of the jigsaw remained unplaced in the penultimate chapter of Maxwell's life. The much-vaunted Maxwell Communications Corporation still existed under the control of Peter Laister.

During December, a team of Price Waterhouse accountants had completed their investigations. To no one's surprise, the intangibles which, five months earlier, Coopers & Lybrand had valued at $2 billion, were now reported to be worth at most $180 million. Since Maxwell had diverted £763 million from shareholders' funds and £240 million had been lost after revaluing its property and foreign-exchange trading, MCC's audited debts of $1.8 billion doubled.

At 10 a.m. on December 16, Laister and the MCC board explained to two hundred bankers their strategy for recovery. Meanwhile in New York, lawyers for Laister and his fellow directors were secretly and successfully seeking protection under Chapter 11 for the British company. The bankers in London would only discover Laister's ploy later that evening. "I'm still the bloody chairman," fumed Laister to those who enquired about the unexpected and unprecedented move. "The bankers were spitting mad when they discovered the directors' duplicity," recalls one accountant. Laister claims that he relied upon the financial advice of Lazards and the legal advice of Robert Hodes of Wilkie, Farr Gallagher. Twenty-two years earlier, Hodes had represented Saul Steinberg against Maxwell. "We spent a fortune on that advice," insists Laister in self-defense. "The behavior of those Price Waterhouse people is worth a chapter in a book."

The bankers' fury had not abated when, two days later, on December 18, they gathered again at Price Waterhouse's glass palace headquarters beside the River Thames. "They were still bloody shocked," recalls one of the accountants who openly accused the directors who had approved MCC's accounts five months earlier of "extensive misfeasance." Alan Wheatley, the senior partner responsible for the investigation, presented a gloomy scenario to the bankers. "A shoddy piece of work," stormed Laister when he saw the analysis. His intemperance curtailed his last hopes of employment. The Chapter 11 application had plunged the company into chaos which the banks, with a vengeance, sought to neutralize. On December 20, by joint applications in London and New York, MCC's management was placed under duel supervision. Laister was fired.

Like the Thousand Year Reich, the Maxwell Empire had survived only a fraction of its intended life span. And like the Führer, Maxwell's greatest humiliations were suffered after his death by his family. The video of his autopsy in Israel, showing in explicit detail the pathologists undertaking their gruesome task, was sold, copied and viewed by hundreds of gawkers, among them many *Daily Mirror* readers. One can only speculate whether Maxwell would have appreciated the initiative of the Israeli technician who sold the video to a French magazine.

The video included the examination by Dr. Iain West, the pathologist from Guy's Hospital in London. Despite his eminence, West has been controversial in Britain. In 1980 Colin Wallace, a senior British Intelligence officer who exposed a catalogue of "dirty tricks" organized by the British government in Northern Ireland, was accused of murder. In the investigation that followed, Dr. West, who performed the autopsy on the victim, was accused of changing the cause of death at the behest of British Intelligence, though nothing was ever proven.

In Maxwell's case West lacked a virgin corpse to dissect. The consequences of embalming were evident; the incisions by the three Spanish pathologists were obvious; and it was unclear whether the abrasions on the corpse had been caused by the air-sea rescue service, the Spanish pathologists, or the embalmer. Still, West was unwilling to allow the Spanish pathologists' verdict to pass unchallenged. He reported that injuries to Maxwell's left hand and torn left shoulder muscles were consistent with a person "clinging to something." West theorized that Maxwell did not jump completely overboard but hung on to the yacht's railing before falling into the sea. Yet West conceded that Maxwell's lungs contained no water. This is the weakness of West's theory: he could present no conclusive cause of death. "The physical injuries," he reported, "while not conclusive with suicide, certainly do not exclude it, and are more compelling than any other cause." The opposite was equally true: namely, that Maxwell had suffered a seizure, fallen overboard, and then tried to save himself. West dismissed the notion of a heart attack, which, according to the Spaniards, he could have suffered while leaning over the rail—explaining that Maxwell would have fallen onto the deck and could not have rolled into the sea. West also ignored the Spanish finding that Maxwell had vomited shortly before his death.

Accordingly, the insurance companies favored suicide on the basis of nonmedical evidence, pointing to Maxwell's financial crisis; his "unusually pleasant manner" to many before his death; his "unusual" solitary presence on the yacht; and, most important in West's opinion—that he locked his bedroom cabin before going on deck. West placed great emphasis on the failure to find the cabin's key. The mystery of Maxwell's death was, therefore, compounded by conjecture.

The greatest humiliation occurred on January 20. Eighty journalists and photographers—those who in Maxwell's opinion were the reptiles of society, deserving only to be bullied, humiliated and dismissed— poured into his London home at the invitation of the administrator seeking publicity for the forthcoming auction of his chattels. Just as forty-six years earlier, the young British lieutenant had walked through Hitler's bunker in Berlin, the enemies of that same lieutenant marched through his former sanctuary, bellowing and chortling about his ultimate defeat.

Little had given Maxwell greater pride than his elegant penthouse apartment on the tenth floor of Maxwell House, adjacent to the *Mirror* building. With panoramic views over London, the helipad on the roof just above, the overstocked kitchen, the vast bath, Swedish sauna with a built-in television and access to the most sophisticated communications system to reach the far-flung outposts of an empire, it was a symbol of his wealth and power. Now every chair, curtain, book and cooking pot was for sale. At a packed auction on Valentine's Day, February 14, eager souvenir hunters paid a hefty premium for a slice of nostalgia: $2,000 for Maxwell's four baseball hats! The "Max Factor" had assumed an unexpected meaning.

The curtain had fallen forever on an astonishing era.

EPILOGUE

Maxwell never imagined that he would bequeath a debt-ridden conglomerate, at the mercy of those whom he despised, as his memorial. Nor would he have expected to be remembered as a fraudster. But, by the nature of the man, it could never have been different. Fixated by a conviction about his own abilities, reckless about the consequences of his deeds and ultra-sensitive to criticism from others, Maxwell's flaws were so obvious and so unmistakable that his survival was only possible because few dared to challenge his overbearing animality. Rarely was Maxwell more perceptive about himself than during his confession in 1967 that he was a "jungle man."

Contemptuous of society's rules and mores and looking to profit from their avoidance or exploitation, Maxwell personified the impoverished refugee who, hungry for success and recognition, became admired as an immigrant buccaneer. In Britain he found a tolerant and genteel society which was first unwilling and then unable to challenge his self-promotion. Some interpreted that inactivity as evidence of Britain's innate sense of fair play. Others condemned the paralysis as proof that Britain's Establishment was amateur and even unintelligent. For it is hard to imagine how any other Western nation, having condemned a businessman in 1971, could praise his virtues twenty years later, just as he perpetuated one of modern history's most enormous frauds. Yet that was the enigma which Maxwell cunningly created: the impossibility of disentangling the right from the wrong. The gulf between Maxwell's morality and his critics' was irreconcilable.

Most accepted that Maxwell was unique because his ambition, tenacity, energy and competence, combined with an unusual blend of talents and interests, had twice helped him overcome official condemnation for his financial misdeeds and enabled him to build a £1 billion publishing empire which apparently was profitable.

Those who aided, profited and praised his accumulation of wealth willingly ignored the fissures which permeated his character—especially his dishonesty. None could have been in any doubt about his past transgressions. The evidence was presented in cogently argued official documents in 1954 and 1971. The motives of those who deliberately ignored the evidence were mixed. His family and close associates loyally accepted his pleas of victimization. But the growing army of business contacts who disregarded the proof were either ignorant or greedy, and often both.

Some might argue that Maxwell's resurrection during the eighties was only possible because of the peculiarities of that era. The extraordinary conviction that the world's economy was destined for perpetual expansion intoxicated a broad swathe of bankers, brokers and lawyers. Their self-esteem dissolved any caution and sense of inquiry which they, as professionals, asserted as reward for epic salaries. Apparently sane, serious and highly paid experts were willingly lured by Maxwell into the unknown.

Maxwell thrived upon secrecy, distortion, menace and contradiction. For any society not to have questioned the integrity of a socialist who consorted with communist tyrants and based his business empire in a tax haven is amusing. For statutory regulators to have perpetually ignored the intrinsic secrecy of that operation is puzzling. For journalists and others to have accepted his employment is pitiful. For professionals like bankers and lawyers to have served his interests without question is shameful. For his auditors, Coopers & Lybrand Deloitte, to have regularly authenticated his bogus accounts is actionable. All of them willingly cast aside rational doubts, accepted his bullying and became committed disciples, unwilling to question their paymaster.

None of those individuals were innocent victims. Only the 20,000 pensioners who lost part or all of their life savings deserve pity, although some might argue that those executives who worked close to Maxwell deserve to suffer.

Had Maxwell embarked upon his career in America, his success would have been limited. But in Britain he was a big fish. Unshackled by British inhibitions and limited horizons, he played on a world's stage, watched by his adopted countrymen with a mixture of bemusement and awe. Yet Americans eventually embraced Maxwell more than Britons ever had. Ignoring his past, New York bankers and lawyers flocked to serve his cause. Initially, they had good reason; there was nothing crooked about Maxwell's businesses in 1985. Nor in 1987. Wall Street undoubtedly warmed to Maxwell's theme that he was the victim of prejudice in London. Of course, that was only partially true. The British Establishment had granted him a third chance, and the British withheld proper controls over a notorious recidivist. Should New York have realized that Britain's regulatory authorities are not staffed by young, ambitious lawyers but by exhausted failures awaiting their pensions? Maxwell's ambitions succeeded because he exploited that flaw.

Of course, the American banks were not naive. The fuel for Maxwell's ambitions was his ability to identify and pander to the vanities of those self-important individuals who controlled the fortunes which he sought to borrow. Attracted by his undoubted magnetism, they joined a bandwagon whose master genuinely believed that what was good for Robert Maxwell was good for the world.

Goldman Sachs, Shearson Lehman Brothers and Salomon Brothers aggressively supported Maxwell when some British banks cautiously held back. The French banks were even more brazen. Flushed with the excitement of being selected the chosen ones, individual bankers, brokers and lawyers yearned to be on the inside of the Big Deal. Their best excuse is that his folly only began in the last months of his life and that the unpremeditated acts of a desperate man cannot immediately be detected and controlled. Their stockholders must now pay the price for the pleasures of Concorde and helicopter rides and a day out on the *Lady Ghislaine*.

For all of his victims and his friends, the final account is of an accomplished trader, a brilliant salesman, an astute financial technician, a masterful printer, a tireless gambler and an appalling journalist. A man who will, at best, be remembered in equal measure for his failures and successes—but most of all for his success in overcoming his failures which would have crushed other mortals forever.

The indictment against Maxwell is lengthy and proven. But beyond the grave, there is an element of Maxwell which, despite the dishonesty, still evokes sympathy. For those who have not experienced the Holocaust and the loss of their family, and the probability of instant death serving in the front lines of an army against a ruthless enemy, it is all but impossible to imagine the influence such experiences exacted upon a young man's life.

Maxwell was unusual in many ways, not least because he sought to write his own epitaph in his lifetime and enjoy his assessment for many years to come. There are many mortals of Maxwell's kind who have sought in their lifetime to ensure a secure place in posterity. Some have succeeded, but Maxwell's weakness was his impatience, vanity and lack of intellect. Among the several privileges of the rich is their freedom to indulge in fantasy and frivolity without accounting to their critics. Maxwell sought to sit in the eye of the world on his own terms. To an astonishing extent, in his own lifetime, he succeeded. Practically every newspaper, including the *New York Times, Wall Street Journal* and *Newsweek,* reported Maxwell's life and exploits in the uncritical terms which Maxwell desired and demanded. That alone proves the force of his personality.

His great dream of a permanent worldwide communications group bearing his name is dead. His wish to be of political consequence was unfulfillable because there was no philosophy to sustain his influence. When asked to choose his own epitaph, Maxwell replied that he hoped to leave the world a slighter better place. Whether he succeeded is questionable. Certainly there are those who benefitted from his generosity and equally there are those who suffered, but not physically. At worst, excepting the pensioners, they suffered a bruised ego.

Whatever his weaknesses and regardless of his sins, his achievements were sufficiently creditable for him to properly expect a special place in the history of post-war Britain. If he was tortured by public humiliation and disbelieving of the criticism he attracted it is understandable. The impressive breadth of his commercial activities was eclipsed only by the intensity of his family bonds. The public image was of a larger than life, occasionally laughing bully whose public successes, crushing failures and flashes of generosity eluded most of mankind and created unpalatable suspicions. What greater accolade could he expect than the attention which the poor Jew made good attracted, and continues to enjoy beyond his three score and ten years?

Now that nature has taken its course and Maxwell has traveled to the next world, his parting message to those left behind is "You haven't understood me." Resounding from the earth is the reply, "But did you understand yourself?"

"For all is vanity. All go unto one place; all are of the dust, and all turn to dust again. Who knoweth the spirit of man that goeth upward, and the spirit of the beast that goeth downward to the earth? Wherefore I perceive that there is nothing better, than that a man should rejoice in his own works; for that is his portion; for who shall bring him to see what shall be after him?"

Ecclesiastes 3: 19–22

Sources

The principal sources for this book were interviews with over three hundred and fifty people, access to a wealth of private papers, the three reports issued by the Department of Trade and Industry about the status of Mr. Maxwell's private and public business affairs between 1971 and 1973, the annual reports of Pergamon and BPC/BPCC and the voluminous newspaper and magazine coverage since 1951. Mr. Maxwell consistently challenged many of the conclusions of the DTI reports, but they are quoted as they contain the evidence given by the people involved at the time.

During May and June 1973, I spent considerable time with Mr. Maxwell filming a long profile for BBC television. It was a critical period in Mr. Maxwell's career, and during those weeks we discussed at great length his ambitions, values and attitude to most of the criticisms which had been leveled at him. Nearly two hours of interview were recorded on film and the many other hours of conversation with him were noted. I retained those records and have drawn upon them for this book. Mr. Maxwell also gave me access at that time to his huge collection of scrapbooks and some papers which were pertinent to his business affairs. These have also been very valuable.

In making the film, I asked Mr. Maxwell to refer me to people who he thought could contribute to presenting a full account of his life. Most of them agreed to be filmed and their interviews, both on and off camera, have also been used. The most important were Mrs. Elizabeth Maxwell, Richard Crossman, Walter Coutts and Philip Okill.

We also interviewed in 1973 Saul Steinberg, the chairman of Leasco, Robert Hodes, his lawyer, and other Leasco executives. In the event, only the interview with Mr. Steinberg was transmitted, but other interview notes were kept. At the time, Mr. Steinberg also made available a quantity of documents concerning his negotiations during 1969 with Mr. Maxwell and Robert Fleming, the merchant banker. These papers were clearly of great help in the descriptions of those events nearly twenty years later. All the quotations from Mr. Steinberg and other Leasco executives date from 1973.

The interviews which I conducted are clearly quoted and sourced. Inevitably, many requested that their comments be off the record and therefore I have not listed any acknowledgments for the enormous help, encouragement and kindness I have received from so many people.

One person who deserves special mention, however, is Michael Shaw of Curtis Brown, whose support has been invaluable.

The individual sources for each chapter do not separately mention newspapers or interviews. These are either apparent from the text or were off the record.

CHAPTER 1

7 According to a historical survey. Herman Dicker, *Piety and Perseverance: Jews from the Carpathian Mountains,* Sepher Hermon, New York, 1981, page 58

The best descriptions of the Jewish communities in Carpo-Ruthenia are in the third volume of S. Y. Goss and Y. Cohen, *The Jews of Czechoslovakia; The Marmos Book*; a special historic memorial about the Jews of Slatinske Doly (or Szlatfina) published by the Yad Vashem Institute, Jerusalem.

CHAPTER 2

I have drawn upon the detailed records of Ferdinand Springer Verlag for the relationship between Maxwell and the publishers; and on interviews with the surviving but retired staff who negotiated with Maxwell during those years.

34 Maxwell's offer was "the only hope for rebuilding our company." Lange letter, February 18, 1955

34 Maxwell's own account. LSE Seminar, February 25, 1969

36 Von Eugen's protest to Kirkness. Public Records Office FO371 1056/250

39 Springer's contract with EPPAC dated September 16, 1949; cf. Lange letter, February 18, 1949, and Maxwell, April 14, 1951

40 He threatened to renege on the whole deal. Historic summary of Maxwell's relationship with Springer, page 11

40 Maxwell sent Otto a menacing letter. Letter, March 15, 1949

43 Maxwell, wrote Tönjes, seemed to ignore any advice and was even signing letters as "chairman." Letter, February 18, 1955

44 "Maxwell gave us enormous and valuable help over those years." Summary, page 14

48 "For Maxwell, it was the means to build for himself a huge business in London." Summary, page 14

51 By November 1950 the outstanding bills amounted to £115,000. Letter, November 25, 1950

52 Maxwell had overcharged Springer's old customer. Summary, page 24

54 "I deeply regret having to write this letter." October 10, 1951

CHAPTER 3

56 The various histories of Maxwell's companies have been obtained from the records at Companies House.

56 The best sources for the Simpkin Marshall affair are the Receiver's Report, 1955; the reports in the *Bookseller,* March 6, 1941; November 3, 1951; March 3 and June 18, 1956; and the Public Record Office, 37034/5/6. The *Sunday Times* in 1969 interviewed Kurt Wallersteiner at length and took several sworn statements from him.

68 terminate the juggling act profitably. Springer letter, April 14, 1951

70 In 1969 Maxwell explained his motives in long interviews with journalists from the *Sunday Times.*

72 "Maxwell has proved to be a difficult person to do business with." Springer letter, September 21, 1953

73 "a wide range of Soviet scientific books is now available." Springer letter, June 21, 1954

CHAPTER 4

91 Philip Wade's letter to the *Lancet,* April 27, 1963

92 "I do it because it ought to be done." *Sunday Times,* January 9, 1966

93 Betty Maxwell has described those years of running a home. *She* magazine, 1987

CHAPTER 5

94 I have relied upon the Buckinghamshire local newspapers—the *Wolverton Express* (later the *Wolverton and Milton Keynes Express*) and the *Bletchley District Express*—for general coverage of Maxwell's local political career. Only a few contemporaneous documents of the Labour Party survive. Local members, however, retain a vivid memory of their experience.

96 ". . . I don't have any specific time or date." *Midweek,* BBC TV, 1973

103 Christopher Booker's phrase, that he would be part of "the dream after the storm." *The Neophiliacs,* Fontana, 1970, page 64

105 "Now," he bitterly complained, "our prized workshops are going to Steptoe's Knacker's Yard for pennies." *Wolverton Express,* March 6, 1964

107 "I thought I was the cleverest thing on two legs there . . ." *Desert Island Discs,* BBC Radio, July 1987

110 "I have watched him frequently." *Hansard,* November 21, 1967

111 Bernard Levin, *The Pendulum Years,* Cape, 1970, page 302

114 "has been pestering Hugh Cudlipp with phone calls." *The Cecil King Diary 1965–70,* Cape, 1972, page 171

115 "That's the thing about me. I'm quick off the mark." *Sunday Times,* March 3, 1968

CHAPTER 6

128 Marriott's query, *Sunday Times,* January 9, 1966

129 Cecil King said subsequently. DTI, page 210

129 Their opposition was supported by Ansbachers. DTI, page 215

130 Maxwell ignored them both. DTI, pages 210/211

130 Maxwell felt that he had "bought a bargain." DTI, page 233

130 A "satisfactory return." DTI, page 20

133 He was to "knock off the Caxton sales force." DTI, page 11

135 ILSC's accounts were in a "deplorable state." DTI, page 74

135 its profits had, on its own admission, increased only "marginally." H. Kay Jones, *Butterworths, History of a Publishing House,* Butterworths, 1980, page 196

136 "to get lost." Kay Jones, op. cit., page 226

136 the absence of reliable information about ILSC's finances. DTI, page 74

136 "irregular and insufficient." DTI, page 73

137 "I was entirely at fault in not getting that as a copy for my own records." DTI, page 73

137 "No accounts had been produced of any nature," he said three years later. DTI, pages 78/9

138 Maxwell recalled that he had "honestly believed." DTI, page 234

138 "Mr. Bennett took the initiative in these matters." DTI, page 232

138 "heavily influenced by Mr. Maxwell." DTI, page 237 (and cf. DTI, page 231)

138 "Tell me where the £200,000 profit is." DTI, page 268

138 the profits were considerably lower than officially anticipated. DTI, page 137

138 "was absolutely disastrous." DTI, page 87

138 Maxwell fired both men and three other senior officials for alleged incompetence. (Although the DTI inspectors stated that Maxwell's allegations were erroneous: DTI, pages 138 and 154)

139 "The Board of ILSC has informed Pergamon that sales and profits . . . are running at the level forecast . . ." DTI, pages 48 and 143. The *Sunday Times*'s cautiously favorable comment was typical; cf. October 20, 1968

144 the profile concluded, he was "surprisingly mild." *The Times,* October 23, 1968

146 "This is a disgraceful affair and it is up to the Take-over Panel to do its proper job." *The Times,* October 26, 1968. For Murdoch's attitude, see Michael Leapman, *Barefaced Cheek,* Hodder, 1983

147 Maxwell had suggested in his circular sent to shareholders on May 15. DTI, pages 143/148

147 ILSC's accounts were "unreliable." DTI, page 160

148 complied with the take-over code. DTI, page 435

148 "the price would rise very substantially." DTI, page 448

148 he would repurchase the shares at any time up to January 31, 1969. DTI, page 518

CHAPTER 7

152 "I just used to think I was part of it." *The Times,* June 19, 1969

154 "I wasn't sure that we needed his particular expertise." BBC TV, May 1, 1973

157 "Maxwell knew more people there than I did." Steinberg, BBC TV, 1973

158 "as we reduce our administration costs." DTI, page 163 and private

161 MSI(DS) was owned by Maxwell, his wife and Tom Clark. DTI, page 364

161 to collect Pergamon's debts, a task which had previously been undertaken by MSI(DS). DTI, page 365

161 for the benefit of Maxwell's sister. DTI, page 352

162 "They made a good case out to me and I was very happy . . ." DTI, page 602

162 "I certainly had no knowledge about terminating it." DTI, page 602

163 Pergamon's profits were unaffected. DTI, page 607

163 "no ability and no experience and no know-how in this area." DTI, page 610

165 "might be inflated or deflated as a result of such relationship." DTI, page 600

165 he also managed Maxwell's private companies' accounts from the same office. DTI, page 462

165 with those of the private companies as "basically impossible." DTI, page 595

165 because all the accounts were chaotic. Pergamon *Annual Report,* 1970

166 one-third of Pergamon's total profits in 1968 would be derived from those two sales. DTI, page 492

166 the exact terms of credit between Pergamon and MSI Inc. DTI, page 483

167 "before the end of the year." DTI, page 887

167 "on a royalty basis if issues no longer available." DTI, page 577

167 the second was a confirmatory telex from MSI Inc.'s auditors. DTI, page 540

168 Maxwell's assurances that Pergamon had received a "firm" order. DTI, page 579

168 a close watching brief on Pergamon's financial management. DTI, page 578

168 personally had the right to vet all major schemes. DTI, page 578

169 soon after his first meeting with Steinberg. U.S. Court of Appeals Docket Nos. 72-1638-41, 72-1654, page 9

170 he had disagreed with Maxwell's views of how the accounts should be prepared. DTI, page 200

170 a "change of practice" in the valuation of stocks. DTI, page 578

171 "and I won't let you steal it." U.S. Court of Appeals Docket Nos. 72-1638-41, 72-1654, page 9

171 a forecast of $1.4m profit if Pergamon owned ILSC completely. U.S. Court of Appeals Docket No. 71-1563, page 9

CHAPTER 8

177 "I was amazed that it was so significant." BBC TV, 1973

178 "Maxwell, Crook or Paranoiac." A three-volume record of the correspondence and negotiations between Maxwell and the *Sunday Times* was compiled in 1973 by Alex Finer.

180 "fair game to try to bring them down." BBC TV, 1973

183 "Maxwell was used to bullying people which our people didn't like." BBC TV, 1973

184 "It was amazing that everyone else thought it was so significant to the world." BBC TV, 1973

188 "But then Maxwell showed us the photo." BBC TV, 1973

188 This was a huge proportion of Pergamon's profits. DTI, page 619

188 the piles of old journals and books stacked on shelves. DTI, page 575

189 no distinction was made in the ownership of the stock between Pergamon, MSI Inc. and Robert Maxwell & Co. DTI, page 598

189 Anderson saw that Pergamon's major customers for back journals were the two private family companies. DTI, page 565

190 had the right to return all the stock it had bought from Pergamon and demand repayment in full. DTI, page 448

190 "no noise, no loss of face, just let's slide out." BBC TV, 1973

193 "The internal management accounts show that ILSC is now trading profitably." DTI, page 183

193 trading profit of just £40,000 at the end of the first eighteen months. DTI, page 174

194 to give ILSC £42,000 credit for services it had been charged for the use of the offices at Fitzroy Square. DTI, pages 176/7

194 "full information available and the points were not at issue." *The Times*, August 22, 1969

194 The amount specified was just £40,000. DTI, page 185

195 Pergamon's recent purchases from ILSC worth £356,895. DTI, page 188

195 the accounts were proven to be in shambles. DTI, page 187

195 "I and my financial advisers are completely at a loss to understand why Leasco acted the way it did." *Sunday Telegraph,* August 24, 1969

199 "has conducted himself with courage throughout the proceedings." *The Times,* August 29, 1969

CHAPTER 9

208 "I and my family have been through hell." Transcript of EGM, page 10

213 Leasco would have had difficulty in establishing control over PPI. DTI, page 616

214 Ross, financed by Leasco, attempted to call a special shareholders' meeting. Supreme Court of the State of New York: *Ross* v. *PPI* and circular from Maxwell to PPI shareholders dated November 4, 1969

219 The issue, and Maxwell's reputation, were left dangling. See Select Committee on House of Commons (Services). Accounts of Refreshment Department 1965 to 1971; *Hansard,* complaint of privilege, October 13, 1969, column 44; First Report from the Committee of Privileges, Session 1969–70, March 3, 1970

CHAPTER 10

224 were quite intentionally private meetings. All England Reports, 1971, page 398

226 "up to two years . . . until the company was on its feet again." *Financial Times,* June 29, 1970

228 When the Price Waterhouse report was finally published, it mentioned a further problem of a government export guarantee issued by the ECGD. This was also discussed by the DTI, page 75

229 Maxwell insisted that Pergamon had agreed to underwrite its massive debts. DTI, page 546

230 he told the *Daily Telegraph* after he returned. November 21, 1970

233 Price Waterhouse, the treatment of 1969 accounts was "fair." Report, paragraph 76

234 The inspectors prided themselves that they never sprang any surprises upon him. DTI, page 91

234 "I can see the value of these enquiries." DTI, page 69

235 Maxwell, according to the inspectors, made no mention of that crucial sale. DTI, page 156

235 ". . . in the warranty period which ended on the 30th June 1968." DTI, page 159

235 Maxwell vigorously denies. *They Must Be Fair,* page 11

236 ILSC which was "misleading and untrue." DTI, page 44

236 he allowed important documents to be destroyed. DTI, page 105

236 that proper records were not kept. DTI, page 119

236 that he must have known that the letter to Bernard Schwartz was not true. DTI, page 169

236 "mislead." DTI, page 187

236 "with the occasional statement which was untrue and calculated to mislead." DTI, page 172

236 at a meeting in Fitzroy Square. DTI, page 85

236 "It is incomprehensible to me." DTI, page 84

236 "I can recollect clearing the document with the BPC directors of ILSC." DTI, page 94

236 not a single original or carbon copy was found of the draft document. DTI, page 86

236 "Not yet." DTI, pages 92 and 96

236 "Mr. Maxwell's assertion . . . is inaccurate." DTI, page 87

236 throughout the questioning, sought to "justify the statement." DTI, page 97

236 "an element of desperation." DTI, page 176

237 admitted ever having seen [the contract] or been aware that Pergamon had made this purchase. DTI, page 176

237 Le Bas and Jenman. DTI, pages 154 and 166

237 "Flemings too had lost faith in Mr. Maxwell and his integrity." DTI, page 185

237 "Mr. Briggs, due to a severe impediment in his speech." DTI, page 186

237 BPC's directors . . . were censured but with considerably less emphasis. DTI, pages 58/9 and especially page 73

237 "I am constantly being amazed by the evidence from the BPC side." DTI, page 135

237 "the complaint." DTI, page 14

240 Maxwell bullied them into recording profits which they disputed. DTI, pages 235, 237/8 and 231

240 "there is a limit how far one can argue when one is an employee." DTI, page 251

240 Maxwell had forced him to record unrealistic profits. DTI, page 251

240 Chalmers Impey. DTI, pages 312 and 318ff.

240 Maxwell had submitted to them as evidence. DTI, page 237

240 invoices to justify. DTI, pages 279, 285ff. and 299

240 "Mr. Silkin, a letter dated July 14, 1971 . . ." DTI, page 330

244 back-dated invoices. DTI, page 568

244 board minutes. DTI, page 555

245 ". . . and R. M. & Co. refused to be bound by this arrangement." DTI, page 502

245 "to whitewash everyone else." *They Must Be Fair,* page 112

CHAPTER 11

On Labour Party affairs, I have used the local newspapers and the report issued by the Labour National Executive.

CHAPTER 12

262 ". . . give the boys a break." *Scottish Daily News,* R. McKay and Brian Barr, Canongate, 1976, page 8

265 The council wanted to pay an additional £16,000, nearly double Maxwell's deal. McKay, op. cit., page 64

269 "Since Maxwell is pivotal to all the changes taking place." The documents obtained by the *Bookseller* during litigation initiated by Maxwell for defamation against the magazine included all the *News's* Council minutes and working papers. This was also the source for the documents regarding the industrial dispute at Pergamon.

292 sought to rescue Oxford United. John Ley, *Rags to Riches, The Rise and Rise of Oxford United,* Queen Anne Press, 1985

293 John Waddington. Victor Watson kept a diary throughout the battle and subsequently wrote various descriptive pieces.

CHAPTER 13

298 thirteen trade unions. Simon Jenkins, *The Market for Glory,* Faber and Faber, 1986

CHAPTER 14

348 The Edinburgh Games. Derek Bateman and Derek Douglas, *Unfriendly Games, The Inside Story*, Mainstream, 1986
356 *Private Eye. Malice in Wonderland*, Macdonald, 1986

CHAPTER 15

387 "That's what they're made for." *Le Matin*, February 16, 1988
388 "he is a mammoth . . ." *Le Point*, October 31, 1988
390 the winners had conspired. *Le Monde*, February 19, 1988
392 "it won't happen again." *L'Expansion*, February 1988
393 "a hiccup in the market." *Wall Street Journal*, May 9, 1988
401 "stupid price for it." *Financial Times*, August 4, 1988
402 "not because you like him." *Business News*, October 24, 1988
406 "I did notify you . . ." *Le Point*, October 31, 1988

CHAPTER 16

411 Bunn, personal interview
412 Mogg, personal interview
419 indispensably contributed to saving eastern Europe." *Guardian*, March 5, 1990
419 "I did no business with eastern Europe before the Berlin Wall came down." *Independent*, May 13, 1990
422 "clearly dancing on the edge." *Financial Times*, August 6, 1990
422 "I treat them like a Field Marshal." *Independent*, May 13, 1990
423 ". . . I'll throw away the big bit." *Sunday Times*, May 13, 1990
427 although some suspected a higher amount. *Financial Times*, September 13, 1990
433 "When I pass a belt, I can't resist hitting below it." *International Herald Tribune*, March 18, 1991
437 the loan was immediately disclosed. *Financial Times*, August 15, 1991
437 ". . . one of the most outstanding performers of the year." John Jay, April 14, 1991
438 because the sale of assets was proving difficult. Sale of Pergamon Press, April 24, 1991
440 "Over the previous five years." Interview with *Sunday Times*, April 14, 1991

441 "secrecy, deviousness and refusal to conform to expected behavior." *Financial Times,* April 18, 1991

442 as set out in the prospectus. Part IV (5) (ii); *see also* page 12 "Related parties"

442 since 1984 compared to the *Sun's* 10 per cent. *Guardian,* November 7, 1991

447 an actual loss of £6.35 million. *Independent,* September 24, 1991

452 Brookes, personal interview

452 Laister, personal interview

459 Guest, personal interview

460 marveled an admirer. *Sunday Times,* September 29, 1991

460 unsettled his New York bankers. *Wall Street Journal,* September 13, 1991

461 observed an eyewitness in Maxwell's office. *Financial Times,* October 5, 1991

INDEX

525

PICTURE ACKNOWLEDGMENTS

PLATE I
Top left, private collection; *top right*, private collection; *bottom*, private collection.

PLATE II
Top left, J. H. Kisch; *bottom left*, Gunther Heyden; *bottom right*, private collection.

PLATE III
Top, Springer Verlag; *bottom left*, Gunther Heyden; *bottom right*, Gunther Heyden.

PLATE IV
Top left, Times Newspapers Ltd; *top right*, Central Press photos; *bottom*, Keystone Press Agency Ltd.

PLATE V
Top, BBC Hulton Picture Library; *bottom*, Times Newspapers Ltd.

PLATE VI
Top left, Daily Telegraph; *top right*, BBC Hulton Picture Library; *center*, Times Newspapers Ltd; *bottom right*, Hill Samuel Group.

PLATE VII
Top left, Financial Times Photography; *top right*, Financial Times Photography; *bottom left*, Daily Telegraph; *bottom right*, Express Newspapers.

PLATE VIII
Top, F. Delafosse, Sygma; *bottom*, Sven Wackstrand, Popperfoto.